The Other in Jewish Thought and History

New Perspectives on Jewish Studies

A Series of the Philip and Muriel Berman Center for Jewish Studies
Lehigh University, Bethlehem, Pennsylvania

General Editor: Laurence J. Silberstein

The Other in Jewish Thought and History

Constructions of Jewish Culture and Identity

Edited by
Laurence J. Silberstein and Robert L. Cohn

NEW YORK UNIVERSITY PRESS
New York & London

Library of Congress Cataloging-in-Publication Data

The Other in Jewish thought and history : constructions of Jewish culture
    and identity / edited by Laurence J. Silberstein, Robert L. Cohn.
      p.   cm. -- (New perspectives on Jewish studies.)
      Includes bibliographical references and index.
      ISBN 0-8147-7989-1 -- ISBN 0-8147-7990-5 (pbk.)
      1. Judaism--Relations. 2. Jews--Identity. 3. Gentiles. 4. Jews-
    -Attitudes. 5. Women in Judaism. 6. Jewish-Arab relations.
    7. Outsiders in literature. 8. Jewish literature--History and criticism.
    I. Silberstein, Laurence J. (Laurence Jay), 1936- . II. Cohn, Robert L.
    III. Series.
    BM534.O84 1995
    305.8'924--dc20   94-10880
                                                                 CIP

New York University Press books are printed on acid-free paper,
and their binding materials are chosen for strength and durability.

Contents

This volume is dedicated to my father-in-law, Charles Berenson of blessed memory, and to my mother-in-law, Bessie Berenson, in appreciation for their unceasing love and support.

L.J.S.

For my parents-in-law, Dr. Samuel and Gertrude Levine, in gratitude for their devotion and encouragement.

R.L.C.

Acknowledgments

The editors wish to thank the Lucius N. Littauer Foundation for providing a grant for publication of this volume. Most of the chapters were presented in earlier versions at the Berman Center conference on "The Other in Jewish Thought and History," held at Lehigh University in May 1992.

This volume, and the series of which it is a part, would not be possible without the continuing support and generosity of Philip and Muriel Berman. We are deeply indebted to Shirley Ratushny for her diligent supervision of the overall preparation of the manuscript and for her meticulous editing. In this task she was ably assisted by Erica Nastasi and, in the final stages, by Julie Miller. All of us at the Berman Center appreciate the continued assistance and counsel of Despina Papazoglou Gimbel and Niko Pfund of New York University Press.

The editors wish to thank the following for granting us permission to reprint or cite material: The University of Minnesota Press for a revised version of "The Other Within and the Other Without," which appeared in *Storm from Paradise: The Politics of Jewish Memory* by Jonathan Boyarin, copyright 1992 by the Regents of the University of Minnesota; and Routledge, Inc., for an expanded version of chapter 7 of *The Jew's Body* (1991) by Sander L. Gilman.

A special thanks to Eitan Notev (alias Shraga Gafni) for permission to publish a translation of his short story "The Battle of Fort Williams," which is included as an appendix to chapter 10 of this volume.

Chapter 1

Others Within and Others Without: Rethinking Jewish Identity and Culture

Laurence J. Silberstein

Introduction

The emergence of Zionism precipitated a radical rethinking of Jewish identity. Transforming Jewish discourse from a religious to a secular mode, Zionism challenged the basic legitimations that had theretofore operated to ground collective Jewish self-understanding. A crisis of identity, which was both a condition for and a result of the rise of Zionism, is clearly evident in a question submitted to Ahad Haam, a founder of secular Jewish discursivity, by an anonymous reader:

> What do we call a Jew who loves his people, its literature and its cultural heritage, and who yearns for its renewal . . . but who at the same time is a free thinker in the fullest sense of the term? While he believes in nature and natural law, he does not believe in a creator God, or the providential God [who watches over His people] and who is the Giver of the Torah. . . . Is such a person a Jew or isn't he (*Halanu hu o'lezarenu*)?[1]

This question is a clear indication of the confusion over the parameters of Jewish identity felt by a growing number of Jews at the end of the nineteenth century. In response, Ahad Haam privileged the secular Jew over the religious Jew. Not only was the person described Jewish, but his form of Jewishness, insofar as it was freely chosen rather than performed as a divine command, was on a higher plane than that of the religious Jew. Thus, Ahad Haam opened the way for a secular Jewish identity.

In Ahad Haam's view, the new secular Jew was not obligated to accept the theological assumptions that legitimated prior forms of Jewish identity. To be Jewish now meant to identify with the Jewish people and its cultural heritage.[2]

In the new discourse of Jewish nationalism, of which Ahad Haam was a major founder, Judaism was transformed from a divinely ordained body of beliefs, norms, and practices into a secular culture created by Jewish people. So long as Judaism was conceived as a divinely ordained mode of existence, its distinctiveness was defined by its divine/transcendent legitimation. However, as the center of gravity of Jewish life shifted from the theological and metaphysical spheres to the realm of the social and cultural, more and more attention was given to those social and cultural traits and characteristics that differentiated this group and this culture from others.

Ahad Haam was fully aware that a significant, far-reaching change was occurring in the sphere of Jewish identity. In previous generations, he argued, it was unthinkable for a Jew to question his/her Jewish identity: "It never occurred to them to ask: 'Why am I a Jew?' Such questions would have not only been considered blasphemy, but would have been seen as the highest level of stupidity."[3]

However, as a result of social, cultural, and political changes, many Jews were now experiencing pervasive doubts concerning their identity:

> In the last few generations, this condition has changed. The new Jew, entering into the mainstream of Western culture, no longer sees himself as superior, as a member of a unique group, distinct from the rest of humanity. On the contrary, he does all that is in his power not to be different. . . . It is no wonder, therefore, that one hears him uttering the powerful question: Of what advantage is my Jewishness to me? Why should I continue to suffer for it? Why should I continue to cherish it?[4]

For Ahad Haam, Zionism had to provide a discourse that would enable these new secular Jews to continue being Jewish. What Ahad Haam did not foresee, however, was that the emergence of secular Jewish discourse rendered the notion of Jewish identity essentially contested. No sooner had Ahad Haam proclaimed the compatibility of Judaism and intellectual freedom than other, more radical voices arose to push the parameters of Jewish identity far beyond the limits he had anticipated. From the outset, Zionist discourse was characterized by ongoing debate over the character and parameters of Jewish identity, a debate that continues to the present.

The issue of identity continues to be a central concern in Jewish public and academic discourse. Every year, a plethora of studies concentrates on the problems of Jewish identity. With few exceptions, these studies assume the natural givenness of Jewish group identity.[5] Focusing on the social-psychological processes by means of which identity is produced, they speak of Jewish identity in terms of a coherent set of values, beliefs, attitudes, and behaviors. Informing most of these inquiries is an anxiety over the precariousness of Jewish life. Analyzing the processes that threaten to undermine the survival of this identity, many studies outline strategies for combating this erosion.

While the concept of identity is a major concern in the writings of sociologists and social psychologists, it also plays a major, albeit implicit role in historical studies of Judaism. While acknowledging ongoing cultural change and development, historical studies of Judaism presume the existence of a sociocultural constant seen as the subject/bearer of that change and development. Like social scientists, historians presuppose the existence of an entity identified alternately as the Jewish people, the Jewish nation, or the Jewish community, the major parameters of which can be identified, isolated, and described. Studies of Jewish history, like the social-scientific studies of contemporary Jewry, assume as given some essential group, body of thought, or set of cultural values and practices that are taken to be essentially "Jewish."[6] To speak of Judaism, the Jewish people, Jewish culture, and Jewish society is, therefore, to speak of a coherent, identifiable entity.

In recent years, writers in a variety of fields, including literary theory, philosophy, cultural criticism, social theory, and women's studies, have called into question the notion of fixed, stable identities, on both the individual and group levels. According to these critics, the notion that individuals and groups are "fixed, bounded entities containing some essence or substance that is expressed in distinctive attributes" is a product of a "substance metaphysics" that has dominated Western thought down to the contemporary period.[7] Stuart Hall has summarized this essentialistic way of thinking about identity as follows:

There are at least two different ways of thinking about "cultural identity." The first position defines cultural identity in terms of one shared culture, a sort of collective "one true self," hiding inside the many other, more superficial or artificially imposed selves, which people with a shared history and ancestry hold in common. Within the terms of this definition, our cultural identities reflect the common historical experiences and shared cultural codes which provide us, as "one people," with stable, unchanging and continuous frames of reference and meaning, beneath the shifting divisions and attitudes of our actual history.[8]

According to this view, which informs most scholarly writings on Judaism, we can uncover, excavate, and bring to light cultures such as Judaism by asking such questions as, What is the essence/ structure of Jewish culture? What is Jewishness? What are the essential teachings, values, and ideals of Judaism? How did Judaism emerge, develop, grow?

However, taking issue with this conventional notion of cultural identity, Hall argues for a dynamic, nonessentialistic, positional conception that talks in terms of process, movement, flux, change, and conflict:

Cultural identity . . . is a matter of "becoming" as well as of "being.". . . It is not something which already exists transcending place, time, history, and culture. Cultural identities come from someplace, have histories. But, like everything else which is historical, they undergo constant transformation. Far from being eternally fixed in some essentialized past, they are subject to the continuous play of history, culture, and power. . . . Far from being grounded in a "mere" recovery of the past, which is waiting to be found, and which, when found, will secure our sense of ourselves into eternity, identities are the names we give to different ways we are positioned by, and position ourselves within the narratives of the past.[9]

To Hall, identity is a "production which is never complete, always in process, and always constituted within, not outside, representation."[10]

As a concrete example of this positional conception of identity, Hall, who is Jamaican born and would conventionally be identified as Black, deconstructs the concept of blackness:

The fact is "black" has never been just there either. It has always been an unstable identity, psychically, culturally, and politically. It, too, is a narrative, a story, a history. Something constructed, told, spoken, not simply found. . . . Black is an identity that had to be learned and could only be learned in a certain moment.[11]

The growing emphasis on the socially constructed nature of cultural identity has been accompanied by a growing awareness of the central role of power, struggle, and conflict:[12]

Individual identities are contextually constructed within fields of power and meaning and cannot easily be separated from specific situations, from culturally specific narrative conventions, or from abstractions we label history, politics, and economics. Identity here is not a unified essence, but a mobile site of contradiction and disunity, a node where various discourses temporarily intersect in particular ways.[13]

The relationship of culture and power is clearly evident in the practices of exclusion and othering that characterize ethnographic practices. As James Clifford argues, "cultural poesis—and politics— is the constant reconstitution of selves and others through specific exclusions, conventions, and discursive practices."[14] This distinction between us and the Other is clearly evident in the letter to Ahad Haam which I cite above. The phrase "Is such a person a Jew or isn't he?" could also be translated "Is he one of us, or is he Other?"

Postmodernism and the Concept of the Other

The concept of the Other is basic to the revised interpretations of cultural identity. According to these theories, we form our sense of self, our identity, in relation to Others over and against whom we define ourselves. Thus, in order to understand identity, both individual and group, we must attend to the Others over and against whom the self is positioned/constructed/constituted.

The Other is, as we have seen, the medium by which we all but consciously define ourselves. Such is the identity/otherness dialectic which must be brought into full consciousness.[15]

The concept of the Other, of otherness, is particularly prominent in the writing of that family of thinkers and writers commonly identified as postmodern.[16]

Among those thinkers commonly identified as central to postmodern discourse, Jacques Derrida and Michel Foucault have been particularly concerned with calling our attention to the ways in which othering and exclusion are imbricated in the process of identity formation. Derrida, a leading theorist of antiessentialistic discourse, argues that difference, rather than unity, simultaneity, or sameness, is the appropriate starting point for understanding Western culture in general, and the notion of identity and self in particular.

Criticizing the prevailing Western views that see cultures as unified, self-contained, and autochthonous, Derrida insists that a culture can only be understood in relation to the cultural Others over and against which it defines itself:

> No culture is closed in on itself, especially in our own times when the impact of European civilization is so all-pervasive. Similarly, what we call the deconstruction of our own Western culture is aided and abetted by the fact that Europe has always registered the impact of heterogeneous, non-European influences. Because it has always been thus exposed to, and shadowed by, its other, it has been compelled to question itself. Every culture is haunted by its other.[17]

To both Derrida and Foucault, the process of identity formation is far from benign. Insofar as identity presupposes alterity, any effort by a group to establish the parameters of its own identity entails the exclusion and/or silencing of the voices of Others. Consequently, the process of identity formation entails acts of violence against the excluded Other:

> The rapport of self-identity is itself always a rapport of violence with the other; so that the notions of property, appropriation and self-presence, so central to logocentric metaphysics, are essentially dependent on an oppositional relation with otherness. In this sense, identity presupposes alterity.[18]

Derrida considers these processes of marginalization and exclusion to be endemic to Western thought and culture. The subject, argues Derrida, can only be understood in relation to the Other that calls it into being. Accordingly, as many of Derrida's interpreters have observed, the basic starting point for his deconstructive activity is the concern for the voices of alterity that have been silenced, the voices of those Others who have been marginalized, expelled, cast out, or excluded:

We can read Derrida as showing us, over and over again, that the devious tactics and strategies designed to exclude, outcast, silence, and exile the contaminating "Other" have never been quite successful. This drive toward exclusion and exile is evidenced not only in logocentrism and phonocentrism, but in the history of the West. Some of Derrida's most moving and passionate prose shines forth in his perceptive descriptions of the dynamics of exclusion and his apologia for what is exiled.[19]

Concern for the marginalized, silenced voices of the Other is also basic to the writings of Michel Foucault. In a series of studies, Foucault has explored the discursive processes and practices by means of which select groups have been marginalized or otherized, and the "regimes of truth" by means of which this marginalization and otherizing was generated, dispersed, and perpetuated.[20] Of particular interest to Foucault is the intricate relationship between these processes and the way in which we construct knowledge and truth.[21]

Like Derrida, Foucault has challenged essentialistic notions of self, subject, and identity. Calling our attention to the practices through which subjects are constructed as objects of knowledge, Foucault has emphasized the seminal role of discourse in shaping the ways in which we conceptualize and think about self and Other.[22]

Feminism and the Other

Postmodernist discussions of identity/difference/otherness have been of particular interest to members of marginalized or excluded groups such as women, Blacks, and colonialized peoples. In an effort to resist and counter the hegemonic notions of gender, ethnicity, and race that currently prevail in Western culture, feminists and postcolonialist critics have sought to uncover the processes by means of which these notions have been socially constructed, disseminated, and institutionalized. Among cultural critics and postcolonialist theorists, Edward Said has been a seminal figure in uncovering the processes as they relate to the victims of otherizing discourses and practices. Of particular concern to Said have been the ways in which scholarly discourse, operating in conjunction with imperialistic enterprises, has objectified and otherized entire cultures.

In his most recent writings, Said has emphasized the inter-actional, polyphonic character of cultures: "Far from being unitary or monolithic or autonomous things, cultures actually assume more 'foreign' elements, alterities, differences, than they consciously exclude."[23] Thus, Said argues for a contrapuntal reading of culture in which we "see several cultures and literatures together, contrapuntally."[24] To read a culture contrapuntally is to read it "with a simultaneous awareness both of the metropolitan history that is narrated and of those other histories against which (and together with) the dominating discourse acts."[25]

Focusing on the knowledge-power nexus depicted by Foucault, Said has helped us to see the processes by means of which Western culture has structured entire scholarly discourses around reified, stereotyped images of the Other. Analyzing literary, social-scientific, and historical discourses, he has alerted us to the role and responsibilities of scholarly and literary communities in the colonializing enterprise. To Said, divisions and differences between cultures "not only allow us to discriminate one culture from another, but also enable us to see the extent to which cultures are humanly made structures of both authority and participation, benevolent in what they include, incorporate, and validate, less benevolent in what they exclude and demote."[26]

Recently, Julia Kristeva, a French feminist and literary theorist, has applied the concept of the Other to the exclusionary practices associated with the construction and perpetuation of national identity, a topic that has also been of concern to Said.[27] Applying psychoanalytic theory, Kristeva draws a parallel between a nation's response to foreigners and the individual's response to the Other within—the foreigner, the uncanny within ourselves: "The foreigner is within us. And when we flee from or struggle against the foreigner, we are fighting our unconscious—that 'improper' facet of our impossible 'own and proper.'"[28]

Others, whether within or without, threaten our sense of distinctiveness, coherence, and stability. As we encounter the foreigner, the external Other, we feel threatened with a loss of self. Thus, the Other is viewed as a threat to our own precarious sense of self, on both the individual and group levels. Only by thoroughly investigating "our remarkable relationship with both the Other and strangeness within ourselves"[29] can we reach a point where we no longer attempt to elevate ourselves by making the Other into a scapegoat. Similarly, we can counter chauvinistic, ethnocentric, exclusivistic nationalism through a demystified, constructionist conception of a nation that acknowledges and accepts differences among individuals and groups.

Elaborating on the initial insights on identity and otherness articulated in the writings of Simone de Beauvoir, feminist theorists have undertaken to reconfigure the prevailing, essentialistic notions of gender, self, and identity. Selectively appropriating many basic arguments from the writings of Derrida and Foucault, these feminists interpret identity in terms of the ongoing discursive and material practices by means of which we are positioned or situated. Seen in this light, identity is

> a posit or construct, formalizable in a non-arbitrary way through a matrix of habits, practices, and discourses. Further, it is an interpretation of our history within a particular discursive constellation, a history in which we are both subjects of and subjected to social construction.[30]

Insofar as identity is contingent, it should be understood "relative to a constantly shifting context, to a situation that included a network of elements involving others, the objective economic conditions, cultural and political institutions, ideologies, and so on."[31] Thus, identity is the product or effect of the social and cultural processes through which it is produced, disseminated, and maintained.[32]

In a recent study of Japanese women factory workers, Dorinne Kondo uses Far Eastern conceptions of self to question the essentialistic conceptions prevailing in the West. Stressing the discursive character of identity, Kondo argues,

> Selves are not referential symbols, the Transcendental Signified, but strategically deployed signifiers. Rather than universal essences, selves are rhetorical assertions, produced by our linguistic conventions, which we narrate and perform for each other. Identities on the individual level resist closure and reveal complicated, shifting, multiple facets. And selves were never separable from context; that is, from the situations in which they were performed, the audience to whom the narrative production of self was addressed, the exclusions implicit in any construction of "self," the historical and political/economic discourses and the culturally shaped narrative conventions that constructed "the self."[33]

In a cogent critique of essentialistic notions of identity, Joan Wallach Scott has highlighted the relationship between identity and experience. Like identity, what we understand as experience is a product of the discourses within which we are situated:

> Subjects are constituted discursively, experience is a linguistic event (it doesn't happen outside established meanings), but neither is it confined to a fixed order of meaning. Since discourse is by definition shared, experience is collective as well as individual. Experience is subject's history. Language is the site of historical enactment. Historical explanation cannot, therefore, separate the two.[34]

As opposed to those who understand agency in terms of autonomous individuals exercising free will, Scott argues for a contingent, situational view. Seen in this light, to be a subject means to be "subject to definite conditions of existence, conditions of endowment of agents and conditions of exercise. These conditions enable choices, although they are not unlimited."[35]

As we would anticipate, feminist theorists situate identity, particularly gender identity, within the power-knowledge nexus that generates, disseminates, and legitimates our current notions of gender. Insofar as experience and identity are related to discourse, and discourse, as Foucault argued, is both the site of and the object of power struggles, the construction of experience and identity "is always contested, always therefore political."[36] Only through the exercise of power do particular identities emerge as hegemonic:

> If the subject is constituted by power, that power does not cease at the moment the subject is constituted, for that subject is never fully constituted, but is subjected and produced again and again. The subject is neither a ground nor a product, but the permanent possibility of a certain resignifying process, one which gets detoured and stalled through other mechanisms of power, but which is power's own possibility of being reworked. . . . The subject is an accomplishment regulated and produced in advance. And is as such fully political.[37]

Some feminists have articulated the concern that the deconstruction of the substantive conception of identity poses a danger to the feminist political project. If the category of woman or female is a social construct, how can one claim rights on behalf of women?

> If gender is simply a social construct, the need and even the possibility of a feminist politics becomes immediately problematic. What can we demand in the name of women if "women" do not exist

and demands in their name simply reinforce the myth that they do? How can we speak out against sexism as detrimental to the interests of women if the category is a fiction? How can we demand legal abortions, adequate child care, or wages based on comparable worth without invoking a concept of "woman"?[38]

However, feminists like Scott, Kondo, and Judith Butler reject the claim that an antiessentialistic notion of gender is incompatible with a positive notion of subjectivity/agency. What is needed, they argue, is a new, positional view of the subject that nevertheless leaves room for action. As Lorraine Code formulates it, "positioned subjects can be self-conscious and creative in reconstructing their situations."[39] Moreover, as Scott has argued, although we are formed as subjects through the narratives and discourses that position us, "these conditions enable choices although they are not unlimited."[40]

Thus, far from subverting the feminist project, the nonessentialistic view of identity has the effect of opening new possibilities regarding what it means to be a woman. By deconstructing essentialistic notions, feminists help to emancipate the concept woman from the "material or racialist ontologies to which it has been restricted."[41] Moreover, the powerful critique of essentialism made by such thinkers as Derrida and Foucault places the burden of proof on those who wish to defend essentialistic notions of identity or subjectivity.[42]

It should be emphasized that neither the feminists discussed here nor social theorists like Stuart Hall deny the reality of identity. They object only to essentialistic notions of identity that are grounded in outmoded assumptions about language, experience, and culture. Thus, the concept of identity continues to play a significant role in their writings. At the same time, they remain deeply concerned that it not be used to occlude the complex realities, the fluid, contested processes that shape the ways in which individuals and groups come to perceive themselves.

Jews and Their Others:
Postmodernism and the Interpretation of Jewish Identity

The theories of identity discussed above are, I would argue, particularly significant for Jews and members of other cultural groups who, rejecting essentialistic notions of identity and culture, nonetheless remain committed to the perpetuation of a distinct community and culture. Unwilling to rest content with the deconstructive moment in the critique of essentialistic notions of Judaism and Jewish identity, they, like the feminist writers, seek alternative conceptions of subject, agency, and community.

Studies of Jewish culture and history regularly emphasize the ways in which Jews have been marginalized, excluded, and oppressed as the Other. Only recently, however, have scholars begun to pay attention to the ways in which Jews, in the process of constructing their cultural identity, construct and define Others. In a pioneering study, *Jewish Self-Hatred*, Sander Gilman explores the dynamic processes whereby stereotypical images of Jew as Other have contributed to the shaping of Jewish self-understanding and the formation of Jewish identity.[43] Focusing on the psychodynamic dimension, Gilman describes the ways in which Jews have internalized and subsequently projected outward the stereotyped notions of otherness that have been applied to them by diverse groups. "As Jews react to the world by altering their sense of identity, what they wish themselves to be, so they become what the group labeling them as Other has determined them to be."[44]

While Gilman examines the stereotyping processes through which other nations and cultures have defined the Jews, as well as the impact of these processes on the Jewish psyche, the anthropologist Virginia Dominguez focuses on the social and cultural processes by means of which Jewish cultural identity is constructed in Israel.[45] Insofar as Israel constitutes the most concentrated example of Jewish culture, Jewish identity formation, and the Jewish exercise of power, the significance of Dominguez's book is by no means limited to Israeli society.

Utilizing a postmodern approach to identity and culture similar to the one discussed above, Dominguez analyzes the ongoing discursive processes through which Israeli-Jewish identity is produced, revised, represented, perpetuated, and imposed. Accordingly, she attends to the processes of representation and objectification that shape, mold, alter, and perpetuate what we call Israeli identity. In contrast to conventional scientific studies of Israeli culture that emphasize shared meaning, common symbols, and common values, Dominguez stresses tension, conflict, struggle, difference, and otherness.[46] In her view, identities do not derive from "natural" qualities or divisions. Instead, they are continually being produced, disseminated, and struggled over.

Dominguez's analysis of cultural identity as a site of conflict and power struggle brings to light the political implications usually overlooked in the prevailing, essentialistic studies of Jewish identity. Far from being benign, the process of identity construction, in which some voices are privileged while others are excluded or marginalized, is infused by power:

> How we conceptualize ourselves, represent ourselves, objectify ourselves, matters not just because it is an interesting example of the relationship between being, consciousness, knowledge, reference, and social action, but at least as much because it is a statement about power. They are simultaneously descriptive and prescriptive, presupposing and creative.[47]

In contrast to the overwhelming majority of Jewish historians and social scientists, who assume Jewish peoplehood as a natural given, Dominguez problematizes the category. Peoplehood, she argues, far from being an objective given, is a discursive process that, like culture and cultural identity, must be continually disseminated and sustained. Thus, to speak of Jewish peoplehood is to speak of a process involving "the objectification of specific collective identities— Israeli Jews' objectification of each other, their objectification of Jewishness, their objectification of Israeli society."[48]

> I think the evidence points toward a dynamic interrelationship between selfhood and otherness in which selfhood is very dependent on the identification (or assumption) of otherness but in which, just as integrally, the boundaries between self and other—semantic as well as referential—are neither fixed nor determinate.[49]

Dominguez is particularly concerned with the issues of otherness and exclusion that form an integral part of the ongoing construction of Jewish peoplehood.[50] Within Israeli society the major Others are Sephardic Jews from Middle Eastern countries.[51] Ashkenazic Jews, Jews from European countries, having achieved cultural hegemony, relate to the Sephardim as "outsiders" who must be integrated or assimilated into the dominant (Ashkenazic) Israeli culture. According to Dominguez, the very terminology used to refer to the cultural traditions of Ashkenazic and Sephardic Jews reveals the process whereby the Ashkenazic culture (*tarbut*) has been privileged over Sephardic tradition (*Morashah*).[52]

For all Israeli Jews, the major external Other is the Arab, including Arabs living outside the country as well as those living inside as citizens. Thus, Ashkenazic and Sephardic Jews alike construct their own sense of Israeliness over and against the more "matter of fact on the surface" Other, the Arab.[53] According to Dominguez, the ways in which Israeli Jews view Arabs is an index of the way they view themselves. Seen in this light, Arabs are the significant Others "not just in terms of the limits of their individual tolerance or what they individually perceive their culture to be, but even more importantly in terms of how uncertain they are about who they are as a 'people.'"[54]

Dominguez has encountered strong resistance to her deconstructive approach on the part of Jewish academicians and nonacademicians alike. In her view, this resistance is indicative of a group's natural reluctance to acknowledge and assume responsibility for the exercise of power: "To see ourselves as constituting others is to acknowledge our having more power than we may wish to have or be comfortable having."[55] Moreover, to the extent that we become aware of our role in the process of constituting Others, we become vulnerable to "calling into question some of the arguments we ourselves frequently use for claiming the 'fact' and the legitimacy of our collective identity."[56]

Jewish feminists, like feminists in general, have found the concept of the Other to be seminal to their struggle to deconstruct the rigid social and cultural patterns by means of which Jewish culture has marginalized and excluded women. In *Standing Again at Sinai*, a forceful statement of contemporary Jewish feminist thinking, Judith Plaskow cites de Beauvoir's analysis as key to understanding the position of women in Judaism. The recognition of the systematic ways in which Judaism has relegated woman to the position of Other is a starting point for her feminist interpretation of Judaism:

> Like women in many cultures, Jewish women have been projected as Other. Named by a male community that perceives itself as normative, women are part of the Jewish tradition without its sources and structures reflecting our experience. Women are Jews, but we do not define Jewishness. We live, work, and struggle, but our experiences are not recorded, and what is recorded formulates our experience in male terms. The central categories of Torah, Israel, and God all are constructed from male perspectives.[57]

In the history of Judaism, women have been marginalized, excluded, and silenced. Insofar as this otherness is systemic, it can only be overcome by means of a far-reaching revision of the system, including its myths, its memories, its conceptions of divinity, its understandings of community, and its conceptions of sexuality. Only such a revision of prevailing interpretation of Jewish society and culture will, argues Plaskow, make possible the recognition of the full humanity of women within Judaism.

Seeking the Other:
Identity Formation and Cultural Construction in Jewish Life

The writings of Plaskow and other Jewish feminists, together with the studies by Gilman and Dominguez, have paved the way for new approaches to the interpretation of Jewish culture and history. Yet the overwhelming preponderance of writings in these areas continues to perpetuate essentialistic notions. However, by disregarding or denying the dynamic processes and power relations that constitute individual and group identity, Jews, like members of any community, run the risk of perpetuating the acts of violence and exclusion about which critics like Derrida, Said, and Foucault have warned us. This volume, focusing on the concept of the Other and on the processes of othering within Jewish society and culture, represents an effort to formulate an alternative approach to Jewish culture and history. In the invitation to the conference at which most of the chapters in the volume were first presented, the editors formulated the theme as follows:

> As increasingly recognized in fields such as anthropology, social thought, and literary theory, groups forge their own cultural boundaries and establish their identities through their definitions of the "Other." Such conceptions of otherness, which often reflect a group's fears and vulnerabilities, also generate and support discourses of inclusion and exclusion. This conference will explore the discourse, categories, and images by means of which Jews have defined other groups and, simultaneously, themselves.

By focusing on the Other, we seek to call attention to the discursive processes by means of which what we call Jewish identity and Jewish culture are generated, disseminated, and perpetuated. It is the hope of the editors that this volume, the first collective effort known to us that uses the concept of the Other to frame Jewish historical and cultural experience, will contribute to a much-needed rethinking of the parameters of Jewish identity and Jewish culture.

The authors, some of whom are not sympathetic to the forms of postmodernist thinking described above, represent a variety of disciplines and areas of specialization within the broad field known as Jewish studies. Not surprisingly, they approach the concept of the Other from a variety of perspectives. Thus, these chapters exemplify diverse ways in which the concept of the Other can shed light on Jewish self-understanding and identity formation.

Most of the chapters focus on particular moments in the history of the construction of Jewish cultural identity. Thus, chapters 2, 3, and 4 explore the processes by means of which biblical writers constructed their own sense of group identity. Of great significance in any nation's image of itself is its myth of beginnings.[58] Such myths enable us to better understand the dynamics of a nation's identity formation or, as Peter Machinist refers to it, a nation's processes of "remembering and appropriating."[59] Of particular interest to Machinist is the fact that, according to the biblical texts, "Israel arrived in Palestine as outsiders,"[60] or, to use the language of this volume, biblical writers conceived of Israel as Others in relation to the land.

According to Machinist, the motif of outside origins provided the emerging Israelite nation with "an important pole around which a collective identity could be segregated and consolidated"[61] during its early formative years. Emphasizing the "protean adaptability"[62] of the biblical tradition to changing problems and crises, Machinist suggests three different ways in which the memory of Israel's outside origins functioned in the life of the community. During the formative stages, it conveyed a message of hope, "from disaster to triumph or, if you will, from marginality to centrality."[63] Later, in the mid-eighth century B.C.E., the story functioned to support the prophet's critique, thereby underscoring "its importance to his Israelite listeners as a mark of their distinctive identity and destiny."[64] Finally, in the period of the Babylonian exile, this tradition provided both hope and motivation to the exiles in Babylonia. Just as they had done before, Israel could once again be transformed from outsiders to insiders, from strangers to home-dwellers.

Archaeology provides one of the major independent sources of information about those groups whom the biblical writers perceived as Others. One of the primary Others in biblical literature, the Philistines, forms the topic of Trude Dothan's and Robert Cohn's jointly authored chapter. What do we find, they inquire, when we compare the image of the Philistines preserved in the biblical texts with the image that emerges from the interpretation of archaeological remains?

In the biblical texts, the Philistines are presented as a warlike, idolatrous people who threaten the survival of the Israelites, their culture, and their religion. Biblical writers ridicule the Philistine gods, as they do the gods of all other peoples with whom the Israelites came into contact, as no match for YHWH's power.[65] However, the material evidence uncovered by archaeologists provides a very different image of the Philistines. This evidence reveals a nation of "accomplished architects and builders, highly artistic pottery makers, textile manufacturers, dyers, metal workers, silver smelters, farmers, soldiers, and sophisticated urban planners" who "played no small part in influencing the culture and political organization of their neighbors."[66]

According to Dothan and Cohn, the conflicting images can best be understood in the context of Israel's identity formation. Confronted by a religiously and culturally sophisticated people with superior military prowess, the biblical writers sought to legitimate their own identity by emphasizing their religious and moral distinctiveness. Perceiving the Philistines as a clear and present danger, the Israelite writers, in the face of the Philistine's military and material superiority, comforted themselves with the belief that they, the worshippers of the true god, YHWH, would be protected. Moreover, in the face of the true God, whose followers they were, the Philistine gods were no match.

In the following chapter, Robert Cohn focuses on another of Israel's earliest Others, the Canaanites, "the Other that is close by."[67] According to Cohn, the tradition of the Israelites as outsiders, a tradition examined by Machinist in chapter 2, made it necessary "to explain why the supposedly indigenous peoples were dispossessed and how the people Israel came into being in contradistinction to them."[68] The result, he argues, was the literary construction of the Canaanite Other. According to Cohn, rather than reading these literary traditions as historical memory, we should see them "as signifiers to carry the image of the Other that defined Israel's cultural boundary."[69]

Cohn finds two distinct constructions of the Canaanites in the biblical texts, one that portrays them as "decent hosts, sometimes even sympathetic individuals,"[70] and another that portrays them negatively as deserving of dispossession. According to Cohn, the difference can best be explained by viewing each construction in terms of the particular myth of origins, or *arche*, in which it is set.

While chapters 2, 3, and 4 provide us with insights into the processes of identity formation during the earliest stages of Israelite history, chapters 5 through 9 take up the issue of Jewish identity construction in classical Jewish texts. Whereas the chapters on biblical Israel, like most of the chapters in the book, focus on Others without, chapters 5 and 6 introduce discussions of Others within, specifically women.

Miriam Peskowitz, analyzing gender construction in Roman-period Judaism, argues the need for an alternative approach to rabbinic sources as they relate to gender. However, while her focus is on the interpretation of tannaitic sources, her concerns apply as well to all historical texts that address issues of gender difference. Of particular concern to Peskowitz is the prevailing scholarship that treats rabbinic sources, particularly their depiction of gender roles and differences, as valid reflections of social and ideological realities. Drawing on contemporary gender and social theory, Peskowitz articulates and demonstrates an alternative approach, one that inquires into the processes by means of which gender roles and images are constructed in tannaitic texts and the cultural conditions that made such roles possible. To demonstrate the cogency of her approach, she analyzes two selections from the Mishnah, the collection of tannaitic texts, and seeks to uncover the ways in which gender and gender differences are constructed in each.

While accepting the metaphor of woman as Other as a valid depiction of the place of women in Jewish religious history, Peskowitz warns about the tendency to overlook complexities embedded in this concept. In particular, she urges us to recognize that otherness itself is a construct, to inquire who has the power to generate and disseminate such constructs, and to attend to the multiple positions, the multiple forms of otherness embedded within the concept of the Other.

Ross Kraemer, focusing on the role that gender played in the formulation of the Other in the Greco-Roman world, takes a different approach to this issue. Through a comparative study of texts, Kraemer focuses not on woman as Other but on "the characterization of the Other as woman,"[71] a common motif in Jewish, Christian, and pagan sources. *The Conversion and Marriage of Aseneth*, according to Kraemer, reveals how Jews, like Christians and pagans, viewed the collective Jewish self in masculine terms. Conversely, they projected onto the pagan Other characteristics conventionally linked to women. A second Jewish text, Philo's *On the Contemplative Life,* reveals the author's tendency to feminize the Other by assigning feminine characteristics to non-Jewish males.

Similarly, in the writings of the Christian polemicist John Chrysostom, Kraemer finds that the author, through terms such as "effeminate" and "harlot," projects onto the Jews many characteristics commonly associated with women. The ubiquity of the feminization of the Other in Jewish, Christian, and pagan communities alike, argues Kraemer, suggests that "the entire notion of a major distinction between the Self and the Other may be a product not of universal experiences, nor even of the universal male, but of particular male experience."[72]

Juxtaposing analysis of both narrative and legal rabbinic discourses, Steven Fraade explores Jewish cultural identity, particularly as it relates to the gentile Other. Rather than view legal texts as reflecting the linear application of fixed rules, Fraade sees such texts as reflecting "intersecting lines of categorical identity and difference that continually reconfigure a culture's sense of solidarity with itself and separation from others."[73] In the act of configuring the gentile Other, these rabbinic texts simultaneously configure Israel's understanding of itself.

According to Fraade, for legal discourse to be effective in configuring Israel's own sense of self, it must intersect "the narrative accounts of Israel's life among those nations."[74] Both of these discourses, addressing the legal and ethical relations between Jew and gentile, reveal the shifting, "anomalous place of the gentile within the Jewish *nomos*."[75] There are, he argues, "three intersecting, and sometime contradicting trajectories in the early rabbinic navigation of that anomaly."[76] These trajectories range from "exclusivity and self-sufficiency of the Jewish *nomos*"[77] to the inclusion of the gentile Other in the Jewish *nomos* to a mediating position between these two extremes.

The kabbalah, the Jewish mystical tradition in which the feminine aspect of the divine receives much attention, is often seen as providing a viable source for feminist Jewish theology. However, examining the form and function of gender types in theosophic

period. This conclusion, argues Peleg, is supported by an analysis of the discourse of right-wing leaders and followers alike, in social-scientific studies, and in Israeli fiction.

Focusing on the highly controversial figure of Meir Kahane, Gerald Cromer sees him as a prism through which to view the processes of constructing Others both within and outside of Israeli society. On the one hand, in Kahane's rhetoric, the Arab was depicted as the demonized Other. Utilizing the cosmic discourse of messianic redemption, Kahane sought to theologically legitimate policies based on the mass exodus of the Arab population from Israel.

At the same time, Kahane otherized Jews within Israeli society, both on the right and the left, who rejected his radical racist solution. Frequently employing the image of the Holocaust, he accused Israeli politicians of pursing Nazilike policies in their treatment of ultranationalist Jews. At the same time, Kahane's opponents utilized the same rhetoric of Nazism, the same discourse of otherness, accusing him of disseminating a Nazilike racism. Thus, as Cromer shows, the language of otherness was heard in both Kahane's camp and that of his opponents.

Combining film theory and feminist theory, Orly Lubin analyzes the mechanisms, such as the "penetrating gaze" and social positioning, through which women are relegated to the margins and designated as Other in Israeli film. At the same time, she describes several ways in which the patriarchal system is subverted, particularly in films directed by women.

Lubin sees a clear relationship between the positioning of women in Israeli culture and the hegemonic Zionist ideology. While valuing the body insofar as it contributed to the Zionist project of reclaiming the Land, Zionism remained silent about the sexual body. This silence, Lubin argues, created a space that made it possible to challenge the dominant phallocentric system. Moving into this space, female writers and directors, focusing on the female sexual body, were able to subvert the cultural assumptions that positioned women on the margins of Israeli society.

In passing, Lubin briefly discusses the ways in which Israeli cinema portrays such Others as Sephardim and Palestinian Arabs. In the process, she shows how some films, by revealing the complex power relations embodied in colonialism and cultural hegemony, subvert these very same processes of social and political positioning and marginalization.

In chapters 14 and 15, Naomi Sokoloff and Elizabeth Fifer turn their attention to the formation of Jewish identity in America and, in the case of Sokoloff, in Israel. One of the significant Others in Zionist discourse is the diaspora Jew, depicted as embodying all of those negative characteristics that Zionism wished to eliminate through the creation of the new Hebrew. In her analysis of novels by the Israeli Natan Shaham and the American Philip Roth, Sokoloff depicts the ways in which diaspora Jews and Israelis each function as Others for one another. Employing categories derived from Bakhtin, Sokoloff finds in the polyphonic, conflicted discourse employed by both Roth and Shaham an indication of the complex attitudes and emotions that currently prevail in the relations between American Jews and Israeli Jews. Just as Shaham's protagonist encounters the otherness of American and American Jews, Roth's protagonist confronts the otherness of Israel. In each book, however, deeply rooted stereotypes of the Other break down, and strongly entrenched oppositions "unravel and dissipate."[83] To Sokoloff, not only do these novels provide "arresting case studies of relations between American Jews and Israeli Jews, but, insofar as they thematize otherness, these fictions also serve as studies in the nature of stereotyping and constructions of identity."[84]

In short stories by American Jewish writers Bernard Malamud and Stanley Elkin, Elizabeth Fifer finds insights into the significance of the Jewish-Black encounter for the construction of American Jewish identity. Estranged from the "approved and sanctioned faces of White America,"[85] the Jewish protagonist in each story turns to Blacks in a futile search for confirmation of his own identity. In each instance, Blacks respond to the Jews' overtures by turning away, an action Fifer interprets as an attempt "to protect their sense of dignity and self-worth."[86] In both instances, therefore, the confrontation with the black Other only serves to threaten the Jews' own sense of identity.

Both of the Jewish protagonists are fragmented people, "fragments of the diaspora, scattered where they cannot root."[87] To Fifer, these stories represent a reenactment of "the sad history of Blacks and Jews."[88] Intertwined in each are the stereotypical anti-Semitic and anti-Black images. Internalizing these images, each group sees the Other as stereotypical, reified Others: "Each sees only a depersonalized fragment of the other, a fiction that denotes distance and separation."[89]

Many of the essays in the volume suggest alternative theoretical approaches to the interpretation of Jewish culture and history. A theoretical dimension is particularly evident in the chapters by Peskowitz, Ophir, Lubin, Hever, and Peleg. In the last three chapters of the book, Sander Gilman, Jacob Meskin, and Jonathan Boyarin, from the perspectives of cultural/literary studies, philosophy, and critical ethnography, respectively, provide alternative theoretical approaches to the meaning and significance of the Other in contemporary Jewish culture.

Gilman, like Derrida, Hall, and the feminist theorists discussed above, emphasizes the fluid, dynamic, processual character of identity construction. "There is," he argues "no such thing as a 'purely' Jewish identity."[90] Throughout their history, "Jews, like all people—have formed themselves within as well as against the world that they inhabited, that they defined, and that defined them."[91] In this chapter, Gilman, who, as noted above, has pioneered in exploring the cultural-psychological significance of otherness, turns his attention to the role of physical characteristics in the social construction of identity/otherness. While not denying that there are genetic differences between groups, Gilman emphasizes the socio-cultural processes by means of which we construct the meaning of and define and interpret the significance of these differences.

Gilman focuses on the ways in which "the representation of the Jewish body is shaped and, in turn, shapes the sense of Jewish identity."[92] Like Hall, Gilman emphasizes the fluid character of so-called racial characteristics, describing how Jews were once categorized as black or swarthy, supposedly an indication of racial inferiority. "By the mid-[nineteenth] century, being black, being Jewish, being diseased, and being 'ugly' came to be inexorably linked."[93] By the late nineteenth century, however, the focus had shifted from skin color to the Jewish nose.

Gilman is here particularly interested in the ways in which Jews internalized anti-Semitic rhetoric, particularly the stereotypical negative meanings attributed to the Jewish nose. Internalizing society's image of the Jewish nose as a sign of ugliness, deficiency, and inadequacy, Jews came to see surgery as a way of overcoming the physical signs of otherness. Interestingly, Gilman observes, the desire to change the Jewish nose is frequently not an indication of a desire to flee from one's Jewishness. Committed Jews, too, often undergo this procedure. Instead, it is simply an attempt to avoid looking "too Jewish."[94]

Emmanuel Levinas, a contemporary French-Jewish philosopher, has formulated one of the most powerful arguments for the positive role of otherness in the construction of human society. Unlike Jacques Derrida, whose starting point is "this ongoing differenti- ation—or fissuring—within the apparent solidity and unity which it in fact makes possible,"[95] Levinas begins with the relation of self to Other. For Levinas, identity results not from our confrontation with or differentiation from the Other, but from our response to the call of the Other: "To be me is already to be *for* the other: I am for the other before I am for myself."[96]

As Meskin interprets Levinas, "insofar as I am I, I stand in a position of responsibility for the Other."[97] To Levinas, political and social forms are not alternatives to our direct encounter with the Other, but rather are already embedded in that encounter. Thus, Levinas offers us a different reading of otherness than we have discussed up to now. Rather than viewing otherness as a socio- cultural construct, Levinas sees it as an inherent part of human consciousness and as the basis for ethical behavior. According to Meskin, Levinas's alternative interpretation of the Other "offers us an important new way to understand concrete societal forms such as tradition, political institutions, and social institutions."[98]

Whereas Gilman focuses on the formation of Jewish identity, and Meskin suggests an alternative approach to social ethics and philosophy, Jonathan Boyarin explores the possibilities for a postmodern, critical Jewish ethnography. Articulating the distinctly Jewish voice with the voices of such postcolonialist critics as Edward Said and Gayatri Spivak, Boyarin criticizes postcolonialists for insufficiently grasping the distinctive otherness of the Jew. While emphasizing the colonized non-European Other, contemporary theorists neglect the Jewish Other inside Europe.

To Boyarin, the strategy of "assimilation," the fetishization of the Holocaust, and the uncritical attitude toward the Jewish state have all served to occlude the distinctive fault lines of the Jews' situation within European society and culture, that is, the otherness of the Jew. Accordingly, any adequate Jewish critical theory presupposes a critical confrontation with each of these forms of occlusion.

Boyarin finds in Kafka "an unprofessional, 'unscientific' model for a Jewish ethnography that could restore Jews to their cultural specificity within Europe and reinforce the critical Jewish voice still contending against supersessionism and progress."[99] Kafka's writings exemplify a relation to the Other that does not occlude the

unique otherness of the Jew. In Kafka's *Letter to His Father* and in
"The Animal in the Synagogue," Boyarin finds the seeds of a critical
Jewish cultural theory that unromantically confronts the past, that
does not privilege space over time, and that does not transform
"persons into exemplars of a reified culture."[100]

Rethinking Jewish Identity: The Next Stage

The revised notions of identity and culture discussed above have, I
would argue, far-reaching implications for the contemporary
interpretation of Jewish identity and culture. Rather than taking
the distinctions between insider/outsider, self/other, Jews/non-Jews
as natural, we would, following the theorists discussed above, treat
them as the products of ongoing discursive processes and cultural
conflicts. Decentering and destabilizing previously held conceptions,
this approach entails a radical shift in focus. Those employing a
postmodernist approach to identity and culture do not ask, Who is a
Jew? What is Jewish identity? What are its essential components,
parameters? What common attitudes, beliefs, practices make up
Jewish identity? Is Jewish identity eroding? Instead they ask, What
are the discursive processes, political as well as social, by means of
which what we understand as Jewish identity has been generated,
disseminated, and perpetuated? Who are the significant Others,
internally and externally, over and against whom hegemonic notions
of Jewish identity have been formed? How have they perceived them
and interacted with them? What characteristics have they ascribed
to them as a means to differentiate Them from Us, Self from Other?
At any given period, who is being marginalized or excluded by
prevailing notions of Jewish identity? What is the relationship of the
processes of otherizing, marginalizing, and excluding to Jewish self-
understanding?

Understandably, there are many who view this contingent,
discursive interpretation of identity as threatening to Jewish
survival. According to this view, conceiving Jewish identity, culture,
and history as dynamic, antiessentialistic, processual, and contested
destabilizes Jewish identity and culture. However, as Judith Butler
has argued, the deconstructive approach to group identity is not a
destructive approach:

To take the construction of the subject as a political problematic is not the same as doing away with the subject; to deconstruct the subject is not to negate or throw away the concept; on the contrary, deconstruction implies only that we suspend all commitments to that to which the term "the subject" refers, and that we consider the linguistic functions it serves in the consolidation of authority. To deconstruct is not to negate or dismiss, but to call into question and, perhaps most importantly, to open up a term, like the subject, to a reusage or redeployment that previously has not been authorized.[101]

Like Butler, I would argue that an antiessentialistic, constructionist approach to Jewish identity opens the way to new possibilities of Jewish discourse, "to a reusage or redeployment that previously has not been authorized."[102]   In light of the problems and criticisms discussed above, the burden of proof falls on those who wish to preserve an essentialistic notion of culture and identity.

NOTES

I would like to thank my colleagues Robert Cohn and Chava Weissler for their valuable comments and suggestions.

1. Ahad Haam, *Collected Writings* (Hebrew) (Tel Aviv: Devir, 1947), 292.
2. This description of the effects of Zionism on Jewish identity applies primarily to Ashkenazic Jews of European origin. The impact of Zionism on the Jews from Middle Eastern countries is a complex phenomenon that is only recently being told. During the writing of this chapter, I encountered two books, Ella Shohat's *Israeli Cinema: East/West and the Politics of Representation* (Austin: University of Texas Press, 1989) and Amiel Alcalay's *After Jews and Arabs: Remaking Levantine Culture* (Minneapolis: University of Minnesota Press, 1993), both of which emphasize the marginalization/otherization of Sephardi Jews and their culture under the Ashkenazic hegemony in the Zionist movement and, subsequently, in Israel. I refer to this process briefly in my discussion below of Virginia Dominguez, and it is also touched upon in chap. 13 by Orly Lubin. As the approach to identity espoused in this chapter should make clear, a comprehensive attempt to address the Other within Judaism remains incomplete without a chapter on Sephardim as Other. The fact that none of us participating in the conference for which the majority of the chapters were delivered remarked about this omission is

indicative of the Western, Eurocentric ethos that permeates the scholarly community.

3. Ahad Haam, *Collected Writings*, 150.

4. Ibid.

5. See David M. Gordis and Yoav Ben-Horin, eds., *Jewish Identity in America* (Los Angeles: Wilstein Institute of University of Judaism, 1991); and Simon Herman, *Israelis and Jews: The Continuity of an Identity* (New York: Random House, 1970). A more dynamic, historical-sociological conception has been developed by Calvin Goldscheider and Steven Cohen. See Steven Cohen, *American Assimilation or Jewish Revival* (Bloomington: Indiana University Press, 1988), especially chaps. 1 and 8; Calvin Goldscheider, *The American Jewish Community: Social Science Research and Policy Implications*, Brown Studies on Jews and Their Societies (Atlanta: Scholars Press, 1986); and Calvin Goldscheider and Alan Zuckerman, *The Transformation of the Jews* (Chicago: University of Chicago Press, 1984). A recent work that addresses the philosophical issues surrounding a postmodern, antiessentialistic Jewish identity is David Theo Goldberg and Michael Krausz, eds., *Jewish Identity* (Philadelphia: Temple University Press, 1993). Many of the articles in that volume complement those of the present volume.

6. In recent discussions, more attention has been paid to the dependence of concepts such as identity and assimilation on the benchmarks or baselines that the scholar takes as his or her starting point. Thus, as Goldscheider and Cohen have argued, the way one construes Jewish identity as well as assimilation depends upon the context that one takes as a starting point (i.e., which geographic, historical, and cultural context serves as the baseline for measuring Jewish identity?). However, neither Cohen nor Goldscheider pushes the discussion as far as the postmodernist critics discussed below. Their methodological concerns notwithstanding, they, like other social scientists studying contemporary Jewry, still assume that in talking about identity, we are talking about some object that can be analyzed, scrutinized, and compared. This is in sharp contrast to social scientists like Clifford whom I quote below. On the idea of a unified Jewish people sharing a common set of cultural and religious symbols, see Charles Liebman and Steven A. Cohen, *Two Worlds of Judaism: The Israeli and American Experiences* (New Haven: Yale University Press, 1990), especially chap. 7.

7. Dorinne K. Kondo, *Crafting Selves: Power, Gender, and Discourses in a Japanese Workplace* (Chicago: University of Chicago Press, 1990), 33. To Kondo, this essentialistic notion of self is embedded in the English language:

The English language encourages an assumption that "the self" is a whole bounded subject who marches through untouched and unchanged from one situation to the next. If openness and multiplicity are admitted as possibilities, if self and world are not separable, the "I" is revealed in its referential emptiness. "The self," "the whole subject," the irreducible "I," the bounded essence separable from "society" is at least partially, then, the sediment of our own history, language, and linguistic ideology, elaborated in myriad ways in everyday and academic discourses. (32)

8. Stuart Hall, "Cultural Identity and Diaspora," in *Identity, Community, and Cultural Difference*, ed. Jonathan Rutherford (London: Lawrence & Wishart, 1990), 223.
9. Ibid., 225. Hall does not deny that identity exists. He is, however, arguing that we ought to replace the prevailing essentialistic model with a dynamic one that emphasizes the social and cultural processes by means of which we come to understand and preserve a sense of who we are, both individually and communally. A similar kind of process-oriented, constructionist conception of group identity has been applied to the concept of national identity in the writings of such scholars as Benedict Anderson, Eric Hobsbawm, and Anthony Smith. See Benedict Anderson, *Imagined Communities*, rev. ed. (New York and Oxford: Verso, 1991); Eric J. Hobsbawm, *Nations and Nationalism since 1780* (Cambridge: Cambridge University Press, 1990); Anthony D. Smith, *Ethnic Origins of Nations* (Oxford and New York: Blackwell, 1986); and idem, *National Identity* (Reno: University of Nevada Press, 1991).
10. Hall, "Cultural Identity and Diaspora," 222.
11. Stuart Hall, "Minimal Selves," in *The Real Me: Postmodernism and the Question of Identity* (London: ICA, 1987), 45.
12. James Clifford has been one of the most vocal among ethnographers in insisting on the contested nature of culture: "Cultures are not scientific 'objects' (assuming such things exist, even in the natural sciences). Culture, and our views of 'it,' are produced historically, and are actively contested. . . . Culture is contested, temporal, and emergent" (James Clifford and George E. Marcus, eds., *Writing Culture: The Poetics and Politics of Ethnography* [Berkeley and Los Angeles: University of California Press, 1986], 18).
13. Kondo, *Crafting Selves*, 47. In response to those who find this discursive view of culture objectionable and dehumanizing, Clifford asserts that it is, in fact, liberating, for it assumes "that no one can write about others any longer as if they were discrete objects or texts" (Clifford and Marcus, *Writing Culture*, 25).
14. Clifford and Marcus, *Writing Culture*, 24.
15. Thierry Hentsch, *Imagining the Middle East* (Montreal and New York: Black Rose, 1992), 192.
16. "We can, rather brutally, characterize postmodern thought (the phrase is useful rather than happy) as that thought which refuses to turn the Other into the Same. Thus it provides a theoretical space for what postmodernity denies: otherness. Postmodern thought also recognizes,

30   *Laurence J. Silberstein*

however, that the Other can never speak for itself as the Other" (Simon
During, "Postmodernism or Post-colonialism Today," in *Postmodernism:
A Reader*, ed. Thomas Docherty [New York: Columbia University Press,
1993], 449).

17. Jacques Derrida, "Deconstruction and the Other," an interview with
    Jacques Derrida, in *Dialogues with Contemporary Continental Thinkers*,
    ed. Richard Kearney (Manchester: University of Manchester Press,
    1984), 116.
18. Ibid., 117.
19. Richard Bernstein, "Serious Play: The Ethical-Political Horizon of
    Jacques Derrida," *Journal of Speculative Philosophy* 1, 2 (1987): 101.
    Thus, in contrast to those who view deconstruction as a nihilistic
    enterprise, Derrida conceives of it as a positive, affirmative mode of
    thinking undertaken as a response to the Other:

    Deconstruction always presupposes affirmation, as I have frequently attempted
    to point out, sometimes employing a Nietzschean terminology. I do not mean
    that the deconstructing subject of self affirms. I mean that deconstruction is, in
    itself, a positive response to an alterity which necessarily calls, summons, or
    motivates it. (Derrida, "Deconstruction and the Other," 118)

20. See, for example, Michel Foucault, *Madness and Civilization: A History
    of Insanity in the Age of Reason*, trans. from the French by Richard
    Howard (New York: Random House, 1965); and idem, *Discipline and
    Punish: The Birth of the Prison* (New York: Random House, 1979).
21. "The history of madness would be the history of the Other—of that
    which, for a given culture, is at once interior and foreign, therefore to be
    excluded (so as to exorcise the interior danger) but by being shut away
    (in order to reduce its otherness); whereas the history of the order
    imposed on things would be the history of the same—of that which, for
    a given culture, is both dispersed and related, therefore to be distin-
    guished by kinds and to be collected together into identities" (Michel
    Foucault, *The Order of Things: An Archaeology of the Human Sciences*
    [New York: Random House, 1970], xxiv; cited in Robert Young, *White
    Mythologies: Writing History and the West* [London and New York:
    Routledge, 1990], 73).
22. Richard Terdiman describes discourse as "the social and linguistic
    processes by means of which we make, disseminate, legitimate, and
    preserve meaning," and as "the complex of signs and practices which
    organize social existence and social reproduction" (*Discourse/Counter-
    Discourse* [Ithaca, N.Y.: Cornell University Press, 1985], 54).
23. Edward Said, *Culture and Imperialism* (New York: Knopf, 1993), 15.
24. Ibid., 43.
25. Ibid.
26. Ibid., 15.

27. The studies by Anderson, Hobsbawm, and Smith, referred to in n. 9, have highlighted the fluid, dynamic processes by means of which national identity is constructed, transmitted, and maintained. These studies by historians and sociologists contribute significantly to a revised, nonessentialistic understanding of nations and national identities. See also Homi Bhabha, ed., *Nation and Narration* (London and New York: Routledge, 1990).

28. Julia Kristeva, *Strangers to Ourselves*, trans. Leon S. Roudiez (New York: Columbia University Press, 1991), 191.

29. Julia Kristeva, *Nations without Nationalism*, trans. Leon S. Roudiez (New York: Columbia University Press, 1993), 51.

30. Linda Alcoff, "Cultural Feminism versus Post-structuralism: The Identity Crisis in Feminist Theory," *Signs: Journal of Women in Culture and Society* 13, 3 (1988): 431.

31. Ibid., 433.

32. In her analysis of Hannah Arendt's conflict with Gershom Scholem following the Eichmann trial, a conflict she sees as revolving around issues of Jewish identity, B. Honig argues for a performative notion of identity. In her view, identity is constructed through our actions, that is, we become who we are through the actions we perform. According to Honig, the self is an "agonistic, differentiated, multiple, nonidentified being that is always becoming, always calling our for augmentation and amendment" (B. Honig, "Towards an Agonistic Feminism: Hannah Arendt and the Politics of Identity," in *Feminists Theorize the Political*, ed. Judith Butler and Joan W. Scott [New York and London: Routledge, 1992], 232). In contrast to the unified, homogenizing notion of identity as a form or framework into which we place ourselves, a view that she attributes to Scholem, Honig argues that the performative notion opens up new possibilities and could lead to "the empowering discovery that there are many ways to do one's Jewishness" (231).

33. Kondo, *Crafting Selves*, 306–7.

34. Joan Wallach Scott, "Experience," in *Feminists Theorize the Political*, 34. In spite of the penchant for essentializing inherent in the current interpretation of experience, we cannot, Scott insists, do without the concept, so imbricated is it in our narratives. However, we must never lose sight of "the discursive nature of 'experience' and . . . the politics of its construction. Experience is at once always already an interpretation and is in need of interpretation" (37). At the same time, Scott rejects the criticism that her discursive orientation introduces a new foundationalism grounded in linguistic determinism: "Treating the emergence of a new identity as a discursive event is not to introduce a new form of linguistic determinism, nor to deprive subjects of agency. It is to refuse a separation between 'experience' and language, and to insist instead on the productive quality of discourse" (34).

35. Scott, "Experience," 34.

36. Ibid., 37.

37. Judith Butler, "Contingent Foundations: Feminism and the Question of 'Postmodernism,'" in *Feminists Theorize the Political*, 13.

38. Alcoff, "Cultural Feminism," 421.

39. Lorraine Code, *What Can She Know? Feminist Theory and the Construction of Knowledge* (Ithaca, N.Y.: Cornell University Press, 1991), 298.

40. Scott, "Experience," 34.

41. Butler, "Contingent Foundations," 16.

42. For a lucid and cogent critique of essentialistic thought, particularly as it relates to gender, see Dianne Fuss, *Essentially Speaking: Feminism, Nature, and Difference* (New York and London: Routledge, 1989).

43. Sander L. Gilman, *Jewish Self-Hatred: Anti-Semitism and the Hidden Language of the Jews* (Baltimore and London: Johns Hopkins University Press, 1986).

44. Gilman, *Jewish Self-Hatred*, 12.

45. Virginia Dominguez, *People as Subject / People as Object: Selfhood and Peoplehood in Contemporary Israel* (Madison: University of Wisconsin Press, 1989).

46. Most Israeli social scientists employ a version of structural functionalism. See Yonatan Shapiro, "Political Sociology in Israel: A Critical View," in *Politics and Society in Israel*, ed. Ernest Krausz, Studies in Israeli Society 3 (New Brunswick and Oxford: Transaction, 1985), 6–16.

47. Dominguez, *People as Subject*, 190. William E. Connolly argues that "if difference requires identity and identity requires difference, then politics, in some sense, pervades social life" (*Identity / Difference: Democratic Negotiations of Political Paradox* [Ithaca, N.Y.: Cornell University Press, 1991], ix).

48. Dominguez, *People as Subject*, 20.

49. Ibid., 169.

50. For other works that depict the role of otherness as an identity-shaping force in Israeli society, see Amos Oz, *In the Land of Israel*, trans. Maurie Goldberg-Bartura (New York: Random Books, 1983). Moving among diverse groups within Israel, including Arabs, Sephardim, Haredim, and Gush Emunim, Oz recorded conversations that reveal the extent to which each of these groups defines its own self/its own identity against both internal and external Others. A different perspective on the processes of otherizing within Israeli society is found in the writings of Anton Shammas, a Palestinian citizen of Israel now living in the United States. In a series of articles and in his book *Arabesques* (New York: Harper & Row, 1988), Shammas poignantly depicts the effects of processes of marginalization and exclusion on the self-understanding and the cultural identity of the Palestinian citizens of Israel. See Anton Shammas, "Diary," in *Every Sixth Israeli: Relations between Jewish Majority and the Arab Minority in Israel*, ed. Alouph Hareven (Jerusa-

lem: Van Leer Foundation, 1983), 29–44; idem, "Kitsch 22: On the Problems of the Relations between Majority and Minority Cultures in Israel, *Tikkun* 2 (September/October 1987): 22–26; idem, "A Stone's Throw," *New York Review of Books*, 31 March 1988, 9–10; idem, "At Half-Mast—Myths, Symbols, and Rituals of the Emerging State: A Personal Testimony of an Israeli Arab," in *New Perspectives on Israeli History: The Early Years of the State*, ed. Laurence J. Silberstein (New York: New York University Press, 1991), 216–24.

51. Other Others within Israeli society include "Goyim" (gentiles), non-Orthodox groups, Jewish ethnic minorities, and marginal groups within the Jewish community whose legitimacy has been questioned such as the Benei Israel (India), the Karaites, Beta Yisrael (Ethiopia), and the Samaritans. For more on Others within Israeli society, see chapters by Ophir, Hever, Cromer, Peleg, Lubin, and Sokoloff.

52. See the works by Shohat and Alcalay cited above, n. 2.

53. Dominguez, *People as Subject*, 157.

54. Ibid., 164–65.

55. Ibid., 191.

56. Ibid.

57. Judith Plaskow, *Standing Again at Sinai: Judaism from a Feminist Perspective* (San Francisco: Harper & Row, 1990), 3.

58. On the relationship of myth of origins to the creation of national identity, see Anthony Smith, *Ethnic Origins of Nations*; and idem, *National Identity*, cited above, n. 9.

59. See Peter Machinist in this volume, 36.

60. Ibid., 42.

61. Ibid., 52.

62. Ibid., 54.

63. Ibid., 52.

64. Ibid., 52.

65. See Trude Dothan and Robert L. Cohn in this volume, 63–64, 72.

66. Ibid., 71.

67. See Robert L. Cohn in this volume, 75.

68. Ibid., 75.

69. Ibid., 86.

70. Ibid., 75.

71. See Ross S. Kraemer in this volume, 123.

72. Ibid., 139.

73. See Steven D. Fraade in this volume, 146.

74. Ibid., 152.

75. Ibid., 158.

76. Ibid., 158.

77. Ibid., 158.

78. See Elliot R. Wolfson in this volume, 170.

79. See Adi Ophir in this volume, 228.

80. Ibid., 208.
81. Ibid., 206.
82. See Hannan Hever in this volume, 249–50.
83. See Naomi B. Sokoloff in this volume, 328.
84. Ibid., 329.
85. See Elizabeth Fifer in this volume, 357.
86. Ibid., 354.
87. Ibid., 357.
88. Ibid., 358.
89. Ibid., 355.
90. See Sander L. Gilman in this volume, 365.
91. Ibid.
92. Ibid., 367.
93. Ibid., 370.
94. Ibid., 394.
95. See Jacob Meskin in this volume, 408.
96. Ibid., 407.
97. Ibid., 411.
98. Ibid., 402.
99. See Jonathan Boyarin in this volume, 443–46.
100. Ibid., 446.
101. Butler, "Contingent Foundations," 14–15.
102. Ibid.

Chapter 2

Outsiders or Insiders: The Biblical View of Emergent Israel and Its Contexts

Peter Machinist

I. Introduction

The last two decades have witnessed an outpouring of scholarly work on the origins of Israel in Palestine. The traditional biblical sources have been reexamined, and examined yet again; archaeological excavation and surface survey have produced an increasing torrent of new material; and the horizons, historical and geographical, within which all of these are to be placed have been enlarged and made more complex. Throughout, however, the three perspectives— or as many would say these days, models—for understanding Israelite origins, established already by the late 1960s, have remained: (1) conquest from the outside, associated especially with William F. Albright and many of his disciples; (2) infiltration of pastoral nomads, which Albrecht Alt and his pupils put forward; and (3) indigenous revolution, proclaimed by George Mendenhall and then, with variations, Norman Gottwald.[1]

The third and newest of these models has gained most of the scholarly attention in recent years, at least in North America, though it is clear that the other two, especially the second, from Alt, are still very much alive. However one may judge this situation— and certainly it is a consequence of larger contemporary cultural and social trends as well as of the discovery of hitherto unknown ancient evidence[2]—accompanying it are two changes in scholarly approach with much broader ramifications. The first is an increasing focus on nonbiblical data for the study of ancient Israelite history: an effort, in more radical formulations,[3] to try to write this history primarily, if not exclusively, from such data. The second point follows from the first. Given that the nonbiblical data at issue are largely of a nonwritten archaeological kind—artifacts, architecture, settlement patterns—they yield less political history (i.e., the establishment of particular events and personalities, and of their chronological sequence) than social and ecological history: what Fernand Braudel, a looming presence in such discussions, called, respectively, *histoire de la conjoncture* and *la longue durée*.[4]   In other words, in the discussion of Israel's origins in Palestine especially, but of other periods of Israelite history as well, efforts have begun to center less on a narrative account of the course of events, which the archaeological data themselves cannot sustain, than on an examination of the shape of emergent Israelite society and culture in their ecological setting.[5]

The common element behind both these changes has been a progressive disenchantment with the historical value of the biblical sources on the period of Israelite origins—the books of Joshua and Judges, but also Exodus, Numbers, and Deuteronomy—which had for so long been the backbone and principal concern of the discussion, and the basis for any narrative political account. This increased sense of their inadequacy has come from an increased appreciation of their late dating and tendentious perspectives—their remoteness, thus, from the events they purport to record—and the consequent despair over separating, or even learning how to recognize, archaic elements, authentic survivals, in them.

This leaves, then, the obvious question: what should an historian do with the Bible in the study of Israel's origins in Palestine? It seems foolish to abandon it—and no one has really done so—because whatever its problems, it still defines the arena within which the nonbiblical data have finally to make sense, by opposition or integration, and wherein, finally, they acquire a specific, concrete historical identity. Moreover, the Bible is the only means at our disposal for determining how Israel remembered and appropriated the experiences of its origins. And if, in fact, these origins lie in revolution, the third of the historical models noted above, then, it must be said, the act of remembering and appropriating becomes especially important as a test of the revolution's ultimate success.

It is on this issue of remembering and appropriating that I wish to focus here. Directly put: what did Israel have to say about its origins in Palestine, and why did it remember them as it did?

II. The Biblical Sources on Origins

Let us begin by sorting out and briefly surveying the relevant biblical texts. In terms of literary corpora, they fall into six groups:[6]

1. *Deuteronomy and the Deuteronomistic History*
   Deuteronomy 1–3 (resume of Egyptian Exodus, Wilderness wanderings, Transjordan conquests). 4:5, 14, 20, 21, 22, 26, 34, 37–38, 40, 46–49; 5:33; 6:12, 18–19, 21–23; 7:1–2, 8, 16, 17–26; 8:1–4, 7–10, 14–16, 20; 9:1–10:11; 11:2–6, 9–12, 23–24, 31; 12:1–3, 9–10, 29; 13:5, 10, 12; 15:15; 16:2, 3; 17:14; 18:9, 12, 14; 19:1, 14; 20:1, 16–18; 21:1, 23; 23:3–4, 20; 24:9, 18; 25:15, 17–19; 26:1, 3, 5–9; 27:2–4, 12–13; 29:1–7, 15, 24; 30:18, 20; 31:2–5, 7, 13, 16, 20, 23; 32:49–52; 34:1–4 (references to Egyptian Exodus, and/or Wilderness, and/or conquest of Palestine, viz., Transjordan or Cisjordan; note 8:22, where conquest will be gradual).
   Joshua 1–12 (narrative of conquest of Cisjordan). 13–22 (tribal allotments in conquered Palestine, with notices of land not yet taken and enemies still present). 23:1–13 (references to conquest of Palestine). 24:1–13, 17–18 (resume of Egyptian Exodus, Wilderness wanderings, conquest of Transjordan and Cisjordan).
   Judges 1; 2:1–5, 20–23; 3:1–6 (narrative of conquest of Cisjordan by tribes, with notices of land not yet taken and enemies still present). 6:8–9, 13; 10:11 (reference to Egyptian Exodus and conquest of Palestine). 11:13–24 (resume of Egyptian Exodus, Wilderness wanderings, and conquest of Transjordan). 18 (narrative of conquest of Laish by tribe of Dan). 21:24 (reference to tribes taking inheritance in Palestine).
   1 Samuel 2:27; 8:8; 12:6, 8; 15:2, 6 (references to Egyptian Exodus, and secondarily to Wilderness and arrival in Palestine).
   2 Samuel 7:6, 23 (references to Egyptian Exodus and to conquest of Palestine).
   1 Kings 8:9, 16, 21, 34, 36, 40, 48, 51, 53, 56; 9:9, 20–21; 12:28 (references to Egyptian Exodus and/or possession of Palestine; note 9:20–21, which lists enemies still present whom Solomon put to forced labor).
   2 Kings 17:7–8, 16, 36; 21:2, 9 (references to Egyptian Exodus and/or conquest of Palestine).

2. *J, E, and P, and R(edactor) in the Pentateuch*
   Genesis 15:13–14 (J[?]), 46:4 (E) (promise of Egyptian Exodus).
   12:1 (J); 15:18–21 (J); 17:8 (P); 26:3 (J); 28:4 (P), 13–14 (J); 35:12
   (P) (promise of possession of Palestine). 22:17 (E) (promise of
   possession of gates of enemies [Palestine]; cf. 24:60 [J]). 34 (J)
   (conquest of Shechem).

   Exodus 1–19 (J, E, P, R); 24 (E, P); 32 (E); 40:34–36 (P)
   (narrative of Egyptian Exodus and Wilderness wanderings to
   Sinai). 20:2 (E[?], P); 23:15, 23, 27–33 (E); 29:46 (P); 33:1–3 (E);
   34:11–13 (J) (references to Egyptian Exodus and/or promise of
   conquest of Palestine; note 23:29–30 [E], where conquest will be
   gradual).

   Leviticus 7:38 (P); 26:46 (P); 27:34 (P) (references to Wilderness sojourn in Sinai; these, with 1:1 [P], designed to show that
   all of book is record of what occurred at Sinai). 11:45 (P); 18:3,
   24–25, 27–28 (P); 19:36 (P); 20:23–24 (P); 22:33 (P); 23:43 (R);
   25:23, 38, 42, 55 (P); 26:13 (P), 45 (R) (references to Egyptian
   Exodus and/or conquest of Palestine).

   Numbers 1:1 (P); 3:1 (R), 14 (R); 9:1, 5 (P) (references to
   Wilderness at Sinai, also to Egyptian Exodus; these designed to
   show that 1:1–10:10 record what occurred at Sinai; note 9:15–23
   [R], describing Wilderness journeying with divine cloud). 10:11–
   12:16 (E, P, R); 13–14 (J, P); 16–17 (J, P, R[?]); 20–25 (J, E, P,
   R); 27 (P); 31–32 (P, J[?]) (narrative of journeys through Wilderness from Sinai to Kadesh, then from Negev to plains of Moab in
   Transjordan and tribal allotments there). 15:41 (P); 26:4 (P),
   9–11 (R), 61, 64–65 (P) (references to Wilderness and/or to
   Egyptian Exodus). 33:1–49 (R) (summary itinerary of journeys
   from Egypt through Wilderness to plains of Moab). 33:50–36:13
   (P) (promise of conquest of Cisjordan and descriptions of tribal
   allotments there, with references to those taken in Transjordan).

3. *"Archaic Poetry"* (all found in J, E, D, and Deuteronomistic
   History as noted above; but cf. related Habakkuk 3; Psalms 68,
   77, 78 cited below)[7]
   Exodus 15:2, 4–10, 12 (drowning of Pharaoh's army in
   Egyptian Exodus), 13–17 (conquest of Palestine).

   Numbers 23:9–10; 24:5–7 (Israel encamped in Wilderness),
   24:8 (Egyptian Exodus and allusion to Israel's future conquests),
   17–19 (conquest of Transjordan).

Deuteronomy 32:10–14 (allusions to Wilderness wanderings and conquest; see further below).

Deuteronomy 33:2 (Yahweh marches from Sinai/Seir/Paran [Wilderness journey]).

Judges 5:4–5 (Yahweh marches from Seir/Edom [Wilderness journey]).

4. *Nehemiah, Chronicles*
Nehemiah 1:10 (allusion to Egyptian Exodus). 9:9–25 (from review of Israelite history in speech of Ezra, here including Egyptian Exodus through conquest, both Transjordan and Cisjordan). 13:2 (mention of Israel in Wilderness incident of Ammon, Moab, and Balaam).

1 Chronicles 1–9 (tribal genealogies; see discussion below). 16:18 (//Psalm 105:11) (promise of land of Palestine). 17:5, 21 (//2 Samuel 7:6, 23) (references to Egyptian Exodus and to conquest of Palestine).

2 Chronicles 5:10; 6:5, 25, 27, 31, 38; 7:22; 8:7–8 (//1 Kings 8:9, 16, 34, 36, 40, 48; 9:9, 20–21) (references to Egyptian Exodus and/or possession of Palestine; note 8:7–8 [//1 Kings 9:20–21], which lists enemies still present whom Solomon put to forced labor). 20:7–8 (reference to conquest of Palestine). 20:10 (reference to Wilderness journey around Ammon, Moab, and Seir). 33:2, 9 (//2 Kings 21:2, 9) (references to conquest of Palestine).

5. *Prophets*
Amos 2:9–10 (references to Egyptian Exodus, Wilderness wanderings, and conquest of Palestine). 3:1; 9:7 (reference to Egyptian Exodus). 5:25 (reference to Wilderness wanderings).

Hosea 2:16–17; 9:10; 11:1; 12:9, 13 (references to Egyptian Exodus and/or Wilderness wanderings). 8:13; 9:3; 11:5 (allusion to Egyptian Exodus in threat of return to Egypt).

1 Isaiah 10:24–26; 11:16 (references to Egyptian Exodus and/or Wilderness wanderings).

Micah 6:4–5; 7:15 (references to Egyptian Exodus and/or conquest of Palestine).

Jeremiah 2:2–3; 31:2 (reference to Wilderness wanderings). 2:6–7 (references to Egyptian Exodus, Wilderness wanderings, and possession of Palestine). 7:7; 35:15 (reference to possession of Palestine). 30:3 (reference to conquest of Palestine). 7:22, 25;

16:14; 23:7; 31:32; 34:13 (references to Egyptian Exodus). 11:4–5 (reference to Egyptian Exodus and promise and fulfillment of possession of Palestine). 32:20–23 (reference to Exodus and conquest of Palestine).

Habakkuk 3:3 (God comes from Teman/Mt. Paran [Wilderness journey (?); cf. Deuteronomy 33:2; Judges 5:4–5; Psalm 68:18]).

Ezekiel 16: especially 3, 45 (Israelite Jerusalem and origins in Palestine as child of Amorite and Hittite). 20:6–26 (resume of Egyptian Exodus and Wilderness wanderings). 23:8, 27 (references to Oholah/Samaria and Oholibah/Jerusalem, representing Israel and Judah, and their sins committed when under Egyptian oppression; cf. Exodus 4:1; 14:11–12; Psalm 106:7). 33:24 (reference to Abraham being given possession of the land [in Palestine]). 36:28; 37:25 (references to possession of Palestine).

2 Isaiah 35: especially 8–10; 40:1–11; 43:16–21; 49:8–12; 51:9–10; 52:11–12; 55:12–13 (return to Zion [from Babylonia] described implicitly as a "new Exodus and Wilderness wandering," i.e., without explicit mention of Egypt or events of Wilderness).

3 Isaiah 62:10–12 (perhaps implicit allusion to Egyptian Exodus, in describing return to Zion). 63:11–14 (reference, explicit, to Egyptian Exodus).

Haggai 2:5 (reference to Egyptian Exodus). (Deutero-) Zechariah 10:10–11 (return to Zion here explicitly as a "new Exodus").

Malachi 3:22 (reference to Moses receiving Law at Horeb, thus, to events of Wilderness).

6. *Psalms*[8]

44:3–4 (reference to conquest of Palestine). 66:6 (allusion to Egyptian Exodus and perhaps crossing of Jordan [Joshua 3–4]; cf. 114:1–6). 68:8–11, 18–19 (reference to Wilderness journeys; note in v. 18 [cf. 9] Yahweh marching from Sinai). 77:17–21 (reference to Egyptian Exodus). 78:12–31, 40–55 (resume of Egyptian Exodus, Wilderness wanderings, and conquest of Palestine). 80:9–10 (reference to Egyptian Exodus and conquest of Palestine). 81:8, 11 (references to Wilderness wanderings and Egyptian Exodus). 95:8–11 (references to Wilderness wanderings). 99:7 (reference to Wilderness wanderings). 105:26–45 (resume of Egyptian Exodus, Wilderness wanderings, and conquest of Palestine). 106:7–39 (resume of Egyptian Exodus,

Wilderness wanderings, and conquest of Palestine; note v. 34, that Israel did not destroy peoples of Palestine, but mingled and sinned with them). 111:6 (perhaps reference to conquest of Palestine). 114:1–6 (reference to Egyptian Exodus and perhaps crossing of Jordan [Joshua 3–4]; cf. 66:6). 135:8–12 (references to Egyptian Exodus and conquest of Palestine). 136:10–22 (references to Egyptian Exodus, Wilderness wanderings, and conquest of Palestine).

III. The Viewpoint(s) of the Biblical Sources

The above survey makes it clear that Israel's origins in Palestine form a subject with wide resonance in the biblical corpus, covering all three parts of the canon. To be sure, not all books are included— missing are the Wisdom books of Proverbs, Job, and Ecclesiastes, which otherwise, as is well known, refer little or not at all to Israel's history, but also others where the absence is not always easy to explain: the five *megillot*, Ezra (unless we consider Ezra with Nehemiah, where origins are discussed), and certain minor prophets, viz., Joel, Obadiah, Jonah, Nahum, and Zephaniah, as well as Daniel. Nonetheless, the texts in which Israel's origins are mentioned represent a great variety of literary types: extended prose narratives, laws, lists, speeches, hymns, prayers, etc.

This material also appears to reflect a diversity of periods and places within Israel. Thus, north (e.g., Hosea and perhaps Judges 5) and south (e.g., J, Jeremiah, Psalm 78) are represented. And while complete and certain dating of all the passages is, like the Hebrew Bible in general, out of reach, there are enough indications to suggest that we have here much of the range of Israelite history: the premonarchic period of settlement, ca. twelfth–beginning of tenth centuries B.C.E., if we follow the dating of certain of the so-called archaic poetry proposed especially by W. F. Albright and his pupils (Exodus 15, Judges 5, Numbers 23–24, Deuteronomy 33);[9] perhaps the tenth–ninth centuries B.C.E. of the United and early Divided Monarchies (J[?], Deuteronomy 32); the eighth century B.C.E. (e.g., Amos, Hosea—at least in parts); the seventh century B.C.E., from Hezekiah to Josiah (e.g., Deuteronomy); the collapse of Judah and Babylonian Exile of the late seventh and first half of the sixth centuries B.C.E. (e.g., Jeremiah, Ezekiel, 2 Isaiah, final version of the Deuteronomistic History; Psalm 106); and the post-Exilic period, late sixth–fourth centuries B.C.E. (3 Isaiah, Haggai, Zechariah, Malachi, Nehemiah, Chronicles). Prominent in this chronology, it should be noted, are the seventh and sixth centuries B.C.E., centering especially on Deuteronomy and the Deuteronomistic History, in which the most elaborate account of Israel's origins in Palestine can be found.

What is most striking about all this material is its point of view. Virtually unanimously—some possible exceptions will be examined presently—the texts agree that Israel arrived in Palestine as outsiders. The picture is one of invasion, normally of a united tribal confederation coming into Palestine from Egypt by way of the Sinai and Negev around the Dead Sea and the Transjordan (e.g., Joshua 1–12), but occasionally in blocks of already-formed tribal units, which take the land in a series of partially successful attacks over time, concluding only with King David's conquests (see especially Judges 1; cf. also 2 Chronicles 8:7–8). To and around these tribes, in turn, the native Canaanite elements are understood to revolve and attach themselves. Yahweh Himself, at least in what seem to be the older attestations of this view, is an outsider to Palestine, arriving from the southern deserts and mountains (Deuteronomy 33:2; Judges 5:4; Habakkuk 3:3; Psalm 68:9, 18). Occasionally in the Pentateuch (e.g., Genesis 12:1; 15:18–21), the point is made that this outside conquest is the return of the Israelite tribes to a land in which their patriarchal forefathers had dwelled and that God had promised their descendants. But in that return Israel is never portrayed as a native of Palestine; indeed, one hardly needs to be reminded that its forefathers are themselves clearly marked as outsiders. It should be noted as well that not infrequently our texts refer to only a part of the invasion process: thus, to the Egyptian Exodus, the Wilderness journeys, or the conquest of Palestine, whether of Transjordan or Cisjordan separately or together. Sometimes this is because the author wishes to focus on a particular incident in this story or because he is at a point in his narrative where he has not yet reached the end of the story and so will not mention the end. But sometimes, one part of the story is meant to serve *pars pro toto*, and if so, it is normally the Egyptian Exodus that is mentioned as the initial and key stage of the story, when the community of Israel was understood to have been organized (e.g., Amos 9:7).[10]

When set against the three models that currently dominate discussion of Israel's emergence in Palestine, the biblical viewpoint just discussed fits best with the first, conquest from the outside, although it could also be accommodated by the second, infiltration of pastoral nomads, insofar as this is understood as movements of groups outside of the Palestinian city-state networks into the land. Clearly, however, this biblical view will not really harmonize with the third of the models, indigenous revolution. Proponents of revolution more or less admit this, even as they look long and hard for at least some supporting biblical evidence. It is instructive that the passages that are usually brought forward—principally, the Rahab story in Joshua 2, 6; the Gibeonites in Joshua 9; the informer and friends at Bethel/Luz in Judges 1:22–26—while they do refer to local groups, Canaanites if you will, who join the nascent Israelite community, nowhere speak of these as part of some mass revolutionary movement. That context has to be supplied by the modern interpreter. Indeed, the context as the biblical sources present it is always that of natives joining the victorious newcomers from the outside.

It would not be fair to conclude this discussion of the biblical material without asking whether it offers any exceptions to the view of Israel as outsiders entering and taking over Palestine.[11] Three possibilities, in fact, need to be considered, to which a fourth can be added from an extrabiblical text. The first is Ezekiel 16, which says of Jerusalem, "Your [place of] origins and [circumstances of] birth are of the land of the Canaanite; your father was an Amorite, your mother a Hittite" (16:3; cf. v. 45).[12] But if this statement implies some sort of aboriginal status in the land of Palestine, note that it is predicated not of all Israel but of Jerusalem, whose anomalous position and late entry into the Israelite fold were still known in the period of Ezekiel.[13] In other words, what we have here is polemic: the prophet condemns the sins of Judah that have brought on exile by linking them with the "pagan" aboriginal city at Judah's center. The argument is of a piece with other statements in Ezekiel portraying Judah's sins as rooted in a tradition that goes back to the very beginning of the community (cf., e.g., 20:4–31). That otherwise Ezekiel recognized and affirmed the standard story of Israel's outside origins is made clear in 20:9–26; 36:28; and 37:25 (cf. also 23:8, 27). To be sure, one might still argue that Ezekiel's polemic in chapter 16 is not simply against a sinful Judah but against those in Judah who argue for Israel's origin in the land, a view he stigmatizes by associating it with the notion of a "pagan" Jerusalem. But if so, this is so buried in Ezekiel's rhetoric as to be unclear and uncertain.

A second possible exception to the motif of outside origins is a passage in the probably old poem, the Song of Moses, Deuteronomy 32:10–14:

> [10] He (Yahweh) found him (Jacob; cf. v. 9) in a land of
>   wilderness;
>   In a formless waste where howling [is to be heard].
>   He surrounded him and showed him understanding,
>   He preserved him as the pupil of his eye.
> [11] Like a vulture he aroused his nest,
>   Over his young he hovered,
>   He spread his wings and took him,
>   He carried him on his pinions.
> [12] Yahweh alone led him,
>   There was no foreign god with him.
> [13] He had him ride on the back[s] of the earth,
>   And had him eat[14] the fruit of the field.
>   He suckled him with honey from the crag,
>   With oil from the flinty rock.
> [14] Curds from the herd, milk from the flock,
>   With the fat of lambs and rams, animals of the
>   Bashan, and he-goats,
>   With the kidney-fat (choicest[?]) of wheat,
>   And from the blood-grape you drank wine.

Whitelam has recently suggested that this passage "may reflect an alternative tradition which locates Israel's origins in the steppes and highlands."[15]   Clearly, as commentators have noted,[16] it recalls, especially in verse 10, Hosea 9:10—and, one might add, Hosea 2:16–17—where Yahweh's special relationship with Israel is said to be founded or reconsummated in the Wilderness. If our passage means to place Israel's origins in the Wilderness, in ignorance or exclusion of an Egyptian Exodus, this wilderness is not, as our passage and the parallels in Hosea show, a part of the promised land of settlement in Palestine. Israel's origins, then, would still be viewed as outside of Palestine, and that would appear to be confirmed by verse 12, which describes Yahweh's guidance of Israel through the Wilderness, viz., toward a more favorable environment, which should be the Palestine of its settlement.[17] Indeed, it may well be that verses 13–14 no longer describe the Wilderness, but the next stage, movement into Palestine,[18] at least into the Transjordanian plateau, where Israel can now eat sufficiently as it could not before (note here, however, that there is no indication of any violent conquest). Thus, if our Deuteronomy 32 passage touches on both the Wilderness and the initial entrance into Palestine, the question is whether it is really ignorant of the Egyptian Exodus. In other words, is our passage the "alternative tradition" Whitelam claims, or docs it, in fact, assume the dominant story of Exodus-Wilderness-Conquest, simply focusing on its Wilderness and perhaps initial Palestinian segments, as do other biblical passages,[19] to illustrate aspects of Yahweh's power and care for Israel? A definitive decision here is not possible, but the burden of proof, it would seem, rests on Whitelam's shoulders.

The third possible exception to the view of Israel as outsiders is the most complex. It has been advanced especially by Sara Japhet, and involves a subtle analysis of 1 Chronicles 1–9, though with attention to other parts of Chronicles as well.[20] Japhet argues that 1 Chronicles 1–9, with its genealogical lists from Adam down through the descendants of the twelve sons of Jacob in the period of the Divided Monarchy and then in post-Exilic times,[21] is meant to provide a kind of history of Israel, which assumes its autochthonous association with Palestine. That is, for the Chronicler, Israel (i.e., Judah) originated and grew up in Palestine, remaining there until the Babylonian Exile of the early sixth century B.C.E. There was, in short, no Exodus, Wilderness, or outside invasion. As proof of this thesis, Japhet points to various divergences in Chronicles especially from the Pentateuchal accounts of J, E, P, and D and from the Deuteronomistic History, where the standard story of Israel as outsiders is found. (This also serves as one point of difference from Ezra-Nehemiah, which likewise maintains the standard view.) For example, in 1 Chronicles 7:14–29, which lays out the genealogies of the sons of Joseph, there is a short story about the son Ephraim (vv. 20–24), describing him as an individual, not as a tribal eponym, whose activities take place in Palestine. But this, observes Japhet, is diametrically opposed to the Pentateuchal accounts, which have Ephraim and his brother Manasseh born in Egypt and dying there before the Exodus takes place (Genesis 41:50–52; Exodus 1:6). If Ephraim, thus, is living in Palestine according to Chronicles, then Joshua, whom Chronicles lists in the tenth generation after Ephraim (7:25–27), must also be a Palestinian, i.e., one who was born there:

the absence in the genealogy of any note of Joshua's involvement in the outside invasion pictured in the book of Joshua only confirms the point.[22]

The assertion of autochthonous origins is not confined, in Japhet's view, to 1 Chronicles 1–9, but extends to other parts of the Chronicler's work. Thus, she notes, 1 Chronicles 16 quotes only the first part of the historical Psalm 105, which reviews the history of Israel from Abraham to Jacob, leaving out the next parts, which deal with Joseph in Egypt, the Egyptian captivity, and the Exodus.[23] And Keith Whitelam, who follows Japhet, notes, among other examples, 2 Chronicles 6, which duplicates the prayer of Solomon in 1 Kings 8, but in verse 16 omits the mention of the Egyptian Exodus that is in the Kings version.[24]

It will be apparent that the passages mentioned by Japhet and Whitelam (and others not summarized here) all represent *indirect* support for the thesis that Chronicles views Israel as insiders, not outsiders to Palestine. There is, in fact, no clear statement of such a view in Chronicles; and Hugh Williamson has noted several other passages in the books—not very many, to be sure, and none in 1 Chronicles 1–9—that mention parts of the dominant story of Egyptian Exodus, Wilderness, and Conquest of Palestine.[25] Most of these are reproductions of the accounts in the Deuteronomistic History (1 Chronicles 17:5, 21; 2 Chronicles 5:10; 6:5, 25, 27, 31, 38; 7:22; 8:7–8; 33:2, 9); but a couple of occurrences are not (2 Chronicles 20:7–8, 10). The question, then, is how does the Chronicler view Israel's origins?

One cannot ignore the passages in Chronicles to which Japhet and Whitelam have drawn attention and the pattern of avoidance or, better, minimalization of the Exodus-Wilderness-Conquest story that they exhibit. To be sure, the case may have been overstated in at least one place, for in 1 Chronicles 7, Ephraim is not said explicitly to be active in the land (of Palestine). Rather, he mourns the deaths of his sons, slain by the men of Gath, "who were born in the land" (7:21).[26] We are then told about the building activity and possessions of Ephraim's children, which are situated specifically in Palestine (7:24–29). One could infer from these details that Ephraim was in Palestine, but it could just as well be that he, and perhaps his family, were outside or at least born outside, in deliberate contrast with the men of Gath "born in the land." Not until verses 24–29, then, would the children be clearly in the land themselves. Whatever location one chooses for Ephraim, the point is that

our passage is ambiguous about it; and that ambiguity only underscores how very muted is the Chronicler generally about the issue of
Israel's autochthony in Palestine, and, indeed, about the whole
history of Israel's origins in the premonarchic period. What the
Chronicler does make clear, on the other hand, is that David represents the decisive first stage in Israel's history, for it is with the fall
of Saul and the kingship of David in Hebron and then, in a quick
jump, in Jerusalem that the Chronicler starts his historical narrative (1 Chronicles 10–11). The genealogies of 1 Chronicles 1–9, thus,
establish that this David is the culmination of the "proto-history"[27]
that began with the first human, Adam. But it is David who, in the
Chronicler's view, gives Israel its form and identity as a community,
who is the base with whom all later Israel—and especially the
Judah of the Chronicler's own day—must make contact. In this
scheme, then, it is not that the Exodus-Wilderness-Conquest doesn't
exist: it does for the Chronicler; it may even be that autochthony
should be worked in for at least some of Israel. But these are all in
the "proto-history"; they are not "history" as they are in the Pentateuchal sources and the Deuteronomistic History, and thus not
directly constitutive of the community of Israel.[28]

We must look at one last text that may raise the autochthonous
issue. It is an extrabiblical source, the stela of Mesha, king of
Moab.[29] Commenting on the Transjordanian holdings of the Israelites before his own successful conquest, Mesha notes, "The men ('š,
literally *man*, but used collectively) of Gad had dwelled in the land
of Atarot (*m'lm*), and the king of Israel had [re]built for himself
Atarot" (10–11). The question here is, what precisely does *m'lm*
mean? As the major studies have made clear,[30] *'lm* refers, in the
Hebrew Bible and contemporary West Semitic inscriptions, to a very
remote, if not the remotest period of time—here, as made explicit by
the preposition *min*, in the past. Sometimes this can be specified as
"from the very beginning of creation" (e.g., Proverbs 8:23); in other
passages, the meaning is more vague: simply "from (very) long
ago/from of old," i.e., a period that it is enough to indicate is (far)
beyond the reach of the writer (e.g., Joshua 24:2; Jeremiah 2:20). In
the Mesha stela, as Jenni has observed,[31] the remoteness of time is
emphasized by contrast. That is, Atarot, in lines 10–11, is said to
have been inhabited by the Israelite tribe of Gad "from *'ôlām*,"
whereas in the parallel description, in lines 7–9, the possession of
Medebah by the northern Israelite kingdom is fixed in the much
more recent past of the writer, namely, of Omri and "his son."[32] In

other words, the phrase *m'lm* signifies that Gad had been in Atarot so long by the time of Mesha's conquest that if it had a point of origin, it could no longer be determined. If we choose to understand this as indicating that Mesha regarded the Gadites, for all practical purposes, as the aboriginal inhabitants of Atarot, we have to remember that the Israelites themselves, at the least the P/J(?) traditions, had a different opinion, for in Numbers 32:3, 34, Atarot is built by the tribe of Gad as part of its share of the invasion and conquest of the Transjordan, all within the Exodus-Wilderness-Conquest story.

Let us now summarize. Of the four possible passages that might espouse a view of aboriginal origins, none can definitively be dismissed. Yet in each, the aboriginal view is obscure and uncertain, and the passage can be interpreted in other ways. This, of course, does not deny that aboriginal views could have existed; but it does underscore how pervasive in the Hebrew Bible, if not in ancient Israel as a whole, was the opposite view, of origins as outsiders.

IV. Why Israel as Outsiders?

The question now before us is why this should be so. We could, of course, answer that it is because that's what, in fact, occurred in history: Israel, already formed into some kind of community, did enter Palestine largely violently from the outside. But stated so baldly, such an answer would find few if any serious adherents today. Archaeological work of recent years, while not ignoring the breaks, has made increasingly clear the cultural continuities between the Late Bronze II and Iron I periods in Palestine,[33] the chronological span within which the emergence of Israel should still be placed. And while this does not eliminate the possibility that outsiders entered into this emergence—indeed, even Mendenhall, Gottwald, and other "revolutionists" allow for them[34]—it does point to the strong role played by indigenous groups.

But debate about whether and how fully outsiders were involved in the actual historical process of Israel's emergence is not finally the point here.[35] For even if it could be settled, it would at most yield only part of the answer as to why the view of outside origins became dominant in biblical, and perhaps in Israelite, tradition. Remembering and recording history, we cannot forget, is never a neutral enterprise. It always tells us at least as much about the recorders as about the events, persons, and institutions it purports to record. So trying to explain the dominance of the outsider view in Israel must entail an effort to see just what values and problems in the society and culture of postemergent Israel—the Israel that coalesced into statehood—this view resonated with and so reinforced and resolved.

In this light, two features of the outsider view and its expression in the biblical corpus compel our attention. First is the assumption that the land that the Bible understands as home had to *become* Israel and, thus, that the community of Israel can exist apart from this land, as its experience in Egypt and the Wilderness demonstrates. Second is the sharp differentiation between Israel and other inhabitants of the land, whether understood as autochthonous or also as outsiders. In this perspective, as we have seen, Israel enters the land already as a distinctive social and cultural group—in other words, as a group formed outside of the contamination emanating from the other inhabitants of the land. Contamination, thus, is a basic fear, perhaps most pervasive in, but by no means exclusive to, the Deuteronomic corpus; and interestingly, that fear centers not really on the other inhabitants that the Bible recognizes as outsiders and new—Philistines, Aramaeans, etc.—but on those denominated as old, if not autochthonous, and often broadly categorized as Canaanites.[36]

Now stories of outside origins are not peculiar to ancient Israel. Whitelam has pointed to various examples,[37] of differing degrees of similarity to our Israelite case, from cultures beyond the ancient Near Eastern and Mediterranean worlds. Here, too, as he summarizes some of the scholarly discussion, the importance is not in the historical validity of the stories told—they may in comparison with other evidence often be largely inaccurate—but in the ways they are used in the communities that tell them to justify current social, political, and other public needs. What about such stories from Israel's own cultural environment? On present evidence, they appear to be rather few, but instructive. One set may be contained in the curious passage in Amos 9:7, where the prophet portrays to his audience the God of Israel rejecting the uniqueness of the Exodus: "'Are you not like the Ethiopians to me, O Israelites?' says Yahweh. '[If] I brought Israel up from the land of Egypt, did I not [also] the Philistines from Caphtor, and Aram from Qir?'" But does this passage really allow us to deduce that outsider stories like the Israelite Exodus were actually being told in Philistine or Aramaean towns?[38] Or is it more likely that we have here the prophet's projection of an Israelite view upon that of certain neighbors for polemical purposes—a kind of reverse ethnocentrism?[39]

A better-established example of outsider stories from regions close to Israel has recently been discussed by Moshe Weinfeld. In several articles,[40] he has drawn attention to the tales of the founding of cities and other settlements in the Greek and then the Roman world, exemplified most elaborately by Vergil's *Aeneid*. These tales, Weinfeld points out, typically focus on two stages of founding: the first involving the arrival of a hero, with family and associates, at a new place, coming usually from an old, established culture; the second describing the actual founding of a new settlement at this new place by the descendants of the hero, under the leadership of a founder (Greek *ktistes*). These two stages, which may sometimes be combined into one story and cast of characters, bear, as Weinfeld has demonstrated, a number of striking similarities to the biblical narratives of Abraham and family, the correlate of the first, heroic stage, and of Moses, Joshua, and the conquest, which echo the second, founding stage. Central to them, for example, is a deity who sends the hero and/or founder off and guides him in his journey, as well as the sanctuary established by the settlers to that deity in the new land.

What is interesting about all these stories, Greek and Roman and biblical, as Weinfeld underlines, is that they concern newcomers, new groups, formed in the wake of the Late Bronze–Iron I transition in the ancient Near Eastern and eastern Mediterranean world, when the old condominium of powers of the Late Bronze Age had broken up. And just like the biblical, the relationship of the Greek and Roman stories to other lines of evidence as to what really occurred is often problematic: new communities and community patterns there seem to have been, but the stories focus on them as made up of new populations arriving from outside, while the archaeological materials and other written sources suggest also, and sometimes even primarily, the continued presence of indigenous groups.[41]

These newcomer stories seem to be a new phenomenon, in the Near East and eastern Mediterranean—at least they are unattested earlier—matching the new communities that they seek to explain. But, significantly, they turn out to be the reverse of tales long told by various older cultures of the region about newcomers that they had to face. Perhaps the best known of such tales are the Mesopotamian, describing the Amorites, and the Egyptian, describing the "Asiatics," both from the early second millennium B.C.E.[42] In them the Amorites/Asiatics appear as uncouth denizens of the steppe or the sand, ignorant of and unable to share in the refinements of Mesopotamian or Egyptian urbanism, and regularly hostile to it. Now in describing Amorites or Asiatics in this way, the Mesopotamian and Egyptian tales, just like the biblical and classical outsider stories, oversimplify a complex reality, obscuring a whole range of interaction, indeed interpenetration, that the Asiatics and especially the Amorites shared with the native populations.[43] Equally to be noted, the two sets of stories, those by the new cultures and those by the old, mirror each other in values. For whereas for Mesopotamia and Egypt, the status of new and outsider assumed the connotation of barbarian, immoral, chaotic, for the biblical and classical, this same status became the mark and proof of a special divine chosenness—its very marginality vis-à-vis the older cultures constituting the basis for replacing them.

These stories, thus, are not reliable history in the sense of a documentary account, though authentic information bearing on the events they depict may well be preserved in them. But they have great historical value in their function as ethnic and cultural boundary markers, asserting for their respective authors that there really is an "us" over against a "them." The more sharply they affirm the boundary, the more we can be certain that the reality was muddier and more fragile. Indeed, we may say that the sharpness was there precisely to make sense of the reality—to affirm an "us" whose existence its members (at least those involved with the stories) felt was threatened, and that they may well have been hard put to distinguish from a host of "others."

Can we specify, then, the contexts in Israelite history when group identity was an issue and for which the outsider stories would have been useful? Whitelam[44] and others[45] point to the Babylonian Exile and return from exile, and there is no question of the importance of these periods, as we shall see. But if the scatter of dates and places noted above for our stories is correct, then there should be other contexts as well, from the pre-Exilic periods. To be frank, these are not easy to locate or to connect with the stories, given the lack of explicitness in the source material, largely biblical. But two examples may be suggestive of the larger picture. The first is the premonarchic period itself of Israel in Palestine, roughly the thirteenth through the eleventh centuries B.C.E. The growing inclination to label this the period of Israel's "emergence" is an acknowledgment that all the sources taken together, archaeological, biblical, and other textual sources, indicate that no simple entity

"Israel" existed then. There was only a fitful process of aggregation and differentiation of groups that from a later vantage could be claimed as Israelite because Israel came out of them. On the other hand, the Merenptah stela and the "archaic" biblical poetry—the part of it that may be premonarchic in date—point to the currency of the label "Israel" among one or more premonarchic groups and to their worship of Yahweh as a key integrating factor.[46] Clearly, whatever "Israel" there was/were premonarchically, it/they existed within a complex and shifting web of relationships to other Palestinian groups. A story of outside entrance into Palestine, then, to which the "archaic" poetry alludes, would have served as an important pole around which a collective identity could be segregated and consolidated. Recall particularly in some of these poems how the nodal issue of Yahweh worship is defined as the cult of a god who is an outsider to the land, and who enters it as a conquering warrior (Deuteronomy 33:2; Judges 5:4; and the archaic-like Habakkuk 3:3; Psalm 68:9, 18).

A second historical context for our outsider stories brings us down to the middle of the eighth century B.C.E., when the prophet Amos was active. As we have seen, he and the tradition gathered up in his book knew the Exodus-Wilderness-Conquest narrative, but in 9:7–8a—which seem to be genuine to him[47]—that narrative is used in reverse: the Exodus is not distinctive of Israel, and it and the rest of the story justify God's judgment on Israel for its sins, not His grant of security and prosperity.[48] Obviously, these assertions would have no point if the audience did not believe exactly the opposite, and Amos's need to use the story of outside origins to argue for coming judgment only underscores its importance to his Israelite listeners as a mark of their distinctive identity and destiny. Yet in denying their positive, self-satisfying interpretation of the story, Amos does not deny the story's social importance. He shows, rather, that this social importance consists in its negative side. In other words, what Amos is suggesting is that the story can be told not only from Exodus to Conquest, i.e., from disaster to triumph or, if you will, from marginality to centrality, but also the other way, from Conquest to Exodus, i.e., from triumph to disaster or centrality to marginality—that just as God let Israel come in from the outside cold to the promised land of Palestine, so He can take Israel back to the outside, in exile, to punish her. This, of course, is exactly what the Assyrians accomplished against Israel, after Amos. It is thus no accident that what in Amos is more an implicit suggestion becomes in his later fellow prophet Hosea, who lived through the first stage of the Assyrian advance, an explicit point.[49]

The premonarchic period and the eighth century of Amos and Hosea offer, then, two contexts in which the Israelite outsider story tradition was useful and productive. But if Whitelam and other scholars have looked to the Babylonian Exile and post-Exile as their context,[50] this is no accident, given, as we have discussed, that the outsider stories in the Bible are most fully attested for these periods. The situation, however, is more complicated and varied than Whitelam presents. For in Deuteronomy and the Deuteronomistic History, the Priestly writer, and Exilic and post-Exilic prophets and narratives, spanning the late seventh through the sixth and early fifth centuries B.C.E., we have actually several contexts in which our outsider tradition operated. Together these contexts comprise a historical record of pronounced vicissitudes for Judah/Israel: from King Josiah's major effort to break Judah out of its marginal political status and to reorganize the community on a scale of political and cultural integration that in some ways was unprecedented in Israelite history; through the rather quick, total collapse of this effort and return to marginality at the hands of Babylonian conquerors, and then, in the Babylonian exile, on to a marginality far worse than before Josiah; and finally to a release from exile and possibility for renewal, but in a situation fraught with uncertainty and tension. These violent swings of the historical pendulum proved good fodder for our outsider tradition. For Josiah's reforms, with which the Deuteronomistic corpus is to be associated in perhaps its decisive phase,[51] the prominence of the outsider tradition there should have provided the sharp distinction between "us"—the chosen conquerors of the land and founders in it of the worship of Yahweh: read Josiah and his reformers—and "them"—the "Canaanites" and other aboriginals of the land: read the rural religious and lay leadership whose power Josiah sought to break.[52] For a Judah conquered and then exiled by Babylonia, one can begin to understand the importance of a tradition that affirms that Israel's formation lay outside of the land and by implication, therefore, that the land, however important, was not indispensable to the very structure and existence of the community. Additionally, the "us"-"them" boundary of the tradition would have remained helpful, although now with different referents, in alien Babylonia, where the exiles, though allowed to remain together, felt at the mercy of their conqueror's might and culture.[53] And yet to these same exiles still in Babylonia and then returning to Palestine in the wake of Cyrus's victory, our outsider tradition appears to have given hope and legitimacy: hope that another Exodus from Egypt to a promised land was possible and would be successful,[54] and legitimacy—which is what Whitelam chooses to emphasize[55]—that those making the journey were indeed the chosen of God, with the rights to the land and its governance, not the ones who had stayed behind and not gone to Babylonia in the first place.

V. Conclusion

In sum, the biblical story tradition of Israel entering as outsiders to take over Palestine should not be dismissed historically, despite the buffeting it has taken in the wake of recent study of Israelite origins. If its historical value is at the most partial as a documentary witness on how Israel emerged in the land, it remains nevertheless vital for understanding how Israel came to understand its origins and itself, and came to deal with its present and future. The pervasiveness of this tradition in the Hebrew Bible, and the multiple historical contexts in which it seems to occur there, suggest a protean adaptability to the problems and crises that ancient Israel had to face. Particularly crucial in this regard, as we may now see, was the sense of marginality and contingency inherent in the tradition. For so viewed it came to mirror the actual course of Israel's history, offering hope that crises are never permanent, yet caution that triumph and security can never simply be taken for granted, and finally, a heightened awareness of the boundaries necessary for group survival. This explanatory power of our story tradition, it may be added, did not cease with the end of the biblical period. As the Passover Haggadah makes clear, Israel in a sense is always emerging from Egypt and the Wilderness to enter its promised land; the desire is only that it should stay there and live an exemplary and prosperous life.

NOTES

This paper went through several hearings and revisions prior to the Lehigh conference on "The Other in Jewish Thought and History," which forms the basis of the present volume. I had already worked out an outline and partial draft of it when I received Keith Whitelam's article on "Israel's

Traditions of Origin: Reclaiming the Land," *Journal for the Study of the Old Testament* 44 (1989): 19–42. To my delight, and partial dismay, I found that we had a very similar appreciation of the problem and the treatment of it. At the same time, as is not unexpected in a field that has always had more questions than its fragmentary and difficult sources allow clear answers, there were differences in some of our conceptions, analyses, and particular sources used. Because of these differences, I decided to proceed with my paper, and in what follows, will try to indicate at least the major differences as well as agreements between us.

1. For a concise guide to these three models and other issues of the Israelite settlement, see J. A. Callaway, "The Settlement in Canaan: The Period of the Judges," in *Ancient Israel: A Short History from Abraham to the Roman Destruction of the Temple*, ed. H. Shanks (Washington, D.C.: Biblical Archaeological Society, 1988), 53–84, 243–45. In more detail: I. Finkelstein, *The Archaeology of the Israelite Settlement* (Jerusalem: Israel Exploration Society, 1988), especially chap. 8; and N. P. Lemche, *Early Israel*, Supplements to Vetus Testamentum 37 (Leiden: Brill, 1985).

2. See, e.g., the dedication (vi) and the preface (xxv) of N. Gottwald, *The Tribes of Yahweh* (Maryknoll: Orbis, 1979).

3. E.g., N. P. Lemche, *Ancient Israel: A New History of Israelite Society*, Biblical Seminar (Sheffield: JSOT Press, 1988); R. B. Coote and K. Whitelam, *The Emergence of Early Israel in Historical Perspective*, Social World of Biblical Antiquity Series 5 (Sheffield: Almond, 1987).

4. Fernand Braudel, *On History* (Chicago: University of Chicago Press, 1980), 25–54, 64–82, especially 74.

5. As examples, see Lemche, *Ancient Israel*; Coote and Whitelam, *Emergence of Early Israel*; and L. E. Stager, "Archaeology of the Family in Ancient Israel," *Bulletin of the American Schools of Oriental Research* 260 (1985): 1–35.

6. For discussion of some of these texts, see Lemche, *Early Israel*, chap. 6. In the following survey, the analysis into the Pentateuchal sources is guided generally by R. E. Friedman, *Who Wrote the Bible?* (Englewood Cliffs, N.J.: Prentice Hall, 1987), 246–60, as one of the latest complete and most convenient statements. Friedman supposes the work of a final redactor, different from the authors of J, E, D, and P, who with some additions of his own put the Pentateuch essentially into its present form; for Friedman this redactor is Ezra. There are, of course, other treatments of the Pentateuchal sources, especially that of Martin Noth, translated as *A History of Pentateuchal Traditions* (Englewood Cliffs, N.J.: Prentice Hall, 1972), 17–19, 28–32, 35–36, with the translator Bernhard Anderson's own table on 262–76. These analyses differ in various details, as complete unanimity on the source attributions is impossible. The point here is to offer a reasonable statement and

general profile that would reflect the majority of biblical scholars, not to debate—ad nauseam—every detail.

7. The basic treatment of this poetry as archaic, that is, as premonarchic and United Monarchic in date, comes from W. F. Albright and his students, especially D. N. Freedman and F. M. Cross. See the joint dissertation of the latter two, "Studies in Ancient Yahwistic Poetry" (1950; Missoula, Mont.: Scholars Press, 1975), with an appendix updating their work. A more recent statement by Freedman tries to synthesize what the archaic poems might offer on the nature of early Israelite religion ("'Who Is Like Thee among the Gods?' The Religion of Early Israel," in *Ancient Israelite Religion: Essays in Honor of Frank Moore Cross*, ed. P .D. Miller, Jr., P. D. Hanson, and S. D. McBride [Philadelphia: Fortress, 1987], 315–35). It should be noted that while the above scholars focus on the poems in the Pentateuch and Judges, they have also recognized other archaic or archaic-like poems elsewhere in the Bible, like Psalms 29 or 77:17–21, or Habakkuk 3.

8. On these, see specifically E. Haglund, *Historical Motifs in the Psalms*, Coniectanea Biblica, Old Testament Series 23 (Uppsala: CWK Gleerup, 1984), 102–6.

9. See n. 7.

10. To be sure, the rest of the unstated story may not in all instances have included the straight Wilderness–march around Dead Sea–across Jordan conquest, but at least the Exodus episode supposes an outside entrance into Palestine.

11. That there are exceptions, with which the outsider story stands in express opposition, is the thesis of K. Whitelam ("Israel's Traditions of Origin: Reclaiming the Land," *Journal for the Study of the Old Testament* 44 [1989]: 29–36; see unnumbered note above), who builds partly on S. Japhet, "Conquest and Settlement in Chronicles," *Journal of Biblical Literature* 98 (1979): 205–18. The following represents an effort to raise doubts about particular elements of their discussions.

12. The word *'emōrî* should be read without the definite article, in parallel with the following *ḥittît* and in agreement with *'emōrî* in verse 45.

13. See the several notes about Jerusalem preserved in the Deuteronomistic History: Joshua 15:63; Judges 1:21; 2 Samuel 5:6–9.

14. Read here not the *qal wayyō'kal*, but the *hiphil wayya'akîlēhū*, perhaps even without the conjunction though with the 3 m.sg. suffix (unless the 3 m.sg. suffix on the parallel verb *yarkîbēhū* does double duty for both verbs). This reading as *hiphil* is in conformity with the ancient versions (cf. K. Elliger and W. Rudolph, eds., *Biblia Hebraica Stuttgartensia* [Stuttgart: Deutsche Bibelstiftung, 1977], ad loc.) and with the *hiphil* forms of the preceding and following parallel cola.

15. Whitelam, "Israel's Traditions of Origin," 38 n. 15.

16. E.g., A. D. H. Mayes, *Deuteronomy*, New Century Bible Commentary (Grand Rapids, Mich.: Eerdmans, 1981), 385.

17. In verse 12 this guidance is expressed by the verbal root *nḥh*, which elsewhere in the Bible can be used to refer to aspects of the Exodus-Wilderness-Conquest story: e.g., Exodus 15:13; Psalm 77:21; Nehemiah 9:12, 19.

18. So, e.g., Mayes, *Deuteronomy*, 385; and S. R. Driver, *Deuteronomy*, International Critical Commentary (1895; Edinburgh: Clark, 1965), 358.

19. Hosea 9:10; 2:16-17 (cf. the connection with the Egyptian Exodus in 2:17); Amos 5:25; Jeremiah 2:2-3; 31:2.

20. Her main presentation is listed above, my n. 11. I thank Norman Gottwald for bringing to my attention Japhet's work, which I had unfortunately overlooked in my first presentation of this paper.

21. It is hard to know how much time the genealogies in chaps. 2–8 are intended to cover, but they do not, at least for the most part, appear to reach the Babylonian Exile: cf., e.g., H. G. M. Williamson, *1 and 2 Chronicles*, New Century Bible Commentary (Grand Rapids, Mich.: Eerdmans, 1982), 2 and passim. Chap. 9 seems to set a terminus with the Babylonian Exile, and then goes on to list the names and genealogical affiliations of the returnees; note that verses 2–17 in this list are largely paralleled by Nehemiah 11:3–19 (Williamson, *1 and 2 Chronicles*, 87).

22. Japhet, "Conquest and Settlement in Chronicles," 213–15.

23. Ibid., 217–18.

24. Whitelam, "Israel's Traditions of Origin," 33.

25. Williamson, *1 and 2 Chronicles*, 27, 80–81, 217, 296–97.

26. Ibid., 81.

27. This term was introduced into the study of biblical history by A. Malamat, "The Proto-History of Israel: A Study in Method," in C. L. Meyers and M. O'Connor, eds., *The Word of the Lord Shall Go Forth: Essays in Honor of David Noel Freedman in Celebration of His Sixtieth Birthday* (Winona Lake, Ind.: American Schools of Oriental Research/Eisenbrauns, 1983), 303–13.

28. The above discussion builds on, but represents a different formulation from, the position of Williamson, *1 and 2 Chronicles*, 27–28, 217, and passim; and earlier, idem, *Israel in the Books of Chronicles* (Cambridge: Cambridge University Press, 1977), 64–66.

29. See text in, e.g., H. Donner and W. Rollig, *Kanaanäische und Aramäische Inschriften* (Wiesbaden: Harrassowitz), vol. 1[4] (1979), 33; vol. 2[3] (1973), 169, 174–75. I thank Dr. E. A. Knauf for reminding me of this passage in the present connection.

30. E. Jenni, "Das Wort *'olam* im Alten Testament," *Zeitschrift für die alttestamentliche Wissenschaft* 64/NF 23 (1952), 197–248; 65/NF 24 (1953), 1–34; idem, in *Theologisches Handwörterbuch zum Alten Testament*, vol. 2, ed. E. Jenni and C. Westermann (Munich: Kaiser, 1979), 228–43; H. D. Press, in G. J. Botterweck, et al., eds., *Theologisches Wörterbuch zum Alten Testament*, vol. 5 (Stuttgart: Kohlhammer, 1986),

1144–59; and J. Barr, *Biblical Words for Time*, Studies in Biblical Theology 33 (London: SCM Press, 1962), 117–20 and passim.

31. Jenni, *Zeitschrift* 64/NF 23, 207.
32. On the problem of identifying this son, see, e.g., Donner and Rollig, *Kanaanäische und Aramäische*, vol. 2³, 174.
33. Thus, while new settlement patterns, particularly in the central hill country, are increasingly clear for Iron I, continuities in material culture from the Late Bronze are also evident. See, e.g., W. G. Dever, *Recent Archaeological Discoveries and Biblical Research* (Seattle: University of Washington Press, 1990), chap. 2, especially 62–79; A. Mazar, *Archaeology of the Land of the Bible: 10,000–586 B.C.E.*, Anchor Bible Reference Library (New York: Doubleday, 1990), 328–55.
34. G. E. Mendenhall, "The Hebrew Conquest of Palestine," *Biblical Archaeologist* 25 (1962): 73, 79; Gottwald, *Tribes of Yahweh*, 453–59, 493–94, and passim.
35. What follows represents a development of some ideas in P. Machinist, "The Question of Distinctiveness in Ancient Israel: An Essay," in *Ah, Assyria . . . Studies in Assyrian History and Ancient Near Eastern Historiography Presented to Hayim Tadmor*, ed. M. Cogan and I. Eph'al, Scripta Hierosolymitana 33 (Jerusalem: Magnes, 1991), 196–212, especially 207–11.
36. E.g., in Leviticus 18, especially verses 24–30. Cf. various listings of these older inhabitants as in Genesis 15:18–21 and Deuteronomy 7:1, with discussion by T. Ishida, "The Structure and Historical Implications of the Lists of the Pre-Israelite Nations," *Biblica* 60 (1979): 461–90.
37. Whitelam, "Israel's Traditions of Origins," 22–27.
38. This conclusion is rather too quickly drawn, e.g., by M. Weinfeld, "The Pattern of the Israelite Settlement in Canaan," in *Congress Volume: Jerusalem 1986*, ed. J. A. Emerton, Supplements to Vetus Testamentum 40 (Leiden: Brill, 1988), 270; idem, "The Promise to the Patriarchs and Its Realization: An Analysis of Foundation Stories," in *Society and Economy in the Eastern Mediterranean (c. 1500-1000 B.C.E.)*, ed. M. Heltzer and E. Lipiński, Orientalia Lovaniensia Analecta 23 (Leuven: Uitgeverij Peeters, 1988), 366.
39. I thank my former student John Huddlestun for this insight.
40. See Weinfeld, "Pattern of Israelite Settlement," 270–83; idem, "Promise to the Patriarchs," 353–69. Weinfeld then offered his assessment of the historical reality behind these stories in "Historical Facts behind the Israelite Settlement Pattern," *Vetus Testamentum* 38 (1988): 324–32.
41. Among the large scholarly literature, see A. D. Snodgrass, *Dark Age of Greece* (Edinburgh: Edinburgh University Press, 1971); K. Lewartowski, *The Decline of the Mycenean Civilization: An Archaeological Study of Events in the Greek Mainland*, Archiwum Filologiczne 43 (Wrocław: Polska Akademia Nauk, 1989), especially 64–182; and F. Schachermeyr, *Die griechische Rückerinnerung im Lichte neuer Forschungen*, Öster-

reichische Akademie der Wissenschaften, Philos.-hist. Klasse, Sitzungs-
berichte 404 (Vienna: Österreichische Akademie der Wissenschaften,
1983).

42. There are, in addition, stories from the first millennium B.C.E., in Mesopotamia, about Aramaeans/Suteans. On these and the Amorite and
other stories of the late third and early second millennia B.C.E., see the
brief discussion with references in P. Machinist, "On Self-Consciousness
in Mesopotamia," in *The Origins and Diversity of Axial Age Civilizations*, ed. S. N. Eisenstadt (Albany: State University of New York Press,
1986), 188–89, 513–14 nn. 20–27. On the Egyptians and the "Asiatics,"
for which one well-known Egyptian term was '*3mw* (vocalized approximately as *Amu*), see the overview of R. Giveon, "Asiaten," in *Lexikon
der Agyptologie*, vol. 1, ed. W. Helck and E. Otto (Wiesbaden: Harrassowitz, 1975), 462–71.

43. See the discussions listed in the previous note.

44. Whitelam, "Israel's Traditions of Origin," 30–36.

45. E.g., the stimulating article by H. Tadmor, "The Origins of Israel as
Seen in the Exilic and Post-Exilic Ages," in *Le Origini di Israele: Roma,
10–11 Febbraio 1986* (Rome: Accademia Nazionale dei Lincei, 1987),
15–27.

46. Pace G. W. Ahlström (*Who Were the Israelites?* [Winona Lake, Ind.:
Eisenbrauns, 1986], especially chap. 40), who argues for the originally
purely geographical sense of "Israel," which he finds in the Merenptah
stela. See the defense and qualification of his position by D. Edelman
and the critical response to them both by A. F. Rainey in *Biblical
Archaeology Review* 17, 6 (November/December 1991): 60, 93; 18, 2
(March/April 1992): 21, 72–74.

47. For a defense of the genuineness of these verses, see my brief comments
in Machinist, "Question of Distinctiveness," 207–8 n. 37.

48. A similarly negative use of the Exodus story can be found in Amos
3:1–2. The problem is that 3:1b, which contains the reference to the
Exodus, is commonly understood to be a gloss dating after Amos: see,
e.g., H. W. Wolff, *Joel and Amos* (Hermeneia; Philadelphia: Fortress,
1977), 174–75 (a Deuteronomistic addition); and S. M. Paul, *Amos*
(Hermeneia; Minneapolis: Fortress, 1991), 100 (non-Deuteronomistic
addition). On the other hand, 3:2 does seem to be genuine to Amos, as
Wolff, Paul, and many other commentators agree. And here at least is
a critique of Israel's use of the covenant as a security blanket, not
unlike what we see in the genuine 9:7–8a, which do deal with the
Exodus.

49. See Hosea 11:5; also 2:14–17, which take the argument further by
bringing the destroyed Israel back to the Wilderness for a new regeneration and thus a new return to the land—a view that is then elaborated
in Exilic and post-Exilic uses of the outsider story, as discussed below.

50. See Whitelam, "Israel's Traditions of Origin," especially 31.

51. For one persuasive version of the connection between this corpus and the reign of Josiah, see Friedman, *Who Wrote the Bible?* chaps. 5–6.

52. Cf. especially the account of Josiah's reforms in 2 Kings 23 and the recent discussion of B. Halpern, who properly traces the policy of breaking the rural elites back to Hezekiah: "Jerusalem and the Lineages in the Seventh Century B.C.E.:   Kinship and the Rise of Individual Moral Liability," in *Law and Ideology in Monarchic Israel*, ed. B. Halpern and D. W. Hobson, JSOT Supplement Series 124 (Sheffield: Sheffield Academic Press, 1991), 11–107, especially 77–79.

53. Cf., e.g., Psalm 137 and the plaintive hope of the exilic editor that echoes through the last episode he reports in the Deuteronomistic History, 2 Kings 23:27–30.

54. This, of course, is one of the central themes of the Exilic prophet known to scholarship as the Second Isaiah: cf. the list of passages from him given above in the chapter, under section 2, number 5.

55. Whitelam, "Israel's Traditions of Origin," 30–36, as well as other scholars like Tadmor, "Origins of Israel." For Whitelam, thus, those who had stayed behind in Judah and avoided Babylonian Exile would have promoted the ideology of aboriginal origins.   Tadmor, while basically in agreement, has a more nuanced view of that ideology, seeing its focus on Israel's bond to the land, into which both indigenous and outside elements were absorbed (Tadmor, "Origins of Israel," 25–26).   Whitelam or, better, Tadmor may well be correct about the association of land/aboriginal views with the non-Exilic Judaeans. But as I have tried to explain, the biblical evidence, at least for aboriginal origins, is obscure and highly uncertain, crowded out as it is by the outsider view.

Chapter 3

The Philistine as Other: Biblical Rhetoric and Archaeological Reality

Trude Dothan and Robert L. Cohn

Archaeologists spend a good deal of time close to the ground, sometimes even under it. If they indulge in speculation, as all scientists must, it is closely connected with tangible material remains. Biblical scholars, on the other hand, try to reconstruct the ideology and ethos of ancient Israel by staying close to the biblical text and listening to its voice. This paper examines the Philistines from both perspectives. While the Philistines have long been known from the Bible as the Israelites' implacable enemy, only the modern archaeologist's spade has revealed the Philistines on their own terms, or at least through their own remains. After a survey of the major images through which biblical literature depicts the Philistines as Other, we turn to the archaeological reconstruction of the Philistine culture. Finally, we ask whether and why the two images converge or diverge.

The term *philistine* in English or *Philister* in German or *Philistin* in French has had an "otherly" existence in Judeo-Christian culture since the seventeenth century, and especially since Matthew Arnold, the English essayist and critic, gave it considerable currency in the nineteenth century. Any respectable dictionary will tell you that a philistine is "a person lacking in or smugly indifferent to culture, aesthetic refinement, etc."[1]

But this is not the philistine we want to talk about—although he is a blood relation to be sure. Our philistine is the Philistine of the biblical scribes, and we will examine him first as he was portrayed in the Bible and then as we see him emerge as a different kind of Other in our archaeological research.

The Biblical Image of the Philistines

There are over 250 references in the Bible to the Philistines, most of them in the books of 1–2 Samuel and those parts of it utilized in 1 Chronicles, though there are scattered references to the Philistines in the Pentateuch and the Prophets. Their appearance in the biblical account of the rise of monarchy in Israel thus accurately reflects their historical encounter with the Israelites during the eleventh and tenth centuries B.C.E. Biblical historiography depicts Philistine attacks on Israelite territory as a major impetus for the Israelite request to the prophet Samuel for a king: "Let the king rule over us and go out at our head and fight our battles" (1 Sam. 8:20). And the parallel between Philistine oppression and Egyptian slavery is made clear in God's words to Samuel about the king (Saul) he is to appoint: "He will deliver my people from the hands of the Philistines; for I have taken note of my people, their outcry has come to me" (1 Sam. 9:16; cf. Exod. 2:23–25).

In the biblical battles between the Israelites and the Philistines, the Philistines have the upper hand until the victories of David guarantee the supremacy of the united Israelite kingdom. Yet the disputes between them were mainly over border territories and control of major trade routes. For the most part, during the six hundred years of their coexistence in the country, the Philistines came, settled, and built their cities—Gaza, Ashdod, Ashkelon, Ekron, and Gath—and the Israelites did the same. Apparently, they each even adopted some aspects of the other's culture and religious practice. Both were eventually subdued by the Assyrians and exiled by the Babylonians.

Although biblical sources reveal no awareness of the modern archaeological finding that the Philistines settled the coastal regions of Canaan at about the same time that Israelite hegemony was crystallizing in the hill country, they do distinguish between the Philistines and those peoples identified as indigenous inhabitants of the land. The Philistines are not included in the formulaic list of the "seven nations of Canaan" to be dispossessed in the conquest (e.g., Deut. 7:1; Josh. 3:9). While biblical writers show no real knowledge of these "nations" (e.g., Canaanites, Perizzites, Hittites,

Amorites) and likely preserve traditional names to refer to pre-Israelite inhabitants,[2] Israelites had continuous historical interaction with Philistines. But is that interaction reflected in the biblical image of the Philistines?

On the one hand, biblical writers preserve certain historical memories of the "otherness" of the Philistines. The often-repeated epithet "uncircumcised," for instance, refers to the most notable physical mark distinguishing Philistines from Israelites. When Saul demands one hundred Philistine foreskins from David as a bride price for his daughter (1 Sam. 18:25), he identifies the symbol of Philistine potency that he is confident that David will never get his hands on. As well, another text sees the Philistines as the Other in industrial terms, for they are credited with a monopoly on iron (1 Sam. 13:19–21). This biblical allegation can be coordinated with archaeological evidence that the Philistines played an important role in introducing ironworking to Palestine.[3]

On the other hand, in biblical narratives in which Philistines figure prominently, their image is constructed less from historical memory than from ideological necessity. The Philistines represent an enemy that must be brought to bay, yet their defeat, unlike that of the Canaanites and their brethren, is not taken for granted. Rather, as a people firmly planted on the seacoast with formidable weapons and culture, the Philistines must be repeatedly challenged by the Israelites and their power contested and bested. The tales about the Philistines are designed to show that despite their power, it is no match for the power of YHWH and his people. The image of the Philistines as the threatening Other emerges from examining the representation of the Philistines in the three narratives in which they have a prominent voice: the Samson cycle (Judg. 13–16), the Ark narrative (1 Sam. 4–7), and the Goliath episode (1 Sam. 17).

In the Samson cycle the sexual power of the Philistines is paramount. Samson has a sexual hankering for the Other and so three times goes after Philistine women. In each case, however, the women prove to be the agents of Philistine men who want to defeat the Israelite hero. The woman of Timnah and Delilah both use their sexuality to unman him: to find the answer to his riddle and the secret of his strength. Though he becomes impotent in the houses of Philistine women, he is a wild man outside and accomplishes feats of strength that ultimately witness to YHWH's hand over the Philistines. But the image of the Philistines projected here reveals Israelite fears of seduction by the Other, of the horror of exogamy, and of the cracking of those internal codes and secrets that keep Israel distinct.

In the Ark narrative the power of the Philistine gods is challenged, ridiculed, and finally defeated. When the Philistines capture the Ark, YHWH's throne, their gods come into direct conflict with YHWH. The tale describes the panic in the Philistine cities as the Philistines come to recognize that the Ark has the power to topple their god, Dagon, and to spread a plague wherever it goes. Though benighted in their own worship, the Philistines can learn from experience and eventually realize that the Ark must be banished. If YHWH's people are too weak, he will fight his own battles even in enemy territory. Like the Egyptians, to whom the Philistine priests and diviners compare their own people (1 Sam. 6:6), the Philistines must acknowledge YHWH's power in order to stop the plague, and they do so by sending the Ark back to Israel. Here the Philistine Other is seen as powerless before Israel's God, yet capable of recognizing the truth.

The last narrative foregrounds in the person of Goliath the image of the Philistines' military power. His gigantic size, the biblically unusual description of his armor, and his ultimatum to Israel stamp him as the symbol of "otherly" force. Moreover, the use of animal rhetoric in reference to Goliath marks him as a nonhuman Other. When David defends his bold challenge of Goliath by reporting that "if a lion or a bear came and carried off an animal from the flock, I would go after it and fight it and rescue it from its mouth" (1 Sam. 17:34–35), he implicitly compares Goliath, "that uncircumcised Philistine" (1 Sam. 17:36), to an animal who has captured and terrorized Israel, the lamb of God. And Goliath's own question to David, "Am I a dog that you come against me with sticks?" (1 Sam. 17:43), reinforces the animal imagery. But Goliath's prowess and bravado are no match for David, who fights with YHWH's backing. Though depicting the Israelites as threatened by the military power of the Philistines, biblical writers claim that it cannot stand against YHWH.

Common to all three narratives is the motif of bodily mutilation. In the Samson story, the Philistines finally succeed in cutting Samson's hair, the symbol of his status as a Nazirite, and they proceed to gouge out his eyes (Judg. 16:21). In the Ark narrative, when the statue of Dagon falls before the Ark, its head and hands are severed (1 Sam. 5:4). Moreover, the Philistines are stricken with hemorrhoids. Finally, in the David cycle, David decapitates the dead Goliath to mark his victory (1 Sam. 17:51) and soon thereafter mutilates a horde of presumably dead Philistines in order to acquire two hundred foreskins for a bride price (1 Sam. 18:27). If, as the anthropologist Mary Douglas argues, a culture's concerns about the human body reflect its concerns about the social body, the repetition of this motif may be significant.[4] Among Israel's neighbors the Philistines stood out from the rest because of their culture, their economy, their weapons, and their physical appearance. The Philistines on the coastal plain and the Israelites in the hill country clashed repeatedly in the undefined border area between them. Might the attention to bodily extremities, the "borders" of the body, in some way reflect the fear of territorial invasion? When Samson's hair and the Philistines' foreskins are clipped, they are rendered impotent. Might this mutilation of the human body symbolize the effect of the incursion of the Other across the border? Surely David's acquiring two hundred Philistine foreskins shows his ability to violate Philistine territory at will. And the ultimate triumph of YHWH over the Philistines is represented by the decapitation of their chief god, Dagon, and their chief warrior, Goliath.

The Archaeological Image of the Philistines

When we turn from the biblical text to the field, from the measured words that we hear with our ears to the naked remains that we see with our eyes, quite a different image of the Philistines emerges.[5] The Philistines arrived in Canaan at the beginning of the twelfth century B.C.E., conquering the Canaanite cities and settling on their ruins. There is also evidence that they were mercenaries in Egyptian-controlled garrison towns at the end of the Late Bronze Age. This has been verified by finds at the cities of the Philistine Pentapolis: Ashdod, Ekron-Tell Miqne, Tell el-Safi (Gath), and Ashkelon. It is also known that the Philistines founded settlements on virgin soil, as in the case of Tell Qasile.

During its first period of settlement, Philistia extended from the Yarkon River to the northwestern Negev, and from the western slopes of Judea to the Mediterranean. From the end of the twelfth century through the eleventh century, the Philistine cities underwent expansion and consolidation. The fact that they built houses outside the city walls indicates that defense was not then a serious problem. Yet, at the same time, Philistine material culture was beginning to lose its uniqueness. The Aegean traditions they had brought with them were gradually being diluted by new cultural influences—especially Egyptian and Phoenician.

It is clear from layers of ash and debris that the Philistine cities were destroyed around the beginning of the tenth century, either by King David or by the Egyptian pharaoh Siamun. They were eventually rebuilt, sometimes on a smaller scale. The Philistines' wars with the Israelites had, apparently, been only a temporary setback (or perhaps the Bible exaggerates their submission to David). Later, with the weakening of the Israelites after the division of the united monarchy into two kingdoms, the Philistines again asserted themselves as a commercial power.

With the rise of Assyria as the controlling power over all of Palestine in the middle of the eighth century B.C.E., some of the Philistine cities enjoyed a renaissance. Ekron reached the acme of its economic growth and prosperity at the end of the eighth or beginning of the seventh century B.C.E. Ashdod still had its own king and maintained its cultural distinction until the sixth century. But by the end of the seventh century, Babylonian ascendancy over the ancient Near East was taking its toll in Philistia. There was a wave of conquest and mass deportations that changed the political, economic, and social landscape of the country forever. It is true that Gaza, Ashkelon, and Ashdod again became flourishing cities in the Persian, Hellenistic, and Roman periods, but their traditions were no longer even faintly Philistine.

Economic Life

The Philistines were capable farmers and artisans, as can be seen from the discovery of underground silos, flint sickle blades, millstones, oil presses, loomweights, and wine jars. But they were not only farmers. They were largely urban dwellers. Their cities were well planned and well fortified, and they traded their industrial products with the rest of the Mediterranean world.

It is clear from all of the Philistine cities excavated that the Philistines were sophisticated town planners. The earliest strata of their cities show that they were divided into different zones: industrial, public and cultic, and domestic. This general plan was more or less followed in succeeding levels as the cities expanded. Fortifications of the cities were built of thick layers of mudbrick.

In Tell Qasile, for example, the uppermost level pointed to the full development of a symmetrical city plan. The private dwellings consisted of inner courtyards, around which were kitchens with ovens, living quarters, and storerooms. That city residents carried on a bulk trade in wine or oil was evident from a storeroom filled with rows of large, heavy store jars. There was also evidence at Tell Qasile of textile dyeing.

Ashdod also had houses with courtyards, a citadel, cultic installations, a drainage system, a municipal garbage dump outside the city walls, and the most extensive pollers' workshop ever found in the region.

From documents discovered at Ugarit, it is apparent that Ashdod was famous as a trade center during the Late Bronze Age, known particularly for the production and export of royal purple cloth, dyed apparently at the nearby harbor town of Tel Mor from murex shells. The fact that the Philistines continued this commercial tradition could be seen from one of the storerooms inside the city gate: in addition to a hoard of iron carpenter's tools, it contained the bronze pans of a scale and a collection of thirty-one stone and metal weights, indicating extensive commercial links with Egypt, Mesopotamia, and the cities of the Phoenician coast.

At inland Ekron, the early Philistines established a large and well-fortified city with a flourishing ceramic industry. Near their square and horseshoe-shaped pottery kilns, there were large quantities of locally made Mycenaean-style pottery. They produced fine tableware as well as everyday kitchenware, such as cooking pots and large, undecorated *lekane* (large, deep bowls). In Ekron there was also evidence that the Philistines introduced pork and beef into the diet, in place of goat meat and mutton. By the seventh century B.C.E., Ekron was the largest producer of olive oil in the ancient Near East. They also had an area for metalworking. Furnaces for copper, bronze, and silver smelting were also found at Tell Qasile.

Philistine Cults and Cult Practices

According to the Bible, the Philistines worshipped male deities, the foremost among them being Dagon. But the fact is that Dagon was a Canaanite god, famous long before the Philistines even arrived in Canaan. It was only when they began to assimilate local customs in the eleventh century B.C.E. that they began to worship Dagon. Until then, they were faithful to the Great Mother goddess of the Aegean world.

The first well-defined Philistine temple was found at Tell Qasile. There was a series of three buildings, all built on the same spot. The first was from around 1150 B.C.E., the second and larger, from around 1100 B.C.E.; and the third, from after the Israelite destruction. These buildings provide a picture of Philistine religious practices, in one place, over a period of about two hundred years.

The temple was oriented more or less on an east-west axis, with an altar and storeroom for ritual objects facing in the direction of the sea. This temple provided the most complete picture of the nature of the Philistine cult. A *favissa*, or pit for burial of discarded religious artifacts, was discovered in an adjoining courtyard, and it contained an incredible assortment of pottery stands, ceremonial masks, libation vessels, and figurines, many of which preserved elements from the earlier stages of the culture of the Philistines.

The first two temples were similar for the most part, containing a "holy of holies" in the form of a plastered platform. The last structure was still close in form to the cult places of the Aegean, reminiscent of those in the sacred area of the Cypriot city of Kition. The ceiling of the large central sanctuary was supported by cedar columns, like Solomon's cedar beams in the Temple of Jerusalem. As in the previous buildings, there were benches along the walls for offerings. But what had once been an open courtyard around the temple was now enclosed by a wall, within which was a square stone base, apparently the foundation for a sacrificial altar. The bones of goats, sheep, camels, cattle, and even hippopotamuses, common in the marshes of the Yarkon Valley in the Early Iron Age, were found around the altar and provided clues to the nature of the Philistine rituals practiced here. Nearby there were also cylindrical cult stands with ritual bowls on them.

It is evident that the strong Aegean cult traditions of the Philistines had been compromised by other influences: the tall cylindrical cult stands were Canaanite; there was a pottery plaque representing the facade of an Egyptian-style temple, framing the fragmentary figures of two deities; the kernos rings with attached pomegranates, birds, and animal heads had parallels in both Canaan and the Aegean, as did a lion-shaped rhyton, or flagon, and a large libation vessel in the form of a woman, her breasts serving as spouts. A number of composite and multispouted vessels, however, seemed to be uniquely Philistine.

The identity of the deity worshipped in the Tell Qasile temples is not entirely clear although the large libation vessel in the form of a female may suggest that the central deity might have been an adaptation of the Great Mother of the Mycenaean world.

The Philistine cult findings in Ashdod were somewhat different. There a building was uncovered whose center was occupied by a rectangular courtyard, on the surface of which were the stone bases of two columns and a plastered brick structure that seemed to be an altar for offerings. In the two rooms adjoining the courtyard, there was a rich assortment of artistic and cultural artifacts. Nearby was a highly unusual platform of mud bricks with an outer apsidal outline and a rectangular depression within, its surface covered with the characteristic black and red painted decoration. No temples with apses were known in this period, yet its proximity to the small courtyard with the altar suggests a cultic connection. But the most interesting cultic artifact found at Ashdod was certainly the highly stylized image of a seated female Philistine deity merged into the form of a high-backed throne or chair, whom the excavators dubbed "Ashdoda."

Over the heavy white slip that covered the clay figurine were alternating zones of horizontal bands and elongated triangles, a stylization of the Egyptian lotus flower motif. And between the small clay breasts was a tiny painted lotus flower, in the form of a pendant, suspended from a painted necklace. The veneration of a seated deity continued, apparently, until the time of Sargon's conquest in 712 B.C.E. although eventually the merged deity showed a *male* cultic image rather than a female.

The most interesting feature of the temple at Ekron—an airy, elegant, and monumental palace—was a massively built "hearth room," dated to the twelfth century B.C.E. Only one other hearth had been found in Israel—at Tell Qasile. The hearth reflected the social structure and habits of everyday life in the Aegean (and Cypriot) palaces and shrines. Crude figurines in the Mycenaean tradition, whose spreading headdresses and birdlike faces prefigured the style of "Ashdoda," were also found at Ekron in great quantities.

The remains of a square cultic stand on wheels was also found at Ekron: three bronze wheels with eight spokes each, a design known from Cyprus in the twelfth century B.C.E. The shape, workmanship, and decorative repertoire of the cult stand are not dissimilar to those of the biblical *mechonot*, or laver stands, made for

Solomon's Temple in Jerusalem by Hiram, King of Tyre (see 1 Kings 7:27–30).

In all the Philistine temples excavated so far, there has been an abundance of artifacts linking cult with industry, a connection well known from the Aegean tradition.

Burial Customs

Although no burial grounds have been found in the major Philistine cities, several cemeteries that can be related to Philistine culture on the basis of tomb contents have been explored, at Tell Aitun in the Lachish area and at Azor near Jaffa. They show great diversity in the manner of interment. Two Philistine burial customs borrowed from foreign traditions are the use of anthropoid clay coffins, from the Egyptian, and rock-cut chamber tombs, from the Mycenaean. There is also evidence from Azor that cremation may have been employed.

It is possible to adduce some picture of Philistine mourning customs from the terra cotta female mourning figurines found in burial sites. The figurines show both hands on the top of the head or one hand on the head, the other on the breast. They are often attached to the rims of Philistine kraters and are similar to Aegean models.

Arts and Crafts

There are four different influences that can be discerned in the decoration of Philistine pottery: most important the Mycenaean, then the Cypriot, Egyptian, and local Canaanite. Although Philistine decoration began with monochrome ware, "classical" Philistine pottery was red and black bichrome on white slip, and most of the motifs—birds, fishes, spirals, concentric semicircles, chevrons, etc.—were borrowed from the Mycenaean IIIC:1b repertoire. At a later stage, the white slip gave way to red slip, hand burnished with dark brown decoration.

The Philistine potters were well versed in the Mycenaean tradition, but they were no mere copiers. The artistic style of their pottery is unique and reflects the cultural traditions acquired during their long migration from the Aegean to Canaan.

Types of Philistine pottery include the bowl, the krater, the stirrup jar, the *pyxis* (cosmetic box) and *amphoriskos* (vessel with globular body and cylindrical neck, ring base, and two horizontal handles on the shoulder), the three-handled jar, the strainer-spout, and the juglet with pinched-in girth.

Philistine cult vessels include ring kernoi, kernos bowls, zoomorphic vessels, rhyta, cup-bearing kraters, and terra cotta figurines.

Among other artifacts discovered were an ivory-handled iron knife; the elaborately incised ivory lid of a pyxis, depicting animal combat among a griffin, a lion, and two bulls, executed in thirteenth- and twelfth-century Aegean style; delicate finger rings, carefully crafted from extremely thin sheets of beaten gold; gold and faience jewelry; and goldleaf dagger pommels ornamented with delicate punctured decoration, in a technique reminiscent of Mycenaean metalsmiths.

Writing

There are few examples of Philistine inscriptions, yet it is inconceivable that they lacked a written language. Some scholars have suggested that the Deir Alla clay tablets, discovered in Transjordan by H. J. Franken in 1964, may represent Philistine script. At the Ashdod excavations were found two stamp seals with several cryptic signs, similar to the Deir Alla script and to the still-undeciphered Cypro-Mycenaean script of Cyprus in the Late Bronze Age. Nonetheless, the nature and alphabet of the Philistine language continues to be a subject of scholarly controversy.

Conclusion

The significance of the Philistines and the other Sea Peoples in the history of the ancient Near East stems from the role they played in furthering the connections between Canaan and the rest of the Mediterranean world and from the developed material culture they brought to the ancient Near East. They were accomplished architects and builders, highly artistic pottery makers, textile manufacturers, dyers, metalworkers, silver smelters, farmers, soldiers, and sophisticated urban planners. They played no small part in influencing the culture and political organization of their neighbors.

Yet from the biblical record, one would never guess their significance in the history of the ancient Near East. In the Bible, as we have seen, their image is primarily a negative one; the Philistines are the hated enemy that threatens Israelite territory and worships false gods. Is there any link, then, between the biblical representation of the Philistines as Other and the archaeological rehabilitation of this ancient people? Does the archaeological record aid us in understanding why biblical authors constructed their image of the Philistines as they did?

In an important way, the archaeological findings confirm the repeated biblical perception that the Philistines threatened Israelite hegemony. The material evidence that Philistia had a long history as an independent people helps us to understand why the Philistine Other assumed such importance in the biblical imagination. With its strong economic base and rich culture, able to absorb elements of Canaanite culture while retaining its own distinctiveness, Philistia represented an ongoing challenge to Israelite culture. At the same time, the Philistine world undoubtedly offered certain attractions to Israelites as both Samson's romantic and David's military flirtations (1 Sam. 27) with the Philistines suggest. Although David eventually defeated and confined the Philistines, their presence in the biblical text indicates a persistent fascination with this uncircumcised Other.

The Philistines' superior material culture may well have contributed, albeit indirectly, to Israel's effort to demonstrate its own superiority in the spiritual realm. That Samson with YHWH's spirit within him could destroy Dagon's temple, that the Ark of YHWH could topple the idol of Dagon, and that David with his slingshot and faith in YHWH could fell Goliath all testify to YHWH's power over religious and military symbols of Philistine strength. Just as in the Exodus narrative the plagues demonstrate YHWH's superiority to the culturally advanced Egyptians, so too do YHWH's plagues on the Philistines convince them that it is YHWH's power, not Dagon's, with which they must reckon (Judg. 6). The Philistines' great skill at smelting, revealed by archaeology, is mocked in Judges when they create golden hemorrhoids and mice as an indemnity to YHWH in the hope that he will lift the plague.

Although the biblical image of the Philistines is very different from the one that emerges from the archaeologist's spade, the material remains contribute a vision to the voice of the biblical text. Seeing with our own eyes the traces of the daily lives of the Philistines, we are better able to understand why this formidable foe became a principal Other in the Israelite worldview.

NOTES

1. Random House, 1987 ed., s.v. "Philistine."
2. See Niels Peter Lemche, *The Canaanites and Their Land*, Journal for the Study of the Old Testament Supplement Series 100 (Sheffield: Sheffield Academic Press, 1991), 84–100.
3. Trude Dothan and Seymour Gitin, "Ekron of the Philistines," *Biblical Archaeology Review* 16, 1 (1990): 33–35.
4. Or as Mary Douglas states it, "bodily control is an expression of social control" (*Natural Symbols* [1970; Harmondsworth: Penguin, 1978], 93–112, quotation at 99).
5. For additional information, see Trude Dothan, *The Philistines and Their Material Culture* (Jerusalem: Israeli Exploration Society, 1982); and Trude Dothan and Moshe Dothan, *People of the Sea: The Search for the Philistines* (New York: Macmillan, 1992).

Chapter 4

Before Israel: The Canaanites as Other in Biblical Tradition

Robert L. Cohn

Introduction

In their images of the Other, cultures reveal much about themselves.
If they are to develop and retain distinctive identities, cultures, like
individuals, must distinguish between "us" and "them." Recognition
of difference is crucial for the maintenance of a stable sense of self.
Cultural perceptions of difference often crystallize into group stereotypes, establishing vocabularies or images through which outsiders
are defined. Sometimes these images project onto the Other those
negative qualities that we fear in ourselves and want to deny; sometimes they depict those estimable features that we desperately want
to appropriate but fear we never will. Our stereotypes of the Other
thus give shape to our own anxieties and vulnerabilities. When
those anxieties are projected onto the Other, we can more easily
identify and control them.[1]

The Other is less an objective reality than a product of our own
naming and classification system. "Otherness," says Jonathan Z.
Smith, "is not a descriptive category, an artifact of the perception of
difference or commonality. . . . It is a political and linguistic project,
a matter of rhetoric and judgment."[2] That is, we create the Other
as a way of defining our cultural boundaries, as an exemplar of
everything that we do not want to or cannot be.

In the study of religions, the Other can serve as an important
interpretive category, for the rhetoric of inclusion and exclusion is
endemic to religious discourse: we believe this and you don't; we

observe this and you won't; we're saved and you're not. In the anachronistic Hebrew Scriptures, generations of Jews and their Israelite forebears constructed a continuous religious identity over against an equally constructed realm of idolatry. The book tells the story of a small people emerging in a world already divided into nations and attempting to develop and sustain its culture in the face of apostasy and exile. As the narrative plots the course of this people in history and the prophets dramatize its distinctiveness among the nations, a variety of other peoples come into view against whom Israel defines itself, including Edomites, Philistines, Assyrians, Babylonians, and Persians.

Among these, the Canaanites present a special challenge, for they are the nearest Other, identified in the Bible as the former inhabitants of the land that Israel came to occupy. While the geographically distant Other need not impinge upon cultural identity, the Other that is close by is always problematic.[3] In the Bible, the tradition that the Israelites began their existence as outsiders who migrated to the land of Canaan gave rise to an equally persistent need to explain why the supposedly indigenous peoples were dispossessed and how the people Israel came into being in contradistinction to them.[4] This need is addressed through the literary construction of the Canaanites as Other.

More precisely, two very different constructions of the Canaanites emerge. In the legal corpora of the Pentateuch and in the account of the conquest and settlement in Joshua and Judges, the Canaanites as a group are stigmatized as horrendous sinners, justly dispossessed. Yet in the narratively earlier tales of Israel's ancestors in Genesis, the natives of Canaan appear as decent hosts, sometimes even sympathetic individuals. They are not the object of polemical attacks either by the ancestors or by the narrator. Why, we are led to ask, should the Canaanites as Other be constructed in two different ways? What function do these constructions serve?

I want to argue that the image of the Canaanites in each case serves the needs of the particular myth of origins, or *arche*, in which that image is embedded.[5] An *arche* is never simply speculation about beginnings but is rather the means by which a group explains the conditions of its own emergence and shapes and fixes those events with which it claims continuity. The conquest *arche* and the ancestor *arche* described above make different sorts of claims about how Israel emerged and so portray the Canaanite Other as threatening in different ways. In the process of biblical compilation, these *arches* were brought together in sequence, but by focusing on the image of the Other, we can see them as separate and even competing accounts of Israelite identity.

Canaanites as Other in the Conquest *Arche*

Even before the military battle with the Canaanites is joined, their image looms large in the narratives of Israel's wandering in the wilderness. Prior to the ratification of the covenant at Mount Sinai in the book of Exodus, the voice of God warns that once in Canaan, the Israelites must not worship the gods of the indigenous peoples (Exod. 23:23–25). And the spies sent into Canaan report that the land is inhabited by Anakites, a race of giants, and Nephilim, hybrid divine-human beings.[6]   Although the Torah claims that Israelite identity was forged in the crucible of the wilderness, apart from civilization, a subtext thus defines Israel against the monstrous and threatening Other that awaits at the end of the journey.[7]

The Torah's legal codes indicate more directly the Canaanite behaviors that Israel must avoid. As Sander Gilman's work on the basic categories of stereotypes would lead us to expect, the Canaanites are portrayed as sexually and religiously perverse.[8]   The priestly code of Leviticus, for instance, opposes the practices and statutes of Canaan to those commanded by the God of Israel and particularly emphasizes the Canaanites' lack of sexual control. At the end of a lengthy list of statutes detailing forbidden sexual relationships, including incest, homosexuality, and bestiality, the divine voice concludes, "For all those abhorrent things were done by the people who were in the land before you, and the land became defiled" (Lev. 18:27). The book of Deuteronomy, for its part, emphasizes perverse Canaanite cultic practices such as child sacrifice, necromancy, resorting to soothsayers and diviners (Deut. 18:9–14), and worshipping images at hilltop fertility shrines (Deut. 12:2–3) and warns, "For anyone who does such things is abhorrent to the LORD, and it is because of these abhorrent things that the LORD your God is dispossessing them before you" (Deut. 18:12).

By representing the Canaanites stereotypically as people sunk in depravity, the biblical writers provide a moral justification for the conquest of their land by a just deity. Moreover, this depiction provides a rationale for the genocide of the Canaanites commanded in Deuteronomy (Deut. 7:1–2) and purportedly accomplished by Joshua (Josh. 10:40). However, alongside the claim that the

Canaanites were wiped out, that the Other ceased to be, another tradition insists that the Canaanites were not wholly destroyed, but continued to live among the Israelites in all of the major areas of the country (Josh. 15:63–17:12; Judg. 1). According to the Deuteronomist, the former inhabitants remained in order to "test Israel," to see whether or not Israel would obey God's commandments and survive or fall into the practices of the Canaanites (Judg. 3:1–4) and be destroyed.

So the Canaanites fulfill two different, seemingly contradictory functions in the ideology of the conquest *arche*. They are the Other "before," the antithesis of Israel, the paradigm of pollution, that had to be swept away if the land were to be reclaimed by God for his people Israel. But they are also the Other "within," not wholly destroyed but still living among the Israelites. As survivors, they witness the incompleteness of the conquest as a consequence of the Israelites' disobedience while tempting Israel to forsake its God and thereby lose its identity. Significantly, in early Christian thought the Jews fulfill the same paradoxical functions.[9] On the one hand, the Church claimed to displace and supersede the old Israel whose legalism and hypocrisy God abhorred. On the other hand, the survival of the Jews witnessed to the incompleteness of the Church's triumph and tempted good Christians to "judaize." In both cases the Other, whose dispossession and disappearance ideology demanded, remained, nonetheless, alive and the object of polemical attack. Sander Gilman notes that "the group defining the Other has projected its insecurities concerning its potential loss of power onto the world in the shape of that Other through which it imagines itself threatened."[10] Just so, the biblical writers understood Israel's existence to be fragile, based on a conditional covenant with a jealous God. They thus shaped the Canaanites as the Other whose sin justified their dispossession, but who also threatened to take Israel down the same path. As outsiders who became insiders, the Israelites in the conquest *arche* seem never quite secure in their land. The Canaanites as the insiders who became outsiders serve as the symbol of that insecurity.

Canaanites as Other in the Ancestor *Arche*

In the book of Genesis, the image of the Canaanites is altogether different. The natives are not depicted as perverse either morally or culticly. With the exception of the sinful citizens of Sodom and

Gomorrah, which the text places outside the land of Canaan (Gen. 13:12), the indigenous inhabitants of Canaan are shown to be pretty decent folks. If anything, they often occupy the moral high ground as victims of the subterfuge of the fathers.

The Canaanites in Genesis do not worship idols, build pillars, consult sorcerers, or engage in any of the other nefarious practices attributed to them in the conquest *arche*. Moreover, the narrative of Genesis entirely lacks the polemic against the Canaanite religious world found elsewhere in the Bible. The ancestors themselves do not rail against idolatry as Moses and Joshua do, and native practice receives no special attention. As Yehezkel Kaufmann, the Israeli biblical scholar, noted long ago, in the biblical representation of what he called the "patriarchal age," "there is no *religious* contrast between the patriarchs and their surroundings."[11] Abram accepts without flinching a blessing from King Melchizedek of Salem in the name of the king's god, El Elyon, and the only idols mentioned do not belong to the natives but to the matriarch Rachel, who steals her father's *terafim* (domestic images) when she leaves home with Jacob. The rabbis, sensing a problem in this portrayal of the ancestors, formulated in the midrash a more conflictual picture of the relationship of patriarchs to those around them. Abraham the first Hebrew, for instance, is depicted as destroying the idols in his father's house. And Sarah, his wife, is said to have sent Ishmael away because she saw him worshipping idols (Rashi on Gen. 21:9). But the biblical text is quite innocent of any such motifs.

Seeking to account for this silence about Canaanite religious difference, Kaufmann argued that it is not that the Canaanites were not pagans, but rather that the ancestors were not monotheists. Monotheism, in Kaufmann's reconstruction of the history of Israelite religion, begins with Moses, four hundred years after the patriarchal age. Only then did the idea of the jealous God emerge and only then did the polemic against idolatry begin. That both are absent from Genesis, Kaufmann argues, shows that the texts dimly reflect the religious reality of the pre-Mosaic period when the religion of the clans whose descendants were to become Israel really was much like that of the Canaanites.[12]

But Kaufmann's historical explanation for the lack of religious contrast presupposes a number of assumptions about the reliability of oral transmission and the dating of texts upon which recent scholarship casts doubt. Surely the ancestor legends in Genesis were shaped, if not created, by Israelites well after the attack on idolatry became a hallmark of Israelite religion. Surely their

authors could have depicted the Canaanites as Other in the stereotypical fashion we have seen in the conquest *arche*. That they did
not do so bespeaks an ideological motivation different from that
reflected in the image of the Canaanites as sexually and culticly
depraved. To ascertain that motivation, we must delineate the ways
in which the otherness of the Canaanites *is* expressed in Genesis.

Genesis depicts the fathers (or patriarchs) coming into the land
of Canaan with their wives and retinues and wandering with their
herds unimpeded. They build altars to their god and pitch their
tents outside the main cities. On several occasions the narrator
remarks, "The Canaanites were then in the land" (e.g., 12:6; 13:7),
reminding us whose land this was at that time and suggesting that
in the author's own time they were no longer there.[13]

These early gentle reminders establish the basis for the relationship between natives and ancestors: the natives have power and the
ancestors have none. The power relationship between them is just
the reverse of what it was in the conquest *arche*. Although God
repeatedly promises the land to the descendants of Abraham, for the
present, the Canaanites control the land on which the ancestors
must tread softly. Confrontations between the ancestors and the
locals are few and the accounts of them underscore the fragile
balance that exists between the two sides.[14]

The difference between the ancestors and the Canaanites in
Genesis is a matter of family and destiny. For the present the
Canaanites are the landowners, the rulers, the entrenched, while the
ancestors are the aliens, the wanderers, the endangered. Yet the
ancestors carry the blessing of God, which will make of their
descendants a great nation in this land. The issue of Genesis is how
God's promise to Abraham can be sustained and transmitted to his
descendants without being derailed or defeated by the *power* of the
Other. Can the family of Abraham prosper in the land of Canaan
but remain separate from its inhabitants?

These questions are implicit in a number of episodes that depict
encounters between the ancestors and the locals. In all of these
encounters, the peoples of Canaan exercise sexual or economic power
over the ancestors that threatens to submerge the chosen line and
end its separate identity.[15] Yet the outcome of each episode is the
rejection of alliances with the natives through marriage or property.
The combined forces of divine intervention and the ancestral sense
of destiny keep the Other at bay and permit the family of Abraham
to survive and prosper in the land promised to them.[16]

The wife-sister episodes are one illustration of the narrative's rejection of sexual compromise with the Other. Three times a patriarch, fearing for his own life in a new territory, has his wife claim that she is his sister, in order to permit the local king to take her for his pleasure without having to kill her husband. In return for his "sister," the king rewards the patriarch with possessions. In two versions of this type-scene, Abraham hands over Sarah in this way, and on one occasion, Isaac attempts the same ruse with Rebekah. What lies behind this literary topos, according to the anthropologist Julian Pitt-Rivers, is the ancient Mediterranean practice of using women to establish a relationship between an alien and a host population, which he calls "sexual hospitality."[17] A host might incorporate a guest into his household by offering his daughter to him, or a guest might establish a relationship as a client of a settled clan by offering his women to the clan in return for protection or grazing rights. In this reading, then, the patriarch uses his wife to forge a bond with the local population so that he and his retinue may dwell in the land unmolested.[18]

The aim of the biblical episodes, however, is to reject "sexual hospitality" as an acceptable arrangement for the ancestors who must dwell apart from the Other. Taken in their narrative order, the three episodes show increasingly greater moral sensitivity to the fate of the matriarch and the cause of the patriarch's enrichment. In the first episode, Abram, forced to leave Canaan for Egypt because of a famine, prepares his wife, whom the narrator notes is sixty-five years old, with these instructions: "Look, I know that you are a good-looking woman, and that if the Egyptians see you and say, 'that's his wife,' they will kill me and let you live. Please say that you are my sister, that it may go well with me because of you, and that I may remain alive thanks to you" (Gen. 12:12). Sarai is taken into Pharaoh's "house" (*beit par'oh*) (12:15) and Abram is rewarded with flocks, herds, and slaves.[19] But though Abram has no reported moral compunction about this arrangement, God reacts by plaguing Pharaoh and his household. Pharaoh in turn furiously reprimands Abram for his lie, apparently having figured out the cause of the plagues, and sends him, his wife, and his riches packing. This expulsion not only foreshadows the expulsion by a later pharaoh of Abram's descendants in the "exodus" but also shows how divine intervention got the foremother of Israel out of an alien bed and prevented permanent entanglement of the ancestors in the local scene.[20]

In the second episode, separated from the first by twenty-five years in narrated time and eight biblical chapters, Abraham tries the same ruse on a different king, Abimelech of Gerar. This version seems to be a kind of midrash on the first, for the author is at pains to make it clear that Sarah was not really bedded by the king and that Abraham didn't really tell a lie. God comes to Abimelech in a dream and warns him that he has taken a prophet's wife. And Abraham, when the king challenges his lie, claims that Sarah is indeed his half-sister (20:12). However lame this explanation may seem—the narrator offers no independent confirmation of it—the outcome is that Abraham is given land and silver *after* Sarah is returned. Abraham is not rewarded as a result of his lie, as in the first version, but to compensate him for the indignity caused to Sarah. This time Sarah has not been sexually compromised and Abraham not politically compromised; he can keep his wife (Abimelech, with more than a little irony, calls Abraham Sarah's "brother" [20:16]) and still dwell peacefully on the land.

In the third version Isaac, Abraham's son, forbidden by God to leave the land of Canaan, again resorts in a time of famine to King Abimelech. Like his father in his day, Isaac tells the locals that his wife, Rebekah, is his sister. But this time the matriarch never even enters the palace. Instead Abimelech sees Isaac *meṣaḥek*—"sporting with" (JPS) or "fondling" (RSV)—Rebekah when he looks out the window. Shocked by this public display of affection between brother and sister, the king quickly figures that Rebekah is Isaac's wife and orders his people not to molest either of them. And then it is the God, not the king, who rewards Isaac with plentiful crops, flocks, herds, and wealth, so that the locals envy him. Again, the chosen family remains unmixed with foreigners despite the sexual hospitality in which the patriarchs are willing to engage in return for peace and pasture.

The three versions thus chart an increasing resistance to the custom of sexual hospitality and increasing clarity that God, not sexual exchange with local kings, brings about the enrichment of the chosen family. Far from being sexually depraved, these local kings are shown to be morally responsible. Though fearing for their lives, the patriarchs remain alive even after their ruses are discovered. The stories make the claim that the patriarchs should not have exchanged and did not need to exchange their women for land and flocks and herds; if they are to beget the chosen people, not human nature but divine nurture will see to it.

If Genesis rejects temporary sexual alliances with the Canaanites, it rejects intermarriage all the more.[21] A second set of episodes portrays the ancestors refusing to marry any but their own kin. Only by strict endogamy, Genesis claims, could Israel develop *in* the land of Canaan but not *of* it, attached to its geography but not to its people.

The issue is first joined in the case of Abraham's son Isaac. In order to prevent him from marrying a Canaanite and, at the same time, to guarantee that he does not leave the promised land, Abraham charges his servant to return to his homeland and get a wife for his son. Fortuitously, as the tale has it, back in the old country the servant encounters Abraham's great-niece, Rebekah, who gladly returns to Canaan with him. Isaac's brother Ishmael, on the other hand, son of the Egyptian maidservant Hagar, weds an Egyptian and thereby expresses through marriage his exclusion from the blessed line.

In the next generation, Isaac's twin sons, Esau and Jacob, symbolically choose their destinies through their choices of brides. Esau, it is reported, marries two Hittite women, prompting his mother's woeful complaint: "I am disgusted with my life because of the Hittite women. If Jacob marries a Hittite woman like these, from among the women of the land, why should I go on living?" (27:46). Isaac then sends Jacob back again to Rebekah's brother Laban to find a wife, admonishing him, "You shall not take a wife from among the Canaanite women" (28:1). Thus Jacob marries Laban's two daughters, his first cousins, while Esau, seeking to reingratiate himself in his parents' eyes, marries a daughter of his uncle Ishmael. But this choice only confirms his separation from the chosen line, because the line of Ishmael has already been rejected. Through their marriages, then, the twins cement their destinies.[22] Kinship is here used as a symbolic structure through which the divine promises flow to the right people and admixture with the people of the land is avoided.

The threat of the Other to ancestral endogamy reaches a climax in the episode of the rape of Dinah. Here the violation of Jacob's daughter by Shechem, son of the Hivite chieftain Hamor, sets off a series of reactions that breaks the peace between the chosen ancestors and the natives and illustrates the ultimate impossibility of assimilation.[23] The introductory exposition reports both Shechem's rape of Dinah and his subsequent love for her (Gen. 34:2-3). When Shechem orders his father, Hamor, to "Get me this girl as a wife"

(v. 4), Hamor uses the occasion to make a broader offer. In his public invitation Hamor sees intermarriage as the prerequisite to economic integration of the landless family of Jacob into Canaanite society: "Intermarry with us: give your daughters to us, and take our daughters for yourselves. You will dwell among us, and the land will be open before you; settle, move about, and acquire holdings in it" (34:9–10). Jacob's sons, Dinah's brothers, though furious about their sister's rape, guilefully (the narrator reports) agree to the marriage and the merger. But they set one condition: all of the male Hivites must be circumcised, "that you will become like us" (v. 15). The Hivites consent but lose more than their foreskins. Once they are disabled by the circumcision, Simeon and Levi, two of the brothers, massacre them all and retake their sister and capture as well the Hivite women, children, and wealth. When Jacob complains to his sons that they have broken the peace between him and the natives and made him easy prey, they answer, "Should our sister be treated like a whore?"

This provocative story lends itself to many readings, but several elements of the story bear on my topic. First, by their vengeance, the sons of Jacob reject not only the offer of intermarriage but also the chance to settle down in the land and acquire property. Although they ostensibly act to punish a rapist and preserve their honor, the brothers' action also expresses the recognition that exchange of women would lead to economic and political subordination to the Canaanites. Second, by insisting that not even circumcision can domesticate the Other, the story underscores the necessity of remaining distinct from the natives. The cultural boundary cannot be crossed. Third, by granting the reader but not Jacob's sons privileged access to a meeting of the Hivites, the author permits us to see that the real motivation of the natives is sinister. At this assembly Shechem and his father urge their men to become circumcised by promising, "Their cattle and substance and all their beasts will be ours, if we only agree to their terms, so that they will settle among us" (v. 23). Thus, the story claims that the aim of the Other is to swallow up Jacob and family, to submerge them in their own fiefdom.

Pitt-Rivers points out that this tale can be understood as the conclusion to the wife-sister stories that we have previously examined. Those stories imply that if the matriarch was really a sister and not a wife, she could legitimately be given away for the sake of establishing a political alliance. But in the Dinah story, Dinah is

really a sister and only a sister, and yet she cannot be given away at
all.[24] Honor and divine blessing demand endogamy, sexual separation from the people of the land.

As in the case of the wife-sister stories, it is not a matter of the
immorality of the Other. The initial rape by Shechem is more than
balanced by the capture of all the women of the town by Simeon and
Levi.[25] And though we may be skeptical that a rapist can turn
lover, the narrator, at least, seems not to be. Moreover, the reader-
elevated perspective from which the episode is written allows us to
see that both sides conceal more than they reveal in their negotiations with each other. All in all, the portrayal of the Canaanites
here is as morally nuanced as that of the brothers. The problem
from the Israelite perspective of the narrator is not that this Other
is inherently wicked, but that any sexual accommodation will lead to
the end of Israel's separate identity, its national suicide.

A final case that proves the point is that of Judah, whose
physical separation from his brothers following their conspiracy
against Joseph ("Judah went down from his brothers" [Gen. 38:1])
sets the stage for his marriage to a Canaanite woman, a marriage
that results in disaster.[26] Of the three sons who issue from this
union, the two eldest, Er and Onan, die of unnatural causes at God's
hand, while the fate of the third, Shelah, remains unresolved within
Genesis. Marriage with a Canaanite woman has resulted only in
death. When the unnamed Canaanite wife herself dies, Judah's
twice-widowed daughter-in-law, Tamar, determined to carry on the
family line, takes matters into her own hands. By posing as a
whore, Tamar turns a quick trick with the sex-starved, newly
widowed Judah and later forces him to acknowledge her righteous-
ness and his responsibility for her resulting pregnancy. Tamar,
whom Judah saw as the femme fatale to be blamed for his older
sons' deaths, instead becomes the agent of his redemption. Without
her intervention, the tale implies, Judah's marriage to a Canaanite
would have ended his family line.

Although the rejection of economic ties with the Canaanites is
implied in several of the sex and marriage encounters, a third set of
episodes focuses on the economic independence of the ancestors.
Genesis is eager to demonstrate that the patriarchs, though dwelling
in the land of Canaan, owe nothing to the Canaanites. Both
Abraham and Jacob buy property from local land barons, and the
texts carefully reveal the amount paid in both cases to underscore
that the land was purchased, not taken or given. Indeed, in the case

of Abraham's purchase of the cave of Machpelah for the burial of his wife, the story has Abraham protesting when Ephron the Hittite offers him the property as a gift: "Let me pay the price of the land; accept it from me, that I may bury my dead there," Abraham insists. Ephron, like a true Middle Eastern bargainer, replies, "A piece of land worth four hundred shekels of silver—what is that between you and me? Go and bury your dead." Having not so subtly revealed the price of the land, Ephron accepts payment from Abraham, exorbitant payment by the way, for the cave and the field around it. And the narrator also assures us that all of the Hittites who entered the town witnessed the transaction. By implication the tale thus insists that the ancestors' claim on the land derives not from the sufferance of the locals but from a fully legal purchase validated by the locals themselves.

A similar claim is suggested by Abram's refusal to accept booty from the king of Sodom after the battle against the kings of the East. In the form of an oath, Abram *renounces* all debt to the king: "I swear to YHWH, El Elyon, creator of heaven and earth: I will not take so much as a thread or sandal strap of what is yours; you shall not say, 'It is I who made Abram rich'" (Gen. 14:22–23). Similar too are the mutual oaths sworn by both Abraham and Isaac with Abimelech. In the first, to warrant that a well that Abimelech's servants had seized had really been dug by Abraham, the patriarch gives the king seven ewes and they both swear that the well is Abraham's (21:25–31). In the second, when Isaac redigs the wells at the same site, Isaac and Abimelech sign a mutual nonaggression pact that recognizes Isaac's claim to the wells (26:17–33). In both cases, not only have the locals acknowledged by oath the ancestors' claims on particular territories, but they also have retreated before them. "We now plainly see that YHWH has been with you," Abimelech's servants declare (26:28). The ancestors stake out their own connection with the land of Canaan, while the peoples of the land, in turn, though holding the balance of power for the present, permit them a wide berth and even recognize the blessing of God within them.

Conclusion

The image of the Canaanites in the ancestor *arche*, we have seen, is startlingly different from their image in the conquest *arche*. In the latter, it is the moral depravity and cultic abominations of the natives that both justify their displacement and explain their survival as a test for Israel. In contrast, the otherness of the Canaanites in Genesis is expressed by their potential sexual and economic power over the ancestors, which must be rejected at all costs. The ancestors forge no lasting bonds of kinship or alliance with the Canaanites despite their apparent moral and religious decency.

What I have tried to show is that neither *arche*, neither story of how the outsider Israelites encountered the natives, preserves historical memories of actual Canaanites but rather each presents its own construction of the Other. For each story, the names of no-longer-surviving peoples—Canaanites, Amorites, Hittites, Hivites, etc.—served as signifiers to carry the image of the Other that defined Israel's cultural boundary. To understand why the conquest and the ancestor traditions constructed Israel's cultural boundary differently, we must look more closely at the purpose of the two traditions.

In this regard I find a recent article by Moshe Weinfeld most suggestive.[27] Weinfeld compares the origin traditions in the Bible with those of the *Aeneid* and finds that in both, a chronological gap separates the tale of the ancestor who leaves a great civilization for a new land with a divine promise from the tale of the fulfillment of that promise by the descendants who settle the new land. These two parts of the genre that he calls the "foundation story" depict the wandering ancestor, on the one hand, and the establishment of law and order, on the other.

I want to extend Weinfeld's argument by suggesting that the two foundation stories represent two rather different kinds of myth even though, in the process of compiling the Bible, the compilers have brought them together in sequence. The ancestor *arche* is a *family* myth claiming that all Israel descended from one man and woman, Abraham and Sarah, by means of the careful preservation of endogamy. Kinship is the structure that explains how all Israel descends from one family that the Other threatens simply by being there.[28] To protect the family line and yet to stake out a claim to the promised land, the ancestors must steer clear of Canaanite cities, not intermarry with the natives, and reject economic integration. The basic decency of Pharaoh, Abimelech, and even the rapist Shechem shows how intermarriage, which might be convenient and profitable, must be resisted nonetheless if a holy, separate people is to come into existence in the promised land.

The conquest tradition, on the other hand, represents a *political* myth. The covenant established at Mount Sinai, which links the conquest of the land of Canaan to Israel's observance of God's commandments, presupposes that Israel is *not* a family but a collection of people who must be legally bound together if they are to constitute a nation. Families do not need covenants; they are bound by kinship. Accordingly, throughout the covenant and conquest stories the Canaanites are depicted as threatening the *political* order. Their cultic abominations, represented by both the false means and the false objects of their worship, strike at the bond between God and Israel established by the covenant. Their moral depravity, represented by their practice of forbidden sexual relationships, strikes at the basis of the social order established by the covenant. The Other thus threatens the very basis of national life, the covenant that binds Israel to God and Israelites to each other.

The two images of the Canaanites as Other thus reflect two different constructions of Israelite identity: Israel as a family of outsiders secure in God's promise and Israel as a nation of insiders insecure in God's covenant. In the first case, the Canaanites threaten to derail the promise by absorbing the family. In the second, they threaten to derail the covenant by tempting the nation into sin. As the Other before Israel and the Other within Israel, the old nations of Canaan remained alive in the biblical imagination to define the border of vulnerability.

NOTES

1. See Sander Gilman, *Difference and Pathology: Stereotypes of Sexuality, Race, and Madness* (Ithaca and London: Cornell University Press, 1985), 13–29; and idem, *Jewish Self-Hatred: Anti-Semitism and the Hidden Language of the Jews* (Baltimore and London: Johns Hopkins University Press, 1986), 1–21.
2. Jonathan Z. Smith, "What a Difference a Difference Makes," in *"To See Ourselves as Others See Us": Christians, Jews, "Others" in Late Antiquity,* ed. Jacob Neusner and Ernest S. Frerichs (Chico, Calif.: Scholars Press, 1985), 46.
3. Ibid., 5.
4. For the biblical idea of Israel as outsider, see Peter Machinist, "The Question of Distinctiveness in Ancient Israel: An Essay," in *Ah, Assyria*

. . . *Studies in Assyrian History and Ancient Near Eastern Historiography Presented to Hayim Tadmor*, ed. Mordechai Cogan and Israel Eph'al, Scripta Hiersolymitana 33 (Jerusalem: Magnes, 1991), 208–9. See also Peter Machinist in this volume (chap. 2).

5. I borrow the term *arche* and its usage in this sense from Marilyn Waldman, "Playing the Ownly Game in Town: The Study of Islam and the Idol of Origins; or, Can Historians Be Neutral about Change?" (paper presented at conference on "Religion and History," Prouts Neck, Maine, October 1991), 1–5.

6. For a study of the way in which the Other is seen as monstrous in fifth-century Greece, see Page duBois, *Centaurs and Amazons* (Ann Arbor: University of Michigan Press, 1982).

7. In *The Shape of Sacred Space: Four Biblical Studies* (Chico, Calif.: Scholars Press, 1981), 7–23, I examine the wilderness period in terms of Victor Turner's notion of "liminality" as a time and space between Egypt and Canaan.

8. See Sander Gilman's analysis of "Stereotypes of Sexuality," *Difference and Pathology*, 37–127.

9. Jon Levenson explores the parallel between anti-Canaanite polemic in the Hebrew Bible and Jew hatred in the New Testament in "Is There a Counterpart in the Hebrew Bible to New Testament Antisemitism?" *Journal of Ecumenical Studies* 22, 2 (1985): 242–60. He does not, however, deal with both Testaments' effort to explain the survival of the supposedly dispossessed people. The parallel paradox deserves further study.

10. Gilman, *Jewish Self-Hatred*, 3.

11. See Yehezkel Kaufmann, *The Religion of Israel*, trans. and abridged by Moshe Greenberg (Chicago and London: University of Chicago Press, 1960), 222.

12. Ibid., 221–31.

13. Interestingly, individual natives who encounter the ancestors are never identified as Canaanites but rather by other gentilics: Mamre the Amorite, Ephron the Hittite, Hamor the Hivite. (These ethnic designations are among those listed formulaically as the seven nations of Canaan in the conquest tradition. The way that these names are used suggests that the biblical authors had no knowledge of these as separate peoples but only used the traditional names to populate pre-Israelite Canaan.) Here, as in the covenant-conquest tradition, the term "Canaanite" appears to be an ideological label rather than an ethnic or national designation. On the names of the pre-Israelite population in Canaan, see Niels Peter Lemche, *The Canaanites and Their Land: The Tradition of the Canaanites*, Journal for the Study of the Old Testament Supplement Series 110, ed. David J. A. Clines and Philip R. Davies (Sheffield: Sheffield Academic Press, 1991), 83–100.

14. See the brief discussion of the relationship between patriarchs and host

peoples in Arnold Eisen, *Galut: Modern Jewish Reflection on Homeless-ness and Homecoming* (Bloomington and Indianapolis: Indiana University Press, 1986), 8–12.

15. For a similar reading of these episodes, see ibid., 8–12.
16. The issues of family and destiny in Genesis are analyzed in an illumi-nating way in Devora Steinmetz, *From Father to Son: Kinship, Con-flict, and Continuity in Genesis* (Louisville, Ky.: Westminster/John Knox, 1991).
17. Julian Pitt-Rivers, *The Fate of Shechem or the Politics of Sex* (Cam-bridge: Cambridge University Press, 1977), 94–125.
18. Ibid., 159.
19. By using the ambiguous term *beit par'oh* ("house of Pharaoh"), the narrator temporarily leaves open the exact fate of the matriarch. The term may denote simply a physical house ("Pharaoh's palace") but may also refer to a household, in this case including Pharaoh's harem. Nahum Sarna is typical of modern commentators in opting for the first meaning and insisting that Sarai "returns to her husband unviolated" (*The JPS Torah Commentary: Genesis* [Philadelphia: Jewish Publica-tion Society, 1989], 94). Yet only two verses later (12:17), as the object of God's plagues, the term clearly denotes not a building but persons. The implication is that Sarai became a sexagenarian sex object in the pharaoh's harem!
20. Although Egypt, and not Canaan, is the venue for this episode and Pharaoh, rather than a Canaanite king, is depicted, the easy transfer of the type-scene to the city of Gerar and to King Abimelech in chaps. 20 and 26 suggests that the issue of all three episodes is the need to keep the ancestors and the landed locals apart.
21. See Steinmetz, *From Father to Son*, 89–101.
22. Ibid., 100.
23. Eisen makes this point, *Galut*, 11–12.
24. Pitt-Rivers, *Fate of Shechem*, 156.
25. The narrative means by which sympathy for the brothers is constructed has been thoroughly analyzed by Meir Sternberg, *The Poetics of Biblical Narrative: Ideological Literature and the Drama of Reading* (Blooming-ton: Indiana University Press, 1985), 445–75. See also the recent critique of Sternberg: Danna Nolan Fewell and David M. Gunn, "Tipping the Balance: Sternberg's Reader and the Rape of Dinah," *Journal of Biblical Literature* 110 (1991): 193–211; and Sternberg's forceful reply: "Biblical Poetics and Sexual Politics: From Reading to Counter-Reading," *Journal of Biblical Literature* 111 (1992): 463–88.
26. Sternberg, "Biblical Poetics," 485–87.
27. Professor Peter Machinist suggested this article to me: Moshe Wein-feld, "The Promise to the Patriarchs and Its Realization: An Analysis of Foundation Stories," in *Society and Economy in the Eastern Mediter-*

ranean (c. 1500–1000 B.C.), Orientalia Lovaniensia Analecta 23, ed. M. Heltzer and E. Lipinski (Leuven: Uitgaeverij Peeters, 1988), 353–69.

28. "Kinship . . . is a symbolic structure which represents the ability of the society to survive and to continue to transmit its cultural heritage" (Steinmetz, *From Father to Son*, 148).

Chapter 5

Spinning Tales: On Reading Gender and Otherness in Tannaitic Texts

Miriam Peskowitz

The study of gender is a study of how roles and possibilities
are conceptualized.
— Carolyn Bynum, *Fragmentation and Redemption*

The formative mechanism of culture thus amounts to a
reification of human activities which fixates the living and
models the transmission of experience from one generation
to another on the transmission of commodities; a reification
which strives to ensure the past's domination over the
future.
—Pierre Canjuers and Guy Debord, "Preliminaries
toward Defining a Unitary Revolutionary Program"

Within the vicissitudes of Jewish religious history, women have been
the Other. That is, women have not occupied positions of centrality,
nor have female Jews been allowed a proactive part in defining the
rituals and legalities known collectively as Judaism. Once this basic
point of otherness has been recognized, however, we must also
acknowledge that otherness is a contingent position. *Other*, in
discussions of women's lives, describes a gendered and sexualized
status that is socially constructed. To call one group of humans
Other and to focus critical attention on their otherness can obscure
at least several points. First and foremost, this focus can obscure
the understanding that the material conditions of women's lives are
quite "real" and that these conditions of otherness are culturally

91

constructed. Furthermore, and significantly, Others are constructed by someone/some group with the power to effect cultural processes and with the power to declare others as Other. This point raises the question of agency, the question of who constitutes Others. In mapping out the lives of Others, such as female Jews, it is necessary to clarify who places them in positions of otherness in the first place.

Augmenting the focus on the material conditions of daily life experienced by Others with an analysis of the process that makes them into Others generates this central question: by what mechanisms can some groups make others into Others? In the case of gender and gendering, by which I mean the process of making men into men, making women into women, and defining the differences that separate one from the other, the central question becomes *how?* *How* has this been done effectively and powerfully in various historical communities?

Theories concerned with the social construction of gender take as a starting point the premise that notions of femininity and masculinity, as well as their social consequences, are neither natural nor essential qualities. Rather, genders are social constructions that can be both modified and reified in time. Thus, as powerful and unjust as conditions of female otherness may be, this subject position is neither essentially nor naturally female, but is made into such. In this essay, then, *gender* refers to the cultural processes that create and enact specific notions about what men and women ought to be and ought to do. Hence, we need to ascertain how an anatural position of female otherness becomes natural*ized.* If, as Canjuers and Debord suggest, the reification of roles and activities is one mechanism of domination, then we need to ascertain how certain notions about the roles, activities, and characters of men and women became reified at various historical moments.[1]

The second point potentially obscured when we rely heavily on the binary relation of Self and Other is that there are usually many Others. The position marked by the term *Other* is fluid and movable.[2] By way of example of what I mean by fluidity, let me present an exchange from my classroom. The course was Introduction to Judaic Civilization. At the five-week mark, my students and I were reading and discussing Albert Memmi's book *The Pillar of Salt.*[3] In this text, certain subject positions keep changing, taking on new moral valences and different relations to colonial power and to the authority of traditional Jewish practice. The person and identity of Alexandre Mordechai Benillouche was transformed as we watched

and read. In our classroom discussion, we had sorted out the
various relationships among religions, ethnicities, and colonial
positions; but we had not yet talked about gender. And so I posed
the question, how are women positioned in this text? What are
women in this text? After a moment, a student suggested with a
degree of assurance that women are the Other. I thought for a
moment and gathered words for the reply. "Yes and no," I said.
"It's not that easy." I directed the class to look at where and how
women are positioned in and around Alexandre's life: his mother,
who represents traditional Jewish culture and religion; the prostitutes, who embody his aspirations for normative masculine sexuality; the girlfriend, in whom rest Alexandre's desires for Frenchness,
for a station of empowerment within colonialist culture. Women are
Other in that they are not Alexandre, in that they are not the center
of the story, in that they are controlled by Memmi's authorship, and
in that they are generally Other in the masculinist society upon
which Memmi's narrative relies.

However, within Memmi's narrative, women do not consistently
represent specific kinds of marginalized and disempowered statuses
of otherness. Positions of otherness can be occupied variously by
women, Jews, or North African natives. In fact, women are positioned by Memmi to represent various stabilized powers. Female
characters are crafted and recrafted to function as stable identities,
against which Alexandre sees, loses, and reshapes pieces of himself.
In other places, for instance in the work camps at which Alexandre
finds for himself fragments of the coherent identity he desires,
women disappear from the narrative.

Thus, while women are generally Other, Memmi's textual
strategy at times repositions them to represent points of cultural
empowerment. At these moments, then, Memmi makes Alexandre—
the multiply colonized subject—into a conceptual "woman." In
response to this discussion of gender as destabilized, and in response
to hearing the sentence "Alexandre is sometimes a 'woman,'" some
confused looks traveled around the classroom. Gender, I reminded
them gently, is complicated.[4]

Common references to the Other may reify that person/place/
position as more unified and stable than it really is or was. This
reification can hide the complex human acts of constructing and
crafting gender culture, especially the gender culture represented in
written texts, texts that are so commonly the focus of our analysis.
Perhaps the formal element of the definite article—*the* Other—may

hide the truism that there are many Others and that Others and images of Others are used, manipulated, and represented. This use and representation of Others is accomplished by those with power to do so. Thus, in the case of the mechanics of gender production, we need to examine closely who represents what, and how. For instance, in the paragraph that precedes this one, I discussed how Memmi represented women, and I claimed that Memmi used femininity to signify power in different ways. That is, I represented Memmi's representation, for my own purposes, much as Memmi represented women for his, much as I told a partial story in which I represented my classroom and a certain student's remarks. As Memmi crafted and storytold, so too do I.[5] So too did the Tannaim of Roman Palestine, a small Jewish scholarly elite who produced their first religio-legal texts around the year 200 C.E., participate in crafting certain notions about women, men, and the difference between the two. In their texts, the Tannaim orchestrate details, arrange partial truths, and choreograph women's lives, words, and actions. Their texts produced the myriad legalities of Jewish ritual and civil life in the post-Second Temple period. Simultaneously, these texts and these sages produce gender culture. Putting the tannaitic sages and redactors in the subject position, we see them as agents of gender culture.[6]

To think further about the relation of these theoretical issues in relation to the production of gender culture in Roman-period Judaism, I will analyze two passages from the Mishnah, a religio-legal text attributed to the Tannaim. These passages share a common theme in that both are about spinners—men and women who turn raw fibers into usable threads and yarns. I choose these passages—Moed Qatan 3.4 and Sotah 6.1—because they include material that helps to us to theorize about the construction of Others, gender, and difference, and thus to rethink the making of masculinity and femininity in Mishnaic texts from the Roman period of Jewish religious history.

In my analysis of one of these passages, Moed Qatan 3.4, I examine how the tannaitic sages constructed male and female spinners as different through the gendered representation of tools and technology. In my analysis of the second passage, Sotah 6.1, I show how these sages produced two types of women, each counterposed as different from the other.[7] In analyzing these two passages, I articulate some concepts that enable us to see how some texts from one variety of Roman-period Judaism produced notions of otherness and sexual difference with regard to gender. Yet, in concentrating on the social construction of notions about gender difference, we must be careful not to lose sight of the power relations of difference, not to decontextualize, belittle, or hide power relations of hierarchy and inequity by analyzing them as relativized "differences."[8]

Since these passages are about male and female spinners, let me begin with a discussion of some tendencies that have informed modern scholarly interpretations of men, women, and the production of spun thread in Jewish communities during what is commonly called the rabbinic or Talmudic period of Jewish religious history, but which I prefer to designate as Roman-period Judaism. I begin this excursion into the territory of gender culture in Roman-period Judaism in Palestine with analyses of modern interpreters for one major reason: that world and its gender culture are not blank slates. We approach and conceptualize the foreign country of Roman-period Judaism with the preconceptions of both intellectual inheritances and the culture around us.[9] Accordingly, an analysis of some selective, but I think representative, examples of these inherited preconceptions (I leave to each reader the project of figuring out their local cultural influences on reconstructions of the past) can help clarify some problems with the histories we scholars have produced. This analysis also reveals how our scholarly practices themselves reify inherited notions of gender culture. This is ironic, since the necessary intellectual project demands precisely that these notions be made visible. Until the invisibilities of gender culture can be made visible, and until we see the cultural specificities of that which is reified, and acknowledge it as reified, our abilities to see how gender was made in Roman-period Judaism and in twentieth-century interpretive scholarship are constrained.[10]

The Transmission of (Gendered) Commodities

In the common, although mostly unarticulated, practice of historicizing early rabbinic texts, scholars have treated these texts as straightforward descriptions of how (rabbinic) Jews in Palestine organized their society with regard to the roles of men and women. On the basis of these roles and of more abstract ancient statements about the complex mire of bias, love, prejudice, disdain, and admiration voiced by male writers about females, scholars have proposed conclusions about the status of women. These conclusions are most often couched in binary terms: images of women are positive or negative; women's status is either high or low.

Most of these studies—characterized by vague, unexamined, and problematic methodologies, a haphazard use of ancient sources, and a lack of attention to social structures that constrained and restricted women's lives—often rely on overgeneralizations based on literary sources from a range of centuries and places. None of the available studies on women's lives and notions about women in early rabbinic Judaism raises the question of how these gender roles and images of women were made culturally possible.[11]

Two examples may be introduced to analyze the interpretive frames through which we scholars view ancient constructions of gender. The first comes from Samuel Krauss, author of the classic *Talmudische Archäologie* (1910), an encyclopedic narrative grounded in the positivist tradition of scholarship that exemplified the *Wissenschaft des Judentum* (science of Judaism), a nineteenth-century movement that emphasized the history and development of Jewish texts, legal tradition, and religion. In his *Archäologie*, Krauss culled rabbinic references to reconstruct aspects of daily life, food, clothing, machines, and families characterizing Jewish life in the "period of the Talmud." Krauss writes, "Spinning is the appropriate occupation of housewives, a work which she was not allowed to forego even when her dowry compensated amply for the cost of her maintenance, and she worked both by moonlight and lamplight."[12]

I am interested particularly in the last phrase, and in the process by which Krauss reconstructed female work from the available ancient sources. In claiming that spinning was the primary work of women and particularly indicative of women's household work, Krauss built on a prevalent ancient discourse that divided labors among men and women, crafted certain labors into "women's work," and assigned to "women's work" a range of values and meanings. The values and cultural meanings ascribed to "women's work," as represented through the icons of spinning, weaving, and woolwork, included marital allegiance, sexual restraint on the part of unmarried women, domesticity, and household industriousness.

As much as some elements of Roman-period culture used female woolwork to signify and approve a narrow range of feminine character traits, these symbols invoked as well a wider range of meanings. For instance, the conjunction of "women's work" and woolwork had different meanings when applied to elite women and to women of lower classes. When the elite Sulpicia, daughter of Servius Sulpicius Rufus, described and derided her beloved Cerinthus's new lover, she portrayed this woman as having a lower social status than herself. To do so, Sulpicia described Cerinthus's new lover as a "strumpet loaded with a woolbasket." In this case, woolworking was used to denote the female nonmarital sexuality in the case of a woman portrayed as lower class.[13]

Other images of female and feminized woolworking from this period appear in a variety of monumental, funerary, burial, and other archaeological evidence. Investigating Others and the construction of otherness often demands that we use "other" types of evidence. This is especially true in the field of rabbinic studies, which has relied so heavily and exclusively upon the rabbis' own documents, often without reference to material culture and excavated archaeology, and in large part without reference to Roman cultural contexts. The expansion of the pool of evidence facilitates the reading of primary documents—predominantly those produced by religious elites—against the grain and in new ways; through these strategies we can posit more nuanced accounts of historical gender culture within Judaism.[14]

Epitaphs for women used woolworking images to memorialize women's qualities. These funerary commemorations are one of the more accessible kinds of material evidence. The following inscription promotes the woolworking imagery of an elite woman:

> Stranger, what I have to say is short. Stop and read it through. This is the unlovely tomb of a lovely woman. Her parents named her Claudia. She loved her husband with her whole heart. She bore two sons, one of which she leaves on earth; the other she has placed beneath the earth. She was charming in conversation, yet her conduct was appropriate. She kept house, she made wool (*domum servavit, lanam fecit*).[15]

In other social settings, funerary references to female woolworkers deployed alternate meanings. In contrast to the highly stylized portrayal of the industrious woolworking wife, an epigraphical inscription by a female slave or freedworker that mentioned explicitly her work as a spinner, weaver, or woolworker could have functioned as a claim to a positive identity within a society that denigrated manual labor and the lower classes.[16]

These few examples establish that a range of meanings were available in Roman-period literary and material culture for the conjunction of femininity, women, and woolwork.[17]   From this repertoire the early rabbis in Palestine could shape their own images of femininized woolwork and could craft particular and local notions about gender culture, about what male and female should mean, and about what men and women should do.

The word I wish to stress is *craft*, especially in the double sense of the economic activities and crafts of ancient artisans and workers on the one hand, and the cultural process of crafting mundane activities of everyday life into early rabbinic legal discussions on the other.   Krauss's final sentence tells us that as a matter of social-historical commonplace, these female spinners worked both by moonlight and lamplight.   Yet, by the time it appeared in Sotah 6.1, this literary topos of women spinning far into the night was a centuries-old mode of illustrating female industriousness.[18]   The existence of a gendered discourse that codes female industriousness through these images should raise concern regarding their facile use as information for historical and sociological realities.

Krauss's reconstruction presumes, problematically, that rabbinic texts "tell it like it is." Like many historians of ancient and rabbinic Judaism before and since, Krauss reconstructed aspects of female work by decontextualizing references in religio-legal documents. Krauss's reference to spinning by moonlight is based on a reading of Sotah 6.1, a text that refers to women who spin and talk in the moonlight. This text is used commonly as evidence for one aspect of the socioeconomic lives of women in early rabbinic texts. But, as I will show below, in Sotah 6.1 the female spinners are important to their tannaitic authors precisely because they might speak of other women's adulteries. The fact that they are spinners evokes a range of contemporary meanings that help the Tannaim establish certain meanings. To extract from this passage—one highly implicated in debates about female gender and sexuality—a declarative statement about the habits and places of female workers involves a mode of *Wissenschaft* interpretation that, although normalized in Krauss's day, seems strangely one-dimensional (although still practiced) today.

This interpretive practice ignores the cultural work of constructing gender being done by the Mishnah. It assumes that the texts tell truths but does not ask what kinds of truths are being told. It ignores the fact that in this passage, the Tannaim do more than

provide a tidbit of information about where women spun—outside
—and when they spun—by night. As I argue elsewhere, the
ideological context and import of these symbols is that they encode
female productivity in imagery that enables the restriction and
control of female work, within the family and marital economy, in
such a way as to make the restriction and control seem natural.[19]
Ignoring the ideological context of spinning symbols in the Roman
world and in other Jewish texts, this kind of historical reconstruction, however widespread, presumes wrongly that the text's legal
concerns—the validity of women's testimonies about other women's
possible adulteries—did not influence the kinds of symbols—women
spinning—that the sages chose to use as they made law into
language.[20]

Another text by a scholarly interpreter of rabbinic Judaism
shares problems similar to those of Krauss. The following passage
comes from an article on the image and status of Jewish women by
Judith Romney Wegner, published in 1991. Wegner's work exemplifies a related and common tendency in rabbinic studies, namely, the
acceptance of certain reconstructions of male and female as true and
natural. Wegner writes,

> Just as most women in Greek society stayed by their spindle or
> loom while men went out to talk politics in the public square or to
> wage war in foreign lands, so Talmudic culture approves women
> who stay home spinning or weaving while men go to the synagogue
> to pray and the academy to study Torah.[21]

That women stay home spinning and men go to war was as common
a trope in the ancient world as its related class stereotype—the
public man and the private woman—became in parts of the industri-
alizing Western world. One need only recall Livy's tale of Lucretia.
The princes had failed to capture Ardea easily, and so began what
would be a long siege of Ardea. One night they sat together,
drinking and boasting of the virtues of their wives back in Rome.
The men's boasts grew more heated, and more irresolvable, until
Tarquinius Collatinus suggested that they ride horseback to Rome,
where they could judge together which prince's wife was best.
Reaching the palace several hours later, the princes surprised the
wives, only to find that all the princesses save Lucretia, the wife of
Tarquinius Collatinus, were banqueting drunkenly, engaged in the
feminized decadence that first-century Roman writers used to

exemplify the downfall of their society's culture. Only Lucretia, set apart from this feminized decadence, "was busily engaged upon her wool, while her maidens toiled about her in the lamplight as she sat in the hall of her house." In Livy's text, and in other retellings of this story, the woolworking Lucretia is displayed as the quintessential virtuous wife of the elite class. She spins and through spinning demonstrates her domesticity, her sexual chastity, her marital loyalty, and her role in preserving the simplicity of "true" Roman culture.[22]

But what does it mean for Wegner, if not for the Tannaim, to invoke this trope of the domestic woolworking wife and the public husband as a historical description of a Talmudically approved system of gender? Most men in Roman antiquity, like most women in Roman antiquity, spent their time working, producing the commodities and services necessary to sustain themselves and their families. Most people in antiquity—men and women—were poor; most were largely illiterate.[23] Men of most classes did not spend their days talking politics in the public square or waging war.[24] Similarly, the imagined Jewish man who could spend the majority of his time in study or in prayer constituted only a small minority.[25] His illusory companion, the Jewish woman who stayed indoors at home with her distaff, spindle, and yarn basket, is likewise a fanciful representation of Jewish women's gender roles in the Roman period. Instead of asking how certain sets of images—spinning women and public men—are used to create notions about masculinity and femininity, Wegner, following a common scholarly practice, takes the images to be truthful and historically accurate descriptions. Herein lies the problem; this kind of analysis inscribes contemporary gender mythologies onto the ancient world, instead of critically analyzing how certain myths were perpetuated as truths.[26] The repetition of this gender stereotype by contemporary interpreters ignores the variety of meanings encoded in this imagery, especially those meanings associated with class distinctions. These repeated stereotypes mask the fact that since it was neither universal nor natural for women to work wool, the image's meaning was not essentially given, but rather was in constant need of being constructed and maintained in the Roman world.

Furthermore, woolwork was not performed exclusively by women in Roman-period societies, including Jewish societies, during that period. In the Roman world, the textile trades, of which spinning and weaving were only two components, were staffed by both male and female workers, free and slave. Similarly, tannaitic sources from Palestine refer to both men and women who spin and weave wool. The textile trades posed difficult problems for cultural elites concerned with the clarification of sexual difference. Such problems confronted the tannaitic sages, concerned as they were with the institution of the gender division of labor within these trades. This concern with instituting policies of gender difference in the structures and systems of workplaces, a concern shared by other Roman-period writers, sets the stage both for my analysis of Moed Qatan 3.4 and, I argue, for the Roman-period gender-cultural meaning of that passage.[27]

My critique of Krauss and Wegner suggests a significant change in the practices by which we do "women's history," a history of one set of Others with regard to Roman-period Judaism. Rather than accept these textual statements at face value as evidence for gender roles and the status of women, we need to ask how these texts go about constructing gender in the first place. Seen in this way, traditional scholarly analyses that presume reified and stable binary gender roles in "Talmudic culture" assume the veracity of precisely that which needs to be questioned. Rather than ask about the approval given by the rabbis to women who stay home filling workbaskets with yarn, we need to ask how they created this image and constructed these subjects and realities.[28] Approbation of such a woman requires as its precondition the creation of such a woman; the subject of the woolworking woman must be constructed before the abstracted elites of "Talmudic culture" can go about the business of approving or disapproving of her.

If we take seriously the axiom that gender is culturally and socially constructed, then we scholars need to inquire how the Tannaim constituted "women" and "men" into recognizable and meaningful categories; we need to explore the mechanisms by which they attached certain cultural meanings to "her" and to "him" and how these meanings were manipulated; and we need to entertain the possibility that the Tannaim created more than one type of woman. This perspective marks a purposeful orienting of Jewish women's history toward a history of gender culture within Judaism, with an emphasis on the mechanisms of how this gender culture worked.[29] The guiding question becomes, how were certain ideas and social structures turned into knowledge and legitimated as "natural" and "true"? This perspective is indebted to the landmark work by Joan Scott, as presented in *Gender and the Politics of History* (1988). Her explanation of the construction of gendered knowledges and knowledge about gender will serve well to situate this new analysis of early rabbinic passages.   Scott suggests that feminist history "becomes not just an attempt to correct or supplement an incomplete record of the past but a way of critically understanding how history operates as a site of the production of gender knowledge."[30] In her 1988 essays, the term "gender"

> means knowledge about sexual difference.   I use knowledge, following Michel Foucault, to mean the understanding produced by cultures and societies of human relationships, in this case those between men and women. Such knowledge is not absolute or true, but always relative. It is produced in complex ways within large epistemic frames that themselves have an (at least quasi) autonomous history. Its uses and meanings become contested politically and are the means by which relationships of power—of domination and subordination—are constructed. *Knowledge refers not only to ideas but to institutions and structures, everyday practices as well as specialized rituals, all of which constitute social relationships.* Knowledge is a way of ordering the world; as such it is not prior to social organization, it is inseparable from social organization.
>
>   It follows then that *gender is the social organization of sexual difference*. But this does not mean that gender reflects or implements fixed and natural physical differences between women and men; rather gender is the knowledge that establishes meanings for bodily differences. . . . Sexual difference is not, then, the originary cause from which social organization ultimately can be derived. It is instead a variable social organization that itself must be explained.[31]

In what follows, I attempt to untangle and explain this perspective with regard to evidence from Roman-period Judaism and provide examples of the difference it makes.

Signifying Difference

One way in which Others are created and their positions maintained is through the persuasive construction of differences. Ideologies of difference influence modes of social organization; men's lives and women's lives are arranged in ways that establish and perpetuate these separations in everyday life. Thus, labor can be divided into

the gendered categories of men's work and women's work; space in
settlements and homes might be divided by gender; personality
traits might be assigned to each gender. The creation of "woman" as
other than "man" in tannaitic Judaism relies on a continuous
explanation of how these two social entities differ, and on the
marking out of the boundaries that separate the behaviors, attributes, and activities of each from the other.[32]

An example of how distinctions of gender were made and
marked can be inferred from a passage about male spinning.
Several passages in the tannaitic-period Mishnah and Tosefta refer
to men who spin.[33] Only one of these passages, Moed Qatan 3.4,
both refers to a male spinner and describes the technology he used
to spin. These passages about men who spin are especially interesting in light of the Roman discourse that both feminized spinning
and feminized the spindle—the tool used to spin fibers into thread.
Furthermore, the passages about spinning are significant in that
they show everyday, habitual acts; in these passages, we can discern
how gender was constructed into and reproduced through the realm
of the ordinary.

Tractate Moed Qatan, in which this passage is placed, addresses
the legal problems of performing work acts, and hence of generating
and distributing material commodities, during the intermediate days
of festivals.[34] From the tractate's examples and brief explanations
of permitted work, it may be said that, in general, work considered
necessary to prevent impending loss was permitted, with several
conditions developed to demarcate the interrelated definitions of
loss, needs, and intention. Furthermore, certain kinds of work
performed on the intermediate days were to be done discreetly
and/or in ways that *differed* from the normal and customary procedures that governed the production of a specific object. In one
example given, an unskilled person might sew in the usual manner,
but a tailor must sew only with rough, irregular stitches.[35]

These legal principles for doing work provide some conceptual
contexts for interpreting the following translated passage, Moed
Qatan 3.4.

> They must not write notes of debt [credit agreements] during the
> intermediate days. But if he is not trustworthy, or he has nothing
> to eat, then he may write [the note].

They must not write Sefarim, Tefillin, or Mezuzot during the
intermediate days, and they must not correct a single mark [in
these documents], even on the *sēfer 'ăzārāh*.
R. Judah says: a man may write Tefillin and Mezuzot for himself,
and he may spin *těkēlet* upon his thigh for [his] *ṣîṣît*.[36]

The final phrase of this passage, "and he may spin *těkēlet* upon his
thigh for [his] *ṣîṣît*," refers to a specific spinning method. The
reference to a man spinning tekelet using the technology of thigh
spinning makes meaning in (at least) two significant ways: first, in
terms of the legal principles and logic it assumes and assembles; and
second, with regard to the short passage's representational value
among the corpus of early rabbinic literatures. Technologically, the
depiction of thigh spinning marks a difference from the more
common and efficient spinning method of the period, which employed the drop spindle—a tool that combined a spindle rod and
spindle whorl—in order to provide weight, tension, and twirling
momentum that would assist a spinner's fingers in drawing out
thread from fibers.[37] That drop spindles were used in Palestine
during the Roman period is supported by the abundance of excavated examples of this tool.[38]

Thigh spinning—on the other hand—is a much older technology
of spinning. Replaced by the drop spindle around the fourth
millenium B.C.E., thigh spinning is a markedly slower and more
tedious process by which a spinner rolls out fibers using the fingers
and upper thigh.[39] Moed Qatan 3.4 dates to the Roman period:
the reference to thigh spinning stands out as a retrograde and
antiquated spinning method. This invocation of a retrograde
technology represents a difference from the more feminized method
of drop spinning with a spindle.[40] Read in this way, the text and
its authors construe the division of genders through tools and
technology. This division, I will argue, is a mechanism that would
distinguish male spinners (at least male spinners of tekelet threads)
from female spinners.

I maintained in my critique of Krauss and positivism that it is
necessary to interpret references to material and everyday realia as
they are constituted within legal and other ideological contexts. The
reference to spinning tekelet upon one's thigh ensues from some
ambulations of tannaitic legal argument. As mentioned above,
within the constraints of immediate need, the principle of doing
work differently is operative. Second, a notion that objects can be

produced for oneself, that is, not for sale or trade, is assumed by and argued by the permission to produce tekelet through thigh spinning.

In the case of Rabbi Judah's dissent and the example of thigh spinning, assessing the specific and exclusive logic that orients the halakhah is complicated. The certainty of any assessment is undermined by critical problems in the Hebrew manuscript itself: the manuscript tradition contains two variations. One variant reads "upon his thigh for *ṣiṣit*"; the other variant reads "upon his thigh for *his ṣiṣit*." The first reading would suggest as central the principle of doing work differently than usual, including using nonnormative technology and techniques. The second would emphasize the condition of doing work for oneself and not for the direct market economy. These readings are not exclusive: the second reading— that of producing an object for one's own use—would not preclude the first apparent principle—that of doing work differently—from operating in the argument attributed to Judah.

According to my reading of the legal ideas with which this passage deals, the reference to the antique technology of thigh spinning seems appropriate and easily explainable. No other spinning technique or spinning tool available to Roman-period spinners would have illustrated as much difference from the normative use of the spindle as would thigh spinning. Even the inclusion of tekelet for *ṣiṣit* makes sense within these logics, following as it does a list of ritual objects that includes tefillin, mezuzot, and Torah scrolls. Based on this reading, which isolates the logic of the halakhah, the passage Moed Qatan 3.4 makes no overt excursions into the manufacture of gender differences. In fact, if we use these legal principles to unravel the passage's logic, it would seem that from a social-historical perspective, male spinners of tekelet threads did use similar spinning techniques and tools as female spinners, so long as such men did not spin their tekelet threads during the intermediate days of Pesaḥ or Sukkot.

This analysis and conclusion, insofar as it would seem to make the representation of gender invisible and beside the point, highlights precisely the conceptual fallacy of reading these texts in isolation only for their legal logic and argumentation. If we want to determine how differences and otherness are culturally constructed and represented, other and additional methods of reading these early rabbinic texts are required. A reading that places this one passage into the context of a larger corpus of literary and/or oral production and a reading that acknowledges gender culture and gendered society more generally can yield alternate conclusions.

Most texts convey multiple and simultaneous meanings. In the course of transmitting halakhah regarding performances of work during the intermediate days, Moed Qatan 3.4 interjects a curious anomaly of technology and gender. Its curiousness as well as its status as anomaly become visible only in light of contextual social information. Spindles and drop spinning were thoroughly feminized and construed as the work of females, despite the fact that men did spin. "Women's work" was depicted most commonly with the image of "woolwork." In such a cultural environment, it becomes more significant that in the entire early rabbinic corpus, the only text that mentions male spinners with their spinning technique describes them as using a technique that differs from the feminized mode of spinning. The most vivid image recorded by the Tannaim of a male spinner spinning—that is, a man participating in a phase of one of the top three industries of Roman Palestine—associates him with a nonfeminized technology. The fact of this passage's function as a textual image that represents how work was to be done marks the gendering mechanisms of this text. In this way, the passage uses spinning tools and technologies to denote and debate festival-related difference concerning productive work, and in doing so, signifies gender difference.

Others within Others

This discussion of Moed Qatan 3.4 has provided an example of how seemingly obscure tannaitic passages present images that create and contribute to cultural notions about gender difference. In this case, gendering was done by means of the representation of a technology related both to textile production and to a pervasive feminizing trope. In a second passage, Sotah 6.1, the Tannaim use similar imagery of spinning and spinners to construct difference and otherness in the service of the social control of sexuality. In this passage, tannaitic authors employ the feminized imagery of spinning to portray women in several different positions with regard to the masculinist order. Yet the categories "woman" and "man" are neither singular nor cohesive. There are many types of women, many types of men. In the Roman world of which Judaism was part, an elite free-born woman was a different social entity than a slave woman, or a freedwoman. A senator or equestrian was a distinct type of man, with distinct types of masculinity, as was an artisan or other worker, whether slave, free, or freed. In early rabbinic documents, a sage was construed as a different kind of man from the unlearned, the *am ha-aretz*. Genders were crosscut and constituted by class categories, both in the way that a certain individual could be understood by others and in the ways that certain individuals could understand and present themselves.

Central to my interpretation of Sotah 6.1 is the theoretically based and empirically grounded position that the categories "woman" or "man" are unstable and multiple, that neither man nor woman is a singular construct. Men can be different kinds of "men," depending on configurations of power and social relations. So too, women. This analysis of Sotah 6.1 is meant to show the gendering mechanism that divides females into several types of women, Others within Others, each with a different relation to ideas of the appropriate social order. The passage reads,

> Whoever had voiced suspicions concerning his wife [with regard to her extramarital sexual actions], and she continued [her actions] secretly: even if he heard [about her secretive sexual actions] from a flying bird (an unnamed, transient source), he must divorce her and give [her] the ketubbah, [this is the] opinion of Rabbi Eliezer. Rabbi Joshua says: [he must divorce her and give her the ketubbah] when the spinners (*môzĕrôt*) argue and repeat [tales] about her [sexual actions as they spin] by the moonlight.

These are the same spinners, the *môzĕrôt*, that formed the basis of Krauss's reconstruction of women who spin beneath the moon.[41] In reading this passage, located within a legal discussion about ascertaining guilt, we need to ask why Rabbi Joshua's brief anecdote employs the image of women spinning under the light of the moon. Rather than assume, as Krauss did, that this passage transposes transparently a true story about women's "real" activities (despite the ever-present possibility that some women, at some times, may have spun yarn with other women outside at night using the light of the moon), we must raise the question of how and why certain female subjects were created through and by and for the law. In light of the conventional and widespread Roman-period meanings associated with women, femininity, and spinning, we cannot assume that any "real" women spinning and talking under the moonlight stood behind or before the textual image of these women in this passage.[42]

The Mishnaic tractate Sotah builds upon Num. 5:11–31 to establish the procedures that a husband may implement when he suspects his wife of adultery. The Mishnah schematizes this series of events as follows. When suspecting his wife of adultery, the husband must first warn the wife of his suspicions, and his warning must be made in front of two witnesses. He must warn her to stay away from and refrain from talking with her suspected partner. If, after this initial warning, the husband still suspects that his wife is having a sexual affair, he may accuse her formally of adultery. Once the accusation is articulated, any of several things may happen. If neither evidence nor witnesses exist, the wife must either admit guilt or claim innocence. If the wife admits guilt, the husband must divorce her, and she loses her *ketubbah*, or marriage settlement. If the wife claims innocence, in the absence of evidence or witnesses, the husband must subject her to drink the *mê hamārîm*, the bitter waters, to be administered by priests at the temple.

According to recorded Jewish traditions, this potion would either sustain the wife's innocence by causing no ill effects on her body or it would establish her guilt by distorting and maiming her body. If the wife is proven guilty as accused, her marriage is ended, she forfeits her *ketubbah*, and the man is free to remarry.

The ritual of bitter waters represented the ultimate recourse by which a husband and the community could ascertain the accused wife's guilt or innocence; if these could be established through other means, the ritual would be legally superfluous, and could be avoided. The development of alternate methods to ascertain the guilt of an accused wife is, of course, indicative of the creation of post-Temple rabbinic methods for adjudicating truth. The search for evidence of the wife's adultery, then, provides the direct legal context for Sotah 6.1. The passage raises the question of the minimum standards of reliable evidence. One side of the debate over standards for reliable evidence is found in the opinion ascribed to Rabbi Eliezer, the euphemistic "flying bird." In the sentence following, Rabbi Joshua presents an additional, and explicit, standard and gives legal authorization to the words of women who talk as they spin yarn by the light of the moon. Rumors, gossip, and second- and third-hand reports that would reach these women would all serve as sufficiently valid evidence. On the basis of these accounts, the accused wife could be proven guilty, and the ritual of bitter waters avoided.

Any discussion of tractate Sotah as an ideological text from early rabbinic Judaism must recognize its optative qualities. Scholarly interpreters have shown an abiding curiosity about the fact that after they present the legal details for the rite, and after they create violently pornographic images of the bound and tied woman, the sages announce that the rite is inoperable.[43] Textually situated as it is within a text that dates to the post–Second Temple period, tractate Sotah is a legal fiction about an archaic ritual. The rite's obsolescence may have resulted in part from the cessation of an active priesthood to administer the bitter waters following the destruction of the temple. But in fact, Mishnah Sotah offers a glimpse into the early rabbinic reorientation from temple-based ritual practice to rabbinic systems. In this extended moment of cultural/religious reorientation, close readings of some tannaitic texts reveal some contexts for the sages' realignment of gender. But what exactly does this fiction tell us about tannaitic visions of women and about their (textual) strategies for controlling gender and sexuality?[44]

In this passage, women spin by moonlight. That the women in Sotah 6.1 are depicted as spinning is significant. They are spinning —in the tangible sense of spinning fibers into thread—and they are spinning for themselves female identities that were approved by their society. This imagery summons the topos of feminized wool-work as a safeguard against female transgression of cultural sexual codes, evoking the woolworking matron of Ketubot 5.5 as well as the Lucretian figure of marital excellence. The quality and trustworthiness of these women's characters is supported by their activity of spinning. Spinning signifies that their actions fall within the moral and sexual boundaries approved by the Tannaim. Hence, the testimony by these women about an "other" woman, a woman whose accused actions have moved her beyond the boundaries of socially approved female actions, is deemed reliable by Rabbi Joshua.

Tractate Sotah, and Sotah 6.1 in particular, sets out the legal sequences and the rules of evidence that would determine successfully and accurately whether an accused woman was in fact adulterous. The legal texts resolve the ambiguities of guilt and innocence and, in doing so, perhaps intend to restore broken sensibilities of a (gendered) social order. Yet, the Mishnaic description of the ritual serves additional purposes besides the legal exposition of evidentiary regulations. Paramount among these is the presentation of a warning to all women. The image of the Sotah is used to apprise other women of the consequences of illicit and extramarital sexuality. This is pronounced most clearly in Sotah 1.5–6 where the sages describe how the priests would prepare the woman for the rite of the bitter waters.

The tannaitic sages imagined the rite in this way: When a suspect wife claims that she has not violated the rules of marital sexuality, her husband brings her to the Jerusalem temple, to the specific place where suspect wives were to be given the drink of bitter waters. There, the wife is given over into the custody of a priest. The priest then siezes hold of the woman and tears her clothing in order to expose her breasts. He loosens the woman's hair and reclothes her in black garments. The priest procures a special type of rope and ties the rope on top of her breasts. Then, the tannaitic imagination places the accused wife on public display.[45] Concerning her display, the sages write, in Sotah 1.6,

> And all who want to see her, may see her, except for her male servants and her female servants, because she [might consider herself] higher than them.
> And all the women are permitted to view her;
> As it is said,
> *And all the women shall be taught not to follow your lewdness.*
> (Ezek. 23:48)

The tannaitic fantasy of the accused wife warns all women of the consequences of illicit female sexuality. It is worth noting that the sexually disloyal wife envisioned by the tannaitic sages comes from the class of elite woman; she is a woman of sufficient means to have servants. The public display and humiliation of the accused wife warns other women to stay within the confines of culturally approved rules of sexual and marital conduct.

Thus, the *sotah* is created to represent illicit female sexuality and its consequences. She exemplifies the opposite of appropriate female behavior, and as such she is contrasted to the women who come to view her. In a gender culture in which women generally are Other, the sexually suspect *sotah* become the new Other. Women, denoted by the spinners beneath the moonlight, are sexually pure. The *sotah* is singled out; the female spinners are depicted en masse. The accused woman's torn clothing and exposed breasts contrast with the supposition that women's bodies should be clothed and covered, as was the *sotah*'s body initially. Her bound and immobile body may be viewed by women with the freedoms to move and to walk. The *sotah* breaks rules and her representation by the Tannaim in tractate Sotah demarcates the boundary between good women and bad women.

In Sotah 6.1 the sages place words into the mouths of women who *spin*. By doing so, they create a second type of woman: the absent woman who is not spinning. The accused woman is absent from the group of spinning women. She shares neither in their activity nor their character traits. The accused wife does not spin.

Images and icons of spinning and woolwork are used in Roman-period Jewish culture in various ways to differentiate men and women from each other. Here, the image of spinning is used to separate some women from another, to create an Other in and among women. If women are generally Other in a religio-legal text written by elite men to protect their interests, then this analysis of Sotah 6.1 suggests how multiple Others are created and how these authors of legal texts fluidly deployed and redeployed statuses of otherness.

What does the construction of Others within Others accomplish? Without greater knowledge of the actual communities within which these texts were read and given meaning, it is difficult to know exactly. The spinning women depicted in Sotah 6.1 become part of social systems that would enforce the regulation of women's sexual behavior. Women themselves are portrayed as reporting on the legal transgressions of other women. Women take on policing powers— over other women. The report of positive rumors about the accused by the female spinners would, hypothetically, save her from the (obsolete) ritual of bitter waters. Incorrect or false information passed on by the spinners would end the woman's marriage and deny her opportunities to resist testimony that called into question her claims to innocence.

Through the words attributed to Rabbi Joshua, the tannaitic texts engage females to police female transgression from a masculinist set of rules. By creating the *sotah* as an Other among women, the sages separate women into two groups. They adopt one group into the structures of masculinism by giving the female spinners temporary powers of legal witness. The spinners are positioned, temporarily, as adult men (when male is defined as having the

power to witness), in contrast to the other female, the *sotah*.[46]
Within the general othering of women, Other women are created.[47]

Concluding Thoughts

"Gender," writes Joan Scott, "means knowledge about sexual
difference."[48]　By reading these two Mishnaic passages in new
ways, I hope to have contributed to the process of making visible
some ways that the tannaitic sages, through the production of the
various passages and tractates that comprise the Mishnah, produced
knowledge and notions about gender difference and cultural otherness.　Recognizing that, in a general sense, woman and femininity
are Other in societies whose cultural production is dominated by
men and masculinism, I examined some mechanisms by which
specific notions about differences between male and female were
created in the Mishnah and, we may speculate, among communities
of tannaitic sages.　These mechanisms included the gendering of
tools and the construction of females into several kinds of "women,"
each serving different functions with regard to the presentation,
protection, and perpetuation of the text's masculinist order.

The guiding impulse of this essay was to generate a move
beyond the common but facile concession that cedes to certain
tannaitic passages that sound "true" the authority of social-historical
"truth."　This move requires the articulation of problems with the
inherited frameworks through which we look at and imagine the
historical past.　Instead, these two passages about spinners were
contextualized into a general Roman-period discourse about femininity, gender difference, and the symbols of spinning and woolwork.　It
is possible to reorient our understandings of the truths of these
tannaitic passages.　These brief passages may carry pieces of true
information about what men and women did in Roman-period
Jewish communities, as well as information about how the lives of
men and women differed.　But more significantly for the writing of
a history of gender, difference, hierarchy, and otherness within
Judaism, these passages present us with evidence about how the
early rabbis used gendered images and icons from the ordinary
world of craftsworkers to conceptualize certain kinds of truths and,
in particular, how these sages crafted truths about gender.

NOTES

I wish to express my appreciation to Lisa Hazirjian and David Gutterman for critical readings and help in the production of this essay.

1. Pierre Canjuers and Guy Debord, "Preliminaries toward Defining a Unitary Revolutionary Program," in *Situationist International Anthology*, ed. Ken Knabb (Berkeley, Calif.: Bureau of Public Secrets, 1989), 305. See the second epigraph that begins this chapter.
2. This insight about multiple otherness is increasingly common in cultural criticism; see, for example, the essays in Toni Morrison, ed., *Race-ing Justice, En-gendering Power* (New York: Pantheon, 1992). Relying on the polar conception of Self and Other reinscribes the binary relations that make otherness seem so acceptable and familiar in the first place.
3. Albert Memmi, *The Pillar of Salt* (Boston: Beacon, 1992). I use the oral record of classroom exchange explicitly to make the point that as intellectuals one of our most constant mirror rooms is found in the classrooms in which we perform. Using the classroom as an authentic and authorized site of intellectual work is not, unfortunately, readily acknowledged in today's academic culture. A small but growing number of thinkers are taking seriously classrooms as sources of knowledge. See Jean O'Barr, *Turning Ideas into Actions: Building Feminist Institutions and Community through Women's Studies* (Chapel Hill: University of North Carolina Press, 1994); Gail Griffin, *Calling: Essays on Teaching in the Mother Tongue* (Pasadena, Calif.: Trilogy, 1992). I am also indebted to Lee Humphreys and Phyllis Kaminski for emergent examples of how to take classroom voices seriously in research, and to the students in Introduction to Judaic Civilizations, Duke University, Spring 1993.
4. This text by Memmi has not received much critical attention from Anglo-American thinkers. On Memmi's practice of simultaneously making "woman" analogous to the colonized subject and excluding "woman" from this category, see the brief note by Judith Butler in "Contingent Foundations: Feminism and the Question of 'Postmodernism,'" in *Feminists Theorize the Political*, ed. Judith Butler and Joan Scott (New York: Routledge, 1992), 14 and 21 n. 9.
5. Since theories of representation are always already theories about power, it is worth reminding readers of the following matrix of power between representer and represented: Memmi's "women" cannot respond to his portrayal of them; Memmi cannot respond to my portrayal of him; my students cannot respond, in this context and to this readership, to my representation of them.
6. There is a possible problem, of course, in falling into a dualistic

framework that sees only agents (male tannaitic sages) or victims (female Jews). By using the example of Memmi's representation of women, I do not wish to reify the tendency to see women, to see Others, as passive. Although we lack much of the historical documentation from Roman Palestine that would allow us to reconstruct the lives of Others, especially aspects of struggles against and agreements with hegemonic culture (whatever that may have been), we can posit their existence while noting the gaps in the sources.

7.   These examples, with additional documentation and argumentation, are taken from my study of gender imagery and everyday work lives in Roman-period Judaism in Palestine: "'The Work of Her Hands': Gendering Everyday Life in Roman-period Judaism in Palestine (70–250 C.E.), Using Textile Production as a Case Study" (Ph.D. diss., Duke University, 1993).

8.   The works of anthropologist Virginia Dominguez are helpful here. As she writes, "The perception of otherness is not just one of difference but inherently one of hierarchy." In her contribution to "The Politics of Representations. Of Other Peoples: Beyond the 'Salvage' Paradigm," in *Discussions in Contemporary Culture*, ed. Hal Foster (Seattle: Bay Press, 1987), 131.

9.   On the relations of otherness between researcher and topic, I am indebted to work by Rey Chow, *Writing Diaspora: Tactics of Intervention in Contemporary Cultural Studies* (Bloomington: Indiana University Press, 1993); Jonathan Z. Smith, "No Need to Travel to the Indies: Judaism and the Study of Religion," in *Take Judaism, for Example: Studies toward the Comparison of Religions*, ed. J. Neusner (Chicago: University of Chicago Press, 1983); and to James Clifford and George Marcus, ed., *Writing Culture: The Poetics and Politics of Ethnography* (Berkeley: University of California Press, 1986).

10. My concurrent interest in scholarly texts ("secondary" literature) and ancient texts ("primary" literature) means to highlight our tendencies to read ancient texts through unexamined modern constructs. We scholars create chains of representation as we tell histories, build arguments, and reconstruct the past. Going about these scholarly practices, we reify and reinscribe notions of gender at all turns. Examining the scholarship not as an evolution of guides to the ancient sources but as sources for gender culture themselves is, of course, related to the Foucauldian genealogical project (Michel Foucault, "Nietzsche, Genealogy, History," in *Language, Counter-Memory, Practice: Selected Essays and Interviews*, ed. Donald Bouchard (1971; Ithaca, N.Y.: Cornell University Press, 1977). Note also the irony that Teresa de Lauretis discerns: "The construction of gender also goes on, if less obviously, in the academy, in the intellectual community, in avant-garde artistic practices and radical theories, even, and indeed especially, in feminism" ("The Technology of Gender," in *Technologies of Gender: Essays on*

Theory, Film, and Fiction [Bloomington: Indiana University Press, 1987], 3).

11. See Peskowitz, "'The Work of Her Hands,'" for bibliography and extended critique. A sampling of works that come under these criticisms include L. Swidler, *Women in Judaism: The Status of Women in Formative Judaism* (Metuchen, N.J.: Scarecrow, 1976); S. Fuchs, "The Expansion of Women's Rights during the Period of the Mishnah" (M.A. thesis, Hebrew Union College, 1974); G. Mayer, *Die Jüdische Frau in der Hellenistich-Romischen Antike* (Stuttgart: Kohlhammer, 1987); L. Archer, *Her Price Is beyond Rubies: The Jewish Woman in Graeco-Roman Palestine* (Sheffield, U.K.: Sheffield Academic Press, 1990); idem, "The Role of Jewish Women in the Religion, Ritual, and Cult of Graeco-Roman Palestine," in *Images of Women in Antiquity*, ed. A. Cameron and A. Kurht (Detroit: Wayne State University Press, 1983); J. Hauptman, "Women's Liberation in the Talmudic Period: An Assessment," *Conservative Judaism* 26 (1972): 22–28; idem, "Images of Women in the Talmud," in *Religion and Sexism*, ed. R. R. Reuther (New York: Simon & Schuster, 1974); J. R. Wegner, *Chattel or Person: The Status of Women in the Mishnah* (New York: Oxford University Press, 1988); P. Flesher, "Are Women Property in the System of the Mishnah?" in *From Ancient Israel to Modern Judaism*, ed. J. Neusner, et. al (Atlanta: Scholars Press, 1989).

12. Samuel Krauss, *Talmudische Archäologie,* vol. 1 (Leipzig: Fock, 1910), 148: "Das Spinnen ist das eigenste Geschäfte der Frau des Hauses, dem sie sich auch dann nicht entziehen durfte, wenn ihr eingebrachtes Heiratsgut die Kosten ihres Unterhaltes reichlich aufwog, und sie arbeitete auch bei Mondshein und Lampenlicht."

13. Sulpicia [Tibullus], *Elegies* 3.16. The small corpus by Sulpicia, containing about forty lines of elegies, comprises the only Roman-period (Augustan period) Latin poetry written by a woman. See Tibullus, *Elegies: Introduction, Text, Translation, and Notes*, ed. Guy Lee (Liverpool: Cairns, 1982); and H. M. Currie, "The Poems of Sulpicia," *Aufstieg und Niedergang der Römischen Welt* 2.30.3 (1983): 1751–64.

14. This argument has been made by others in the course of using nonliterary materials to pursue the study of women and gender in this period. See Bernadette Brooten, *Women Leaders in the Ancient Synagogue: Inscriptional Evidence and Background Issues* (Chico, Calif.: Scholars Press, 1982); and Ross Kraemer, "Jewish Women in the Diaspora World of Late Antiquity," in *Jewish Women in Historical Perspective*, ed. Judith Baskin (Detroit: Wayne State University Press, 1991), 43–67. For similar methods and successes with regard to an earlier historical period, see Carol Meyers, *Discovering Eve: Ancient Israelite Women in Context* (New York: Oxford University Press, 1988).

15. CIL 1.(2).1211. M. Durry, ed., *Eloge funèbre d'une matrone romaine* (Paris: Budé, 1950). This translation is from S. Pomeroy, *Goddesses,*

Whores, Wives, and Slaves: Women in Classical Antiquity (New York: Schocken, 1975), 199. The date of the inscription is debated: Kampen dates this inscription to the first century B.C.E., whereas other scholars place it in the second century B.C.E.

16. See Sandra Joshel, *Work, Identity, and Legal Status at Rome: A Study of the Occupational Inscriptions* (Norman: University of Oklahoma Press, 1992), for a wonderfully sophisticated reading of funerary epitaphs to see the construction of identity by slave, freed, and free workers.

17. See also Eve D'Ambra, *Private Lives, Imperial Virtues: The Frieze of the Forum Transitorium in Rome* (Princeton, N.J.: Princeton University Press, 1993).

18. See, for instance, Proverbs 31:18–19, with regard to the woman whose lamp stays lit all night, as she works with distaff and spindle; and Apuleius, *Metamorphosis* 9.5–7, in which the construction worker's wife declares her virtuousness by means of the argument that all day and all night she wears her fingers to the bone spinning wool.

19. Peskowitz, "'The Work of Her Hands,'" chaps. 2 and 3.

20. Krauss's inclusion in his *Archäelogie* of topics that deal with (rabbinic notions about) women's lives is worth noting. This feature of scholarship on Judaism done during the late nineteenth and early twentieth centuries corresponds to the first wave of feminism in England, Germany, and the United States. Thus inclusion stands in contrast to a marked indifference to and absence of these topics in most scholarship produced from the 1940s onward.

21. Judith Romney Wegner, "The Image and Status of Women in Classical Judaism," in *Jewish Women in Historical Perspective*, ed. J. Baskin (Detroit: Wayne State University Press, 1991), 83.

22. Livy, *History (Ad Urbe Condita)* 1.57. On the political symbology of the rape of Lucretia set up by this portrayal of the chaste, virtuous wife, see Sandra Joshel, "The Body Female and the Body Politic: Livy's Lucretia and Verginia," in *Pornography and Representation in Greece and Rome*, ed. Amy Richlin (New York: Oxford University Press, 1992), 112–30.

23. On work, poverty, and illiteracy as ubiquitous in Roman antiquity (allowing, of course, for regional variations), see representative works by Keith Bradley, *Discovering the Roman Family* (New York: Oxford University Press, 1991); and Gildas Hamel, "Poverty and Charity in Roman Palestine, First Three Centuries C.E." (Berkeley: University of California Press, 1990).

24. Although "talking politics" should not be presumed the domain of only the elite classes.

25. Studies of named rabbis suggest a remarkably low number of religious elites, about one hundred men, during the tannaitic period. See Lee Levine, *The Rabbinic Class of Roman Palestine in Late Antiquity* (New York: Jewish Theological Seminary, 1989); and Shaye Cohen, "The Place

of the Rabbi in Jewish Society of the Second Century," in *The Galilee in Late Antiquity*, ed. Lee Levine (New York: Jewish Theological Seminary, 1992). Neither does the excavated material culture of Palestine suggest a local population of Jews with the accumulated wealth to support a large upper class.

26. By contrasting "myth" and "truth," I do not mean to suggest that myths are untrue while truths are true. Rather, I mean to point up the relative nature of both designations of truth value. See Michèle Barrett, *The Politics of Truth* (Stanford, Calif.: Stanford University Press, 1991).

27. Qiddushin 4.12, t.Qiddushin 5.14; Clement of Alexandria *Paedagogus* 2.11–12.

28. It is problematic at times to speak of "the rabbis" as a uniform group; my terminology here follows Wegner's generalization.

29. In articulating a project about gender—the construction of masculinities and femininities—I take for granted that women and women's lives remain central to this intellectual project. I am concerned that much recent work on gender and bodies in ancient and rabbinic Judaism has concentrated so totally on the construction of masculinity and the male body, thereby perpetuating the traditional masculinism of research in these field.

30. Joan Wallach Scott, *Gender and the Politics of History* (New York: Columbia University Press, 1988), 10.

31. Scott, *Gender and the Politics of History*, 2. See also her subsequent articles and responses to critics, including "The Evidence of Experience," *Critical Inquiry* 17 (1991): 773–97.

32. William Connolly's understanding of the cultural dynamics of identity and othering are helpful: "An identity is established in relation to a series of differences that have become socially recognized. These differences are essential to its being. . . . Identity requires difference in order to be, and converts difference into otherness in order to secure its own self-certainty" (*Identity/Difference: Democratic Negotiations of Political Paradox* [Ithaca, N.Y.: Cornell University Press, 1991], 64, cited in David Gutterman, "Taking on Masculinity: Sexuality, Gender, and Cultural Performance Anxiety" [unpublished manuscript, 1993]).

33. On men who spin: t.Berakot 7.5, t.Shehihot 10.5. Other Roman-period texts about men who spin include Pliny, *Naturalis Historia* 19.3; Josephus, *Antiquities* 18.310–70. But note the rhetorical and demasculinizing elements of Josephus's description of the brothers Anilaios and Asinaios as woolworkers, in Peskowitz, "'The Work of Her Hands.'" Note the text-critical analysis by Naomi Cohen, "Asinaeus and Anilaeus: Additional Comments to Josephus' Antiquities of the Jews," *Annual of the Swedish Theological Institute* 10 (1976): 30–37, which argues that in case of any historical truth to the text's description, textual corrup-

tions and mistranslations from Aramaic to Greek would suggest that the brothers were not really woolworkers but metalworkers.

34. The festivals of Pesaḥ and Sukkot. The following analysis of Moed Qatan 3.4 appears as chap. 5 in Peskowitz, "'The Work of Her Hands.'" It also was part of a paper, "And Spinning Flax Is a Respectable Occupation even for Men (Pliny, HN 19.3.18): The Gendering of Work in Roman-period Palestine," delivered to the section, "Rethinking Roman-period Judaism," at the 1992 SBL/ASOR annual meetings. I am indebted to critical remarks by Shaye J. D. Cohen on the delivered paper, and by Kalman Bland on the chapter. Any remaining problems are due only to my own convictions and stubbornness.

35. Moed Qatan 1.8.

36. On ṣîṣît, or fringes, see Num. 15:37–39. Note that the MS tradition includes two variations: la-ṣîṣît, for "fringes"; and lĕ-ṣîṣîtô, for "*his* fringes."

37. See Georges Lafaye, "Fusus," in *Dictionnaire des Antiquites Grecques et Romaines*, ed. Ch. Daremberg and E. Saglio (Paris: Hachette, 1877–1919), 1424–27.

38. The technology of drop spinning at this time is uncontested. On Palestinian excavations of spindles and whorls: Caesarea, Tell el-Ful, Gush Halav, Jalame, Meiron, Nessana, Samaria, Jerusalem, and other published and unpublished sites.

39. E. J. W. Barber, *Prehistoric Textiles: The Development of Cloth in the Neolithic and Bronze Ages* (Princeton, N.J.: Princeton University Press, 1991); R. J. Forbes, *Ancient Technology*, vol. 4 (Leiden: Brill, 1956), 170; J. Bird, "Handspun Yarn Production Rates in the Cuzco Region of Peru," *Textile Museum Journal* 2–3 (1968): 9–16.

40. I make this argument contra Yigael Yadin, *The Finds from the Bar Kokhba Period in the Cave of Letters* (Jerusalem: Israel Exploration Society, 1963), 182–87, pl. 59, who argues that in Roman Palestine, Jewish men as a matter of course, and not only on intermediate days, spun their own tekelet using the method of thigh spinning. For a critique of how Yadin interprets material culture to support this reconstruction, see Peskowitz, "'The Work of Her Hands.'"

41. Regarding the terminology of môžĕrôt: The usual root used in tannaitic documents to denote spinning and spinners is ṭ-w-h (cf. Ketubot 7.6 and t.Tohorot 4.11). Several explanations for the more specific meaning of môžĕrôt are possible, although none is yet fully compelling to me. The term could signify the fiber being spun, following distinctions made in some parts of the Hebrew Bible between the spinning of flax (š-z-r) and the spinning of wool (ṭ-w-h). See Exodus 26–28, 35–38. On Egyptian evidence for different spinning techniques for these fibers, see Barber, *Prehistoric Textiles*, 46–51, who suggests that the linguistic distinctions refer historically to different methods of spinning yarn, namely, to the specific technique of linen splicing. Yerushalmi Sotah 6 (20d) makes

some distinctions between variants of the term *môzĕrôt* and the spinning of linen or wool fibers, assigning *m-z-r* to flax production. This could suggest that the women in Sotah 6.1 spun flax; however, such a distinction is not carried through systematically in the tannaitic literature, where *t-w-h* is linked explicitly with flax spinning.

Other uses of the related roots (*š-z-r*) in rabbinic Hebrew would suggest a physical action that involves twining, twisting, or plying, perhaps to make yarn for uses other than eventually weaving, such as ropes, cord, heavy-duty threads, and twine that require multi-ply methods of production. See b.Eruvin 96b. I would lean toward this second explanation, although the ambiguities are not problematic for the argument put forth in this essay.

42. This, despite the ease with which we imagine women gathering and doing work "informally." The stereotypes of female labor marked by this ease need to be examined critically. See Vicki Schultz, "Telling Stories about Women and Work: Judicial Interpretation of Sex Segregation in the Workplace in Title VII Cases Raising the Lack of Interest Argument," *Harvard Law Review* 103 (1990): 1749–1844. It is worth quoting Judith Butler on the construction of female subjects through law, upon which both Schultz and I rely: "Juridical power inevitably 'produces' what it claims merely to represent; hence, politics must be concerned with this dual function of power, the juridical and the productive. In effect, the law produces and then conceals the notion of 'a subject before the law' in order to invoke that discursive formation as a naturalized foundational premise that subsequently legitimates that law's own regulatory hegemony. . . . Indeed, the question of women as the subject of feminism raises the possibility that there may not be a subject who stands 'before' the law, awaiting representation in or by the law. Perhaps the subject, as well as the invocation of a temporal 'before' is constituted by the law as the fictive foundation of its claim to legitimacy" (*Gender Trouble: Feminism and the Subversion of Identity* [New York: Routledge, 1990]).

43. Sotah 9.9.

44. I stress that these are textual strategies due to the growing tendency to recognize the lack of rabbinic influence in Galilee at the purported time that the Mishnah was promulgated. See Levine, *Rabbinic Class of Roman Palestine*, and Cohen, "The Place of the Rabbi." For the insight that moments of reorientations and periods of national and cultural crisis are particularly opportune times to see the realignment of notions about gender, see Judith Bennett, "Feminism and History," *Gender and History* 1 (1989): 251–72.

45. On suggested symbolic values for these ritual acts and others associated with the ritual of bitter waters, see Adriana Destro, *The Law of Jealousy: Anthropology of Sotah* (Atlanta: Scholars Press, 1989).

46. This mechanism of assigning to women the power to police is articu-

lated elsewhere in tannaitic sources. In the description of the tomb of Helena of Adiabene, the convert to Judaism, Helena was said to have commissioned a gold tablet engraved with the words of Num. 5:12–31, the scriptural discussion of the Sotah. See Yoma 3.10, t.Yoma 11.3, t.Sukk 1.1 and Naz 3.6.

47. I disagree with Destro, *Law of Jealousy*, that the description of the *sotah* is meant to place her beyond the boundaries of tannaitic culture. Rather, this representation of women serves *within their imagined culture* to define and construct appropriate femininity. On the use of the Other within, note Edward Said, relying heavily on Foucault: "Certain alterities, certain Others, have been kept silent, outside or—in the case of his study of penal discipline and sexual repression—domesticated for use inside the culture" (*The World, the Text, and the Critic* [Cambridge: Harvard University Press, 1983], 10).

The construction of Others among women has been articulated acutely and powerfully by feminist writers who are constructed as Other to white heterosexual women who have dominated the production of feminist thought. See Audre Lorde, "The Master's Tools Will Never Dismantle the Master's House," in *Sister Outsider* (Trumansburg, N.Y.: Crossing Press, 1984); Trinh T. Minh-ha, "Difference: 'A Special Third World Women Issue,'" in *Woman, Native, Other* (Bloomington: Indiana University Press, 1989); Evelyn Torton Beck, *Nice Jewish Girls* (Boston: Beacon, 1989).

48. Scott, *Gender and the Politics of History*, 10.

Chapter 6

The Other as Woman: An Aspect of Polemic among Pagans, Jews, and Christians in the Greco-Roman World

Ross S. Kraemer

In her introduction to *La Deuxieme Sexe*, first published in 1949, Simone de Beauvoir argued that the quintessential expression of otherness is woman.

> [Woman] is defined and differentiated with reference to man and not he with reference to her; she is the incidental, the inessential as opposed to the essential. He is the Subject, he is the Absolute— she is the Other.[1]

Among the supporting evidence she offers is a stunning quotation from Emmanuel Levinas, a small portion of which I reproduce here:

> I think that the feminine represents the contrary in its absolute sense. . . . Otherness reaches its full flowering in the feminine, a term of the same rank as consciousness but of opposite meaning.[2]

But if it is true that for men, women are the Other, the reverse is not obviously the case. De Beauvoir herself addresses precisely this question. The presentation of the Other as woman is not an objective description of reality but is in fact the expression and assertion of male privilege. She insists that the duality of Self and Other is not inherently a gendered duality, but is rather a human universal to which gender was only subsequently attached.[3]

The irony and the enigma de Beauvoir seeks to explain is, in part, how and why it is that women have generally acquiesced in

121

this male perception that we are the Other. My choice of the first person plural here is deliberate. De Beauvoir herself observes that of all the groups represented as the Other by the white male bourgeois, only women do not appropriate the language of the first person for themselves:

> Regarding themselves as subjects, they [these various groups] transform the bourgeois, the whites, into "others." But women do not say "We," except at some congress of feminists or similar formal demonstration; men say "women," and women use the same word in referring to themselves.[4]

The work of de Beauvoir, as well as that of many subsequent feminists such as Nancy Chodorow, Sherry Ortner, and Carol Gilligan,[5] suggests that gender is either a crucial component in male characterizations and constructions of the Other or, at the very least, a major component. Yet, at least in my own field, it is an aspect that has received virtually no attention. The otherwise excellent anthology of essays edited by Jacob Neusner and Ernest S. Frerichs, *To See Ourselves as Others See Us: Christians, Jews, "Others" in Late Antiquity*,[6] contains no reference to the work of de Beauvoir or to the role that gender plays in the formulation of the Other in the Greco-Roman world.

This neglect is all the more surprising given the role that gender and gendered characteristics play in the depiction of the Other in Greco-Roman authors, regardless of whether those authors (all either male, anonymous, or pseudonymous) or the Other were Jews, Christians, or pagans. In the second century, for instance, the pagan Celsus, a critic of both Judaism and Christianity, characterized Christians as "the foolish, dishonorable and stupid . . . slaves, women, and little children."[7] The author of 2 Tim. 3:6–8, probably writing in the same century, characterized women as particularly susceptible to false teachings because they are "overwhelmed by their sins and swayed by all kinds of desires, [they] are always being instructed and can never arrive at a knowledge of the truth." In the fourth century, the Christian Jerome not only leveled Celsus's accusation against pagans but also pointed to a causal connection between women and heretics.

> It was with the help of the harlot Helena that Simon Magus founded his sect. Bands of women accompanied Nicolas of Antioch

that deviser of all uncleanness. Marcion sent a woman before him
to Rome to prepare men's minds to fall into his snares. Apelles
possessed in Philumena an associate in his false doctrines. Mon-
tanus, that mouthpiece of an unclean spirit, used two rich and
highborn ladies Prisca and Maximilla first to bribe and then to
pervert many churches. Leaving ancient history, I will pass to
times nearer to our own. Arius intent on leading the world astray
began by misleading the Emperor's sister. The resources of Lucilla
helped Donatus to defile with his polluting baptism many unhappy
persons throughout Africa. In Spain, the blind woman Agape led
the blind man Elpidius into the ditch. He was followed by Priscil-
lian, an enthusiastic votary of Zoroaster and a magian before he
became a bishop. A woman named Galla seconded his efforts and
left a gadabout sister to perpetuate a second heresy of a kindred
form.[8]

These examples pose an interpretive dilemma. Given their potential
as evidence for women's religions, I am much intrigued by references
that suggest that heretics and other Others really were women, and
I have dealt extensively with such passages in my recent book.[9] Is
there a meaningful difference between accusations that the Others
(here identified with one's opponents) are real women and accusations that the Others have feminine attributes? Perhaps, as in
Jerome's insistence that behind all male heretics stood a female
agitator, the two may sometimes be related. It is not entirely clear
to me whether accusing heretics of being women (or of being
influenced by women) is a statement in which women's religion is
labeled as heresy or a statement by which heresy is feminized and
thereby denigrated.

However, this essay is not about women as the Other. It is
rather about something subtler and regrettably far more elusive:
the characterization of the Other as woman, and the role that
gender plays in the construction of the Other in religious propaganda of the Greco-Roman world. And I should emphasize that my
interest here is not with the kinds of philosophical and theological
debates that sometimes constitute the exchanges among Jews,
Christians, and pagans, but rather with the characteristic ways in
which they portray each other, both explicitly and implicitly, in the
images and symbols that are employed.

In those portraits, certain elements appear repeatedly. Jews,
Christians, and pagans alike routinely characterize the Other in
terms of sex, food, worship, dress, and knowledge or intellectual

acumen, though this by no means exhausts the list. In rabbinic characterizations, not only do gentiles eat problematic food and engage in the wrong sort of worship, that is, idolatry, but they are also presumed to engage in all sorts of sexual impropriety. In the Mishnaic tractate Ketuboth, the sages imply that gentiles (gentile men, though the rabbis do not see this distinction) are quite likely to have sex with any female in their control over the age of three years and one day.[10]

The typical cluster of characteristics is amply illustrated by a wild story that the first-century C.E. Jewish historian Josephus attributes to Apion of Alexandria. The author of a history of Egypt that appears to have contained considerable anti-Jewish material, Apion opposed the Jews of Alexandria (represented by Philo) before the Emperor Gaius ca. 41 C.E.[11] Supposedly, when Antiochus IV Epiphanes entered the temple in Jerusalem during the Maccabean crisis, he encountered an astonishing scene. Reclining on a couch within the temple was a Greek man; in front of him was a table laden with fish, meat, and fowl. Falling on his knees before the king, the man recounted a most piteous tale. Traveling about Judea on business, he had been kidnapped by foreigners (*ab alienigenis hominibus*: literally, men of a foreign race) who abducted him to the temple and fattened him up with lavish meals. Ultimately, those waiting on him told him the grim news: annually, the Jews kidnapped a Greek (*Graecum peregrinum*), fattened him up, slaughtered him in the woods, sacrificed his body, and ate the appropriate portions of the flesh, while swearing an oath of hostility to the Greeks.[12] At the end of this gruesome tale, this year's victim implores Antiochus to free him, out of respect for the gods of the Greeks.

Jews are thus accused in this story of misanthropy, murder in the form of human sacrifice, cannibalism, and impiety. Just before this story, Josephus also attributes to Apion a related tale in which Antiochus found a gold representation of an ass's head in the temple, thus revealing the true object of Jewish impiety.[13]

A vicious tale about Christians attributed to Marcus Cornelius Fronto (second century C.E.), now related in the *Octavius* of Minucius Felix (late second or early third century C.E.?), replicates slanders of misanthropy, ritual murder, and impiety, adding to them accusations of sexual deviance, both promiscuity and incest.[14] Christians are accused of the ritual murder and consumption of an infant, followed by sexual orgies in which men have intercourse with their mothers and sisters. Apion's claim that the Jews worshipped the head of an ass is a charge also leveled against Christians.[15] Jews do not escape accusations of sexual impropriety: Tacitus claims that although Jewish men abstain from sexual relations with foreign women, they are nevertheless "prone to lechery," and "among themselves nothing is banned."[16]

In Tertullian's several treatises against gentile characterizations of Christians, accusations identical or very similar to those in the *Octavius* are disputed in a most intriguing manner.[17] Not only does Tertullian refute these claims, but he also stands the accusations on their heads, accusing the gentiles themselves of precisely the illicit and erroneous food, sex, and worship that gentiles attribute to Christians. Christians, Tertullian insists, eat only holy and proper food, while the gentiles consume vile substances. Christians engage only in lawful, marital sex, abstaining from all other sexual intercourse, while the gentiles engage in all sorts of illicit sexual acts, from adultery to homosexuality, often compounded by incest.[18] As proof, Tertullian offers his own repugnant tale that demonstrates the tragic and evil consequences of gentile sexual practices.[19] A young boy of aristocratic family was once kidnapped and eventually sold back as a slave to his own father, who, not recognizing him, engaged in sexual intercourse with him. Ultimately, when the truth became known, the parents committed suicide. Tertullian insists that it is Christians who offer the proper worship to the one true God, gentiles who proffer the wrong rites to the wrong gods.

It is sometimes suggested that pagan misperception of Christian rites accounts for the distorted portrait of Christian practices. Pagans knew that Christians had a feast called *agapē* (literally: love): what else could a "love-feast" entail but acts of feasting and sexual license? Pagans heard that Christians partook of the body and blood of their god: could this not easily be transformed into accusations of ritual sacrifice and cannibalism? But these categories are by no means unique to gentile characterization of Christians: they appear with remarkable consistency in "orthodox" Christian characterizations of heretics, such as Epiphanius's account of the Phibionites or his denunciation of the Kataphrygians,[20] Philo's characterization of gentiles,[21] to which I shall return, and many others. Hence I am more and more inclined to think that any causal relationship between actual Christian practice and pagan characterization of Christians is likely to run in the opposite direction. That is, widespread, widely held preconceptions about Others provided the lenses through which pagans viewed and construed Christian ritual and belief (rather than the other way around). While it is quite apparent that communities use rules about sex, food, and worship to establish, maintain, and confirm boundaries between themselves and others, the actual correspondence or similarity of anyone's practices to the constellation of characteristics assigned to the Other would simply have been seen as confirmation of the rightness of the categories in the first place.

How we begin to comprehend and analyze the significance of the categories routinely employed by ancient writers to define the Other over against the Self is a complex matter. One aspect of these accusations that particularly intrigues me is the extent to which the characterizations of the Self and the Other can be sorted out into a series of binary oppositions that are consonant with the distinction of nature and culture articulated by Claude Levi-Strauss. Levi-Strauss's theory that the nature/culture dichotomy is a universal phenomenon leads us to expect a general association of the Self with culture and the Other with nature. In the examples I have offered, together with those I will shortly discuss in more detail, every one of these accusations proclaims that the Self is aligned with culture and the Other, with nature.

This is particularly relevant in a paper on the Other as woman, for gender is a central component of the nature/culture dichotomy, as the work of anthropologist Sherry Ortner has shown, most notably in her often-cited and much-critiqued 1974 essay "Is Female to Male as Nature Is to Culture?"[22] Working from Levi-Strauss's proposition that all societies not only distinguish between nature on the one hand and culture on the other but also ascribe negative values to nature and positive ones to culture, Ortner proposed that all societies associate men more with culture and women more with nature, since women's bodily processes of menstruation, pregnancy, and lactation lend themselves to such an identification. Ortner further argued that the universal devaluation of women relative to men had its roots in the universal devaluation of nature relative to culture.[23] Ortner's development of Levi-Strauss's theory suggests that gender will be, at the very least, a significant component in the construction of the Other.

Both Levi-Strauss and Ortner's revision of his model have been subject to extensive criticism for their claims that the nature-culture dichotomy (and its associated gendered dualism) is universal.[24] At least for the present, however, I am less interested in the universal nature of the nature-culture opposition and more concerned with whether it offers a useful analytical tool for understanding ancient polemic about the Self and the Other.

Since the focus of the conference at which this essay was originally read was "The Other in Jewish Thought and History," I have chosen to devote the remainder of my discussion to three ancient texts in which Jews are either the Self or the Other and in which gender figures significantly in the construction of the Other. Utilizing the first of these criteria narrowed my choices considerably, particularly since I wanted to include texts written from a Jewish perspective, not merely Christian or pagan anti-Jewish sentiment. I am not yet prepared to say whether these texts are broadly representative of the phenomenon under study, but taken together, these three examples allow me to make some significant observations and to pose some important initial questions.

The first text is an anonymous work usually titled *Joseph and Aseneth*, which I prefer to call *The Conversion and Marriage of Aseneth*.[25] Partly because I know this text extremely well and partly because it lends itself easily to such analysis, this text receives the majority of my attention here. My second text, Philo of Alexandria's *On the Contemplative Life*, allows me to explore the use of gendered language in a Jewish author about whom we know a reasonable amount, relatively speaking. We are also relatively well informed about the social and historical context of my third example, which constructs Jews not as the Self but as a highly denigrated Other, namely John Chrysostom's *Against Judaizing Christians*.

The Conversion and Marriage of Aseneth

The Conversion and Marriage of Aseneth is a highly problematic text for a multitude of reasons, not the least of which is its unknown authorship and provenance and its uncertain date. Virtually all recent scholarship considers the text Jewish, with a probable date between 100 B.C.E. and 100 C.E., although both of these assessments are far less secure than most discussions acknowledge. The story is extant in several textual traditions, and scholars are divided in their judgments about which of two major reconstructions, if indeed either, represents the earliest form of the story. My analysis here utilizes the text reconstructed by Marc Philonenko in preference to that of Christoph Burchard.[26]

The story of Aseneth and Joseph is set in the time of the seven years of plenty, when Joseph traveled Egypt collecting corn against the forthcoming famine. On his travels, he comes to Heliopolis, the city of the sun, where Aseneth lives with her father, Pentephres (an Egyptian priest), her mother, and their large household of servants. A virtuous virgin, Aseneth has had no contact with any males outside her family and has spent all of her eighteen years in the family compound, notably in a high tower sumptuously decorated and appointed. Her only fault seems to be her worship of Egyptian idols.

When Pentephres learns that Joseph is coming to his household seeking rest and refreshment, he calls his dutiful daughter and proposes that she marry Joseph. But Aseneth refuses, recounting the local gossip that Joseph is an abandoned son who, sold into slavery, had sex with his master's wife—and who is therefore clearly an unsuitable husband.

But when Aseneth actually sees Joseph, she is thunderstruck with his glorious appearance and with the power of God that emanates from him. Now, perceiving the error of her judgment and the error of her idolatry, Aseneth renounces her worship of Egyptian gods and flees to her high chamber, where she spends the next seven days in weeping, ashes and sackcloth, and general repentance. At the conclusion of her self-mortification, a figure resembling Joseph, but who is clearly an angelic being, appears miraculously in her chamber. Informing her that her repentance has been accepted, he instructs her to rise up from the floor, to wash herself, and to put on clean, fresh clothing. When she does so, he shows her a mystery involving bees and a honeycomb. When the angel finally departs, Aseneth returns to her family and marries Joseph, her preordained spouse, and they live, more or less, happily ever after.[27]

The portraits of both Aseneth and Joseph in this text afford us insights into the author's characterization of both Egyptians (who may or may not be equated with gentiles as a whole) and the community of Joseph, which we may equate with the author's understanding of Self. Interestingly enough, the author does not use the word *Jew*: the term *Hebrews* is used once, Joseph is called a Canaanite (though by Aseneth before her conversion), and he worships the God of Israel. Conceivably, this simply points to a careful pseudepigrapher, since the equivalents for *Jew* do not appear in either the Hebrew or the Greek Genesis.

The term that the author most frequently uses as a form of self-identification is *theosebēs*, a troublesome Greek word that literally means "one who fears or reveres God." Many scholars take the use of *theosebēs* in various Jewish funerary and donative inscriptions to designate non-Jewish participants in Jewish rituals and synagogues, in contrast to non-Jews who have undergone some formal rite of conversion to Judaism (designated as *proselytes*).[28] Since *theosebēs* is used first and foremost of Joseph himself, and secondarily of Aseneth after her conversion, it is apparent that here, at least, *theosebēs* carries connotations other than those supposed for most of the epigraphical examples. Despite the prevalence of *theosebēs* as a term of self-designation, in this discussion I will refer to the communal Self of this text as Hebrews. Scholars have generally been quite comfortable referring to the author's community as Jews, but it strikes me as not inconceivable that the distinction the author establishes between *theosebeis* and Egyptians might not be so easily extended to all Jews and all gentiles.

While the figure of Joseph unambiguously represents the ideal Hebrew, the figure of Aseneth is a little more complicated, for the author announces at the outset that "[Aseneth] was in no way like the daughters of the Egyptians but was in all ways like the daughters of the Hebrews."[29] This qualification notwithstanding, a comparison of the portraits of Joseph and Aseneth demonstrates that each exemplifies, respectively, the characteristics of Hebrew and Egyptian.

Within the opening chapters of the book, the central components of Aseneth's otherness are apparent: she eats foods unacceptable to Hebrews, she worships Egyptian gods, she wears emblems of her idolatry on her clothing and jewelry, and she is "contemptuous and disdainful of all men,"[30] a charge reminiscent of, though certainly not equivalent to, that of general misanthropy. Although she is initially presented as a loving and dutiful daughter, this image dissolves quickly when Aseneth refuses, obstinately, to acquiesce to her father's proposal that he marry her to Joseph.[31] Only in the matter of sexuality does Aseneth not conform to the pattern of the Other, for she is, like Joseph himself, a virgin.

The contrast between Joseph and Aseneth, Hebrew and Egyptian, Self and Other is illuminated brilliantly in Joseph's response to Aseneth when she comes forth to kiss him in greeting, as instructed by her father. Joseph puts his hand out against her breast, keeping her at a distance, and says,

> It is not appropriate for a *theosebēs anēr* (a man who reveres God),
> who blesses the living God with his mouth and eats the blessed
> bread of life and drinks the blessed cup of immortality and is
> anointed with the blessed ointment of incorruptibility, to kiss a
> foreign woman, one who blesses dead and deaf idols with her mouth
> and eats the bread of strangling from their table and drinks the cup
> of ambush from their libations and is anointed with the ointment of
> perdition. But a *theosebēs anēr* (a man who reveres God) kisses his
> mother; and his sister, who is of his own tribe and family; and his
> wife, who shares his bed; those women who with their mouths bless
> the living God. Similarly, also it is not appropriate for a *theosebēs
> gunē* (a woman who reveres God) to kiss a strange man, because
> such is an abomination before God.[32]

Proper food, worship, and physical contact, including sexual relations, differentiate us, here designated *theosebēs*, from them, here
designated *allotrioi* (Others, strangers).

That these characteristics are determinative is seen also in the
portrait of Aseneth after her conversion experience, which begins in
6:1, when Aseneth sees Joseph from her balcony and recognizes
instantly that he is in reality the son of God, whom she has slan-
dered foolishly. Aseneth divests herself of all the elements of
otherness: not only her idolatrous clothing and food but also her
pride and arrogance, and her hatred of men. Having insolently
refused her father's offer to become Joseph's bride, she now seeks
nothing more than the ultimate subordination of becoming his
slave.[33]

By the end of chapter 21, Aseneth has been wholly transformed
from an Egyptian to a Hebrew, from the Other to the Self. Now she
worships the living God, eats the proper foods, wears a primordial
wedding garment, and displays the proper humility toward her
parents and affection and subordination to her husband, Joseph.
Once the antithesis of a *theosebēs*, she is now worthy of that label
herself.

Throughout the text, gender plays a subtle but significant role.
First is the very fact that the Other, the gentile, is here represented
by a woman; the Self, the Hebrew, by a man. One may legitimately
note that this assignment accords with the passages in Genesis on
which this story almost certainly depends, but this begs the question
of whether the gentile is a woman because Joseph is said to have
married an Egyptian, or whether the story of Joseph and Aseneth
receives such extensive articulation precisely because it offers the

opportunity to elaborate upon the conversion of a woman. Here, I wish to propose that the choice of a woman as the exemplar of a convert, more familiar to readers in the biblical story of Ruth, may reflect the idea of the Other as woman and the Self as male, where a complete transformation of identity from the Other to the Self requires the element of gender as well.[34] This is clearly a complicated question. Stories about the conversion of women to Judaism may have their roots in various social realities. But recognition of real historical and social circumstances behind a text does not preclude other forms of analysis.

Second, both Joseph and Aseneth are described with important gender-specific language. Joseph is repeatedly called Powerful, *dunatos*, the very attribute of God in 8:10: he is not only the Powerful One of God (*ho dunatos tou theou*)[35] but also *anēr dunatos en sophia kai epistēmē*: a man strong (or powerful) in wisdom and knowledge.[36] Such language is not used to describe any of the female characters. Joseph is also called *sōphrōn*, wise, temperate, reasonable: one of the paramount virtues of the Greek male philosopher.[37] Aseneth, on the other hand, is described in certain stereotypical ways: in terms of her physical beauty, for instance.[38] In contrast to Joseph's wisdom and discernment, Aseneth is miserable and foolish.[39] Her initial failure to perceive the truth about Joseph and her acceptance of false Egyptian gossip about him exemplify her ignorance, a stereotypical trait of women in ancient sources.

Gender also figures in Aseneth's transformation from an Egyptian to a Hebrew. Though the narrative content of the story precludes Aseneth from becoming male, several details of the text point in this direction. First, she acquires wisdom and knowledge, discerning the truth about Joseph and understanding, though we do not, the mystery of the bees. More specifically, when Aseneth returns to the mysterious angelic figure after washing off the residue of her mourning and donning new clothing and a veil, the figure says, "Lift off the veil from your head, because today you are a holy virgin and your head is as a young man's."[40] This passage has ramifications far beyond this text, as those acquainted with the discussions of women's headcoverings in early Christianity and early Judaism will recognize,[41] but in any case, it is apparent that here, at least, Aseneth's transformation is accompanied by a suggestion of gender transformation as well.

Gender plays yet another role in Aseneth's transformation. In her preconversion state, Aseneth is not only a woman but also, in certain respects, the wrong sort of woman. True, she is a virgin, and true, she allegedly resembles the daughters of the Hebrews in all respects. But this can hardly be, for Aseneth is portrayed as arrogant, unsubmissive, and disdainful of men. After her transformation, Aseneth is the epitome of the good woman: submissive, willing if necessary to be servile, appropriately affectionate toward men, the ideal wife and mother. This, I think, points not so much toward a conception of the Other as woman but to another characterization of the Other in which what distinguishes Them from Us is that their women are not properly submissive and do not conform to appropriate gender categories, whereas our women are and do.[42]

Interestingly, the tale of Aseneth contains another presentation of the Other, in the form of Aseneth's initial and, of course, ultimately inaccurate portrait of Joseph. When her father, Pentephres, proposes marriage with Joseph, Aseneth is quick to catalogue Joseph's deficiencies: he is a foreigner, a fugitive sold into slavery, the son of a Canaanite shepherd who abandoned him, a slave who has illicit sex with the wife of his owner, and an interpreter of dreams. This is clearly an allusion to Genesis 37–39, particularly to Gen. 39:6–20, where the unnamed wife of Potiphar, Joseph's owner, attempts unsuccessfully to seduce Joseph and accuses him of attempted rape when she fails, resulting in Joseph's imprisonment. Joseph, depicted thus, is hardly an appropriate spouse for the aristocratic virgin daughter of an Egyptian priest.

The aspect of this that intrigues me most is the accusation of illicit sexuality. Sander Gilman, in his introduction to *Difference and Pathology*, points out that "the sexual dimension of human experience is one of those most commonly divided into the 'normal' and the 'deviant'." Obviously, "normal" or "proper" sexuality is most likely to be associated with the Self and "deviant" or "improper" sexuality, with the Other.[43] Eva Keuls has argued that in ancient Greece, sexuality was integrally linked with hierarchy and dominance, a view endorsed by an increasing number of scholars. Natural, proper sex was defined as a male penetrating a social inferior with his penis. Thus, sexual behavior necessarily expressed hierarchy and dominance, and the constitutive elements of hierarchy could be several, including gender, class status, and so forth. Proper sex expressed and reinforced concepts of superiority and inferiority, whereas improper sex was that which subverted those norms.[44]

Although Keuls's study focused on ancient Greece, her analysis offers much potential for the construction of sexuality among Jews and non-Jews alike in the Greco-Roman period. Viewed from this perspective, what is wrong with Joseph's alleged sexual misconduct is not simply that it violates (anachronistic?) biblical prohibitions against sex with the wife of another man but also that in having sexual relations with his hierarchical superior, Joseph symbolically and perhaps actually violates the categories of hierarchy and dominance.

It is important to note that while gender here is clearly a component in the construction of both the Self and the Other, the text itself, at least at an explicit level, refrains from attaching strong value judgments to either gender. At least in Philonenko's reconstruction, the text is remarkably free of any explicit misogyny or denigration of women.[45] Why this should be so is beyond the scope of this paper. But I think it is not irrelevant that the text of *Aseneth* is not explicitly polemical or even apologetic. It would be difficult to demonstrate that the main concern is the denigration of gentiles, a term the author never uses, or even of Egyptians.

It is possible to argue that at a more subtle level, the text intentionally refutes the images of Jews that we find, interestingly, in Egyptian authors such as Apion. At the conclusion of his treatise *Against Apion*, Josephus recapitulates both Apion's charges and his own refutations. Apion's accusations include the following: Jews are not an ancient people; they were originally Egyptians; they were expelled from Egypt for "bodily impurity"; Jewish law teaches impiety; and Jews hate other peoples. Though any connection between Aseneth and Apion seems impossible to demonstrate, it is noteworthy that the text asserts Joseph's Canaanite origins and presents Aseneth as a woman who hates men yet renounces that hatred, as an impious person who, through acceptance of the God of Joseph, becomes *theosebēs*.

Philo of Alexandria, *On the Contemplative Life*

Interestingly, though we can only speculate about the relationship between Aseneth and Apion, Apion played a much more central role in the life of the author from whom my next example is drawn, Philo of Alexandria. Handbooks routinely assert that Philo lived from ca. 20 B.C.E. to 50 C.E., but all we know for certain about Philo is that he represented the interests of the Jews of Alexandria in that same dispute before Gaius around 40–41 C.E., and that at the outset of his treatise against Gaius, he describes himself as aged and grey. A philosopher and mystic whose writings were not transmitted by Jews but rather by Christians, Philo is best known for his allegorical interpretations of Torah, which he appears to have known only in Greek.

Though it is not my intention to do so here, it would be relatively simple, I think, to demonstrate that for Philo, as for other Greco-Roman male authors, women were the prototypical Other. His assignment of feminine characteristics to men he considered Other is perhaps more subtle than his depiction of women as the Other, but it is nevertheless apparent in Philo's treatise *On the Contemplative Life*, which describes a monastic community of male and female solitary contemplatives, called Therapeutics, living on the shores of Lake Mareotis outside Alexandria.[46]

Virtually half the text[47] is devoted to a description contrasting the Therapeutics' banquets to those of others (literally! *ta tōn allōn sumposia*).[48] A comparison of Greek and Roman banquets to those of the Therapeutics displays the common constellation of nature/culture oppositions. Improper food, sex, dress, and concern for the body typify foreign banquets, while proper food, abstinence from sex, modest dress, and concern for the soul characterize those of the Therapeutics.

Within this constellation, gender plays a significant role. The drunken behavior of some banqueters is described in language reminiscent of bacchic frenzy, a phenomenon closely, though certainly not exclusively, identified with women.[49] Young male slaves are made up, like women, with cosmetics and braided hair.[50] What is particularly offensive about these banquets, for Philo, is that they lead some to abandon the masculine virtues of athletes, which they display in daylight, for debauched night-time revelries that many ancient authors associate with women's rites.[51] His greatest criticism is reserved for Plato's symposium, for its emphasis on what Philo interprets as pederasty, which robs men of *andreia* (manly virtue) and "sets up the disease of effeminacy in their souls."[52] Philo's translator in the Loeb series, F. H. Colson, argues that Philo has wrongly interpreted Plato here, which bolsters a reading of this passage as Philo's own feminization of the Other.[53]

Whereas foreign banquets feature boy slaves dressed as girls and sex between older men and younger boys, the Therapeutics are all ascetics who abstain from sexuality, an abstention made easier, perhaps, by the fact that most of the female Therapeutics are old and virgin and by the fact that the men and women sit divided from one another (women predictably on the left and men on the right) by a barrier that prevents visual and physical contact.[54] Philo thus portrays the foreign banqueters as feminized men, while the Therapeutics are presented as exemplars of classical masculine virtues. As I have demonstrated elsewhere, even the women of the Therapeutics are, for all intents and purposes, men: they are asexual, neither wives nor mothers, highly educated, devoted to philosophy and the pursuits of the soul.[55]

In comparison with the tale of Aseneth, Philo's characterization of the foreign banqueters has a much sharper edge, and his characterization of both the Self, here identified with the Therapeutics, and the Other has both clearer gendered components and stronger value judgments attached to masculinity and femininity. But both of these texts are relatively tame when compared with my third and last example, John Chrysostom's *Against Judaizing Christians*.

John Chrysostom, *Against Judaizing Christians*

In the fall of 386 C.E., John Chrysostom, later to become bishop of Constantinople but then a priest in Syrian Antioch, preached a series of vicious sermons intended to dissuade his congregants from their apparent habits of flocking to Jewish synagogues. The imminent onset of the fall festival season was clearly an impetus. Although the sermons were written for a Christian audience, much of their vehemence is directed at Jews, who clearly constitute the Other for Chrysostom. In his characterization of the Jews, gender plays a major role.

In the first place, Chrysostom identifies real women as prominent among the Judaizers, women whose husbands fail to prevent their impiety.[56] "Now that the devil summons your wives to the Feast of Trumpets and they turn a ready ear to his call, you do not restrain them."[57] Although blaming women for the idolatry of men is a tactic with ample precedent in Jewish scripture, Chrysostom seems to be doing more than utilizing an ancient stereotype. But in virtually the same breath, he goes on to insult and feminize even male Judaizers: "As a rule, it is the harlots, the effeminates, and the whole chorus from the theater who rush to that festival."[58] In the previous sermon, Chrysostom has made much the same accusation: "These Jews are gathering choruses of effeminates and a great rubbish heap of harlots; they drag into the synagogue the whole theater, actors and all. For there is no difference between the theater and the synagogue."[59]

Chrysostom's choice of language is particularly telling. The word that Harkins translates as "effeminates" is *malakoi*, which literally means "soft ones." Paul uses the same term in a list of those who will not inherit the kingdom of God, where it seems to designate males who are the receptive partners in sexual intercourse between men.[60] The same adjective describes the couches rejected by the virtuous, masculinized Therapeutics in favor of plain wood ones covered only with shredded papyrus.[61]

Many of the characteristics Chrysostom assigns to Jews are typically associated with women. They are sensual, slippery, voluptuous, and greedy: they are also associated with folly (*anoia*), madness (*mania*), and godlessness (*asebeia*).[62] Christians, by contrast, possess those classic male characteristics of *sophrosune* (moderation; temperance) and *aretē* (excellence; virtue, this last a translation itself derived from the Latin *vir*, man).[63] Drawing on the language of Hosea, Chrysostom compares Israel to an obstinate heifer.[64] The gluttony of the Jews gives birth to their ungodliness (*asebeia*), another feminizing metaphor.

Chrysostom's simultaneous feminization and denigration of Jews extends to the synagogue itself, a term that is conveniently feminine in Greek. Not only are the Jews prostitutes, but the synagogue itself is a brothel, "for where a whore is, that place is a whore house."[65] It is important to emphasize that Chrysostom here is not particularly talking about Jewish *women*, though I am confident he knew that some Jews were women. The insult is all the more effective if it is aimed primarily at men, although to call women prostitutes was certainly no compliment.

Chrysostom's inventory of invective and insult is by no means confined to the accusations presented here. By now, it will be no surprise that they, too, constitute a catalogue of nature/culture oppositions. The Jews are dogs, pigs, and goats, consumed with bodily concerns, lustful and savage. They are possessed by demons, which also inhabit the synagogues, and to dance with the Jews on their festival days is to dance with demons. Christians, on the other hand, either explicitly or implicitly, are rightly concerned with matters of the soul, properly controlled in their bodily concerns, chaste, and civilized. Demons have no truck with Christians.

Although it is certainly true that Christians believed that both men and women could be possessed by demons, the very metaphor of possession is a sexualized one, in which the model of a male demon and a female victim works far more easily than the reverse. In cultures where possession is a widespread form of religious experience, those possessed are almost uniformly either women or feminized men.[66]   Thus, it may be that Chrysostom's characterization of the Jews as possessed by demons is itself a further allusion to their femininity. In any case, the connections between women and demons, while hardly simple, warrant additional investigation.

There is much more to be said about the use of gender in the characterizations of the Other by pagans, Jews, and Christians in the Greco-Roman period than is possible in this paper. Indeed, the more I read for this essay, the more I realized I had undertaken a project of enormous scope. Many questions suggest themselves, both historical and theoretical, that I can do little more than pose at the moment.

One that particularly intrigues me is that the tendency to feminize the Other creates a particular dilemma for Christian writers as the metaphor of the Church itself as feminine becomes more and more prominent. Just how insulting can it be to call the Other female, if the Church, at least the so-called orthodox church, has already appropriated that metaphor for itself? I suspect that the problem already exists for Chrysostom, who does not merely label Jews female but who also chooses particular female imagery, especially that of the whore. That such a metaphor was already present to hand in Jewish scripture itself was convenient, but Chrysostom's use of it still constitutes a conscious choice. Thus, for many Christian writers, it would no longer be sufficient to label Jews female—a further distinction would have to be made, and this is precisely what we find, particularly in the overtly polemical literature such as the *Dialogue of Timothy and Aquila* or the *Dialogue between Synagogue and Church*. These texts profitably exploit the Christian splitting of woman into Mary and Eve, virgin and whore, identifying the church with Mary's virginity and the synagogue with Eve's pernicious sexuality.

Further, it is apparent to me that ancient writers, Jews, Christians, and pagans alike, employed the metaphor of gender very differently in their constructions of the Other. The texts that I have surveyed here suggest that the more the Other is characterized as feminine, and the more that characterization is construed as negative, the more real social conflict lay at the heart of the rhetoric. Thus we know that Chrysostom, whose language is both the most feminized and the most negative, was deeply concerned to differentiate between his own community and the Jews at a time when many of his congregants did not so discriminate. The Jewish community of fourth-century Antioch was vibrant and flourishing at this time, posing a real threat to Christian efforts to convert pagans, a threat made even worse only twenty-five years earlier by Julian's support of the Jews and his animosity towards Antioch's Christians.

By comparison, the gendered language in *Aseneth*, while present, is relatively mild. If the story of Aseneth reflects any real social circumstances, and this is a major question, they would seem to be those in which relations between Jews and Egyptians are generally cordial, where intermarriage is an option, provided the Egyptian becomes *theosebēs*. Philo's description seems to constitute a kind of median, whose social circumstances we can also ground to some extent. Philo is well known for his concern to harmonize classical Greek philosophical culture with his understanding of Judaism, and it is apparent that despite the recurrent tensions between Jews and non-Jews in Alexandria and elsewhere in Egypt, in which Philo himself played a significant part, there was also considerable toleration and accommodation between the two. Perhaps this correlates with the degree of his characterization of the Other as feminine and the value judgments he attached to that identity, at least in this text. Elsewhere, of course, Philo has some fairly nasty things to say both about the feminine and about real women.[67]

At the theoretical level, many questions remain. None of the ancient examples from which this chapter draws are known to have been authored by women, and most are known to be the work of men. This leads us to wonder what women in antiquity did with the constructs of woman as Other and male as Self. A handful of Christian texts suggest that some women internalized these categories and did indeed think of themselves as male, but we have so little evidence about the perceptions and constructs of women in the Greco-Roman world that such questions are difficult to approach except by analogy.

De Beauvoir herself pursued the question of why women do not appear to construe men as the Other. Unquestionably, women are socialized into dominant male values, but this is nothing more than a further observation, not an explanation.

Feminist research subsequent to de Beauvoir suggests that the very notion of Self and Other may not be universal, but may be the product of male experience in many, but by no means all, cultures. In her essay "Family Structure and Feminine Personality,"[68] Nancy Chodorow sought an explanation for the universal devaluation of women in the psychological ramifications of what she took to be a universal culture fact: infants initially identify with the nurturing agent, and in all human societies that initial nurturing agent is always a woman, though not always the biological mother. Positing the identification of the mother or nurturer with the female child, Chodorow suggested that girls grow up with an easily available gender and role identification. For boys, on the other hand, the socialization process consists of understanding what it means to be male primarily in opposition to what is feminine.

Although Chodorow's argument, like those of Levi-Strauss and Ortner, has come under attack for her attempts to isolate a single and universal origin for the widespread devaluation of women in human societies, her hypothesis remains intriguing for those communities in which primary responsibility for child care does fall to women, regardless of how such divisions are made and justified. It suggests that the idea of the feminine as Other is rooted in childrearing practices (and therefore might not exist in cultures where childrearing is not a gender-specific activity). Further, it suggests that in societies where all children are initially raised by women, both sexes will come to construct the concepts of Self and Other quite differently. Women may not conceptualize men as the Other not merely because we have been socialized to accept the dominant male constructions of reality without recognizing them as such but also because the entire notion of a major distinction between the Self and the Other may be a product, not of universal experience, nor even of universal male experience, but of particular male experience.

In the future, I hope to explore the utility of further analysis of the nature/culture aspect of the portraits of Self and Other in Greco-Roman polemic, as well as to consider correlations between the use of such rhetoric and the social location of the authors on the grid/group matrix of Mary Douglas, whose model I have previously employed in my work on women's religions in antiquity.[69]   These are tasks, however, for another time.

NOTES

1. Simone de Beauvoir, *The Second Sex*, trans. and ed. H. M. Parshley (1953; repr. New York: Knopf, 1974), ix.   A recent issue of *Signs: Journal of Women in Culture and Society* (18, 1 [1992]) contains a cluster of retrospective essays on de Beauvoir, several of which address her analysis of otherness, including Mary G. Dietz, "Introduction: Debating Simone de Beauvoir" (74–88); and Sonia Kruks, "Gender and Subjectivity: Simone de Beauvoir and Contemporary Feminism" (89–110).   For a useful summary and critique, see also Susan J. Hekman, *Gender and Knowledge: Elements of a Postmodern Feminism* (Boston: Northeastern University Press, 1990), 73–79.
2. Emmanuel Levinas, *Temps et l'Autre*, cited in de Beauvoir, *The Second Sex*, xix, n. 3.
3. De Beauvoir, *The Second Sex*, xix.
4. Ibid., xxii.
5. Nancy Chodorow, "Family Structure and Feminine Personality," in *Woman, Culture, and Society*, ed. Michelle Rosaldo and Louise Lamphere (Stanford, Calif.: Stanford University Press, 1974), 43–66; idem, *The Reproduction of Mothering: Psychoanalysis and the Sociology of Gender* (Berkeley: University of California Press, 1978); and idem, *Feminism and Psychoanalytic Theory* (New Haven, Conn.: Yale University Press, 1989).   Carol Gilligan, *In Her Own Voice* (Cambridge: Harvard University Press, 1982).   For references to Ortner, see below, nn. 22 and 23.
6. Jacob Neusner and Ernest S. Frerichs, eds., *To See Ourselves as Others See Us: Christians, Jews, "Others" in Late Antiquity* (Chico, Calif.: Scholars Press, 1985).
7. Origen, *Against Celsus*, 3.42.
8. Jerome to Ctesiphon, Letter 33.4.
9. Ross S. Kraemer, "Heresy as Women's Religion: Women's Religion as Heresy," in Ross S. Kraemer, *Her Share of the Blessings: Women's Religions among Pagans, Jews and Christians in the Greco-Roman World* (New York and Oxford: Oxford University Press, 1992), 157–73.
10. M. Ketuboth 1:4, where the *Ketubah* (marriage-contract) of a convert, a captive, or a slave who was converted, redeemed, or freed after the age of three years and one day is that of a nonvirgin, and virginity suits cannot be lodged against them, obviously because they cannot reasonably be expected to be virgins, having lived among gentiles.
11. Josephus, *Jewish Antiquities*, 18.257 ff.; Philo, *Embassy to Gaius*.

12. Josephus, *Against Apion*, 2.89–96.
13. Ibid., 2.80; see also 2.112–14.
14. Minucius Felix, *Octavius*, 9.5–7.
15. Tertullian, *Against the Nations*, 14; *Octavius*, 9.3.
16. Tacitus, *Histories*, 5.5.2.
17. There is considerable scholarly dispute over the dating of the *Octavius* and its relationship to Tertullian. For a brief recent summary, see the entry under Minucius Felix in *The Encyclopedia of the Early Church* (New York: Oxford University Press, 1992), 2:562–63.
18. Tertullian, *Apology*, 7, 8, 15; idem, *Against the Nations*, 7.
19. Tertullian, *Against the Nations*, 16.
20. Epiphanius, *Medicine Box*, 26.4–5, on the Phibionites, who engage in ritual sexual intercourse and eat an offering of semen and menstrual blood; 78.23 and 79.1 on women who celebrate improper Eucharists to Mary.
21. Philo, *On the Contemplative Life*, on which see below.
22. Sherry B. Ortner, "Is Nature to Culture as Female Is to Male?" in *Woman, Culture, and Society*, ed. Michelle Rosaldo and Louise Lamphere (Stanford, Calif.: Stanford University Press, 1974), 67–88.
23. "Men will tend to be culturally aligned with 'culture' and women with 'nature'" (Sherry B. Ortner and Harriet Whitehead, "Introduction: Accounting for Sexual Meanings," in *Sexual Meanings: The Cultural Construction of Gender and Sexuality*, ed. Sherry B. Ortner and Harriet Whitehead [Cambridge: Cambridge University Press, 1981], 7).
24. See especially Carol MacCormack and Marilyn Strethern, eds., *Nature, Culture, and Gender* (Cambridge: Cambridge University Press, 1980). Hekman, *Gender and Knowledge*, devotes an entire chapter (105–51) to the nature/culture issue; 118–19 deal specifically with Ortner's thesis and critique.
25. The original title of the work is not known, and the manuscripts assign it various titles. The more common *Joseph and Aseneth* has been preferred for its similarity to the titles of ancient Hellenistic romances, but I dislike it for its bias in favor of Joseph, who is in fact absent for much of the story.
26. Two significantly different reconstructions of the text have been proposed by Marc Philonenko (*Joseph et Aseneth: Introduction, texte critique, traduction, et notes*, Studia Post Biblica [Leiden: Brill, 1968]) and Christoph Burchard (*Joseph und Aseneth*, Jüdische Schriften aus hellenistisch-römische Zeit [Gütersloh, 1983]). Burchard translated his own provisional text in James H. Charlesworth, ed., *The Old Testament Pseudepigrapha* (Garden City, N.Y.: Doubleday, 1985), 2:177–247. English translations of Philonenko's text may be found in H. F. D. Sparks, ed., *The Apocryphal Old Testament*, trans. D. Cook (Oxford: Oxford University Press, 1984), 465–502; and in Ross S. Kraemer, *Maenads, Martyrs, Matrons, Monastics: A Sourcebook on Women's*

Religions in the Greco-Roman World (Philadelphia: Fortress, 1988), 263–79.

    Aseneth was the topic for the 1991–92 Philadelphia Seminar on Christian Origins, chaired by myself and Robert A. Kraft; it was also the focus of Kraft's doctoral seminar that same year. Although recent scholarship on *Aseneth* has tended to accept Burchard's provisional reconstruction, our work, still in progress, raised significant questions about this consensus. In correspondence, Burchard expressed his agreement with many of our concerns. For a brief discussion of the gendered dimensions of the different reconstructions, see Kraemer, *Her Share of the Blessings*, 110–13.

27. This summary is taken from Kraemer, *Her Share of the Blessings*, 110.
28. The debate over whether *theosebēs* is a technical term for a "partial proselyte" has a long history. With the discovery of an inscription from the ancient city of Aphrodisias in western Asia Minor, where the term does have a technical connotation of some sort, many scholars consider the matter closed, though others, including myself, are not as convinced. The Aphrodisias inscription, with extensive commentary and discussion of prior arguments, was published by J. Reynolds and R. Tannanbaum, *Jews and Godfearers at Aphrodisias*, Cambridge Philological Society Supplementary Vol. 12 (Cambridge: Cambridge Philological Society, 1987). Two recent discussions, with extensive bibliography, may be found in P. W. van der Horst, *Ancient Jewish Epitaphs: An Introductory Survey of a Millenium of Jewish Funerary Epigraphy (300 B.C.E.–700 C.E.)* (Kampen: Kok Pharos, 1991), 68–72; and Paul R. Trebilco, *Jewish Communities in Asia Minor*, SNTS Monograph Series 69 (Cambridge: Cambridge University Press, 1991), 145–66. Interestingly, none of these discussions has taken into account the prevalence of *theosebēs* in *Aseneth*.
29. *Aseneth* 1:7. All translations are mine, published in *Maenads*.
30. *Aseneth* 2:1; also 3:9–11; 2:5.
31. Ibid., 4:11–16.
32. Ibid., 8:4–7.
33. Ibid., 6:8.
34. In the case of Ruth, the story may be a response to Persian-period attempts to dissolve marriages with outsiders and to discourage future ones.
35. *Aseneth* 3:6; 4:7; 18:1–2.
36. Ibid., 4:9.
37. Ibid., 4:8.
38. This is true also of Joseph, whose physical appearance and beauty receive considerable attention.
39. *Aseneth* 6:7.
40. Ibid., 15:1.

41. See Kraemer, *Her Share of the Blessings*, 146–49, with further bibliography in the notes.

42. I would especially like to thank Jacqueline Z. Pastis for her comments at a 1991–92 Philadelphia Seminar on Christian Origins session on *Aseneth*, which suggest this reading. In addition, the figure of Vashti in the book of Esther springs to mind as another example of this.

43. Sander L. Gilman, *Difference and Pathology: Stereotypes of Sexuality, Race, and Madness* (Ithaca, N.Y.: Cornell University Press, 1985), 24. Gilman also writes here, "For a secure definition of self, sexuality and the loss of control associated with it must be projected onto the Other."

44. Eva Keuls, *The Reign of the Phallus: Sexual Politics in Ancient Athens* (New York: Harper & Row, 1985). See also John Winkler, "Unnatural Acts: Erotic Protocols in Artemidoros' Dream Analysis," in *The Constraints of Desire: The Anthropology of Sex and Gender in Ancient Greece* (New York and London: Routledge, 1990), 17–44.

45. I suggest that this is one of the many ways in which the Philonenko text differs from that of Burchard: for a preliminary discussion, see Kraemer, *Her Share of the Blessings*, 110–13.

46. The categorization of the Other as female may occur elsewhere in Philo. I have not had time to study this.

47. Philo, *On the Contemplative Life*, 40–90.

48. Ibid., 40.

49. Ibid.

50. Ibid., 51.

51. E.g., Livy's account of the Bacchanalia in *Annals of Rome*, 39.8–18; in Kraemer, *Maenads*, 247–56; Juvenal, *Satire 6*, excerpted in the same, 39–42.

52. Philo, *On the Contemplative Life*, 60: *theleian de noson tais psychais enapergazomenos.*

53. F. H. Colson, *Philo*, Loeb Classical Library (Cambridge: Harvard University Press, 1941), 9:521–22.

54. Philo, *On the Contemplative Life*, 68–69.

55. Ross S. Kraemer, "Monastic Jewish Women in Greco-Roman Egypt: Philo Judaeus on the Therapeutrides," *Signs* 14, 2 (1989): 342–70.

56. John Chrysostom, *Against Judaizing Christians*, 2.3.4–6. Unless otherwise noted, the translation here is from Paul W. Harkins, *Saint John Chrysostom: Discourses against Judaizing Christians*, Fathers of the Church 68 (Washington, D.C.: Catholic University of America Press, 1979).

57. Ibid., 2.3.4. In 4.7.3, he suggests that slaves and women are particularly vulnerable to the allure of Judaism.

58. Ibid., 2.3.4.

59. Ibid., 1.2.7.

60. 1 Cor. 6:9. For the debate on its meaning, see D. F. Wright, "Homosexuals or Prostitutes? The Meaning of *Arsenokoitai* (1 Cor. 6:9, 1 Tim.

1:10)," *Vigiliae Christianae* 32 (1984): 2:125–53; W. L. Petersen, "Can *Arsenokoitai* Be Translated by 'Homosexuals'? (1 Cor. 6:9, 1 Tim. 1:10)," *Vigiliae Christianae* 40 (1986): 2:187–91; and Wright, "Translating *Arsenokoitai* (1 Cor. 6:9, 1 Tim. 1:10)," *Vigiliae Christianae* 41 (1987): 4:396–98. If, as some suggest, *malakoi* means "masturbators" (as it does in modern Greek), the text here has a somewhat different cast.

61. Philo, *On the Contemplative Life*, 69.
62. Chrysostom, *Against Judaizing Christians*, 1.5.1; 1.6.5.
63. Ibid., 1.6.2 (a man of sound and prudent mind).
64. Ibid., 1.2.5, also to an untamed calf.
65. Ibid., 1.3.1; translation mine, paraphrasing slightly!
66. E.g., contemporary Zar possession. In antiquity, this seems true of some forms of Dionysian possession. In Euripides' *Bacchae*, for example, Dionysus possesses all the women of the house of Cadmos and two males, the former king Cadmos and the blind seer Teiresias, both of whom are described in feminized terms. See Kraemer, *Her Share of the Blessings*, 36–49.
67. See Kraemer, "Monastic Jewish Women." See also Dorothy Sly, *Philo's Perception of Women*, Brown Judaic Studies 209 (Atlanta: Scholars Press, 1990).
68. Chodorow, "Family Structure."
69. Particularly in Kraemer, *Her Share of the Blessings*.

Chapter 7

Navigating the Anomalous: Non-Jews at the Intersection of Early Rabbinic Law and Narrative

Steven D. Fraade

I. Introduction

Rabbinic legal writings are preoccupied not simply with defining categories and sorting their contents, but with navigating the brackish waters among them—the anomalous areas where boundaries either overlap or leave gaps. Such human discourse shares in the divine work of separation, or *havdalah*, by which the world was created. What is more important, it facilitates the necessary yet anxious commerce across the permeability of such categorical boundaries: between holy and profane, pure and impure, male and female, land of Israel and the Diaspora, people of Israel and the nations. Here I wish to focus on the last pair, in particular on the problem of the adjudication of civil claims between Jew and gentile, each of whom inhabits a different but intersecting nomian world.[1] Even more particularly, I shall examine the "double standard" by which the gentile's goring ox and his lost or robbed property are treated when they fall within the Jewish *nomos*. To those who might think that I have whittled down my topic too much, let me quote Maimonides, who, in commenting on just one Mishnaic passage central to this subtopic, says, "Discussion of this subject would require a separate book." Indeed, the volume of traditional treatment of this topic is so great that I will have to omit from consideration not only most of what Maimonides has to say but also many of the Babylonian Talmudic texts and the subsequent history of commentary and codification. Here I shall focus my attention on the earlier, formative Palestinian rabbinic texts that lie at the base of that subsequent legal history of interpretation.[2]

Although a convenient excuse, space constraints alone do not dictate my strategy of concentrating on the earlier texts. Past treatments have tended to subsume these earlier formulations under later, more systematic codifications for two interconnected reasons. First, the earlier formulations often appear incommensurate with one another, being more ambivalent in their treatment of the gentile and hence more difficult to domesticate to a unified Jewish view of the non-Jew, or even to a linear progression toward the same. Second, many of these earlier formulations, in their "discriminatory" treatment of the gentile, are embarrassingly foreign to the more "liberal" sensibilities of later interpreters. We must attend to this polysemic and problematic navigation of the anomalous position of the non-Jew in Jewish law in its own historical and ideational right.[3]

Legal discourse is not simply the linear application of fixed rules to changing cases and circumstances but is the dynamic interplay of intersecting lines of categorical identity and difference that continually reconfigure a culture's sense of solidarity with itself and separation from others. To begin with, Israel is uniquely circumscribed by its reception and practice of the divinely authorized, if not authored, rules of Torah, whereby it is set apart from other peoples. The internal government of Israel's collective life by the words of Torah aligns it with a sacred historical scheme to which other peoples are ancillary at best. According to this conception, Israel inhabits a nomian world exclusive of other peoples.

But the divine author of Israel's *nomos* is also the creator and governor of the nations among whom Israel dwells and to whom Israel is destined to be, by virtue of its distinctive life of Torah, a sharer of light and blessing. According to this conception, Israel and the nations inhabit a shared nomian world, or at least interlocking nomian worlds that share, ultimately at least, a common governor. In the more immediate historical interim, however, Israel is governed by the rules and rulers of other peoples, whether de jure or de facto. According to this reality, Israel's nomian life depends on and may be threatened by a gentile *nomos* whose authority it must acknowledge but whose religious legitimacy it must oppose in order to preserve its own sense of nomian solidarity and separation.

Navigating these intersecting and interfering concepts and realities requires a variety of discursive strategies. Therefore, while our topic is legal (halakhic), several of our texts will be narrative (aggadic). Although Jewish studies, both traditional and academic, have suffered a bifurcation of interest in rabbinic halakhic and aggadic literary formations, the two are closely interconnected and interdependent in rabbinic textual practice.[4] The enunciation of rules and the telling of stories *together* contribute, albeit in very different ways, to the rhetorical construction of a Jewish nomian world in which the anomalous may be safely, if not simply, navigated. In order to highlight this diversity and interdependence of navigational textual practices, we shall examine them according to their documentary settings.

II. Ruling and Crossing Categorical Lines: Mishnah and Tosefta

The following passage from the Mishnah is the locus classicus for discussion of the "double standard" applied to the non-Jew in Jewish law.

1. *Mishnah Baba Qamma* 4:3:

> (A) If an ox of an Israelite gored an ox dedicated to the Temple, or an ox dedicated to the Temple gored an ox of an Israelite, neither owner is culpable, as it is said, "[When a man's ox injures] the ox of his neighbor (*rēʿēhû*) [and it dies, they shall sell the live ox and divide its price; they shall also divide the dead animal]" (Exod. 21:35).

> (B) If an ox of an Israelite gored an ox of a gentile, the owner is not culpable. But if an ox of a gentile gored an ox of an Israelite, regardless whether it is harmless (*tām*) or an attested danger (*mûʿād*), the owner pays full damage.[5]

The biblical law of an ox goring another ox makes a single distinction between two types of goring oxen: If the goring ox was not previously known to be a danger, the owners share the loss equally, each one receiving half the price of the sold goring ox and half the carcass of the dead gored ox (Exod. 21:35). If, however, the goring ox was previously known to be a danger and its owner had been forewarned to restrain it, the owner of the goring ox is culpable for the loss, making payment to the owner of the gored ox for the full value thereof, but receiving its carcass (Exod. 21:36).

The Mishnah, in understanding the biblical word "his neighbor" (Exod. 21:35) to denote two Israelites of similar status, enunciates other possible distinctions between the owners, thereby introducing two anomalous situations that it treats in strikingly different ways. In the first example (A), "his neighbor" is taken to exclude from the biblical rule cases in which one ox has been dedicated (presumably by an Israelite) to the temple, and hence is now owned formally by the temple, while the other ox is owned by an Israelite. Even if the goring ox is a known danger (*mûʿād*), its owner bears no culpability for injury done by his ox to the other. The two cases of this rule are symmetrical: Regardless of whether the temple ox or the Israelite ox did the goring, there is no culpability. However, in the two cases where one of the owners is a gentile (B), only when the owner of the gored ox is a gentile does the owner of the goring ox (a Jew) bear no culpability. Conversely, if the owner of the goring ox is a gentile, he is culpable for full damage, even if his ox is a first-time offender (*tām*) and the owner has not been forewarned to restrain him.

Rabbinic commentators from the Talmuds on have recognized the asymmetry of this rule, and its departure from the biblical model, and have sought to justify it with various logical and exegetical arguments, some of which we will meet below.[6] Here we may simply note that the Tosefta (*Baba Qamma* 4:2), in dealing with the case of *two* gentile ox owners who desire to be judged according to Israelite law, requires full-damage payment regardless of whose ox does the goring and regardless of whether the goring ox has gored before, since "there is neither *tām* nor *mûʿād* [as categories] in gentile laws of damages."[7] Although the gentiles desire to be judged according to the rules of the Jewish *nomos*, in which full damages are only paid by the ox owner who failed to restrain his previously attested goring ox (*mûʿād*), they are judged even by Jewish judges according to the rules of their own *nomos*, wherein this allowance is not made.

Thus, in the anomalous cases of either two Israelite oxen of different status or two gentile oxen of (presumably) similar status that come before an Israelite court, a single principle can be applied regardless of whose ox has done the goring: in the first no culpability, in the second full culpability. But in the cases of damages between an Israelite and a gentile ox, which principle is applied depends on whose ox has done the goring. These cases are more deeply anomalous than the others because the two parties belong to entirely different nomian worlds that must now be crisscrossed. Can a Jew be held legally culpable for damages to a non-Jew according to a rule that is understood to govern intranomian Israelite relations? Conversely, can a non-Jew expect favorable treatment within the Jewish *nomos* if he has not accepted, and is understood to have rejected, its norms?[8] If the non-Jews' legal status cannot be predicated on their acceptance of the terms of the Jewish *nomos*, perhaps they might be thought to inhabit a *nomos* of their own whose religious legitimacy could be acknowledged in its own right. This brings us to the rabbinic idea of a separate, but interlocking, *nomos* of the descendants of Noah.

2. *Tosefta ʿAbodah Zarah* 8(9): 4–5:

> Concerning seven commandments were the descendants of Noah commanded: concerning adjudication, and concerning idolatry, and concerning blasphemy, and concerning sexual immorality, and concerning bloodshed, and concerning robbery, and concerning a limb torn from a living animal. . . . Concerning bloodshed, how so? A gentile against a gentile or a gentile against an Israelite is culpable (*ḥayyāb*), [whereas] an Israelite against a gentile is exempt (*pāṭûr*). Concerning robbery, whether stealing or robbing, or taking a beautiful woman captive (Deut. 21:11), or the like: a gentile against a gentile or a gentile against an Israelite is prohibited (*ʾāsûr*), [whereas] an Israelite against a gentile is permitted (*mûtār*).[9]

Since both the Jewish *nomos* (the Torah) and the gentile *nomos* (the seven Noahide laws) prohibit robbery and bloodshed, the members of each are prohibited from such acts against their fellow members and would be presumed to be tried for such by their respective courts.[10] However, what happens when the boundary between these two nomian worlds is crossed? We may presume that a gentile who so acts against a Jew could be found guilty in a Jewish court since he has been prohibited from such actions by the seven Noahide laws, which are also binding upon, and hence adjudicable by, Jews.[11] But the converse case—a Jew so acting against a gentile— does not necessarily follow. Although our text does not provide an explanation, we may infer one from other texts to be considered below. Since the gentile has not accepted the norms of the Jewish *nomos*, or Torah, he is not entitled to its protection. Similarly, since gentile courts do not rule according to the norms of that Jewish *nomos*, they could not hold a Jew legally culpable according to the terms of the Torah. As the Mekilta, in the name of R. Eleazar b. Azariah, interprets Exod. 21:1, "You may judge theirs, but they may not judge yours."[12] Before we become too disturbed by the moral implications of this juridical asymmetry, let us look at another passage from the Tosefta, which stakes out a very different position.

3. *Tosefta Baba Qamma* 10:15:

> One who robs from a gentile is liable to return [what he robbed]. Robbing from a gentile is viewed more strictly than robbing from an Israelite . . . because of profanation of the divine name.[13]

If the argument here strikes us as contradicting that of the preceding passage, we need to recognize that it is set on an entirely different foundation: Jewish behavior toward and before the gentiles can result in their commendation or condemnation of the Jewish *nomos* and its divine governor. Although the Jewish *nomos* is, in one sense, exclusive of the gentile who lives outside its norms and bounds, it is in view of and responsive to the reaction of the gentile, especially at those points at which Jewish behavior directly intersects that of the gentile. Jewish practice, especially beyond what is juridically required, that occasions gentile praise of the Jewish *nomos* is deemed sanctification of God's name, whereas the opposite is deemed profanation of God's name. The former is to be encouraged, the latter to be discouraged, but either is difficult to legislate.[14]

III. Reconfiguring Scriptural Rules: Midrash Halakhah

The Tosefta is not alone, however, in combining seemingly incommensurate representations of the status of non-Jews in Jewish law. The Sifra, the earliest rabbinic commentary to the Book of Leviticus, similarly enunciates two colliding tacks through the anomalous waters of Jewish-gentile legal relations. It orients both to the words of Scripture:

1. *Sifra Wayyiqra' pereq* 22:1:

> ["When a person sins and commits a trespass against the Lord by dealing deceitfully with his fellow (*'ămîtô*) with regard to a deposit or a pledge, or robbery, or by defrauding his fellow, or by finding

something lost and lying about it; if he swears falsely regarding any one of the various things that one may do and sin thereby—when he has thus sinned and realized his guilt, he shall restore that which he got through robbery or fraud, or the deposit that was entrusted to him, or the lost thing that he found, or anything else about which he swore falsely. He shall repay the principal amount and add a fifth part to it. He shall pay it to its owner when he realizes his guilt" (Lev. 5:21–24)]: What does Scripture signify by "his fellow" "his fellow" [two times]? The first "his fellow" comes to exclude the Most High (*haggābôah*). The second "his fellow" comes to exclude others (*'ăḥērîm*) [non-Jews].[15]

The commentary understands the repetition of "his fellow" to emphasize that Scripture is legislating behavior between "fellows" of a shared *nomos*, excluding thereby the obligation to restore and pay a penalty for that which has been wrongfully obtained or misused of God (involving property dedicated to the temple) or non-Jews. For our present purposes, we may presume that the Sifra's exclusions of culpability apply to robbery and the retaining of lost property, as scripturally specified. Note that the two excluded classes of owners are the same as in *Mishnah Baba Qamma* 4:3, with reference to a goring ox: property dedicated to the temple and property of a gentile. The Sifra passage, however, is more consistent in applying its exclusionary principle, since it is only dealing with the Israelite behavior toward the Other and not, as in the Mishnaic passage, with the behavior of the Other toward the Israelite.[16] In striking contrast to this exclusionary exegesis, let us now consider the following inclusionary interpretation of another verse from Leviticus:

2. *Sifra Behar pereq* 9:2–3:

["If a resident alien among you has prospered, and your brother, being in straits, comes under his authority and gives himself over to the resident alien among you . . . , after he has been sold he shall have the right of redemption. One of his brothers shall redeem him . . . ; or, if he prospers, he shall redeem himself. He shall compute with his purchaser the total from the year he gave himself over to him until the jubilee year. . . . If he has not been redeemed by any of those ways, he shall go forth in the jubilee year, he and his children with him" (Lev. 25:47–55)]: R. Simeon says: From whence can we derive that the robbery of a gentile is [indeed] robbery? Scripture teaches, "after he has been sold." Is it possible that he [the Israelite] shall [forcibly] seize him in order

that he shall go forth? Scripture teaches, "he shall have the right
of redemption (*gĕ'ûlâ*)" [for money].[17] Is it possible that he [the
Israelite] shall set an arbitrary [low] price for him? Scripture
teaches, "he shall compute with his purchaser." He shall reckon
precisely with him. But perhaps this only speaks of a gentile who
is not subject to your authority? And if so, what can you do with
him [but reckon with him precisely]? When it says "he shall go
forth in the jubilee year, he and his children with him," behold,
Scripture speaks of a gentile who is subject to your authority.[18] If
Scripture speaks thus of [redeeming through precise payment] a
gentile who is indeed subject to your authority, how much more so
with regard to a gentile who is not subject to your authority. If the
Torah has thus ruled strictly concerning the robbed property of a
gentile [that it is forbidden], how much more so concerning the
robbed property of an Israelite.[19]

The commentary places the biblical legislation in a setting in which
the non-Israelite to whom the Israelite has been sold in servitude
lives under Israelite jurisdiction. If so, it is presumed that the
Israelite could have forced the non-Israelite to release his Israelite
brother from servitude. The fact that Scripture requires the
Israelite to reckon exactly the time remaining until the jubilee so as
to pay the non-Israelite justly, without taking advantage of his
weaker position, is understood to imply a prohibition of Israelite
robbery of a gentile in all cases. This exegesis comes, therefore, to
a diametrically opposite conclusion regarding the Israelite robbing of
a gentile than does the previously cited passage of the Sifra that
excluded Israelite culpability for robbing a gentile since the latter is
not his "fellow." However, lest we think that our present passage is
totally nondiscriminatory, we should note that underlying its final a
fortiori argument is the assumption that robbing an Israelite is still
more severe than robbing a gentile, in contrast to *Tosefta Baba
Qamma* 10:15, which stated the opposite.[20]

IV. Reconfiguring Scriptural Narratives: Midrash Aggadah

For legal discourse to be rhetorically effective in configuring Israel's
self-understanding vis-à-vis the non-Jewish nations, it must intersect the narrative accounts of Israel's life among those nations, both
biblical and postbiblical. The following passage, from the earliest
rabbinic commentary to the Book of Deuteronomy, comments on a

biblical passage that is rabbinically understood to denote God's favoring of Israel at the time of His giving of the Torah to them at Mount Sinai, but now exegetically juxtaposed to a narrative of an encounter between rabbinic and Roman authorities of a much later time:

1. *Sifre to Deuteronomy 344*

> Another interpretation: "Lover, indeed, of the people(s)" (Deut. 33:3): This teaches that the Holy One, blessed be He, did not dispense love to the nations of the world as He did to Israel. Know that this is so since they [the sages] have said: "The robbed property of a gentile is permitted, while the robbed property of an Israelite is forbidden." It once happened that the government [of Rome] sent two officers, instructing them as follows: "Go and disguise yourselves as converts,[21] and find out what is the nature of Israel's Torah." They went to Rabban Gamaliel at Usha,[22] where they recited Scripture and studied Mishnah: Midrash, Halakot, and Aggadot.[23] As they were taking their leave, they said, "All of the Torah is pleasing and praiseworthy, except for one thing, and that is your saying, 'The robbed property of a gentile is permitted, while the robbed property of an Israelite is forbidden,' but we will not report this to the government."[24]

The cited clause from Deut. 33:3 is understood to signify God's favored relationship with Israel. As proof of this, the rule is cited whereby a different standard is applied to the robbed property of a gentile than to that of an Israelite.[25] A story is then related to exemplify this rule and to recount an instance of gentile reaction to it. The Roman officials who come to study with Rabban Gamaliel are particularly bothered by this discriminatory rule and do not hesitate to say so to their rabbinic hosts. But they are so impressed with the totality of Israel's (rabbinic) Torah that they choose not to report this unfavorable rule to their superiors. Since the story in its present form can be presumed to be fictional,[26] it may be argued that its rabbinic "authors" have projected onto the non-Jewish officials their own countervoice of discomfort with the rule permitting robbed gentile property. But they have also projected what they would like to hear from non-Jews about their *nomos*: (1) It is in sum pleasing and praiseworthy. (2) Its expression of God's unique love for Israel, to the disadvantage of the non-Jews, would not be so bothersome to the non-Jews if they would only cross the boundary into that *nomos* to experience it from within. This version of the story (we shall next see a different one), while expressing rabbinic ambivalence toward the disfavored status of gentiles in Jewish law, manages to decenter that ambivalence.

V. Interlacing Rabbinic Rules and Narratives with Scripture: Palestinian Talmud

In the the continuing career of this narrative, that ambivalence becomes stronger again, as we shall see in the following reworked version of the story in the Palestinian Talmud, now commenting not on Scripture but on the Mishnaic passage with which we began (*Baba Qamma* 4:3). The Talmudic unit juxtaposes several of the formulations we have seen expressed separately in the antecedent rabbinic corpora.

1. *Palestinian Talmud Baba Qamma* 4:3 (4b):

(A) Rab said: "[God] looked and loosened the nations" (Hab. 3:6): He loosened [permitted] the property of the nations of the world.

(B) Hezekiah said: "and [God] showed himself from Mt. Paran" (Deut. 33:2): He showed his face against the nations of the world.

(C) R. Yose b. Ḥanina said: He lowered them from their property.

(D) R. Abbahu said in the name of R. Yoḥanan: [The Mishnah] is in accord with [the gentiles'] laws [according to which it matters not whether the ox was an attested danger].

(E) R. Hela said: [The previous statement] was not said with regard to this [Mishnah] but with regard to what R. Ḥiyya taught: If the ox of one gentile gored the ox of another gentile, his fellow, even if he elected to be judged according to the laws of Israel, whether [the ox was] harmless or an attested danger he pays full damage.[27] It is with regard to this [*barayta*] that R. Abbahu said in the name of R. Yoḥanan: It is in accord with their laws.

(F) It once happened that the wicked government [of Rome] sent two officers to learn Torah from Rabban Gamaliel. They learned from him Scripture [and] Mishnah: Talmud and Aggadah.[28] At the end they said to him: "All of your Torah is pleasing and praiseworthy, except for these two things that you say: 'An Israelite woman cannot serve as a midwife to an gentile woman but a gentile woman can serve as a midwife to an Israelite woman, and an Israelite woman cannot nurse the child of a gentile woman but a gentile woman can nurse [the child of] an Israelite woman."[29] [Secondly,][30] 'the robbed property of an Israelite is prohibited while the robbed property of a gentile is permitted.'" At that moment, Rabban Gamaliel decreed that the robbed property of a gentile be forbidden because of profanation of the divine name. "'If an ox of an Israelite gored an ox of a gentile, [the Israelite owner] is not culpable.' Concerning these matters we will not inform the government."[31] Even so, they did not get so far as the Ladder of Tyre when they forgot all of it.[32]

The first three statements (A-C), by third-century sages, seek to justify the unequal treatment accorded the gentile ox owner of the Mishnah. Their citation and interpretation of Hab. 3:6 and Deut. 33:2 allude to aggadic traditions spelled out more fully elsewhere:[33] When God is about to reveal the Torah at Mount Sinai, he surveys the nations, offering them the Torah in terms of the Noahide laws that they previously were commanded and accepted, but now reject. These include the prohibition of stealing/robbing, which is rejected by the descendants of Ishmael, associated with Paran (Gen. 21:21). Rebuffed by the nations, who now renege on their previous acceptance of the minimal Noahide laws, but welcomed by Israel who accept the entire Torah unconditionally, God turns from Paran to Sinai, from the nations to Israel. Since the nations' behavior has shown disregard for the property of others (their denial of the Noahide law against robbery), God loosens (through a word-play on *wayyattēr* of Hab. 3:6) their legal claims to their own property.

R. Abbahu, in the name of R. Yoḥanan (D), takes a juridical rather than exegetical tack: The nations should be judged according to their own laws of damages, which draw no distinction between previously harmless and harmful oxen. But R. Hela (E) sees the danger that lies before this tack: If we predicate the Mishnah on the principle of applying gentile law to damages between Israelites and gentiles, how is it possible to absolve totally the Israelite of culpability when his ox gores that of a gentile? So instead, he applies R. Abbahu's statement to the *barayta* (*Tosefta Baba Qamma* 4:2) concerning the case of two gentiles who come before a Jewish court, who are judged irrespective of the categories *tām* and *mû'ād*, without either being absolved of culpability.

This discomfort with the discriminatory aspect of the Mishnah is now (F) given more poignant expression through a subtly yet significantly different version of the story of the two Roman officials who visit the court or school of Rabban Gamaliel. Two other discriminatory rules are added to the protest of the officers (one being that of the Mishnah being commented upon). However, it is that of the robbed property of a gentile that is the most offensive of all since it alone is now abrogated by Rabban Gamaliel so as to prevent profanation of God's name in the eyes of the non-Jews.[34] Once again, the officers promise not to reveal the remaining discriminatory rules to their superiors, but even so they forget them on their return route, leaving them nothing negative to report (or recall).[35] They cross over to their own *nomos* with only positive impressions of their sojourn within the Jewish *nomos*. The problematic rules regarding the crossing of boundaries between Jewish and gentile nomian worlds remain safely contained within the Jewish *nomos*, except for the most problematic of them, which has been abrogated in response to the objection of gentiles who crossed that boundary.[36]

However, we should not presume that now at last we can expect rabbinic unanimity regarding the status of the robbed property of the gentile. Our final passage, once again a web of *nomos* and narrative, suggests otherwise.

2. *Palestinian Talmud Baba Meṣi'a* 2:5 (8c):

> Simeon b. Shetaḥ labored in flax. His disciples said to him, "Rabbi, rid yourself [of this work] and we shall buy you an ass so you will not have to work so hard. They went and bought him an ass from a certain Sarkean [Ishmaelite]. Hanging on it was a pearl. They came to him and told him, "From now on you do not have to work any more." He said to them, "Why?" They told him, "We bought you an ass from one of the Sarkeans and hanging from it was a pearl." He said to them, "Did its master know about it?" They said, "No." He said to them, "Go and return it." But did not R. Ḥuna say: R. Bibi bar Gozlon, in the name of Rab, stated: They replied before Rabbi, "Even in the view of one who says, 'the robbed property of a gentile is forbidden,' all parties agree that his lost property is permitted [to be retained]"? [He replied to them:] "Do you think that Simeon b. Shetaḥ is a barbarian? Simeon b. Shetaḥ prefers the pronouncement [from a gentile], 'Blessed be the God of the Jews' above all the wealth of this world."[37]

Although the sages disagree whether the robbed property of a gentile must be restored, they all agree that there is no such legal obligation to restore the lost property of a gentile. Simeon b. Shetaḥ does not dispute this seeming legal consensus, but rather argues in terms of the metalegal principle (although he does not enunciate it by name) of *qiddush hashem* ("sanctification of the divine name"). Crossing the boundary between Jewish and gentile nomian worlds for the sake of a purchase, governed by the shared laws of the market, is one thing, but crossing it again to restore a lost property entails a degree of risk from and confers a degree of nomian legitimacy (or comparability) upon the other. But such boundary crossing also presents a metalegal opportunity, one that cannot be measured in purely legal terms, of winning gentile praise for the Jewish *nomos* and its divine governor.

However laudatory is Simeon ben b. Shetaḥ's example, it does not become the legal norm, or *required* behavior. Rather, the negatively stated version of the same principle, as attributed to the *tanna* R. Pinḥas ben Ya'ir, eventually assumes that position: "In a place where there is [the possibility of] profanation of the divine name, even the lost property of a gentile is forbidden."[38] In other words, a Jew *may* retain the stolen property of a gentile, *except* where by so doing, he would bring disrepute to the Jewish *nomos*. Legally, the gentile's lost property falls outside the scriptural obligation to return the lost property of one's "brother" (Deut. 22:3), but metalegally, under certain circumstances (which cannot be fully predetermined), it should be treated as if within.

VI. Conclusions

Rabbinic rules that treat non-Jewish Others other than they treat their own have troubled interpreters of rabbinic thought from early rabbinic times until the present. From medieval until most recent times, such troubled interpreters have sought to explain away these embarrassing rules: (1) They represent a merely *theoretical* position that was never accepted in practice. (2) They represent a *minority* view but not the halakhah (as first expressed in medieval codes). (3) They represent a necessary short-term response to gentile economic or political oppression of the Jews at a very specific time and place in history.[39] These reductive explanations, whatever their apologetic advantages, fail to engage the diversity and complexity of early rabbinic constructions of our problematic: the anomalous place of the gentile within the Jewish *nomos*.

That complexity may be denoted as three intersecting, and sometimes contradicting, trajectories in the early rabbinic navigation of that anomaly:

1. The gentiles have *no* juridical status within the Jewish *nomos* since they are not parties to its contractual terms. Not having accepted its obligations they have no claim to its protections.

2. To be sure, the gentiles have their laws, and therefore may be said to inhabit a *nomos* of their own, but their laws are not divinely revealed or commanded—the very foundation of the Jewish *nomos*. What happens, however, when two such incommensurate nomian worlds overlap and require mediation, as in a case of damages between a Jew and a gentile? In such a case, social and political contingencies may require a Jewish court to acknowledge gentile laws and gentile claims under Jewish laws, but without granting them any constitutive bearing on the Jewish *nomos*.

3. Since gentiles, like all creatures, are subjects of the single deity who is the originary source of the Jewish *nomos* and is acknowledged as such by its inhabitants, they too should be brought to a recognition of His beneficent governance of the Jewish *nomos* at the points at which they intersect it.

The first trajectory denotes the axis of complete exclusivity and self-sufficiency of the Jewish *nomos*. It heightens the distinctiveness of Jewish self-understanding but does not allow for the reality of interlocking nomian worlds. We saw it narratively enunciated through the story of the nations' rejection of God's laws at the very moment Israel accepted them, thereby sealing the boundary between Israel and the nations.

The third trajectory denotes the opposite axis of drawing the nations to (and eventually into) the Jewish *nomos*. It heightens the attractiveness of Jewish self-understanding but risks the blurring of Jewish nomian boundaries. We saw it narratively enunciated in a story of supererogatory rabbinic behavior of sanctification of the divine name.

The middle trajectory denotes the no-less-risky, yet historically necessary, dialectical course between the two: self-confirming boundaries, which may in places be pierced or stretched to facilitate commerce with the Other. We saw this narratively enunciated in the Palestinian Talmud's story of the visit of two Roman officers to Rabban Gamaliel's school and his selective bending of the Jewish *nomos* to accommodate their complaint.

Finally, we have seen that each of these perilous tacks through the Scylla and Charybdis of adjudicating contact with the nomian Other employs *multiple* modes of discourse: rule making and story telling, and the interpretation of words of Torah that joins them within a *single*, divinely governed yet humanly constructed nomian world.

NOTES

1. For my use of "nomos" and "nomian world" here and in what follows, I am indebted to Robert Cover, "Nomos and Narrative," *Harvard Law Review* 97, 1 (November 1983): 4–68.
2. For a treatment of Maimonides on our general topic, see Dov I. Frimer, "Israel, the Noahide Laws, and Maimonides: Jewish-Gentile Legal Relations in Maimonidean Thought," in *Jewish Law Association Studies II: The Jerusalem Conference Volume*, ed. B. S. Jackson (Atlanta: Scholars Press, 1986), 89–102. There are surprisingly few critical treatments of the topic of Jewish attitudes to non-Jews in ancient times. For recent literature, in some cases with respect to the conversion of non-Jews to Judaism, see Naomi G. Cohen, "Taryag and the Noahide Commandments," *Journal of Jewish Studies* 43 (1992): 46–57; Shaye J. D. Cohen, "Crossing the Boundary and Becoming a Jew," *Harvard Theological Review* 82 (1989): 13–33; S. D. Fraade, *From Tradition to Commentary: Torah and Its Interpretation in the Midrash Sifre to Deuteronomy* (Albany: State University of New York Press, 1991), 25–68; Martin Goodman, "Proselytising in Rabbinic Judaism," *Journal of Jewish Studies* 40 (1989): 175–85; Aaron Lichtenstein, *The Seven Laws of Noah*, 2d ed. (New York: Rabbi Jacob Joseph School Press, 1986); David Novak, *The Image of the Non-Jew in Judaism: An Historical and Constructive Study of the Noahide Laws* (New York: Edwin Mellen Press, 1983); Gary G. Porton, *Goyim: Gentiles and Israelites in Mishnah-Tosefta* (Atlanta: Scholars Press, 1988); idem, *The Stranger within Your Gates: Converts and Conversion in Rabbinic Literature* (Chicago: University of Chicago Press, 1994); Nahum Rakover, *Hammišpat ke'erek 'univesali: dine bibne noah* (Jerusalem: Ministry of Justice, 1987); idem, "The 'Law' and the Noahides," *Jewish Law Association Studies IV: The Boston Conference Volume*, ed. B. S. Jackson (Atlanta: Scholars Press, 1990), 169–80.
3. For examples of attempts at explaining away this embarrassing otherness, see below, n. 39.
4. For rabbinic statements on the unity and interdependency of halakhah and aggadah, and admonitions not to abandon one for the other, see, for example, *Sifre Deuteronomy* 48, 306, 317 (ed. L. Finkelstein, 113, 339,

359); *Abot deR. Natan* 8 (ed. S. Schechter, 18a–b). Of course, such admonitions must reflect the opposite tendency among some to favor, and hence attend to, one at the expense of the other. Note, for example, the story recounted in *Babylonian Talmud Soṭah* 40a, about two sages, a teacher of halakhah and a teacher of aggadah, who come to a town and compete with each other for the people's attention (which goes to the latter). For a modern essay on the interconnections between halakhah and aggadah, see Hayyim Nahman Bialik, *Law and Legend; or, Halakah and Aggadah*, trans. Julius L. Siegel (New York: Bloch, 1923). See also Judah Goldin, "The Freedom and Restraint of Haggadah," in *Midrash and Literature*, ed. Geoffrey H. Hartman and Sanford Budick (New Haven, Conn.: Yale University, 1986), 57–59.

5. This rabbinical distinction derives from Exod. 21:29: "and warning has been given (*wĕhûʿad*) to its owner."

6. Note in particular the critique of this inconsistency, narratively projected into the mouths of gentiles, in *Babylonian Talmud Baba Qamma* 38a: "his neighbor" cannot be differently understood depending on whose ox is doing the goring, exempting from culpability in one case but not in the other.

7. For the text, see *The Tosefta according to Codex Vienna, with Variants from Codex Erfurt, MS. Schocken and Editio Princeps (Venice, 1521): The Order of Nezikin*, ed. Saul Lieberman (New York: Jewish Theological Seminary of America, 1988), 14. For discussion of the text and its variants, see Saul Lieberman, *Tosefta Ki-Fshuṭah: A Comprehensive Commentary on the Tosefta; Part IX: Order Nezikin* (New York: Jewish Theological Seminary of America, 1988), 35–36. The same passage is cited as a *barayta* in *Palestinian Talmud Baba Qamma* 4:3 (4b).

8. For an exegetical attempt at grounding this internomian anomaly, see *Mekilta Mishpatim* 12 (ed. H. S. Horovitz and I. A. Rabin, 290), where *rēʿēhû* of Exod. 21:35 is interpreted to *exclude* the gentile as the owner of the gored ox, while *ʾîš* (person) of the same verse is interpreted to *include* non-Jews as the owners of the goring ox. Hence, a gentile owner of a goring ox is culpable for damages done by his ox to that of a Jew, but not vice versa. But this exegetical argument is not sufficient to determine that the gentile must pay full damage to a Jew whose ox his has gored, regardless of whether the gentile's ox was *tām* or *mûʿād*. For an extreme justification, see Maimonides' commentary ad loc: "Do not find this matter difficult in your eyes and do not be surprised by it, just as you should not be surprised by the slaughter of animals even though they have not done any wrong. For whoever lacks the human qualities is not a true person, and his purpose is only to serve the true person."

9. *Tosephta Based on the Erfurt and Vienna Codixes*, ed. M. S. Zuckermandel, with a supplement by Saul Lieberman (Jerusalem, 1937; repr. Jerusalem: Wahrman, 1970), 473. This tradition is also cited and

discussed in *Babylonian Talmud Sanhedrin* 56a–57a, where the difference in language between exemption from culpability with respect to bloodshed and permission (to retain property) with respect to robbery is noted.

10. For a comprehensive treatment of the seven Noahide laws of the gentiles, see Novak, *Image of the Non-Jew in Judaism*, as well as other treatments referred to above, n. 2. For the Torah's prohibition of robbery between Israelites, see Lev. 19:11, 13, where the words "fellow" and "neighbor" are used.

11. For the possibility, whether real or hypothetical, of claims between Jews and gentiles being tried in a Jewish court, according to the rules of whichever *nomos* would favor the Jew, see *Sifre Deuteronomy* 16 (ed. L. Finkelstein, 26–27), as well as the following: *Babylonian Talmud Baba Qamma* 113a (but note R. Akiba's demurral); *Midrash Haggadol* Exod. 23:6; Maimonides' commentary to *Mishnah Baba Qamma* 4:3. On the relation of Noahide laws to Sinaitic revelation, see Novak, *Image of the Non-Jew in Judaism*, 53–74. On the question of overlapping jurisdictions between Jewish and Roman civil legal systems in Palestine during the first two centuries, see Bernard S. Jackson, "On the Problem of Roman Influence on the Halakha and Normative Self-Definition in Judaism," in *Aspects of Judaism in the Graeco-Roman Period*, vol. 2 of *Jewish and Christian Self-Definition*, ed. E. P. Sanders, et al. (Philadelphia: Fortress, 1981), 159–72; and more generally and less critically, Shemuel Safrai, "Jewish Self-Government," in *The Jewish People in the First Century*, Compendia Rerum Iudaicarum ad Novum Testamentum, sec. 1, vol. 1, ed. S. Safrai and M. Stern (Assen: Van Gorcum; Philadelphia: Fortress, 1974), 404–12.

12. *Mekilta Mishpayim* 1 (ed. H. S. Horovitz and I. A. Rabin, 246).

13. For the omitted text, also omitted in MS Ehrfurt, see *The Tosefta . . . : Order Nezikin*, ed. S. Lieberman, 53, and Lieberman's discussion of this passage and its variants in *Tosefta Ki-Fshuṭah; Part IX: Order Nezikin*, 121–22.

14. For this concept, see Ephraim E. Urbach, *The Sages: Their Concepts and Beliefs*, trans. Israel Abrahams (Jerusalem: Magnes, 1979), 356–60, 842–44. In addition to the texts cited below, see *Babylonian Talmud Baba Qamma* 113a–b. Compare *Damascus Document* 12:6–8: "No one shall stretch out his hand to shed the blood of any of the gentiles for the sake of property and gain. Nor shall he carry off anything of their property, *lest they blaspheme*, unless by the counsel of the company of Israel." For discussion, see Lawrence H. Schiffman, "Legislation concerning Relations with Non-Jews in the *Zadokite Fragments* and in Tannaitic Literature," *Revue de Qumran* 11 (1983): 382–84.

15. *Sifra on Leviticus*, vol. 2, ed. Louis Finkelstein (New York: Jewish Theological Seminary of America, 1983), 211. For *'āḥērîm* as non-Jews, see Saul Lieberman, *Tosefta Ki-Fschuṭah; Part III: Order Mo'ed* (New

York: Jewish Theological Seminary of America, 1962), 294 (top), as well as Rabbenu Hillel's commentary to our passage. For similar uses of *'āḥēr* and *'āḥērîm*, see *Tosefta Baba Qamma* 4:2; *Mekilta Mishpaṭim* 12; *Midrash Haggadol* Exod. 23:6.

16. Some commentators, being uncomfortable with the *Sifra's* exclusion of the Jew's obligation to restore wrongfully obtained or used property to a gentile, suggest that the *Sifra* is only excluding the Jew's obligation to pay the added fifth and to bring a guilt offering to the priest (Lev. 5:25). See Lieberman, *Tosefta Ki-Fschuṭah; Part IX: Order Nezikin*, 121–22; Maimonides, *Mishneh Torah Gezelah Wa'abedah* 7:7.

17. "Redemption" denotes being released in exchange for a payment rather than by force.

18. The law of the jubilee year only applies to the land of Israel when it is under Israelite sovereignty.

19. *Sipra' debe rab hu' seper torat kohanim*, ed. I. H. Weiss (Vienna, 1862; repr. New York, 1947), 110b; *Sifra or Torat Kohanim according to Codex Assemani LXVI* (Jerusalem: Makor, 1972), 206. The passage is cited in part as a *barayta* in *Babylonian Talmud Baba Qamma* 113b, where R. Simeon (bar Yohai) is said to attribute the interpretation to his teacher, R. Akiba, and where an ensuing debate concerns whether it applies to any gentile or only to a *gēr tôšāb* (resident alien). Our text itself makes no such distinction. Compare as well *Midrash Tanna'im* ad Deut. 20:14 (ed. D. Hoffmann, 121).

20. For another exegetical argument against robbing from a gentile, see the interpretation of Deut. 7:16, attributed to Rab Huna, in *Babylonian Talmud Baba Qamma* 113b. For other rabbinic texts that prohibit the robbing or robbed property of a gentile, see *Seder Eliahu Rabbah* 16, 26 (ed. M. Friedmann, 75, 140). More commonly, scriptural exegesis is employed to argue *against* extending the prohibition of robbery to the gentile. On the relation of exegesis to edict (*gezerah*), in this regard, see Eliezer S. Rosenthal, "Dyssoi logoi—Sheney debarim," in *Isac Leo Seeligmann Volume: Essays on the Bible and the Ancient World*, ed. Alexander Rofé and Yair Zakovitch, vol. 2 (Jerusalem: Rubinstein's, 1983), 475–76.

21. For this reading and its significance, see my book, *From Tradition to Commentary*, 214 n. 129.

22. There is a problem here in that Rabban Gamaliel (presumably II) was the Patriarch at Yabneh and not at Usha. For different attempts to resolve this contradiction, see my book *From Tradition to Commentary*, 214 n. 130, 214–15 n. 137.

23. On this formulation, see my book, *From Tradition to Commentary*, 244 n. 111; Jackson, "The Problem of Roman Influence," 357 n. 50. Note that it is the full curriculum of written and oral (rabbinic) Torah that the Roman officers study and not simply the Jewish system of civil law,

as some have presumed (see citations, *From Tradition to Commentary*, 214–15 n. 137, especially the article by Saul Lieberman).

24. *Siphre ad Deuteronomium*, ed. Louis Finkelstein (New York: Jewish Theological Seminary of America, 1969), 400–401. I have treated this passage more fully in *From Tradition to Commentary*, 51–54. For another version of the commentary, see the text published by Menahem Kahana as *Mekilta to Deuteronomy* in *Tarbiz* 57 (1988): 196–98, as well as *Midrash Haggadol* Deut. 33:3. The version there, however, is much closer to that in *Babylonian Talmud Baba Qamma* 38a.

25. Although we have not yet seen exactly this formulation, compare *Tosefta 'Abodah Zarah* 8(9): 5 (passage II.2 above), in contrast to *Sifra Behar pereq* 9:2–3.

26. Previous scholars have gone to great lengths to reconcile the details of the story with one another and with a particular historical setting on the assumption that the story is a simple historical representation rather than a rhetorical construction. For bibliography and further discussion of the question of the historicity of this story, see my book, *From Tradition to Commentary*, 214–15 n. 137; Jackson, "On the Problem of Roman Influence," 163, 358 nn. 54, 55; Catherine Hezser, "Form, Function, and Historical Significance of the Narratives in Yerushalmi Neziqin" (Ph.D. diss., Jewish Theological Seminary of America, 1992), 39–42.

27. Cf. *Tosefta Baba Qamma* 4:2, cited above, and n. 7 above for reference to discussion of the variants thereto.

28. MS Leiden, like the version of the story in *Sifre to Deuteronomy* has "Halakot and Aggadot."

29. MS Leiden adds *biršûtāh*, "with her permission" or "in her domain," as in *Mishnah 'Abodah Zarah* 2:1; *Babylonian Talmud 'Abodah Zarah* 26a. For other formulations of the rules for Israelite and gentile midwives, see *Tosefta 'Abodah Zarah* 3:3, which in the view of R. Meir maintains a symmetry of exclusion, prohibiting a gentile woman from being a midwife to an Israelite woman, but in the view of the sages permits such service so long as there are others (Israelites) in attendance. Cf. *Palestinian Talmud 'Abodah Zarah* 2:1 (40c) for other views that permit a gentile woman to be a midwife to an Israelite woman, but only under certain restrictive conditions. Finally, *Babylonian Talmud 'Abodah Zarah* 26a attributes to R. Joseph the view that an Israelite woman may serve as a midwife to a gentile woman if she does so for pay, because of fear of causing enmity between Jews and gentiles. Our text, in citing *Mishnah 'Abodah Zarah* 2:1, states the dissymmetry between Israelite and gentile women in the starkest terms. For further discussion, see Christine E. Hayes, "Between the Babylonian and Palestinian Talmuds: Accounting for Halakhic Difference in Selected Sugyot from Tractate Avodah Zarah" (Ph.D. diss., University of California, Berkeley, 1993), 39–54.

30. For a different understanding of "two things," see Rosenthal, "Dyssoi logoi—Sheney debarim."
31. Others interpret this to mean that the Roman emissaries decided not to tell Rome the justifying reasons for this seemingly discriminatory law. But this reading cannot be sustained by the text. See the commentary *Peney Mosheh* ad loc., as well as Rashi ad *Babylonian Talmud Baba Qamma* 38a. MS Leiden has "this matter," presumably referring to the last-mentioned rule of the gentile and Israelite oxen.
32. It is unclear whether they forgot everything they learned or only the discriminatory rules to which they objected. My translation is based on MS Escorial in *Yerushalmi Neziqin*, ed. E. S. Rosenthal (Jerusalem: Israel Academy of Science and Humanities, 1983), 12, but MS Leiden concludes "all of them," presumably referring to the aforementioned rules.
33. See my book, *From Tradition to Commentary*, 28–49, 216–17 nn. 142, 143, 145; Novak, *Image of the Non-Jew in Judaism*, 257–73; Israel Lewy, *Mabo' uperush letalmud yerushalmi baba' qamma' I–VI* (Jerusalem: Kedem, 1970), 112 (reprint from *Jahresbericht des jüdisch-theologischen Seminars: Fraenckel'scher Stiftung* [Breslau, 1895–1914]).
34. For this sentence as an awkward editorial addition to the story, see Rosenthal, "Dyssoi logoi—Sheney debarim," 475 n. 48, following Lewy, *Mabo' uperush letalmud yerushalmi*, 114. This presumes that Rabban Gamaliel's edict was not necessarily an historical act but a literary accretion, no less historically significant but perhaps so for a later period in the history of the transmission of the story. In this light, Reuven Hammer's comment to the *Sifre* version of the story (*Sifre: The Tannaitic Commentary on the Book of Deuteronomy*, trans. Reuven Hammer [New Haven, Conn.: Yale University Press, 1986], 507 n. 3) is anachronistic: "It is strange that [R. Gamaliel's] prohibition is not mentioned here." The whole point of the *Sifre* version of the story, as I have argued, is that the rule permitting the robbed property of the gentile remains in place, notwithstanding gentile protest.
35. Note that in the version of the story in *Mekilta to Deuteronomy* (ed. M. Kahana, 198) and *Midrash Haggadol* (ed. S. Fisch, 756) to Deut. 33:2, their forgetting of the laws comes in response to Rabban Gamaliel's prayer, and hence appears to be divinely effected.
36. The "Ladder of Tyre" refers to a mountain range on the coastal route to Syria between Keziv (Akhziv) and Tyre. Its southern end (modern-day Rosh Haniqra) marked the northern boundary of Jewish settlement in the land of Israel on the officers' return route. Cf. 1 Macc. 11:59; Josephus, *Jewish War* 2.10.2 (§188); *Genesis Rabbah* 39:8 (ed. J. Theodor and Ch. Albeck, 371); *Tosefta Pesahim* 2:16 (1:29) (ed. S. Lieberman, 147); *Palestinian Talmud 'Abodah Zarah* 1:9 (40a); *Babylonian Talmud Shabbat* 26a; *'Eruvin* 64b; *Leviticus Rabbah* 37:3 (ed. M. Margulies, 863). See Michael Avi-Yonah, *Historical Geography of the*

Land of Israel (Hebrew) (Jerusalem: Bialik Institute, 1951), 34; Samuel Klein in *Studies in the Geography of Eretz Israel* (Jerusalem: Mossad Harav Kook, 1965), 154 (Hebrew trans. of "Das tannaitische Grenz-verzeichnis Palestinas," *Hebrew Union College Annual* 5 [1928]); idem, *'Ereṣ Haggalil*, rev. ed. Y. Elitzur (Jerusalem: Mossad Harav Kook, 1967), 131; Lewy, *Mabo' uperush letalmud yerushalmi*, 115; Adolphe Neubauer, *La Géographie du Talmud* (Paris, 1868; repr. Hildesheim: Olms, 1967), 39; Eshtori Haparḥi, *Caftor va-pherah* 11, ed. A. M. Luncz (Jerusalem, 1897), 247.

37. Once again, my translation follows MS Escorial, from *Yerushalmi Neziqin*, ed. E. S. Rosenthal, 48, but with the corrections suggested by Saul Lieberman in his notes to the same, 135. For parallels, see *Deuteronomy Rabbah* 3:3; *Deuteronomy Rabbah 'Ēqeb* 3 (ed. S. Lieberman, 85); *Yalquṭ Shim'oni Mishle* 947.

38. *Midrash Tannaim* Deut. 22:3 (ed. D. Hoffmann, 134); *Babylonian Talmud Baba Qamma* 113b; *Midrash Haggadol* Deut. 22:3 (ed. S. Fisch, 486). For medieval codifications, see Maimonides, *Mishneh Torah Gezelah Wa'abedah* 11:3; *Shulḥan Aruk Hosen Mishpaṭ* 266.1–4. For further discussion, see Lieberman, *Tosefta Ki-Fshuṭah; Part IX: Order Nezikin*, 121.

39. For (1) and (2) see, for example, H. Freedman's note to his translation of *The Babylonian Talmud Seder Nezikin Baba Meẓi'a* 87b (London: Soncino, 1935), 506: "The robbery of a heathen, even if permitted, is only so in theory, but in fact it is forbidden as constituting a 'hillul hashem,' profanation of the Divine Name. But the consensus of opinion is that it is biblically forbidden too, i.e., even in theory." He then cites for support significantly later medieval codifications: *Mishneh Torah Gezelah Wa'abedah* 1:2, 6:8; *Shulḥan Aruk Hosen Mishpaṭ* 348.2. For (3) note especially Heinrich Graetz's commonly adduced argument (*Monatsschrift für Geschichte und Wissenschaft des Judentums* 30 [1881]: 495) that any permission to retain the robbed property of a gentile was directed against the *fiscus Judaicus* imposed by Vespasian and rigorously exacted by Domitian (ca. 90). In other words, permission was granted to circumvent this oppressive Roman tax. This explanation is cited approvingly by Novak, *Image of the Non-Jew in Judaism*, 78 n. 41. Cf. H. Freedman's note to his translation of *The Babylonian Talmud Seder Nezikin Sanhedrin* 57a (London: Soncini, 1935), 389: "Not a few of these harsh utterances (where they do not reflect the old Semitic tribal law . . .) were the natural result of Jewish persecution by Romans, and must be understood in that light. In actual practice, these dicta were certainly never acted upon." Israel Lewy (*Mabo' uperush letalmud yerushalmi*, 115) states that the robbed property of a gentile was only permitted in times of war when the Jews took booty from their gentile enemies. For critiques of these historicizing attempts, see references above, n. 26.

Chapter 8

Woman—The Feminine as Other in Theosophic Kabbalah: Some Philosophical Observations on the Divine Androgyne

Elliot R. Wolfson

In recent years various writers have attempted to find a place for the voice of the feminine in Jewish religious expression. Some of these writers have naturally turned to the rich legacy of medieval Jewish mysticism, known in scholarly literature as theosophic kabbalah, which characterizes the nature of the divine in terms of masculine and feminine attributes. In the search for a traditional corpus in which to ground feminine images of God, this has been a logical avenue of constructive theology. However, while I am not unsympathetic to such a project on a personal level, I would raise a question regarding the viability of using the kabbalistic literature to cull images of the feminine God without taking into consideration the precise nature of the cultural context that produced that literature. It is not sufficient to lift descriptions of the masculine and feminine out of their particular religious and sociocultural milieu, as the issue of gender (and body more generally) cannot be isolated from such contexts.

The same critique may be leveled against most scholars who have discussed the role of gender in kabbalistic symbolism and myth. Little attention has been paid to the specific cultural contexts wherein the different kabbalistic ideas were expressed. Previous scholarship on this issue has tended to take for granted the use of gender without analyzing the way that gender functions in a larger environment.

In line with contemporary anthropologists, I assume that sex/gender types are sociocultural constructs that are often expressed in biological terms.[1] When the discussion is cast in this light, it will be seen how precarious is the attempt to base current feminist theology in Judaism on these medieval sources. Such a project will succeed only when it is understood that the feminine images of God that inform one's theological posture must reflect current cultural concerns and cannot simply be extracted from sources rooted in an entirely different context that is thoroughly androcentric. A critical, even deconstructive, orientation must be applied to images of the feminine in theosophic kabbalah before they can be utilized in contemporary feminist approaches to Judaism.

This presentation brings together two essential elements in kabbalistic theosophy: on the one hand, the issue of femininity or femaleness, particularly as it relates to the Godhead, and on the other, the problem of otherness, that which is distinct from or independent of the divine. The decidedly monistic tendency of kabbalistic metaphysics as it has developed over the centuries, in some cases even leaning toward panentheism, pantheism, or acosmism, makes positing an Other in any ultimate sense highly problematic. In a universe where all is God, what is other than God? Thus, in its classical formulation, theosophic kabbalah cannot tolerate a concept of absolute otherness as posited by standard ontological dualism. If we are to speak of an Other within the theoretical framework of kabbalah, it must be a relative Other, i.e., otherness in relation to something that may ultimately be dissolved.

From its incipient stages, kabbalistic speculation links the issue of otherness to the feminine. The accepted gender stereotypes in medieval European society wherein theosophic kabbalah flourished,[2] enhanced by the patriarchal norms of rabbinic culture,[3] associates the masculine with holiness, light, the right side of grace, and the feminine with impurity (even the demonic), darkness, the left side of judgment and severity. These stereotypes were by no means unique to Jewish mysticism, but they gained added currency through kabbalistic literature insofar as the issue of gender in this corpus intruded into theological discourse more profoundly than it did in the multiple currents of rabbinic Judaism. Even though feminine images were employed in the classical aggadic and ancient esoteric texts to describe things pertaining to the divine, the fact remains that only in theosophic kabbalah does the male-female polarity become a central tenet that informs the theological imagination on the level of ritual and belief, symbol and myth.

In this study, I shall approach the problem of the feminine as Other in kabbalah by exploring in detail a relatively neglected aspect of the myth of the primordial androgyny. To do this, I shall select kabbalistic texts from the formative period of kabbalah in the twelfth and thirteenth centuries. Before proceeding to the analysis of the relevant material, let me offer the following disclaimer: It is no less a mistake to think of a single kabbalistic perspective on the topic of woman as Other than it is to think of a singular attitude with respect to any of the essential ideas in theosophic kabbalah. There is a great deal of diversity in kabbalistic texts related to the issue of gender; here I propose to deal with one motif that has not, in my opinion, received sufficient notice by scholars: the monistic framework of the kabbalistic myth of the divine androgyny.

In the following pages, I shall argue that a basic tension lies at the heart of kabbalistic speculation regarding the androgynous nature of the divine and its reflection in the human sphere: on the one hand, insofar as the divine is characterized by a male-female syzygy, the task of *homo religiosus* is to unite these two aspects in order to restore the primal unity of God; on the other hand, as a consequence of the androcentric orientation that colored the socio-religious environment of the kabbalists, the divine androgyny is primarily male.[4] That is, not only are the masculine characteristics regarded as positive and the feminine as negative, but the latter is itself ultimately absorbed by the former. Despite the larger role accorded the female in kabbalistic mythology, the female continues to be subordinated to the male.[5]

The redemptive task (proleptically realized by kabbalists in the performance of normative rituals with the proper mystical intentions) is to reintegrate the female in the male or, to put the matter in terms of the well-known gnostic motif expressed in the *Gospel of Thomas*, to "make the female male."[6] In the state of *conjunctio oppositorum*, the two are unified in a manner that the female becomes male. Conversely, when the female is separated from the male, or when the female is treated as an autonomous power divorced from the upper nine emanations, the female either comes under the dominion of the demonic or it assumes a demonic character.[7] It is an act of heresy to worship the feminine in isolation from the masculine, and therein lies the psychological root of idolatry.[8]

The demonization of the female is also expressed in terms of the male becoming female, i.e., the impotent or celibate male—mythically depicted in the *Zohar* and other kabbalistic works from the late-thirteenth-century Castile as the Edomite kings who symbolically represent Christianity on the historical plane[9]—has the same ontic status as the female. This point is expressed in striking terms at the very beginning of one of the more recondite textual units included in the zoharic anthology, the *Sifra di-Zeniuta* ("Book of Concealment"): "Before there was a balance[10] they did not look face to face, and the primordial kings died, their weapons were not found and the land was destroyed."[11] It is evident that the word "weapons" in this passage functions as a metaphor for the *membrum virile* and the word "land" for the feminine potency. Before there was a balance in the Godhead, there was no union of male and female—signified by the face-to-face glance—and hence the primordial kings, elsewhere identified as the kings of Edom,[12] died and the earth was destroyed. These kings were emasculated and thus have the symbolic valence of females, i.e., untempered forces of judgment.

As will be argued more fully below, although kabbalists (and later Hasidim drawing upon the kabbalistic tradition) strove to discover the underlying unity of reality, this quest did not lead to a breakdown of either the social divisions between men and women within the Jewish community or the religious-cultural boundaries between Jew and non-Jew. Nowhere in kabbalistic literature, as far as I am aware, do we hear of a tendency to harmonize or equalize the social roles of men and women.[13] It is certainly the case, moreover, that despite occasional references to women's spiritual visions, the circles of Jewish mystics through the ages (including the Hasidic groups in Eastern Europe of the eighteenth and nineteenth centuries)[14] were exclusively male fraternities.[15] Thus, there is an essential homology between the structure of the myth of divine unity predicated on the transcendence of sexual opposites, on the one hand, and the structure of social relationships, on the other. That is, just as in the former case the female is subordinated to the male, so too in the latter.

In the worldview of the medieval theosophic kabbalists, as in a variety of ancient Gnostic sources, especially of Valentinian provenance, the cultic retrieval of sexual unity is in fact a "reconstituted masculinity," i.e., the union of the sexes results in making the female male.[16] The yearning to transcend otherness and separation (signs of exile and death) manifests itself in a reunification (redemption or salvation) of male and female in which the female is absorbed in the male and the polarity of male and female is abolished. The myth of the divine androgyne in kabbalistic sources, as in the

Gnostic compositions of Late Antiquity, is yet another expression of a socially dominant androcentrism. The ultimate goal of religious behavior is the containment of the feminine left in the masculine right[17] or, to put the matter in slightly different terms, the neutralization of the female power in the unity of the androgynous male.

In earlier strands of Jewish esotericism, as one finds in more exoteric modes of aggadic discourse, the anthropomorphic characterizations of the divine are decidedly masculine. Thus, for example, in the *Hekhalot* texts it is evident that the central image is that of the divine king sitting upon his throne of glory.[18]   In the more radically anthropomorphic texts of the *Shi'ur Qomah* tradition, the visible and measurable enthroned form is male in nature; indeed, explicit reference is made to the phallus even though its exact measure is not given.[19] Finally, in another work of ancient Jewish esotericism, the *Sefer Yezirah*, reference is also made to the divine anthropos, depicted in terms of the ten *sefirot* corresponding to the ten fingers, five against five, with the covenants of the tongue and phallus set in the middle as the covenant of oneness.[20] Here the masculine nature of the imagined form of the divine in the pleroma of *sefirot* is unparalleled by other texts, for the phallus itself is singled out as one of two foci of divine unity. It has been suggested by some scholars that an underlying component of the ancient Jewish esoteric tradition posited an androgynous element in the divine pleroma, but the dominant characterization of the enthroned and measurable glory is masculine. The move to an elaborate characterization of the divine anthropos as androgynous is distinctively the patrimony of theosophic kabbalists in the High Middle Ages, although allusions to such a theological posture are found in the writings of the Rhineland Jewish pietists as well.[21]

There are a variety of basic structures that inform the ideational character of theosophic kabbalah. One such structure is that of the divine androgyny, referred to in the literature of the kabbalists as *du-parzufim*, two-faced, the technical locution employed in the rabbinic aggadah to characterize the nature of Adam at creation.[22] In kabbalistic parlance, this term denotes the idea that God is simultaneously male and female, i.e., that there is a masculine and feminine aspect to the divine. Bracketing for the moment the question of the antiquity of this idea (or related images) in the history of Judaism, it is unquestionable that the notion of a divine syzygy is a critical component of kabbalistic speculation.

Consider, for example, the following testimony of Todros ben Joseph Abulafia regarding the aggadic motif of *du-parzufim*: "Know that all the elements of the proper tradition (*ha-qabbalah ha-nekhonah*), in their principles and details, are all built upon this foundation, and they revolve around this point. It is a deep secret upon which are hanging very high mountains."[23]

The first composition that espouses an elaborate and sustained theosophic position characteristic of medieval kabbalah is the *Sefer ha-Bahir*. In that work, the idea of the syzygy is contextualized in terms of the primordial anthropos. Indeed, the *Bahir* unqualifyingly interprets the divine image (*zelem elohim*) by means of which Adam was created in terms of the correspondence between human and divine limbs. Thus, in one instance seven limbs are specified: two hands, head, body, two thighs, and the male and female sex organs, which are considered as one (*berit milah we-zugo hashvinan had*).[24] In another passage eight extremities are mentioned: two hands, two feet, head, body, phallus, and the female who is the counterpart to the male.[25] Unlike the former passage wherein the female was considered as one entity with the male, in the latter passage the female complements the male and is enumerated as an autonomous force.

Just as the divine anthropos was characterized in these androgynous terms, so the human below was expected to emulate this state of harmony by the man cleaving to the woman and becoming one flesh, as stated in Gen. 2:24, which is cited in the bahiric context under investigation. In another passage, the *Bahir* speaks of seven holy forms of God that correspond to seven limbs in the human being: the two thighs, two hands, head, body, and phallus,[26] and of the woman as a counterpart to the male.[27] The language of the text makes it clear that the female is considered part of the male in the same way that Eve was part of Adam. Thus, the bahiric authorship comments after delineating the six limbs:

> You said there were seven! The seventh is his wife, as it is written, "[Hence a man leaves his father and mother and clings to his wife] so that they become one flesh" (Gen. 2:24). Thus she was taken from his rib, as it is written, "He took one of his ribs."[28]

The androgynous nature of the divine is also implied in another verse cited in this section, "in the image of God He created him, male and female He created them" (Gen. 1:27). According to the understanding of the *Bahir*, reiterated in subsequent kabbalistic literature, the divine image by means of which Adam was created comprises male and female. Yet, it is evident that the feminine element is contained within the masculine, and not vice versa. This point is elucidated by the parable of the king's seven sons that introduces the text just cited. These sons are the seven holy forms that are compared to seven limbs that include either the full form of a woman or the female genitals that complement the phallus. The primordial androgyny is further illustrated by a second parable in the same context:

> To what may this be compared? To a king who decided to plant in his garden nine male trees, and all of them were to be palm-trees. He said, If all of them will be of the same species, they will not be able to exist. What did he do? He planted a citron-tree (*etrog*) amongst them, and it is one of the nine that arose in his mind to be male, but the citron is female.[29]

The fact that the tree that is female was initially one of the males symbolizes that the female aspect of the divine pleroma is itself part of the masculine. The point is emphasized once again in the *Bahir* where the citron is associated symbolically with the beloved described in Song of Songs 6:10: "On account of her the female was taken from Adam, for the upper and lower worlds could not exist without the female."[30]

While other passages from the *Bahir* dealing with the syzygy could be cited, the texts discussed above permit the following conclusions: Just as the human below comprises male and female, so too the divine image above, and just as below the female is comprised within the male, so too above the female aspect is part of the male. Hence one cannot really speak of the female as Other in any absolute sense. This point is epitomized in another bahiric passage where a parable is offered to explain why the glory (*kavod*) is blessed independently when it is one of the divine potencies:

> To what may this be compared? To a man who has a beautiful garden, and outside the garden and close to it there is a beautiful field.[31] . . . At the beginning he irrigated his garden and the water went all over the garden but not upon that field which is not connected, even though everything is one. Therefore he opened a place for it and irrigated it separately.[32]

Just as the field is unified with yet separate from the garden, so the feminine potency of the divine is distinct from yet unified with the other, masculine potencies. The ultimate task of *homo religiosus*, and the final goal of the historical process itself, is to achieve a state wherein the female is reintegrated into the male.

In one section of the *Bahir*, a reworking of the aggadic interpretation of the word *yinnon* in Ps. 72:17 as a reference to the proper name of the Messiah,[33] the kabbalist author reflects, "[The word *yinnon*] has a double *nun*, the bent *nun* and the straight *nun*, for [the redemption] must happen through the masculine and the feminine."[34] Commenting on this Scholem noted, "This is Jewish gnosis, in pronounced contrast to antinomian and encratist tendencies."[35] Scholem goes on to contrast the idea of redemption implied in the bahiric text with an apocryphal remark of Jesus in the *Gospel of Thomas*, alluded to above, to the effect that redemption is marked by a

> triumph over the masculine and feminine . . . that reestablishes their original unity, but says nothing of redemption itself resulting from the union of the masculine and feminine. The conjunction of the two principles is certainly not the same as overcoming them in the reestablishment of an original androgynous state.[36]

I am not certain that Scholem's attempt to contrast the Christian gnosis and the Jewish on this score can be upheld. That is, it seems to me that the Jewish gnosis as expressed in the *Bahir*, and developed further in subsequent theosophic kabbalah, is predicated on a notion of redemption that signifies a return to an original unity in the divine pleroma. In this unity, sexual differentiation is either transcended or the feminine is reintegrated in the masculine, in contrast to the continual coupling of the two potencies.[37]

The view that I have attributed to the bahiric authorship is confirmed in one of the few kabbalistic texts that may have been authored by R. Abraham ben David of Posquiéres, widely regarded by subsequent kabbalists as one of the first links in the chain of transmission of this esoteric knowledge. The passage, a sustained reflection on the rabbinic notion that Adam was created *du-parzufim* (two-faced), has been studied by various scholars.[38] However, given the central importance of this text to the thematic of this analysis, it would be prudent to cite it in full:[39]

The Rabad explained that the reason for the creation [of Adam] as double-faced (*du-parzufin*) was so that the woman would obey her husband for her life depends on him, and they should not each go his or her own way, but rather there should be a closeness and friendship between them without separation. Then there will be peace between them and harmony in their abode. Thus one finds with respect to the "agents of truth, whose action is truth."[40] The reason for the [two] faces indicates two things. First, it is known that two opposites were emanated, one of pure judgment (*din gamur*) and the other of pure mercy (*rahamim gemurim*). If they had not been emanated as double-faced, each of them would act in accordance with its own attribute. It would then appear as if they were two [separate] powers, and each one would act without any connection to the other and without its assistance. But now that they were created double-faced, all their actions take place together, in an evenly balanced manner and perfect unity, without any separation. Moreover, if they had not been created double-faced, no perfect unity could emerge from them, and the attribute of judgment could not rise to that of mercy, nor that of mercy to judgment. Now that they have been created double-faced, each of them draws close and unites with the other, and yearns and desires to be joined to the other, so that the tabernacle will be one. You find a proof of this in the fact that each of the [divine] names refers to the other. Thus you find that the Tetragrammaton [the attribute of mercy] indicates the attribute of judgment, and Elohim [the attribute of judgment] the attribute of mercy, as in "the Lord rained upon Sodom and Gomorrah sulfurous fire" (Gen. 19:24); He passed from one attribute to the other.

The two attributes of God, expressed in more or less standard rabbinic terminology, are here correlated with the masculine and feminine aspects of the divine, which correspond to the earthly man and woman. The author of this text emphasizes that the attributes should not act independently but rather in concert, for to separate the attribute of judgment and that of mercy would be akin to creating a division in the Godhead between male and female or, in traditional terms, positing two divine powers. The union or conjunction of the two attributes enables the one to pass into the other so that acts of judgment can be ascribed to the name associated with mercy (YHWH) and acts of mercy to the name associated with judgment (Elohim). This is the mystical significance of the legendary account of Adam's having been created double faced, the male and female emerging simultaneously.

The point that I wish to underscore, however, is the hierarchical relationship established in this passage: while the focus clearly is on the union of the two attributes, the masculine is privileged over the feminine. This is evident at the very beginning of the text: "The reason for the creation [of Adam] as double-faced was so that the woman would obey her husband for her life depends on him, and they should not each go his or her own way, but rather there should be a closeness and friendship between them without separation." While any rupture in the divine is detrimental, the severance of the female from the male is more problematic insofar as the female cannot survive without the male. The unity of the male and female within the pleroma is ultimately predicated on the role of subordination or passivity on the part of the female. When the theosophic structures are applied anthropologically, the woman expresses the union of the relationship by serving the man because ontically she draws her life force from him.[41]

The conjunction of male and female, so central to theosophic kabbalah in terms of both doctrine and practice, is predicated on the reestablishment of the original androgynous state wherein the female aspect of judgment is contained in the male aspect of mercy. Such a view is reflected in the following description of primordial Adam found in the *Zohar*: "When the Holy One, blessed be He, created man He created him perfect, as it says, 'God made man straight' (*asher asah elohim et ha-adam yashar*) (Eccles. 7:29). 'Man' (*et ha-adam*): male and female, and the female was contained in the male; thus it is written straight."[42] The perfect human form is one wherein the female is contained within the male. The union of masculine and feminine is predicated on the reintegration of the latter in the former. This is also depicted in the containment of the attribute of judgment (the left) in that of mercy (right).

To cite two pertinent examples, both of which deal with the hierogamy in the divine pleroma:

> When the Matrona sits with the King and they are joined face-to-face, who will come between them? Who will come close to them? When they are joined the one is sweetened[43] by the other. . . . Therefore the judgments are sweetened, one in the other, and the upper and lower beings are perfected.[44]

> The feminine emanates in her side and cleaves to the side of the masculine until she is separated from his side and comes to join

with him face-to-face. When they are joined they appear indeed as
one body. From here it is learnt that the male alone appears as
half-a-body (*pelag gufa*), all merciful, and so it is with the female,[45] but when they are joined as one everything appears indeed
as one body. . . . So too when a male unites with a female everything is one body, and all the worlds are joyous, for everything is
blessed from the complete body. . . . From here [it can be deduced]
the one who is not found as male and female is called half-a-
body.[46]

Without a mate of the opposite sex neither man nor woman is
complete. Yet, true equality (signified by the oxymoron "same but
other") between male and female is envisioned only when the sexual
duality is finally overcome and the negative aspect of the feminine
is neutralized or ameliorated by her containment in the masculine.
Hence, the alterity of the feminine in relation to the masculine is not
an irreducible otherness; on the contrary, the passage in the *Zohar*
presumes the possibility of effacing the Other of the feminine by
absorbing her within the masculine.[47] The roots for such a state
may be projected in the preemanative stage, i.e., before the process
of emanation unfolds, represented here by the double-faced Adam.
Again, one confronts the fact that the androgyny in kabbalistic
theosophy is primarily and essentially male, the female being a
secondary entity with a lower ontological and axiological status.

In apparent contrast to the texts discussed above, an alternative
view may be derived from the following remark of the sixteenth-
century Safedian kabbalist, Moses Cordovero:

The emanation of Understanding (*Binah*, the feminine element or
the Mother) did not take place after the completion of the emanation of Wisdom (*Hokhmah*, the masculine or the Father), but rather
before Wisdom completed its stature (*shi'ur qomatah*) Understanding was emanated. And this is precisely the reality with respect to
the *du-parzufin*, Beauty (*Tif'eret*, the Son) and Kingdom (*Malkhut*,
the Daughter), for Kingdom was emanated before the completion
of the stature of the masculine (*shi'ur qomat ha-zakhar*). The
reason for this was so that the feminine could be face-to-face with
the masculine, for if the masculine completed the entire emanation
of its limbs and afterwards the feminine would begin, she would
have always been [in the status of a] stool under his feet. Rather
the feminine began [to emanate] its stature before the completion
of the stature of the masculine, and they were emanated together,

this one [according to] its stature and the other one [according to] its stature, and they were face-to-face.[48]

This is a noble attempt by Cordovero to assign an equal value to the masculine and feminine. Here he argues that the feminine forms (*Binah* and *Malkhut*) emanate before the males (*Hokhmah* and *Tif'eret*) so that they may unite face-to-face with their respective mates rather than being subservient to them as symbolized in the image of the footstool.[49]

Nevertheless, the weight of textual evidence indicates that Cordovero's formulation represents a departure from the earlier tradition that viewed the feminine as ontologically inferior to the masculine.[50] In contrast to Cordovero, most kabbalists, following the aggadic sources that interpreted Ps. 139:5 as referring to the androgynous nature of Adam, referred to the masculine potency as the face and the female as the back. While the union of male and female involves a face-to-face encounter,[51] in the ontic situation reflected in the emanation of these forces, the male is the front and the female the back. In classical kabbalistic theosophy, the back (*ahor*) is clearly the Other (*aher*) and never quite attains the same status as the male in the way that Cordovero suggests.

The masculine nature of the divine androgyne is further highlighted in the following anonymous text, apparently representing an early Geronese tradition. Here, the morphological correspondence of the divine anthropos and the limbs of the human body are established in relation to Gen. 1:26, "Let us make Adam in our image and in our likeness":

> The head of man corresponds to the Supreme Crown (*Keter 'Elyon*). . . . The brain and the palate of man correspond to Wisdom (*Hokhmah*). . . . His tongue corresponds to Understanding (*Binah*). . . . The extension of the body corresponds to Beauty (*Tif'eret*). . . . The arms correspond to Love and Power, Love is the right and Power the left. Love is [the quality of] mercy and Power judgement. His feet correspond to Endurance (*Nezah*) and Majesty (*Hod*), Endurance on the right and Majesty on the left. Foundation (*Yesod*) corresponds to the phallus which is set in the middle. This is the form that we have explained . . . and it corresponds to the human body, for the nine *sefirot* are portrayed as an anthropos. A person should not err when he does not see the tenth *sefirah*, for when Beauty was mentioned there was enough [of an allusion] and the intelligent one will understand. When Aher saw the completion of

the [sefirotic] edifice and he saw as well Kingdom (*Malkhut*), the tenth attribute, he cut the shoots and said, "Heaven forbid, perhaps there are two powers."[52] He did not consider in his heart that the wife of a man is set aside and prepared for him all the time, in a perfect union without any separation, like the heart of a man which is prepared. Concerning it the verse said, "And the Lord spoke to His heart" (Gen. 8:21).[53]

This text, which graphically illustrates the point that I was making above regarding the dominant masculine nature of the divine androgyny, represents one of the earliest attempts on the part of thirteenth-century kabbalists to depict the divine anthropos in terms of its correspondence to human limbs. One is immediately struck by the fact that the divine image is depicted here as a male anthropomorphic form. The feminine aspect of the divine, the tenth attribute or Kingdom, is treated either as the spouse of the sixth emanation, Beauty, or as the heart of this form, but not as an autonomous entity. While other names of the tenth emanation are given at the end of the passage, they are not related directly to the image of the anthropos. The critical point is that this image is primarily masculine, for the feminine element is comprised within the male.

A passage in the *Zohar* provides the conceptual underpinning of the mythic nature of the androgyny in zoharic theosophy and, by implication, of the ontic status of the feminine as Other. In the opening comment at the very beginning of the *Zohar* on the first word of Scripture, *bereshit*, "in the beginning," we read,

> In the beginning of the will of the King, the hardened spark engraved engravings in the supernal splendor, and there emerged from within the concealed of the concealed, the beginning [or secret] of the Infinite, a vaporous mass fixed in a ring, not white, black, red or green, or any color at all. When the measure extended it produced colors to shine within. Within the spark there emerged a spring whence the colors were formed below. The concealed of the concealed, the mystery of the Infinite, broke and did not break through its aura. It is not known at all until from the force of its penetration a single point shone, the supernal concealed one. Beyond this point nothing is known at all. Therefore it is called *reshit*, the first of all the *logoi*.[54]

This text offers a profound mythical depiction of the process of emanation from the state of undifferentiated oneness to the differentiated many. By concentrating on the implicitly sexual elements in this mythic portrayal, we can delve more deeply into the principle of the feminine as Other in kabbalistic symbolism. The key to understanding the sexual dynamic implied in the myth of divine autogenesis is the notion of the *bozina de-qardinuta*, which I have translated above as the "hardened spark."[55] This spark, also referred to, on the basis of Jer. 31:39, as the *qav ha-middah* (line-of-measure), serves as the divine tool that gives shape and dimension to the *sefirot* in the emanative process.[56] Scholars, following the lead of kabbalists themselves, including a key passage in *Zohar* 3:48b,[57] generally consider this aspect of the Godhead to be a vehicle of divine judgment. They derive this interpretation from the connection with limitation and boundary, characteristics that are associated in the standard kabbalistic symbolism with divine judgment and hence the feminine aspect of the divine persona.

Yet, it seems clear that several of the essential characteristics attributed to the spark are decidedly phallic in orientation and thus should be associated with the principle of masculinity or the attribute of mercy. Indeed, the inherent nature of this spark is outward projection or elongation (*hamshakhah*) and spreading out (*hitpashtut*), attributes of the male potency.[58] Particularly telling in this regard is the expression *meshiha* (or *mishhata*) associated in several contexts with this spark.[59] While the principal meaning of this expression is "measure," a second connotation is implied, insofar as the root *mashah* can also mean "to anoint." Both meanings have decidedly phallic implications, for it is the nature of the phallus to be erect (hence related to *meshiha* in the sense of "to measure, extend, or stretch") and to emit seminal fluid (*meshiha* in the sense of "to pour oil").

The above zoharic passage describes the Infinite's breaking through its own aura and thereby producing the first point of emanation. The aura, as traditional commentators on the *Zohar* have noted, is the first *sefirah* or the Crown (*Keter*), which is coextensive with the Infinite, while the point is Wisdom (*Hokhmah*). The aura, it seems, is a principle of femininity vis-à-vis the Infinite, which is the masculine element.[60] More specifically, it is the *bozina de-qardinuta*, the hardened spark, which exemplifies the principle of masculinity in relation to the ether or aura that surrounds the divine light.[61] Given the phallic nature of this entity, the reading *bozina de-qardinuta* as opposed to *bozina de-qadrinuta* (the black or dark flame) seems preferable, thereby conveying the notion of an erect penis.

Perhaps it would be more accurate to speak here not of the phallus, but rather of the aspect of the brain that functionally corresponds to it.[62] The hardened spark, therefore, may be referred to as the upper phallus in a functional rather than ontological sense. This is the implication as well of the further identification of the spark as the line-of-measure, i.e., the extended line, sometimes also associated with the letter *waw*, or in one case in *Tiqqune Zohar*, the *waw* that extends from the *yod*, i.e., the line that is drawn out from the point.[63]

To return to the zoharic passage: The spark is characterized as engraving engravings within the supernal luster. It can be shown from a number of other passages in the *Zohar* that the act of engraving or inscription is viewed as a decidedly phallic activity,[64] sometimes designated by the more overtly phallic terms "striking" or "knocking."[65] A nexus is thus established between writing and intercourse such that the hardened spark or line-of-measure functions as a kind of (phallic) stylus and the supernal luster, the *sefirah* of *Keter*, as a (feminine) tablet or writing surface upon which the inscribing is accomplished.[66] Other phalliclike activities applied to the spark include its extending forward to produce colors, the emergence of a spring, the paradoxical breaking through and not breaking through of the aura,[67] the penetration that results in the illumination of a point.

The continuation of the text highlights the erotic nature of this activity in the divine:

> And the enlightened will shine like the splendor of the sky and those who turn the many to righteousness like the stars forever and ever (Dan. 12:3). *Zohar*, the Concealed of the Concealed struck against its aura, for it touched and did not touch this point. Then this Beginning emanated and made itself a palace for its glory and praise. There it sowed the seed of holiness to give birth for the benefit of the universe. . . . *Zohar*, it sowed a seed for its glory, like the seed of fine purple silk, for it wraps itself within and makes itself a palace which is its praise and benefit to all.[68]

The erotic dynamic between the (masculine) spark and the (feminine) aura is thus repeated in the next stage wherein the first point of emanation, the *sefirah* of Wisdom (*Hokhmah*), produces for itself a palace, the *sefirah* of Understanding (*Binah*) wherein it places its seed.

This text shows, moreover, that the kabbalists, designated as the righteous (*zaddiqim*), are illuminated or enlightened by the splendor (*zohar*), which is the concealed spark that strikes against the aura. Of the many interpretations of the eschatalogical promise of Dan. 12:3 in zoharic literature, the verse that provided the title for the work, the one that is particularly relevant to this discussion interprets the splendor as *Yesod* (Foundation), the gradation that corresponds to the phallus of the divine anthropos.[69] This text thus links the kabbalists specifically to *Yesod*, the splendor with which they are illuminated and by means of which they interpret the text of Scripture.[70] Indeed, this correlation is essential as the spiritual worldview of the *Zohar* (including mystical, theurgical, and messianic elements) is completely dominated by the correspondence of the kabbalist below and the *Zaddiq* above.

It is no mere coincidence that the *zohar* that enlightens the kabbalist is related either to the *bozina de-qardinuta* or to *Yesod*; on the contrary, the characterizations of the two are extremely close. Indeed, according to one passage, it is evident that the one parallels the other: just as the *bozina de-qardinuta* is described as the flashing spark that strikes against the ether or the brain in order to produce a scattering of light, so *Yesod* is depicted as a spark of light that strikes or overflows in various directions. Moreover, just as the *bozina de-qardinuta* is paradoxically associated with concealment and manifestation, shining and not shining, striking and not striking, so *Yesod* is at once hidden and revealed, visible and invisible.

This dialectic of concealment and disclosure—to reveal in the concealing and to conceal in the revealing—is attributed by the *Zohar* to *Yesod*, on the one hand, and to the master of esoteric gnosis, on the other. Finally, it is precisely some such phallic activity that underlies the following zoharic passage from the section *Qav ha-Middah*, an extended meditation on Deut. 6:4:

> Fortunate are those who know how to bring out upper secrets from the faith and they know how to enter to the right and left as is appropriate without embarrassment. Thus it is written, "And the enlightened will shine like the splendor of the sky." When the hardened spark produces a measure it is gathered into them, and it is in each and every grade in that gathering, and it establishes them. Afterwards it rises concealed until they rise, and it is hidden and concealed and unknown, and everything remains as it is. Then

what shines shines and it emits rivers and water to irrigate everything. Until here is the secret of the hardened spark to unify in it all aspects of faith. The hardened spark exists in those which are concealed, it rises and descends. The one who knows the secret of wisdom can comprehend and can produce a measure in all aspects, until he knows the supernal secrets, the secrets of his master, the secrets of wisdom so that he may know and comprehend. Fortunate is the portion of one who knows and contemplates in this world and in the world-to-come, for by means of this principle a person should arrange his feet such that he enters [from behind] the curtain and walks in a straight way. Fortunate is he in this world and in the world-to-come.[71]

Interestingly, the gnosis attained by the mystics as a result of the illumination by the hardened spark is characterized in terms of the measure applied by the kabbalists themselves to the form of the divine anthropos. As Yehuda Liebes has noted, the praise at the end of this citation betrays the influence of the well-known statement contained in some of the recensions of the *Shi'ur Qomah* regarding the virtue of one who knows the measure and praise of the Creator: "Whoever knows the measure of our Creator and His praise is guaranteed to be in the world-to-come."[72] It thus follows, as Liebes astutely observes, that the *bozina de-qardinuta* is not only a tool in the hands of the Creator, but it is at the same time "a tool in the hands of the kabbalist who contemplates and seeks to comprehend the secrets of the divine attributes."[73] The kabbalist is entrusted with the task of constructing the divine form either through scriptural expositions[74] or through specific mystical intentions in prayer.[75] In both cases the act of measuring is linked especially to what one might call the phallic imagination of the mystic.

The interpretation of the *bozina de-qardinuta* that I have offered challenges a generally accepted impression reflected in the scholarly literature. It is often assumed that sexual characteristics are inapplicable to the highest recesses of the Godhead.[76] To be sure, such a view is expressed occasionally in the writings of the kabbalists themselves. Yet, the mythical account of the zoharic authorship, which had a profound impact especially on Lurianic kabbalah, is predicated on the presumption of a primordial androgyne that is a *complexio oppositorum*, a symbol of the fusion of male and female. The primeval androgyne is composed not of a father and mother, but rather of a single androgynous parent who is primarily male.[77]

The first gradation (coextensive with the Infinite) is feminine in relation to the Infinite, whose masculine principle is represented by this hardened spark or line-of-measure. The next stage of emanation, the shining forth of the point (*Hokhmah*) encased within a palace (*Binah*), represents a further unfolding or splitting of the androgynous nature of the divine, for the point is the masculine projection (symbolized in some parts of the *Zohar* as the Father) and the palace the feminine receptacle (the Mother). The androgyny is represented on yet a third level when *Tif'eret* and *Malkhut*, the Son and Daughter, are emanated. The unfolding of the androgyny in this threefold process is well captured in the following passage from the *Idra Zuta* ("Lesser Assembly"), where it is designated as a matter that should not be revealed except to the supreme holy ones who are adept at entering and exiting the orchard of mystical speculation:

> It has been taught: When the Holy Ancient One, Concealed of the Concealed (*Keter*), desired to fix the order [of reality], he arranged everything as male and female, in the place where male and female were merged (*itkelilu*). They did not exist except in another state (*qiyyuma ahra*)[78] as male and female.[79] When this Wisdom (*Hokhmah*), the principle of everything, emerged and was illuminated from the Holy Ancient One, it did not shine except as male and female. For that Wisdom emanated and there came forth from it Understanding (*Binah*), so that there was male and female. Wisdom as Father and Understanding as Mother. Wisdom and Understanding are weighed on the one scale (*be-had matqela itqalu*), male and female. . . . When they were joined they gave birth and Faith[80] (i.e., Beauty and Kingdom, male and female) emanated. . . . The two (Wisdom and Understanding) are joined together and the Son is in them, the principle of everything, containing male and female. Through their arrangment is the perfection of everything, the containment of everything: Father and Mother, Son and Daughter.[81]

The significant point for this study is that in the primary stage the principle of femininity, that which is Other, is itself part of the masculine divine rather than a distinct reality. In the Infinite all opposites coincide, as the *Zohar* itself in one place puts it:

> R. Isaac said: When the Holy One, blessed be He, created the world and wanted to reveal the depth out of the hiddenness and the light from within the darkness, they were contained within one

another. . . . And all things were contained one within the other, the good inclination and the evil inclination, right and left, Israel and the nations, white and black. All things were dependent on one another.[82]

Although the imagery of male and female is not employed here, it is evident from other passages in the *Zohar* that the gender types are correlated with the other items listed in the asymmetrically valued pairs. Within the infinite depths of the divine, therefore, male and female were perfectly balanced. The beginning of the process of emanation is marked by a disrupture of this balance, or the activation of the sexual play between masculine and feminine, the separation of right and left, Israel and the nations, holy and profane.

The implications of the zoharic idea are fully drawn by the author of *Tiqqune Zohar*, who in one place comments,

> In the beginning of the will of the King, when the hardened spark begins to produce a measure (*madid meshiha*), a line comes forth from that point, for the [divine] Thought is hidden like a final *mem* (i.e., a square closed on four sides). Initially it is a closed *mem*, but when the line, which is a *waw*, extends from the measure, it opens up and becomes a *bet* (i.e., three sides closed and one open). And this is *bereshit, bet reshit*, the point in its palace.[83]

The primordially androgynous quality of the divine is graphically represented by the final *mem*, which is a square closed off on all four sides. The square represents wholeness, the perfect balance, and unity of masculine and feminine. In the ultimate state, gender differences are overcome rather than held in dialectical tension. The activity of the phallus, symbolized by the hardened spark or the letter *waw*, creates a rupture in the Godhead, symbolized by the final *mem* being broken into a *bet* and *waw*, but this rupture is necessary for the creative process to unfold. Hence the *bet* formed from the final *mem* itself becomes the receptacle to receive the masculine point, which contains the semen that will produce the lower *sefirot* in the ontological chain. In the primary state male and female are inseparable and ultimately indistinguishable. The logical implication of this is drawn in a small text on the mystery of the *du-parzufim* composed by David ben Yehudah he-Hasid.[84]

After describing the sexual polarity that characterizes the lower seven *sefirot*, R. David cautions the reader:

> But in the primordial world (i.e., *Keter*) there is no loss or division,
> and the feminine power is not separate from the side of the mascu-
> line. This is sufficient for the one who understands. For all the
> souls emerge from there in pairs, and they return there. Since they
> go out from there male and female, it is evident that they go out
> from the absolutely simple force . . . and they do not separate. If
> they were separated there would be, as it were, a loss and division.
> This is sufficient for one who understands and to the wise an
> allusion [is enough].

The secret transmitted by this kabbalist concerns the fact that in
the primordial world of *Keter* the masculine and feminine elements
are completely unified in the simple unity of the divine wherein all
opposites coincide. Only in the lower realm of the sefirotic edifice
are the masculine and feminine distinguished as distinct powers.

It goes without saying that for the theosophic kabbalist, the
purpose of religious life is to restore the harmony of the masculine
and feminine aspects of God. On the basis of a careful reading of
the relevant biblical passages, the zoharic authorship, following
other theosophic kabbalists, maintained that the divine image (*zelem
elohim*) with which Adam was created—i.e., the form of the sefirotic
pleroma—comprises both maleness and femaleness: "Any image
wherein male and female are not found is not a supernal image."[85]
Herein lies the foundation of the kabbalistic understanding of divine
unity that the *Zohar* refers to in any number of contexts as the
secret of faith[86] or the perfection of everything.[87] "This is the
praise of the supernal faith to know that YHWH is Elohim, the male
is completed in the female, the one contained in the other, the male
is built within the female, and this is the perfect union, for there is
no perfection except when male and female are one."[88] All human
activity, especially the conjugal union of a man and his wife, is
empowered with the theurgical capacity to affect the union of the
masculine and feminine attributes above.[89]

It is a commonplace that the motif of *hieros gamos* is central to
kabbalistic anthropology and theology, for the ultimate function of
prayer, Torah study, and indeed all the traditional commandments
is to promote the union of masculine and feminine attributes of the
Godhead. In the absence of such unity the divine is ruptured and
consequently impotent. As the zoharic authorship in another
passage succinctly expresses it, "a king without a matrona is not a
king."[90] One can go even further and say that the messianic

impulse reflected in the *Zohar* and other theosophic writings invariably turns on the issue of unification of masculine and feminine: The historical state of exile signifies division in the Godhead and redemption marks a restoration of that union.[91]

The issue that I have raised, however, concerns the nature of this hierogamy: does the kabbalistic emphasis on sexual union and coupling in the divine realm imply the conjunction of two principles that nevertheless remain distinct, or the reestablishment of an original androgynous state wherein gender differences are transcended? I cited above Scholem's remark, which contrasted Jewish and Christian gnosis on this very score. A careful examination of the relevant sources indicates, however, that the image of union affirmed in kabbalistic texts is predicated on the overcoming of sexual differences achieved by the containment or reintegration of the feminine left side in the masculine right. On occasion the dualistic language of male and female gives way to a more monistic approach. A striking example of that is found in the kabbalistic treatment of the rite of circumcision. Following normative rabbinic halakhah,[92] the kabbalists distinguish two stages in this ritual, *milah* (cutting the foreskin) and *peri'ah* (uncovering the corona), each one symbolically corresponding to one of the last two of the ten emanations. According to some kabbalists, the corona of the penis corresponds to the Diadem (*'Atarah*), i.e., the *Shekhinah* or feminine Presence. The feminine aspect of God, therefore, becomes localized as part of the phallus itself. Thus, to cite one of many relevant examples, the *Zohar* comments on the verse, "Blessings light upon the head of the righteous" (Prov. 10:6): "The head of the righteous (i.e., the *sefirah* of *Yesod*, which corresponds to the phallus) is the holy corona."[93] The act of uncovering the corona is mystically transformed into an occasion for the revelation of the divine Diadem; indeed, the ritual of circumcision is understood in kabbalistic literature as a theophanic moment.

The following account is given by Moses de León:

> And contemplate that the secret of the covenant (*sod ha-berit*) is the way of comprehensive faith (*derekh kelal emunah*). When the foreskin is removed from the phallus—this is the secret of faith. Yet the removal of the foreskin to enter into the secret of the faith [is not complete] until one pulls down [the membrane] and the corona is revealed. When one reaches the corona one enters into the mystery of the way of faith and is bound to faith.[94]

In a second work Moses de León returns to this motif, but there he emphasizes the visionary element of the experience:

> The foreskin is the shell standing on the outside and the phallus is the core on the inside. . . . This is the secret of the proper matter when a person enters the secret of faith. Concerning this secret it says, "All your males shall appear before the Lord your God" (Deut. 16:16). For one must cleave [to the divine] and show that place [the phallus] in its source, the branch in its Root, to unite everything in the bond of the secret of His unity, with one bond and in one secret, so that "the Lord will be one and His name will be one" (Zech. 14:9).[95]

Through the mechanism of the circumcised phallus, Jewish males cleave to the divine Presence so that there will be unity above between the masculine and feminine, the Lord and His name. In the first text it is especially evident that the corona of the phallus, disclosed in the second act of the circumcision ritual, symbolizes the feminine Presence. This indicates quite convincingly that within the kabbalistic tradition there is a conception of the feminine that is an integral part of, rather than distinct from, the masculine. To borrow the formulation of Mircea Eliade, it may be said that circumcision from the kabbalistic perspective is a ritual of symbolic androgynization.[96] The phallus is not merely the signifier that concomitantly marks the difference between sexes and effaces that difference by acting as the copula that connects them;[97] the paradox in kabbalistic symbolism is more profound, for the phallus is the locus of both masculinity and femininity.

For the kabbalist the phallus provides access to the (feminine) Other not only by filling in the lack by its erectile form but also by absorbing the feminine as part of its very physiological (and, by implication, semiological) structure. Hence, as a result of the ritual of circumcision the corona is disclosed and an opening is created in the male body that corresponds to the opening in the divine realm, i.e., the feminine Presence, the gate through which the mystic enters to approach the masculine king. By virtue of the circumcised penis, therefore, the male Jew can unite with the Presence; in this relationship the mystic is valorized as male and the divine as female.

Yet, the same ritual has a feminizing aspect as well: The Presence can dwell on the male who has been circumcised because the circumcision has opened the male to receive the divine efflux;

thus the male is female vis-à-vis the divine.[98] The feminizing of the masculine effected by circumcision is predicated on the ontological fact that femaleness is part of maleness. It is the same ontic assumption that allows for the masculinization of the feminine. Thus, in a variety of contexts the feminine aspect of the divine is treated as masculine, i.e., there is a transmutation of gender characteristics such that the female becomes male.

Indeed, the third gradation, *Binah*, is identified as the Mother, or the female consort to *Hokhmah*, the Father; yet that very gradation is referred to on any number of occasions as the king (*melekh*), for when she overflows and produces the lower gradations she assumes the posture of a male.[99] "Even though that supernal world (*Binah*) is feminine, it is called a male when it emanates all the goodness and all the light comes out from it."[100] "Even though [*Binah*] is the supernal king it is feminine in relation to the supernal point (*Hokhmah*) that is most concealed, but it is masculine in relation to the king who is below (*Shekhinah*)."[101] The feminine Presence is designated *melekh*, king, or sometimes *Malkhut*, kingship, for she too is considered a king vis-à-vis the lower realms of being insofar as the latter emanate out of and are sustained by her.[102] In one passage the *Shekhinah* is explicitly described as the

> angel that sometimes is male and other times female. When it bestows blessings upon the world it is male and is called male like a man who bestows blessings upon a woman. So too it bestows blessings upon the world. When it stands in judgement upon the world it is called female, like a woman who is pregnant she is filled with judgement, and then she is called female. Thus it is sometimes masculine and sometimes feminine. It is all one mystery.[103]

This inversion of gender attribution is related to a larger principle in kabbalistic ontology that is predicated on the valorization of the masculine: In relation to what is above it, a particular attribute is feminine for it receives; but in relation to what is below it, that same attribute is masculine for it overflows. The feminine attributes, *Binah* and *Malkhut*, become male when they overflow to the grades beneath them. Only when they abolish their own femaleness and assume the characteristic of the male are they viewed positively.

Just as the spiritual ideal, the secret of faith, is one in which the female is united with the male, the root of idolatry is the separation of the female from the male. This is expressed in two ways that I alluded to above: the reification of the feminine as a distinct divine power or the emasculation of the masculine. The former state is related exegetically to various sins recorded in the Bible, including the sin of Adam and Eve eating from the tree of knowledge, Noah's drunkenness, the building of the Tower of Babel, and the construction of the golden calf, to name some of the better-known episodes. The separation of the female from the male in all these cases involves the last of the emanations, the *Shekhinah*.[104]

In this connection it is important to recall that according to the zoharic tradition there is a profound ambivalence with respect to the *Shekhinah* and its relationship to the demonic realm. While the zoharic authorship sometimes sharply contrasts the *Shekhinah* with her demonic feminine counterpart, Lilith, on other occasions the line separating the two is blurred and the characteristics of Lilith are applied to the *Shekhinah*.[105]

In the latter state, i.e., the emasculated male (symbolized as well as the celibate), the primeval forces of unbalanced judgment are eliminated from the economy of the divine before the splitting of the primeval androgyne into masculine and feminine. These forces are designated by various names in zoharic theosophy, including that of the Edomite kings who rule before Israel (based on Gen. 36:31–39). This designation is significant for it casts the discussion in an historical and polemical light: the ontic source of Christianity is viewed as deriving from the demonic, symbolized as the unbalanced forces of the Edomite kings that must be eliminated before the holy forces of the Godhead, symbolized as the androgynous Israel, unfold. To be sure, even here one must be careful about not lapsing into a rigid dualism, for the judgmental powers are themselves part of the divine. This is highlighted in one particular text in terms of imagery that calls to mind Esau and Jacob, i.e., the elder is Esau, Christianity or the demonic force, and the younger is Jacob, Israel, the side of holiness, the androgynous that is expressed as a balance of right and left, male and female.[106] However, when discussed in relation to Israel, the nations are associated with the left or demonic, and Israel with the right or holy. The following passage from the *Zohar* may be considered exemplary:

> Israel is from the right side and they do not cleave to the left nor are they mixed together with it. When they sin they cause the right to be subdued and the left to be aroused. . . . It has been

taught: there is a right and a left, mercy and judgement, Israel on
the right and the idolatrous nations on the left.[107]

Given the further association of the left with the feminine and the
right with the masculine, it is plausible to assume that the gentile
nations take on the status of the woman vis-à-vis Israel, which is
the male.

This introduces still another dimension of the feminine as Other
in kabbalistic symbolism, a dimension reflected in still another
zoharic passage.[108] There, the nations of the world, symbolized by
the woman, derive from the demonic, other side characterized as
severity or harsh judgment. Hence, the gentile woman is Other in
relation to the male Jew; if the latter should cross the boundary and
have relations with her, then the demonic force overpowers the holy.
By contrast, the Jewess, who is also by nature judgmental, can
exercise mercy if she cleaves to a male Jew through sexual intercourse, symbolized by the metaphor of tasting. Once more we see the
subordinate function accorded the woman, for she is merely a vessel
that assumes the character of that which is poured into it. In the
final analysis, the union of man and woman is to facilitate the male
so that he may be united with the *Shekhinah* and to ameliorate the
judgment of the female, i.e., to eradicate the femaleness of the
female; even in sexual intercourse the goal is to masculinize the
feminine.[109] This is not to deny the fact that sexual ethics in
kabbalistic literature reflect a genuine concern for the dignity and
well-being of the woman.[110] The relevant texts indicate that the
man is not to treat the woman as a mere sex object, but rather as a
partner in the task of realizing the sacred union above and maintaining the divine image by prolonging the chain of being.[111]
Nevertheless, the fact is that the woman is assigned a passive role
in relation to the active male, and in those instances where she does
assume a more active role she takes on the persona of a male.

Thus, we are led to conclude that, despite the larger role
assigned to the feminine in kabbalistic spirituality, the androcentric
emphasis of medieval rabbinic culture had a profound impact on the
depiction of the woman as Other in this major trend of Jewish
mysticism. The woman is indeed the Other, the back side of divine
judgment that, in the moment of union, is turned around so that she
stands face-to-face with the masculine attribute of mercy. In this
facing, however, her otherness is effaced as she becomes reintegrated
into the male. The element of female otherness vanishes as the

feminine left is absorbed in the masculine right.[112] In the absorption of the female in the male, the union is consummated so that there is only one body in actuality and otherness is dissolved in totality.

NOTES

1. See the review of this problematic in the introduction of Julia Epstein and Kristina Straub, *Body Guards: The Cultural Politics of Gender Ambiguity* (New York and London, 1991), 1–28.

2. For the misogynist tendencies in medieval Christian culture, cf. Caroline Walker Bynum, "'. . . And Woman His Humanity': Female Imagery in the Religious Writing of the Later Middle Ages," in *Gender and Religion: On the Complexity of Symbols*, ed. Carol Walker Bynum, Stevan Harrell, and Paula Richman (Boston, 1986), 257–88, and other references given on 280–81 nn. 1–2. See also Kari Elisabeth Børresen, "God's Image, Is Woman Excluded? Medieval Interpretation of Gen. 1,27 and I Cor. 11,7," in *Image of God and Gender Models in Judaeo-Christian Tradition*, ed. Kari Elisabeth Børresen (Oslo, 1991), 208–27. See, however, Maryanne Cline Horowitz, "The Image of God in Man—Is Woman Included?" *Harvard Theological Review* 72 (1979): 175–206. For a general survey on the status of women within medieval Jewish societies, see Judith R. Baskin, "Jewish Women in the Middle Ages," in *Jewish Women in Historical Perspective*, ed. Judith R. Baskin (Detroit, 1991), 94–114.

3. The literature on this topic is already quite extensive and growing rapidly. Here I cite only some representative studies listed in chronological order. Cf. Saul Berman, "The Status of Women in Halakhic Judaism," *Tradition* 14 (1973): 5–28; Leonard Swidler, *Women in Judaism: The Status of Women in Formative Judaism* (Metuchen, N.J., 1976); Judith Hauptmann, "Images of Women in the Talmud," in *Religion and Sexism: Images of Woman in the Jewish and Christian Traditions*, ed. Rosemary Radfort Ruether (New York, 1974), 184–212; Jacob Neusner, *Method and Meaning in Ancient Judaism* (Missoula, Mont., 1979), 80–86; Blu Greenberg, *On Women and Judaism: A View from Tradition* (Philadelphia, 1981); Rachel Biale, *Women and Jewish Law* (New York, 1984); Judith R. Baskin, "The Separation of Women in Rabbinic Judaism," in *Women, Religion, and Social Change*, ed. Yvonne Yazbeck Haddad and Ellison Banks Findly (Albany, N.Y., 1985), 3–18; Judith Romney Wegner, *Chattel or Person? The Status of Women in the Mishnah* (New York, 1988); Blu Greenberg, "Female Sexuality and Bodily Functions in the Jewish Tradition," in *Women, Religion, and Sexuality: Studies on the Impact of Religious Teachings on Women*, ed.

Jeanne Becher (Philadelphia, 1990), 1–44; Judith Romney Wegner, "The Image and Status of Women in Classical Rabbinic Judaism," in *Jewish Women in Historical Perspective*, 68–93. All of these studies attempt to paint a portrait of the social role of women within Jewish society in Late Antiquity on the basis of rabbinic literature that stems from an androcentric elite. For a different methodological approach, cf. Ross S. Kraemer, "Jewish Women in the Diaspora World of Late Antiquity," in *Jewish Women in Historical Perspective*, 43–67, and references to other relevant studies on 62–63 n. 5. See also Ross Kraemer in this volume, chap. 6.

4. My formulation here has been influenced by Wendy Doniger O'Flaherty, *Women, Androgynes, and Other Mythical Beasts* (Chicago and London, 1980), 28–29, 284, 286, 331, 333–34. Regarding the one-sex theory in the primarily androcentric Western culture, see Thomas Laqueur, *Making Sex: Body and Gender from the Greeks to Freud* (Cambridge and London, 1990).

5. A similar claim has been made for ancient Gnosticism. See the evidence adduced by Michael A. Williams, "Uses of Gender Imagery in Ancient Gnostic Texts," in *Gender and Religion: On the Complexity of Symbols*, 197–98; and cf. reference to study of MacDonald cited below, n. 16. Williams's own position is more nuanced, however, arguing for a variety of different opinions in Gnostic literature.

6. Cf. *Gospel of Thomas*, logion 114, in *The Nag Hammadi Library in English*, ed. J. M. Robinson, 3d ed. (San Francisco, 1988), 138. See, however, logion 22, op. cit., 129, where the formulation for entering the kingdom is to "make the two one . . . so that the male not be male nor the female female." In the latter case too, however, the issue is abolishing the polarity of male and female so that the latter could be absorbed in the former. Cf. Philo, *Quaestiones et Solutiones in Genesin* 2.49; *Quaestiones et Solutiones in Exodum* 1.8; Clement of Alexandria, *Stromateis* 3.13.92; 6.12.100. Cf. Jacob Jervell, *Imago Dei. Gen. 1:26f. im Spätjudentum, in der Gnosis, und in den paulinischen Briefen* (Göttingen, 1960), 161–63; Robert M. Grant, "The Mystery of Marriage in the Gospel of Philip," *Vigiliae Christianae* 15 (1961): 129–40; Mircea Eliade, *The Two and the One*, trans. J. M. Cohen (Chicago, 1965), 103–8; Richard A. Baer, Jr., *Philo's Use of the Categories Male and Female* (Leiden, 1970), 45–49, 69–71; Wayne A. Meeks, "The Image of the Androgyne: Some Uses of a Symbol in Earliest Christianity," *History of Religions* 13 (1973–74): 195–96; J. M. Sevrin, "Les Noces spiritueles dans l'Évangile selon Philippe," *Le Muséon* 87 (1974): 143–93; Carl G. Jung, *Mysterium Coniunctionis*, trans. R. F. C. Hull (Princeton, N.J., 1977), 373–74; M. W. Meyer, "Making Mary Male: The Categories 'Male' and 'Female' in the Gospel of Thomas," *New Testament Studies* 31 (1985): 554–70; Peter Brown, *The Body and Society: Men, Women, and Sexual Renunciation in Early Christianity* (New

York, 1988), 103–21; Kari Vogt, "'Becoming Male': A Gnostic and Early Christian Metaphor," in *Image of God and Gender Models in Judaeo-Christian Tradition*, 172–87; Kari Elisabeth Borresen, "God's Image, Man's Image? Patristic Interpretation of Gen. 1,27 and I Cor. 11,7," op. cit., 188–207; Elizabeth Castelli, "I Will Make Mary Male": Pieties of the Body and Gender Transformation of Christian Women in Late Antiquity," in *Body Guards*, 29–49.

7. Cf. *Zohar* 1:35b, 52a–b, 53a–b, 75a–b, 83a, 221a–b, 262a; 2:191a, 237a; 3:42a. Cf. Isaiah Tishby, *The Wisdom of the Zohar*, trans. David Goldstein (Oxford, 1989), 373–76.

8. Cf. Alexander Altmann, *Studies in Religious Philosophy and Mysticism* (Ithaca, N.Y., 1969), 193 n. 60.

9. Cf. Yehuda Liebes, "The Messiah of the Zohar," in *The Messianic Idea in Jewish Thought: A Study Conference in Honour of the Eightieth Birthday of Gershom Scholem* (Hebrew) (Jerusalem, 1982), 194–97, 219–21.

10. The word I have rendered as "balance" is *matqela*, which means "weight" (in Hebrew: *mishqal*), from the root *teqal*, "to weigh." Cf. *Zohar* 2:255a. Regarding this term in its zoharic context and a possible precedent in the writings of R. Isaac the Blind, see Yehuda Liebes, *Peraqim be-Millon Sefer ha-Zohar* (Jerusalem, 1976), 329–30; idem, "The Messiah," 199.

11. *Zohar* 2:176b.

12. Cf. *Zohar* 3:128a, 135a, 142a, 292a.

13. Another way of expressing this is that there is no explicit ritual by means of which the socioreligious division between men and women in Jewish communities is transcended such as one finds, for example, in the baptismal rite of certain early Christian churches as may be adduced from Gal. 3:27–28 (cf. Col. 3:9–11). Cf. Meeks, "The Image of the Androgyne," 166, 180–85. (For a different reading of the Pauline claim in Gal. 3:28, cf. n. 16.) See op. cit., 189–97, where Meeks discusses other rituals in Gnostic sources, including most importantly the mystery of the Bridal Chamber, intended to renew or restore the androgynous Image. Nor am I aware of any rituals of bisexual behavior in the case of Judaism as a means of uniting the masculine and feminine. For examples of such a phenomenon in the history of shamanism, cf. Eliade, *The Two and the One*, 116–17.

14. Following the conjecture of S. A. Horodecky (*Ha-Hasidut we-ha-Hasidim*, vol. 4 [Tel-Aviv, 1951], 68–71), many scholars have maintained that in Hasidism women were accorded a more positive and equal social role due to the popularization of esotericism and the overcoming of rabbinic intellectualism by pietistic emotionalism. For a critique of this romantic portrait of Hasidism, cf. Jacob Katz, *Tradition and Crisis: Jewish Society at the End of the Middle Ages* (New York, 1977), 243; Ada Rapoport-Albert, "On Women in Hasidism, S. A. Horodecky and the

Maid of Ludmir Tradition," in *Jewish History: Essays in Honour of Chimen Abramsky*, ed. Ada Rapoport-Albert and Steven J. Zipperstein (London, 1988), 495–525. For a more positive assessment of women in Hasidic spirituality and a partial rejoinder to Rapoport-Albert, see Nehemia Polen, "Miriam's Dance: Radical Egalitarianism in Hasidic Thought," *Modern Judaism* 12 (1992): 1–21.

15. On the conspicuous absence of women in the Jewish mystical tradition, a seeming anomaly in the history of religions, see the oft-cited formulation of Gershom Scholem, *Major Trends in Jewish Mysticism* (New York, 1956), 37–38. Several scholars have already challenged Scholem's assumption that the exclusion of women from Jewish mystical groups is tied to the theoretical correlation of the feminine and the demonic. See Rapoport-Albert, "On Women in Hasidism," 523 n. 80; and Polen, "Miriam's Dance," 17–18 n. 26. While this is not the appropriate context to enter into a lengthy discussion of this issue, let me briefly note that the literary evidence attests that women did have visionary experiences that should qualify as mystical in nature. Thus, e.g., we find that such visions are attributed to women in Hayyim Vital's diary, *Sefer ha-Hezyonot*, ed. A. Aescoli (Jerusalem, 1954), 6–7, 10, passim. There is also evidence that in the context of the Sabbatian movement women had prophetic visions together with men. Cf. Gershom Scholem, *Sabbatai Sevi: The Mystical Messiah*, trans. R. J. Zwi Werblowsky (Princeton, N.J., 1973), 254, 418–23. However, as Rapoport-Albert points out, "On Women in Hasidism," 496, these women were not central to the phenomenon of mass prophecy and certainly were not mystical leaders of the messianic movement. In the case of the Frankist heresy a significant role is accorded to the feminine aspect of God, and there is also evidence of female participants in visionary experiences (cf. Bernard D. Weinryb, *The Jews of Poland* [Philadelphia, 1976], 236–61), but here too we are dealing with isolated incidents and would therefore be ill advised to draw any general conclusion about the role of women's participation in the history of Jewish mysticism. (Some of the examples of women visionaries adduced above were discussed by Chava Weissler in her lecture, "Jewish Mystical Heresy and the Construction of Women as the Other," delivered at the conference whose proceedings are being published in this volume.) For a striking example in popular religious literature of the eighteenth century of a woman appropriating the kabbalistic symbolism of the *Zohar*, see Chava Weissler, "Woman as High Priest: A Kabbalistic Prayer in Yiddish for Lighting Sabbath Candles," *Jewish History* 5 (1991): 9–26. As the author readily admits, however, for the woman to assume an active role in the cosmic drama, she becomes a male according to standard kabbalistic symbolism and thus there is no significant transformation of the accepted gender valences (see especially 18–20). See idem, "For Women and for Men Who Are Like Women: The Construction of Gender in Yiddish Devo-

tional Literature," *Journal of Feminist Studies in Religion* 5 (1989): 7–24, especially 16–22. The same may be said about the material studied in idem, "Women in Paradise," *Tikkun* 2 (1987): 43–46, 117–120. Finally, let me note that the recognition of women visionaries in the history of Jewish mysticism does not alter my view regarding the essentially phallic nature of visionary experience in terms of the phenomenological structures of kabbalistic thinking. Cf. Elliot R. Wolfson, "Circumcision, Vision of God, and Textual Interpretation: From Midrashic Trope to Mystical Symbol," *History of Religions* 27 (1987): 189–215. The pattern that I discussed in that context is not challenged by the fact that women too have visions, for the nature of these visions would be judged (from within the standpoint of the tradition of theosophic kabbalah) qualitatively different from the ecstatic vision of the feminine Presence that was the subject of my study. The seeing of the divine from the circumcised phallus (derived exegetically from Job 19:26, "This, after my skin has been peeled off, but from my flesh I will see God") is, *ex definitio*, limited to male Jews. Consider the formulation in *Zohar* 3:14a: "Thus R. Simeon said, The human being who is born a son [alternative reading: the infant who is circumcised] is bound to the Presence for she is the opening of all the supernal openings [or: crowns], the opening that is bound to the Holy Name." The valorization of the phallus as the locus of seeing God privileges the masculine and relegates the feminine to a secondary status. On the other hand, it should be noted that to some extent the kabbalistic treatment of the rite of circumcision involves a feminization of the masculine insofar as the incision of the penis results in an opening of the body that corresponds to the feminine aspect of the divine; cf. Wolfson, "Circumcision, Vision of God, and Textual Interpretation," 204–5. On the possibility that this is already adumbrated in Midrashic texts, see Daniel Boyarin, "'This We Know to Be the Carnal Israel': Circumcision and the Erotic Life of God and Israel," *Critical Inquiry* 18 (1992): 493–97.

16. Cf. Dennis R. MacDonald, "Corinthian Veils and Gnostic Androgynes," in *Images of the Feminine in Gnosticism*, ed. Karen L. King (Philadelphia, 1988), 283–85. MacDonald claims that even Gal. 3:28 proves only that the overcoming of sexual differentiation results in the constitution of one male person. For a different approach to Paul's attitude toward women, see William P. Walker, Jr., "I Corinthians 11:2–16 and Paul's Views regarding Women," *Journal of Biblical Literature* 94 (1975): 94–110.

17. Cf. Elliot R. Wolfson, "Left Contained in the Right: A Study in Zoharic Hermeneutics," *AJS Review* 11 (1986): 27–52.

18. Cf. Scholem, *Major Trends*, 54–56.

19. Cf. Martin S. Cohen, *The Shi'ur Qomah: Liturgy and Theurgy in Pre-*

Kabbalistic Jewish Mysticism (Lanham, Md., 1983), 210–11 n. 47, and 217 n. 6.

20. Cf. Ithamar Gruenwald, "A Preliminary Critical Edition of Sefer Yezira," *Israel Oriental Studies* 1 (1971): 141. The reading of *Sefer Yezirah* that I have here proposed is a radical departure from most scholarly interpretations that do not interpret the doctrine of *sefirot* in *Sefer Yezirah* theosophically. See, e.g., Gershom Scholem, *Origins of the Kabbalah*, trans. Alan Arkush, ed. R. J. Zwi Werblowsky (Princeton, N.J., 1987), 81, 139. For a more elaborate presentation of this interpretation, see my forthcoming book, *Through a Speculum That Shines: Vision and Imagination in Medieval Jewish Mysticism*, end of chap. 2.

21. Cf. Scholem, *Origins*, 184–87; Alexander Altmann, "Eleazar of Worms' *Hokhmath Ha-'Egoz*," *Journal of Jewish Studies* 11 (1960): 101–12, reprinted in idem, *Studies in Religious Philosophy and Mysticism* (Ithaca, N.Y., 1969), 161–71; Joseph Dan, "Hokhmath Ha-'Egoz, Its Origins and Development," *Journal of Jewish Studies* 17 (1966): 73–82, especially 77; idem, *The Esoteric Theology of Ashkenazi Hasidim* (Hebrew) (Jerusalem, 1968), 116–29; idem, "A Reevaluation of the 'Ashkenazi Kabbalah'" (Hebrew), *Jerusalem Studies in Jewish Thought* 6, 3–4 (1987): 125–39, especially 137–39. Dan's insistence that sexual symbolism does not play a significant role in the more developed stages of Pietistic theosophy has been challenged recently by several scholars. Cf. Asi Farber, "The Concept of the Merkabah in Thirteenth-Century Jewish Esotericism: Sod ha-Egoz and Its Development" (Hebrew) (Ph.D. diss., Hebrew University, 1986), 101–23, and the copious notes to this section, 533–657, which contain many important insights for the study of gender imagery in ancient Jewish mysticism, German Pietism, and theosophic kabbalah; Elliot R. Wolfson, "The Image of Jacob Engraved upon the Throne: Further Speculation on the Esoteric Doctrine of the German Pietists," *Ephraim Gottlieb Memorial Volume* (Jerusalem, 1994). See also the passing comment of Moshe Idel, "Sexual Metaphor and Praxis in the Kabbalah," in *The Jewish Family: Metaphor and Memory*, ed. David Kraemer (New York and Oxford, 1989), 221 n. 79. Cf. idem, "Additional Fragments from the Writings of Rabbi Joseph Hamadan" (Hebrew), *Da'at* 21 (1988): 47–55, especially 51–52; idem, *Kabbalah: New Perspectives* (New Haven, Conn., 1988), 130, 193–97.

22. Cf. B. Berakhot 61b; Eruvin 18a; Genesis Rabbah 8:1; Leviticus Rabbah 14:1. Cf. Charles Mopsik, "Recherches autour de la Lettre sur la sainteté. Sources, texte, influences. Tome I: La Dualité masculin/feminin dans la cabale. Tome II: La Secret de la relation entre l'homme et la femme" (Ph.D. diss., Sorbonne, Paris, 1987), 29–73 (my thanks to Hananya Goodman for providing me with a xerox of Mopsik's dissertation); Idel, *New Perspectives*, 128–36.

23. *Ozar ha-Kavod ha-Shalem* (Warsaw, 1879), 9b.

24. *Sefer ha-Bahir*, ed. Reuven Margaliot (Jerusalem, 1978), par. 82.

25. Ibid., par. 168.

26. That is, the body or torso and the phallus are counted together as one of the seven holy forms that correspond to bodily parts. See, however, the reading of MS Munich 209, fol. 33a, the body of the phallus, *guf biberito*.

27. Ibid., par. 172.

28. Ibid., par. 21.

29. Ibid., par. 172.

30. Ibid., par. 173; my translation follows the reading in MS Munich 209, fol. 33b.

31. On the image of the field as a metaphor for the feminine in classical Greek writings, cf. Page duBois, *Sowing the Body: Psychoanalysis and Ancient Representations of Women* (Chicago and London, 1988), 39–64. See also O'Flaherty, *Women, Androgynes, and Other Mythical Beasts*, 29–30.

32. *Sefer ha-Bahir*, par. 133.

33. Cf. B. Sanhedrin 98b.

34. *Sefer ha-Bahir*, par. 86.

35. Scholem, *Origins*, 142.

36. Ibid.

37. For a different opinion, cf. Idel, "Sexual Metaphor and Praxis," 211: "The return to the primal androgyne state of humans, which was commonly described by Gnostics, or the endeavor to transcend the feminine plight by mystic transformations of the female into a 'male,' recurring in ancient Chirstian thought and Gnosticism, is alien to talmudic and theosophical kabbalistic weltanschauung." See also Charles Mopsik, *Lettre sur la sainteté: le secret de la relation entre l'homme et la femme dans la cabale* (Paris, 1986), 324–25 n. 218; and Elliot K. Ginsburg, *The Sabbath in Classical Kabbalah* (Albany, N.Y., 1989), 107.

38. Cf. Scholem, *Origins*, 216–18; Idel, *New Perspectives*, 128–34; Mopsik, "Recherches autour de la Lettre sur la sainteté," 32–46.

39. I have translated the text as published in Gershom Scholem, *Reshit ha-Qabbalah* (Tel-Aviv, 1948), 79 n. 1, from MSS British Museum 768, fol. 14a, and Oxford-Bodleian 1956, fol. 7a.

40. That is, the sun and moon, which here stand symbolically for the male and female aspects of God; cf. Idel, *New Perspectives*, 338 n. 151.

41. In a fundamental sense the kabbalistic perspective is continuous with the androcentric posture of the rabbinic tradition expressed, e.g., in the following statement in B. Yevamot 63a: "R. Eleazar said, Every man who has no wife is not a man (*adam*), as it says, 'Male and female He created them . . . and called them Man' (Gen. 5:2)."

42. *Zohar* 3:18b–19a. For an extended discussion of the motif of containment in zoharic literature, see my study referred to above, n. 17.

43. The zoharic expression reflects a technical Spanish idiom, *endulzar*, as noted by Scholem, *Major Trends*, 388 n. 44.
44. *Zohar* 3:142b–143a (*Idra Rabba*); cf. Liebes, "The Messiah," 191.
45. The text here is elliptical for it should read that the female alone is all judgmental just as the male separated from the female is all merciful.
46. *Zohar* 3:296a (*Idra Zuta*).
47. Interestingly, a similar critique has been made with respect to Emmanuel Levinas's conception of the alterity of the feminine. Cf. Luce Irigaray, "Questions to Emmanuel Levinas on the Divinity of Love," trans. Margaret Whitford, in *Re-Reading Levinas*, ed. Robert Bernasconi and Simon Critchley (Bloomington and Indianapolis, 1991), 109–18.
48. *Elimah Rabbati* (Jerusalem, 1974), 95a.
49. On this image for the Presence, see Elliot R. Wolfson, "Images of God's Feet: Some Observations on the Divine Body in Judaism," in *People of the Book: Jews and Judaism in Embodied Perspective*, ed. Howard Eilberg-Schwartz (Albany, N.Y., 1992), 162.
50. For a different understanding, see Mopsik, *Lettre sur la sainteté*, 93.
51. Cf. Liebes, "The Messiah," 164 n. 273.
52. This reflects, of course, the heretical claim attributed to Elisha ben Abuyah (Aher) in B. Hagigah 15a. Cf. Alan F. Segal, *Two Powers in Heaven: Early Rabbinic Reports about Christianity and Gnosticism* (Leiden, 1977), 60–67.
53. MS Cambridge Dd. 10. 11, fols. 27a–b. See Bahya ben Asher's commentary on Gen. 1:4, ed. Ch. Chavel (Jerusalem, 1981), 1:47.
54. *Zohar* 1:15a.
55. The word *bozina* means lamp or light, and the word *qardinuta* is derived from the Talmudic idiom, *hitte qurdanaita*, "wheat from Kurdistan," which Rashi tells us was very hard; cf. the translation of Hayyim Vital recorded in *Derekh Emet*, ad loc., *nizoz hazaq*. According to another reading, the expression is *bozina de-qadrinuta*, which should be rendered "dark flame," the word *qadrinuta* being related to *qadrut*, darkness. Cf. Tishby, *Wisdom of the Zohar*, 276–77; Liebes, *Peraqim*, 145–51, 161–64.
56. The zoharic notion is based on earlier sources. Thus, e.g., in kabbalistic material from Gerona, mention is made of the *qav ha-yosher* or *qav ha-mishor*, which gives boundary to the otherwise boundless divine light and which extends and emanates. Cf. *Commentary on Talmudic Aggadoth by Rabbi Azriel of Gerona*, ed. Isaiah Tishby (Jerusalem, 1948), 89, and other reference to Jacob ben Sheshet supplied in n. 6 ad locum. Cf. Liebes, "The Messiah," 199 n. 374. Interestingly, the expression *qav ha-yosher* is linked particularly to the *Zaddiq*, the ninth emanation, which corresponds to the phallus, in Yosef ben Moshe Alashqar, *Sefer Zofnat Pa'aneah*, MS Jerusalem 4^0 154, fol. 100a, facsimile edition published with an introduction by Moshe Idel (Jerusalem, 1991).

57. See also the explanation of Isaac Luria cited in Gershom Scholem, "The Authentic Kabbalistic Writings of Isaac Luria" (Hebrew), *Qiryat Sefer* 19 (1942): 199. However, it appears that in an earlier stage of his thought Luria, like Moses Cordovero, posited a phallic interpretation of the *bozina de-qardinuta* as the *yod* or the semen that comes forth from the Ein-Sof. Cf. Ronit Meroz, "Redemption in the Lurianic Teaching" (Hebrew) (Ph.D. diss., Hebrew University, 1988), 112–13.

58. I note, parenthetically, that from the perspective of kabbalistic symbolism it would seem that the quality of time is decidedly masculine, i.e., the ever-flowing stream à la the Bergsonian *élan vital*, whereas space is bisexual, i.e., extension as well as a receptacle. I hope to elaborate on this theme in a forthcoming study on space and time in the Jewish mystical tradition. The issue of time in kabbalistic literature, especially the *Zohar*, seems to me to be tied to narrativity, as one finds in the classical aggadic sources of the rabbis as well (cf. Jonah Fraenkel, "Time and Its Role in the Aggadic Story," in *Binah: Studies in Jewish Thought*, ed. Joseph Dan [New York, 1989], 31–56), rather than any strict philosophic conception of time that is dependent on matter and space. For a different approach, see Martel Gavarin, "The Conception of Time in the Works of Rabbi Azriel" (Hebrew), *Jerusalem Studies in Jewish Thought* 6, 3–4 (1987): 309–36. On the linkage of femininity and space, see L. Shannon Jung, "Feminism and Spatiality: Ethics and the Recovery of a Hidden Dimension," *Journal of Feminist Studies in Religion* 4 (1988): 55–71.

59. Cf. *Zohar Hadash*, ed. Reuven Margaliot (Jerusalem, 1978), 58c–d, 105a.

60. On the first *sefirah*, *Keter*, as feminine in relation to the Infinite, a point overlooked in much of the scholarly literature, cf. Mopsik, "Recherches autour de la Lettre sur la sainteté," 205–6, 209–11.

61. One of the strongest proofs that this feature of the divine is understood in the terms that I have suggested is found in Moses de León's commentary on Ezekiel's chariot. The comment occurs in the context of de León discussing the *Shekhinah* as the lower point that is the center of the circle. After explaining the symbolism of the point in this way, he notes, "The more precise secret concerns another matter, for in truth the secret of their arrangement is in a circle [marked out by] a compass (cf. Isa. 44:13), 'like a calf's hoof' (Ezek. 1:5), and that very point is in the middle, and a way is open in its middle like the foot, and this is the secret of the line-of-measure (*qav ha-middah*). The secret is very deep [known] by the sages, servants of the Supernal" (MS JTSA Mic. 1805, fol. 20b). The line-of-measure is portrayed here as the masculine potency (also symbolized as the foot; regarding this symbol, see my study referred to above, n. 49) that is united with the feminine, the point or space in the middle of the circle. It is instructive that in this case de León does not reflect the zoharic tradition in exact terms, but

rather reinterprets it for his own purposes. From his guarded comments we can nevertheless learn something about the view expressed in the *Zohar* concerning the phallic nature of the line-of-measure.

62. This image is related to a much older idea that is widespread in kabbalistic literature regarding the origin of the semen in the brain. For references, see Elliot R. Wolfson, "Anthropomorphic Imagery and Letter Symbolism in the *Zohar*" (Hebrew), *Jerusalem Studies in Jewish Thought* 8 (1989): 169 n. 98. In this context mention should also be made of another motif that seems to me to be rooted in the same tradition, viz., the image of the dew in the skull of the Godhead (the exegetical basis for this image being Song of Songs 5:2; cf. *Pirqe Rabbi Eliezer*, chap. 34). Within the framework of zoharic theosophy the dew parallels the semen; this lends further support to my interpretation of the spark as an analogue to the phallus. See, in particular, *Zohar* 3:128b, 135b (*Idra Rabba*).

63. Cf. *Tiqqune Zohar* 5, ed. Reuven Margaliot (Jerusalem, 1978), 19b. Cf. *Zohar* 2:177a (*Sifra di-Zeniuta*); *Tiqqune Zohar*, 18, 37b; 19, 38b, 41a.

64. Cf. Elliot R. Wolfson, "Letter Symbolism and Merkavah Imagery in the *Zohar*," in *'Alei Shefer: Studies in the Literature of Jewish Thought Presented to Rabbi Dr. Alexandre Safran*, ed. Moshe Hallamish (Bar-Ilan, 1990), 233 n. 140 (English section). I have elaborated on the phallocentric character of writing in theosophic kabbalah in my study "Erasing the Erasure/Gender and the Writing of God's Body in Kabbalistic Symbolism," published in *Transmission et passages en monde juif* (Paris, 1994). On the phallic character of writing in medieval Christian culture, see Alexandre Leupin, *Barbarolexis Medieval Writing and Sexuality*, trans. Kate M. Cooper (Cambridge, Mass., and London, 1989). See also reference below, n. 66.

65. Cf. Wolfson, "Letter Symbolism and Merkavah Imagery," 232 n. 136. The image of striking is applied to the spark in a number of zoharic passages; cf. *Zohar* 2:133b, 180a, 254b; *Zohar Hadash*, 1b (*Sitre Otiyyot*), 73b, 105a, 121d (*Matnitin*). The word *batash*, "to strike," is employed by the zoharic authorship in other contexts to refer to the activity of the masculine potency (usually *Yesod*) vis-à-vis the feminine (*Shekhinah*). To cite one of countless examples: in one passage the light of *Shekhinah* is said to be "compressed" or "folded" within her "until the other light (i.e., *Yesod*) strikes in her, for it perforates that light and penetrates it" (*Zohar Hadash*, 61d). Cf. Nehemiah Hayyun, *Sefer Ta'azumot*, MS Jews' College, London Heb. 62, fol. 20a: "Every sexual union is [an act of] knocking (*betishut*)." A very likely source for the zoharic terminology is the statement in the text, *Ma'ayan ha-Hokhmah* ("Fountain of Wisdom"), deriving from the 'Iyyun circle, utilizing the image of an artisan striking with a hammer (*makkeh be-fatish*) in order to describe the dispersion of sparks from the Primordial Ether, also identified as the Holy Spirit; cf. MSS JTSA Mic. 1822, fol.

26a; Camb. Heb. Add. 643, fol. 20b; Munich 56, fol. 132a; Vat. 236, fol. 26b. Concerning this work, see Scholem, *Origins*, 321; Mark Verman, *The Books of Contemplation: Medieval Jewish Mystical Sources* (Albany, N.Y., 1992), 49–64, and especially 57 where the aforementioned passage is translated. See below, n. 67.

66. The image of the tablet as a metaphor for the feminine is found in much older sources; see the evidence adduced by duBois, *Sowing the Body*, 130–66. Cf. the statement of Pierre Besuire, "For Christ is a sort of book written into the skin of the Virgin," discussed in Maryann E. Brink, "The Image of the Word: The Representation of Books in Medieval Iconography," in *Transcending Boundaries: Multi-Disciplinary Approaches to the Study of Gender*, ed. Pamela R. Frese and John M. Coggeshall (New York, 1991), 41–53. On the image of bestowing form upon the matter as a metaphor for sexual intercourse between man and woman, see the anonymous kabbalistic work, *Iggeret ha-Qodesh*, in *Kitve Ramban* 2, ed. Ch. Chavel (Jerusalem, 1982), 328, translated in Mopsik, *Lettre sur la sainteté*, 238. Cf. ibid., 336 (Mopsik, 255, 320 n. 200). Despite the basic premise of this composition regarding the ultimate sanctity of the union of male and female, the aforementioned comment indicates again the underlying androcentric orientation that colors this medieval kabbalistic text. On the other hand, it must be noted that the author of this text does assign to the woman an important role in forming the character of the child on the basis of her intentions during intercourse, actualized principally through the imagination; cf. Chavel, 331–32 (Mopsik, 241–42, 300–301 n. 133). Still, even here one can discern an essential difference between man and woman: the task of the woman is to synchronize her thoughts with her male partner but the task of the man is to be mentally bound to the upper realm so that he can draw down the efflux of divine light unto the *semen virile*. Thus the author of this text appropriates a passage from Azriel of Gerona dealing with the mystical *ascensio mentis* (cf. Mopsik, 305–6 n. 149), which applies only to males. The logical implication is drawn explicitly by the author commenting on the statement in B. Berakhot 20a concerning R. Yohanan's sitting by the bathhouses so that the women exiting from ritual immersion could look upon his face and be blessed with offspring as beautiful as he: "Thus with the key that we have placed in your hand you can understand the action of that pious one who would sit at the gates of the bathhouses so that the thought [of the women] would cleave to his form, and his form would cleave to the supernal entities." See also the description of the birth of Isaac in ibid., 336–37: "Abraham had the [proper] intention during the time of intercourse and he cleaved with his mind to the supernal entities; therefore, he gave birth to a son who was worthy for what God, blessed be He, had promised." The course of action required for giving birth to righteous sons (!) is for the males to unite with the

sefirotic realm during the time of sexual union. For the most part in subsequent kabbalistic literature, especially the sixteenth-century Safedian materials, the emphasis is likewise placed on the male to have the proper intentions during sexual intercourse. Nevertheless, women too are assigned specific intentions; see, e.g., the text of Abraham Azulai cited in Daniel C. Matt, *Zohar: The Book of Enlightenment* (New York, 1983), 236–37, and discussed further in Ginsburg, *The Sabbath in the Classical Kabbalah*, 291–92; Hayyim Vital, *Sha'ar ha-Gilgulim* (Jerusalem, 1903), 12a. The whole matter of mystical intentions for women during intercourse requires a separate treatment.

67. I note in passing that here too the zoharic expression is probably based on an image used in another text from the *'Iyyun* circle, *Midrash R. Shim'on ha-Zaddiq* (cf. Scholem, *Origins*, 321–22; Verman, *The Books of Contemplation*, 211–15), regarding the breaking through of a splendor or light, identified as Primordial Wisdom (*hokhmah qedumah*), from the Primordial Ether (*'avir ha-qadmon*) or Darkness (*hoshekh*); cf. MS Munich 54, fol. 293a.

68. *Zohar* 1:15a.

69. Cf. *Zohar* 1:15b–16a, 100a–b (*Sitre Torah*); 2:2a, 23a–b; *Zohar Hadash* 104b–c, 105a, 106b. See Elliot R. Wolfson, "The Hermeneutics of Visionary Experience: Revelation and Interpretation in the *Zohar*," *Religion* 18 (1988): 311–45, especially 320 ff. Also relevant is the discussion in Pinchas Giller, *The Enlightened Will Shine: Symbolization and Theurgy in the Later Strata of the Zohar* (Albany, N.Y., 1993), 21–32.

70. See my study referred to above, n. 15.

71. *Zohar Hadash*, 58c–d.

72. Cf. Peter Schäfer, *Synopse zur Hekhalot Literatur* (Tübingen, 1981), §§ 711, 953.

73. Cf. Liebes, *Peraqim*, 146–47; idem, "The Messiah," 199–200.

74. Cf. *Zohar* 2:258a.

75. Cf. *Zohar Hadash*, 105a.

76. An exception is Mopsik; see reference above, n. 22.

77. My formulation here is indebted to O'Flaherty, *Women, Androgynes, and Other Mythical Beasts*, 333. See discussion in Yoram Jacobson, "The Aspect of the Feminine in the Lurianic Kabbalah," in *Gershom Scholem's Major Trends in Jewish Mysticism 50 Years After*, ed. Joseph Dan and Peter Schäfer (Tübingen, 1993), 242. According to Jacobson's interpretation, the Ein-Sof in Lurianic kabbalah is neither male nor female but rather contains both aspects within itself in an undifferentiated way. In n. 6 Jacobson does acknowledge the view that emphasizes the male aspect of Ein-Sof due to the fact that it is the source of the holy semen. In my opinion the myth of the divine autogenesis expressed in Lurianic texts is predicated on a decidedly male androgyne breaking forth into male and female. According to Jacobson's own

analysis, especially 247 ff., it is evident that the purpose of the emanative process was to balance the negative forces of feminine judgment by
the masculine forces of mercy. From a gender perspective, therefore,
the male is still valorized as the positive force of the Godhead that
keeps the potentially destructive aspects of the feminine in check. The
negative feminine is rendered productive only when its feminine
character is transformed by unification with the male. In a sense the
whole historical process can be seen as the ontic transformation of the
negative feminine into a positive feminine, the latter being attained
most fully when the female is reintegrated as part of the male. See also
Meroz, "Redemption in the Lurianic Teaching," 97–98, 244–45.

78. Cf. *Zohar* 3:135b (*Idra Rabba*).
79. It seems that the point of this difficult passage is that the primordial
    unity of male and female is for the purpose of generating another
    androgyne that then produces other beings. Cf. Mopsik, *Lettre sur la
    sainteté*, 90 n. 200.
80. On the connotation of the word "faith" (*mehemanuta*) in the *Zohar* as
    the union of male and female, see Liebes, *Peraqim*, 398–99; Matt,
    Zohar, 217.
81. *Zohar* 3:290a.
82. *Zohar* 3:80b.
83. *Tiqqune Zohar* 5, 19a.
84. Cf. Moshe Idel, "Kabbalistic Materials from the School of R. David ben
    Judah he-Hasid" (Hebrew), *Jerusalem Studies in Jewish Thought* 2
    (1983): 195–96.
85. *Zohar* 1:55b.
86. Cf. *Zohar* 1:49b, 55b, 101b, 160a, 204b; 2:26b, 161b; 3:264a; Elliot R.
    Wolfson, *The Book of the Pomegranate: Moses de León's Sefer ha-
    Rimmon* (Atlanta, 1988), 68–69 (English section). For a wide-ranging
    discussion of the word *mehemanuta* (faith) in the *Zohar*, cf. Liebes,
    Peraqim, 398–401.
87. See, e.g., *Zohar* 3:214b.
88. *Zohar Hadash*, 90c.
89. Cf. A. E. Waite, *The Holy Kabbalah* (Secaucus, N.J., 1960), 377–405;
    Scholem, *Major Trends*, 225–29; Tishby, *The Wisdom of the Zohar*,
    1355–79; Mopsik, *Lettre sur la sainteté*, 45–163; Idel, "Sexual Meta-
    phors and Praxis," 207–13. See also M. D. Georg Langer, *Die Erotik der
    Kabbala* (Munich, 1989), 41–57.
90. *Zohar* 3:5a; cf. 1:256a.
91. Cf. Gershom Scholem, *The Messianic Idea in Israel* (New York, 1971),
    343 n. 32; Liebes, "The Messiah," 198–203; Moshe Idel, "Typologies of
    Redemptive Activity in the Middle Ages," in *Messianism and Eschatolo-
    gy: A Collection of Essays* (Hebrew), ed. Z. Baras (Jerusalem, 1983),
    266–75.
92. Cf. B. Shabbat 137b.

93. *Zohar* 1:162a.
94. *Sheqel ha-Qodesh,* ed. A. W. Greenup (London, 1911), 67.   Cf. Wolfson, *Book of the Pomegranate,* 227–29 (Hebrew section).
95. Jochanan Wijnhoven, ed., *Sefer ha-Mishqal* (Ph.d. diss., Brandeis University, 1964), 133.
96. Cf. Eliade, *The Two and the One,* 111–14.
97. Cf. Elizabeth Grosz, *Jacques Lacan: A Feminist Introduction* (London and New York, 1990), 117.
98. See reference to my study and that of Boyarin cited above, n. 15.
99. Cf. *Zohar* 1:87a, 151a, 206b; 2:67b, 100b; 3:236b; *Zohar Hadash,* 45c, 62a.
100. *Zohar* 1:163a.
101. *Zohar* 2:4a.
102. Cf. *Zohar* 1:47b, 122a, 235b; 2:4a, 67b.
103. *Zohar* 1:232a. This passage was cited by Gershom Scholem, *On the Mystical Shape of the Godhead: Basic Concepts of the Kabbalah* (New York, 1991), 186, who duly noted the attribution of active, masculine aspects to the feminine *Shekhinah*.
104. For references, see above, n. 7.
105. Cf. Scholem, *On the Mystical Shape,* 191–92; Tishby, *The Wisdom of the Zohar,* 376–79, 469.
106. Cf. *Zohar* 3:48b, and the discussion in Elliot R. Wolfson, "Light through Darkness: The Ideal of Human Perfection in the Zohar," *Harvard Theological Review* 81 (1988): 81 n. 29, 86 n. 46.
107. *Zohar* 3:77a and 119a.
108. *Zohar* 3:259b.
109. Cf. *Zohar* 1:94a.
110. For discussion of some of the relevant sources, see above, n. 66.
111. Cf. Charles Mopsik, "The Body of Engenderment in the Hebrew Bible, the Rabbinic Tradition, and the Kabbalah," in *Zone: Fragments for a History of the Human Body,* ed. Michel Feher, Ramona Naddaff, and Nadia Tazi (New York, 1989), 48–73.
112. See Peter Brown's characterization of Valentinian Gnosticism in *The Body and Society,* 113.

Chapter 9

From Pharaoh to Saddam Hussein: The Reproduction of the Other in the Passover Haggadah

Adi Ophir

I. The Context of Reading

Every culture has its own privileged texts. A privileged text is not simply a text that belongs to a sacred canon, a text that has been canonized in a particular cultural field, such as literature, science, or religion. Rather, a privileged text is part of the very process of acculturation that serves to unify a culture over and above its different, particular spheres or fields. A privileged text resides at the intersection of several cultural mechanisms; for example, the mechanism that authorizes one to speak in the name of a culture, to interpret it for its members; the mechanism that reproduces cultural identity and solidarity among the members of a culture; and the mechanism that demarcates the outer boundaries of a culture and excludes nonmembers.

Usually, a privileged text resides at a privileged cultural place—the theater or the High Court, for example, or the synagogue or the church—and is visited frequently by some or all of that culture's members. Access to such texts is restricted, denied to some but permitted to others, the privileged, who thus possess precious symbolic capital.[1] In addition, this differentiated access is sometimes institutionalized so that the privileged text becomes the authorized property of a privileged community of discourse. And finally, a privileged text has its own limited and authorized modes of material reproduction and dissemination, which are often authorized and

limited differently for members of different classes within the
community, and for community members and nonmembers.[2]

In traditional Jewish culture, the existence of privileged texts is
clearly evident. The Talmud and the prayer book have played this
role for centuries. Also, in a more restricted and concrete way, the
Passover Haggadah, perhaps the most popular text in Jewish
religious literature, has served as such a privileged text.[3]

In modern Jewish culture, outside the ultra-Orthodox community (which has been vigorously striving to maintain its traditional
character despite and against overwhelming processes of moderniza-
tion), among both secular and religious alike, the Talmud has clearly
lost some, if not all, of its privileged position. However, in contemporary Israeli Jewish society, some portions of the prayer books
(especially those used at the High Holidays) and, more conspicuous-
ly, the Passover Haggadah still remain privileged texts in the sense
defined above. Even among secular Jews, the Haggadah occupies a
privileged traditional site and time, the Seder table on Passover,
wherein at least the first section is usually read—sometimes
parodied, but nevertheless read—before the Passover meal is served.

The Haggadah is a multilayered text whose origin is quite
ancient. In essence, the text is a collection of the midrashic interpretations of a few verses from Deuteronomy to which various
passages were added through the years. Scholars—philologists and
historians of Jewish culture—are capable today of reconstructing
more or less precisely the different layers of the text, returning them
to their places of origin and putting them in a proper chronological
order. This order ranges from the late days of the Second Temple to
the early modern era, when the final versions of the text were
consolidated with the advent of printing in different Jewish communities. In this essay, however, I am not concerned with the text's
historical development or with the history of its interpretations.[4]
My concern is rather with the text that appears at a contemporary
Seder table, where it functions as a privileged text par excellence,
playing a key role in contemporary Israeli culture. The Haggadah,
I will argue below, has been adopted into secular Jewish culture in
Israel as a kind of metanarrative that frames and constrains the
account of the relation between Israel and the Nations, i.e., of the
history and logic of separation (*havdalah*, *hibadlut*) of the Jewish
people from all its Others.

Secularization in general and the Zionist revolution in particular
have not affected the Haggadah's popularity; it is by far the most

popular traditional Jewish text among secular Jews in Israel. New editions of the text appear every year, some printed with a high-quality design, some especially designed for special audiences (children, immigrants, soldiers). Fancy facsimile editions using images from old prints have become very popular and are among the favorite Passover gifts. Every year, the main daily newspapers distribute cheap reprints as supplements to their Passover-eve editions. Inexpensive reprints are also distributed by the Ministries of Absorption and Tourism, the Israeli Defense Forces (IDF), and a few other governmental and public agencies.

The kibbutzim, once considered the crown and symbol of modern secular Judaism, have adopted the Haggadah with well-known amendments and have established their own tradition of the Passover ritual. During Passover in 1992 I saw a private edition published by a candidate in a local election in the northern Galilee area. The candidate inserted campaign propaganda in the margin of the page, alongside the verses, without altering the main body of the text or its traditional design.

The most astonishing fact about the status of the Haggadah in Israeli culture, however, is not that the text is so widely distributed but that in the last three or four decades so few attempts have been made to revise it.[5] Thus, secular Jews in Israel, accepting the authority of Orthodox Jews, reproduce only the Orthodox authoritative version. Although sometimes improvising on the graphic design, they leave the main body of the text untouched, acknowledging as it were its "authenticity." This sense of authenticity seems to compensate for a lost, longed-for aura of sacredness.

Moreover, "the text in itself" often serves as a bridge, or a common ground, linking Orthodox (rabbinic) Jews, Zionists as well as non-Zionists, with secular Zionists.[6] From "the text itself" Zionist readers derive nationalist, chauvinist meanings often echoed in contemporary (Israeli) rabbinic interpretations of the Haggadah. It is perhaps because of this common ground of nationalistic hermeneutics that the Haggadah, more than any other product of rabbinic culture, has come to occupy such an important position in Israel's "civil religion"[7] and in the formation of its Jewish identity.

In contemporary Israeli culture, the text of the Haggadah is privileged in all the senses defined above. It has its own privileged sites and time; it is visited frequently by almost all of the culture's members; and there are acknowledged legitimate modes of its material reproduction (to which the use of the Haggadah in an election campaign is still an exception, almost a transgression).

The text currently resides at the intersection of several cultural mechanisms, in three related domains: the production, reproduction, and distribution of collective memory; the production of national identity and social solidarity; and the demarcation of the culture's outer boundaries, which set the limits of inclusion and exclusion, frame the metanarrative of the relation with the Other, and constrain the perception of the Other in both popular and political culture. Unlike the Talmudic text, however, the Haggadah has never become the authorized property of a privileged community of discourse. On the contrary, the symbolic capital acquired through the appropriation of the text is evenly distributed among all the members of the community who take part in the ritual. Thus, for one night, the text turns all members, even those incapable of reading it, into one united community of discourse.

This community of discourse commemorates and reproduces the moment at which Israel became a privileged people. It does that through a rite of separation that reaffirms and reinterprets both the identity of the nation as well as its difference from all other nations. While separation is clearly not the only theme in the Seder and the Haggadah, it is, I would argue, the theme most emphasized in both secular and religious communities in Israel. Moreover, it is certainly the aspect that, more than any other, forges a common ground between Orthodox and secular Jews.

Especially since the Six-Day War, two complementary cultural processes have played a decisive role in shaping the particularist, nationalist character of Jewish society in Israel: (1) the adoption by and incorporation into secular Israeli culture of nationalist motifs drawn from rabbinic culture[8] and (2) the growing nationalistic character of the Orthodox community's response to the Zionist conception of modern Jewish identity.[9] The Haggadah and its ritual, the Seder, both embody and exemplify a unique combination of discursive and ceremonial practices that in the last decades have played a growing role in structuring and reproducing Jewish collective memory and identity in Israel. Thus, the Haggadah and the Seder have had the effect, usually unnoticed, of linking secular Israeli Jews to their traditional, premodern, pre-Zionist, Orthodox forerunners, on the one hand, and to contemporary Orthodox Israelis, on the other hand.

These two nationalistic processes, and the combination of discourse and ceremony they have made possible, should be understood in light of what I consider to be the single most important factor in contemporary Jewish life in Israel: the reversal of power relations between Jews and Gentiles. In Israel, Jews are the ruling party and enjoy cultural hegemony; the Gentiles (i.e., the Palestinians) are the dominated, and their culture is the subordinate, minority culture.

The Haggadah was originally composed by a more or less oppressed minority culture to commemorate its (already lost) triumph over its enemies and its (by then gone) liberation and sovereignty. But today in Israel, the Haggadah is read as a text of the majority culture. Within this culture, it is the Palestinian Other who now occupies the place of the oppressed. This inversion of oppressor and oppressed forms the perspective that frames the following analysis and critique.

I have described the status of the Haggadah and its position as a cultural phenomenon in order to place my study of the Haggadah in its precise sociological and historical context, i.e., the context of contemporary Israeli culture. But I have also presented it as a pretext, a kind of apology. This is the apology of a secular Israeli who, like so many Israelis of his generation, cultural background, and political temper, has often experienced the Seder as a somewhat annoying ceremony and the Haggadah as a somewhat boring, even alien, text that, nonetheless, warrants a close reading. In what follows I am offering neither a playful, sacrilegious interpretation of a sacred text nor a fashionable strategy of tearing down a valued cultural object. In the critical interpretive analysis of the Haggadah below, I attempt to expose within the text itself a structure that, in contemporary Israeli culture, has come to dominate the uses and abuses of Passover's text and ritual. Once this structure is exposed and its presence in the midst of our secular culture is made manifest, it may be easier, I believe, to resist its hidden agenda.

II. Text and Ritual

Like the Mishnah and the Talmud, the Haggadah too is a text that betrays the variety and multiplicity of its sources, announcing from almost any of its pages that no single *author* stands at its origin. Like the Mishnah and the Talmud, the text erases all the traces of the process and historicity of its composition. Yet, unlike the Mishnah or Talmud, and despite its explicit intertextual dimension, the relative unity of the text and its clear closure are strictly maintained. Many voices are heard at the table when the Haggadah is read, yet the text appears as an almost seamless, written substratum for a rite of speaking and eating. It is the Haggadah that organizes the rite from the preliminary ceremony, *Bi'ur Hametz* (the elimination of food forbidden on Passover), occurring on the evening preceding the first night of Passover, to the completion of the Seder. Thus, the Haggadah determines how the table is to be set and the food served. In addition, it designates that which is to be said, prayed, and sung in the form of blessings, games of questions and answers, short stories, and midrashic interpretations.

The ritualized reading of the Haggadah is a rite of recollection that erases most of the traces of the text's composition. Nonetheless, the unity of the text is actualized through the act of the telling itself, during which open-ended passages or loose threads of composition are woven together, overcome. Thus, neither the history of the text nor the continuity of its transmission guarantees its unity for a contemporary reader/user; rather, this unity results from the way the text is interwoven with the Passover ritual. In this sense, the text has always remained unified, at least since its establishment as the written medium of the ceremony providing the directions for the rite.

Actually, the unified text displays hardly any traces of its own history and serves, in fact, as a mechanism for dehistoricizing the Passover rite. Directly linking the participants to the event described and reenacted in the Seder, the exodus from Egypt, the Haggadah dehistoricizes both the actual text and the ceremony. Thus, the contemporary reader is placed on one temporal plane together with the children of Israel who came out from Egypt. He or she experiences the Egyptian redemption as his or her own, for the redemption from Egypt is ongoing, from the time of Pharaoh to ours, stretching over thousands of years in an instant. **We were once the slaves of Pharaoh in Egypt**, and we were rescued by the Lord our God. Had He not **brought our ancestors out of Egypt then we and our children and our children's children might still be enslaved to a Pharaoh in Egypt**.[10] Thus, the event transcends the entire history of the community and is realized in a rite made possible by the text.[11]

At the same time, the text is unified by the rite that it organizes and directs. The text and the rite are inseparable, together comprising one **rite of passage** through a liminal stage of existence, which is also a rite of (textual) passages, a textual event, a ritualized text, a ri/te/xt. It is this ri/te/xt that I would like to subject to a careful deconstruction.

III. Separation

Passover is a holiday of "separation." This fact is already inscribed in the holiday's Hebrew name: *Pesach*, from *pasach*, meaning "passed over." As God passed over the doors of Israel's houses, He separated the marked houses of the Israelites from the unmarked houses of the Egyptians, and the Israelite first-born sons, marked for life, from the Egyptian first-born, marked for death. Although this particular divine act of separation is mentioned only briefly at a late stage of the ri/te/xt, practices of marking throughout the Seder serve as traces of that primordial separation.

Early **on the evening before the Seder night**, a ceremonial **search for leavened food**, *Bi'ur Hametz*, marks the separation of the seven subsequent days from the rest of the year. But even those who come to the Seder table unaware of these preliminary acts are immediately introduced into rites of separation. Through acts of marking, separation permeates the inner core of the Passover text and ritual. As with a Russian doll (*babushka*), these practices are arranged in several layers, forming a more or less symmetrical order, before and after the main body of the ri/te/xt in which the story is unfolded and interpreted.

Those who gather at the Seder table are first separated from their mundane everyday existence through various acts of marking. This is enacted through two series of rites of separation/distinction during the first part of the Seder. Prior to the narrative recounting slavery and redemption, we have a blessing distinguishing Israel from the other nations and sacred time from profane time (*Kadesh*); rinsing of hands (*u-Rehatz*); a blessing over **the fruit of the earth** and the tasting of the vegetable (*karpas*); breaking the middle *matzah* and hiding the *afikoman* (*Yahatz*); **Ha Lachma Anya** (behold the *matzah*, bread of poverty), the first general symbolic interpretation in the Seder; and the **Four Questions** beginning *Mah Nishtanah* (In what ways is this night different from all other nights?) Following the narrative but prior to the meal, we find the recitation of Rabban Gamaliel's statement regarding the three major symbols of Passover; a long blessing over the second cup of wine; a second hand washing (this time with its blessing); a blessing over bread in general and unleavened bread (*matzah*) in particular; the blessing over the bitter herbs (*maror*); and the eating of *matzah* and *maror* together (*korekh*).

All of these acts combine speech and tasting, except for the silent rinsing of hands at the beginning. While the first group serves to introduce and temporally bracket the ceremonial reading of the narrative, the latter group introduces and temporally brackets the festival meal. Between them comes the main body of the Passover narrative, separated twice, from the profane time and everyday practices that precede it, and the meal that follows.

However, prior to being inscribed in the participants' minds through changing and telling, separation is physically inscribed on the table. At this early stage, the ri/te/xt has not yet introduced the *Kadesh*'s metaphysical and transhistorical separations and announces them only by way of anticipation. The main separation at this point is that of the concrete time and place of the Seder in which the rite of separation itself is now beginning to occur. A mute gesture, rinsing hands without a blessing (reference without meaning); a "blind" blessing over a vegetable of the earth (*karpas*, a name without a reference; the real *karpas* is unknown);[12] followed by a deaf word, *afikoman*, a Greek word whose precise meaning had long been forgotten—all create an open space for the approaching story. Only in this space, a space emptied of colloquial expressions and everyday meanings, can the story of origin be properly enacted, a story that confers deep meanings on trivial objects, endows food articles with symbolic import, and, above all, elevates the concrete and historical to a transcendent, metaphysical plane.

After the recitation of the story, just before the meal is served, the movement of suspension is reversed. The symbolic meaning of the ceremonial food is explicitly stated. In fact, the three last speech and tasting acts that precede the meal (*matzah, maror, korekh*) are but a highly condensed version of the story embodied in a few articles of food. At the beginning of the Seder, the food, not yet imbued with symbolic meaning, simply marked the spatio-temporal separation of the rite of separation. Now, however, it symbolizes the merging of two kinds of separation, that of the world of ritual from the everyday world, and the separation, affirmed in the course of the ritual, of Israel from its Others. **This Matzah which *we* eat . . . is because there was not enough time for *our ancestors*' dough to ferment before they were redeemed from Egypt. . . .**

At the same time, the food symbolizes the continuity of the concrete community gathered at the Seder table who, separated from the historical present, form part of the transhistorical community of the separated people. Thus, **in every generation a person should see himself as though he, personally, came out of Egypt.** As speech has been concretized in food, the food becomes an embodied memory, a tangible medium of recollection, which guarantees the transhistorical continuity and unity of the nation.

At this point, as people become aware of their hunger, a gradual transition occurs from the transcendent plane that confers meaning back to the concrete site of the gathering. This transition is completed right after the meal, with the materialistic, sometimes greedy negotiation that usually accompanies the retrieval of the *afikoman*.[13] Between the first act of purification and the latter blessing over hand washing, between the lost *karpas* and the found *afikoman*, lies the ri/te/xt of Israel's separation.

Between *Magid* (the beginning of recitation of the narrative) and *Korech* (the eating of the *matzah* together with bitter herbs), the interplay between tasting and blessing is replaced with another, the interplay between storytelling (recollection) and midrashic commentary (interpretation). With this interplay the separation of the ceremonial event turns into the separation constituted by the ri/te/xt. By telling the story of the exodus from Egypt, the ri/te/xt makes present the first Egyptian separation; by presenting the midrashic commentary, alluding to the story of its formation and ongoing transmission, the ri/te/xt creates the historical continuity that guarantees and reaffirms the separation of the entire nation, past and present, from the other nations. Thus, at the heart of the ri/te/xt, recollection and separation are intrinsically linked.

Recalling the memory of the original separation, the participant reaffirms the ongoing, eternal separation. The present separation derives from the original one and is, in essence, bound up with it; but at the same time, the original separation is reasserted, made present, through present-day acts of recollection, which themselves presuppose an ongoing separation. The told story and the story of the telling are closely linked.

IV. Two Beginnings

In the beginning, when they were redeemed from Egyptian slavery, the people of Israel were separated from their Others, the Gentiles. **We were once the slaves of Pharaoh in Egypt. But the Lord our God brought us forth from there. . . .** Thus, the opening verse of the story presents the three protagonists as well as the fundamental structure of the narrative: we, that is, Israel; Pharaoh, the archetype of all Gentiles to come, the terrible Other; and the ultimate Other, the one who separates, rescues, redeems, the Almighty, **our God**. If He had not rescued *us* from *them*, we would still be there, slaves. Even before His redeeming intervention, there had been a state of separation resulting from the power relations between us, the people of Israel, the enslaved, and Pharaoh, the one who enslaves.

But the merciful God did not simply invert those power relations; He did not put us in Pharaoh's place. Instead, when He rescued us from Egypt, He also rescued us from the type of power relations the Egyptian domination entailed, thus making us different from both masters and slaves. Henceforth, we shall never resemble the slaves we once were even when we again suffer under the yoke of oppression. When better days come and others are placed under our domination, we shall not resemble those Egyptian masters. For we came out of Egypt, and it is our duty (*mitzvah*) to recount this exodus from Egypt. **And whoever dwells on the story of the liberation from Egypt is praiseworthy.** The story, or rather the act of telling the story, guarantees that we too, not only our ancestors, have left Egypt.

The enacted narrative consolidates the first encounter among the three protagonists and transforms it into the eternal structure of Israel's separation. While the *content* of the story asserts the appearance of the transcendent in history and transforms historical reality to a metaphysical reality, the concrete *speech act* connects the historical present to an already sacred history. Thus, the act of telling the story strips away the local and temporal context, turning the events into ephemeral moments in the eternal return of the same: Israel/Gentile/God.

The Haggadah's second story recounting Israel's origins tells of an even earlier moment of separation that precedes the Egyptian exodus. **In the beginning our ancestors were idol worshippers**. Thus, the Egyptians' separation is placed in a wider historical context.   Slavery, we are told, has its roots in **ancient times, beyond the river Euphrates**, while the roots of redemption are found in God's promise to Abraham, who was himself led out of Egypt to the land of Canaan.   Now this first exodus from one place to another is seen as the historical source of Israel's separation, of its otherness vis-à-vis the rest of nations.   However, the children of Abraham went down to Egypt and became there the Other of others, **strangers in a foreign land**.   Thus, long before the nation's collective identity, the identity of a nation mediated by God, the Holy One, who endows identities and makes differences, was established in Egypt, another separation had occurred and another identity established—the coercive separation between master and slaves, the oppressed identity of the slaves vis-à-vis their masters.

The double story of origins thus performs a crucial task.   It removes separation from its historically contingent and ontologically meaningless political context and places it, once and for all, in its proper theological context, that of God's presence in history.   By overcoming Pharaoh, God not only rescued Israel but also created the conditions for Israel to recognize Him as the sole and ultimate basis of their separation from all future pharaohs.   The victory over Pharaoh, a radical, totally evil Other, is thus uncompromisable and the nation's separation from him complete.

Thus, recognition of God becomes the true basis for Israel's separation.   While the nation as a whole came to recognize God through His miraculous intervention in Egyptian internal affairs, this was certainly not the beginning.   Nor can the true beginning of Israel's separation be located in history, even if one goes as far back as Terah, Abraham's father.   There, beyond the river, before our forefathers separated from the rest of nations, was a place and a time of *avodah zarah*, idol worship, which literally means foreign or "other" worship.   Although God had not yet revealed Himself to Abraham, the distinction between true and false worship, *avoda zara* and *avodat hashem*, was already drawn.   **I, Adonai . . . no other**, the believers would later say, as they retrospectively fixed the time before the revelation as a time of ignorance and blindness, of illusion and false consciousness.

The distinction between true and false religious consciousness precedes the revelation and, unlike it, needs no particular historical context.   For this distinction follows from the concept of God itself.   God may be an unintelligible unity over and above all separations and distinctions, yet He is the One responsible for all separations, from the separation between darkness and light to that between the holy and the profane. God generates separation and difference in the world through His presence in history: a concealed presence, the presence of an absence. For had He not been absent, had He not required revelation as the constitutive moment of human history, and had He not limited this revelation to His selected, separate people, there would have been no idol worship in this world and every nation and every person would have recognized Him as what He is, worshipping Him alone. The absence of God, which is the mode of God's presence in the world of humans, is the source of all separations.

This means that positive acts of creation, sanctification, revelation, or election, acts that either generate history or traverse it while imbuing it with meaning, acts whose origins are always transcendent, are not the ultimate foundation of divine separation. The primordial origin of separation is, rather, the essential concealment of God, the concealment to be unconcealed in those rare moments of revelation. The God of separation is the god who is absent, that god who is not. His negated presence, that painful hole that God left in the world to be healed temporarily once or twice in the past and once and for all in the future, is the true origin, the source of all sources. Only when this source is asserted as the true origin is it possible to unfold the nation's genealogy.

The opening verse—**In the beginning our ancestors were idol worshippers**—posits a straightforward genealogy within the context of separation and formulates its first principle. Without this opening verse, the story would have been but a simple genealogy, tracing the nation from its founding to the people who came out of Egypt. The distinction between the worship of God and idol worship forms the first distinction between the same and the Other. The first otherness is that of another, false, unreal god, an ephemeral appearance that takes the place of the one, true God. The first Other is nothing, and the recognition of this nothingness for what it is provides the basis for further separations. The first solidarity among human beings is among all those who have recognized the one and only God and learned to separate Him from His Others.

The promise that accompanied the first revelation (of God to Abraham) and the first recognition (of God by Abraham) has **stood by our ancestors and us** and provided the basis for the generalization at the end of that short genealogy: **In every generation enemies rise up against us and seek to destroy us. But the**

Holy One, praised be He, delivers us from their hands. The slavery in Egypt was the first, but by no means the last. *God* saves *us* from *their* hands, the hands of those Others who recognize neither Him nor us as His chosen people. Thus, the relations among the chosen people, their Other, and their God formed during the first slavery and first redemption comprise a persistent pattern within which the genealogy forever unfolds.

But not during the Seder. With the exception of one passage, **If He had merely . . .** , whose subjunctive language clearly serves a different purpose, Israel's genealogy is not going to be retold again in this ri/te/xt. From this point in the Seder onward, the fundamental structure of relations among the three protagonists, God, Israel, and its Other, will be re-presented and elaborated in the context of that formative, originative event. The entire history of Israel is going to be a history of going down to, becoming slaves to, and going out from an Egypt. Henceforth, Israel will have no history, but stories whose beginning and ends are already known, for they are produced as analogies to the story of that first and last event of Jewish history, The Historical Event. Each particular story will be but a reflection of that first story and a realization, in different times and places, of the eternal return of the same: Israel/Gentile/God (I/G/G).[14]

V. Revelation

After the general outline of the formative story and its lesson has been firmly established, the Haggadah again tells, through midrashic interpretations, the story of Egypt.[15] At each stage of the plot, God and Gentile appear embraced back to back, holding each other's heel. When the one is concealed, the other reveals himself, and vice versa. When one occupies center stage, the other recedes into the background. In the middle are the people of Israel, surviving through the power of the One and being separated by the force of the Other; or, vice versa, surviving on account of the word of the Other and being separated by the word of the One.

As the Haggadah tells it, Jacob's original descent to Egypt is the wandering of a nomad who escapes from one Gentile seeking to persecute him, Laban (**A Syrian tried to destroy my father**), only to become a guest, and later a hostage, of another Gentile, Pharaoh. As the text implies, permission to remain in Egypt was granted in response to an explicit request (**The Sons of Jacob told Pharaoh: We have come to the land to dwell here temporarily**).

At the same time, Jacob's descent to Egypt is read as a response to a divine decree, as implied by the phrase **compelled by the word** (*anus al pi hadibur*), interpreted by traditional commentators as well as English translators to mean God's command. While the Gentile, Laban the Syrian, who planned to destroy Jacob, is depicted as powerful, cruel, and ill meaning, God's presence is only hinted at indirectly.

In Egypt, however, Israel becomes **a great and mighty people**, yet their suffering and future redemption are already implied: **I have caused you to multiply as the buds of the field . . . your breasts were formed and your hair grew long, yet you remained naked and bare . . . .** At this point, the God previously referred to through allusion appears center stage as speaking on behalf of His people and giving expression to their suffering. The Gentile, who previously appeared on center stage, now recedes into the background, momentarily suppressed, referred to only as the unspoken cause for Israel's terrible situation.

But almost immediately, the Gentile returns to center stage, reemerging in a display of power and cruelty: **and the Egyptians treated us harshly, and oppressed us, and imposed hard labor upon us.** Now it is God who recedes into the background, temporarily absent. His absence, a condition for the cruel "revelation" of the Gentile, sets the stage for and provides the pretext for this cruel "revelation." Conversely, repressing or destroying the Gentile is the purpose and justification (and an implicit precondition as well) of God's miraculous revelation.

In Egypt the Gentile is revealed to Israel as the one who imposes hard labor. Between Pithom and Raamses, in a setting of torture and hard labor, the oppressing Gentile appears. Now the distinction between master and slave, oppressed and the oppressor, clearly emerges, together with the distinction between good and evil. The fundamental demarcation between the collective, national subject, Israel, and its Other, the enemy, is represented in the text through the opposition of the first- and third-person plural. (**Let *us* outwit *them*, lest *they* multiply; . . . *they* will join *our* enemies and fight against *us*. . . .**)

They have started all the trouble, when they posited us as their significant Other who might conspire with their enemies. *Our* response was to reify the relation of otherness. Thus, *we* have turned otherness into a fixed, persistent, unchanging quality, eternalizing the Other as totally wicked: **and the Egyptian treated us harshly** [*vayareu otanu*, ill-treated us] (this is the decree of the newborn boy), **and oppressed us** (this is the decree of taskmasters), and **impressed hard labor upon us** (this is the decree of *avodat parekh*, hard labor). Between idol worship (*avoda zarah*, foreign work), and the worship of God (*avodat hashem*, the work of God), lies the site of genuine hard work, the site of hard labor. This kind of work does not produce goods in order to fulfill needs, relieve material scarcity, or alleviate psychological burdens. This work, born out of the Other's display of wicked power, produces scarcity and intensifies hardship and suffering. At the site of hard work, the Other is marked as radically evil and his domination portrayed as the source of all evils. At this site, the absence of God is most depressingly evident.

From that place, *min ha-avodah*, from the place of hard labor, Israel's **cry . . . came up to God**, as they sought to replace one revelation with another. Because of their bondage, that is, from the perspective of the oppressed, God is an invisible observer and listener, an absent addressee to whom the cry of the oppressed is directed. But the perspective of the ri/te/xt changes rather suddenly. In the next verse God becomes the subject of the story, portrayed as an active observer and listener, one who **hears** the **voice** of the oppressed and **sees** their **misery and toil**.

Suddenly the play of appearance and disappearance, revelation and concealment, between God and Gentile, comes to a stop. For a short moment, the two seem to appear together, facing one another, set at each other's throat by a text that celebrates Israel's revenge. The text places the two on a course that will lead to their terrible, unavoidable clash, the outcome of which is known in advance. God, not yet seen but already seeing and listening, watches the oppressive Gentile, while the Gentile watches only his slaves, deaf to their outcry.

God's impending revelation would soon be a display of wonders to be interpreted, a last moment of truth for the Gentile, who is doomed to perdition and an educating process for the benefit of all other nations as well as all other Gentile nations witnessing the event from afar. **Has any god ever tried to remove one nation from the midst of another by trials, signs, wonders, war; with a mighty hand, outstretched arm, and with great awe?** Redemption occurs through the unmediated appearance of God, the

Divine Being revealing **Himself**. Israel is saved neither by **an angel** nor by **a seraph**, nor by **a messenger**, but by Him alone. And He did it with **trials and signs**, lest there be any doubt, **He and none other**.[16]

But in truth, He Himself, almighty, with outstretched arm and strong hand, was never seen. What actually appears to the human eye-witnessing the scene of revelation is a horrible show of destruction, the destruction of the Gentile who is now tortured, robbed, and murdered in that series of plagues brought upon him by the Almighty. Each scene of horror is a sign of and testimony to God's presence, and is immediately interpreted as one of His faces, or one of His more conspicuous traces. The dead Egyptian first-born signify the march of the Almighty **through the land of Egypt**; the **heavy pestilence** that strikes Egyptians' **horses, donkeys, camels, cattle, and flocks** is God's **mighty hand**; His **outstretched arm** is a **drawn sword**; His **signs** refer to the **rod** Moses used to terrify the Egyptians; and His **wonders** [*moftim*, demonstrations] refer to the **blood** that ran in their rivers. The Egyptian catastrophe thus sets the stage for the appearance of God, who, even in the moment of His revelation, remains invisible. He, rather than His angels or messengers, inscribes His imprint on the world by means of awful plagues that He pours upon the poor Egyptians and through the screams that rise from their stricken land.

These screams, however, are not going to be heard by anybody. As the Egyptians drown in the sea, everyone watches but nobody hears. The famous, oft-cited midrashic critique, "How can you sing while my creatures are sinking in the sea?" is not found in the Haggadah, but forms a counterdiscourse that challenges the dominant discourse.

Thus, the Haggadah turns the presence of the Other into a mere function of divine revelation and reduces the presence of the Other to an effect of God's absence. Once God appears, the Gentile loses his position as a possible speaker and listener. The Gentile's suffering, justified as it may be, is but a testimony to the concealed presence of the Holy and Blessed One.

Every year that awful drowning of the creatures of God is solemnly reconstructed in the Passover rite, with its symbolic display of **blood and fire and pillars of smoke**. Through this drowning, the God who made Israel holy and separated them is revealed. From this rite, Israel emerges as a holy people and a kingdom of priests (*kohanim*), chosen and separated from all other peoples.

From the point of view of the participant immersed in the ceremony and engaged in ri/te/xt through both interpretation and action, the distinctive identity of the nation is reasserted and reaffirmed each year, mediated through the memory of God's revelation and Pharaoh's destruction. From the point of view of the critic engaged in the work of deconstruction, God seems ever more absent and the Gentile ever more present. The memory of the appearance of the One is the promise for the disappearance of the Other; the memory of the destruction of the Other is the promise for the revelation of the One. Together, the two make possible the coming into being, the formation and separation, of the chosen people.

If these two were separated, that is, if God were represented and understood independent of the mediation of the Gentile and vice versa, the entire structure would collapse. However, in order for that structure, the discursive formation that endows the nation of Israel with unity and identity, to survive, the image of God destroying the Gentile and being revealed through this destruction must be continually reproduced. Henceforth, all—or almost all—Gentiles will be seen as the terrible Pharaoh, the Other who is essentially evil, the source of evil. Since evil and otherness are essentially linked, Israel can do little except pray for a recurrence of that awful midnight, the night in which **Thou didst destroy Egypt's first-born**. Thus, the recollection of God's miraculous intervention in the history of the Jewish people determines and severely restricts the scope of the people's historical expectations.[17]

At this point the ri/te/xt becomes more rhythmic, broken into shorter passages, and the pace of alternation between quotation and interpretation quickens. The allusion to the drowning through the spilling off of drops of wine adds emphatic force to the text. As the wine is spilled from the cup three times, the room is filled with shouts of **blood, fire, and pillars of smoke**. After each plague is mentioned, the participants spill more drops of wine and recite the initials of the plagues, their multiplications, and the interpretation of the calculus of evils. Perhaps all this additional noise and activity is but a way to draw one's attention away from the disaster that, in the ri/te/xt, is pouring down upon the late Egyptians, whose plagues are multiplied by five and twenty and twenty-five, up to

two hundred and fifty plagues at the sea, besides **the fifty they received in Egypt**.

This continues until God's **wrath** and **fury** and the terror of His **messengers of evil** fill the room. The Gentile himself has not been removed, of course. There he waits, outside the door, still to be mentioned several times in the ri/te/xt, from **He punished the Egyptians** to **Pour out Thy wrath**. But something essential to the Gentile's mode of being and representation has been erased: he has lost his position as a speaker or listener, as an interlocutor in the discourse, while the children of Israel have lost the ability to identify with his suffering. At the risk of anachronistically employing modern language, one may say that what has been erased is the Gentile's humanity. For what is the plague calculus if not the final erasure of the humanity of the Gentile, the reduction of the Gentile to radical Other, capable of radical evil, beyond understanding, compassion, punishment, and forgiveness.

The peculiar midrash that calculates the number of plagues actually excludes the Gentile from the domain of legitimate interaction and exchange among individuals and nations. The midrash implies that the ten plagues brought upon the Egyptians were not adequate punishment for the evil done to Israel. So terrible was that evil that it is neither intelligible, punishable, nor forgivable.[18]

Thus, the plague-stricken Egyptians are objects of an unrestrained exercise of power that knows no limits. This exercise of power cannot be justified by the wickedness of the Gentile (or by Israel's suffering, for redemption was postponed until the tenth plague had stricken); this unrestrained exercise of power can only be explained as the mode of God's presence in history. God's presence seems somewhat dialectical to the presence of the Gentile, the latter appearing as radical Other precisely at the moment in which God exercises unrestrained power.

No normative value or moral principle limits the Gentile's exercise of coercive power, only his limited, finite nature. According to the inner logic of the situation formed by the relation of master and slave, the power of the Gentile is unlimited. The same goes for God, whose power seems to be limited only by the limited imagination of the interpreting rabbis who quite arbitrarily stopped at two hundred and fifty plagues. But by the same logic, the logic of unlimited power, God could have inflicted more plagues.[19] Between God's omnipotence and the unlimited power of the Gentile, the people of Israel is powerless, totally impotent, entirely dependent either on the contingent, ephemeral, unreliable mercy of a seemingly kind Gentile or upon the grace of a benevolent God who **keeps His promise**.

A twofold binary structure henceforth shapes the Jewish reception of historical experience, the experience of exile, of being a separate nation dispersed among the nations. On one axis, the binary opposition is between passive and active positions in power relations. From Israel's perspective, power is always exercised upon Israel from without by an Other, either God or Gentile. Israel is but the passive victim or beneficiary of power exercised by an Other. On the second axis, the binary opposition is between slavery and redemption. Within this redemptive framework, power is exercised from without in order to enslave or to redeem, but never in pursuit of everyday interests.

From Israel's perspective, power belongs to the domain of the holy, or rather to the moment of the appearance or disappearance of the holy within the realm of the everyday. In any case, Israel remains outside the historical realm of power clashes. From Israel's point of view, only two historical situations are possible: either the Gentile is beating Israel to death or God is beating the Gentile to death; either God covers His face and the Gentile appears in a cruel display of power, or God appears on the ruins of a destroyed Gentile.

The two binary axes are clearly expressed as the plague calculus comes to its arbitrary end, in the song "Dayeynnu" (it would have been enough for us): **If He had merely rescued us from Egypt but had not punished the Egyptians, it would have been enough for us. . . . If He had merely brought us to the land of Israel but had not built the Temple for us, it would have been enough for us. All the more then—doubled and redoubled— are the blessing the Eternal has done for us! For He rescued us from Egypt . . . and built the Temple for us.**

The slavery-redemption axis is expressed in the content of the song, which is a linear progression beginning with the exodus from the abyss of Egyptian domination and concluding with the worship of God at the temple, the pinnacle of freedom. The active-passive axis is twice expressed in the grammatical form of the passage. First, each sentence is divided into explicitly active and implicitly passive forms: He is the one who rescued us and split the sea for us, supplied us in the desert and gave us the Sabbath, etc., and we are the ones to whom all this was done, was given, happened. Moreover, that axis is expressed by the subjunctive form of the whole song: **If He had . . . but had not . . . it would have been enough. . . .**

"Dayeynnu" actually closes the story of the exodus from Egypt, the story that begins in idol worship, concluding with the worship of God in His temple, **where we could atone for all our sins**. "Dayeynnu" also provides, with utmost precision, the final shape for the overall structure of the narrative: presence-absence, appearance-disappearance; slavery-redemption; passive-active; Israel/Gentile/God.

VI. Pour Out Thy Wrath

After the meal the text continues with the blessing after the meal (*Birkat Hamazon*) and the psalms of praise (*Hallel*), which are chanted on every holiday. After these two standard prayers, the unity of the text, which up to now has been strictly maintained, is abandoned. Now we encounter different songs and prayers from different Jewish communities. Now, when the rite of separation has been completed and the unity of the transhistorical nation that transcends each concrete historical community has been reaffirmed, a multiplicity of versions, no longer threatening, can be safely recited at the level of folk culture.[20]

Only one passage from this section merits serious consideration and close reading, **Pour Out Thy Wrath** (*Shefokh Hamatkhah*). This passage is exceptional is several respects. While apparently seamless, it is actually made up of three different verses: **Pour out Thy wrath. . . . Pursue them in anger. . . . Destroy them. . . .**[21] Moreover, the passage seems to fall outside the narrative structure described above, for it contains neither a recollection of a past redemption nor the promise of a future one. Instead, it is a cry for help, or rather, adhering closely to the wording of the text, a curse and a call for revenge: take revenge, O Lord, on those Gentiles who **have devoured Jacob and laid waste his dwelling place.**

Linked to this exceptional outcry is an exceptional gesture: The door is opened and the curse is pronounced aloud while a glass of wine is poured for Elijah, the prophet and redeemer. Despite the playful, amusing quality of the act, the appeal to Elijah and the curse upon the Gentiles dampens the joyful tone engendered by the praises for the glory of the Almighty who saved His people and destroyed their enemies. The sweet taste of utopia has been embittered, the upward movement from the mundane, historical present to the transhistorical separation of the chosen people abruptly interrupted, and the participants brought down to earth. Now, without warning, an explicit reference to actual power relations between concrete communities of Jews and Gentiles introduces real politics into the ri/te/xt.

Now the separation is between those Gentiles, **heathen nations who do not know** God and **do not call upon His name**, and the children of Jacob who have known God throughout the ages. While the Gentiles still live in darkness, Israel has seen the light emanating from the reproduced memory of the miracle of revelation. And now there arises between the two typical power relations of oppression and persecution. And the time is, as always, a time of the hidden face. As the Gentile appears in a display of power and cruelty, God is absent, as always, leaving no historical trace. And there is no sign, no hint, of His possible coming revelation, except for that old promise of a second redemption that the Haggadah mentions.

Nevertheless, this passage does not transgress the fundamental structure of Israel's separation established in the first part of the Seder. Rather, it embodies that structure in a partial manner. The text does not invert the visible-invisible, present-absent oppositions, nor does God replace the Gentile as the active agent in the scheme of power relations. What we hear is a call for such an inversion, for such a displacement. In other words, in the period between the Egyptian redemption and the messianic redemption, Israel remains in this world without any concrete, tangible evidence of the utopia promised in the rite of separation. Instead, there is suffering, sorrow, lust for revenge, and the painful sense of God's absence from history.

This painful sense of absence can be relieved neither by the symbolic opening of the door, when Jews act *as if* they are not afraid of the Gentile, nor by the glass of wine poured for Elijah. In fact, only the fact that Passover night is considered to be a *Leil Shimurim*, a night in which Israel is protected from the Gentile's wrath by God's attentive presence, makes it possible for this courageous gesture be played out. Moreover, this playful act—whether or not it is taken seriously by the participants—reflects a common perception of the fundamental Jewish condition: even in times of temporary relief, Jews are continually confronted by the threat of danger and persecution.

It is interesting to note that among secular Jews in Israel, the original meaning of the open door has almost been forgotten. Today, opening the door is associated with Elijah, the always-expected invisible guest. A simplistic, benign messianic interpretation suppresses the original hostile attitude toward the Gentile. Nobody takes that appeal to Elijah seriously, however. To some, it serves to amuse the children who participate in the ceremony. In some Jewish communities, which have adopted certain Christmas customs, it may also serve as an occasion for the distribution of gifts.

The appeal to Elijah, the legendary savior, also serves to intensify a sense of absence. While the children are sent to open the door, someone may drink from the cup of Elijah, who, like a Jewish Santa Claus, hovers over Israel's houses, flying from one Seder to another, paying a short visit to each household. And in each house, small children may be excited but somewhat fearful. Nevertheless, as every adult sitting at the Seder table knows full well, Elijah's cup is a cup of absence, the concrete presence of an absence in the second part of the ceremony. Once it is painfully realized, everyone turns back to the regular proceedings and sings to the glory of the absentee, **for his kindness is everlasting**. His kindness is forever, only not for now, at this difficult moment, in these hard times.[22]

While most scholars agree that this late addition is a response to persecutions, they are unable to relate that response to a particular event. Rather than traces of a concrete historical context, the verses of the curse provide a general relational pattern between Israel and its Other, a pattern of constant threat, coercion, and persecution. Instead of a particular Jewish response to a particular case of Gentile persecution, we encounter a general prescription for such a response, a topos of complaint and appeal to God.

This topos still follows the fundamental structure of collective memory that we have found to be manifest in the Haggadah. Israel faces the Gentile passively, waiting for salvation. God mediates Israel's reception of the Gentile presence in history, deferring any active Israelite intervention in that history, directing Israel's attention from the pressing present to the remote past and the promised future.

The Gentile, whose face is always drawn in the image of Pharaoh, separates Israel out with force **by means of the harsh labor**, the slavery, and humiliation. That separation is immediately projected onto a different separation, which precedes it in principle and justifies it a-posteriorly, the separation by means of the knowledge of God. Those who recognize God, which now means those who belong to the community separated through recollection of the first moments of recognition, are distinguished from those who have been denied the opportunity to share in this collective memory. Separation by means of recognition becomes separation by means of recollection, collective memory, and the duty to remember. Facing the Gentile through the prism of this memory, the Jew wishes for nothing but reversal of the wheel of suffering. Once again, God is expected to become manifest through the destruction of the Gentile and Israel is expected to grow and become holy (*yitgadal veyitkadash*) and be separated as they were in ancient times as a result of the particular way God has chosen to exercise His power in history.

In the constitutive event of Jewish history, there was a series of violent clashes between the Gentile and Israel and their God, in the course of which God was revealed, the Israelite nation separated from all nations, and the Gentiles drowned in the sea. The memory of that event, shaped by the central ceremony of Jewish life, the Seder, constitutes the collective memory of the community of believers as an antihistorical memory.[23] It erases the traces of the actual present, subordinating ongoing events, their antecedents and consequences, to the paradigmatic moment of origin, and shapes them in the form of that moment, coercing each particular historical recollection into the structure dictated by the memory of origins. Moreover, this memory determines the dominant structure of historical consciousness as a result of which the historical present is perceived as an ephemeral moment between the Egyptian redemption and the coming messianic one. And this moment is always, that is, in the meantime, till God will pour out His wrath, placed somewhere between Pithom and Raamses.

The historical Gentile who thus appears on stage is always perceived in the image of Pharaoh. Being a poor imitation of the Egyptian arch Other or a monstrous refinement of him, he is always between Pithom and Raamses. God, who no longer appears with the Gentiles on the same stage, is perceived through the image of the ten plagues, which will again strike when the Holy and Blessed One reappears on stage. In the meantime, He is addressed **by means of the harsh labor** and the hard times, that being the permanent mode of existence for the Jew addressing God. In that meantime, the people of Israel remains on stage as the eternal witness to the Gentile's revelation and God's absence. Witnessing their two

Others, waiting for salvation, they perceive themselves under the shadow of that old clash between the two—a clash that has long been but a myth of a golden age, indeed, but one that is doomed to return someday. This is the clash that constituted the origin of Israel's separation, the separation between material and spiritual slavery, that is, between being subjects of the One or of the Other.

VII. If There Is an IDF, Let It Appear at Once

This is not the end of the story. Later, as everyone knows, came the Zionists, who refused to wait any longer and generated another exodus, from Europe and from Arab lands. They resettled Canaan, gained control over the labor market, and revived the Hebrew language, which could now serve to curse God as well as praise Him, to announce His death as well as worship Him. The Zionists have, in principle, created the conditions for the development of new attitudes towards the Gentiles and a new type of interaction with Gentile nations. During that same period, there came Gentiles who allowed a new, most terrible pharaoh to emerge, the most horrible, systematic and sophisticated Pharaoh ever to have existed. Old Pharaoh, the Egyptian, now seems almost benign and obsolete, while the new, most sophisticated one belies comparison, he and no other. He turned the Nile into gas chambers and threw into them not only newborn Jews but all born Jews.

Nevertheless, the old forms of memory have been neither replaced nor enlarged; they have been simply filled with new blood, stamped in ashes. And when the German pharaoh sent the children of Israel to their death, God saw the **blood and fire and pillars of smoke** and remained silent. Perhaps He died long ago, perhaps He too suffocated together with His children, perhaps He revealed Himself to His people, as in ancient times, out of the smoking ashes.[24] However, just as in ancient times, now too, whether God is temporarily or totally absent, the Gentile still occupies the same position between God and His People.

Meanwhile, the Zionists have built Hebrew armed forces that have their own mighty hand and outstretched arm. Those forces have called upon the mercy of God and succeeded in inverting, in some crucial historical moments at least, the power relations between the Gentiles and the Jews. Their outstretched arm can now gain a hold over the nation's enemies and visit upon them **anger and wrath, indignation, trouble, and messengers of evil** at a time and place that mighty Israel deems fit. And one need no longer wait forever for that power, which is now revealed or concealed strategically, according to the law of supply (of Gentiles' atrocities and hostilities against Jews) and demand (for revenge).

Nevertheless, despite the transformation of power relations between Jews and Gentiles brought about by the Zionist movement, the main structure that produces and reproduces Jewish collective memory, which the Haggadah embodies more than any other Jewish text, remains dominant. Many Israeli Jews, and not only Israeli, perceive the Jewish state apparatuses, its armed forces first and foremost, as substitutes for God's outstretched arm, just as they perceive enemy leaders, from Nasser through Arafat to Saddam Hussein, as modern embodiments of ancient pharaoh. And when a threatening Gentile appears, he is viewed within the crossed shadows projected by the Pharaoh of the Nile and the Pharaoh of the Gas Chambers. When a Gentile appears, Israelis call upon the mighty power that protects them. They call upon it to appear immediately and pour its wrath upon the Gentiles who have not known it, or have not yet understood the meaning of its presence in history.[25]

In the meantime, between the Gentiles' Pithom and Raamses, between Nablus and Gaza and Ossirac, many Jews continue to pour wrath upon Gentiles. Some of them do it while in the tents of Torah, others while in the corridors of power and halls of science; some are engaged in overt missions of wrath pouring, others in secret ones. Or at least, this is how the story is being told, obeying the rules of one grand narrative into which all stories of heroism and glory and torture have been woven. And the people of Israel have grown and expanded, and have become blessed and holy, yet they close their ears to the groaning and curses of their subjugated Others. And each year families gather in order to tell their sons and daughters on that night, at one long stroke, long as the entire exile, the miracles of exodus and the split sea, and the conquered land, and national independence, and immigration, and the seven last wars, and all those still to come.[26] And above all, they once again affirm, reproduce, and reestablish the miracle of separation.

NOTES

This chapter is part of a larger research project in progress.

1. For the notion of symbolic capital, see Pierre Bourdieu, "The Production of Belief: Contribution to an Economy of Symbolic Goods," *Media, Culture, and Society* 2 (1980); idem, *Questions de Sociologie* (Paris: Minuit, 1984).
2. I acknowledge here the influence of Foucault's concept of discourse as developed in the *Archaeology of Knowledge* (New York: Pantheon, 1972) and *"The Order of Discourse"* (in *Untying the Text: A Post-Structuralist Reader*, ed. R. Young [Boston and London: Routledge & Kegan Paul, 1981]). The notion of a privileged text, however, is my own.
3. Goldstein counts twenty-seven hundred editions since the fifteenth century (*Encyclopaedia Judaica*, s.v. "Haggadah").
4. However, I accept as authoritative Daniel Goldschmidt's *Passover Haggadah: Its Sources and History* (Jerusalem: Mosad Bialik, 1960).
5. Although the kibbutzim emend their Haggadot from year to year, they rarely print them, preferring in most cases cyclostyled forms. In any case, their main contribution belongs to a previous era. In the last three decades the Seder ritual in many kibbutzim has become more traditional. On the kibbutzim's Haggadah and its changes, see Avshalom Reich, "Changes and Development in the Passover Haggadot of the Kibbutz Movement" (Ph.D diss., University of Texas, n.d.).
6. One may distinguish three types of attitudes of Orthodox Jews toward the Zionist movement and the institutions of the state: the Orthodox Zionist (or national-religious); the Orthodox non-Zionist (most Haredi Jews, Agudat Israel, Shas); and ultra-Orthodox anti-Zionist (Neturei-Karta). I refer above to the two first types.
7. Cf. Charles Liebman and Eliezer Don-Yehiya, *Civil Religion in Israel: Traditional Religion and Political Culture in the Jewish State* (Berkeley: University of California Press, 1983). Liebman and Don-Yehiya distinguish three phases of civil religion in Israel according to the degree of conflict between secular and orthodox-religious cultures, and they observe a transition from a "confrontational" stage to a more reconciliatory, "interpretationist" one. If such a transition has indeed taken place, the central position of the Haggadah was maintained throughout it; however, the nationalist-ethnocentric tendencies in Haggadah's interpretations are more characteristic of the last, contemporary stage.
8. For an affirmative interpretation of the presence of national-religious motives in secular culture, see, for example, E. Schweid, *Ad Mashber: Yahadut ve-Tsionut Ba-medina Ha-Yehudit* (On the verge of crisis: Judaism and Zionism in the Jewish state) (Jerusalem: Zack, 1969); idem, *Emunat Am Israel ve-Tarbuto* (The faith of the people of Israel and its culture) (Jerusalem: Zack, 1976). For a critical view, see, for example, S. Yizhar, "Haoz Lihyot Hiloni" (The courage to be secular), *Shdemot* 79 (1981): 74–80; Boaz Evron, *Ha-heshbon Ha-Leumi* (The

national account) (Tel Aviv: Dvir, 1988); Adi Ophir, "On Sanctifying the Holocaust: An Anti-Theological Treatise," *Tikkun* 2, 1 (1987): 61–67.

9. I mainly have in mind here the emergence and institutionalization of Gush Emunim, the success of its messianic ideology and settlement practices, the more extreme religious nationalism of Rabbi Meir Kahane, but also clear nationalist tendencies among non-Zionist Orthodox in the Sephardic community (that find political expression in the Shas party) and in the Hasidic community, especially in the Chabad movement. Cf. Tsvi Raanan, *Gush Emunim* (Hebrew) (Tel Aviv: Syphriaat Ha-Poalim, 1980); Yohai Baruch Rodik, *Eretz Geulah* (Land of redemption) (Jerusalem: Institute for the Study of Rabbi Kook's Teaching, 1989); Menachem Freidman, "Medinat Yisrael Kedilemma Datit" (The state of Israel as a religious dilemma), *Alpaiim* 3 (1990): 24–68.

10. The text in bold is part of the Passover Haggadah as translated by Adi Ophir with editorial changes by Laurence J. Silberstein.

11. A similar point is made by Yerushalmi, who emphasizes the link created in the Seder between past and present, text and ritual. "The entire Passover Seder is a symbolic performance of a historical script, and the three main scenes of that script—slavery, liberation, salvation—are the foundation of the Haggadah read aloud" (Yosef Hayim Yerushalmi, *Zakhor: Jewish History and Jewish Memory* [Seattle: University of Washington Press, 1982], 66).

12. The first *poskim* (rabbinic authorities who render legal decisions) mentioned the *karpas* in particular and relied on many hermeneutic and mystical interpretations to justify it. However, either because the vegetable was not available or because its identity was unknown, different vegetables were used in different communities (Adin Steinsaltz, *Passover Haggadah* [Jerusalem: Karta, 1984], 21).

13. The *afikoman* is a piece of *matzah* from the Seder plate that is broken off during the opening section of the Seder and hidden. Custom dictates that the Seder cannot be concluded until everyone tastes from the *afikoman*. Thus, a negotiation takes place between those who have found the *afikoman* and the person leading the Seder. The rules of the *afikoman*'s game vary widely among different communities, and the game itself has not been "commercialized" everywhere. Of special interest is the function of the *afikoman*'s retrieval in official Passover ceremonies in army camps. The game opens channels of communication and exchange between high officers and junior officers on the one hand and rank-and-file enlisted personnel on the other. Almost always the game serves as an opportunity for the rank and file to gain some material benefits, such as a few days off, a television set for the soldiers' club, or other improvements in the living conditions at the camp.

14. The basic structure is maintained even among some contemporary secular Zionists, and certainly among Orthodox-nationalists (*Gush*

Emunim), who tell the story of the birth of Israel and its continuous war against the Arabs. The Zionist narrative exemplifies here an impressive continuity with the traditional narrative of Jewish history, the Haggadah being one of its most important sources and clearest realization. History always lies between total destruction and slavery on the one hand and final redemption on the other hand. Political events are interpreted as indications for the present state of Israel, always lying somewhere between the two extremes, and historical processes are understood as concretization of one of two possible trends, downward to Egypt or upward to the land of Israel—except that among secular Jews, omnipotent God is replaced by a seemingly omnipotent army. About this point see below.

15. According to an explicit mishnah (*Pesahim* 10, 4), every man is commanded to study and interpret the Torah's verses in the Haggadah only from the section beginning, "A Syrian tried to destroy my father. . . ." This abbreviated version of Israel's history was also to be read (without its midrashic commentary, of course) by the Pilgrims to the Temple at the ceremony of Pentecost (Deut. 26:5–9; cf. Yerushalmi, *Zakhor*, 30).

16. This last issue received much emphasis in the midrash:

> Rabbi Meir says, when The Holy and Blessed One revealed Himself to the Egyptians at sea, He was revealed with ninety thousand angels of terror. Some of these angels were angels of Shaking (*ziia*), some of Trembling (*rettet*), some of Hail (*barad*), some of Flame (*shalhevet*). And anyone who sees them is trembling with fear. They [the angels] said to Him, Sovereign of the world, let us do your will in Egypt. He said to them, my anger will not cool down till I myself will take revenge of those who hate Israel. Therefore it was said, *vayanhigehuu bi-kvedut*. (*Mekilta of Rabbi Simon b. Jocahi*, Hoffmann's edition [Frankfurt a.M: Kauffman, 1905], 52).

A different version of the same midrash appears in the *Vitri Machzor* and other manuscripts of the same period and it probably echoes a historical debate concerning the existence of angels (Goldschmidt, *The Passover Haggadah*, 86; Louis Finkelstein, "Pre-Maccabean Documents in the Passover Haggadah," *Harvard Theological Review* 35, 4 [October 1942]: 295–332).

17. This is also the case for many secular Zionists whose historical expectations remain entrapped within the scheme of destruction and redemption. Accordingly, minor terrorist threats are often interpreted as threats to the very existence of the state; major military operations are presented as decisive solutions to the Israeli-Arab conflict; and the so-called peace process is described by opponents as a recipe for destruction, and by supporters as the road to salvation. For these secularists, who are skeptical of divine intervention, the IDF has replaced God's outstretched arm.

18. Of course, not all Gentiles are depicted as being as radically evil as Pharaoh, nor is their otherness presented as being as radical as his. Even Pharaoh would not have been all that radically evil had God not deafened his heart. Thus, one sees an obvious contradiction between the reification of the Other as radically evil and that accumulated historical experience that shows that Gentiles are capable of kindness and repentance and willing to improve and mend their ways. One way of overcoming this contradiction is by interpreting texts in light of historical experience, thereby opening the way for differentiating among Gentiles and empathizing with them. Another way is to impose a literal reading of the Haggadah on the text of historical experience, thereby assuming the Gentiles' essential wickedness. The following example of the second approach is taken from a contemporary preface to a new edition of the manuscript of *Rabbi Eleazar of Worms, Rokeach's Commentary on the Passover Haggadah*:

> Gentiles are closed off from repenting, for they are quick to become excited. Pharaoh had to wonder, for he saw all those miracles and wonders and supernatural events. [Hence God] made an effort to strengthen the point of evil which resides in the Gentiles' inner nature. This point stems from the depth of their hatred to Israel, from the Aggadah that "it is known that Esau hates Jacob," which means the struggle of good against evil. For the people of Israel triumph over evil, but the Gentile draws his strength from it. Since the Gentile is an innate liar (*hesed leumim hatat*), even his outer appearance is covered with deceit in the sense that all Gentiles are uncircumcised. Thus Esau was born with a coat of hair, which is the body's decrements. (Rabbi Moshe Hershler, ed., *Rabbi Eleazar of Worms, Rokeach's Commentary on the Passover Haggadah* [Jerusalem and Chicago: Beit Hamidrash Latorah, 1984], xiv)

19. The plagues calculations have occupied many interpreters for many generations. Cabalists have been especially good at it, as they have deciphered numbers and letters time and again, back and forth, till nothing has remained of the poor Egyptians except for a series of signs of signs, and the entire corpus of the holy scriptures has turned into a scene of divine revelation. Once again I am quoting occasionally (from the Haggadah of *Orah Haim*, Jerusalem, 1963):

> A marvelous remedy to read at Passover eve, which is transcribed from the writing of the Holy Cabalist, Rabbi Shimshon Magid from Astropollea [who quoted what] the ARI, blessed be his memory, wrote in his notebook called *Many Wonders* in the part called "The Outgoing from Egypt," chap. 3, p. 42, side 1, and this is what is written there: "I have already let you know that Pharaoh was stricken in Egypt with those ten plagues by three thousands two hundreds and eighty angels of terror who reign in three spheres (skies) of impurity. One is called *SHARAA*, the other is called *TEMOCH* and the third *BISHEHA*. . . . These things are wonders, opaque and closed and nobody can interpret them. . . . [But] I am going to uncover a secret revealed to me in a dream in a night vision

. . . these are the ten plagues which I have inscribed letter by letter, which make up three thousands two hundreds and eighty angels of terror in charge of the purification of the evil ones, and this is a wonderful literal interpretation, no one has ever seen. And here is the calculation properly set, when we write *CNM* without the Iyota, and also *ARV* without the Waw, and also *HSHECH* without the Waw, and then the sum is indeed no more and no less than three thousands two hundred and eighty angels of terror who punish the evil one. (51–53)

20. Zionist culture, especially Labor Zionist, has contributed a rich reper-toire of songs that are sung at this point. But the most popular songs, even in secular families, remain the traditional "Had-Gadya" and "Ehad Mi Yodea."

21. Ps. 79:6–7; Ps. 69:25; Lam. 3:66.

22. The passage "Pour Out Thy Wrath" was added to the Haggadah sometime during the Middle Ages, and it was probably the last to be fixed. The available manuscripts and early prints contain different versions of curse upon the Gentiles, all of which are taken from different verses from Prophets and Hagiographia (Goldschmidt counts twenty such curses). Different communities have arranged these verses differently. It seems that different communities had first introduced independently a passage of curses to be included in the official cere-mony, and only later, with the advent of printing, the final form of the curse was more or less fixed. Different communities used to pronounce a different number of curses: the Italian Jews, one; the Spanish Jews, two; the Ashkenazic Jews, four; and other communities even more. See Goldschmidt, *The Passover Haggadah*, 62–64.

23. This is Yerushalmi's claim in *Zakhor* regarding the basic patterns of Jewish collective memory in general.

24. Cf. Emil Fackenheim, "The Commanding Voice of Auschwitz," *God's Presence in History: Jewish Affirmations and Philosophical Reflections* (New York: Harper & Row, 1972). For a more critical discussion of the same theme, see Adi Ophir, "On Sanctifying the Holocaust: An Anti-Theological Treatise," *Tikkun* 2, 1 (1987): 61–67.

25. I am not speaking of some lunatics or of a marginal phenomenon, not even about the messianic Lubavitchers, or the nationalist, fascist Orthodox Jews of Gush Emunim, or the racists of Kahane. It is mainstream Zionism that I have in mind here and its most recent expressions. One particular example, Dan Meiron's call during the Gulf War ("If there is an IDF, let it appear at once.") serves as the heading for this section.

26. For a clear example of the theme developed above, see "Haggadat Harel," in which the quite extravagant design consists of a series of straightforward allegories between recent events of Jewish and Israeli history and key moments in the Passover story. On the first page of the text its producers declare:

The traditional text of the Haggadah, which speaks of the way out, from slavery to redemption, is accompanied by illustrations describing the return of the Jewish People to its homeland from the beginning of the Zionist movement to the establishment of the State of Israel. . . . Through this Haggadah the idea of freedom embodied in the holiday of Passover is linked to the modern return to Zion and to the independence of Israel. Thus we add another chapter to the story of the outgoing from Egypt. (David Harel [design] and Chava Harel [text], *Rebirth of Israel: Passover Haggadah* [Israel: Harel, 1987])

Chapter 10

Territoriality and Otherness in Hebrew Literature of the War of Independence

Hannan Hever

Israeliness and the Literary Canon

The question of Israeliness, of Israeli identity, is an ongoing contested issue in Israeli discourse. While some deny the existence of an essential Israeli cultural identity, others proclaim that we are in the midst of an Israeli cultural renaissance. I would argue, however, that Israeliness is best understood as an ongoing process of the construction of subjectivity, and that those who participate in the debate simultaneously participate in this construction.

The Israeliness that is now being forged is part of a continuous narrative. The beginnings of that narrative are located in Jewish history. To many Israelis, Israeliness represents the culmination of that narrative. In the disputes over Israeli identity, we encounter such questions as, Where in that narrative do we now stand? Where should we be? How do we define its stages? What impediments await us? Are we still in the first stages of the transformation of the Jewish entity into a modern national unit? Or are we in the midst of the Zionist era, the era of national liberation? Or, as some would argue, have we already entered a new era, an era that is witnessing the emergence of a post-Zionist "Israeli" identity?

In many ways, the crucial moment in the development of Israeliness was the establishment of the state. At one extreme there are those who see the State of Israel as the culmination of Jewish history. To these people, Israel, as a Jewish state, must be constituted, culturally and politically, in a manner that is consistent with the Jewish cultural tradition and the Jewish historical heritage. At the other extreme are those who view Israel not as a Jewish state but as the state of all of its citizens, Jews and Arabs alike. According to them, the character of Israel should be defined by its citizens, and not, for example, by Jews, past and present, living outside Israel. To both groups, however, the relationship between Israeli Jews and the Palestinian Other has a significant impact on the current definition of Israeliness.

Whether one defines Israel as a Jewish state or as an Israeli state has significant political implications. Thus, to take but one example, one who views Israel as a Jewish state, the state of the Jewish people, would consider the ongoing immigration of Jews from abroad to be a priority. This position is reflected in the massive mobilization of resources to meet the needs of the new wave of Russian and Ethiopian immigrants. However, given the limited resources and the disparity in the allocation of these resources between Israeli Jews and Israeli Palestinians, the impact of this mobilization is particularly felt by Israeli Palestinians. Thus, on the other hand, those who argue that Israel is a state of all of its citizens could very well argue that this immigration policy, which conflicts with the needs of a significant portion of its citizens, is detrimental.

To take a different example, the growing participation of Israeli Palestinians in certain areas of Israeli cultural life has a recognizable impact on the character of Israeli identity.[1] To those who view Israel as a Jewish state, this impact could appear as negative, while those who view it as a state of all of its citizens would view it positively. These are but a few examples of various political and cultural factors affecting the elusive boundaries of Israeliness.

In the ongoing debate over Israeliness, people often turn to literature in search of cultural models. Some of these models are drawn from the ancient past, while others are taken from the recent past. In this chapter I would like to discuss the models of Israeliness that emerged in Hebrew fiction from the period of the 1948 War. My point of departure will be literary works that have conventionally been viewed as either marginal to or outside of the canon of Israeli Hebrew literature. Such an analysis of what has traditionally been marginalized or expelled from the canon of Hebrew fiction and placed beyond its boundaries helps us to identify the borders of Israeliness as they have been defined in works of fiction and in the canonization process itself.

Let me emphasize that in speaking of the canon, we are dealing neither with a fixed entity nor with an essence, but with a dynamic process. Within this process, "other" texts, those that were excluded from the Hebrew canon, serve as indicators of the limits imposed by the dominant groups within Israeli culture at a given point in time. In this chapter, I shall examine the doubly marginalized or excluded; those Others who were marginalized or excluded in texts that were themselves marginalized or excluded from the Israeli literary canon. Specifically, I will focus on the depiction of the Palestinian Arab as Other in the writings of the so-called Canaanite Movement, which was, for several years, an influential noncanonical source of cultural models of Israeliness.

The Canaanite Movement

At the height of the struggle for Israel's independence, when the Zionist vision was being dramatically and enthusiastically realized, a literary and ideological countermovement emerged. Led by the poet and intellectual Yonatan Ratosh, the movement positioned itself in sharp opposition to official Zionist culture. This small, secular, anti-Zionist group emerged when Ratosh, after parting company with the right-wing Zionist Revisionist party at the end of the thirties, established in 1939 the Committee for Formation of the Hebrew Youth. From the beginning of the 1940s, Ratosh and his followers came to be known as Canaanites. The name, given to the group by its enemies, was a reflection of their belief that a new Hebrew nation, separate and distinct from the historical Jewish people, had come into being in the modern land of Israel (Eretz-Israel), the contemporary analogue of the biblical land of Canaan. The historical, cultural, and national outlook of this group, based on the claim that all those who lived within the borders of Eretz-Israel were exclusively Hebrew, was territorial.

The Canaanites wished to sever all links between the new national Hebrew culture in Eretz-Israel and the historical, cultural, and spiritual heritage of Jewish life in the Diaspora.[2] According to the Canaanites, a classic Hebrew nation and civilization had existed in ancient Canaan. This nation and its civilization were to serve as the foundation for a new Hebrew identity, not only for those dwelling in the land of Israel but for all of the residents of the Middle East, the "Semitic space" or "Eretz-Kedem," in Canaanite terminology. The Canaanites thus rejected the basic Zionist claim that the

Jews were a territorial people expelled from their homeland whose goal was to return to their homeland and rebuild the Third Temple. To the Canaanites, the identity of the Jews was based not on national existence but on the existence of a religious congregation with no real connection to the country or its past. In the view of the Canaanites, even the Holocaust was an event that had happened not to the Hebrew nation but to another people, the Jews.

Denying any ties to Jewish historical memory and denying any links between the Jews as a group and Eretz-Isracl, the Canaanites made the concept of territory the primary component of their own national identity. Rejecting the cultural heritage of diaspora Jewry, they developed a concept of culture defined solely by the geographical boundaries of the land of Israel. To them, the true basis for a Hebrew Eretz-Israeli identity was the collective sentiment of nativeness. Whereas the Zionist narrative was grounded in the historical experience of the Jewish people, the Canaanite narrative revolved around territory, the culture that emerged in that territory, and the nation that dwelled in it.

The revolutionary views of the Canaanites extended far beyond the small circle of their movement. Their strong "sense of a Hebrew homeland" permeated the thinking of many of the Eretz-Israeli youth in the 1940s. So extensive was this influence that in the 1950s the Israeli educational authorities became anxious over what they considered to be the Canaanites' dangerous impact on Isracli youth.

While its impact on the Israeli political system remained marginal, the Canaanite Movement emerged as a significant cultural phenomenon and quite a few artists and writers were identified with it.[3] One such artist, the sculptor Itzhak Danzinger, created a new kind of Israeli sculpting style from a fusion of modern and ancient Near Eastern cultures. Moreover, writers like Benjamin Tammuz, Amos Kenan, and Aharon Amir, through their fiction and poetry, were part of an effort to create a new concept of a Hebrew nation, or, in Benedict Anderson's terms, a Hebrew "imagined community."[4]

The cultural and political stance assumed by this extreme, marginal, anti-Zionist Canaanite group in the young Israeli culture diverged sharply from that of the dominant Labor-Zionist movement. Canaanite fiction protested against the norms of the Zionist Hebrew literary canon of the 1940s and 1950s. Moreover, Canaanite fiction parodied the canonical fiction's alienation from the Israeli landscape, its commitment to a Hebrew language that was rooted in Jewish tradition, and its positive characters such as the warrior, the hero, and the moralist. Using a very simple vocabulary and syntax and language charged with so-called pagan allusions, Canaanite fiction, with its flat and cynical characters, challenged the dominant Zionist canon.

Canaanite writers were actually challenging the exclusive, Jewish-ethnic boundaries of the Zionist canon. Thus, for example, Ratosh contrasted the developing "Hebrew literature" to what he called "Jewish literature in the Hebrew language." Whereas the former was the literature of a territorial nation, the latter was the literature of a religious community.[5]

The Contradictory Representation of the Other

The Canaanites clearly repudiated the Jewish dimension of the emerging Israeli identity. In fact, their total negation of the Diaspora and their rejection of any linkage with Jewish history represented an anti-Jewish, anti-Zionist definition of the new Israeliness. Whereas the Zionists linked the Israeli nation to the historical career of the Jewish people, the Canaanites defined the new Hebrew nationality in terms of a "territorial cultural society that is open to any person without race or religious difference."[6]

Given this definition, one might expect that the Palestinian, the Other, would be perceived by the Canaanites as equal to other Hebrews in the Middle East. Indeed, it seems reasonable to expect that the Canaanite anti-Jewish perspective would yield a new inclusive representation of the non-Jewish Other. However, a careful reading of Canaanite fiction of this period reveals a different, more complex picture. In this critical area of Israeli identity, the borders of which are signified by the Palestinian Other, one finds conflicting modes of Canaanite representation.

A typical example of this conflict is found in "The New Morning,"[7] a story by Aharon Amir that was published in *Aleph*, the Canaanite publication, at the end of the War of Independence. On one level, the story condemns the deportation of Palestinian residents from the new Israeli state. Gabriel, a Jew, tries to use his connections in the Israeli establishment to prevent the expulsion of Abu-Hussein, his native Moslem friend, from his land. Abu-Hussein has been designated as a "Present Absentee," an oxymoronic euphemism invented by the Israeli authorities to refer to those

Palestinians who, after fleeing or being expelled during the 1948 War, were prohibited from returning. But Gabriel's efforts are in vain. The Israelis are insensitive to the suffering of the Palestinians, the "Sons of their homeland. Sons of their mountain. Sons of these mountains and this village and this land." Following the battle, the Israelis assemble the villagers who are returning to their homes and expel them to Jordan, from whence they had come. At the end of the story, unrelated to the villagers' actions and their readiness to submit to the expulsion order, they are killed.

In the basic thematic structure of the story, the cynical, powerful, cruel Zionist Jew is contrasted with the persecuted, powerless, and innocent Palestinian, the uprooted European Jew with the rooted Palestinian, who considers it his moral right to continue cultivating his land. However, the text is not consistent. Over and over the reader is confronted with another voice, one that cannot be easily reconciled with the voice of the narrator. Here and there, sometimes in the margins and sometimes at the center of the narrative, one finds suggestions of an alternative reading. For example, Abu-Hussein, the father, in an analogy to Abraham offering up his son Isaac as a sacrifice, is depicted as being full of compassion. But this is balanced by the narrator's comment that this is probably the first time in many years that the father had embraced his son.

Similarly, while the narrator portrays the innocent deportees positively, this is offset by the use of such negative terms as "murderers," "evil people," and "crooks." Moreover, even the positive image of the Palestinian Other is represented more indirectly, through the harsh criticism of the deporting Zionists, than through the direct depiction of his inherent positive qualities. Thus, the negative portrayal of the Other balances the passages that serve to evoke in the reader a full-blown empathy with that suffering Other.

Moreover, Canaanite narrative is not devoid of stereotypical negative depictions of the Other. Thus, in Shraga Gafni's story, "Praise the Lord,"[8] the description of the Israeli conquest evokes a strong identification with the sufferings of the conquered. Through the voice of the narrator, our sympathy for the Palestinian child is aroused. The child hears rumors concerning the Jew's cruelty and, along with the villagers, hopes that the foreign soldiers will help defeat them. He fantasizes about heroic battles against the Jews, but as the Jews conquer the village, all such fantasies are destroyed. The narrator then depicts the senseless cruelty of the Jews.

Although the narrator displays sympathy toward the Palestinian villagers, he simultaneously employs negative stereotypes to describe them. The discrepancy between positive and negative representations of the Palestinians intensifies as the narrative progresses. However, this is offset by harsh descriptions of Palestinians as flatterers who grovel before Jewish conquerors.

The Territorial Solution

How can we explain this tension, this seeming contradiction in Canaanite discourse? How are we to understand this tension between compassion and contempt for the persecuted refugee? To answer these questions, we must contextualize the internal mechanism for representing the Other in the Canaanite literature.

Despite their anti-Zionist ideology, the Canaanites nevertheless wrote from the position of conquerors. As a part of the dominant party in an asymmetrical power relationship, the Canaanites were thus confronted by the basic cognitive and psychological dissonance of a self struggling to remain unified. The discourse of the strong is always trapped in an ambivalent situation between "its appearance as original and authoritative and its articulation as repetition and difference."[9] The problem is how to maintain in the long run an authoritative representation of the Other. The powerful Subject, when representing the Other, is caught between two poles: On the one hand is the Subject's self-image as a powerful, hegemonic Self seeking to control the Other by repetition, which assimilates her and makes her the same as the Subject. But on the other hand there is the dominant Subject's concern to maintain the differences between them, so as to maintain authority and control.

Within these asymmetrical power relations, the subordinated Other is represented through various figures of speech presented as "true representations."[10] Situating the Other in an inferior position, these figures of speech are employed so as to depict universal and objective truths. This figurative apparatus describing the Other marks the continuous struggle of the Self to reconcile two opposite tendencies. On the one hand, the Self, seeking to secure its unity, masks the gap between itself and the Other. This has the effect of creating an "improved" Other, an Other who is similar to the Self and thus less ominous. On the other hand, this masking mechanism preserves the permanent difference between the improved Other and the powerful Self, thereby ensuring the Other's subordinated, dominated position.

However, the powerful can never thoroughly eradicate the anxiety evoked by the threat that the Other poses to her own stable identity. Thus, the fetishistic, simplistic, stereotypical representation of the Other reveals the obsessive anxiety of the representing Self as well as the subjugation of the represented Other. Depicted as a fixed reality that is different from the Self and thus visible, the Other is known in advance and susceptible to control.

This stereotypical repetitive representation serves to control or repress the anxiety that the Other will undermine the Self's original authority. The Canaanite anxiety is especially acute. Like the Zionists, they are in an asymmetrical power relationship with the Palestinian Other. But in contrast to the Zionists, the Canaanites have severed their connection to the historical past that provides the living link to the nation's authoritative origins. All Israeli characters in these stories exist and move without reference to their historical past. Instead, their identity is grounded spatially and territorially. Elements of landscape and even human beings are represented essentially as spatial objects. Roots, in the Canaanite stories, whether of plants, beasts, or human beings, are an exclusively territorial phenomenon.

Thus, in the Canaanite narrative, territorial space substitutes for the original, unbroken authority derived from historical continuity. Through an enhancing repetitive reconstruction of movements on the territory, the Canaanite writers seek to compensate for the insecurity resulting from their rejection of historical continuity. Their protest against the expulsion of the rooted Palestinians notwithstanding, the Canaanites, lacking their own sense of historical continuity, experience the Palestinian Others as a threat. In response, they reduce the identity of the Other to simplified and stereotypical spatial and territorial representations. Through this kind of stereotyping, the Subject is able to express her basic ambivalence toward the Other. Although both sympathetic and hostile at the same time, she simultaneously denies or represses the hostile feelings.

The spatial, synchronic narrative reinforces the truth of this representation of the Other. The result is a reductionistic, essentialistic stereotyping of the Other. This "unchanging abstraction,"[11] to use Edward Said's term, produces a completely ahistorical narrative, one that suppresses the historical context and the conditions that made possible this particular image of the Palestinian Other. In other words: the Canaanites' radical territorialization of national identity erases the historical context of asymmetrical power relationships. At the same time, this process enables the Canaanites to repress the fact that they are stereotyping.

"The Battle of Fort Williams"

As we have seen, the conflicting thematic representation of the Palestinian Other is reflected in the formal structure of the Canaanite plots. In Aharon Amir's "New Morning" we encounter a purportedly linear narrative account of the deportation of the Palestinian Arabs. But here, too, the structure of the story is actually controlled by spatial rather than temporal motifs. The narrative is divided into five units, each containing one or two scenes. However, the narrative transmissions between them are not explicit. For example, there is a sudden jump from the first section (which describes Gabriel's efforts to prevent Abu-Hussein's expulsion) to the second section, which describes the deportation. The jump to the last section in which the Palestinian villagers are killed also remains unexplained. Since they obeyed the soldiers' orders, why were they shot? In the closing phrase, "and a new morning will rise at the edge of the East," we see an allusion to "Hatikvah," the Zionist national anthem, which provides an ironic perspective on the cruel, senseless murder of the Palestinians by the Jews. It is the price of Jewish national independence. This results in an elliptical structure in which every scene is depicted as a repetition of a basic spatial paradigm. This repetition serves to undercut the continuity of time that could have made the discourse more open to rival interpretations, thereby threatening the unity of the representor's viewpoint. The historic time is condensed into the present moment, with no representation of historic movement. Hence, the Other is not depicted as the result of a long process that could be interpreted in different ways. In this way, the spatial representation minimalizes any threat to the coherence and authority of the representor's viewpoint.

In "The Battle of Fort Williams," a story by Shraga Gafni found in the appendix to this chapter,[12] the Canaanite protest against Zionism is conveyed through imagery that systematically displaces the territorial arena of the War for Independence battles against the

Egyptians in the Negev.   The story's setting is the seventeen minutes preceding an attack by an Israeli unit on an Egyptian outpost.   Danny (the commander) imagines his soldiers lying motionless as "hewn stones sown along the slope." Regardless of the outcome of the battle, most of the soldiers will be killed. The cruel fate that awaits them should they be defeated is represented as a cynical parody of the conventional representation of the dead, the "comrades" in the jargon of the period, in which it is assumed that they will receive a dignified burial.

Thinking about his own death, Danny recollects a humorous obituary that Yossi, his friend, had written in his honor. With flowery, empty rhetoric, he had eulogized Danny as having fought in "every major campaign ever fought anywhere in the world," whether by Jews or by others. At no point, however, had the "deceased" been linked to Jewish history. Danny's and Yossi's shared history has had nothing to do with that of the Jewish people. Theirs had been a private history of street battles, fought in their old neighborhood and in the adventure books they had read.

The battles with the Egyptians in which they are now participating as adults seem trivial when compared with the terrible childhood battle fought twelve years ago on Purim. Thus, the memory of their childhood war games eclipses the reality of the actual national war with the Egyptians in which they are now engaged.

As opposed to the Zionist perspective on the Negev that is grounded in historical heritage and historical continuity, the Canaanite links the territory to children's war games, historical tales of exotic peoples, and stories of the Wild West. Thus, while Zionist narrative links the War of Independence to Jewish, and therefore Zionist history, the Canaanite narrative severs these ties. In the words of Ratosh, "The Hebrew War of Independence is as much a struggle over the past as it is a struggle over the formation of the present and the vision of the future."[13]

But there is a price for this representation of the Other in the Canaanite counterdiscourse. This detachment from Jewish history, while undermining the Zionist claim to authority, results in inconsistent depictions of power relationships. In "The Battle of Fort Williams," the fabricated analogy to the American Wild West, the Israeli Sabra is identified alternately as a warrior fighting on the side of the American colonists or as a Comanche Indian warrior. Whether the story positions the Arabs as Indians or as cowboys, it is motivated directly by the reduction to mere territory. The representation of this territory is devoid of historical continuity or national meaning. The positioning of the Arabs as Indians and the Israelis as cowboys eclipses their historical identity. In the end, all identities are reduced to spatial relations. Those relations are materialized in one specific territory (in this case, that of the childhood neighborhood or the outpost in the Negev) over which both sides fight at this specific point in time. For example, "It's too bad," says Danny, the commander, "that these Egyptians are not Indians and the Negev is not the Wild West." In other words, the historical context of the war is displaced. This Canaanite protest by displacement is achieved by entwining actual territory with the repression of historical memory. In the end, the platoon joker's suggestion—"let's take that enemy position and forget it!"—conveys the sense that as soon as they carry out their territorial mission, it will be immediately repressed and forgotten. Thus, the territorial achievement is to play no role in the shaping of a historical identity. Thus, when Danny can no longer endure the Zionist message he had tried to impart to his soldiers before the battle, he laughingly agrees to just "take that enemy position and *forget it*."[14]

Minority Discourse versus Majority Discourse

The party who is subjected to moral judgment in the Canaanite narrative is a localized, stereotyped object rather than a morally responsible, autonomous being who has a history. In the story "Praise the Lord," the behavior of the Jewish conquerors is condemned. But this criticism is accompanied by the revelation that one of the Palestinian prisoners had been involved in the cruel murder of Jews. The critical perspective on the behavior of the Jews resumes when they are described as guilty of a massacre of Palestinian Arabs. Yet this is followed by the criticism of a Jewish soldier for not killing a Palestinian boy. One explanation suggested to account for this inconsistency argues that, from the Canaanite point of view, the Palestinian Arabs deserve their fate. As the story implies, instead of aligning themselves with the native population, both Hebrew and Palestinian, they joined forces with foreigners such as Arabs from other countries in the region and Englishmen.[15] But this political explanation alone cannot explain the fragmented moral vision. While criticizing Jewish cruelty against Palestinians, the Canaanite literature also praises the Jewish warrior who takes part in the war against the Arabs without moral qualms, feelings of shame, or any reflection on the meaning of his acts.[16]

This nonmoralistic Canaanite attitude conflicts with the underlying assumptions of the Zionist Israeli canon of that time. As opposed to the canonical "major literature," the Canaanites created what Deleuze and Guattari call "minor literature."[17] As is typical of national "major literature," the Israeli literary canon from the period of the War for Independence was "directed toward the production of an autonomous ethical identity for the subject" who represents the nation as a whole.[18] Unlike the "minor" Canaanite fiction, the "major" canonical works spoke in a universalistic voice, representing themselves as "autonomous," that is, "both self-contained and original," seeing themselves as engaged in the "recreation at a higher level of the original identity of the race."[19] "Minor literature," on the other hand, as reflected in the Canaanite contempt for moral doubts and qualms, tends "to undermine the priority given to distinctive individual voice in canonical criticism."[20]

The Israeli canon of that time is exemplified in the fiction of the major writer S. Yizhar, who has been praised for his great sensitivity to the Palestinian Other. In two of his stories, "The Prisoner"[21] and "The Story of Hirbet Hiz'ah,"[22] Yizhar represents the Palestinian as a victim of the war. In "The Prisoner" the protagonist-narrator follows an Israeli platoon that takes an Arab shepherd as a prisoner of war. Although the shepherd poses no danger to anyone and carries no important information, Israeli soldiers engage in acts of excessive cruelty. The narrator, assigned to accompany the prisoner to another camp, experiences inner conflict—he is torn between his obligation to follow orders and the voice of his conscience telling him to release the prisoner. Just before the end of the story, he justifies disobeying orders and releasing the prisoner by emphasizing his common humanity with the prisoner.

But at the very end of the story, he does not release the prisoner. There is a very short interval in which the narrative suppresses the universalistic motif of the shared humanity. Momentarily disregarding his doubt and his inner conflict, the narrator, again focusing on space, begins to describe the beautiful landscape. But he soon resumes his inner struggle and again employs a universalistic analogy based on "some waiting woman." However, unable to resolve his inner conflict, he cannot bring himself to release the prisoner. But despite this, the Other is still represented as sharing a common humanity with the Jewish Subject. In "The Prisoner" the representation of the Other, controlled by the Jewish narrator, is also stereotypical. But it also includes a universalistic characterization of the Other that derives from the Israeli's Jewish perspective. Moreover, as the Israeli asks, "Who knows what else there may be even more universal, which the setting sun is going to leave here, among us, without end?"[23]

In "Hirbet Hiz'ah," Yizhar's representation of the Palestinian Other is far more extreme. This story depicts the deportation of women and children from an Arab village at the end of the War of Independence. It is clear that for the narrator-protagonist, the deportation signifies the Israeli rejection of Jewish values, which, ironically, are then adopted by the Palestinians. The Palestinians own the future and now have God on their side. At the end of the story, God descends into the valley in order to determine, as He did in the case of Sodom, "whether they have acted altogether according to the outcry that has come to me" (Gen. 18:21).[24]

In Yizhar's stories, the biblical setting, infused with Jewish historical memories, contrasts with the Wild West setting in "The Battle of Fort Williams." Moreover, Yizhar, while sharply critical of the behavior of the Israeli Jew, never abandons the commitment to the historical continuity of the Jewish Israeli Subject. Ironically, it is the Palestinian refugees rather than the Israeli Jews who are the bearers of Jewish values. Thus, although the Israeli Jew fails to live up to Jewish moral standards, the chain of Jewish tradition is not broken. Thus, Yizhar replaces the failed Israeli Jew with Palestinian refugees, who become the new Jews.

This Jewish commitment to universal, humanistic values is reflected in many other canonical stories of the period. Even when the Israeli warriors (called Hebrews, as in Canaanite writings) reject, with anger and contempt, the Jewish diasporic mentality, they do this in the context of a dialogue on the problem of Jewish values. This kind of dialogue, found in Natan Shaham's story "On Line,"[25] differs significantly from the total alienation from Jewish identity one finds in a story such as "The Battle of Fort Williams." In contrast to Canaanite fiction, which surrenders the historical dimension in favor of the spatial, Yizhar's stories continue to emphasize the Jewish historical dimension.

The contrasting attitudes of the canonic writers and the Canaanites to the historical dimension is reflected in their contrasting representations of the Other. Negating the unbroken continuity of Jewish history, Canaanite writers simultaneously negated the history of the Palestinian Other. Accordingly, while accusing the Zionists of subordinating the native Hebrews to Jewish tradition for their own nefarious purposes, the Canaanites also criticized Pan-Arabism as the creation of foreign imperialist interests in the region. Abandoning historical continuity in an effort to create a new identity, the Canaanites eliminated historical memory as well. Thus, Canaanite ideology espoused a plan to force Hebrew culture on the Arabs by drawing out from the Arabs the real Hebrew hidden within.

In conventional interpretations, Canaanism is depicted as the radical culmination of the Zionistic negation of the Diaspora and the Zionist effort to normalize Jewish existence. But the Canaanite perspective of the Other renders this interpretation problematic. The problem arises because the Canaanites did develop a discourse that unknowingly shared characteristics of exilic discourse. In rejecting the historic past and insisting on transforming the present into the sole determinant of Hebrew identity, the Canaanites elevated the present to the level of an absolute.[26] This mirrored, albeit unconsciously, the position of those Zionists at the beginning of the century who, acknowledging the long-term survival of the Diaspora to be a given, advocated "work that was present oriented (*Gegenwartsarbeit*)." Intertwined with this position was a conception of the Jews as a national minority in a diaspora land with its own Hebrew culture.

Like the Canaanite literature, much of the Hebrew literature created by the advocates of "present-oriented activity"—such as that which arose in Poland between the two world wars[27]—subverted the mainstream Zionist literary canon. Basically, the object of this subversion is the Zionist utopian conception of time. But in contrast with the cultural and literary practice of a national minority literature, which acknowledges the limits of its power, the Canaanites were part of an emerging sovereign state. Consequently, theirs was a situation of false consciousness of those who, although in a position of power, retain the attitude of a powerless exiled minority. On the one hand, as part of the hegemonic group, they tended to legitimate the uncontrolled use of power in an effort to enhance what they perceived to be their own weak position. On the other hand, like the relatively powerless national minority in exile, they were committed to a territorialist vision.

On the basis of the foregoing discussion, I would argue that the specific nexus of territory, history, and narrative within Zionist discourse made a genuine confrontation with the Palestinian Arab Other more likely than did the noncanonical Canaanite literature. Zionist literature always privileged the historical perspective over the spatial, territorial one. Thus, although like the Canaanite literature, the Zionist literature occasionally denied the full humanity of the Palestinian Other, it never totally denied to the Palestinian Arabs their link with their own historical past.

The Zionists could, of course, oppose the Other as an enemy and defer responding to the Other's claim to civil rights and territory. Nevertheless, the Zionist commitment to its own national historical past makes it difficult to deny the national history of the Other. For better or for worse, both Jews and Palestinians have a common history in Palestine. For better or for worse, both participate in the same narrative and are, therefore, subject to the same criteria of judgment.

By reducing the Other to the spatial dimension alone, the Canaanites rendered him/her a convenient object for manipulation. For it is far easier to deny claims to authority that are grounded in space and territory than it is to deny those grounded in history. Thus, the Canaanites and their heirs in contemporary Israel, denying historical continuity and defining the collective identity of the Other in terms of territorial connections, consider it legitimate to transform, even do violence to, the Other's collective identity in order to preserve their own unified sense of self.

While Zionists have used their own reading of history to justify repressing the history of the Palestinian Other, that repression can never be total. For those like the Zionists, who acknowledge their own historical continuity, it is difficult to totally deny the Other's claim to historical continuity. However, a conqueror who, like the Canaanites, denies his own historical continuity can more easily deny the historical heritage of the subordinated Other and thereby justify refusing to engage in dialogue with him.

Thus, if the subordinated minority has to choose between an occupier committed to its own unbroken history and one who is not so committed, it would do better to choose the former. For those like the Canaanites who deny their own historical continuity can deny that of the Other as well. But a victorious conqueror like the Zionist, who accepts the legitimacy of his own historical heritage, however ethnocentric that heritage may be, is vulnerable to the Other's claim to historical continuity and, consequently, to legitimacy.

NOTES

1. Hannan Hever, "Israeli Literature's Achilles' Heel," *Tikkun* 4, 5 (September/October 1989): 30–33.
2. Ya'acov Shavit, *Me-Ivri Le-Knaani* (Jerusalem: Domino, 1984), 10.
3. Boaz Evron, "Ha-Maase U-bavuato Ha-Akademit," *Yediot Aharonot*, 2 March 1984.
4. Benedict Anderson, *Imagined Communities* (London and New York: Verso, 1991).
5. Yonatan Ratosh, *Sifrit Yeudit Ba-Lashon Ha-Ivrit* (Tel Aviv: Hadar, 1982).
6. Shavit, *Me-Ivri Le-Knaani*, chap. 6.
7. Aaron Amir (Yariv Eitam), "Ha-boker Ha-hadash," *Aleph* (October 1949).
8. Eitan Notev (Shraga Gafni), "Praise the Lord," *Aleph* (May 1950): 9–12.
9. Homi Bhabha, "Signs Taken for Wonders: Questions of Ambivalence and Authority under Tree outside Delhi, May 1817," in *Europe and Its Others*, vol. 2, ed. F. Barker, et al. (Colchester: University of Essex Press, 1985), 93.
10. Gayatri Chakravorty Spivak, "Imperialism and Sexual Difference," *Oxford Literary Review* (1984): 226.
11. Edward Said, *Orientalism* (London and Henley: Routledge & Kegan Paul, 1978), 7–8.
12. Shraga Gafni, "Ha-Krav Al Mivzar Williams," *Aleph* (April 1950). Translation in appendix.
13. Yonatan Ratosh, "Sifrut Yeudit Ba-Lashon Ha-Ivrit," *Sifrut Yeudit Ba-Lashon Ha-Ivrit* (Tel Aviv: Hadar, 1982), 41.
14. Emphasis by the copyist.
15. Nurit Gertz, "Ha-Kevuza Ha-Knaanit—Bein Ideologia Le-Sifrut," in *Ha-Kevuza Ha-Knaanit bein Ideologia Le-Sifrut*, ed. N. Gertz and R. Weisbord (Tel Aviv: Open University, 1986), 220.
16. Amos Kenan, "Ivrim Ve-lo Zabarim," *Aleph* (1949): 2.
17. Gilles Deleuze and Felix Guattari, *Kafka: Toward a Minor Literature*, trans. D. Polan (Minneapolis: University of Minnesota Press, 1986), 16–27.
18. David Lloyd, *Nationalism and Minor Literature: James Clarence Mangen and the Emergence of Irish Cultural Nationalism* (Berkeley: University of California Press, 1987), 19–21.
19. Ibid., 19.
20. Ibid., 23.
21. S. Yizhar, "The Prisoner," in *The New Israeli Writers*, ed. Dalia Rabikovitz (New York: Funk & Wagnalls, 1969), 107–28.
22. S. Yizhar, "The Story of Hirbet Hiz'ah," trans. Harold Levi, *Caravan—A*

Jewish Quarterly Omnibus, ed. Jacob Sonntag (New York: Yoseloff, 1962), 328–34.

23. Yizhar, "The Prisoner," 128.
24. Nurith Gertz, *Hirbet Hiz'ah Ve-Haboker She-Lemaharat* (Tel Aviv: Ha-Kibutz Ha-Meuhad Press and Porter Institute Publications, 1983), 77.
25. Natan Shaham, "Ba-Tor," *Ha-Elim Azelim* (Merhavia: Sifriat Poalim, 1949), 51–52.
26. Baruch Kurzweil, "Mahuta U-Mekorotea Shel Tnuat Ha-Ivrim Ha-Zeirim (Knanim)," *Sifrutanu Ha-Hadashah—Hemsech O Mhapecha?* (Jerusalem and Tel Aviv: Schocken, 1971), 278.
27. Hannan Hever, "From Exile without Homeland to Homeland without Exile—A Guiding Principle of Hebrew Fiction in Inter-War Poland," in *The Jews of Poland between the Two World Wars*, ed. Israel Gutman, et al. (Hanover and London: University of New England Press, 1989), 334–67.

The Battle of Fort Williams

Eitan Notev (alias Shraga Gafni)

It was seventeen minutes to zero hour and Danny closed the leather cover over his phosphorescent watch and crouched as comfortably as he could behind the rock, leaning his back against the rough, cool surface. The platoon was deployed behind him, squad by squad, in attack formation. By the pale starlight, the men, lying still and evenly spaced (except for squad three! These fellows will never learn to spread out properly—all piled up in a bunch, once again!), seemed to him like hewn stones sown along the slope by some mysterious hand. This reminded him of tombstones in a graveyard, and the accuracy of the comparison made him grin, since his platoon was spearheading the attack and many of the men would soon become inmates of just such an institution. That is, he reflected, in the best case scenario, if they capture the position and can collect their dead and move them to the rear. Things will be quite different if the attack fails and they have to retreat under enemy fire. In that case there would be no way to pay their comrades their last respects. Actually, though, it didn't make any difference. How did Shimshon put it? "The earth can use manure anywhere."

On the left flank, some twenty paces away, the second-wave platoon lay huddled together, looking in the dark like a huge creature fast asleep yet slightly quivering, its limbs apparently shaking all over with tiny shocks.

The darkness obscured the rest of the platoon, who took positions near the wadi. From his position by the rock, Danny could only barely see the team providing cover on his right, where their khaki dress contrasted with the dark-red soil. Well, he concluded, everyone got there safe and sound and so far everything was proceeding according to plan. This was quite amazing, since it was customary for them to be two or three hours late and no operation on record ever commenced at the planned zero hour.

As Shimshon often put it: "Either artillery is too slow, or the infantry lags behind, or the enemy has moved to another address and you, our good buddies from reconnaissance, have been blind!"

Danny listened to the silence which now reigned. Rather than break the silence, the sporadic fire from a nearby enemy stronghold and the occasional thud of distant artillery only accentuated it, making it seem closer and more palpable. The silence seemed to him filled with the noise of what was about to happen: the rattle of machine guns, the screeching of shells, the booming of explosions, and the roaring of the attacking men.

Will I be killed? he wondered, and immediately recalled the eulogy which Yossi had written for him against any such eventuality, produced for general entertainment during one of the long, boring days they had spent holding the line. Yes, Yossi acquired quite a reputation as a first-rate specialist in mock-elegies of this type . . .

How did that eulogy go? . . . One of the dearest, most devoted lads of Israel, who gave up his life in the defense of the Yishuv and the cause of the Zionist endeavor—such was platoon leader Daniel Zehavi, who died at _____ (the blank was for the place to be specified later). He was an outstanding commander, a man of many talents, who, in spite of his tender age, had a great deal of combat experience, having taken part in every major campaign ever fought anywhere in the world, from the Jewish rebellion against the Romans to Genghis Khan's invasion of Europe, from the Hundred Years War to the Chmielnicki uprising, from the capture of the Wild West from the Indians to the Civil War of North against South (here let it be noted that he always fought alternately for either side) . . .

The boys around him guffawed gleefully at this discourse, but only Yossi and he could fathom the subtle allusion it contained. They were childhood friends, having grown up in the same neighborhood. One was a cheerful, happy-go-lucky fellow, as befitted his yellow, sheep-like hair and long nose, whereas the other, Danny, was a dreamer and a visionary, a man with great, daring projects, a result of his having devoured all of the great classics by authors such as Jules Verne, Henric Senkevic, Walter Scott, and Moyne

Reed. He read them day and night, devouring them again and again. He perused them at school under his desk, pored over them during meals, memorized them during the day before falling asleep late at night, still holding them. And after digesting a sufficient quantity of battles, journeys, and adventures, he carved himself a wooden rifle, buckled on a sword made of scrap metal, mounted a broomstick and, after gathering every last urchin in the neighborhood and urging them to follow suit, he explained to their eager ears what it was all about. Then, he and his daredevil warriors dedicated their considerable dramatic skills to reenacting the bloody, desperate battles of Poles against Swedes, Tartars against Russians, red men against white.

Once, Yossi had objected: "Listen, Danny! After all, this is nothing but a game, just make-believe."

"Fool!" he had replied after a brief reflection. "If we don't take this seriously, there won't be any point to it."

And now he is a platoon leader and Yossi is his sergeant. Instead of a wooden rifle he has a real one with a bayonet, a pistol in his belt, and two grenades, but no horse. In order to fire a shot he does not have to yell "boom!" but simply flip the catch and press the trigger. Instead of *By Fire and by Sword* he now reads operation orders, and rather than fight the Mehdi's Sudanese under Lord Kichener and General Gordon, he is now fighting King Farouk's Sudanese under Givati.*

The watch now showed five minutes to zero hour. Without shifting his body position, Danny could feel it gradually filling with tension, like a sprinter in expectation of the starting gun. Very soon artillery would start booming and shells would fly screeching through the air, machine guns would rattle, their bullets sounding like a thousand switches whipping by your ear. An acrid smoke would settle on the hills through which men would run shooting, stabbing, and throwing grenades, killing and being killed, shouting and groaning. But one thing was certain: what was about to happen here would pale compared to that horrible battle he and his cohorts had waged some twelve years ago following a certain Purim celebration. They had unanimously resolved not to waste a single cork-gun shot on Haman and his ten Jew-hating sons during the reading of the Megilla, saving all their ammunition in order to

---

*   Givati was the code name for Shimon Avidan, commander of the
    "Givati" Brigade during the War of Independence.—ED.

repulse the Indian attack led by Chief Flying Dogtail against Fort Williams, that precarious, isolated outpost deep in the Delaware forest. The fort had been properly built on a vacant lot at the edge of the neighborhood and the force divided in two. One half took off most of their clothes, stuck chicken feathers from the butcher in their hair, and, uttering blood-curdling shrieks, galloped on long sticks, circling the fort walls continuously, harassing the beleaguered defenders with a constant barrage of poison arrows. The other half took up positions behind the old crates and construction beams covered with dried cement that made up the walls of the fort, countering the bold attack with heavy cork-gun fire. No less than four hundred corks were fired within a single hour, and no salvo by any gun battery today would even come close to causing the din they had made. For what are our petty skirmishes here and now compared to the horrors of our childhood wars? The blasts of gunfire and the howls of the attackers and the wounded had been a thousandfold more real and sincere then than they were today. At least one had more faith in them. After many months of war, after the offensives and the retreats, the shelling and the sniping, he still couldn't imagine a more dangerous situation than the one he had faced when the Indians mounted a daring frontal attack on the fort. The wall had tumbled down and he had found himself face to face with six-year old Zvi wielding a Delawarean spear while his own gun had not a single cork left in it. Standing at the very brink of death, he had felt with all his being the boundless despair of a doomed man.

"Give up!" Zvika demanded.

"No!" he answered proudly.

The spear came down.

And if in appearance he survived and was now here, behind that rock, in actual fact he had fallen heroically then in the exercise of his duty and his scalp still hung triumphantly on little Zvika's wigwam pole.

As Shimshon would put it: "Only once hath my mother given me birth!"

No! It was not Shimshon who said that, but Pan Zglowa, who had fought the Cossacks and drank whey. It must be admitted, though, that the two were very much alike.

"What are you grinning about?"

The whisper of the radio man lying next to him snapped Danny out of his meditation. "I'm not grinning, just airing the inside of my mouth," he answered jokingly in a low voice.

"What are you thinking about?" asked the radio man.

"I was thinking how great it would be if we all grew beards, packed pistols, and wore cowboy hats. I'm being quite serious," said Danny in a whisper.

"Get off it," the radio man grumbled incredulously.

"But I am being perfectly serious," Danny whispered. "And it's too bad these Egyptians are not Indians and the Negev is not the Wild West. Were it so, we might do great things."

"Quit pulling my leg. We have one more minute."

They settled once more into waiting, which was as stubborn and tangible as the rocky terrain underneath. Danny surveyed the still platoon, remembering how a few hours earlier these men had stood before him among orange trees in the staging area in the rear and heard from him the things they had to do as part of the attack plan. These things were very tough to do and plainly reeked of death, so he went on to give the kind of pep talk one gives on the eve of a battle, a speech full of Zionist ideology. As the boys listened, he spoke of flourishing settlements and national aspirations, of the moral code of battle and the inhumanity of the enemy. As he continued to speak, they grew more attentive, and when he was finished, they remained thoughtful, looking up at him. He, too, felt that the last word had not been said.

There was a moment of silence, interrupted suddenly by Yossi, the platoon joker: "Come on, Danny, you're talking like one of the eulogies I make up. Why don't you just say, the hell with life, the main thing is to stay healthy, so let's take that enemy position and forget it!"

Everyone laughed. He did too, in relief. The last word had been said.

But later he pulled Yossi aside and said: "Still, we must take Zionism seriously, or else there won't be any point to the whole thing."

Artillery thundered nearby on their left. Shells sailed through the air, followed by explosions. The radio man next to him said, "Here we go," and Danny and his men stood up and stormed down the front slope of the small hill shouting and screaming like a bunch of wild Comanches.

The tradition of the battle of Fort Williams lives on!

TRANSLATED FROM HEBREW BY MOSHE RON

Chapter 11

Otherness and Israel's Arab Dilemma

Ilan Peleg

Since its inception in 1948, the State of Israel included within its boundaries a large number of non-Jews, most of them Arabs. The mixed population has presented thorny questions to the new state, which defined itself from the very beginning as a Jewish homeland. Yet, the demographic dimensions of the problem in the first nineteen years of Israel's existence were quite small. From 1948 to 1967 the proportion of non-Jews under Israeli jurisdiction averaged about 13 percent, and virtually all of these were Israeli citizens.[1]

Israel's demographic picture changed dramatically following the Six-Day War in 1967, with potential far-reaching and long-term implications. The occupation of the West Bank, the Gaza Strip, and the Golan Heights increased the proportion of Arabs living under Israeli jurisdiction by about three-and-one-half-fold, with only a small minority of them enjoying Israeli citizenship. Demographically, socially, and politically, the post-1967 political order became, de facto, a binational order. The length of the occupation (by the time of writing, over twenty-six years) has only deepened the binational character of the new sociopolitical reality.[2]

The emergence of intensive communal cleavage in Greater Israel (the pre-1967 state plus the West Bank and Gaza) is, of course, not unique. Such a cleavage characterizes many societies in the contemporary world. Yet, the depth of the Arab-Jewish rift has been among the most serious anywhere. The two groups differ ethnically, religiously, linguistically, and culturally, and their conflict has been fed by a deep-seated tendency, on both sides, to negate the opponent's claim for legitimate rights in the land.

This multifaceted conflict has been studied through the years from a variety of angles: broad historical analysis,[3] legal perspective,[4] personal observations of policy makers and others,[5] exploration of security dilemmas,[6] and analysis of the attitudinal prisms.[7]

The current essay deals with the perceptions that Jews and Arabs in Israel have had of each other, examining these perceptions as a crucial element in the web of complex relationships between the two groups. My argument is that following the events of 1967, the perceptual matrix defining Jewish-Arab relations has become even more negative than before and that it became a prism dominated by mutual and intense hostility, estrangement, hatred, and rejection. Relatively small numbers of Arabs and Jews have rejected their society's negative stereotype of the other society. This essay focuses primarily on the Jewish perception of the Arab, inside Israel and in the occupied territories. It attempts to demonstrate that while Arab-Jewish relationships have been negative for a number of generations, the negativity of the pre-1967 era was considerably more benign, superficial, and passive than that of the post-1967 era, when it became more destructive, deep rooted, active, and intense. Political events, public opinion polls, and literary works have reflected the emergence of a new structure of negativity and rejection.

The Six-Day War reshaped not only the strategic balance and the geopolitical map of the Middle East but also the intercommunal relationship in the land, creating a new reality of hostility and rejection. The 1967 conflict and other events that followed it in rapid succession (particularly the 1973 War, the 1982 Lebanese invasion, and the Intifada) triggered a process that some have called the "Palestinization" of the Israeli Arabs, in which Palestinian identity became considerably more attractive to many members of Israel's Arab minority.[8]

At the same time, the traumatic experiences of 1967 and 1973 revived the dormant forces of ultranationalism and expansionism within the Jewish community in Israel, forces that had been marginalized and delegitimized within the Israeli political system after 1948 and within the Jewish community of the prestate days. Thus, the last generation has seen the emergence of a growing distance between the two ethnic groups in Greater Israel, Israeli Jews and Palestinian Arabs, both inside and outside the so-called

Green Line, and among citizens and noncitizens of the State of Israel. Put differently, "while the political focus of the Arab community had moved to the left, there was a shift to the right in the Jewish community,"[9] a process resulting in a condition of alienation and estrangement or, in the language of this essay, "otherness." Only in 1992 and 1993 did a trend in a different direction become apparent.

The process of radicalization among both ethnic groups was nourished by growing structural polarization of Israel's party system, a phenomenon associated with the disintegration of the consensus on foreign policy and security issues. While prior to the Six-Day War Israel was generally a comparatively united polity and highly cohesive with regard to most questions of foreign and security policy, this momentous event resulted in the emergence of a deeply divided society. The division, which occurred at both the level of the political elite and that of the masses, was most evident in the country's policy toward the newly conquered territories and its relationship to its Arab inhabitants. The political differences within the Israeli-Jewish body politic, triggered by the 1967 earthquake, quickly became unbridgeable and irreconcilable: while some Israelis wanted to use the territories to negotiate peace with the Arabs and effect a grand historical compromise, others saw the permanent incorporation of the territories into Israel as a national and even religious mission far more important than a negotiated settlement with the Palestinian Arabs.[10] This fundamental rift is still the major feature of Israel's political landscape.

Some analysts believe that the polarization within the Jewish camp in Israel resulted not in the decline in the power of the Arabs but, to the contrary, in an increasing "solicitousness" toward the Arabs, particularly on the part of Jewish politicians.[11] Yet, it can be argued that the polarization within the Jewish majority in Israel created a powerful impetus to perceive, describe, and even treat the Arab minority—the subject of that polarization—as the ultimate enemy of Israel, Israelis, and Jews in general.

Indeed, there are numerous indications that in large segments of the Israeli society the "otherization" and even demonization of the Arabs as an inalterably hostile enemy has occurred. Ideologically and politically, viewing the Arab as the Other is a natural (although not quite inevitable) outgrowth of a right-wing position on the future of the territories. The demonization of the Arab, after all, provides the most effective rationalization for territorial annexation.

Solicitousness and "otherness" may, indeed, be quite compatible insofar as they relate to different aspects of the Israeli political process. While political leaders in search of votes and other forms of political support may have indeed been conciliatory in their approach to Israel's Arab population, in the day-to-day life of rank-and-file Israelis the fundamental rejection of the Arab and his depiction as the ultimate Other has grown dramatically over the last two decades. This process of "otherizing" has influenced the country's political life and affected politicians, even those who have shown solicitousness toward the Arabs.

The Dimensions of Otherness: The Ethnic Context

Otherness is an abstract concept. To make it an analytical tool useful for understanding political phenomena, we must identify its dimensions and describe its operationalization. In some ways, otherness is the end result, the product and the consequence of perceiving someone else as the complete negation of oneself, the perceiver.

Otherness is a social condition in which certain individuals or groups are perceived, described, and treated as fundamentally and irreconcilably different from the reference group (often the majority). Any and all negative qualities are projected onto the Other, often the very qualities that the perceiver fears or even recognizes in himself.

Albert Memmi, in his study of the relationships between groups in a colonial setting, maintains that the colonizer perceives the colonized as everything that the colonizer is not.[12] Put differently, not only is the colonized different from the colonizer, but every negative quality is projected onto him, and even his humanity is questioned. Individuals belonging to a group defined as the Other are not seen as individuals, but rather as part of a chaotic, disorganized, and anonymous collectivity.

In trying to depict the process through which otherization occurs, it might be useful to focus on the concept of the "barbarian" in ancient Greek civilization. Although the origin of he word itself is not quite clear,[13] some scholars speculate that it was initially used by the Greeks to denote what was perceived as the unclear speech of non-Greeks, mocked as "bar-bar-bar" (similar to the

English usage of the colloquial "blah-blah-blah" to denote insignificant or nonsensical speech).

Whatever the exact origin of the concept, it was surely applied to foreigners, non-Greeks, and over time it assumed the connotation of inferiority. Observes Julia Kristeva, "The word barbarian no longer refers to a foreign nationality but exclusively to evil, cruelty, and savageness."[14] In other words, the concept assumes a new and different meaning, significantly more negative and more general than the original one.

The process through which the notion of the "barbarian" assumed a new meaning for the Greeks is identical to the process of otherization in other ethnic contexts, including the Arab-Jewish one. The process begins with differentiating between people on the basis of ethnic origin, religion, language, culture, race, or any other attribute assumed to be of social significance. The initial differentiation is based on what many people in society would regard as "objective," clear-cut differences among social groups in such areas as physical appearance, religious practices, or language. As the intergroup differentiation deepens, a process that can be influenced by numerous factors,[15] the Other is perceived in increasingly negative terms.

At an advanced stage of otherization even a mere reference to the Other is considered negative; in fact, the term(s) used to denote the Other become synonymous with a highly negative, socially undesirable set of characteristics. Thus, terms such as "Jew," "Negro," "Arab," or "Creole," which might have originally been innocent descriptive terms applied to certain individuals or groups, can become (and have become in certain social and historical contexts) highly negative, emotionally charged terms. To Yael Feldman, otherness is a process in which the self talks to the image, and not to the person, a condition in which there is a split between signified (the person) and signifier (his image), between the subject and one's perception of what he or she might be.[16]

This is not the place to offer an extensive theoretical discussion of otherness, but a few of its most pertinent dimensions ought to be identified before we analyze otherness in the Arab-Jewish context. Accordingly, a brief theoretical analysis of some of the parameters of otherness, especially those relating to ethnic conflict, is in order. Otherness is a perceptual device through which an intergroup conflict is sustained. It is a normal, expected outgrowth of such a conflict, particularly a severe one. In fact, *not* to view an adversary as the Other often produces painful ambiguity, a serious and unsettling cognitive dissonance. Perceiving an adversary as a totally negative, evil entity is thus not an unreasonable solution for people locked into conflict.

Nevertheless, otherness cannot be seen merely as a psychological device, for it is a condition characteristic of groups as well as individuals. Otherness—the identification of others as fundamentally different and as highly negative—is organically linked to the social status enjoyed by different groups within society. Most often, those who are seen as Others in society occupy low status, a status that certain non-Others in society might want to sustain and perpetuate. Thus, otherness is not only a device that maintains the emotional well-being of those who define the Other; it is also an instrument for sustaining a social and political order in which the Other is a victim.

When otherness characterizes a society, it is inevitably disseminated through the process of socialization in which one generation transmits values, norms, and beliefs to other generations. A high degree of intergenerational congruence is likely to exist in societal attitudes toward the Other, particularly in a situation of severe ethnic conflict. At the same time, since otherness is not a fixed condition but a dynamic one, psychologically or socially, significant intergenerational differences might emerge regarding attitudes toward the Other.

A long list of variables may affect otherness: demographic trends, economic changes, and dramatic political events, for example, could lead to an increase or decrease in the level of alienation. Moreover, and very important in the context of this essay, public policy choices may also influence the degree of hostility between populations and thus affect the intensity of the condition of otherness. In a society in conflict, there is an ongoing political struggle over the public's attitude toward the adversarial group. In this struggle, powerful cultural symbols are often used to convince the public to reject the out-group, the Other. At the same time, a government committed to the resolution of existing conflicts between in- and out-groups could adopt policies that might help to de-otherize the out-group. Although fundamental attitudes, of which otherness is one, are not entirely susceptible to governmental and political manipulation, they are not entirely immune to political influence either.

In the treatment of a minority perceived as the Other, the government and other political actors have available to them a range of choices that not only immediately affect the minority in question but also influence the intensity of the negativity toward this minority in the long run. At the passive pole of this spectrum of choices, political actors may decide to ignore the Other. At the active pole, they may choose to harass, persecute, expel, and even annihilate the Other. In an ethnic conflict, the nationalist right wing within each of the opposing groups is likely to endorse racist, expulsionist, and sometimes annihilationist positions, reflecting a strong sense of otherness toward the adversary.

Moreover, in a situation of acute ethnic conflict, not only could otherness be easily translated into a policy of oppression and coercion toward the out-group (the Other), but it could also turn into a campaign against "disloyal" members of the in-group. Otherness not only depends on a high degree of generalization—every member of the "other" group is *assumed* to have the negative traits of his/her collectivity—but also requires total conformity from all members of the in-group. Cracks in the wall of hostility toward the out-group are considered to be extremely dangerous to the mental structure and the political order on which otherness is erected. Therefore, deviant elements within the in-group are likely to be exposed to a variety of sanctions, with the "penalties" for deviation increasing with the heightening of the conflict.

In the final analysis, otherness is as much about an internal conflict within the in-group as it is about an external conflict between the in-group (the perceiver) and the out-group (the Other). Although otherness may characterize entire societies, the degree of the individual's rejection of the Other varies. In an ethnic conflict, one of the most important distinctions is between those in the in-group who are willing to entertain the notion of a possible change in the Other's position, character, or behavior and those who assume that such change is entirely impossible. Otherness in its extreme form entails a denial that the adversary is capable of changing and an insistence that the essential *nature* of the adversary is not only highly negative but also fixed. It is interesting to note that in an effort to maintain the "order of otherness," the fundamental rejectionist belief system of a society, a variety of terms (psychological, religious, cultural, etc.) could be used to describe the Other.

Those who emphasize the fixed nature of the Other have two available strategies: (1) deny any difference between the individual

Other (perceived as highly negative) and the wider collectivity of which he is a part, that is, perceive all members of the collectivity as virtually identical; or (2) deny that those designated as the Other are capable of or inclined toward changing over time. The first strategy is based on the denial of *spatial differentiation*, the second on the denial of *temporal differentiation*. The end result of both strategies, especially when they are used together (as often is the case), is to prevent any change in the perceiver's perspective.

Denial is an important psychological mechanism that facilitates the perception of uniformity on the other side of a social divide, such as in the case of an ethnic conflict. In its extreme form, denial amounts to negating the other side's very existence or, at the very least, its claims to be recognized as a relevant entity in an existing conflict. Referring to humans as animals, a fairly common occurrence in interethnic conflicts, also is indicative of a high level of denial.

Otherness and the Arab-Jewish Conflict

The growing role of otherness in the Middle East conflict has been influenced not only by the dynamics of that conflict but also by the historical legacy of the Israeli Jewish community. The vast majority of the leaders of that community from virtually all of Israel's major political parties were raised in Europe or in homes of European Jews. The traditional, powerful rejection of the Jew in Christianized Europe and the resulting lack of integration into European society has not been lost on these leaders and on the Israeli society in general. In fact, the seemingly permanent status of the Jew as the ultimate Other was among the most important factors contributing to the emergence of the Zionist movement and, subsequently, to the establishment of Israel as an independent state.

The historical otherness of the Jew—his widespread, long-term depiction by gentiles as the Other and his own, equivalent tendency to see them as Others—has created fertile conditions for the emergence of a new structure of otherness, fed and sustained by the Arab-Jewish rivalry. The rivalry, starting in the late part of the nineteenth century, intensified during the mandatory era, a period that saw the strengthening of the tendency of Jews to view the Arabs as Others and the tendency of the Arabs to view the Jews similarly.[17] Thus, the seeds for the mutual rejection by Arabs and

Jews of one another were sown in Palestine in the last years of
Ottoman rule and during the British Mandate.

The establishment of the State of Israel did not resolve the
tension of otherness in the land. In fact, the presence of a significant Arab minority within the borders of the Jewish state has
accentuated this tension, especially in times of growing hostility
between Israel and its neighboring Arab countries.

The events of 1967 and beyond sharpened existing divisions
within Israel's Jewish community, divisions that were evident
already in the prestate days. According to Yoram Peri, two ideological schools of thought emerged in Israel regarding the essential
definition of the Jewish state. One school of thought, *political
nationalism*, defined the state in national-political terms. To this
group, there was no difference between Jews and non-Jews within
the Israeli collective: both groups were citizens with identical rights
and duties. The second school of thought, *ethnonationalism*,
subscribed to the idea that a nation is a community based on blood
relations, language, culture, and tradition and that the state is
merely a "tool of the ethnic community."[18] According to the ethnonationalists, one who does not belong to the ethnic community
cannot be an equal member of the state. Similarly, Don Peretz
distinguished between "the universalist outlook of left-labor Zionism
and the particularism of national territorialists."[19]

The differentiation between the two perspectives is essential for
understanding not only the legal status of Arabs in Israel but also
their positioning as the Other by large segments of the Israeli
society. The tribalist approach of ethnonationalism *requires* the
depiction of all non-Jews as Others; the statist approach does not.
According to the ethnonationalists, only Jews can be members of the
Israeli collective. To them, the Arabs are the Others, individuals
who do not belong and cannot fully belong to the body politic.

Many of the specific positions taken by right-wing Israeli
politicians over the years make sense only within the broader
context of their ethnonationalist philosophy. Thus, some of these
politicians continuously maintain that an Israeli government that is
supported by Arab members of the Knesset is illegitimate, as if
Arabs are noncitizens or citizens whose votes are not quite equal to
those of Jews. Similarly, some of these politicians attempted to
introduce changes in the penal code that would have given Jews an
advantage over Arabs.[20]

Thus the ever-present Arab-Jewish rivalry brought into sharper focus than ever before the conflict between Israel's universalistic tradition, deriving from the country's socialist origins and the ideals of Herzlian Zionism, and nationalistic particularism, with its depiction of those who do not belong to the national group as Others. It is evident that the forces of particularism and otherness have made some important advances over the last generation, particularly since the 1967 and 1973 wars. Thus, the philosophy of *am levadad yishkon* (a people that dwells alone) has grown more and more powerful in contrast to its alternative ideal, *goy kechol hagoyim* (a nation like any other nation), which clearly dominated in the early days of the Zionist movement.

Although the structure of the Arab-Israeli conflict, and certainly the Arab-Jewish dilemma within Israel, is very different from the colonial situation described by Albert Memmi, his analysis of otherness applies rather well to the long-standing Middle Eastern dispute. Arabs and Jews, both inside Israel and in the territories, mutually perceive their adversaries as the Other. This perception, which is extremely widespread, is based on intense hostility toward and rejection of the members of the adversarial groups, both as individuals and as a collective.

Furthermore, the reality of growing hostility, estrangement, and hatred is related to the close contact between Arabs and Jews. Sammy Smooha, an Israeli sociologist who has studied Israeli public opinion for many years, observes, "Most Jews view Arabs as outsiders. Surveys usually uncover virulent anti-Arab feelings of disdain, distrust, and rejection among Jews."[21] Smooha shows that this rejection is widespread not only attitudinally but also behaviorally. Arabs are discriminated against in jobs, education, funding for their local municipalities, land ownership, and other areas.

The widespread existence of the condition of otherness is further documented in a series of studies dealing with the attitudes of Jewish and Arab youth. David Shipler quotes studies that conclude that a large majority of children on both sides believe that war with the other side is always necessary and justified.[22] A high level of anxiety, focused on the other group, was reported among Arab and Jewish children alike. Fear of and aggression toward the Other go hand in hand; they are causally linked. If the Other is genuinely threatening, one feels the necessity of making war on him.

Mina Tzemach and Ruth Tzin, among others, have studied the position of Israeli youth on a number of issues relating to Israel's Arab minority.[23] They demonstrated that even in the pre-Intifada era over one-half of Israeli youth saw the Arabs as people to whom democratic rights do not apply. Thus, 60.2 percent thought that Israeli Arabs should not be given equal rights, and 64.3 percent thought that West Bank and Gaza Strip Arabs should not be allowed to vote even if the territories were annexed.[24] Tzemach and Tzin also reported that 29 percent expressed the opinion that in cases of murder for nationalist causes, an Arab deserves a tougher penalty than a Jew. This position clearly reflects the existence of two incompatible value systems, one for the self, the second for the Other.

Most importantly, the study identified correlations between antidemocratic positions and an annexationist stance,[25] demonstrating the compatibility of a favorable attitude toward annexation with approval of curbing the rights of Arabs. Otherness is, thus, empirically linked to ultranationalism.

The relationships between specific political positions on the future of the territories and more general positions toward the Arabs demonstrate an important characteristic of otherness: its dynamic, ever-changing character, which responds to political events.

Within the context of Greater Israel, I would argue, the dynamics of the relationships between Arabs and Jews is such that each violent or hostile act deepens the interethnic hostility and, therefore, the sense of estrangement and otherness. Moreover, even nonhostile acts by members of one group are likely to be perceived by at least some members of the opposing group as profoundly hostile. Thus, Shipler documents the story of the arrival of some Israeli Arab families at Upper Nazareth, the perception of this process (by Jews) as "Arab penetration," and the formation of an organization called the "Defenders of Upper Nazareth."[26]

This type of event, of which there are many, is paradigmatic for a sociopolitical situation dominated by otherness in the relations between two adversarial groups. Thus, rather than interpreting the movement of Arabs into Jewish neighborhoods in terms of demographic and economic needs of Arab families in search of appropriate homes, the "Defenders" saw these families as the Other, a threat to their very survival. Regardless of his motivation or intention for acting in a specific situation, the Other is typically perceived as a menace.

The awakening of Arab political consciousness and the increase of Arab political activity in post-1967 Israel are important factors contributing to the growing sense of hostility and otherness.

Analysts have noticed that despite the ethnic cleavage within the Israeli society, Israel was spared "most of the consequences of ethnic strife, which came to characterize other ethnically divided societies."[27] Nevertheless, the occupation of the West Bank and Gaza in 1967 and the events that followed for the next generation radicalized not only the Arabs in the territories but also those in Israel. Thus, in 1976 Israeli Arabs declared a general strike on Land Day; in 1982 they protested vehemently the Beirut massacre; and since 1987 they have continuously expressed sympathy with the Intifada. A dynamic of otherness, substantially more severe than before, set in.

The deepening hostility between Arabs and Jews has also been reflected in Israeli literature, as noted by literary critics such as Yael Feldman and Gilead Moragh.[28] In the early period of Zionist settlement in Palestine, Jewish writers "shared a romantic fascination with the mystique of Arab primitivism" and "their works were informed by an overriding sense of innate separateness between Jews and Arabs."[29] Arabs were almost ignored by Jewish writers, and, to the extent that they were dealt with, their characters were merely "stereotypical abstractions."[30]

The literature emerging following the Six-Day War reflected a different approach, offering a much more extensive description of Arab characters, focusing on their unique personalities, and detailing the complexity of their relations with Jewish characters. In terms of the current essay, the explanation seems clear. Responding to the dramatic intensification in the relations between Jews and Arabs in the period following the 1967 War, Israeli authors felt moved to deal with the Arab in less stereotypical fashion. Thus, much of this post-1967 literature could be interpreted as a protest against the otherization of the Arab.

Moragh believes that the new Israeli literature, viewing the current form of Arab-Jewish relations as "damaging to both sides," describes "the general indifference of Jewish society to the personal and national identity of Arabs." In it, the Arab ceases to be "an object of emulation."[31] Modern Israeli fiction has fully reflected the reality of otherness evident in the everyday political and social life of the country.

Behavioral scientists have also analyzed the increasing interpersonal contacts between Arabs and Jews in Israel. Yehuda Amir, a psychologist, specifically studied contacts between Jews and Arabs.[32] He reports that "negative attitudes [toward Arabs] were found to be prevalent among all levels of the Israeli population."[33]

More importantly, however, Amir concludes that, above and beyond differences in culture, religion, customs, and traditions, "the main reason for the distance [between Israelis and Arabs] is the political conflict between them."[34] The fundamental ethnic cleavage in Israel creates conditions that are conducive to the development of extreme intergroup hostility. Moreover, Amir quotes sociopsychological research indicating that intergroup contact will induce a positive attitude change "only if there is equal-status contact between members of the interacting groups." Contact between ethnic groups of different social status such as Jews and Arabs in Israel tends to support the *perception* of differences between the groups.[35] Consequently, Amir expects an increase in the negative attitude toward the Arabs, an expectation that has indeed been evident since the publication of his important article in 1979.

It is interesting to note that Amir believes that interpersonal contact, when carefully planned, can positively affect antagonistic attitudes of one people toward another. He questions the fixed nature of the hostility, and rightly so.

While Amir approached Arab-Jewish relationships from the perspective of interpersonal contacts, John Sullivan and others have approached the dilemma from the perspective of political tolerance.[36] Their findings proved to be remarkably similar to those reported by Amir. Shamir and Sullivan found that both Arabs and Jews have shown "focused intolerance" toward each other, selecting certain groups in the other ethnic camp as targets of their hostility. The authors believe that this type of intolerance does not allow for the counterbalancing effect of the abstract norms of democracy. They conclude that "there is a dynamic feedback relationship between these two publics [the Arab and the Jewish]: intolerance on either side no doubt breeds intolerance on the other."[37] Furthermore, in line with the argument promoted in this article, they believe that the political sources of intolerance are the most critical and that should the political context change, levels of tolerance could change as well.[38]

Sullivan, et al., found that in comparison with the United States and New Zealand, Israel has the highest potential for translating intolerant attitudes into action. Moreover, they conclude, "The political context of the Arab-Israeli conflict, with the threat it involves, seems to be the major source of Israel's high score" of intolerance.[39] Put differently, and in terms of the present article, the Arab-Israeli conflict creates intolerance that is directly linked to the rejection of the Other.

Otherness, as well as intolerance, both in general and in the Arab-Jewish context, is related to a tendency to stereotype, to deny reality, and to block knowledge of and emotions toward the Other. Radicals on both sides of the Arab-Jewish divide have difficulty recognizing large or even small nuances in the other side's attitudinal or behavioral position. Thus, many right-wingers in Israel have dismissed any reported changes in the Palestinian position. Otherness implies a strong tendency to generalize about members of the adversarial group and to look at all of them as identical.

Thus otherness, in the Arab-Israeli context, has become fixed, frozen in time. As a fixed condition, it has been used in very different contexts from the one in which it had originally emerged. What might be called "otherness by displacement" has been evident in the Arab-Israeli conflict.

A good example of this process is the place of the Holocaust in the collective mind of Israeli Jews. To some Israelis, particularly those whom Sprinzak refers to as the "Radical Right,"[40] the Holocaust emerged as a metahistoric event, symbolizing the otherness of all adversaries, even those entirely unconnected with the event. For them, the Holocaust has become an instrument for transferring otherness from one context to another. In the case of the Arab-Israeli conflict, the Holocaust facilitates the transference of European Jewry's deep sense of estrangement to a new, Middle Eastern milieu. A generalized sense of otherness can, by its very nature, be easily applied to any and all adversaries, regardless of historical circumstances.[41]

Psychological mechanisms such as denial facilitate the reification of the Other and the resistance to any change in the depiction of the Other. In its extreme form, denial within the Arab-Israeli context has amounted to the negation of the other side's very existence. Thus, the Arabs have traditionally insisted on the distinction between "Jews" and "Zionists," claiming that while they accept the legitimacy of Judaism, they reject the legitimacy of Zionism and, consequently, of the State of Israel. Similarly, many Israelis, particularly on the Right, have denied the very existence of a Palestinian nation. For many years the Palestinian Other was simply too great a threat for most Israelis, although this position seems to be changing.

Mutual denial has been sustained by a surprisingly low level of knowledge of and emotional empathy with the adversary on the part of both Jews and Arabs. It is evident that many Israelis have very little knowledge about the Arab minority or very great concern for its well-being. As Robins concludes, "Basically and predominantly, Jews do not want to think about Arabs."[42] This position of animosity, ignorance, and lack of concern is mutual.

In the Arab-Israeli conflict, certain historical events have become strongly imprinted in the collective minds of the combatants. These events could be thought of as mental benchmarks of the highly developed, full-fledged hostility between Jews and Arabs. Undoubtedly, the 1948 and the 1967 defeats have served as such benchmarks for the Arabs. These events left behind a legacy of deep resentment of and hostility toward the Jews and contributed significantly to deepening the attitude of otherness. Similarly, the 1973 Yom Kippur War has reinforced in Israeli Jews the conviction that Arabs are treacherous Others determined to eliminate the Jewish state. It is important to realize that significant events may assume a life of their own, independent of their historical context. When they become focal points for otherness, they are frozen in the group's collective consciousness and create a sense of otherness that is almost indestructible.

The condition of otherness may also be sustained and perpetuated by powerful cultural symbols. Shared values, whatever their origin, often serve as a basis for the rejection of an out-group. Thus, right-wing Israelis frequently refer to Arabs as Amalek, the ancient tribe that God in the Bible commanded the Israelites to destroy. This type of cultural symbol, in which an enemy is transformed into the "primal Other" serves as an instrument for justifying almost any action against the Other.

Otherness and Israel's Nationalist Right

Between 1977 and 1992 Israeli politics were dominated by a coalition of right-wing parties headed by the Likud; for thirteen out of these fifteen years Israel was governed by leaders who saw themselves as representing the country's "National Camp." During this period a series of political, economic, and diplomatic actions was taken to facilitate the eventual annexation of the West Bank, the Gaza Strip, and the Golan Heights by Israel.[43]

The period between 1977 and 1992 saw also a dramatic, unmistakable deterioration of the relationships between Arabs and Jews in "Greater Israel," which includes both proper Israel of the pre-1967 borders and the territories conquered by Israel during the Six-Day War. In this section I will inquire into the relationship between the establishment of a self-declared nationalist government in Israel and the heightened Arab-Israeli hostility and rejection. My argument is that although otherness has been a long-term characteristic of the relationship between Arabs and Jews, the political relationships between the two ethnic groups since 1977 have deteriorated significantly.

In order to understand the policies of Israel's right-wing government toward the Arabs, in Israel and in the territories alike, one has to consider the history of the Zionist Right in the 1920s and 1930s. The leader of the Zionist nationalist Right since 1922 was Vladimir Jabotinsky, a man for whom the national idea, and it alone, was a supreme value. Jabotinsky's fervent nationalism, which first developed in Europe, was further radicalized by the evolving Arab-Jewish dispute over Palestine. His approach to the conflict came to be dominated by popular ideas (at the time) of "blood and soil," a Jewish version of Social Darwinism.[44]

Jabotinsky's major political objective was the establishment of a Jewish state on both sides of the Jordan River. His Revisionist party rejected out of hand the possibility, or even the desirability, of a compromise political settlement with the Arabs. Instead, it demanded a unilateral and total Jewish control of Eretz Israel in its entirety.

This territorial stance reflected an extreme form of otherness, based on the complete rejection of any and all Arab claims for national and political rights in Palestine. To Jabotinsky, the blood feud between Jews and Arabs was inevitable. Some of Jabotinsky's admirers even relished the idea of a violent clash between the two groups. Thus, the important nationalist poet Uri Zvi Greenberg wrote,

> There will come a day
> When from the River of Egypt to the Euphrates
> And from the Sea to beyond Moab
> My young warriors will rise
> Calling my enemies for the final battle,
> And blood will determine
> Who is to rule this land.[45]

Jabotinsky, himself a man of letters, tried to devise a political solution for the Arab dilemma. But while a growing number of Zionist leaders considered partition of the land into an Arab and a Jewish state as a reasonable solution, Jabotinsky adamantly demanded exclusive Jewish control over Palestine. In Avineri's words, "There is no appreciation of the force, authenticity, let alone legitimacy of Arab nationalism in Jabotinsky's writings."[46]

As is typical in a situation dominated by otherness, Jabotinsky and his supporters adopted an either/or approach to the Arab dilemma: "Either the Jews had a right to their state, in which case Arab resistance [to the Jews] was immoral, or they had no argument for such a right, in which case the whole argument for Zionism collapsed."[47] Thus, Jabotinsky's position is based on polarization between the self and the Other in terms of their character, nature, and fundamental rights.

Jabotinsky's simplistic position, which purposely ignored the enormous complexity of the dilemma, made him Weizmann's and, subsequently, Ben-Gurion's main political adversary. While these men recognized the importance of a compromise solution to the ever-escalating conflict with the Arabs, Jabotinsky, as a matter of principle, rejected any compromise. He was inherently incapable of recognizing the rights of the Arabs, just as most Arab leaders were inherently incapable of recognizing the rights of the Jews.

Jabotinsky's position is fully reflected in the attitude of Israel's political right today, particularly the radical Right. Many people who belong to that camp see Israel's Arab dilemma as an extension of the fundamental problem of Jewish existence—anti-Semitism. Thus, the sense of otherness in the attitude toward the Arabs is built on a more general structure of otherness, with even deeper foundations—otherness toward the world at large.

The anti-Arab stance is often reflected in the use of the term "Amalek" in regard to the Arabs. By introducing this powerful symbol, those on the Right attempt to legitimize the idea of unlimited war against the Arabs by providing a religious sanction for it. If the Arabs are, indeed, Amalek, then they are the ultimate Other, a dangerous enemy with whom coexistence is simply unachievable. Israel cannot make peace with them. Not surprisingly, some people on the Right have even called for a "Milchemet Mitzvah [an obligatory war] for the annihilation of Amalek."[48]

Within the right wing, especially among the intellectuals who supported the Likud government, there has been a tendency to present the Arab as an uncivilized savage, the complete opposite of the Israeli. As Moshe Shamir, one of Israel's most accomplished novelists and a former Knesset member of the radical Tehiya party, wrote, "The struggle between Jewish settlements in Eretz Israel and the Arab inhabitants of the country was the struggle between culture and the desert."[49]

Dr. Ahron Davidi, an ex-paratrooper general, went even further in the effort to otherize the Arabs by painting Israel's adversaries as the mortal enemies of the entire world:

> The Arabs deserve the hatred of the entire world and the united action of the entire civilized world against them—a vigorous and extreme action. . . . The Arabs want only to enrich themselves, so that they can control the entire world. They, the Arabs, do not contribute a thing to the world. They are unproductive people, the least productive people in the entire world. They sell petroleum in which they did not invest even one cent. They choke the world . . . they merely steal from the world economy.[50]

There is no doubt that this type of cultural warfare—describing the Arabs as Israel's eternal enemy, the ultimate Other for Jews and the world—fulfilled an important role in the legitimation of Likud's foreign policy, including the settlement policy in the territories. Evidence of the dehumanization of the Arabs could also be found in the language used by the top leadership of the Likud governments. Thus, Prime Minister Begin described persons belonging to the PLO as "two-legged animals,"[51] while General Rafael Eitan, the army's chief-of-staff and the future leader of the radical Tzomet party, called the inhabitants of the territories "drugged cockroaches."

In general, right-wing politicians, ideologues, and intellectuals tended to adopt a fundamentally stereotypical position toward the Arabs. Since Jabotinsky's time, Arabs as Arabs were considered the enemy, an adversary who can only be dealt with by military, coercive means. Given the realities of the Arab-Israeli conflict, it was relatively easy for the Likud to radicalize Israeli public opinion on the Arab question.

Under these circumstances, as could have been expected, Israel's political culture did not have the capacity to resist the evolution of the structure of otherness described in this essay. Given the situation of extreme and continuous national crisis, periodic military confrontations with neighboring countries and the local Arab population, and the legacy of Jewish history, the perception of the Arabs and, to some extent, the world at large as the Other seemed a natural consequence. The words of a highly popular Israeli song reflected this sense of otherness very clearly:

> The entire world is against us,
> it is an ancient melody
> that we have learned from our forefathers.
> We have learned this song from our elders,
> and we sing it as well,
> and after us our children
> and the grandchildren of our grandchildren
> here in Eretz Israel.
> But whoever is against us
> can go to hell![52]

In August 1992, Israel experienced a change in government. The Labor party reassumed the leadership and the Likud returned to opposition. The new prime minister, Yitzhak Rabin, declared his intention to move toward a quick agreement on autonomy for the West Bank and Gaza. A year later, in early September 1993, the PLO and Israel officially recognized each other, and on 13 September 1993, they signed a declaration of principles envisioning Palestinian self-rule in the occupied territories and, eventually, a final settlement.

It remains to be seen whether these dramatic events will lead to full-fledged peace between Arabs and Jews, and whether this new situation will, in turn, succeed in demolishing the long-established structure of otherness. In their efforts to achieve their respective national goals, Arabs and Jews have delegitimized each other for decades. Each group has seen the other as a "negative reference group."[53] The future of peace in the Middle East rests on their ability to change significantly their perceptions. Despite some positive political developments in the region, a recent book by one of Israel's most important writers, David Grossman, leaves serious doubts as to the likelihood of significant perceptual change among Arabs and Jews.[54] The breakthrough of 1993, on the other hand, leaves the analyst with a more optimistic conclusion.

NOTES

The author would like to thank the editors and Professor Jonathan Mendilow for their valuable comments on a previous version of this essay.

1. Ian S. Lustick, "The Political Road to Binationalism: Arabs in Jewish Politics," in *The Emergence of a Binational Israel: The Second Republic in the Making*, ed. Ilan Peleg and Ofira Seliktar (Boulder, Colo.: Westview, 1989), 97.
2. For an assessment of Israel's binational dilemma, see Peleg and Seliktar, *Emergence of a Binational Israel*.
3. See, for example, Fred J. Khouri, *The Arab-Israeli Dilemma*, 3d ed. (Syracuse, N.Y.: Syracuse University Press, 1985); Alvin Z. Rubinstein, ed., *The Arab-Israeli Conflict: Perspectives*, 2d ed. (New York: Harper-Collins, 1991); Avi Shlaim, *Collusion across the Jordan: King Abdullah, the Zionist Movement, and the Partition of Palestine* (New York: Columbia University Press, 1988).
4. See, for example, Alan Gerson, *Israel, the West Bank, and International Law* (London and Totowa, N.J.: Cass, 1978); J. N. Halderman, *The Middle East Crisis: Test of International Law* (Dobbs Ferry, N.Y.: Oceana, 1969); John N. Moore, ed., *The Arab-Israeli Conflict* (Princeton, N.J.: Princeton University Press, 1977).
5. For personal observations by policy makers, see the memoirs of Ben-Gurion, Dayan, Meir, Sadat, and Weizmann, among others. For the observations of others, see, inter alia, Saul Friedlander and Mahmoud Hussein, *Arabs and Israelis* (New York and London: Holmes & Meier, 1975); Sona Hassan and Amos Elon, *Between Enemies: A Compassionate Dialogue between an Israeli and an Arab* (New York: Random House, 1974); Amos Oz, *In the Land of Israel* (New York: Vintage, 1983), as well as a large number of fictional works (some of which are quoted in this essay).
6. See, for example, Shai Feldman, *Israeli Nuclear Deterrence: A Strategy for the 1980s* (New York: Columbia University Press, 1982); Steven J. Rosen, *Military Geography and the Military Balance in the Arab-Israel Conflict*, Jerusalem Papers on Peace Problems 21 (Jerusalem, 1977); Ilan Peleg, "Solutions for the Palestinian Question: Israel's Security Dilemma," *Comparative Strategy* 4, 3 (1984): 249–71.
7. Attitudes and perceptions are the focus of such studies as those by Yehoshafat Harkabi (*Arab Strategies and Israeli Responses* [New York: Free Press, 1977]) and John Edwin Mroz (*Beyond Security: Private Perceptions among Arabs and Israelis* [New York: Pergamon, 1982]).
8. Elie Rekhess, "The Israeli Arabs since 1967: The Issue of Identity" (Hebrew), *Skirot* 45; Mark A. Tessler, "Israel's Arabs and the Palestinian Problem," *Middle East Journal* 31, 3 (1977): 313–29.

9. Ofira Seliktar, "The Arabs in Israel: Some Observations on the Psychology of the System of Controls," *Journal of Conflict Resolution* 28, 2 (June 1984): 257.

10. Amnon Sella, "Custodians and Redeemers: Israeli Leaders' Perceptions of Peace, 1967–1979," *Middle Eastern Studies* 22, 2 (April 1986): 247–48; Ilan Peleg, *Begin's Foreign Policy, 1977–1983: Israel's Move to the Right* (Westport, Conn.: Greenwood, 1987), especially chaps. 3–4.

11. Lustick, "The Political Road to Binationalism."

12. Albert Memmi, *The Colonizer and the Colonized* (Boston: Beacon, 1967), 82.

13. I owe some of these observations to Professor Howard Marblestone of Lafayette College.

14. Julia Kristeva, *Strangers to Ourselves* (New York: Columbia University Press, 1991), 51–52. See also Helen Bacon, *Barbarians in Greek Tragedy* (New Haven, Conn.: Yale University Press, 1961); and Edith Hall, *Inventing the Barbarian,* Oxford Classical Monographs (Oxford: Oxford University Press, 1989).

15. On this question, see Virginia R. Dominquez, *White by Definition: Social Classification in Creole Louisiana* (New Brunswick, N.J.: Rutgers University Press, 1986), especially chap. 4.

16. Yael Feldman, "The 'Other Within' in Contemporary Israeli Fiction," *Middle East Review* 22, 1 (Fall 1989): 47.

17. Interestingly enough, one of the most important structures of otherness within the Jewish community of Palestine prior to and following the establishment of the State of Israel was the division between "Jew" and "Israeli." According to Y. Feldman ("The 'Other Within,'" 52), the Israeli was the "self," and the Jew the "other." Moreover, Feldman even believes that "the basic existential and ideological experience of Israeli culture is that of the Other. Besieged from within and without, contemporary Israeli identity experiences itself as Otherness" (52). As for Arab-Jewish relations, they were dominated by mutual rejection since the late nineteenth century. See, for example, Don Peretz, "Perceptions: How the Israelis and Arabs See Each Other," *The World and I* (April 1992): 469–83.

18. Yoram Peri, "From Political Nationalism to Ethno-Nationalism: The Case of Israel," in *The Arab-Israeli Conflict: Two Decades of Change*, ed. Yehuda Lukacs and Abdallah M. Buttah (Boulder, Colo.: Westview, 1988), 41–52.

19. Peretz, "Perceptions," 475.

20. Thus, in the 1980s, Knesset members from the far Right proposed changing the criminal code so that a Jew who kills an Arab for nationalist reasons would not be prosecuted according to the existing criminal law but would be dealt with preferentially (Peri, "From Political Nationalism to Ethno-Nationalism," 52).

21. Sammy Smooha, "Control of Minorities in Israel and Northern Ireland,"

Comparative Studies in Society and History 22, 2 (1980): 256–80, quotation at 264. See also Sammy Smooha, *Arabs and Jews in Israel.* Vol. 1, *Conflicting and Shared Attitudes in a Divided Society* (Boulder, Colo.: Westview, 1989).

22. David K. Shipler, *Arab and Jew: Wounded Spirit in a Promised Land* (New York: Penguin, 1986), 21–22.
23. Mina Tzemach and Ruth Tzin, *The Position of Israeli Youth in Regard to Democratic Values* (Jerusalem: Van Leer Jerusalem Foundation, 1984), 1–33.
24. Ibid., 17–18.
25. Ibid., 33.
26. Shipler, *Arab and Jew,* 28–30.
27. Ofira Seliktar, "The Arabs in Israel," 247.
28. Y. Feldman, "The 'Other Within'"; Gilead Moragh, "The Arab as 'Other' in Israeli Fiction," *Middle East Review* 22, 1 (Fall 1989): 35–40.
29. Moragh, "The Arab as 'Other' in Israeli Fiction," 35.
30. Ibid., 36.
31. Ibid., 37–39.
32. Yehuda Amir, "Interpersonal Contact between Arabs and Israelis," *Jerusalem Quarterly* 13 (Fall 1979): 3–17.
33. Yochanan Peres, *Ethnic Relations in Israel* (Tel Aviv: Sifriat Po'alim, 1976); Sammy Smooha, "Arabs and Jews in Israel: Minority-Majority Group Relations," *Megamot* 22, 4 (1976): 397–423.
34. Amir, "Interpersonal Contact between Arabs and Israelis," 7.
35. Ibid., 10–11.
36. John L. Sullivan, Michal Shamir, Nigel Roberts, and Patrick Walsh, "Political Intolerance and the Structure of Mass Attitudes: A Study of the United States, Israel, and New Zealand," *Comparative Political Studies* 17, 3 (October 1984): 319–44; and Michal Shamir and John L. Sullivan, "Jews and Arabs in Israel: Everybody Hates Somebody, Sometime," *Journal of Conflict Resolution* 29, 2 (June 1985): 283–305.
37. Shamir and Sullivan, "Jews and Arabs in Israel," 296.
38. Ibid., 303.
39. Sullivan, et al., "Political Intolerance and the Structure of Mass Attitudes," 336.
40. Ehud Sprinzak, *The Ascendance of Israel's Radical Right* (New York: Oxford University Press, 1991).
41. The idea of the generalized Other is incorporated into the Passover Haggadah: "In every generation, they rise to annihilate us, but the Almighty saves us from their hand." See also Yosef Yerashalmi, *Zakor: Jewish History and Jewish Memory* (Seattle: University of Washington Press, 1982); and Adi Ophir's chapter in this volume.
42. Edward Robins, "Attitudes, Stereotypes, and Prejudices among Arabs and Jews in Israel," *New Outlook* 15, 4 (November-December 1972): 46.
43. For a description of these events, see, for example, Ilan Peleg, *Begin's*

Foreign Policy, 1977–1983: Israel's Move to the Right (Westport, Conn.: Greenwood, 1987), especially chaps. 4–6.

44. Zvi Ra'anan, *Gush Emunim* (Tel Aviv: Sifriat Po'alim, 1980), 78.
45. Uri Zvi Greenberg, *Sefer Hakitrug Ve'haemuna* (The book of chastisement and faith) (Jerusalem: S'dan, 1938), 169.
46. Shlomo Avineri, *The Making of Modern Zionism: Intellectual Origins of the Jewish State* (New York: Basic, 1981), 179.
47. Walter Laqueur, *A History of Zionism* (New York: Holt, Rinehart, & Winston, 1972), 349.
48. Israel Hess, "Mitzvat Hagenocide Batorah" (The genocide commandment in the Torah), *Bat-Kol*, February 1980.
49. Moshe Shamir, "La'amod Mineged" (To stand against), in *El Mul Pnei Hamilhame Hachazaka* (Facing the tough war) (Tel Aviv: Shikmona, 1974), 116–28.
50. Ahron Davidi, "Israel's War Aims," in *Sefer Eretz Israel Hashlema* (The greater Israel book), ed. Ahron Ben-Ami (Tel Aviv: Greater Israel Movement and S. Freedman, 1977), 199–203.
51. Knesset speech, 8 June 1982.
52. The song is by Yoram Tehar-Lev. It is quoted in Ilan Peleg, *Begin's Foreign Policy*, 62.
53. Daniel Bar-Tal, "Delegitimizing Relations between Israeli Jews and Palestinians: A Social-Psychological Analysis," in *Arab-Israeli Relations in Israel: A Quest in Human Understanding*, ed. John E. Hofman (Bristol, Ind.: Wyndham Hall, 1988), 217–40.
54. David Grossman, *Sleeping on a Wire* (Tel Aviv: Kibbutz Mehuad, 1992).

Chapter 12

The Creation of Others:
A Case Study of Meir Kahane
and His Opponents

Gerald Cromer

Introduction

Meir Kahane provides an excellent example of the central contention
of this collection of essays—that identity, to quote Derrida, presupposes alterity.[1] Kahane defined himself as the antithesis of his arch
enemies, Arab and Jewish alike. Aviezer Ravitsky's remarks soon
after Kahane's election to the Knesset in July 1984 are, in fact, a
fitting description of his entire political career. "All along the way,"
he pointed out, "Kahane is busy fanning the flames of every confrontation. It would appear that only in this fashion, in the face of
confrontation, the I comes into its own and achieves its full identity."[2] Interestingly, though, Kahane was by no means alone in this
respect. His Jewish opponents were doing exactly the same thing.
They, too, were creating their own identities in—or, to be more precise, against—the image of their staunchest enemy. The process of
"otherizing" was, in short, a reciprocal one.[3]

Throughout his life, Meir Kahane berated American Jews for
their complacency. The apparent dearth of anti-Semitism, he noted
at the beginning of the seventies, should not be allowed to deceive
anyone. He said that the United States was beset by a series of
crises and, as is always the case in such situations, the gentiles
would sooner or later take out their frustrations on the classic
scapegoat—the Jew. Those who believed that America was different
had, according to Kahane, simply failed to learn the lesson of

history—that anti-Semitism is universal. Jews are always in danger because Esau hates Jacob wherever he may be.

Kahane's initial response to this impending danger was to establish vigilante squads to protect New York's elderly Jews from the local street gangs and hoodlums. These were soon augmented by a series of programs designed to teach the art of Jewish self-defense in general, and the use of firearms in particular. According to Kahane, this kind of education was of great symbolic value—it would "change the image of the Jew from one of a timid, frightened creature, to that of one who is quite as prepared to bash the head of a Jew-hater as anyone else is to physically protect his own rights."[4]

Kahane was well aware, however, of the limited practical value of these programs, which could only solve the problem of the "local Hitlers." There was, he argued, only one effective way of dealing with anti-Semitism on a national level: *aliyah* (emigration to Israel). Kahane therefore set up organizations such as Habayta (Homeward) and ZEERO (Zionist Emergency Exile Evacuation Research Organization) to convince American Jews that "a tragedy of massive proportions is coming" and that they should "flee the graveyard of exile and escape to Israel before catastrophe strikes." In short, it was "time to go home."[5]

For Kahane, Jew hatred was by no means the only, or even the most serious, threat to the survival of American Jewry. American Jews, he argued, put their faith in the melting pot because they felt it was the best way to prevent anti-Semitism. "A society that melted, meant a society where the Jew would not be different or singled out for persecution." As time went by, however, the process of the melting pot developed a dynamic of its own within the Jewish community. "The Jew who originally wanted liberalism to save himself, after decades of experiencing it and living it as a lifestyle, began to believe in it for its own sake, and began to disappear as a real Jew."[6]

Kahane regarded the religious leaders of American Jewry as ultimately responsible for the problems of assimilation. By "Reconstructing it, Reforming it, and making a mockery of Conserving it,"[7] they had caused the erosion of Judaism. There was, he insisted, only one way to prevent further assimilation within the Jewish community—a return to Orthodox Judaism or the "authentic Jewish idea." However, even this solution did not guarantee success. "The awesome majority influences of impurity and corruption," Kahane argued, made it very difficult to return to the fold while in exile. Genuine repentance was only really possible in the Holy Land—in an exclusive Jewish society "free of the spiritual and social assimilation of a foreign and abrasive culture."[8] Thus, *aliyah* was the only viable solution to the problems facing American Jewry.

After making *aliyah* himself, however, Meir Kahane began to adopt a much less sanguine view of the situation. He soon came to the conclusion that the same dangers that threaten Jewish survival in the Diaspora are also present in Israel. In fact, on several occasions Kahane argued that both threats—the external one of annihilation and the internal one of assimilation—are even more acute in the Jewish state. He therefore portrayed those responsible for them, Arabs and Jews alike, in the most negative way imaginable. Not only did they become his two personifications of evil; they were both also compared to what is commonly regarded as the absolute evil in Israeli society—to the Nazis.

Arabs as the Other

Christian missionaries and the Black Hebrews of Dimona were the first targets of Kahane's political activities in Israel. Within a very short time, however, they yielded pride of place to the local Arab population. In August 1972, less than a year after having made *aliyah* to Israel, Kahane organized the show trial of Muhamed Ali Jaabari, the mayor of Hebron, for his part in the 1929 massacre of the local Jewish community. Henceforth, Kahane was always at pains to point out the myriad ways in which the Arabs constituted a danger to the State of Israel.

Kahane continually drew attention to the problem of Arab terror and violence. Israeli Jews, he argued, are beset by fear. And this is by no means limited to those in the occupied territories. Even within the Green Line, parents are afraid to let their children go out by themselves, and soldiers are afraid to accept lifts. Kahane therefore urged the government to take more dramatic measures, including applying the death penalty to terrorists and expelling agitators and stone throwers. He took their refusal to do so as a justification for the vigilante activities of his supporters, who organized the euphemistically named Committee for Safety on the Streets. Nevertheless, Kahane argued that it was not Arab terrorism that constituted a threat to the survival of the Jewish state. The real problem lay elsewhere. The otherness of the Arabs resided not in any acts they committed, but in their very being. They were ontologically distinct—a separate or, to be more precise, inferior species.

> The Jewish soul is divine and pure. Its basic disposition is positive. In contrast, the gentile soul is materialistic and its basic disposition is negative. The difference between Israel and other nations is so great that they do, in fact, constitute two completely separate species. In the same way that God differentiated between inanimate and animate objects, He also made a distinction between people . . . and created a higher species . . . the Chosen People, the People of Israel.[9]

To ensure that they fulfilled their divine role, Jews were enjoined to separate themselves from other nations of the world. However, the "plague" of assimilation and intermarriage had not spared even the Jewish state. Less than three months after his election to the Knesset, therefore, Kahane tabled a private member's bill for "the prevention of assimilation between Jews and non-Jews and the holiness of the People of Israel."[10] According to the provisions of the bill, all educational institutions and public beaches were to be segregated, non-Jews would be prevented from living in a Jewish neighborhood except with the consent of the majority of the residents, and Jewish citizens would be forbidden to marry or even to have sexual relations with non-Jews.

But, to Kahane, it was not only marriage or even contact with non-Jews that constituted a threat to the continued existence of the Jewish state. The mere presence of Arabs in the country was a danger. Above all, he argued, Israel was endangered by the exceptionally high birth rate among Arabs on both sides of the Green Line. This, together with a number of demographic trends among Israeli Jews (e.g., a much lower birth rate, a large number of abortions, the continuing decline in immigration, and a steady increase in emigration), threatened the most minimal conception of Zionism—a state with a Jewish majority. If these trends were not reversed, the Arabs would sooner or later "peacefully, quietly, and non-violently become the majority in Israel, and then democratically vote the Jewish state out of existence."[11]

To prevent the growth of an Arab majority, Kahane put forward a number of ideas such as the abolition of child allowances to Arab families and the limitation of Jewish abortions to those cases in which the mother's life is endangered. However, he was always aware of the limited effect of these measures. In the early seventies, therefore, he began to advocate a series of more comprehensive programs, all of which were designed to achieve two broad aims—a reduction of the number of Arabs living in Israel and the "political neutralization" of those who remained.

The first program of this nature included a call for the establishment of an Emigration Fund for Peace that would provide Israeli Arabs with financial inducements to leave the country, as well as tax exemptions to encourage all residents of the occupied territories to opt for noncitizenship.[12] These proposals, however, were only a first step and were followed by more radical ones. Thus Kahane's private member's bill concerning "Israeli citizenship and a population transfer between Jews and Arabs"[13] advocated restricting citizenship to members of the Jewish people. Non-Jews who wished to live in Israel would only be able to do so as "resident aliens" lacking the right to be elected to public office or even to vote in elections. Those who were not prepared to accept this status would have the option of leaving the country willingly and receiving compensation for their property, or being forcibly removed.

Kahane argued that "any Jew with a modicum of an instinct for self-preservation" should support this bill. To him, it constituted the only viable solution to the immediate but seemingly intractable problems posed by the local Arabs[14] and would prevent the growth of an Arab majority in the Jewish state. Kahane also defended the bill on halakhic grounds—as the "embodiment of Jewish law" concerning the conditions under which gentiles are allowed to remain in the Holy Land.[15] More importantly, he regarded the law as a necessary prerequisite for the final redemption.

In order to understand this last claim, it is necessary to look, albeit briefly, at the theological underpinnings of Kahane's attitude toward the local Arab population. The very presence of the Jewish people in exile is, according to Kahane, a Hillul Hashem—a desecration of God's name. The gentiles, persecuting this weak and defenseless people, come to look upon their God with scorn and disdain. This is the derision of which the Psalmist said, "Wherefore shall the nations say: Where then is their God?"[16] While this condition had existed throughout nearly two thousand years of exile, it reached its climax in the horrors of the Holocaust. "The essence of Auschwitz," Kahane argued, "is not in the murder of Jews but in what that murder implied for the existence, power and truth of their God. There was never a greater Hillul Hashem than this."[17] God, therefore, had no choice but to establish the State of Israel in order to reaffirm His presence and dominion.

> And so, a Jewish state arose from the crematoria and the ashes, not because we deserved it, but because the gentile did. Because the punishment and awesome wrath of God were being prepared for a world that had mocked and humiliated the name of the Lord, God of Israel.[18]

Ironically, as Kahane was at pains to point out, God's name had also been desecrated in His own land. The following are just a few examples: Sexual relations with non-Jews not only defiled those involved, but they also "strike at the God of Israel through the daughters of His people." Moreover, Arab terror and violence were not only directed against the Jews; "each stone is directed at the Almighty Himself." And, most importantly, the continuing presence of Arabs was not only a rejection of Jewish rule, but their "rejection of Jewish sovereignty over the Land of Israel constitutes a rejection of the sovereignty and kingship of the Lord God of Israel."[19]

For Kahane, God's establishment of the State of Israel was the beginning of the final redemption. How and when this process would reach fruition, though, depended on the behavior of His chosen people. The Messiah, Kahane argued, will only come when the degradation of the Jews and, in turn, the desecration of God's name are brought to an end. This could be accomplished, in part at least, with the help of specific measures such as the outlawing of sexual relations with gentiles. However, the only way of ensuring complete success would be to rid the country of its Arab population. Consequently,

> Their transfer from the Land of Israel becomes more than a political issue. *It is a religious issue, a religious obligation, a commandment to erase Hillul Hashem.* . . . The great redemption can come immediately and magnificently if we do that which God demands. One of the great yardsticks of real Jewish faith . . . is our willingness to reject fear of man in favor of awe of God, and

remove the Arabs from Israel. . . . Let us remove the Arabs from
Israel and bring the redemption. *They must go.*[20]

But Kahane was pessimistic as to the likelihood of this happening.
The Jews, he felt, were unable to take this leap of faith because
their faith, not only in God but also in themselves, had been
destroyed by the "Arabs within."

Jews as the Other

The Arabs, according to Kahane, threatened the very existence of
the Jewish state. Nevertheless, in Israel as in the Diaspora, the
Jews, he insisted, were their own worst enemies. Motivated by a
deep self-hatred, politicians of all persuasions pursued policies that
endangered both the physical and the spiritual survival of the
Jewish state. To quote one Kahane flier, left and right, secular and
religious were all guilty of "stabbing Israel in the back."

While Kahane accused Israeli theater and movies of "consistently injecting the viruses of guilt, moral confusion and self-hate into
the body politic," he regarded the news media as being particularly
blameworthy in this respect. In his view, Israeli television was a
"fifth column" controlled by

> a small gang of defeatists who poison the minds of Jews, especially
> the young, with distorted stories of Israeli guilt, crimes and
> immoral policy. They corrupt the country from within, eroding the
> confidence and belief of the Jew in the rightness of the Israeli
> cause. They instill guilt over the actions of Israel against the
> "poor" Arab, weak and defenseless. There is a deliberate policy of
> presenting Israel in the worst possible light while burying the
> historical truths of Arab cruelty and slaughter of Jews—thus
> effectively distorting history. They stab Israel in the back, poison-
> ing and destroying that most priceless of weapons—faith in the
> justice of the Jewish cause.[21]

According to Kahane, even those on the right of the political spectrum had been influenced by this "cultural treason." Thus, he
accused Prime Minister Begin of treason since his Likud government
had returned the Sinai Peninsula to Egypt. After the Likud joined
the National Unity Government of the Labor leader, Shimon Peres,

this kind of criticism became even more strident. "Now," Kahane argued,

> it has come down to the final, ultimate betrayal. The party that once sang of both sides of the Jordan, and which had long since given up its ideological deposits from the East Bank, now announced that it was joining with Shimon Peres, the man they had accused for ten years of betrayal of the West one. . . . The last betrayal. The whole spirit of settlements and the whole idea of Jewish sovereignty in Judea, Samaria and Gaza is over. . . . The shameless agreement with Labor guarantees the end of the Jabotinsky vision [of a Greater Israel]. It is a disgusting example of cynical capitulation of ideals to power and money.[22]

Not surprisingly, the clearest expression of Kahane's denunciation of Likud is found in his manifesto for the 1988 Knesset elections.[23] Placing responsibility for the betrayal of the previous four years on what he disparagingly referred to as the "National Calamity Government," he blamed both Labor and Likud for the fact that the country was "falling apart." Consequently, there was no reason to prefer one party to the other. And, Kahane argued, the smaller parties on the right of the political spectrum were no better. They only disagreed with the Likud on minor issues such as the number of settlements to be established in the occupied territories. None of them, however, was prepared to say that the Arabs on both sides of the Green Line should leave or be expelled. Even the newly founded Moledet party only advocated the voluntary transfer of those living in the occupied territories. Consequently, they were all equally unacceptable.

"Dear Jew," Kahane pleaded,

> Consider a 100 meter race in which there are three runners. One of them runs 30 meters and falls. The second runs 50 meters and falls. The third runs 90 meters and falls. Who won? None of them. They all lost because in order to win you have to reach the finishing line. The winner is the one who achieves his aim; the one who was prepared to go all the way from the very beginning. Consequently, there is, in the final analysis, no difference between them. Not Peres, not Shamir, not Sharon and not Geula Cohen. . . . All of them are part of the silence that will, God forbid, bring upon us a disastrous national calamity.[24]

Regarding the danger of spiritual assimilation, those whom Kahane accused of "cultural treason" he also judged to be guilty of engaging in antireligious coercion. Thus, in the mideighties, he expanded his attack on the media to include their coverage of intermarriage and other issues of Jewish identity. In his last book[25] he drew attention to the growing number of plays and movies based on the theme of love between an Arab and a Jew, and in the Knesset he tabled a motion of no confidence in the government for banning a television program about the danger of assimilation and intermarriage in Israel.[26] Although the Israeli media was greatly concerned with these issues in the Diaspora, in the Jewish state it was, Kahane argued, completely oblivious to them.

At times, Kahane portrayed this process of "dejudaization" or "gentilization" as resulting from a kind of cultural diffusion through which Israel had become a "hideous caricature of America." Usually, however, he attributed it to the purposive action on the part of the founding fathers of the state who sought to subvert the Jewish tradition. According to Kahane, this antireligious coercion was most marked during the first decade of the state. "The leftist leaders," he argued,

> understood very clearly the danger that the Sephardi immigrants constituted to the state that they wanted to build. Everything the Middle-Eastern Jews represented conflicted with the aspirations of the "progressives." They were religious, while the leftists wanted to create a non-primitive, modern secular society. . . . Since they constituted a real threat to the continued political hegemony of the Labor party . . . the leftists engaged in a shocking and intentional campaign to spiritually destroy the Middle-Eastern Jews through the brutal use of government power and force. . . . Tens of thousands of youngsters were sent to anti-religious institutions, to the kibbutzim of the Marxist Hashomer Hatzair movement, where the 2000 year old Jewish soul was quickly destroyed. In the transit camps the immigrants were subject to the control of leftist officials . . . who denied them almost all contact with the representatives of the religious and ultra-nationalist parties. If the latter tried to enter the camps they were threatened, banished, and even arrested. The fascist anti-religious left even mobilized the police to enforce the isolation of the Eastern Jews.[27]

After the nationalist camp (those parties that opposed the return of any occupied territories) came to power, it was also criticized for

engaging in antireligious coercion. Thus, Kahane described the
"compulsory meetings" between Israeli Arabs and Jewish schoolchildren as just the latest ploy in the attempt to "remove the
barriers between Jews and gentiles, and thereby destroy the unique
holiness of the Jewish people." And, as he was at pains to point out,
these programs were introduced by a religious minister of education
in a right-wing Likud government.[28]

Not even the religious parties were immune to criticism. They
too were taken to task by Kahane for having "narrowed" or "crip-
pled" traditional Judaism. In fact, they were sometimes singled out
as being particularly dangerous in this respect. "If I were the evil
inclination," Kahane suggested,

> and I wanted to uproot the true and original Torah, I wouldn't
> disguise myself as a member of Mapam or the Citizens' Rights
> Movement. On the contrary, I would assume the role of a moderate
> religious person, a kind of mixture of Torah and foreign western
> culture, and begin to spread my Torah with all its falsehood and
> distortion.[29]

Kahane was often at pains to point out that the struggle against the
secularists, whom he referred to as Hellenists or "Hebrew-speaking
goyim," was even more important than the struggle against the
Arabs. As we have seen, however, Kahane did not limit his attacks
to the Israeli Left or, for that matter, to secular Israelis in general.
Nobody was beyond rebuke. Even the religious parties were chided
for having been infected with the malignancy of "gentilized foreign
culture." According to Kahane, he, and he alone, had remained
faithful to the authentic Jewish idea. Everyone else had falsified it.
They were all beyond the pale.

The Other as Nazis

While acknowledging that the impending rise of anti-Semitism in
the United States was due to the "political, social, economic, and
psychological realities of America today," Kahane often couched his
prophecies of doom in terms of the destruction of European Jewry
nearly half a century earlier.[30] Not only did he emphasize the
similarities between contemporary America and pre–World War II

Germany; he also reminded those who insisted that "it can't happen here" that people had similar opinions in Weimar in the late 1920s—in "the Weimar that could never fall into Hitler's hands but did."[31]

To support his claim that a holocaust could happen in the United States, Kahane emphasized the humanity of the Nazis. Rejecting the "devil theory of Nazism," he argued that "the German had no horns or tails, was not some form of aberration. He was a man and a woman like all others, just as decent and indecent, just as strong or weak." Consequently, it can happen anywhere. "As long as one gentile lives opposite one Jew, the possibility of a holocaust remains."[32]

Kahane did not hesitate to apply his Holocaust rhetoric to the Arab-Israel conflict, often portraying the Arabs as Nazis in a new guise.[33] To take just one example—the following flier was distributed on Holocaust Remembrance Day, 1987:

> Nazis of Bir-Zeit, leave our country!
>
> There will not be a second Holocaust!

> Hundreds of Jews were slaughtered by Arabs in Israel before even one Jew was destroyed in Nazi Germany. Today they continue to run wild with the clear aim of carrying out a new holocaust of the Jewish people. We will not allow the new Nazis to repeat the Holocaust. We come today on Holocaust Remembrance Day, to Bir-Zeit University, the center of incitement of the new Nazis, in order to tell them, "Nazis, leave our country!"

Kahane often legitimated his policies vis-à-vis the terrorists in particular and the Arabs in general by referring to the "mounds of corpses of Auschwitz and Treblinka." Since the Holocaust, he argued, Jewish existence had become not only the highest but the sole moral imperative. Now the yardstick for judging all actions, on both the individual and national level, had to be "Is it good for the Jews?" Political leaders who disregarded this new categorical imperative were guilty of "desecrating the memory of the six million martyrs."[34]

Carrying this line of reasoning a step further, Kahane actually accused Israeli politicians of implementing policies similar to those of Nazi Germany. Thus, he depicted the freeze on new settlements in the occupied territories and the ban on Jews living in certain Arab cities on the West Bank as part of a much more comprehensive program to create a "Juderein Judea and Samaria."[35] Further, he spoke of attempts on the part of Israel's secular leaders to subvert Jewish tradition as equivalent to organizing "a second Auschwitz for all Jews who wish to continue being Jewish."[36] In his *The Black Book: What the Left Did to the Middle-Eastern Jews*, which dealt with the mass immigration of the 1950s, he argued,

> The descendants of the communities that produced Maimonides, Nachmanides, Rav Alfasi, Rav Joseph Caro and an entire army of scholars, who did not know the taste of crime, sit today in the Ramla and Shata prisons. Truly the Jews of our time suffered two terrible holocausts. The first was a physical genocide launched by the gentiles. The second, which is less easily recognized, was the attack of the hellenized and secular Jews on the spirit of Judaism that beats in the hearts of hundreds of thousands of Jews from Arab lands. It is a crime which we are already paying for today, but whose ultimate cost will be frightening.[37]

Kahane also reverted to Holocaust rhetoric when criticizing contemporary educational policies in Israel. The "compulsory meetings" between Arab and Jewish schoolchildren were, he argued, not really designed to create deeper understanding between Jews and Arabs. In truth, they were part of "a deliberate policy of obliteration and assimilation." Like earlier instances of antireligious coercion, this kind of dialogue was likely or, to be more precise, was designed to cause a "spiritual holocaust." In fact, Kahane considered these meetings to be such a serious threat to Jewish survival that he referred to them in even more extreme terms. They were, he claimed, the "final solution."[38]

Kahane as Nazi

Of course, Kahane's opponents read the situation very differently. In fact, they tended to adopt exactly the opposite stance. According to their way of thinking, it was Kahane and his supporters who were beyond the pale. Thus, Noah Moses, the late editor of *Yediot Aharonot*, Israel's most widely read newspaper, argued as follows:

In the same way as the PLO is outside the consensus because of its racist stance that does not recognize the basic right of the Jews to live in the Land of Israel, so the racism of Kahane is outside the consensus because it does not recognize the right of the Arabs to do so. Kahane is beyond the border of Zionism, because Zionism and racism are contradictory concepts. Kahane is not just another, more extreme national movement. There is a red line between Herut, Tehiya, and Kahane.[39]

However, those who placed Kahane beyond the pale, or over the red line, argued not only that he was outside the Zionist consensus but also that his teachings contradicted all the values that the State of Israel held dear. Thus President Herzog explained his refusal to invite a representative of the Kach party to consultations on the formation of a government in terms of Kahane's "abrogation of civil rights and his negation of the principles of the Torah of Israel."[40] And Yitzhak Zamir, the attorney general, attacked Kahanism on the grounds that it "contradicts the principle of international law and the standards of civilized nations" and "distorts Judaism by presenting a biased picture of the tradition and heritage of the Jewish people." As such, he argued, "it also undermines the Declaration of Independence according to which the State of Israel grants complete social and political equality irrespective of race, nationality or religion."[41]

Many of Kahane's opponents also utilized the rhetoric of the Holocaust in attacking him. Comparing his worldview with that of the Nazis, they portrayed Kahane as a modern-day führer. One biography, for instance, bears the title *Heil Kahane!*[42] Kahane's supporters were compared to Hitler Youth, with the only difference between them being the color of their shirts—yellow instead of brown. And, most importantly, Kahane's ideology was depicted as "a Jewish variation of Nazism."

This particular analogy was most clearly expressed in M.K. Michael Eitan's speech to the Knesset Rules Committee in favor of limiting Kahane's parliamentary immunity. The main points of his speech, in which he pointed out the striking resemblance between a number of Kahane's private member's bills and the infamous Nuremburg Laws of 1935, have been summarized in the following table published in the daily paper *Hadashot*.[43]

Subject	Kahane's Proposal	Nazi Legislation
Residential restrictions	Non-Jews may not live within the Jerusalem city limits.	Apartments in Berlin and Munich rented to Jews may not be rented again to the Jew, his wife, or a Jewish undertaking without a special permit.
Prohibition of intermarriage	Male and female Jews, citizens and residents of the state are forbidden to marry non-Jews both in and out of the country. Mixed marriages will not be recognized.	Marriage between Jews and citizens of German blood or related blood is forbidden. Marriages in violation of the law are invalid even if performed outside the country.
Separation of students	All educational institutions in Israel will be segregated between Jews and non-Jews.	It is forbidden for Jewish students to study in German schools. They are only allowed to study in Jewish schools.
Extramarital relations between Jews and non-Jews (in Nazi legislation, between Jews and citizens of the Reich)	A. It is forbidden for male and female Jews who are citizens of the state to have full or partial sexual relations of any kind with non-Jews, including outside marriage. Violation of this provision is to be punished by two years' imprisonment.	A. Extramarital relations between Jews and subjects of the state of German blood or of related blood are forbidden.
	B. A non-Jew who has sexual relations with a Jewish prostitute or a Jewish male is to be punished by fifty years in prison. A Jewish prostitute or Jewish male who has sexual relations with a non-Jewish male is to be punished by five years in prison.	B. Jews are not permitted to employ in their households subjects of the state of German or related blood who are under the age of 45.
Prevention of meetings among youth	All summer camps, community centers, and other mixed institutions will be abolished. Visits by Jewish and Arab students in villages and homes, overseas trips in which Jewish students are guests in non-Jewish homes, and similar visits by non-Jews in Israel will be abolished.	It is forbidden to include non-Aryan students in visits to youth hostels. It is intolerable that Jewish students take part in school events in which they may come into contact with Aryan students.

Invidious comparisons of this nature were often used in an effort to convince political leaders as well as the general public of the need for concerted action against Kahane and his supporters. In many instances, they were reinforced through emphasis both the similarities between the political situation in Israel and in Weimar Germany (e.g., galloping inflation, a failed war) and the failure to take effective action against the Nazis during the early stages of their rise to power.[44] To quote Gideon Hausner, the former attorney general and government prosecutor at the Eichmann trial, "We have long accused the Germans of silence in the face of evil. We, of all people, must each of us speak out [against Kahane]. Not to do so would be a grave mistake."[45]

This train of thought found its clearest expression in a statement published by Yad Vashem, the national memorial to the victims of the Holocaust, immediately after Kahane's election to the Knesset. "We must," it urged,

> condemn these traces (of racism) not only when they appear amongst others, but also where they appear amongst us. Even if they are in response to threats and murder they must be denounced and eradicated while they are still in their prime. . . . The world around us is plagued by racism and the hatred of Israel and anti-Semitism is nourished by it. However, we, as victims of racism, must not be caught up by it. . . . Yad Vashem calls for a cleaning of the air and for a strengthening of education towards values which have been the guiding light of the Jewish people in all generations. This is the heritage of the martyrs of the Holocaust.

Various educational programs were introduced in the wake of Kahane's election to the Knesset. Most of these were based on the premise that a deeper knowledge of the Arabs, their history, culture, and language would undermine stereotypes and, in turn, reduce the hostility toward the Arabs fostered by Kahane. A number of observers, however, suggested a different way of solving the problem. They were of the opinion that a deeper awareness of the Jewish experience—"that you were strangers in the land of Egypt"—was more likely to generate empathy with the Arab minority. Thus, in the following statement, as well as several others, Yitzhak Zamir, the attorney general, drew attention to the following statement made by Justice Berenson in the Supreme Court about the lessons to be learned from Jewish history.

> When we were exiled from our country and banished from our land we were victims of the nations of the world among whom we dwelt,

and in every generation we knew the bitter taste of persecution, repression, and discrimination for no other reason than that we were Jews whose religion differs from all others. Given these bitter and wretched experiences . . . it was hoped . . . that we would not follow the perverse ways of the Gentiles, and that when we gained our independence in the State of Israel, we would take care to avoid any form of discrimination against law-abiding non-Jews who wished to live according to their own faith and religion.[46]

One explanation of the failure of Israeli Jews to put an end to discriminatory practices against Arabs was that, as a result of their history, Jews have always conceived of themselves as victims. Consequently, they never considered it possible that they could join the ranks of the victimizers. Viewed in this light, racism was regarded as "a crime against Jews, not a crime Jews are capable of inflicting on others."[47]

It was for this reason that a number of prominent educationalists bemoaned the fact that the Holocaust is depicted only in its most extreme forms—the death marches, concentration camps, gas chambers, etc.—and is portrayed as the "work of the devil" rather than of "civilized human beings like you and me." Because of this, they argued, it was difficult, if not impossible, to draw any implications from Nazi behavior that would be applicable to the behavior of Jews in Israel. If, however, the Holocaust was viewed as a "human experience," the Jewish majority might be forced to consider whether "it can happen here." In fact, if the Holocaust was seen as "a gradual decline to a criminal society," Israeli Jews might even come to the conclusion that the process of decline had already begun in their own society—that having returned to history, the Jewish people were in danger of repeating its worst excesses.[48] After all, there already was the "first Nazi in the Knesset."

Opponents as the Other

Many of Meir Kahane's opponents, including some of the most adamant, acknowledged that he was not sui generis. They emphasized instead the similarity between Kahane and other right-wing politicians. The sole difference between them, they insisted, was that Kahane said openly what they were only prepared to talk about behind closed doors. Thus, frequent reference was made to

Menachem Begin's description of Palestinian terrorists as "two-legged animals" and Raful Eitan's portrayal of the Arabs in the occupied territories as "drugged cockroaches in a battle." These statements, it was argued, revealed the Israeli Right in its true colors—"as a gallery of Kahanes, of varying but converging views."[49]

Proponents of this point of view not only pointed out the essential similarity between Meir Kahane and other leaders of the nationalist camp; they also drew attention to the interaction between them. Thus, Kahane's entry into the Knesset and subsequent rise in popularity were viewed as a logical conclusion to what one columnist referred to as "the long journey to the right in Israeli society." According to this way of thinking, Kahane was "a rather wild, but legitimate child of the nationalist camp."[50]

The growing ascendancy of right-wing factions within existing parties (e.g., the Likud and the National Religious party) and the establishment of new parties dedicated to the idea of the Greater Israel (e.g., Tehiya and Morasha in the 1981 and 1984 Knesset elections, respectively) were regarded as important manifestations of this trend. So, too, was the drift toward "dangerous violence" within the extraparliamentary group, Gush Emunim—from the establishment of unauthorized settlements in the occupied territories to engagement in civil disobedience against the evacuation of the Sinai Peninsula and the involvement in terrorist activities in the West Bank. As Ehud Sprinzak has pointed out,

> From a historical vantage point, it is not difficult to see how the illegalism of Gush Emunim reached groups with a lower level of idealism, negative motives and a lack of self-restraint . . . groups characterized by a tendency to intensive violence and a complete disdain of the law appeared on the fringes of Gush Emunim. . . . After a long period of failure and inability to attract the attention of the Israeli public, Rabbi Kahane came to the realization that the only way in which he could succeed was to act as a catalyst for the extremist trend that Gush Emunim had begun . . . and he systematically did so.[51]

The trend toward the right was not only thought to have led to the violence of Meir Kahane's most rabid supporters; it was also regarded as the cause of his general rise in popularity. Thus his sudden surge in the public opinion polls after the Knesset elections in 1984[52] was attributed, in part at least, to the failure of other right-wing politicians to censure Kahane or take any concerted action against him.

The leaders of the national religious camp were regarded as particularly blameworthy in this respect. Attention was frequently drawn to the Chief Rabbinate's "very weak statement" about the need for harmonious relations with the Arab minority, the National Religious party's opposition to laws forbidding incitement to racism, and the refusal of the religious school system to adopt programs designed to foster Arab-Jewish coexistence. Together they were interpreted as a seal of approval or, to quote a *Jerusalem Post* editorial,[53] as "a certificate of Kashrut" for Kahane and the ideas that he espoused.

Interestingly, leaders of the nationalist camp insisted that it was the leftist parties that had caused Kahane's entry into the Knesset. Those who voted for the Kach party, it was argued, had not done so because they agreed with his worldview. Rather, they simply wished to register a protest vote against government complacency toward, and leftist sympathy for, Arab troublemakers. Not surprisingly, this point of view found its clearest expression in an editorial of *Nekuda*, the journal of the Council of Jewish Settlements in Judea, Samaria, and Gaza:

> Most of those amongst us, and they are relatively few, who voted Kach, did so in response to what appeared to them as the government's failure to enforce the law against Arab troublemakers, especially those on the roads of Judea and Samaria. . . . There is no doubt that those who voted Kach . . . did so as a response to the attitude of Yossi Sarid, Shulamit Aloni, and others like them, who ridicule any patriotic Jewish stance and, by and large, justify in a sick and anti-nationalist way the Arab viewpoint.[54]

The non-Zionist *haredi* (ultra-orthodox) parties took this argument a step further. They portrayed Meir Kahane and the ideology he espoused as both essentially similar to, and the logical conclusion of, secular Zionism as a whole. According to the Agudat Yisrael daily *Hamodia*,

> Since Zionism is his basic worldview, Kahane is not only closer to Geula Cohen, Yuval Neeman, or Yitzhak Shamir than he is to *haredi* Judaism and Agudat Yisrael . . . he is also closer to Yossi Sarid and Shulamit Aloni . . . the moribund debate between them is not concerned with basic principles, it is just about style and

mode of expression. Kahane does not constitute a deviation from Zionism . . . because he is influenced above all by the idea of establishing and maintaining a Jewish state, and the idea of "taking our future into our own hands."[55]

Thus, each political camp put forward different or, to be more precise, dramatically opposed explanations as to why Meir Kahane had been elected to the Knesset. Interestingly, however, the line of reasoning was always the same. Each group claimed that Meir Kahane's electoral success was due to the fact that his worldview constituted the logical conclusion of its rival's ideology. Moreover, in the case of the nationalist camp, many observers believe that Kahane's entry into the Knesset and his subsequent rise in popularity had prompted other right-wing politicians to adopt similar policies. Thus, in one case, two members of the government (Michael Dekel, the Likud minister of agriculture, and Yosef Shapiro, the National Religious party minister without portfolio) were taken to task for advocating the transfer of the Arab population. Once again, however, it was Gush Emunim that was criticized as being most influenced by Kahane. A series of violent actions carried out against Arabs in the occupied territories were cited as evidence of Kahane's deleterious influence on that group. According to Avishai Margalit, a prominent activist in the Peace Now Movement:

> There are now two approaches in Gush Emunim—settlement and expulsion. . . . The latter is intent on creating a public atmosphere and public pressure that will lead to the expulsion of the Arabs . . . that is the logic behind the demand to outlaw completely the throwing of stones. The only way to achieve this aim is to ensure that there will be no Arab children on the West Bank or, in short, to expel all the Arabs. Daniella Weiss . . . represents a new factor in the occupied territories: the expulsion option. Kahane himself is on the fringes of Israeli society. . . . Whilst Rabbi Levinger and Daniella Weiss are not on the margin, they are, to all intents and purposes, Kahanists. Consequently, that rogue is benefiting from their lawlessness, and his work is being done by others.[56]

This process of radicalization, or what Yehoshofat Harkabi has aptly referred to as Kahanization,[57] was attributed to the fact that Kahane's electoral success had given a certain degree of legitimacy to his policies and the ideology on which they were based. Consequently, those who had previously been wary of expressing such ideas in public now felt free to do so. Several images were used to describe this process (e.g., the opening of a Pandora's box of evil and the breaking of a barrier of shame), but the most vivid one was clearly provided by the satirist B. Michael in the afternoon daily *Hadashot*. "Kahane's strength," he argued,

> is to be found in his lack of shame, in the legitimacy that he gives to other dark forces, in the breaches that he makes in the red line . . . Kahane is the AIDS virus in the weary body of Israeli society . . . . he undermines what remains of its immunity system. We will not die, it seems, from Kahane himself, but he makes it much easier for the fatal illness to develop.[58]

The worst, therefore, was yet to come. As one columnist pointed out in an article aptly entitled "The Law of Relativity,"[59] "In comparison to Rav Kahane, Rabbi Levinger suddenly sounds like the apogee of moderation. In four years' time another monster will arise and Kahane will seem like a moderate. He may even say a few fitting words against extremists."

Conclusions

Meir Kahane not only placed the entire secular establishment beyond the pale, but he also castigated the leaders of the religious parties for having betrayed the "authentic Jewish idea." And, in order to drive this message home, Kahane compared their policies to those of Nazi Germany. Both their sins of omission and their sins of commission were equated with those of the Nazis during the Holocaust. Interestingly, these arguments comprised two of the major themes in the public outcry against the "growing menace of Kahanism." From the time he first entered the Knesset in 1984, Meir Kahane was roundly condemned for distorting Judaism. Despite protestations that "Nazism is unique and a very particular kind of satanic behavior,"[60] his critics, as we have seen, frequently compared his policies with those of Adolf Hitler. According to this way of thinking, Kahane advocated a policy of "Judenrein in reverse."

Clearly, therefore, Kahane's opponents were involved in exactly the same process as he was—creating their own identities by contrasting themselves with the image of their staunchest adversary. However, the situation was somewhat more complicated, as reflected in two debates that took place in the wake of Kahane's entry into the Knesset. One centered on his worldview, while the other revolved around the relationship between his worldview and other political ideologies. Kahane was simultaneously portrayed as both sui generis and essentially similar to other political leaders. This apparent contradiction stems from the fact that the strategy of Kahane's opponents was directed at two "others" at one and the same time. Not only did they try to place Kahane beyond the pale; they also used his electoral success and subsequent rise in popularity to attack and exclude rival ideologies. While this latter strategy was in no way intended to blunt their critique of Kahane himself, it may well have unintentionally had that effect After all, emphasizing the similarity and interaction between Kahane and other political leaders has the effect of blurring the differences between them. If they differ in degree rather than kind, then Kahane can no longer be regarded as evil incarnate. He is, at best, just a little worse than others.

NOTES

1. Jacques Derrida, "Deconstruction and the Other," in *Dialogues with Contemporary Thinkers*, ed. Richard Kearney (Manchester. University of Manchester Press, 1984).
2. Aviezer Ravitsky, "The Roots of Kahanism: Consciousness and Political Reality," *Jerusalem Quarterly* 39 (1986): 96.
3. This essay is only concerned with the rhetorical aspects of this process. For a description of its legal manifestations, see Gerald Cromer, "The Prevention of Racial Incitement in Israel," in *Under the Shadow of Weimar: Democracies Confront Racial Incitement*, ed. Louis Greenspan and Cyril Levitt (New York: Praeger, 1993).
4. Meir Kahane, *The Story of the Jewish Defense League* (Los Angeles: Nash, 1971), 115.
5. For a detailed presentation of this argument, see Meir Kahane, *Time to Go Home* (Los Angeles: Nash, 1972).
6. Meir Kahane, *Why Be Jewish? Intermarriage, Assimilation, and Alienation* (New York: Stein & Day, 1977).
7. It is important to point out, however, that the leaders of modern orthodoxy were also held to task in this regard. See, for instance, *Jewish Press*, 4 January 1985.
8. Meir Kahane, *They Must Go* (New York: Grosset & Dunlop, 1981), 55.
9. *Between Israel and the Nations* (Jerusalem: Kach Movement, n.d.), 40.
10. Meir Kahane, *Law for the Prevention of Assimilation between Jews and Non-Jews and the Holiness of the People of Israel* (unpublished bill,

1984). This proposal is represented in full in Yair Kotler, *Heil Kahane!* (New York: Adama, 1986), 198–203.

11. This argument is most clearly expressed in Meir Kahane, *Uncomfortable Questions for Comfortable Jews* (Secaucus, N.J.: Lyle Stuart, 1987), 59–68. It must be pointed out that on many occasions Kahane actually portrayed the high Arab birth rate as a form of politicization; i.e., they have many children in order to achieve a majority within the State of Israel.

12. For further details of this proposal, see Meir Kahane, *Our Challenge: The Chosen Land* (Rodnor, Pa.: Chilton, 1974), 46–50.

13. Meir Kahane, *Law of Israeli Citizenship and a Population Transfer between Jews and Non-Jews, 1985* (unpublished bill). This proposal is reprinted in full in Kotler, *Heil Kahane!*, 203–8. The name of the bill is based on Kahane's contention that the removal of the Arabs constitutes the "second stage of a population transfer" that began in 1948 with "the flight of Jews from Arab and Moslem lands accompanied by a violent expulsion with no compensation for confiscated property."

14. One flier, for instance, addressed the extent to which the Arab population constitutes a drain on the country's limited economic resources in the following terms:

> The leftists from Peace Now claim there is insufficient money for both settlements and deprived neighborhoods. Lies! Falsehood! It is untrue. The country has enough money for both urban renewal and the establishment of new settlements. So where is all the money? . . . The Arabs swallow it up. . . . Give us the power to deal with the Arabs and then there will be enough money for everything. There is no alternative!

15. For further details, see Kotler, *Heil Kahane!*, 204–5.

16. Ps. 115:2.

17. Meir Kahane, *Forty Years* (Jerusalem: Institute for Jewish Ideas, 1981), 3.

18. Ibid.

19. Ibid., 48–49.

20. Kahane, *They Must Go*, 275–76. Italics in original. For a similar argument concerning the need for "an immediate return of the Jews of the Exile home to the Land of Israel," see Meir Kahane, *Numbers 23:9* (Miami Beach: Block, n.d.), 18–24.

21. *Jewish Press*, 31 August 1984.

22. Ibid., 14 September 1984.

23. For an abridged version of the manifesto in English, see Kahane's column in *Jewish Press*, 20 May 1989.

24.. Ibid. Shimon Peres and Yitzhak Shamir were the leaders of the Labor and Likud parties, respectively. Ariel Sharon was on the right wing of the Likud, and Geula Cohen was a member of the maximalist Tehiya party. At a press conference held immediately after his party was excluded for the 1988 Knesset elections, Kahane urged his supporters not to vote at all. "There is," he argued, "not Kach and nearly Kach; there is Kach and only Kach."

25. Kahane, *Uncomfortable Questions*, 125.
26. *Divrei Knesset* 2 (1986): 1981–82.
27. Ibid., 3440.
28. *Divrei Knesset* 1 (1985): 58.
29. Meir Kahane, "On Joy and Sorrow," *This Is the Way of the Torah* 3 (Sivan 5746): 83. Mapam and the Citizens' Rights Movement are two parties on the left of the Israeli political spectrum that many traditional Jews regard as being antireligious.
30. Paradoxically, the "temporary embargo" on anti-Semitism in the United States was attributed, in part at least, to gentile guilt about the Holocaust. For further details of this argument, see Kahane, *Time to Go Home*, 16–21.
31. Significantly, Kahane's Jerusalem exhibit of Jew hatred in America is called the Museum of the Potential Holocaust. As far as the written word is concerned, these ideas are most clearly expressed in his essay entitled "Once upon a Time" in Meir Kahane, *Writings, 5732–5733* (Jerusalem: Jewish Identity Center, 1973), 81–83.
32. Ibid., 83.
33. Kahane's criticism of the world response to the Arab-Israel conflict was also couched in terms of the Holocaust. In a "campaign of defiance" against the universal condemnation of Israel's response to the Palestinian uprising in the occupied territories, he argued as follows: "Let us not fear the world. Far better a Jewish state that survives and is hated by the world than an Auschwitz that brings us its love and sympathy."
34. Meir Kahane, *Never Again: A Program for Jewish Survival* (Los Angeles: Nash, 1971), 212.
35. *Devrei Knesset* 6 (1985): 489. In contrast, those who took a determined stand against the Arabs were compared to the ghetto resistance fighters; they were regarded as the modern equivalents of Mordechai Anilevitz and Yosef Glasman.
36. Kahane also referred to the gentile missionary efforts in the rhetoric of the Holocaust. "The Jew," Kahane argued, "is destroyed equally through the ovens of Auschwitz and through the loss of the Jewish soul to the missionaries and cults."
37. Meir Kahane, *The Black Book: What the Left Did to the Middle-Eastern Jews* (Jerusalem: Kach Movement, n.d.), 12. In fact, Kahane suggested that this spiritual holocaust be marked by a day of remembrance in exactly the same way as the physical destruction of European Jewry has been commemorated in Israel since 1959.
38. Meir Kahane, *Four No-Confidence Motions* (Jerusalem: Kach Movement, n.d.), 2.
39. *Yediot Aharonot*, 15 September 1985.
40. Statement concerning the decision not to invite a representative of Kach to the consultations on the formation of a government, 1 August 1984.

41. The quotations are taken from the unpublished protocol of the Knesset House Committee's deliberations on the question as to whether Meir Kahane's parliamentary immunity should be restricted.
42. Kotler, *Heil Kahane!*
43. *Hadashot*, 16 November 1984. Interestingly, the Kach movement has recently published a similar table comparing "two murderous covenants"—those of the PLO and those of the Nazis.
44. See, for instance, Yoram Peri, "The Road to Weimar," *Davar*, 25 July 1984, and Dan Horowitz, "Israel Is Ripe for Fascism," *Davar*, 7 December 1984.
45. *Jerusalem Post*, 3 August 1984. Paradoxically, Kahane adopted a similar stance vis-à-vis "extremist groups" in the United States. See, for instance, Kahane, *Never Again!*, 255–60.
46. See, for instance, Yitzhak Zamir's article, "Cracking Down on Kahane," *Jerusalem Post*, 14 December 1984.
47. Charles S. Liebman, "The Religious Component in Israel Ultra-Nationalism," *Jerusalem Quarterly* 41 (Winter 1987): 142.
48. For a more detailed description of this argument, see Arik Carmon, "A Decline along the Continuum of Evil," *Maariv*, 25 November 1984, and Haim Avni's comments on Aviezer Ravitsky, *The Phenomenon of Kahanism: Consciousness and Political Reality* (Jerusalem: Institute of Contemporary Jewry, 1985), 43–44.
49. Allen Shapiro, "Kahanes by Another Name," *Jerusalem Post*, 15 August 1988.
50. *Davar*, 27 July 1984.
51. Ehud Sprinzak, *Every Man Whatsoever Is Right in His Own Eyes: Illegalism in Israeli Society* (Tel Aviv: Sifriat Poalim, 1986), 142–43.
52. Kahane's party, Kach, received 1.2 percent of the votes cast for the eleventh Knesset in 1984. However, by August of the following year, public opinion polls predicted that as many as 9 percent of the electorate would have voted Kach if the elections had been held at that time.
53. *Jerusalem Post*, 7 August 1986.
54. *Nekuda* 76, 8 August 1984.
55. *Hamodia*, 8 August 1984.
56. *Yediot Aharanot*, 12 May 1987. Daniella Weiss was the general secretary of Gush Emunim from 1985 to 1988. Rabbi Levinger was one of its most influential ideologues. They were widely regarded as leaders of the trend toward the extreme right within the settler movement.
57. Yehoshofat Harkabi, *Fateful Decisions* (Tel Aviv: Am Oved, 1986), 231.
58. *Hadashot*, 24 August 1984. Interestingly, this argument was also made after Kach was disqualified from the Knesset election in 1988, and the newly founded Moledet party, which advocated the transfer of the Arabs from the occupied territories, won two seats and its leader subsequently became minister without portfolio in the Likud-led government.
59. *Yediot Aharonot*, 27 July 1984.
60. Aharon Megged, "The Kahane Affair," *Davar*, 17 August 1984.

Chapter 13

The Woman As Other in Israeli Cinema

Orly Lubin

One of the dramatic highlights of Michal Bat Adam's film *Moments* (1979) occurs when the underlying sexual tensions between Yula (Bat Adam) and Ann (Brigette Catillon) hover at the breaking point on a hotel bed in Jerusalem. After touring the unfamiliar city together, the two women, one a Tel Avivian, the other a French tourist, laze indulgently on the bed, opening up emotionally to each other and, perhaps, lightly touching.

The scene develops into a love scene but not before another, apparently necessary, element is introduced—Yula's boyfriend, played by the definitive male of the Israeli cinema, Assi Dayan. What began as the prelude to an intentional and dramatic climax of intimacy and sexual love between two women turns into a trite display of pornography.

It begins with the most basic of all situations in this genre: a man observing two passionately aroused women, partially undressed, about to make love. The act becomes pornographic as it is performed before the penetrating gaze of a man who derives sexual gratification from observing the scene. He is using the women for his voyeuristic pleasure. They are thus transformed from subjects of love into objects of exploitation.

The scene continues as Dayan sleeps with both of them—another model in the genre. As a result of this form of intercourse—and the film does not offer any (lesbian) alternatives—the ultimate connection between the two women is achieved by means of the male organ: the movement of the phallus from one woman to the other.

305

Only the phallus, we are being told, has the power to constitute female *and* interfemale sexuality.

Moments is a film in which the main characters are women, and the main theme is women's experience. The constitution of the female subject is the heart of the narrative and the subject of the dialogue between the women: everyone has told Yula that she has no talent; her boyfriend has told her that she wrecks everything important; Yula goes to Jerusalem to try to fulfill herself by writing, and there she meets Ann.

The film was written by a woman, directed by a woman, and a woman stars in it (and in this specific case, the viewer/critic is also a woman). Yet despite this, the constitution of women's sexuality is achieved through the "penetrating gaze" of the voyeuristic "peeping Tom"—the reifying male. Thus, the representation of women in this film is no different from that of most other films in which women are not the main subjects of the film, are not central to the narrative, and have no part in its creation.

In film theory, the concept of the penetrating gaze has been used to describe the apparatus both for film enjoyment in general and for representing the female in particular. Expounded by Laura Mulvey (1975) in an article that is regarded as a classic, the concept has been discussed, criticized, and updated by, among others, Mulvey herself (1981). According to this concept, woman's specific "otherness" differs from the otherness of other minorities in that the core of her otherness consists in her being subjected to a penetrating gaze. This gaze reifies her as it turns her into the object of the male's voyeuristic pleasure.

Under the penetrating gaze of the male, women are not experienced as active flesh-and-blood persons. Whether under the penetrating gaze of the man in the film, the male viewer in the audience, or the male camera/director on the set, the woman becomes a thing, a displayed object to be used. This is the dominant mechanism through which the cinema marginalizes women as the Other.

In films, as in culture in general, the marginality or otherness of women is not simply the result of specific moments or situations. Rather, the text constructs a normative world in which the woman is always perceived as inferior. Lacking any position at the center, she does not function as an autonomous, coherent self. Instead, her entire existence depends on and is marginal to that which lies at the center, that is, the normative phallocentric system that sees that which the phallus represents as perfection. Thus, the female (margin) is not a counterpart of the male (center), but an object to be used by him. She exists solely to fulfill a function for him: to be the object of his sexual voyeuristic gratification.

The problem raised by feminists scholars is, how is it possible for women to enjoy films like Garry Marshall's *Pretty Woman* (1990) or Luc Besson's *Nikita* (1990), two modern Pygmalion-like tales in which the women are tamed and shaped to fit precisely into the molds required by patriarchal society, or Howard Hawks's *Gentlemen Prefer Blondes* (1953), in which, as in so many other films, the woman's body is commercialized and put on permanent display (the very display of which becomes thematicized) for the enjoyment of the viewer?[1]

Mulvey, in her later article (1981), formulated her psychoanalytic explanation, comprised of three components: "Freud's concept of 'masculinity' in woman, the identification triggered by the logic of a narrative grammar, and the ego's desire to phantasize itself in a certain, active manner" (in Penley 1988, 72). Of course, this explanation presupposes a Freudian view in which woman is defined in terms of absence as an *homme manque*, as devoid of or lacking a penis. However, this Freudian view has been severely criticized through feminist readings of the case of Dora (see Bernheimer and Kahane 1985) and critiques of the Oedipus complex.

A film like *Moments* seems to indicate that women do not necessarily position women in a different way and that the female gaze is not necessarily different from that of the male. It is not the sex of the filmmaker that determines the positioning of the women characters (or the women viewers), but rather the normative world created by the text.

The most potent factor in defining the woman's position in the normative world built by a text is the depiction of the character of women in it. The way the text positions and judges the female characters transmits to me, the female viewer, my position and the way I am to be judged in the "real" world. Through this positioning, I become aware of my otherness. Thus, just as women can create a text in which women are marginal, it is theoretically (and not only theoretically) possible for a man to create a text in which the woman, constituted as an autonomous subject, is positioned at the center.

The opinions of some feminist theoreticians notwithstanding, women do not necessarily read texts differently than men. Reading and viewing are acquired skills and not functions of biological differences. Insofar as women, like men, learn to read and view within the hegemony, any difference between the way that men and women read/view can only emerge within the context of that system.

Therefore, a possible mechanism for a nonpatriarchal form of reading/viewing is the technique of subversive reading, which becomes, ipso facto, feminist reading. In such readings, the woman reads against the grain of the text. Such readings, which challenge the plain meaning of the text, permit the woman a coherent autonomous existence. Nevertheless, just as there are many women who do not write subversive texts, so there are many women readers who, contrary to the opinions of some feminist theoreticians, do not perform subversive readings (see Lubin 1993). A hegemonic text, adhering to a set of norms defined by the center, situates woman at the periphery. A feminist text is not simply a text that focuses on woman's experience but is one in which I, the female reader, can constitute my subjectivity as I read without having to struggle against it. A text can also be subversive. While establishing a hegemonic set of norms, it can simultaneously, through the same words, expose their hegemonic character. Thus, by exposing the norms as humanly constructed rather than naturally given, it can provide the female reader with the means to resist them. Similarly, a text that purports to be feminist can actually be hegemonic.[2] While seeming to position women at the center, it can subvert this positioning through negative judgments and negative consequences.

The focus of this analysis, therefore, is twofold: first, the devices employed by the text, such as the penetrating gaze and the positioning of women, that reify women and establish the otherness of the female character and, through her, the female viewer; and, second, the appropriation and use of these devices by the Other—the female camera/director—in those instances where they subvert the hegemonic norms.

The number of full-length feature films produced in Israel—380 —permits a fairly accurate generalization concerning the way in which women are represented in them (Schnitzer 1993). Virtually all of these films have been made by men. While women have made a large number of short films, the number of feature films made by women is quite small—only fourteen (six of them by Bat Adam).[3]

The device of the penetrating gaze is employed in almost every Israeli film in which there is a female character. In almost all such films, women's sexuality is displayed—not as a central theme or a plot catalyst, but as a contingent prop. However, careful analysis reveals that despite the recurring use of this mechanism to position women as inferior, it is not the dominant one. In Israeli films, the dominant mechanism is not the penetrating gaze but rather social positioning—women's professional standing, their place in the community, and their role in the family: the war widow in Gilberto Toffano's *Siege* (1969), the soldier's wife in Yossi Somer's *Burning Memory* (1989), the girlfriend of the soldier who is killed and who then marries his best friend in Shimon Dotan's *Repeat Drive* (1982), the prostitute and the housewife in endless films, and the helpmate in Shmuel Imberman's *Don't Give a Damn* (1987) and in Amos Gutman's *Himmo, King of Jerusalem* (1987), or women in such stereotyped female professions as teaching or nursing. Frequently, however, no mention is made of a woman's vocation: either she has none, or her working only occurs off-screen.

Even when the woman has a profession (e.g., the physical training teacher in Uri Barbash's *Where Eagles Fly* [1990]), it is irrelevant to the plot and inconsequential to her life and to her relations with the world. Furthermore, as is the case in this film, her profession is only used as an excuse for displaying her body. Even when the woman fulfills an economic function equal to that of her husband, as in Jacob Goldwasser's *Over the Ocean* (1991), where both run a family business, her main function, in terms of plot and theme, is as the sister of a fallen soldier. While her husband, who is responsible for the financial well-being of the family, is anxious to emigrate, she feels prevented from doing so because of her responsibility to visit her brother's grave. Thus, while the husband's actions are based on his central function as a provider, her actions derive from her role as a man's sister.

In short, most Israeli films construct a normative world in which the woman is positioned, socially and professionally, at the margins. There are, however, a few films in which a woman is positioned at the center of the action. These include *The Summer of Aviya* (1988), a joint enterprise of the writer and leading actress, Gila Almagor, and the director, Eli Cohen, which deals with a child (marginal) and a mentally disturbed woman (also marginal) whose heroic past is mentioned and then forgotten; Isaac Zepel Yeshurun's *Noa at Seventeen* (1982), in which strong women deride and emasculate the men; and Avraham Heffner's *Laura Adler's Last Love Affair* (1990), a film about the Yiddish theater and its star actress, both in a state of decline. There are also films in which the women are less stereotypical, such as Eitan Green's *American Citizen* (1992), where, in addition to a stereotypical nymphomaniac groupie, there is a serious career woman, a pianist who initiates all of her professional and romantic pursuits, creating her own world. But in most Israeli films, as already pointed out, women are not central and their marginal positioning is determined by their place in the community.

In Hollywood films, the mechanism of the penetrating gaze is the dominant one used in portraying women. In these films, the objectification of women by using them for sexual pleasure is the dominant mode of marginalizing women on screen and, by extension, in the audience. The mechanism of social positioning is also actively used but is not dominant. In Israeli films, on the other hand, the mechanism of social positioning is the dominant one, although that of the penetrating gaze is very active as well. This results primarily from mainstream Zionist culture's suppression of the sexual body and the privileging of the body of the worker attached to the hoe or the plow.[4] Thus, sexuality and eroticism are subordinated to the national project. When the sexual body again appears in Israeli culture, it functions as an act of subversion. Unable to constitute an autonomous female subject in the spheres privileged by Zionism (i.e., community and work), poets, writers, or those filmmakers discussed in this article who seek to represent female experience will often have to turn to the sphere of sexuality.[5]

However, in the very act of rendering the sexual body as Other, Zionism has provided women artists with a space in which to constitute the female subject. Whereas the power of Zionist culture renders difficult any effort to position women at the center socially and professionally, its silence regarding the sexual body leaves a space into which women artists can move. And, in the case of films, the move to place the sexual body at the center entails the mechanism of the reifying penetrating gaze. Only now, the penetrating gaze serves to subvert the hegemonic, patriarchal culture by representing the woman as a sovereign and autonomous being with her own center.

This is a subversive rather than a revolutionary act. A revolutionary act would be to represent the sovereign autonomous woman functioning professionally and socially. Restoring women to the center by focusing on the sexual body is, rather, an act of subversion (i.e., an action that subverts but does not overthrow the hegemonic system).

A film in which the sexual body and the penetrating gaze is used subversively is Dina Zvi-Riklis's 1984 short film, *Coordania*. This film tells the story of two families left behind in an immigrants' transit camp (*ma'abara*, from the 1950s). The heart of the film is the experience of a female adolescent and the story is told from the young girl's point of view. The young heroine witnesses her mother's rape by her father and her mother's pregnancy and difficult childbirth, and she experiences the loss of childhood love and her first menstrual period. Desire and its absence, sexuality and the beginning of puberty, and the significance of female sexuality fill the world of the young heroine.

The mechanism of the penetrating gaze (which is basically sexual) is evident in a scene showing the awakening of desire between the girl and a boy. In that scene, the girl, bathing alone in her underwear, is unaware of the presence of the boy on a hilltop overlooking the sea. The boy gazes at the girl and, in an act that literalizes the metaphor of the penetrating gaze, uses his hands like binoculars. The camera also literalizes the metaphor as it thematizes the penetrating gaze: no longer an abstract description anymore, the penetrating gaze is now an actual event. This transition from metaphor to literalness uncovers and subverts the power mechanism of the gaze. It is as if the film were saying, If, in order to constitute the female subject, one must abandon the social scene and operate in the realm of the body—constituting a sexual subject and introducing the penetrating gaze—we shall subvert the power of this mechanism (the gaze) by exposing it.

The camera, however, does not focus on the girl from the boy's vantage point, that is, from above to below. Instead, it persistently views the girl at eye level. Furthermore, the camera does to the boy exactly what he is doing to the girl: it gazes on him from below rather than from the height of his eyes. This twofold act—showing him as observer and as the object of observation—exposes the penetrating gaze as a power mechanism. Moreover, Zvi-Riklis integrates the ethnic issue into the film alongside the gender issue. The boy, an Ashkenazi, concentrates his gaze on the girl, a Sephardi.[6] By intersecting the gender-sex axis with the ethnic axis, the camera exposes the penetrating gaze as nothing but a power mechanism, a human construct that can be used to oppress any minority or group. In thematizing the penetrating gaze, the film also reveals its inherent limitations.

Zvi-Riklis uses a similar juxtaposition of axes—this time nation/gender—in another short film, *Lookout* (1991). An Israeli soldier, posted on a roof in a refugee camp in the occupied territories, is preoccupied with a young Palestinian woman living across the street with her family. He follows her fortunes obsessively as she is forced into a marriage and becomes pregnant. Moreover, her father is jailed by the occupation authorities and her husband, involved in radical activities, uses her young brother to carry a grenade, concealed in a shoe box, to another radical outside. Upon seeing his father returning from prison, the boy drops the box and is killed by the explosion. Appalled, the soldier shoots the husband.

From the beginning, the camera follows the soldier manning the lookout as he observes the surrounding area. Besides the family across the way, he also watches people in the street. By using the penetrating gaze simultaneously on a Palestinian woman in the street and another Israeli soldier patrolling the area, the camera/director positions them on the same plane. This thematization of the gaze exposes it as a device that can be turned on whomever the power behind it chooses.

The camera thus maintains its own position of power, filming the world from the soldier's vantage point, and filming him as well. In this way, the camera, in the act of photographing him, subjects the soldier to its own gaze. Thus, the position of power simultaneously lies in the hands of the soldier, who holds both the gun and a pair of binoculars, and those of the director, both of them white Israelis (i.e., citizens of the occupying nation) and apparently heterosexual, bourgeois Jews. On the other hand, one is a man and the other a woman. And the woman, despite her being a citizen of the occupying country, observes the soldier from an alienated position.

The overriding, oppressive power of the gaze derives from its capacity, as already noted, to reduce and reify the object it is observing. If that gaze is turned on me and I stand naked before it, I am both my physical body and an object, as I cannot return the gaze: powerless, I lower my eyes. The gaze represents established power (as Foucault [1977] has pointed out), while I am transformed into an object of gratification.

The female director's subversive act is to thematize the subject. As a result, the film is not about the occupation but about the mechanisms for controlling others. Turning the mechanism of the gaze into the subject thus exposes it as a mechanism, discloses its limitations, and reveals ways in which one can defend oneself against it.

The film presents the major alternative modes for dealing with the penetrating gaze. The first, the simplest and most common, is to continue living under it, aware of its presence but ignoring it. The second is to block the gaze. Thus, in *Lookout*, the shutters of the family's apartment across the way are closed twice in the face of the soldier's binoculars, once by the young Palestinian woman who has aroused the soldier's interest and once by her husband. A third and more rebellious mode of coping with the gaze is to return it, refusing to lower one's eyes. This is done by the young Palestinian woman in an obvious and determined manner at least twice in the film.

But above all, the film exposes the inner contradictions of the colonialist's position of power. The soldier, who apparently occupies an Olympian position of power, seeing and controlling everything, is ultimately revealed as someone who knows nothing and does nothing. In the middle of the film, Israeli troops break into the apartment that has so absorbed the soldier's attention. Having no advance knowledge of the break-in, he contacts the troops to find out why they are doing it. Helpless, he neither takes part in the break-in nor is able to prevent it (although it appears that he would have liked to). Later he will have neither the foreknowledge of, nor the power to prevent, the blast that kills the young woman's small brother. Similarly, he lacks the power to prevent the girl from being married against her will.

The only power he has is the power to react after the fact. Not having generated the events, he can only react to them. Thus, he reacts to the death of the young boy by killing the husband who gave him the grenade. He reacts, just as the soldiers who broke into the apartment react, to something that has apparently happened somewhere else. Thus, the occupying Israeli can only react to that which others around him have caused to happen.

The thematization of the penetrating gaze is a subversive act that reveals the gaze as a mechanism of oppression while at the same time exposing its limitations. One is thus given the prescription for surviving it (even if one is unable to expunge it, cancel it out, or undermine it).

When the soldier kills the person responsible for the child's death, he is making a twofold statement: he is not responsible for the boy's death ("they" kill each other, he had no part in it), and he is the one who restores the moral order by killing in the name of universal justice. The order that he has restored is that of the

Zionist ethos, the ethos of selective killing. While soldiers (the occupation) are responsible for the situation that results in the killing, it is not, the film asserts, the occupier who has bloodied his hands. The occupier can distinguish, even in the heat of battle, between justified and unjustified killing and between moral and immoral killing. It is this order, this code, that the soldier seeks to restore.

From the heights of the lookout, surveying everything except himself, he—and with him the camera—observes the world through a closed, coherent moral system that refuses to consider the Palestinian native's own moral system. The positioning of the native-born Israeli in this lofty moral position thus precludes any criticism of the occupation. Not only is there no discussion of the roots of the situation that led to the killing, but the occupation is presented as providing a foundation for implanting a superior system of moral norms—a traditional position of the colonialist toward the "inferior" native. But the absence of concrete political criticism does not diminish the criticism of the mechanism, the unmasking of the limitations of the power mechanism.

This absence of political criticism is linked to the one power position that cannot be avoided but that is in no way subversive —that of the penetrating gaze of the camera. The power of the camera's eye cannot be nullified. True, the thematization of the penetrating gaze neutralizes its force, subversively exposing the mechanisms of power and oppression contained in the penetrating gaze of the soldier. Nevertheless, the fact that the camera remains with him all the time, seeing everything from his viewpoint alone, never taking the position of those who are subjected to his gaze, makes it into a full partner in the restoration of the Zionist moral order. This is the hegemonic side of this subversion.

The subversive stance in *Lookout* does not, therefore, challenge the Zionist moral or communal ethos. Instead, it works in the space left by Zionism, the space of the sexual body. Although not focused on the sexual body, *Lookout* nevertheless uses the related apparatus, the penetrating gaze, for its subversive ends.

A good example of the subversive use of the sexual body to constitute the female subject while leaving the hegemonic norms intact is the film *A Thousand and One Wives* (1989), adapted by Michal Bat Adam, who also directed the film, from the story of Dan-Benaya Seri (1987). In this film, a woman filmmaker adapts a story written by a man about male experience into a film about female experience. The film centers on the sexual awakening of Flora, Naftali Siman-Tov's third wife. In both the story and the film, Naftali's two previous wives have died before bearing any children (he has apparently murdered them). Anxious about the fate of his third wife, Naftali decides that his dead wives were poisoned by his sperm. With Flora, therefore, he only masturbates into a towel that she brings him every night. Afterward, she wraps herself in the towel, laundering it the next day.

Into Flora's life comes Hamedian, a textile merchant, who gets Flora pregnant, although Flora herself is not entirely aware of what is happening. The rabbi points out Flora's pregnancy to Naftali, who, realizing that he is not the father, murders Flora too, thus restoring order.

Although Seri's original story centers around Naftali, there are also allusions to Flora's desires. Bat Adam's film, on the other hand, centers around Flora's sexual awakening and her subversive actions. In the transition from story to film, the point of view does not change. Both Naftali's and Flora's points of view are represented in each. The difference, as noted, lies in the thematic emphasis.

In the film, the transition in focus from Naftali to Flora is made by the camera alone, without dialogue. We do not hear Flora's voice: the camera merely observes her actions, her face, her movements. And silence is precisely what Naftali wants of Flora: "Why are you never quiet?" he asks. "Shut up!" (Seri 1987, 64). Lacking a voice, Flora cannot tell her own story. Thus, it is not she who constructs her biography but Naftali, and her attempt to digress from the lines of his story brings about her punishment.

It is the camera that makes it possible for Flora to tell her own story (that is, to constitute her own world) and, in so doing, to subvert the original story's intention. However, the camera is used subversively, not rebelliously in a revolutionary manner. The only voice that the film gives the woman (aside from a few irrelevant pieces of scattered dialogue) is through her singing. The film opens and closes with a woman singing. Although the song also provides her with a voice, it is not a speaking voice, a logical voice, a voice that can formulate grievances against the world. It is simply "sound."

The change of focus achieved by the camera, the transition from the "telling" by Seri's omniscient and authoritive narrator (as shown by Hever 1990) to the "showing" in the film, endows the characters with more authority. Insofar as Flora is the film's dominant character, this narrative device enhances her authority. It now becomes her story rather than the narrator's even though it is told wordlessly. The omniscient narrator, whose irony in the story is pitted against Flora's naiveté, is replaced by a camera that, by providing a visual and authoritative presence for the woman's perspective, privileges it over that of the man. Herein lies the essence of the subversive act: in both the story and the film, Flora, even though she does not fully understand what she is doing, seeks sexual satisfaction with another man and becomes pregnant by him. At the same time, the film enhances this subversion by visually representing both the sexual awakening as well as the crystallization of a model of subversive female sexuality—thus bypassing the voicelessness of the heroine.

Flora's first act of subversion is to limit the effectiveness of the penetrating gaze. As Flora undresses on her wedding night, Naftali peeks through the keyhole. But Flora has placed a towel over the handle, thereby blocking his view. It is this same towel that will later absorb his semen. Moreover, Flora gazes at Naftali while he is asleep. Finally, a moment before her death, even as she cries out, she refuses to avert her eyes from his penetrating gaze.

Flora's second act of subversion is to go to another man in order to fulfill her sexual desires. In the story, her sexuality is described in only a few words. Her sexual desire is awakened after the wedding when, on a walk, she finds Naftali's appearance pleasing and notices "that strange superfluous motion in his pants." "A dense smell filled her nose" (Seri 1987, 16), a smell that becomes the main metaphor for male sexuality, which is concretized in the smell of Naftali's semen: "The strange smell which so engrossed her the whole night again filled her nostrils. She believed, without knowing quite why, that this was the sticky smell of aged trees, and indeed, when she brought the towel to her nose, all her hopes were realized[!]—carob jelly" (35).

Naftali quickly hides the towel, "her new possession," under her clothes. The towel becomes a substitute for sex: "She never tired of looking at it . . . she only wanted to stretch out her arm and touch. Each time, excited by her loathsome craving, she would secretly draw the towel across her belly and rush off to the steam of the bath" (37). She demonstrates her strength through a penetrating gaze, and in place of the desired sexual contact she clings to the towel, which smells of carobs and which she takes with her to the bath—to do what?

It is the camera that executes this action: the combination of laundering the towel and masturbating with it provides the main sexual scene of the film. Here Flora vents her sexual desires in a semimasturbatory simulation of the sexual act. When she meets Hamedian, she feels "in her heart the sticky taste of carob jelly" (46). From that moment until she faints after apparently having had intercourse with him, the story presents her point of view: from her joy after the first meeting to her agitation at home in anticipation of the second meeting to her thoughts and her attempts to please Naftali retroactively, and through numerous images of rain, downpours, and droughts that, from the beginning, are constructed as an analogy to intercourse and fertility.

The film builds a much more complex story than the text, introducing an important event that does not occur in the story: Flora's act of injuring herself in anticipation of her second meeting with Hamedian. The act itself is an allusion to a story from the traditional text, *Sefer Hayashar* (Book of the righteous), which recounts the attempted seduction of Joseph by Potiphar's wife, Zuleika. In the film that story is introduced through the character of Zuleika, a spinster who once gave up her lover and subsequently died, an allusion to Potiphar's wife. After falling ill out of longing for him, she invited her friends in to explain her actions:

> She gave them citrons and knives to peel them and eat them with. And she gave the order and they dressed Joseph in fine clothes and brought him before them. And Joseph came before them and all the women looked at Joseph and saw his beauty and were unable to take their eyes from him. And they all cut their hands with the knives they held and covered all the citrons they had in their hands with blood. (Dan 1981, 200)

At the center of this story is the female penetrating gaze. A group of women (a group, and not a singular woman) gazes at a man who has been brought before them as a displayed object. While the text alludes only to Potiphar's wife's name, the film alludes to the entire story: Flora takes a sharp instrument and, intentionally cutting herself, draws blood. Her maddening desire connects her with Zuleika and her friends. Her desire must be satisfied.

Whereas the book alludes to fertility, the film stresses sexuality and desire, thereby undermining the story through images, again, without sound. After the subversive act of constituting the sexual body comes the act of abolishing the body's limits, annihilating the distance between the body and what lies outside of it by mutilation, by the eruption of the body fluids.

At this point one can contrast the positioning of the woman in the story and in the film. In the story it is her social position that is emphasized. In the film it is the sexual body.

Both texts, the written and the visual, are based on commonality and "seriality." The title "The Thousand Wives of Naftali Siman-Tov" (changed in the film to *A Thousand and One Wives*) indicates an undifferentiated and serialized mass of women. The number "one thousand" is equivalent to "unlimited" (the thousand wives of King Solomon) or "unparticularized." "In a thousand tongues people lay in wait for him [Naftali] under the bed" (Seri 1987, 24). And "even if you wait a thousand years you will never see her [Flora] dead," Naftali consoles himself (27).

In the story, Flora attempts to end the cycle, whereas Naftali seeks to thwart this attempt by restoring order by destroying her. Seriality is at the heart of woman's social positioning. To be a good woman means to be one of Naftali's wives, one of a group of undifferentiated women all of whom fulfill the same role, one in a chain of objects designed for his sexual satisfaction and for the constitution of his social position. "You are a good woman," says Naftali to Flora—until she becomes pregnant—and he repeats this before the murder.

Flora disrupts this seriality by going to another man, thereby breaking the chain of "good women" and emerging as a woman differentiated from the mass, but her subversive attempt fails.

Even the seriality itself is a simulation, a substitute, a transformation: all of the women in the series are interchangeable. The very act of placing them in a row is a simulation. The subversive —not revolutionary—act of female survival is an act of substitution: substituting sex for a towel, one man for another, a fetus for the anti-Christ. However, by turning to the body, the singular, the particular, the film brings this process of simulation to an end.

Thus Flora, unable to overcome the power of social positioning, subverts it by "choosing" the sexual body for self-fulfillment. The film, acknowledging the impossibility of overcoming the force of social positioning, chooses, instead, to subvert it through the suppressed region of sexuality.

But the film's subversion is much greater than the story's. Whereas the story focuses on the restoration of order, the film focuses on the sexual body; whereas the story focuses on the positioning of society and family (and, ipso facto, fertility), the film focuses on sexual awakening. In the story, the only threat to seriality is Flora's act of going to another man. In the film, the threat is greater, involving the constitution of the sexual body and sexual awakening.

But the greater the subversion, the greater the failure. First of all the story, unlike the film, leaves open the possibility that the cycle will be broken, if only after the death of Flora. In the story, following the funeral, the rabbi says, "This interest in women, Mr. Naftali, even though the Torah demands it from us, perhaps it would be better to let them alone a little" (Seri 1987, 78). This sentence was cut out of the film, thereby eliminating the hope that the seriality would end. Furthermore, the fact that the film (though not the story) opens and closes with a funeral gives one a feeling of unending repetition: everything that happened after the first funeral will happen after this one, too, ad infinitum.

The second thing that indicates the continuation of seriality in the film is the change in the positioning of Zuleika. In the story, she refuses to marry any of the handsome men who have asked for her hand. After her death, it is revealed that she had been in love with a Torah scholar, who loved her in return. His grandfather, however, begged her to leave him alone, and she died of a broken heart. None of this remains in the film.

In the film, Zuleika, pursuing a married man, refuses to relinquish her earthy life. Gazing at Flora like a vulture, she awaits her turn in the chain of wives. As Flora lies dying inside, Zuleika follows Naftali to his doorstep. Thus, Zuleika serves as an agent for continuing the cycle, ensuring the victory of familial and communal positioning over female sexuality.

In the most subversive act of all, Flora, through her body, allegorically actualizes an act of redemption—the birth of the Messiah—whereas Naftali takes the unborn child to be the devil or the anti-Christ. Naftali notices "something" and, when Rebbi Duak explains to him that Flora is pregnant, Naftali tries to explain it away as something that happens "among the gentiles." He tries to convince Duak that there once was a woman who conceived from a spirit and not from a man. But Duak rejects this explanation, thus denying the possibility that Flora could be the Holy Virgin Mother, uncontaminated by any "snake poison" (as Naftali considers his own semen). Consequently, Flora must die.

Here again, neither the character of Flora nor the film as a whole has the power to overcome the social positioning of women. Any attempt to do so is doomed to failure. If one adds to this the attempt of the film to build upon the suppressed sexual body, the failure is magnified: the seriality that Flora has attempted to break is destined to continue.

In other words, the transition from the male text (of Seri) to the female text (of Bat Adam) is also a transition of focus from the family-society positioning to bodily subversion, from the "good woman" to sexual awakening, which ends in the bodily concretiz-ation of the myth of redemption. The battle of the sexes thus becomes a battle between bodies: that of the Messiah and that of the woman. This intertextual element deflects the discussion to an area in which the body becomes the essential thing: it provides a structural affirmation of an ideological reading that sees the body as central to the gender plot. The female text, which attempts to crystallize a model of female sexuality, to constitute a female subject, is forced to do this in the margins, through suppressed elements: through the sexual body. It has not succeeded in success-fully creating an alternative to the powerful Zionist model of social-professional-familial positioning, which is the dominant mechanism for turning the woman into the Other in Israeli cinema.

In the secular Zionist ethos, the body is mobilized for the historic event of redemption, the core of secular, messianic Zionism. Conse-quently, the body, valued primarily for its social-national function, is deprived of its privacy, its sexuality. However, in the subversive act of turning to the sexual body, Flora privileges a nonsecular Sephardic messianism, a Sephardic otherness, which contrasts with Ashkenazi secular messianism. In this, Naftali, also a Sephardi Other, stands with her. His view of messianic redemption is also opposed to Zionism's secular version. Here, too, as in *Coordania* and *Lookout*, two kinds of otherness are portrayed, female and ethnic. Thus the focus of *A Thousand and One Wives* on the sexual body subverts the Zionist hegemony.

An attempt to challenge directly the dominant mechanism of social positioning is made in the "Divorce" episode of the film *Tales of Tel Aviv* (Ayelet Menachmi and Nirit Yaron, 1992). In earlier episodes, the women's professions are stereotypical. In "Sharona Honey," Sharona is an assistant art director in a country where this is not yet considered a "real" profession. In "Operation Cat," Zofit is both a reporter for a local journal who is fired from her job and a poet with a small modicum of success (one of her poems has been set to music).

The first two episodes of *Tales of Tel Aviv* deal with the constitution of female sexuality ("Sharona Honey") and the constitution of an autonomous female subject ("Operation Cat"). At the end of the first story, Sharona screams "Why don't you listen to me?" at three of her four lovers, who insist on courting her contrary to her wishes. She insists on her right to choose her own sexuality and the kind of relationship she has with them. She does not want them bothering her all the time, making demands and proposals (especially for a common child) while ignoring what she has to say. She insists, in other words, on getting her own voice back, of being able to write her own story even if it does not jibe with that of her friends. And when she does not get what she wants, she leaves on the garbage truck that has come to clean up the city, ridding it (and her) of all the garbage that has accumulated.

But of course this is a film about Sharona's sexuality and her sexual biography. Once again, in order to constitute the female subject, the film turns to the sexual body and the relevant mechanism—the penetrating gaze. Here it takes the form of the gaze of a male friend—through binoculars—on the roof across the street, and Sharona's gaze at the parade of men among whom she functions. While it is too difficult for her to challenge the social structure, she can, however, smash the binoculars, thus eliminating the male gaze and constituting herself as a sexual subject according to her own model.

This is the case in "Operation Cat" as well. Zofit is a stereotypically fragile, passive, helpless woman: she fails at a suicide attempt, loses her bank card, and finds that her job is not only *not* central to her life but also interferes with what has become central—rescuing a cat that has fallen through the grid of a sewer. The fact that the cat has become the focus of her life deflects her attention from far more serious matters such as attending to her job and completing the arrangements for separating from her husband. The cat, which she succeeds in saving, is her only area of success.

Zofit has applied to all the bureaucrats who run the municipal services, all male, except for the woman veterinarian of the S.P.C.A. She, by the way, is the only one whom Zofit dares to threaten. Finally, Zofit realizes that she alone is capable of saving the cat (saving herself?) and she does just that. She reaches this realization with the help of another woman, an assertive, creative career woman who is dying. It is as if the film wants to say that such women have a place in this world only as disembodied mentors and not as real living creatures. Again, the constitution of an autonomous female subject—one who is not dependent upon or subservient to the surrounding male milieu, who is able to choose her own goals and attain them by her own efforts—cannot take place through a woman's social or professional positioning. It can only take place when this kind of positioning is nullified or at least marginalized through female solidarity or through the encouragement of a coveting male (in this case, one who not only covets her body but also appreciates her poetry). And in any event, the constitution of the female subject occurs through an act of simulation: saving the cat instead of herself. Only through the analogy of transformation can the female subject be constituted.

Thus, Sharona constitutes herself as well as her biography around her sexual body and her sexuality. Zofit constitutes her subjectivity by projecting her world onto the travails of a cat. But neither of them can do it directly, just as the film itself cannot, by confronting the dominant mechanism of their marginalization—their social positioning. And then comes Tikva, the protagonist of the third episode, who tries to construct her own mechanism for obtaining a divorce.

Tikva is a policewoman who does her job well, even managing to challenge the patriarchal rules of the game, which dictate sexual submission for job advancement. Tikva refuses to show favoritism in distributing parking tickets. She also performs well in her community role as a mother. Raising her children alone since her husband departed five years ago, she always keeps her promises to them. Thus, her social position is simultaneously that of a "good woman" (a perfect mother, holding an acceptable job) and an "unflawed person" (professionally honest, good parent). In short, she is a success.

Tikva has not seen her runaway husband for five years. Although deserted by him, she cannot (according to rabbinical law) get a divorce without his consent. One day she spots him in a tall office building and begins to chase him. Here, too, she refuses to play by the rules: she steals a gun from a security guard and tries to force her husband to agree to a divorce. When her husband succeeds in escaping, she takes hostages and refuses to release them until her husband is brought back. Thus, she takes her destiny into her own hands and, for the first time in her life, determines her husband's destiny as well. Moreover, she is ready to accept the consequences of her action and pay the price—a jail sentence.

Tikva begins her odyssey by choosing divorce, thereby remaining within the rabbinical system. When the security guard offers her another option—freeing herself from the established order by having an affair—she refuses to consider this option. She wants a divorce, to be set free not by an act of her own volition but by the rabbinical establishment that has imprisoned her in the first place. She tries to create her own mechanism for liberation by forcing the police to find her husband and bring him before the rabbinate. When that does not happen fast enough, the rabbinate—in the person of one of her hostages, a rabbi—gets the religious establishment itself to go after the husband. Returning the husband to the place where she is holding the hostages, they are now willing to perform a divorce on the spot. Although Tikva has succeeded in constituting herself as a social subject and forging the mechanism for her divorce, at the last moment she relents. She is unwilling to undergo an instant divorce and now wants her husband jailed. In the final analysis, she still needs the official sanction of the establishment, which, she feels, is "preferable" to her own.

The female gaze, the female camera/director in "Divorce," attempts to constitute the autonomous female subject but stops short of challenging the dominant mechanism for the reification of woman, the mechanism of community or social positioning. A more accessible option is found in what has been suppressed, the sexual body, with its accompanying mechanism, the penetrating gaze, and its thematization.

At this point, in accordance with the critical traditions of feminist theory, the question arises, how can one eliminate the penetrating gaze of the camera, considering that it is itself the active cinematic apparatus? Is, therefore, the feminist cinematic project doomed to failure, or does an alternative model exist, one that includes the power struggle as a legitimate component? One can assume that it is the second alternative that we are seeking—not to distance ourselves from the penetrating gaze but rather to internalize its operating mechanism and use it to our own ends.

NOTES

1. See also Turin 1990; and Seneca 1990.

2. Most recent Hollywood films in which women play leading roles are of this type. On the one hand, the woman, at the center of the movie, has some feminist traits. She has a nonstereotypical job, is autonomous, and develops as a sexual being. However, these norms are subverted through the normative world of the film. This is accomplished by making negative judgments of the woman or by calling into question her professional abilities. See, for example, *Mermaids* (Richard Benjamin, 1990); *Blue Steel* (Kathryn Bigelow, 1990); *Shirley Valentine* (Lewis Gilbert, 1989); *Always* (Steven Spielberg, 1989); and *Indecent Proposal* (Adrian Lyne, 1993).

3. The reasons for this are not certain. It may be because the number of women who finish higher studies in cinema, and therefore produce short films, do not enter the film industry in as great numbers as men. Or, it may be that fewer funds, national or commercial, are entrusted to women directors. There does appear to be a correlation between the situation in the Israeli film industry and literature worldwide. In general, women seem to choose the short story form over the long novel. Perhaps the amount of time required by the shorter genre is better suited to women's economic and social situation resulting from family and home responsibilities. Similarly, until such time as women's artistic creativity is encouraged, they are not likely to embark on full-time film careers.

4. In Abraham Shlonsky's 1920 poem "Yizrael" (the valley), which praises the *halutz* (pioneer) of the third *aliyah* (coming of the Jews to Israel for permanent residence), he transposes physical identity into the discourse of national rhetoric. And in Bialik's poetry, eroticism was almost always read in terms of national issues. On Zionism and the erotic, see also Biale (1992, 176–203).

5. For an extremely blunt (and controversial) example, see Yona Wallach's poetry.

6. On changes in the balance of the racial power structure between Ashkenazi and Sephardi in this scene, see Ben-Shaul (1987).

BIBLIOGRAPHY

Arbuthnot, Lucie, and Gail Seneca. 1990. "Pre-Text and Text in Gentlemen Prefer Blondes." In *Issues in Feminist Film Criticism*, ed. Patricia Evens. Bloomington and Indianapolis: Indiana University Press.

Ben-Shaul, Nitzan. 1987. "The Politics of the Creator" (Hebrew). In *Sratim* (Films) 3.

Bernheimner, Charles, and Claire Kahana, eds. 1985. In *Dora's Case*. New York: Columbia University Press.

Biale, David. 1992. *Eros and the Jews: From Biblical Israel to Contemporary America.* New York: Basic.

Dan, Joseph, ed. 1981. *Sefer Hayashar* (Book of the righteous). DOROT Library. Jerusalem: Bialik Institute.

Foucault, Michel. 1977. *Discipline and Punish: The Birth of the Prison.* Trans. A. M. Sheridan Smith. New York: Pantheon.

Hever, Hannan. 1990. "On the Fiction of D. B. Seri" (Hebrew). In *Siman Kriah* 20: 394–97.

Lubin, Orly. 1993. "Women Read Women." In *Theory and Criticism: An Israeli Forum* 3:65–78.

Mulvey, Laura. 1975. "Visual Pleasure and Narrative Cinema." In *Screen,* 16, 3 (Autumn).

———. 1981. "Afterthoughts on 'Visual Pleasure and Narrative Cinema,' inspired by *Duel in the Sun.*" In *Framework* 6:15–17.

Penley, Constance, ed. 1988. *Feminism and Film Theory.* New York: Routledge; London: BFI.

Schnitzer, Meir. 1993. *Israeli Cinema: Facts, Plots, Directors, Opinions.* Jerusalem and Tel Aviv: Israel Film Archive, Jerusalem Cinamatheque and Kineret Publishing House.

Seri, Dan-Benaya. 1987. *Birds of the Shade.* Jerusalem: Keter.

Turin, Maureen. 1990. "Gentlemen Consume Blondes." In *Issues in Feminist Film Criticism*, ed. Patricia Evens. Bloomington and Indianapolis: Indiana University Press.

Chapter 14

Israel and America—Imagining the Other: Natan Shaham's "The Salt of the Earth" and Philip Roth's The Counterlife

Naomi B. Sokoloff

Israel has never been one of the major themes of American Jewish literature.[1] And America, for its part, has remained by and large a peripheral concern in Israeli imaginative writing. Given the importance of Israel in American-Jewish political debate, given the pervasiveness of American influence in Israeli culture, and given the existence of shared family and historical roots in the two societies and the increasing familiarity of each with the other, the marginalization of one another in their literatures gives pause for thought.

There have, of course, been exceptions. In the United States, Arthur Koestler's novel *Thieves in the Night* (1946) dealt with the establishment of the State of Israel. Later, Hugh Nissenson wrote a number of stories with Israeli settings (see, for example, *A Pile of Stones* [1965] and *In the Reign of Peace* [1968]). There is no doubt, though, that American literature has relegated Israel primarily to the arena of suspense thrillers, melodramatic potboilers, or pulp fiction, while according it little serious, substantive literary treatment.[2]

In Israel, too, notable attention to America was the exception years ago. In the 1970s, Yehuda Amihai published a series of poems about his travels to the United States, as well as a novel, *Mi yitneni malon* (Hotel in the wilderness) (1971); Yoram Kaniuk's *Hayored lema'alah* (*The Acrophile*) (1961) and *Sus'ets* (*Rockinghorse*) (1973), similarly, are set in the United States; and A. B. Yehoshua's *Bithilat kayits 1970* (*Early in the Summer of 1970*) (1972) introduces an American character. Some stories by Yizhak Ben Ner—"Kokomo"

(1976) and "Mikhtav" (1981)—touch on the topic of America. But few other titles come to mind.

There are signs that in recent years things have begun to change. From the American side, the late 1970s and the 1980s witnessed the publication of quite a few new novels relating to Israel, including E. M. Broner's *A Weave of Women* (1978), Tova Reich's *Master of the Return* (1985), Micha Lev's *Yordim* (1986), Anne Roiphe's *Lovingkindness* (1987), and a number of poems (for example, the 1990 collection edited by Elaine Marcus Starkman and Leah Schweitzer, *Without a Single Answer*). In Israel there have appeared such titles as Hanoch Bartov's *Be'emtsa haroman* (In the middle of it all) (1984); Natan Shaham's *Hutsot Ashkelon* (The streets of Ashkelon) (1985); and Moshe Shamir's *Yaldei hashe'ashu-'im* (Playboys) (1986), all of which boast American settings.[3] A significant number of other texts draw on American characters: among the prominent examples are A. B. Yehoshua's *Gerushim me'uharim* (*Late Divorce*) (1982) and Meir Shalev's *Roman Rusi* (*The Blue Mountain*) (1988). By the same token, America is constantly in the background of Amos Oz's *Kufsah shehorah* (*Black Box*) (1986), if only as the place where the protagonists flee to evade responsibility and as the place from which to write letters home.[4] There is also a growing body of work that defies easy categorization: texts written in Israel in English by North Americans who have come to live there and texts written in Hebrew by Israelis on American shores.

This literature as a whole invites discussion in terms of identity politics, the psychology and history of stereotypes, the semiotics of culture, and issues of narrative voice in representations of diversity. As literary theory turns increasingly to studies of "otherness," this corpus of work would seem to present an alluring case for two reasons. First, Israel and America have been such meaningful (dare one say "significant"?) Others, and, second, their literatures have curiously disregarded or marginalized this topic.

Debate about otherness concerns the relation of discourse to power; many studies explore the ways in which blindnesses of texts ensure the dominating vision of powerful, hence vocal and recognized, social orders at the expense of other classes or groups of people. Much attention has been paid to ways in which respected canonical works encompass, distort, or misrepresent suppressed voices: how majorities portray minorities, for example, or how men have imagined women. This area of study has expanded also to encompass a range of cross-cultural perceptions, reciprocal interpretations by opposing groups, and the concomitant decentering of power that such mutual scrutiny entails.[5]

Two pieces of fiction that offer fertile ground for comparison based on issues of otherness are Natan Shaham's novella "Melaḥ ha'arets" ("The Salt of the Earth") from 1977, and Philip Roth's novel *The Counterlife* from 1986. Though stylistically quite distant from one another, they are thematically parallel in many regards. In addition, these narratives admit multiple voices and perspectives in ways that allow them to play off and play out the issues of kinship and difference that bind their characters. Shaham's tale follows an aging kibbutznik's first trip to America and his encounters there with relatives and new acquaintances. These confrontations occasion a collision of values, primarily between kibbutz pioneer ideals of socialism and the self-satisfactions of a successful capitalistic diaspora. Roth similarly imagines an American's first trip to Israel, one that evolves into a sojourn with Gush Emunim. The character who adopts this counterlife is an affluent dentist from suburban New Jersey, who makes *aliyah* (that is, immigrates to Israel, or, literally, "ascends") to join what his relatives view as the lunatic fringe of religious nationalists in Israeli society. Following in horrified pursuit, hoping to dissuade him, is his brother Nathan Zuckerman, the writer/protagonist familiar from earlier Roth fiction.

In both narratives, the protagonists start out with mixed feelings of indifference and resistance at the prospect of making their overseas trips. Once at their respective destinations, though, they discover an unexpected closeness with the Jews there. As their contact becomes more intimate, immediate, and personal, the stereotypes they had brought with them begin to break down. Some misgivings remain, but they experience new sympathy and new respect for, or collaboration with, values they had once held to be foreign and downright abhorrent.

However, just as the old oppositions unravel and dissipate, a violent crisis leads to disaster and to painful conclusions—in two senses. Each narrative comes to an explosive end, and in each case the devastating events that constitute a painful conclusion to the plot also reconfirm the protagonist's worst fears and suppositions, shocking him into the conclusion that he has been betrayed. The ensuing sense of having been abandoned by the other Jews undoes the intimate ties that had begun to emerge between Israelis and Americans. These developments leave that relationship newly undefined. Perhaps the most unsettling part of the outcome is the metaphysical or existential irresolution that results from the othering of the protagonists. That is to say, these figures, defined by those around them, find themselves at the mercy of others' inventions of them. As this happens, once repressed stereotypes return, painfully reaffirming the radically alienating vulnerability they experience by being Other. These texts therefore not only provide arresting case studies of relations between American Jews and Israeli Jews; but, insofar as they thematize otherness, these fictions also serve as studies in the nature of stereotyping and constructions of identity.

"The Salt of the Earth"

Shaham's protagonist, Meisels, at first resists the idea of a trip to the United States on ideological grounds. He perceives travel as an indulgence, a luxury unseemly for a kibbutznik, and he bristles especially at the thought of accepting private funds—a gift from his citified children—for this purpose. Underlying his arguments is another factor. He has become a creature of routine who is intimidated by the details of travel: how much to tip, how to turn on unfamiliar faucets, and what to order from a breakfast menu in a strange language. To cover up this inertia, he defines running abroad as "provincial," something beneath the dignity of a man whose life goal has been to "plant one Jew" on the land of Israel and so put a redemptive halt to the frantic wanderings of the Jews (Shaham 1983, 213).

Although Meisels's initial reaction is one of hesitation, his second is one of eerie recognition. The text reports that, as his plane lands in New York,

> The encounter with America was as he had expected it to be. Like something being discovered for the second time. Everything was new and yet familiar. As if America had been dormant within him even when it was far away. And was now being roused into an active state. A promise being fulfilled. (233)

That promise at first is a reconfirmation of his expectation—that the Land of Promise will contrast starkly with the Promised Land. He sees the United States as materialistic, dirty, and violent, a place where everything is gigantic and moves at dizzying speed. He buys into all the stereotypes he had acquired at home and sees America as the craven opposite of the kibbutz utopia:

> What he had read about in books he actually experienced here. Everything—the loss of individuality in the unending landscape, solitude in the crowd, alienation, simple fear for one's livelihood, it was all here as expected. (236)

To stereotype is to erect symbolic boundaries that reinforce sharp contrasts between self and Other; Meisels's inclination, at first, is precisely this, and he distances himself from Americans by clinging to negative preconceptions:

> A few he detested profoundly. He could not bear the overweening pride and complacency of property owners who believed the whole world operated according to their values. He hated those smug faces and the lady-bountiful expressions glittering forth out of covetous eyes. As if they were assaulting his own values—life without competitiveness or class symbols, or the drive to dominate, life on a modest scale. (240)

As if to concertize and monumentalize Meisels's feelings of distance and alienation, the narrator also quickly erects a huge symbolic boundary. Describing the skyscrapers of New York, the text depicts a towering emblem of difference. When the protagonist forays into the city for the first time, his host, Dr. Webster, witnesses his astonishment at the sight of Manhattan across the river.

> Taller than tall. A wall at the end of the earth. The beginning of an*other* world. Those were words that struck a chord in Webster: the beginning of an*other* world. (246, emphasis added)

Even so, beyond this encounter with the otherness of America, Meisels does find Jewish kinship. Upon meeting many relatives who live in New Jersey, he feels that he's back in the *shtetl*, a small town in the old country; they speak Yiddish and he concludes that "he's flown halfway across the earth just to go from one country village to another" (234).[6] In Manhattan, despite the awe-inspiring massiveness of the city, he finds familiarity. At YIVO, the offices of a Yiddish newspaper, the site of a sweatshop fire, and Lincoln Center, he and Webster find tributes to famous Jewish artists. Even the tall buildings are subsumed into this familiar Jewish frame of reference:

"What Webster showed him was actually a Jewish city. True, they did go up to the top of the Empire State Building, but that was while they were involved in a lively discussion about Mendele Mokher Seforim" (246).

Given this sense of kinship, it becomes imperative to return to the passage that speaks of Meisels's initial discovery of America and to reassess its formulation of his reaction: "Everything was new and yet familiar. As if America had been dormant within him even when it was far away" (233). While these lines affirm stereotypes and expectations, the polyvalent text can also be read as suggesting that America is an extension of the character himself. Although Israeli Jews and American Jews represent binary oppositions, they are also somehow the same. The boundaries of difference have shifted, for the borders between Israelis and Americans are no longer so easy to identify or locate. Subsequently, the boundaries shift even more as the main character comes to know America more personally, particularly through meeting people, talking, debating, and airing differences.

M. M. Bakhtin's theory of the dialogic imagination provides a model for exploring in more detail the interactions of voice that enable that acquaintanceship and that bring Meisels more closely in contact with the Other. Bakhtin has defined the novel as a polyphonic genre, made up of a plenitude of discourses. His interest lies in the multiple linguistic stratifications—the dialects, jargons, varying registers, and idioms—that make up any cultural setting. As these come into contact they modify one another. One voice or discourse may interpret the other, subsume it, appropriate it, question its assumptions, or retort to it. In so doing, each deprivileges and relativizes the other in a process of mutual modification that Bakhtin defines as "dialogic." And, it is important to note, in the process these voices vie for power; the one that interprets, i.e., defines the other, asserts itself as the center and subsumes the other into its own frame of reference. By the same token, as it conjoins disparate and disruptive voices and views, fiction becomes a site of struggle among varying ideologies. In addition, Bakhtin notes that diverse discourses may collide in a public, external realm—such as a formal debate—or in a more intimate and private realm, in someone's inner thoughts. Psychic life consists of an amalgam of discourses spoken by others and selectively absorbed by the individual. As people assimilate, reevaluate, and so redefine the words of those about them, ideas develop through a struggle within for hegemony among various points of view and various sets of values.

Novels implement dialogic interaction in a number of ways, dialogue in the ordinary sense of directly transcribed verbal exchange being but one possible form. Other possibilities, at the level of narrated events, include interpretations of one character's words by another, reports of another's speech, and parody of statements by others. Even simple juxtapositions of characters can lead two distinct kinds of idiom to expose their contrasting assumptions and reveal each other's ideological underpinnings.

Another, extensive set of dialogic relations arises from all those strategies of narration in which the author or authorial figure coordinates his or her voice with that of a character. Sometimes these narrative strategies underscore boundaries between the two kinds of voices, and sometimes they blur them or generate doubt and indistinctiveness—as is the case with free indirect discourse or related techniques.[7]

All these kinds of dialogue admit plural voices to narration. Shaham's narrative captures multiple voices primarily in the intimate realm of the protagonist's own thoughts, as he listens to, absorbs, and reacts to the words of others. Assimilating public debate and external exchange into Meisels's internal dialogues, the narrative very subtly explores the ways private motives and complexities of personality adumbrate and challenge public ideology. In this way Shaham embodies multiple issues within one character, conveying them through varieties of double voicing that subsume external perspectives within the inner world of the protagonist.

A conversation reported early in the text suggests a commentary on this pervasive strategy of narration in "The Salt of the Earth." The scene takes place at Kennedy Airport. There, Meisels tries to deal with an Israeli El Al manager who ignores him in order to chat with an old army buddy. As Meisels listens to their Hebrew slang and their breezy familiarities, the narrative presents snatches of overheard conversation.

> The familiar words that his sons used with friends. *Salamtak*. Tell us about it. Some friend you are. So help me. We won't let you get away hungry. With the Missus, naturally. How are the little bastards?
>
> A lingo that belonged to a certain time and place. And a few memories of his own associated themselves with it for a while.

Even though he was only a visitor to this idiom. The imitation that
leads to assimilation. He had used it from time to time. With
cautious irony. (197–98)

The words that are cited directly are not presented in dialogue
format. Instead, they are consolidated into a paragraph as the
subject of Meisels's own musings. As occurs in much of the narrative, here the protagonist tries on the discourse of others, listening
to it, absorbing it to varying degrees, always maintaining some
distance from it. And, as he plays with the possibility of imitation,
he is pulled—inadvertently—toward an always ironic assimilation
into their views. This narrative technique proves particularly
effective in depicting Meisels's relations with Americans, because the
subtle pull toward "assimilation" is loaded with implications about
Jewish acceptance of the majority, non-Jewish culture of America.

Consider, for instance, the following passage, which appears
after the protagonist and his host spend an evening at a burlesque,
once a Yiddish theater. There, an old Jewish comedian has told
Jewish jokes to a seedy non-Jewish audience that understands
nothing of his humor.

> When they emerged both were in low spirits. So this is what
> Jewish culture looks like in America, [Meisels] said sadly. An old
> Jew running around among bosomy girls for as long as he can hold
> out trying to be witty. Webster smiled. He liked wit even if it
> lacked real substance. The only hope for the Jewish people lay
> here. Israel was raising soldiers and peasants. In America we had
> been liberated. In America there was no such thing as one kind of
> work being less worthy than another. Whatever led to freedom and
> prosperity was respectable. Only in America could Jews be un-
> afraid of the same things as the goyim.
>
> He did not argue. He only asked: And in Israel? Israel is the
> only country in the world where Jews are killed because they are
> Jews, said Webster. (249)

Emerging in this scene is the pull that American values exert on
Meisels. The two men hold diametrically opposed views—Webster
extols the very prosperity and freedom that Meisels has frequently
denounced as crass materialism and a lack of human values—but
the Israeli declines to argue with his American host. Tired, not open
to energetic exchange, Meisels at this point allows the words and
convictions of others to filter into his own thoughts, through the fog

of his own biases, and does not fight back vigorously against them. Bakhtin suggests that the novel is a genre in which discourse is "contested, contestable, and contesting" (Bakhtin 1981, 332); in "The Salt of the Earth," such contest is central but subdued.

Stylistically, the text reinforces this quality in the dialogic interactions between Meisels and Webster. Even in this passage that evidently reports conversation, there is no direct dialogue in Shaham's prose. The phrases followed by the explicit reports "he said," "Webster said," and "he only asked" are not placed in quotation marks. This omission mutes the otherness of the words. There is no stark demarcation of Meisels's words and those of his companion, and the result is a homogenization of the narrative surface. Consequently, the reader gets the impression that here we have less a polemic than a memory or a perception of a polemic within the consciousness of the protagonist.

Some of the other lines read like free indirect discourse: "He liked wit even if it lacked real substance." This sentence could be an example of psychonarration—a narrator's knowing explanation of Webster's inner thoughts. More probably, we could understand these words as ones vocalized by Webster and then internalized into Meisels's memories. (The whole section is a flashback in which the protagonist reflects on some of the events of his trip.) The difficulty of classifying the discourse is indicative of ways in which Shaham's homogenizing tends to suppress vigorous give and take or dramatic argumentativeness. Debate between an American and an Israeli is crucial here, but the emphasis is less on external polemics than on the main character's psychological adjustments to his acquaintance's opposing views.

This scene is in keeping with direct reports the reader has had about Meisels earlier. He is a character who has avoided conversation and, as he has aged, has "welcomed the onset of deafness, which enabled him to shut himself off from words for which he had no reply" (Shaham 1983, 174). Meisels is fatigued—especially after the dejecting evening at the burlesque but in general as well. He is no longer comfortable with the exacting moral standards of self-abnegation and austerity that he once embraced as kibbutz ideals, and amidst the luxuries and seductions of foreign travel, he is unwilling to engage in battle on behalf of those ideals. In fact, he finds himself gradually, increasingly, seduced into stances and roles he would find repellent at home. Though despising the conspicuous trappings of wealth and the airs of self-importance of American

Jews, he himself succumbs to the pleasures of "simple creature comforts" they offer him: alcoholic beverages, steaks, and even ordinary Coca-Cola (241).

Accepting their hospitality, he also adopts the role they have defined for him: to serve as a kind of unofficial *shaliah*—a representative of Israel—and a pundit who can explain current events when friends come to visit.

> A few had already been in Israel and saw whatever they saw. Others read the papers. A few posed questions just to show how much they knew. Others—in order to give him a chance to say something. He gave them solemn assurances that war was not in the cards. People who want to wage war do not make threats. He did not thoroughly believe every word that he said. But what was wrong with planting a few false hopes? After all, he had not come to America to sow seeds of despair. (235)

As he plays this role that the Americans have invented for him, he tells them what he thinks they want to hear. In the process, boundaries between his opinions and theirs become blurred. Meisels is partially coopted into the Americans' way of thinking. The greatest betrayal of his earlier point of view comes with his formulaic affirmation of their success, in which he seems to deny their differences altogether. As wave after wave of relatives comes to greet him, he repeats time and again that Israel and America are like "two kinds of victory over Exile," facing one another "without Jew-fears or the equivocating of the underdog, proud in their strength, their wealth, their uprightness" (239). The Americans listen and respond, "Amen."

Stylistically, too, Shaham plays down difference. Like the previously cited passages, the one in which Meisels plants "false hopes" also features reports of speech, but diminishes mimetic representation of speech. The phrase, "He gave them solemn assurances," for example, does not reproduce his words. The line closest to a direct quotation ("People who want to wage war do not make threats") probably presents Meisels's exact words, but this sentence is an example of free direct discourse, i.e., not demarcated by quotation marks or by inquit phrases such as "he said." "He did not thoroughly believe" is psychonarration, a report of the protagonist's inner life without the use of his own words, or perhaps free indirect discourse, his thoughts verbalized to himself. All these

events are blended through a smooth narrative surface. There are
no abrupt changes from one sentence to the next, and the result is
to suggest, first, that there is no longer a firm barrier between
Meisels's opinions and the Americans' opinions and, second, that all
the narrated events have been internalized and told in retrospect
from Meisels's perspective. He has dallied with the ideas of others;
their ideas have become part of his memory and are no longer
clearly differentiated from his own.

Meisels is aware of being caught in between two cultures, aware
that he is eliding boundaries, and aware that he is allowing the
language and views of others to encroach on his own values and
dominate his own discourse. His awareness of his complicity is
expressed in this passage:

> He choked on his words in one language he was no longer used to
> and in another that he had not yet mastered. An emissary from
> the Holy Land. Who had sent him? What for? What tidings did he
> bear? With a sense of disgrace he recalled a letter he had written
> to Bronka as empty boasting: something to the effect of his having
> brought the message of Israel to "American Jewry" more effectively
> than those paid to do the job, who demolish more than they build.
> He was ashamed of having fallen into the linguistic trap of those
> dignitaries who go to America to confer with two or three individu-
> als and return to Israel as pleased with themselves as if they had
> sown seeds of hope on foreign soil. (237)

As he falls into their language, his self-confidence sinks, and it sinks
further as contact with America makes him aware of limitations in
his own dearly held views and habits. Until the trip to the United
States, he had been convinced that kibbutz socialism was far
superior to more cosmopolitan but rapaciously capitalistic outlooks.
Once in the United States, however, he finds that he has "the
reflexes of a country bumpkin," just as his children would have
surmised, that any salesperson could "intimidate, cajole, or cheat
him," that "a drop of alcohol could loosen his tongue"—in short, that
he has led a very provincial life (236). An even more startling
revelation comes to him as he watches construction workers scaling
the walls of intimidating skyscrapers in Manhattan. Seeing these
men hard at work, he recognizes that other forms of existence may
be decent, honest, industrious, and—in some ways—even superior to
kibbutz life, because less encumbered by a rigid ideology of self-
sacrifice.

Meisels's new awareness of Others, which whittles away his resistance to American ways of life and puts his own shortcomings into relief, deepens and is then reversed at the end of the novella. Encountering a woman who convinces him to take an impromptu five-day tour of New England, he postpones his return to Israel. In the course of the tour, he opens up even more to America, and then later rejects it. These changes depend on his own oscillating state of mind and the degree to which he feels vulnerable or empowered. Consequently, this episode underscores how slippery are perceptions of Others and how personal uncertainty and insecurity fuel stereotyping. Secure in himself, Meisels acquires sudden new flexibility. Beset with fears and feelings of powerlessness, he suffers strong aversion to those who are different from himself.

It happens this way. Meisels meets Anna Steinhardt at a party. This flirtatious new acquaintance promises him that she can rearrange his flight schedule and take him to see "another" America (258), not the Jewish America he has come to know. Through her he discovers beautiful new countryside and a surprising camaraderie. He feels an attraction to her and also a special affinity, since they both grew up in Poland and share a similar background. Far from home, with someone he barely knows, he bares his soul and enjoys long, confidential talks. However, when she drops him off at the airport and takes her leave, he discovers to his surprise that, in fact, he has no reservation and must remain in New York, alone, for several days. He stays in a hotel, at a loss, unable to reach Anna or his relatives by phone. Finally, he is mugged on the street. In the last paragraphs of the novella, he experiences heart failure, just as the phone rings in his room.

In short, he does find an "other" America—a non-Jewish one. And this is an America ruled by murderous norms of othering, where negative stereotypes and suspicions divide individuals and ethnic groups. As his relative Feinstein had warned him earlier, "New York is hell . . . a city of gangsters and murderers. You never know when you're going to run into a mugger, anti-Semite, psychopath, or just someone who doesn't care for the way you look or the color of your skin" (235). At the end of Meisels's visit to the United States, it is precisely this worst case scenario that comes to pass.

This turn of events sends shock waves through his perception of Others. Meisels had felt rejuvenated by his little adventure with Anna Steinhardt, warming to America because of it. Now, however, as he starts to feel more vulnerable, he reverts back to stereotypes and succumbs to the pull of hatred. As a moderate person, not a fanatic, he tries to be rational and not confuse generalizations with individuals. Under pressure, he struggles against an urge to stereotype. For instance, when he realizes he has missed his flight home, he despises American Jews for their parasitism as an exploiting class. At the same time, he recoils from this feeling within himself. Realizing that he is homesick for little things—familiar smells, simple faucets, his own towel—he chides himself that "it would be ridiculous to hate America all of a sudden. He hadn't come here just to confirm prejudices" (242). However, when he is mugged, he ceases to struggle. Now he feels hatred, pure and simple, for his assailants. As for American Jews, he remembers the warning an Israeli friend issued him before his trip: "They'll greet you like royalty, they'll fuss over you, they'll spoil you with silly presents, and be glad to get rid of you" (207). At the end of the novella, as Meisels readily endorses this stereotyped view, the names of some of the characters take on new resonance and provide further confirmation of the prejudiced image. Feinstein (fine stone) is a man preoccupied with material wealth. Anna Steinhardt (stone hard), abandoning her guest and leaving him in real need, has emerged as a cold and heartless figure.

The denouement dramatizes ways in which fear generates and drives stereotyping. No one can function in the world without stereotypes; beginning with our early childhood needs for self-definition, they help us to distinguish self from the world. In particular, they enable us to externalize that which is threatening or bad. As Sander Gilman explains, adults are never entirely free of stereotypes, but they normally retain the ability to control this tendency rationally:

> Stereotypes can and often do exist parallel to the ability to create sophisticated rational categories that transcend the crude line of difference present in the stereotype. We retain our ability to distinguish the "individual" from the stereotyped class into which the object might automatically be placed. The pathological personality does not develop this ability and sees the entire world in terms of the rigid line of difference. (Gilman 1985, 2)

Highly stressful situations, of course, undermine reason and self-control. As a response to anxiety, the deep structure of the stereotype may emerge to acquire new dominance. When faced with loss of control of the self, adults often need to return to notions of "us and them" and draw those crude lines of division once again. Especially compelling is our need to attribute evil to the Other, so as to stave off "potential disintegration of the mental representations" (Gilman 1985, 3) that the individual has created.

In "The Salt of the Earth," Shaham suggests the degree to which Meisels's view of the Other, his propensity to stereotype, stems from within himself and his own state of mind, rather than from any intrinsic quality in the Others. Through his uses of the Hebrew root *d.m.h.* and words related to it (*to be similar, to seem, to appear, to imagine*), Shaham presents difference as an active psychic process and not as external fact. Each character (*demut*) is constructed by the protagonist in the image of people he has known in the past; that is, they are similar (*domim*). And the Hebrew reverberates with the added meanings of *ledamot le'atsmo* (to imagine to himself): it is he who imagines the Other as similar or as different depending on his own self-confidence. Consequently, when opening up to Anna Steinhardt and her America, he tends to perceive the Other in terms of his own past experiences. He remarks frequently that the landscape reminds him of the Poland where he spent his youth, and that Anna reminds him of his first wife, Silvia ("damtah me'od leSilvia," Shaham 1977, 209). Anna engages in the same practice when she says that he resembles Uncle Sam ("domeh laDod Sam," 196), an image springing from within *her* very American frame of reference. Through this comment, the reader becomes aware of the characters as creating multiple competing inventions of one another.

Meisels is also aware that he is fitting into American images when he plays the part of a *shaliah*, as his hosts expect ("hu nitbakesh la'amod be*dimuyo* — halutz zaken, yehudi kafri" [1977, 184]; "he [had] to take up his role [image]—that of the old pioneer, the country Jew" [1983, 239]). The sense of imagining/inventing Others is clearly indicated when he wanders the streets of New York by himself, surmising that he can tell—just by looking at them—who in a large crowd is going home to dinner and who has more nefarious plans ("*dimah* shehu yakhol lir'ot be'einei ha'anashim" [1977, 210]; "He imagined that he could tell from people's eyes" [1983, 276]). Similarly, when a police car races by, the root *d.m.h.* recurs, suggesting that he imagines to himself that he is the only one who is paying attention to an all-too-common drama: "verak hu kame-dumeh nifnah lehabit" (1977, 210); "he seemed to be the only one who turned around to look" (1983, 276). And he even ascribes to the crowd an indifference and an othering of him. It seems to him that they would be amused to see him hit by a car ("*vedomeh* shehayu merutsim ilu nidras k'an le'einehem vetolesh reg'a ehad mishigrat yomam" [1977, 210]; "He had the impression that they would have been glad to see him get run over and that that would have diverted them from the monotony of their day" [1983, 276–77]).

It is not surprising that words related to the root *d.m.h.* are found in concentration at the end of the novella, where Meisels's feelings of powerlessness greatly intensify. Apparent in this clustering of words is the instability of boundaries between self and Others. Difference is fluid, a projection outward of the self, and toward the close of the narrative, the protagonist is most alone, somewhat wildly and erratically trying to connect with and relate to Others. As his connection with them becomes tenuous, he increasingly imagines them and, because of his uncertainties, projects his suppositions onto them.

The ending is devastating. Meisels collapses in the hotel room and the phone rings., There is no way to know whether help is on the way or whether he has been correct in his negative estimation of Americans. Although he has fought nobly to overcome stereotypical condemnations, it seems either that his nobility has been misplaced, i.e., that the world really is evil, or else that he has led himself, through his own doubts, into a foolish despair and foolish choices. On one hand, he has ignored the commonsense protection that stereotypes afford (i.e., it's not safe to walk alone down unfamiliar dark streets in New York). On the other hand, he has also adhered to a belief in the negative stereotype of American Jews; doubting their sincerity and affection causes him to doubt their warnings. Doubting that they will help him, he wanders off in the streets by himself, straight into danger. Everyone needs stereotypes to function in the world, but misusing his and miscalculating their usefulness, Meisels gravely miscalculates the Other. His heartrending misfortune becomes an indictment of his provincialism and naiveté, as well as a satiric indictment of American shortcomings.

The Counterlife

Like Shaham's "The Salt of the Earth," the "Judea" chapter of Roth's *The Counterlife* begins with a protagonist reluctant to travel. Nathan Zuckerman, an unabashedly secular individual, feels secure in his native United States and feels nothing but aversion for nationalism, religion, and Jewish xenophobia. These he considers unnecessary emotional burdens and hallmarks of Israeli identity, but he remains highly idealistic about America as a land of tolerance and pluralism.

Zuckerman assumes a wall of difference between American Jews and Israeli society. Like Shaham, Roth presents a physical symbol of this barrier: in this case, the Western Wall. Nathan has been skeptical about having an emotional reaction to the Wall, but when he arrives there he notes,

> It *was* more impressive than I'd anticipated, perhaps because the floodlights dramatizing the massive weight of the ancient stones seemed simultaneously to be illuminating the most poignant of history's themes: Transience, Endurance, Destruction, Hope. (Roth 1986, 93)

The capital letters indicate a separate realm, an authoritative world of meaningful collective history, opposed to his own preference for the realm of ordinary, personal, private experience.[8]

The situation is complicated, because within this difference are intimations of similarity. Thus, Nathan's brother, Henry, found at the Wall that its very otherness revealed to him his true mission in life. Upon seeing some children chanting their *heder* lessons there, he identifies fully with Jews and Judaism, decides to make *aliyah*, and discovers a self he had never before recognized as his own.

Having used the setting at the Wall to set up a clear opposition, and having then undermined that opposition, Roth introduces a comic dimension to the scene. Nathan runs into Jimmy, a manic *ba'al teshuva* (a secular Jew who has turned to ultraorthodoxy). Jimmy, from New Jersey, has become a fervent enthusiast of *yeshiva* life, but nonetheless laments that there is no baseball in Israel. "How can there be Jews without baseball" (Roth 1986, 105), he cries, and goes out for an imaginary catch at the Wailing Wall. This piling up of contradictory possibilities for Jewish self-definition is symptomatic of Roth's narrative approach in general. Indeed, cultivating plot juxtapositions and extensive use of direct dialogue, counterpoising all sorts of incongruous characters, Roth advances sharp polemical exchange and fosters a series of collisions between disparate ideologies and perspectives. In other words, he adopts dialogic strategies quite different from those of Shaham. Instead of emphasizing a complex convergence of voices within a single character, Roth revels in the external realm of public debate and dramatic contrast. In this way, though, his text, too, exemplifies Bakhtin's dictum that

> a language is revealed in all its distinctiveness only when it is brought into relation with other languages. . . . Against the dialogizing background of other languages . . . each language begins to sound differently than it would have sounded "on its own," as it were (without relating to others). (411–12)

The primary debate about Israel revolves around Agor, the settlement to which Henry Zuckerman repairs after surviving a dangerous coronary operation and undergoing a spiritual as well as a medical change of heart. Through a series of conversations held in Israel, and through letters exchanged between the Zuckerman brothers, Roth brings out the way in which these characters interpret themselves and one another. Each, in effect, invents the other. That is to say, each explains the other according to his own frame of understanding, while simultaneously striving to choose his own self-definition. At the heart of the novel, then, are proliferating, conflicting inventions of Jewishness. As Robert Alter noted in an early review of the book (July 1987), "After genocide and statehood and the fullest invitation to assimilation of any diaspora in history," it is not easy to imagine what a Jew might be. This novel is constructed as a series of clashing imaginations of the Jewish self in which "no single viewpoint is allowed to cancel out the others."

The most vigorous conflict takes place between champions of the secular, even hedonistic pleasures of diaspora life and of the super-nationalist ideals in Israel. The point of departure is the familiar Zionist accusation that diaspora Jews live an abnormal life of psychic division, in need of the clarity that could be theirs were they to live as Jews in a Jewish land. Nathan defends America as a triumph of Jewish identity. In his view it is in America, not Israel, that Jews enjoy a secure, tolerated existence, equal rights, and freedom from harm.

Henry staunchly opposes such views. Renaming himself Hanoch, he is intent on finding his Jewish roots, recalling a glorious ancient past, and defending the Jewish people by building a Jewish homeland. Henry also maintains that, for the sake of these values, he has overcome a profound selfishness. In New Jersey he had been willing to risk death from the heart operation, largely because he didn't want to jeopardize his sexual potency and an illicit amorous liaison. Now all that past life seems trivial and tawdry. Nathan counters that his brother's actions amount instead to an escape from humdrum propriety; rather than learning selflessness, Henry has indulged himself in a fantasy that allows him to leave his wife and children callously behind. Seen in this light, the mild-mannered dentist has not acquired courage. He has simply been seduced by irresponsibility due to an infatuation with military might and a rhetoric of force.

Each of these arguments gives rise to others, provokes additional comebacks, and so yields more elaborate, conflicting constructions of Israeli and American identity. Members of Gush Emunim, with which Henry has identified, charge that it is American culture that is enchanted with violence (its lionization of Norman Mailer is proof of that), while the use of arms in Israel is but a necessary means of self-defense. To Nathan, his brother's loyalty to Agor's leader, Lippman, is but subjugation to a charismatic father figure. Henry responds by accusing his brother of reducing every historical issue to individual neurosis. The debate encompasses religion, too. Appalled by the lack of sanctity in the secular world, Henry believes that Nathan's life is not genuinely Jewish. Nathan, in turn, feels that Henry's new piety is counterfeit, a kind of play-acting at Jewish devotion that betrays the particulars of Henry's own secular upbringing. In his view the Gush is a dangerous cult that has brainwashed and kidnapped his brother.

These debates entail extensive use of dialogue, many direct quotes, retorts, and counter-retorts. The characters frequently make speeches to one another. Here, for example, is one of Nathan's declarations of his convictions:

> I was the American born grandson of simple Galician tradesmen who, at the end of the last century, had on their own reached the same prophetic conclusion as Theodor Herzl—that there was no future for them in Christian Europe, that they couldn't go on being themselves there without inciting to violence ominous forces against which they hadn't the slightest means of defense. Insomuch as Zionism meant taking upon oneself, rather than leaving to others responsibility for one's survival as a Jew, this was their brand of Zionism. And it worked. (59)

And here is Henry's statement of his stance:

> All you see is escaping Momma, escaping Poppa—why don't you see
> what I've escaped *into*? *Everybody* escapes—our grandparents came
> to America, were they escaping their mothers and fathers? They
> were escaping history! Here they're *making* history! There's a
> world outside the Oedipal swamp, Nathan. (157)

The debate that rages throughout the narrative not only sets up
oppositions, letting each side's argument undermine the absoluteness of the other positions; the exchange also brings Nathan, at
least, to a remarkable degree of compromise, as he comes to acknowledge the finer qualities of the Agor leader. At first Nathan
condemns Lippman simply as a fascist, but later he concedes that
there must be some good in his values, since this man fills his
followers with pride; his wife's "eyes [shine] with love for a life free
of Jewish cringing, diplomacy, apprehension, alienation" (134).
Henry, as self-styled Hanoch, is "freer and more independent" (135)
than Nathan ever expected, and so, Nathan concludes, he is not
entirely mad for giving up his former life. To be sure, Nathan still
dismisses Lippman as a fanatic, but Nathan's own sense of what it
means to be Jewish has clearly been challenged.

If these dialogues internal to the "Judea" chapter unsettle set
definitions and understandings of Jewishness, so on a larger scale
does the overall structure of the novel. "Judea" is but a single
segment of a text that offers alternative imaginings of Henry's and
Nathan's lives. In one version Henry undergoes the heart operation
and dies, a victim of his own hedonism. In another it is Nathan who
has the cardiac problem, survives, and marries a non-Jewish woman.
In this version Nathan, moving to genteel England, finds himself
disenchanted with Christendom and so turns back to his Jewish
origins. Part of the narrative is presented as Nathan's own fiction
writing. Part is his wife's version of events as told to a psychiatrist.
Yet another part takes the form of Henry's reaction to Nathan's
words. Thus, each character creates the other by telling the tale
differently, and so Roth creates a kaleidoscope of possible relations
to Jewishness.[9]

Though this overall organization of the novel questions the very
notion of beginnings and endings, a disastrous ending to Nathan's
Israeli visit serves as a strong vehicle for Roth's depiction of Zionism
and marks that section of the novel with a disturbing final scene.

Significantly, as was true in Shaham's text, the disaster takes place when the protagonist is in transition, just beginning to return home. It occurs when he is most vulnerable—literally without his feet on the ground, in Roth's case, for Nathan is on an airplane.

On the flight Nathan finds himself sitting next to Jimmy, the manic American youngster whom he first met at the Western Wall. In a disturbed state, Jimmy has decided to hijack the plane to make a political statement. He appears as a self-styled terrorist whose slogan is "Forget Remembering." He figures that if everyone forgets Jewish history, gentiles will also forget to persecute Jews. When he pulls out a hand grenade, two guards swiftly arrest him. Nathan is also taken into custody as Jimmy claims that he, too, is involved in the hijacking scheme, and the two of them are stripped down to their skin and interrogated. Nathan's deepest complaint against Israel has been the militarism and violence that threaten the security of the individual, along with his distaste for the guardedness and suspiciousness that can easily turn into paranoia or xenophobia, thereby threatening individual freedoms. This final scenario of his visit brings these issues to life in a way that realizes his worst fears—far more personally than he had ever imagined.

It should be noted that the hijacking is recounted in a short segment of the novel called "Aloft," where the concerns with Jewishness, fictiveness, and invention of the Other converge most intensely. Placing the protagonist in an El Al plane high above the ocean, the narrative formulates the issues of identity and self-conception most loftily, while also leaving them most up in the air. On the flight, before the final denouement, Nathan composes and reads letters to his brother and to a friend. In them he expresses the governing conviction of the novel: "The treacherous imagination is everybody's maker; we are all the invention of each other, everybody a conjuration conjuring up everyone else. We are all each other's authors" (Roth 1986, 164). Nathan even goes further, concluding that we invent one another for our own benefit and fail to achieve genuine communication. Since Henry will probably disregard his comments and his criticisms of Agor, Nathan decides that his letter is directed more to himself than to his brother: "Hadn't I written this for myself anyway, for my own elucidation, trying to make interesting what he could not?" (176). Nathan even entertains the possibility that he, through his own interpretations of Henry, invests his brother's *aliyah* with more heightened meaning than that *aliyah* ever had for Henry.

The free play of imagination, which is the subject of Nathan's rumination, is brought dramatically to the fore thanks to the appearance of Jimmy. The simultaneous power and precariousness of self-invention manifest themselves obtrusively in this character's actions, for Jimmy makes himself up as he goes along. In Jerusalem he had adopted ultraorthodox garb with an astonishing alacrity that could only suggest phony conviction; now a fan of Zuckerman's, he declares his wish to follow his idol to England and celebrate Nathan's latest intermarriage.

Jimmy is a wild card who embraces the most assimilationist values after experimenting with the least assimilationist ones. His zany self-inventions are not dismissed out of hand as foolishness in the novel, for the security agents on the plane take his threat quite seriously. Though Jimmy insists he is a harmless prankster, and while Zuckerman protests that *he* is innocent of collusion, neither has proof of being what he claims. Until the plane lands and they can corroborate their stories, they remain unmoored in space, naked (stripped of a recognized identity), and at the mercy of Others who perceive them quite differently than they perceive themselves. At stake are matters of life and death, grievous injury, and individual rights; but in the midst of such high drama, the issues of interpretation and imagined identities are both powerful and privileged. In the air one feels especially keenly both the flimsiness of the (unsubstantiated) self-conception and the dire consequences attendant on each character's reading of the other.

Conclusions

Altogether, Roth pits a series of myopic projections against one another as he creates multiple inventions of the Jew. Although these foster more extended polemics than are found in "The Salt of the Earth," they also lead to slapstick possibilities for misunderstanding—most clearly at the end of "Aloft" when Nathan, unenthusiastic about Zionism, is transformed into a public enemy of Israel. To be sure, in the colliding worlds Roth describes there are amusing incongruities. It is humorous to find a Nathan Zuckerman in a biblical landscape, and the division evident in the split persona of a Henry/Hanoch is at least in part laughable. Moreover, the connections among different kinds of Jews represented in the novel may well seem tenuous, odd, or downright comic. The sabra, the European Holocaust survivor, the American suburbanite, the taxi driver from Iraq and his soldier son—these characters who have little in common seem to be part of a cockeyed, if not preposterous scheme of things. Roth creates a vision of Jewish history that, its tragic dimension notwithstanding, is a grand joke, the target of satiric exaggeration and attack.

Shaham's "The Salt of the Earth" reverses Roth's hierarchies of opposition. Shaham, too, recognizes comic incongruity in Jewish diversity, the astonishing variety of Jewishnesses in the world today, and the clashes that inevitably will arise among them. While Roth produces a surfeit of contradictory dialogues, Shaham, featuring, locating, and exploring the contradictions of being Jewish largely within a single protagonist, calls attention less to humor than to Meisels's ironic, somewhat bitter self-awareness. In contrast to Roth, Shaham studies his protagonist's pain at finding himself the fool and taking the pratfalls within a complicated scheme of things where there is no clear boundary between self and Other.

By the same token, Roth's juxtaposition of multiple plots, his retorts and polemics that put varying ideological stances into counterpoint, clearly fit in with critical concerns about "how the power to define what is 'obvious' helps to determine who rules" (Kavanaugh 1990, 318). Roth shows how different ideologies vie for the power to interpret one another in order to dominate one another and occupy the center of Jewish life. By contrast, Shaham for his part shows how much a sense of belonging depends on *having* power. As his protagonist feels in control, at the center of things, he interprets America according to his own beliefs. As his sense of power wanes, he either falls very much under the influence of others or falls back on prejudice and—in extremis—into blind hatred.

The titles of these novels put these basic contrasts into relief. Roth's choice, *The Counterlife*, suggests counter-point—i.e., counterparts and oppositions, a doubling or a multiplication of alternatives that puts into question the absoluteness of any one version of Jewishness. As these plural inventions of the Jew put into doubt the authenticity of any one definition, they also imply that any monolithic understanding of Jewishness must be counterfeit. Shaham's title, "The Salt of the Earth," is a phrase that connotes something modest, but genuine. Indeed, this description fits the protagonist, who is provincial but solidly grounded in his humanity —at least at first. He knows who he is, what he believes in, what impact—for better and for worse—his life has had on the people and

institutions connected with him. All those things, however—his
beliefs, his sincerity, his modesty—are challenged as he comes in
contact with Jews different from himself.

At the center of Shaham's narrative is the very personal transformation of a single character. Roth's novel includes one such
story, Henry's transformation into Hanoch, but the text expands well
beyond one episode of intercultural contact and constructs a grand,
abstract scheme of colliding values. This approach draws on Roth's
strengths. He creates grand farce peppered with the vitality,
persuasiveness, and zest of spoken dialogue. Shaham's text similarly exhibits narrative strengths that are typical of the author and
that he has developed elsewhere: Shaham uses a variety of double
voicings, especially free indirect discourse, to show diverse communities interpreting one another, while their mutual zeal to interpret
opens onto an abyss of misunderstandings.[10]

In her remarkable memoir, *Lost in Translation* (1989), Eva
Hoffman discusses cross-cultural encounters in terms peculiarly
applicable to these fictions by Shaham and Roth. Her comments
may serve as an apt summation of the contrast between "The Salt of
the Earth" and *The Counterlife* in their approaches to difference:

> It is no wonder—in our time of mass migrations and culture
> collisions and easy jet travel, when the whole world lies below us
> every time we rise into the skies, when whole countries move by
> like bits of checkerboard, ours to play on—it's no wonder that in
> this time we've developed whole philosophies of cultural relativity,
> and learned to look at whole literatures, histories, and cultural
> formations as if they were toy blocks, ours to construct and decon-
> struct. It's no wonder, also, that we have devised a whole meta-
> physics for the subjects of difference and otherness. (209)

These words are reminiscent of Roth's concerns. Hoffman moves on,
however, to considerations much closer to the issues that motivate
Shaham's text:

> But for all our sophisticated deftness at cross-cultural encounters,
> fundamental difference, when it's staring at you across the table
> from within the close-up face of a fellow human being, always
> contains an element of violation. My American friends and I find
> it an offense to our respective identities to touch within each other
> something alien, unfamiliar, in the very woof and warp of our inner
> lives. [We] are forced to engage in an experiment that is relatively

rare; we want to enter into the very textures, the emotions, and flavors of each other's vastly different subjectivities—and that requires feats of sympathy and even imagination in excess of either benign indifference or a remote respect. (210)

The compelling difference between Shaham and Roth, above all, is that Roth constructs, through literary play, a model of cultural relativity and otherness; Shaham traces more subtly one individual's experience of coming in contact with a different cultural milieu, sometimes entering and sometimes remaining estranged from the textures, flavors, and emotions of the Other's subjectivity.

Both these narratives, however, throwing Israelis and Americans into dialogue with one another, may herald a growing literary dialogue. American Jewish authors, showing new attentiveness to Israel, are no longer so quick to dismiss Israelis as distant Others. Israeli authors, showing new attentiveness to America, have begun to move beyond the impulse to deride the difference of their American kin and to exaggerate the differences between them.

NOTES

1. A few critics have lamented this neglect. See, for example, Fisch (1971), Alter (1987), Solatoroff (1988), and Sokoloff (1991). My own discussion here benefits from suggestions made at the Workshop on Modern Hebrew Literature held in Jerusalem (July 1992) and sponsored by the International Center for the University Teaching of Jewish Civilization. My thanks go to the workshop participants, especially to Gilead Moragh and Rachel Feldhay Brenner.

2. Several famous novels that mention Israel tangentially are Chaim Potok's *The Chosen* (1969), Philip Roth's *Portnoy's Complaint* (1969), and Saul Bellow's *Mr. Sammler's Planet* (1970). The first takes a very positive/idealistic view of Zionism, the second pokes satiric fun at Zionism in its final chapter, and the third observes and then turns away from the violence of military struggle in Israel. None of the novels, however, makes these issues into a major thematic focus. When discussing American writers in this essay, I am referring to authors from the United States. It is well worth looking at these issues also in relation to Canadian authors. In Canada, one major figure centrally concerned with Israel is A. M. Klein. He devoted poetry and a major novel, *The Second Scroll* (1951), to assessments of Zionism as a response to the Holocaust.

3. Menucha Gilboa comments on these three pieces of fiction at some length.
4. Another recent example from Hebrew literature that focuses centrally on an American setting is Anton Shammas's *Arabeskot* (*Arabesques*) (1986), which recounts the adventures of an Arab from Israel visiting Iowa. This fiction falls somewhat beyond the purview of this essay, since there is little attention in it to relations between American Jews and Israeli Jews.
5. Discussions of otherness have drawn on a range of theoretical approaches, including those of Michel Foucault, Jacques Lacan, Julia Kristeva, and Simone de Beauvoir, inter alia. My discussion here attempts to illuminate this text by drawing on the concepts of Bakhtin and Gilman, though no doubt other strategies of reading would yield interesting results as well.
6. One of his literary forebears, surely, is Sholem Aleichem's Mottel (*Mottl Peyse dem khazns*, 1908–1915), who flees Russia with his family but runs into Jews over every border they cross. Even in America Mottel feels he has never left the *shtetl* because he is surrounded by *landsmen*.
7. Bakhtin's ideas most important for this discussion find expression in "Discourse and the Novel" in *The Dialogic Imagination* (1981), 259–422. For extended discussion of the relation between inner dialogue and external voices in the work of Bakhtin and his contemporaries, see Caryl Emerson (1986).
8. Wilson (1991) provides extended discussion on the theme of history in this novel. See also Potok (1987) and Wohlgelernter (1989). My own 1991 essay discusses Roth's novel at greater length and compares it with Anne Roiphe's *Lovingkindness* (1987), as that novel also deals with American perceptions of Israel.
9. On this narrative organization as postmodernist fiction, see Greenstein (1991).
10. This kind of polyvocal narrative portrait is accomplished with comic flair in another novella set in the United States, "Tsion hal'o tish'ali," collected in *Ḥutsot Ashkelon* (1985). For an overview of Shaham's work, his ideological stances, and his artistic development, see Shaked (1990).

BIBLIOGRAPHY

Alter, Robert. 1987. "Defenders of the Faith." *Commentary* 84, 1:52–55.
Amihai, Yehuda. 1971. *Mi yitneni malon* (Hotel in the wilderness). Tel Aviv: Bitan.
Bakhtin, M. M. 1981. *The Dialogic Imagination: Four Essays*, ed. Michael Holquist. Trans. Caryl Emerson and Michael Holquist. Austin: University of Texas Press.

Bartov, Hanokh. 1984. *Be'emts'a haroman* (In the middle of it all). Tel Aviv: Am Oved.

Bellow, Saul. 1970. *Mr. Sammler's Planet.* New York: Viking.

Ben Ner, Yizhak. 1976. *Shki'ah kafrit* (Rustic sunset). Tel Aviv: Am Oved.

———. 1981. *Erets rehokah* (A distant land). Jerusalem: Keter.

Broner, E. M. 1978. *A Weave of Women.* New York: Holt, Rinehart, & Winston.

Emersen, Caryl. 1986. "The Outer World and Inner Speech: Bakhtin, Vygotsky, and the Internalization of Language." In *Bakhtin: Essays and Dialogues on His Work,* ed. Gary Saul Morson. Chicago: University of Chicago Press.

Fisch, Harold. 1971. *The Dual Image: The Figure of the Jew in English and American Literature.* New York: KTAV.

Gates, Henry Louis, Jr. 1985. *Race, Writing, and Difference.* Chicago: University of Chicago Press.

Gilboa, Menucha. 1988. "Amerikah kemakom, kemetaforah ukhesemel bishloshah romanim" (America as place, metaphor, and symbol in three novels). In *Migvan: mehkarim basifrut ha'ivrit uvegiluyeha ha'Amerikaniyim: mugashim leYa'akov Kabakuk bimlot lo shiv'im shanah.* Lod: Mckhon Haberman lemehkerei sifrut.

Gilman, Sander. 1985. *Difference and Pathology: Stereotypes of Sexuality, Race, and Madness.* Ithaca, N.Y.: Cornell University Press.

Greenstein, Michael. 1991. "Ozick, Roth, and Postmodernism." *Studies in American Jewish Literature* 10, 1:54–64.

Hoffman, Eva. 1989. *Lost in Translation: A Life in a New Language.* New York: Dutton.

Kaniuk, Yoram. 1961. *Hayored lema'alah.* Jerusalem: Schocken.

———. 1961. *The Acrophile.* Trans. Zeva Shapiro. New York: Atheneum.

———. 1973. *Sus'ets.* Tel Aviv: Sifriyat Poalim.

———. 1977. *Rockinghorse.* New York: Harper & Row.

Kavanaugh, James H. 1990. "Ideology." In *Critical Terms for Literary Study,* ed. Frank Lentricchia and Thomas McLaughlin. Chicago: University of Chicago Press.

Klein, A. M. 1951. *The Second Scroll.* New York: Knopf.

Koestler, Arthur. 1946. *Thieves in the Night.* New York: Macmillan.

Lev, Micha. 1986. *Yordim: Leaving the Promised Land for the Land of Promise.* Boston: Woodbine.

Nissenson, Hugh. 1965. *A Pile of Stones.* New York: Scribners.

———. 1968. *In the Reign of Peace.* New York: Farrar, Straus, Giroux.

Oz, Amos. 1986. *Kufsah shehorah.* Tel Aviv: Am Oved.

———. 1988. *Black Box.* Trans. Nicholas de Lange. San Diego, Calif.: Harcourt Brace Jovanovich.

Potok, Chaim. 1967. *The Chosen.* New York: Simon & Schuster.

———. 1987. "Potok on Roth." *Tikkun* 2, 2:91–93.

Reich, Tova. 1985. *Master of the Return*. New York: Harcourt Brace Jovanovich.

Roiphe, Anne. 1987. *Lovingkindness*. New York: Warner.

Roth, Philip. 1969. *Portnoy's Complaint*. New York: Random House.

———. 1986. *The Counterlife*. New York: Penguin.

Shaham, Natan. 1977. "Melaḥ ha'arets." In *Kirot'eits dakim*. Tel Aviv: Am Oved.

———. 1983. "The Salt of the Earth." In *The Other Side of the Wall*. Philadelphia: Jewish Publication Society.

———. 1985. *Ḥutsot Ashkelon* (The streets of Ashkelon). Tel Aviv: Am Oved.

Shaked, Gershon. 1990. "Tamid anaḥnu guf rishon rabim? 'al yetsirato shel Natan Shaham" (Always first person plural? On the writing of Natan Shaham). *Hakibbutz* 13:176–204.

Shalev, Meir. 1988. *Roman Rusi*. Tel Aviv: Am Oved.

———. 1991. *The Blue Mountain*. Trans. Hillel Halkin. New York: Aaron Asher.

Shamir, Moshe. 1986. *Yaldei hasha'ashu'im* (Playboys). Tel Aviv: Am Oved.

Shammas, Anton. 1986. *Arabeskot*. Tel Aviv: Am Oved.

———. 1988. *Arabesques*. Trans. Vivian Eden. New York: Harper & Row.

Sokoloff, Naomi. 1991. "Imagining Israel in American Jewish Fiction." *Studies in American Jewish Literature* 10, 1:65–80.

Solatoroff, Ted. 1988. *The New York Times Book Review*. 18 December, 1.

Starkman, Elaine Marcus, and Leah Schweitzer, eds. 1990. *Without a Single Answer*. Berkeley, Calif.: Magnes.

Wilson, Matthew. 1991. "Fathers and Sons in History: Philip Roth's *The Counterlife*." *Prooftexts* 11, 1:41–56.

Wohlgelernter, Maurice. 1989. "Philip Roth: Life and Counterlife: A Review Essay." *Modern Judaism* 9, 3:325–39.

Yehoshua, A. B. 1972. *Bitḥilat kayits 1970*. Merhavia: Hakibbutz Hemeuchad.

———. 1977. *Early in the Summer of 1970*. Trans. Miriam Arad. Garden City, N.Y.: Doubleday.

———. 1982. *Gerushim me'uharim*. Merhavia: Hakibbutz Hameuchad.

———. 1984. *Late Divorce*. Trans. Hillel Halkin. Garden City, N.Y.: Doubleday.

Chapter 15

Black Is Black: Jewish-American Reparations in Bernard Malamud's "Black Is My Favorite Color" and Stanley Elkin's "I Take Care of Ed Wolfe"

Elizabeth Fifer

The Other brings the self into focus. We learn what we are by declaring what we are not. In what way is black "other" to Jew? How has the relation between black and Jew been altered, ruptured, subverted? Can it be restored? How is black "difference," to use Jacques Derrida's term, manifested in Jewish consciousness? Is the black marginalized to the Jew as the Jew is to the rest of society? How has the black been construed and constructed in contemporary Jewish-American fiction? Both Bernard Malamud's "Black Is My Favorite Color" and Stanley Elkin's "I Take Care of Ed Wolfe" investigate these issues in the context of such concerns as Jewish obligation to other oppressed peoples and the burden of black and Jewish history.[1]

In these stories, the Jew bears witness to the suffering of blacks, including his own role in that suffering, and seeks to make reparation for it, but his attempts to do something for them are rebuffed and rejected. In Malamud's story, Nat Lime, proprietor of a liquor store in Harlem and a lonely, middle-aged bachelor, tries vainly to form an attachment to a black woman. His distance from her and from the rest of humanity insures his continued isolation. Elkin's tale of Ed Wolfe, the ex–bill collector's quest for connection, is similarly quixotic—in anger and desperation he thrusts himself into work, and once that ends, randomly moves in crowds, feeling himself attracted to black strangers who distrust and fear him. Although these two stories contrast in their treatment of black characters, they are similar in that their characters fail to realize the Jewish

ideal of *mitzvot*, fulfillment through connection and even identification. The black characters realize their state of otherness to the
Jews and consequently turn away to protect their sense of dignity
and self-worth.[2]   Malamud's story traces the failed love affair
between a white man and a black woman; Elkin's tale explores a
white man's disaffection with the whole society and his attempt to
relate to a black man and woman in order to alleviate his own
depression.   The twin failures of these two otherwise different
attempts suggest something of the complexity and intransigence of
black-Jewish relations in America today.

The Other brings the self into question. It is self-doubt that
fuels the sense of responsibility Malamud's Nat Lime and Elkin's Ed
Wolfe feel toward blacks. They perceive their separation from the
black as a judgment against them. Both feel a pull, a summons to
the black community, to that part of themselves that lies with the
Other, but precisely because they act out of self-interest and in the
context of their own sense of persecution and need for expiation,
they are rudely expelled. By exposing themselves and their needs
they benefit only themselves and are therefore left vulnerable to the
anger of black characters who are similarly caught up in their own
needs and their own history.

Nat's and Ed's obsession with blacks and their desire to have an
emotional and psychological union with them carries within it a
sense of desperation that has little to do with justice or mercy and
that allegorizes and depersonalizes its recipients. It consists of a
sort of substitution—the black stands for something these Jewish
protagonists cannot actualize within themselves.   These black
characters, however, insist on their independent personhood; they
will not allow themselves to be reduced to opportunities for Jewish
self-congratulation or reparation.

These two particular short stories are important because each
contains an encoded history of race relations in America. Despite
their disparate styles—Malamud's earthy, slice-of-life language,
replete with Jewish dialect, contrasts sharply with Elkin's elaborate,
apocalyptic, elegant prose—both present odysseys in which Jewish
characters seek to right the wrongs of American history, to pay back
what has been taken away from blacks. While their attempts might
be considered heroic, the results are predictable. Noble gestures are
perceived as gestures nevertheless.

In both stories Jews see blacks through a veil of difference that
obscures their true identity. Although Jews share an urban geogra-

phy with blacks, the black world is utterly cut off, alien and desperate. For Nat Lime, seeing the way his black friend Buster lived, only a few blocks away, was an admonition and a hellish vision of danger that returns him to the dangers of the Holocaust:

> The Negro houses looked to me like they had been born and died there, dead not long after the beginning of the world. . . . If there can be like this, what can't there be? I mean I caught an early idea what life was about. (Malamud 1984, 75)

Within the same sort of limitation, when Buster finally rejects Nat's friendship, he does not see the person of Nat but only a "Jew bastard" trying to humiliate him with charity (77). Each sees only a depersonalized fragment of the Other, a fiction that denotes distance and separation. Otherness represses identification even as it reflects and preserves identity.

This limitation pervades the most intimate moments of these characters' lives. Even when Nat has become infatuated with Ornita and they are about to make love, he sees not an individual woman but an odd pastiche of black and white:

> Under her purple dress she wore a black slip, and when she took that off she had white underwear. When she took off the white underwear she was black again. But I know where the next white was, if you want to call it white. (80)

Nat sees her as a color combination; to transcend her otherness he imagines her blackness covering an essential whiteness that sexuality alone can discover. In this way he recreates her out of his own need. Her beauty substitutes for his ugliness. By this metamorphosis he seeks to become other than what he is. He can then define himself in relation to this second image. When they are out together, he imagines a passerby admiring her and, by extension, him—the gaze goes from her to him: "If they looked maybe they saw . . . how pretty she was for a man my type" (79). She is an instrument meant to legitimize his sexuality, put into question by his "bald spot" shining under a street lamp, even as she is meant to legitimize his humanity. Her sexuality and humanity are merely adjuncts to his pervasive needs.

It is for this same reason that Elkin's Ed Wolfe finds himself literally unable to see his Other with whom he means to join. Oliver is buried behind a newspaper, the "blind date" Mary Roberta only visible through an alcoholic haze in a speakeasy. Like Nat, Ed is left mainly with colors—Mary Roberta's "luxuriant brown hand" inside his own "pale" one (Elkin 1967, 549). His mind is on the separateness that marks and mocks him, questioning his own vitality. Cherishing the separate identity of a fellow human being is strictly secondary to his own pressing but self-contained needs.

Finding emotional and spiritual concerns to be beyond their ken, both men find it easier to focus on their material status. Money, both decide, is their real problem, their real measure. Ed loses his job and ends up with his life savings, $2,479.03, in a coat pocket. "So, he thought, that was what he was worth" (537). Far from being the acquisitive or even the thrifty Jew, however, Ed's urge is to arrange a renunciation, a throwing off, a Jewish "potlatch"[3] in which all his goods, replete with memory, are auctioned for a fraction of their value. He throws away the money he gets for them. But he cannot throw away his identity.

Nat is a provider, the archetypal good Jewish husband, although he has no wife. He makes a living with his business. He pays his black workers well. Through the giving of a discount, he makes friends with Ornita, the black woman with whom he falls in love. He can treat Ornita to good dinners, dressed in a "new lightweight suit" (Malamud 1984, 79). He uses his economic power to draw Ornita to him, but he does not see his self as valuable. He doubts the validity of his own body. He sees social failure inscribed on his body, a second circumcision. He offers money in the place of a discounted self.

Both Nat and Ed want to enter forbidden territory, to rid themselves of their economic and psychological past. Their need is to escape and recreate their selves. When Nat decides to marry Ornita, he inventories his store, preparing to sell out. Ed, too, sells everything he has and takes his earnings, stuffed in his pocket, to the black speakeasy. Both are divested before their central encounter with the black—Nat has lost his mother to cancer (only to see her again in a black woman's eyes); Ed has lost his job and lives alone in one room.

Their loneliness is horrific. They have not yet been legitimized by an Other. Nat summarizes his few attachments in the past—"I have liked one or two nice girls I used to go with when I was a boy" (Malamud 1984, 80). One day Ed realizes nobody has touched him in six months.

Both Ed and Nat are also outsiders even among other Jews, Nat because of his attraction to blacks, or his lack of attraction to Jews, Ed because he is an orphan, given Jewish identity only by chance: "Ed Wolfe, the Flying Dutchman, the Wandering Jew, the Off and Running Orphan" (Elkin 1967, 527).

Ed goes down to the city's "navel," the origin of all life, to seek the pawnshop with its Jewish owner who will give him money for the last shreds of his possessions. There he sees the Jew as Everyman—"I wouldn't have recognized you. Where's the skullcap, the garters around the sleeves? . . . You look like anybody. You look like everybody" (534). Here the Jew is divested, alone among a hoard of others' possessions, assimilated to the point of anonymity—in other words, he is like Ed himself. Ed almost tells him something sordid—anything to define himself, to claim his own "difference" and identity. Only this contrast, this opposition, can crystallize his own distinct humanity.

Both Nat and Ed are in the pre-mirror stage[4] that Lacan describes. They are fragmented; they have not yet achieved the wholeness, let alone the solidity, of the composite image the mirror stage implies: "a powerful gestalt promising mastery, unity, and substantive stature . . . that idealized totality that grounds the mechanisms of defense" (Muller and Richardson 1982, 6). "The image is a form that in-forms the subject and makes possible the process of identification with it" (28). Ed is the invisible man—clothes fastidious, unmarked, but empty inside, or worse than empty, flayed, unable to cohere: "I don't speak of inside. Inside it's all Band-Aids, plaster, iodine, sticky stuff for burns . . . I feel as if I'm selling my skin" (Elkin 1967, 535). Inside his baggy frame Nat is amorphous, too—he "could lose frankly fifteen pounds" off a body that, even then, nobody would look at twice.

Both are depicted as fragments of the Diaspora, scattered where they cannot root. Nat's store is in Harlem, "between Hundred Tenth and Eleventh" (Malamud 1984, 83). He is the Jew as entrepreneur, "the clever and economically necessary merchant" (Porter 1979, 80) who stands between the blacks and the rest of the society, "economic middlemen in the black ghetto" (80). If Nat is displaced, Ed is doubly so—he has no work community, no family, no friends—"no one calls" (Elkin 1967, 535).

Because they cannot see themselves reflected in the approved and sanctioned faces of white America—they cannot compel the glance—they seek their Other, the societally marginalized black, feeling that here at last is a face that cannot risk turning away. They are both proved emphatically wrong in this assumption. As Stuart A. Lewis has observed, and as both Malamud and Elkin demonstrate, "The Jew has come to realize that on the emotional and personal level he needs the black more than the black needs him" (1973, 330).

Both stories, from a Jewish perspective, reenact the sad history of blacks and Jews. Both Malamud and Elkin add the burden of Jewish self-hatred, the internalization of the anti-Semitic oppressor. As he sells off everything, Ed muses, like Shakespeare's Shylock, "Put money in your purse, Ed Wolfe" (Elkin 1967, 528). Nat remembers his mother "and what she tried to teach me. Nathan, she said, if you ever forget you are a Jew a goy will remind you" (Malamud 1984, 80). In an eerie parody of history, Wolfe starts a mock slave auction in the black club, putting his black companion on the block while insisting he is "not a consumer himself," that "nobody's death can make me that" (Elkin 1967, 547). But the Jew's rejection by white America is not sufficient to support his assumption of common ground with blacks.

Ed may not consider himself to be a consumer, but he is a salesman, "a disposer, a natural dumper" (Elkin 1967, 531). Maurice Charney has noted that in Stanley Elkin's fiction "the archetypal Jewish character . . . is the salesman" whose tone can turn "frantic, obsessive, and manic" (Charney 1987, 185). As he mimes the fearful act of selling another human being, Ed's style is that of the hyped-up auctioneer: "What am I bid? What am I bid for this fine strong wench? Daughter of a chief . . . say, what's the matter with you darkies? Come on, what am I bid?" (Elkin 1967, 547).

In this mirroring of history, Ed transforms the woman into both a commodity and a symbol of the most extreme otherness. Her physical self is the only reality in this exchange value: "Look at those arms. Those arms, those arms. What am I bid?" (Elkin 1967, 547). Because he has no self-image, he misreads his listeners. He cannot mollify the black audience by calling them "masters" (547). The audience begins to mutter threateningly, "You can't make fun of us" (548), and the girl is pulled from the stage.

Here Ed draws a comparison between the Jewish orphan in history, himself once a slave, and the slavery of the blacks. Their mistreatment by the society around them has put them outside the normal bounds of emotional connection and demands. They cannot be expected to love if they have not been treated with love. Rather than seeking to remedy this emotional deficiency, however, Ed seeks to use it to his own advantage. He feels freer when he does not have to be responsive and sensitive to others' feelings: "An orphan doesn't have to bother with love. An orphan is like a nigger in that respect. Emancipated" (548). This perspective may be useful in his self-justification, but it cannot mask the essential ugliness of his sentiments.

To this extent, Nat Lime is different—he needs love and can admit to it. He actively searches for love with blacks and courts Ornita with energy. Yet this reaching out is no more successful than Ed's rejection—both extend the distance between the self and the Other. One night as he is accompanying Ornita home, Nat's courtship is violently interrupted by racial and economic forces he hasn't the strength to oppose. Three men or boys, identifiable only by a black hat with a half-inch brim, a green cloth hat, and a black leather cap—just as traditional Jews might be reduced to their headgear by unsympathetic Christians—confront him. One carries a six-inch switchblade, asking Ornita accusingly, "What you doin' with this white son of a bitch?" (Malamud 1984, 82).

At first the distance is only from black to white. But when Nat speaks, hatred is extended to the Jew as Nat becomes the stereotyped landlord who extorts money from blacks, even as he himself, the impoverished immigrant, had been squeezed in the tenements. "'You talk like a Jew landlord,' said the green hat. 'Fifty a week for a single room. No charge fo' the rats,' said the half-inch brim" (82).

Nat protests, explaining that he owns a liquor store (and in some ways this plays into stereotypes of black need; Nat's identity as a purveyor of a drug that corrupts the black ghetto is doubly damaging): "My store is Nathan's Liquors . . . I also have two colored clerks, Mason and Jimmy, and they will tell you I pay good wages as well as I give discounts to certain customers" (83).

If his attackers fail to gain identities, are flattened into thugs, Nat is flattened into a figure of greed and injustice. Jack Nusan Porter remarks that in the context of black anti-Semitism, "The Jew is no longer neutral. He can be viewed as the enemy" (Porter 1979, 80). "'Shut your mouth, Jew boy,' said the leather cap, and he moved the knife back and forth in front of my coat button. 'No more black pussy for you'" (Malamud 1984, 83).

This ritual is about the transference, and the demonstration, of sexuality. The brandishing of the six-inch knife, the reduction of

Ornita to her organs alone, creates a sexual response to the Jew's power in the outside world. Even as the black man has been, the Jew is reduced to a mere "boy." Anger at the Jew's economic power is translated into a physical response: "I got slapped on the mouth" (Malamud 1984, 83). As the Jew is rendered impotent, his love is devalued: "'Speak with respect about this lady, please.' 'That ain't no lady'" (83).

The scene transfers Nat's love to violence. The men threaten to shave Ornita's hair, the punishment dealt to collaborators with the enemy, the hated Other. Her scream recalls her husband's violent end, "like her husband was falling fifteen stories" (83). Later it is Nat who falls, literally, into the gutter, a man who cannot protect his beloved, a Jew discovered and mocked and, as a last insult, punched and robbed. Ornita, as if to stress his vulnerability, walks him to the subway.

Just as Nat is robbed by the thugs, so Ed fantasizes being robbed by his black companion, Oliver, whom he calls "razor man" (Elkin 1967, 543). Ed is haunted by movie images of blacks and replays old tapes where he is the lovelorn Humphrey Bogart character in a trench coat with his sidekick Eddie. This reinforces the conventions of master and slave, thereby empowering Ed. The black supplies the drama missing from Ed's life. "I'll never smile again,' he sang. 'Mistuh Wuf, you don' wan' ta heah dat al song no maw. You know what it do to you. She ain't wuth it, Mistuh Wuf.' He nodded. 'Again, Eddie.' Eddie played his black ass off" (549). Ed's identity is split between the Jew Ed, the straight man, and Eddie, the black salesman, between "Mr. Wolfe" and "Mr. Woof."

As if to confirm this shattered identity, Ed later tells the black audience that his companion Oliver is "my man. I take him everywhere with me. It looks good for the race" (542). Ed possesses Oliver, ironically imposing distance at the same time with the words "my man" (with all that implies—servant, friend, or master, it depends how you take it).

Historical images block out the reality of the Other in both Malamud's and Elkin's texts. Malamud's Ornita refuses Nat Lime's advances at first, saying wisely, "I don't like white men trying to do me favors" (Malamud 1984, 78). Behind her suspicion is the certain memory, at least historical if not personal, of white men's aggression, of the kind of "favor" white men did for black women.

Nat Lime is fated to be unloved. Either the language of his heart speaks falsely, or it is unheard.[5] His risks in the liquor store business pay off—"I do alright" (74)—but that does not make up for losses in love. Ed Wolfe also wants to give reparation to the blacks. He sells everything and brings his money to the black club as "the going rate for orphans in a wicked world" (Elkin 1967, 537). At the end of his auction he tries to give his money away, but his currency has been devalued; he just hears the sound of "paper tearing" (549).

Nat would like to make reparation through his marriage to Ornita, but first he has to satisfy the ghost of her dead husband. "'My husband woulda killed me.' 'Your husband's dead.' 'Not in my memory'" (Malamud 1984, 81).

If Ornita does not judge, her dead husband will. Memory and language conspire to evict Ed when he walks into the black club: "'Who's the ofay, Oliver?'" (Elkin 1967, 543). Ed feels lifeless beside Mary Roberta, for when he takes her arm, her "muscle leaped . . . filling his palm" (545). He tells Mary Roberta that he is a pusher who can't get hooked himself. It is his torment. This idea of the inability to enter into addiction, the inability to satisfy a need, to make an end of desire, marks Ed's separateness from all humanity and especially the blacks: "'Ach, what would you goyim know about it?'" (546).

Saying "'I got trouble enough of my own'" (Malamud 1984, 84), Ornita leaves Nat. This failed romance is framed by Nat's new infatuation with Charity Quietness, his maid, who reminds him of his mother. But even Charity refuses to eat at the same table with Nat. She comes from Father Divine, she has been saved, and so she can ignore his pleas for equality, eating her hard-boiled eggs in the toilet for privacy. She would rather be there than with Nat. When Ed grasps the hand of the black woman in the club at the end of the story, he says he feels "infinitely free" (Elkin 1967, 549), but is this the same absolute lack of connection that Nat feels alone at his kitchen table?

These characters say they don't want to accept difference but difference remains, nevertheless. The black will always be black, the white will always be white, and the Jew will always be regarded with suspicion by both black and white, regardless of his motive. In other words, rejection of the Jew by white society does not imply Jewish solidarity with blacks, as Nat finds out when he tries to help a blind black man and is rebuffed for the last time. "'I can tell you're white,' he said" (Malamud 1984, 84). It's a vaudevillian ending, but it fits Nat's excessive zeal. Even a blind man can recognize Nat's "otherness." It is the ironically fitting reply to a man who loved Ornita, but could not keep from judging her "lips a little thick and nose a little broad" (78). If these characters cannot embrace their own autonomous selves, how can they hope to construct the face of the Other?

NOTES

1. As articulated by Eugene Borowitz, "We Jews, of all peoples, cannot turn our backs on this sense of human solidarity, for one of its earliest triumphs was our emancipation" (1984, 61). Referring to Abraham Joshua Heschel, Borowitz argues, "Heschel insisted that the Covenant mandated a concern for all humanity and that, wherever human values were seriously at stake, Jewish interests were necessarily involved" (67). No matter how oppressed Jews were, they did not deny the basic unity of mankind (403).
2. Stanley Schatt notes that both Buster and Ornita want to preserve their "self-respect" by "fleeing" from Nat (Schatt 1970, 52).
3. The Indians of the Pacific Northwest, like the Haida, engaged in a ritual giving away of all their goods in a ceremony called the "potlatch," considered a cleansing process, usually performed at intervals of a decade.
4. Muller and Richardson, explicating Lacan, have described this stage as the "infant's jubilant identification with its reflection" (1982, 6).
5. Stuart Lewis observes that "Nat is 'liberal' not because he really believes in the equality of all men—he consistently stereotypes Blacks—but rather because he feels that holding such an attitude is the commendable thing to do. In return, he expects love and gratitude, which are denied to him" (Lewis 1973, 323–24).

BIBLIOGRAPHY

Borowitz, Eugene B. 1984. *Liberal Judaism*. New York: Union of American Hebrew Congregations.

Charney, Maurice. 1987. "Stanley Elkin and Jewish Black Humor." In *Jewish Wry: Essays on Jewish Humor*, ed. Sarah Blacher Cohen. Bloomington: Indiana University Press, 178–95.

Elkin, Stanley. 1967. "I Take Care of Ed Wolfe." In *Contemporary American Short Stories*, ed. Douglas Angus and Sylvia Angus. New York: Fawcett, 519–49.

Lewis, Stuart A. 1973. "The Jewish Author Looks at the Black." *Colorado Quarterly* 21:317–30.

Malamud, Bernard. 1984. "Black Is My Favorite Color." In *The Stories of Bernard Malamud*. New York: New American Library, 73–84.

Muller, John P., and William J. Richardson. 1982. *Lacan and Literature: A Reader's Guide to Ecrits*. New York: International Universities Press.

Porter, Jack Nusan. 1979. "John Henry and Mr. Goldberg: The Relationship between Blacks and Jews." *International Migration Review* 13, 3:73–86.

Schatt, Stanley. 1970. "The Faceless Face of Hatred: The Negro and the Jew in Recent American Literature." *Western Review: A Journal of the Humanities* 7, 2:49–55.

Chapter 16

The Jewish Nose: Are Jews White?
Or, the History of the Nose Job

Sander L. Gilman

When the Lubavitcher Manis Friedman, the dean of the Bais Chana
Women's Institute in St. Paul, preaches that "Jews are different.
Let's accept it and be thrilled," one can only agree.[1] But his sense
of difference is cast in a language that itself is contaminated with
the sense of a negative Jewish difference, a difference of the Jewish
body. He continues: "For 2,000 years we have denied our uniqueness. *We have tried to come to the world as if we were normal. Well,
guess what? The world hasn't bought it, and they never will.*"
According to Friedman, Jews are not normal.

What is the antithesis of "normal"? It certainly is not "different"
or "special" or "chosen." Rather, it is abnormal, diseased. What
does it mean, therefore, when those who celebrate a particular
Jewish difference can only speak of it as being positioned at the far
end of the scale reaching from the normal to the abnormal, the
deviant, the different? One consequence is that the celebration of
Jewish difference (whether of the religious or the secular mode)
assumes a fixity in relation to that primary referent of difference.
And that fixity is understood in terms of its fictive polar alternative—collapse, decay, destruction. Thus, difference is commonly
understood as a fixed, rather than a fluid equation, and it is often

This chapter is a much-expanded version of chapter 7 of *The Jew's Body* by
Sander L. Gilman, 1991; and is reprinted here by permission of the
publisher, Routledge, Inc.

possible so to repress the perils of this dichotomy that one finds oneself on the wrong side of "normal."

Yet, viewed from a different perspective, identity is a combination of internal and external, psychological and social qualities—you are always where you are, not who you are. Identity is always interactive, never separate from the world—either in a developmental or a cultural sense. Identity is a dynamic process—not a fixed point. Seen in this light, there is no such thing as a "purely" Jewish identity; from the prebiblical world to the Babylonian Diaspora to the world of Sepharad or Askenaz, Jews—like all people—have formed themselves within as well as against the world that they inhabited, that they defined, and that defined them.

Gilles Deleuze and Félix Guattari began to sketch a dynamic, constructive model of the process of identity formation in their description of "becoming-Jewish." They wrote in *A Thousand Plateaus*,

> Jews . . . may constitute minorities under certain conditions, but that in itself does not make them becomings. . . . Even Jews must become-Jewish (it certainly takes more than a state). But if this is the case, then becoming-Jewish necessarily affects the non-Jew as much as the Jew. Becoming-woman necessarily affects men as much as women. Conversely, if Jews themselves must become-Jewish . . . , it is because only a minority is capable of serving as the active medium of becoming, but under such conditions that it ceases to be a definable aggregate in relation to the majority. . . . Becoming-Jewish, becoming-woman . . . therefore imply simultaneous movements, one by which a term (the subject) is withdrawn from the majority, and another by which a term (the medium or agent) rises up from the minority.[2]

This merging of the identity of the majority that defines and the minority, the Other, that is defined and thus redefines the majority is a process of constant construction and reconstruction of identity.

Now such identity transformations have been conventionally understood as being internal, purely psychological in their representation. Thus, "becoming-Jewish," in the sense of Gilles Deleuze and Félix Guattari, is understood as a process of identity formation. However, what is often overlooked in this psychological view of identity formation is the role of the physical.

In this essay, I wish to illustrate the complex, physical reconstitution of the Jewish body within the past century, not only its perception and internalization but also the actual physical alteration of the body. I hope to show how this "becoming-Jewish" is a slipperier locus of difference than even Gilles Deleuze and Félix Guattari have imagined—that the common wisdom after the Shoah about the power of assimilation totally to destroy Jewish identity is not only false but provides yet another simplistic attempt to deal with the complexity of identity formation not only in the Diaspora but also in contemporary Israel—for Israeli identity is in part a reflex of diaspora Jewish identity. The view that states that the pressures of assimilation in the European and American Diaspora lead to perversions of the self and to a model of self-hatred so intense that its fire can destroy the very fabric of sanity is but one end of this spectrum—for identity is a complex thing and its deformations and reformations are many in their form and their direction.

The personals columns in the *Washingtonian*, the local city magazine in Washington, D.C., are filled with announcements of individuals "in search of" mates. ("In search of" is the rubric under which these advertisements are grouped.) These advertisements are peppered with various codes so well known that they are never really explained: "DWM [Divorced White Male] just recently arrived from Boston seeks a non-smoking, financially secure 40+ who loves to laugh," or "SJF [Single Jewish Female], Kathleen Turner type, with a zest for life in search of S/DJM for a passionate relationship." Recently, I was struck by a notice which began "DW(J)F [Divorced White (Jewish) Female]—young, 41, Ph.D., professional, no kids, seeks S/D/WWM, exceptional mind, heart & soul."[3] What fascinated me were the brackets: advertisements for "Jews" or for "African Americans" or for "Whites" made it clear that individuals were interested in choosing their sexual partners from certain designated groups within American society. But the brackets implied that here was a woman who was both "White" and "Jewish." Given the racial politics of post–civil rights America, where do the Jews fit in? It made me ask the question that the woman who placed the personals advertisement clearly was addressing: are Jews white? and what does "white" mean in this context? Or, to present this question in a slightly less polemical manner, how has the question of racial identity shaped Jewish identity in the Diaspora? I am not addressing what the religious, ethnic, or cultural definition of the Jew is—either from within or from without Judaism or the Jewish community—but rather I am asking how the category of race present within Western, scientific, and popular culture has shaped Jewish self-perception.

My question is not merely an "academic" one—rather, I am interested in how the representation of the Jewish body is shaped and, in turn, shapes the sense of Jewish identity. My point of departure is the view of Mary Douglas:

> The human body is always treated as an image of society and . . . there can be no natural way of considering the body that does not involve at the same time a social dimension. Interest in its apertures depends on the preoccupation with social exits and entrances, escape routes and invasions. If there is no concern to preserve social boundaries, I would not expect to find concern with bodily boundaries.[4]

Where and how a society defines the body reflects how those in society define themselves. This is especially true in terms of the "scientific" or pseudoscientific categories such as race that have had such an extraordinary importance in shaping how we all understand ourselves and each other. From the conclusion of the nineteenth century, the idea of "race" has been given a positive as well as a negative quality. That we belong to a race and our biology defines us is as true a statement for many groups as is the opposite: you belong to a race and your biology limits you. Race is a constructed category of social organization as much as it is a reflection of some aspects of biological reality. Racial identity has been a powerful force in shaping how we, at the close of the twentieth century, understand ourselves—often in spite of ourselves. Beginning in the eighteenth century and continuing to the present, there has been an important cultural response to the idea of race, one that has stressed the uniqueness of the individual over the uniformity of the group. As Theodosius Dobzhansky noted in 1967,

> Every person has a genotype and a life history different from any other person, be that person a member of his family, clan, race, or mankind. Beyond the universal rights of all human beings (which may be a typological notion!), a person ought to be evaluated on his own merits.[5]

Dobzhansky and many scientists of the 1960s dismissed "race" as a category of scientific evaluation, arguing that whenever it had been included over the course of history, horrible abuses had resulted.[6]

At the same time, within Western, specifically American, culture of the 1960s, there was also a transvaluation of the concept of "race." "Black" was "beautiful," and "roots" were to be celebrated, not denied. The view was that seeing oneself as being a part of a "race" was a strengthening factor. We at the close of the twentieth century have, however, not suddenly become callous to the negative potential of the concept of "race." Given its abuse in the Shoah[7] as well as in neocolonial policies throughout the world,[8] it is clear that a great deal of sensitivity must be used in employing the very idea of "race." In reversing the idea of "race," we have not eliminated its negative implications; we have only masked them. For it is also clear that the meanings associated with "race" impact on those included within these constructed categories. It forms them and shapes them. And this can be a seemingly positive or a clearly negative response. There is no question that there are "real" (i.e., shared) genetic distinctions within and between groups. But the rhetoric of what this shared distinction comes to mean for the general culture and for the "group" so defined becomes central to any understanding of the implications of race.

Where I would like to begin is with that advertisement in the *Washingtonian* and with the question that the bracketed "J" posed: are Jews white? To begin to answer that question we must trace the debate about the skin color of the Jews, for skin color remains one of the most salient markers for the construction of race in the West over time. The general consensus of the ethnological literature of the late nineteenth century was that the Jews were "black" or, at least, "swarthy." This view had a long history in European science. As early as 1691 François-Maximilien Misson, whose ideas influenced Buffon's *Natural History*, argued against the notion that Jews were black:

> 'Tis also a vulgar error that the Jews are all black; for this is only true of the Portuguese Jews, who, marrying always among one another, beget Children like themselves, and consequently the Swarthiness of their Complexion is entailed upon their whole Race, even in the Northern Regions. But the Jews who are originally of Germany, those, for example, I have seen at Prague, are not blacker than the rest of their Countrymen.[9]

But this was a minority position. For the eighteenth- and nine-teenth-century scientist the "blackness" of the Jew was not only a mark of racial inferiority but also an indicator of the diseased nature of the Jew. The "liberal" Bavarian writer Johann Pezzl, who traveled to Vienna in the 1780s, described the typical Viennese Jew of his time:

> There are about five hundred Jews in Vienna. Their sole and eternal occupation is to counterfeit, salvage, trade in coins, and cheat Christians, Turks, heathens, indeed themselves. . . . This is only the beggarly filth from Canaan which can only be exceeded in filth, uncleanliness, stench, disgust, poverty, dishonesty, pushiness, and other things by the trash of the twelve tribes from Galicia. Excluding the Indian fakirs, there is no category of supposed human beings which comes closer to the orangutan than does a Polish Jew. . . . Covered from foot to head in filth, dirt and rags, covered in a type of black sack . . . their necks exposed, the color of a Black, their faces covered up to the eyes with a beard, which would have given the High Priest in the Temple chills, the hair turned and knotted as if they all suffered from the *plica polonica*.[10]

The image of the Viennese Jew is that of the Eastern Jew, suffering from the diseases of the East, such as the *Judenkratze*, the fabled skin and hair disease also attributed to the Poles under the designation of the *plica polonica*.[11] The Jews' disease is written on the skin. It is the appearance, the skin color, the external manifestation of the Jew that marks the Jew as different. There is no question for a non-Jewish visitor to Vienna upon first seeing the Jew that the Jew suffers from Jewishness. The internal, moral state of the Jew, the Jew's very psychology, is reflected in the diseased exterior of the Jew. *Plica polonica* was a real dermatologic syndrome. It results from living in filth and poverty. But it was also associated with the unhygienic nature of the Jew and, by the mid-nineteenth century, with the Jew's special relationship to the most frightening disease of the period, syphilis.[12] For the non-Jew seeing the Jew it mirrored popular assumptions about the Jew's inherent, essential nature. Pezzl's contemporary, Joseph Rohrer, stressed the "disgusting skin diseases" of the Jew as a sign of the group's general infirmity.[13] And the essential Jew for Pezzl was the Galician Jew, the Jew from the eastern reaches of the Hapsburg Empire.[14] (This late-eighteenth-century view of the meaning of the Jew's skin color was not only held by non-Jews. The Enlightenment Jewish physician Elcan Isaac Wolf saw this "black-yellow" skin color as a pathognomonic sign of the diseased Jew).[15]   Following the humoral theory of the times, James Cowles Pritchard (1808) commented on the Jews' "choleric and melancholic temperaments, so that they have in general a shade of complexion somewhat darker than that of the English people."[16]   Nineteenth-century anthropology as early as the work of Claudius Buchanan commented on the "inferiority" of the "black" Jews of India.[17]   By the midcentury, being black, being Jewish, being diseased, and being "ugly" came to be inexorably linked.   All races, according to the ethnology of the day, were described in terms of aesthetics, as either "ugly" or "beautiful."[18] African Blacks, especially the Hottentot, as I have shown elsewhere, became the epitome of the "ugly" race.[19]   And being ugly, as I have also argued, was not merely a matter of aesthetics but was a clear sign of pathology, of disease.   Being black was not beautiful.   Indeed, the blackness of the African, like the blackness of the Jew, was believed to mark a pathological change in the skin, the result of congenital syphilis.   (And, as we shall see, syphilis was given the responsibility for the form of the nose.)   One bore the signs of one's diseased status on one's anatomy, and by extension, in one's psyche. And all of these signs pointed to the Jews being a member of the "ugly" races of mankind rather than the "beautiful" races.   In being denied any association with the beautiful and the erotic, the Jew's body was denigrated.[20]

Within the racial science of the nineteenth century, being "black" came to signify that the Jews had crossed racial boundaries.   The boundaries of race were one of the most powerful social and political divisions evolved in the science of the period.   It was held that the Jews, rather than being the purest race, were, because of their endogenous marriages, an impure race and therefore a potentially diseased one and that this impurity was written on their physiognomy.   According to Houston Stewart Chamberlain, the Jews were a "mongrel" (rather than a healthy "mixed") race, who interbred with Africans during the period of the Alexandrian exile.[21]   They were "a mongrel race which always retains this mongrel character."   Jews had "hybridized" with blacks in Alexandrian exile.   They were, in an ironic review of Chamberlain's work by Nathan Birnbaum, the Viennese-Jewish activist who coined the word "Zionist," a "bastard" race, the origin of which condition was caused by their incestuousness, their sexual selectivity.[22]

The blackness of the Jew was associated very early with the meaning of the Jew's physiognomy.   At the close of the eighteenth century, the Dutch anatomist Petrus Camper came to describe the meaning of the facial angle and its reflex, the nasal index. The nasal index was the line that connected the forehead via the nose to the upper lip; the facial angle was determined by connecting this line with a horizontal line coming from the jaw. This line came to be a means of distinguishing between the human and the other higher anthropoids. The importance of Camper's distinction between the line that determines man from ape is that it was also used, by many of his contemporaries, such as Theodor Soemmering, and by most of his successors, as a means of distinguishing between the races on the basis of the perceived aesthetics of the facial angle. Camper himself presented criteria for the beautiful face in his study. Indeed, he defined the "beautiful face" as one in which the facial line creates an angle of one hundred degrees to the horizontal.[23] The African is the least beautiful because he/she is closest to the ape in his/her physiognomy, went the later reading of Camper. And the Jew was virtually as ugly because the Jew's physiognomy was understood to be closer to that of the African than to that of the European. Camper also saw the physiognomy of the Jew as immutable:

> There is no nation which is as clearly identifiable as the Jews: men, women, children, even when they are first born, bear the sign of their origin. I have often spoken about this with the famed painter of historical subjects [Benjamin] West, to whom I mentioned my difficulty in capturing the national essence of the Jews. He was of the opinion that this must be sought in the curvature of the nose. I cannot deny that the nose has much to do with this, and that it bears a resemblance to the form of the Mongol (whom I had often observed in London and of which I possess a facial cast), but this is not sufficient for me. For this reason, I feel that the famed painter J[acob] de Wit has painted many men with beards in the Meeting Room of the Inner Council [in Amsterdam] but no Jews.[24]

It is the nose that makes the Jewish face, and it is this quality that is closest to that of the face of the African. It is the nose that relates the image of the Jew to the image of the Black, not because of any overt similarity in the stereotypical representation of the two idealized types of noses, but because these qualities are seen as racial signs and as such reflect as much the internal life ascribed to Jew and African as their physiognomy. The most widely read physiognomist of the eighteenth century, Johann Caspar Lavater, quoted the Storm and Stress poet J. M. R. Lenz to the effect that

> it is evident to me the Jews bear the sign of their fatherland, the orient, throughout the world. I mean their short, black, curly hair, their brown skin color. Their rapid speech, their brusque and precipitous actions also come from this source. I believe, that the Jews have more gall than other people.[25]

It is the character ascribed to the Jews that is written in the nose and on their skin. Jews bear the sign of the Black, "the African character of the Jew, his muzzle-shaped mouth and face removing him from certain other races," as Robert Knox noted at in the mid-nineteenth century.[26] The physiognomy of the Jew is like that of the Black: "The contour is convex; the eyes long and fine, the outer angles running towards the temples; the brow and nose apt to form a single convex line; the nose comparatively narrow at the base, the eyes consequently approaching each other; lips very full, mouth projecting, chin small, and the whole physiognomy, when swarthy, as it often is, has an African look."[27] This assumption that the Jewish prognathism was the result of the Jew's close racial relationship to or intermixing with Blacks became a commonplace of nineteenth-century ethnology. Both Aryan and Jewish anthropologists of the fin de siècle wrote of the "predominant mouth of some Jews being the result of the presence of Black blood" and the "brown skin, thick lips and prognathism" of the Jew as a matter of course.[28] It is, therefore, not only the color of the skin that enabled the scientist to see the Jew as black but also the associated anatomical signs, such as the shape of the nose. The Jews were quite literally seen as black. Adam Gurowski, a Polish noble, "took every light-colored mulatto for a Jew" when he first arrived in the United States in the 1850s.[29]

This view dominated the readings of the Jew's nose well into the early twentieth century. The German popular physiognomist Carl Huter, who evolved his "psycho-physiognomy" at the turn of the twentieth century under the influence of spiritualism, presented his representation of the scale of the nose (1904).[30] It was the "socially dangerous" nose that marked the Jew. In 1941 one of Huter's most ardent followers, Walter Alispach, described the nose as reflecting "coarse and bad character."[31] According to the interpretation, the nose shows an exaggerated "sexual area." The cropped image is a photograph of the German-Jewish novelist Stefan Zweig.

The immutability of the Jew was tied to the Jew's physiognomy, which reflected the Jew's mentality. If the Germans (Aryans) were a "pure" race—and that was for the turn-of-the-century science a positive quality—then the Jews could not be a "pure" race. But what happened when Jews attempted to stop being Jews, to marry out of the "race"? Their Jewishness, rather than being diminished, became heightened. Their status as a mixed race became exemplified in the icon of the *Mischling*, the member of the mixed race.[32] The term *Mischling* in late-nineteenth-century racial science referred to the offspring of a Jewish and a non-Jewish parent. The Jewishness of the *Mischling* "undoubtedly signifies a degeneration: degeneration of the Jew, whose character is much too alien, firm, and strong to be quickened and ennobled by Teutonic blood, degeneration of the European who can naturally only lose by crossing with an 'inferior type.'"[33] They could have "Jewish-Negroid" features.[34] Language and, therefore, thought processes were a reflex of the racial origin of the "black" Jew. And their "blackness" appeared even more strikingly in mixed marriages, almost as nature's way of pointing up the difference and visibility of the Jew. This "taint" could appear among families "into which there has been an infusion of Jewish blood. . . . [It] tends to appear in a marked and intensely Jewish cast of features and expression."[35] As early as Edgar Allan Poe's "The Fall of the House of Usher" (1839), itself indebted to German literary models, the description of Roderick Usher, the last offspring of a highly inbred family (Poe hints at an incestuous relationship between him and his sister), is visualized as degenerate:

> A cadaverousness of complex; an eye large, liquid, and luminous beyond comparison; lips somewhat thin and very pallid, but of a surpassingly beautiful curve; *a nose of a delicate Hebrew model*, but with a breadth of nostril in similar formations; a finely moulded chin, speaking, in its want of prominence, of a want of moral energy.[36]

It is in the "mixed" breed, therefore, that these negative qualities are most evident. As an anti-Semite said to the German-Jewish writer Jacob Wassermann during the 1920s,

Whether, after conversion, they cease to be Jews in the deeper sense we do not know, and have no way of finding out. I believe that the ancient influences continue to operate. Jewishness is like a concentrated dye: a minute quantity suffices to give a specific character—or, at least, some traces of it—to an incomparably greater mass.[37]

Crossing the boundaries of race presented the potential of highlighting the inferiority of the Jews.

So even when the Jew wished to vanish, by marrying out of the "race," his or her blackness was not diminished. Indeed, it was heightened. The power of the image of the "Black Jew," the product of crossbreeding Jew with Black, was a powerful one in nineteenth-century Europe, especially for those Jews who desired to see themselves as "white." When, for example, Sigmund Freud, half a century after Knox's work, compared the unconscious with the preconscious, he evoked the image of the *Mischling* or "half-breed": "We may compare them with individuals of mixed race who, taken all round, resemble white men, but who betray their colored descent by some striking feature or other, and on that account are excluded from society and enjoy none of the privileges of white people."[38] The Jew remained visible, even when the Jew gave up all cultural signs of his or her Jewishness and married out of the "race." It was the inability to "pass" that was central here as well as the image of the mixed race. But what was the "striking feature" that marked the Jew as different? What marked the Jew as visible, even in the Jew's desired invisibility?

Jews looked different, they had a different appearance, and this appearance had pathognomonic significance. Skin color marked the Jew as both different and diseased. For the Jewish scientist, such as Sigmund Freud, these "minor differences in people who are otherwise alike . . . form the basis of feelings of strangeness and hostility between them."[39] This is what Freud clinically labeled as the "narcissism of minor differences." But are these differences "minor" either from the perspective of those labeling or from the perspective of those labeled? In reducing this sense of the basis of difference between "people who are otherwise alike," Freud was not only drawing on the Enlightenment claim of the universality of human rights but also on the Christian underpinnings of these claims. For this "narcissism" fights "successfully against feelings of fellowship and overpower[s] the commandment that all men should love one another." It is the Christian claim to universal brotherly love that Freud was employing in arguing that the differences between himself, his body, and the body of the Aryan are trivial. Freud comprehended the special place that the Jew played in the demonic universe of the Aryan psyche. But he marginalized this role, relegating it to a matter of the Jew's function "as an agent of economic discharge . . . in the world of the Aryan ideal" rather than recognizing it as one of the central aspects in the science of his time.[40] What Freud was masking was that Jews were not merely the fantasy capitalists of the paranoid delusions of the anti-Semites; they also mirrored within their own sense of selves the image of their own difference.

By the close of the nineteenth century, the "reality" of the physical difference of the Jew as a central marker of race had come more and more into question. Antithetical theories, such as those of Friedrich Ratzel, began to argue that skin color was a reflex of geography and could and did shift when a people moved from one part of the globe to another. Building on earlier work by the president of Princeton University at the close of the eighteenth century, Samuel Stanhope Smith (1787), scientists came to see the Jews as the adaptive people par excellence: "In Britain and Germany they are fair, brown in France and in Turkey, swarthy in Portugal and Spain, olive in Syria and Chaldea, tawny or copper-colored in Arabia and Egypt."[41] William Lawrence commented in 1823 that "their colour is everywhere modified by the situation they occupy."[42] The questionability of skin color as the marker of Jewish difference joined with other qualities that made the Jew visible.

By the latter half of the nineteenth century, Western European Jews had become indistinguishable from other Western Europeans in matters of language, dress, occupation, location of their dwellings, and cut of their hair. Indeed, if Rudolf Virchow's extensive study of over ten thousand German schoolchildren published in 1886 was accurate, they were also indistinguishable in terms of skin, hair, and eye color from the greater masses of those who lived in Germany.[43] Virchow's statistics sought to show that wherever a greater percentage of the overall population had lighter skin or bluer eyes or blonder hair, there a greater percentage of Jews also had lighter skin or bluer eyes or blonder hair. But although Virchow attempted to provide a rationale for the sense of Jewish acculturation, he still assumed that Jews were a separate and distinct racial category. George Mosse has commented, "The separateness of Jewish schoolchildren, approved by Virchow, says something about the course of Jewish emancipation in Germany. However, rationalized, the survey must have made Jewish schoolchildren conscious of their minority status and their supposedly different origins."[44] Nonetheless, even though they were labeled as different, Jews came to parallel the scale of types found elsewhere in European society.

A parallel shift in the perception of the Jewish body can be found during the twentieth century in the United States. In 1910 the famed German-Jewish anthropologist (and the founder of modern American anthropology) Franz Boas authored a detailed report for Congress on the "Changes in Bodily Form of Descendants of Immigrants."[45] This report documented the change in body size, cephalic index, even hair color of the offspring of Jewish, Sicilian, and Neapolitan immigrants born in the United States. Unlike their siblings born abroad, first-generation immigrants were bigger, had greater brain capacity, and had lighter hair color. Boas attempted to argue that racial qualities, even to the color of hair, changed when the environment shifted and that racial markers were at least to some degree mutable. Needless to say this view was contested in the science of his time. Arguments against this view ranged from the contention that the impact was merely a result of the shift from rural to urban life to the view that the "degenerate" types that developed in Europe underwent reversal in America, resulting in the reemergence of the "pure" and therefore healthier original European types. The image that there could be a "new human race" evolving under American conditions startled European scientists. But it was not only that these Eastern European Jewish immigrants were physically becoming more and more like other Americans; it was also that they were growing into American culture.[46] As the body type altered, their culture also changed.

It is not merely that second- and third-generation descendants of Eastern European Jewish immigrants do not "look" like their grandparents; it is also that they "look" American. The writer and director Philip Dunne commented on the process of physical acculturation of Jews in Southern California during the twentieth century:

> You could even see the physical change in the family in the second generation—not resembling the first generation at all. Of course, this is true all across the country, but it is particularly noticeable in people who come out of very poor families. . . . One dear friend

and colleague of mine was a product of a Lower East Side slum. He was desperately poor. And he grew up a rickety, tiny man who had obviously suffered as a child. At school, he told me, the goyim would scream at him. Growing up in California, his two sons were tall, tanned, and blond. Both excelled academically and in athletics. One became a military officer, the other a physicist. They were California kids. Not only American but Californian.[47]

But the more Jews in Germany and Austria at the fin de siècle looked like their non-Jewish contemporaries, the more they sensed themselves as different and were so considered. As the Anglo-Jewish social scientist Joseph Jacobs noted, "It is some quality which stamps their features as distinctly Jewish. This is confirmed by the interesting fact that Jews who mix much with the outer world seem to lose their Jewish quality. This was the case with Karl Marx."[48] And yet, as we know, it was precisely those Jews who were the most assimilated, who were passing, who feared that their visibility as Jews could come to the fore. It was they who most feared being seen as bearing that disease, Jewishness, that the mid-nineteenth-century German-Jewish poet Heinrich Heine said the Jews brought from Egypt. For Heine, too, in his memorial of the German-Jewish writer Ludwig Börne, it was the body, specifically the "long nose which is a type of uniform, by which the King-God Jehova recognizes his old retainers, even if they had deserted."[49] Conversion was not an answer to this immutable marking of the Jewish body and the Jewish soul.

In the 1920s, Jacob Wassermann chronicled the ambivalence of the German Jews toward their own bodies, their own difference. Wassermann articulated this difference within the terms of the biology of race. He wrote,

> I have known many Jews who have languished with longing for the fair-haired and blue-eyed individual. They knelt before him, burned incense before him, believed his every word; every blink of his eye was heroic; and when he spoke of his native soil, when he beat his Aryan breast, they broke into a hysterical shriek of triumph.[50]

Their response, Wassermann argued, was to feel disgust for their own body, which even when it was identical in *all* respects to the body of the Aryan nonetheless remained different:

> I was once greatly diverted by a young Viennese Jew, elegant, full
> of suppressed ambition, rather melancholy, something of an artist,
> and something of a charlatan. Providence itself had given him fair
> hair and blue eyes; but lo, he had no confidence in his fair hair and
> blue eyes: in his heart of hearts he felt that they were spurious.[51]

There are older examples of the Jew's internalization of the image of
his/her body, an image that is "dark and ugly." In the *Nizzahon
Vetus,* the high medieval Jewish response to the Christian discourse
about Judaism, the author wrote, "The heretics ask: Why are most
Gentiles fair-skinned and handsome while most Jews are dark and
ugly?" The Jewish author, while never countering this assertion,
answered that the Jews were "dark and ugly" because of their more
hygienic and more discreet sexual practices:

> Gentiles are incontinent and have sexual relations during the day,
> at a time when they see the faces on attractive pictures; therefore,
> they give birth to children who look like those pictures, as it is
> written, "And the sheep conceived when they came to drink before
> the rods."[52]

The Jew's experience of his or her own body was so deeply impacted
by anti-Semitic rhetoric that even when that body met the expectations for perfection in the community in which the Jew lived, the
Jew experienced his or her body as flawed, diseased.[53]

If only one could change those aspects of the body that marked
one as Jewish! For it was these aspects that were associated with
specific qualities. Thus the famed German artist and poet Wilhelm
Busch, in his best-known work, *Pious Helene* (1872), read the Jew's
usurious soul into the image of the Jew's nose:

> Und der Jud mit krummer Ferse
> Krummer Nas' und krummer Hos',
> Schlängelt sich zur hohen Börse
> Tiefverderbt und seelenlos!
>
> [And the Hebrew, sly and craven,
> Round of shoulder, nose, and knee,
> Slinks to the Exchange, unshaven
> And intent on usury.][54]

The nose was a sign not merely of the difference and illness of the body but also of the social illness represented by the Jew in German society, an illness of the body politic. The Jew's nose came to represent the Jew's sick soul.

This awareness was projected not merely onto but also into the Jew. In a startling series of studies undertaken during the 1940s and 1950s in the United States concerning the visibility of the Jew, the question was raised as to who and why the Jew could be seen. Raphael Isaacs in 1940 had discussed the "so-called Jewish type" in a Jewish medical journal and his focus was on the "so-called 'hooked' nose." For him the "hooked nose, curling nasal folds (ali nasal)" were the salient markers in the representation of the Jew. He cites a University of Michigan study in which "only 51 percent showed a definite convex nasal outline." Isaacs's work, like earlier work by Jacobs and Fischberg, argued against the centrality of "nasality" as a marker of the Jew while illustrating the central importance of this sign for the culture in which he lived. The more analytic work of the Harvard psychologist Gordon Allport in 1946, followed by a series of papers, attempted to understand what was being measured when Jewish and non-Jewish judges were asked to sort images into the category "Jewish" and "non-Jewish."[55] It was clear that Jews had a higher rate of positive identification, as did those non-Jewish judges who showed a higher index for anti-Semitism. Was it that these two groups were more closely attuned to what the subliminal signs of Jewishness were or was it that they simply judged more of the images to be Jewish? The former seemed to be the case.[56] What was clear was that the Jewish judges "tended to give more false positives and were more accurate than non-Jews." The conclusion was that they "were particularly sensitive to possible cues in others which would enable them to ascribe group membership to these others and that this disposition was directly related to the degree of acceptance of the majority stereotype."[57] In other words Jews were attuned of the meaning of the image of the Jew because of the culture in which they lived. As Nietzsche noted, one is never aware of one's own body until one is ill; one is also never aware of the difference of one's body—whether it is real or constructed—until one learns about it. This difference is associated with the exotic and the distanced, as the contemporary British novelist Julian Barnes has his protagonist note in one of his early novels about one of his Jewish friends:

Toni far outclassed me in rootlessness. His parents were Polish Jews and, though we didn't actually know it for certain, we were practically sure that they had escaped from the Warsaw ghetto at the very last minute. This gave Toni the flash foreign name of Barbarowski, two languages, three cultures, and a sense (he assured me) of atavistic wrench: in short, real class. He looked an exile, too: swarthy, bulbous-nosed, thick-lipped, disarmingly short, energetic and hairy; he even had to shave every day.[58]

Barnes romanticizes all of the negative images associated with the Jew but still associates them with the physical difference of the Jew. This is not all that far from the aspect of Dickens's Fagin (with his "villainous and repulsive face") or du Maurier's Svengali (whose "Jewish aspect [was] well featured but sinister"). It is associated with the difference and the distance of the Jew in British society.[59] The actual acculturation of the Jew into British society could in no way mask the Jew's visibility.

But nothing, not acculturation, not baptism, could wipe away the taint of race. No matter how they changed, they still remained diseased Jews. And this was marked on their physiognomy. Moses Hess, the German-Jewish revolutionary and political theorist, commented in his *Rome and Jerusalem* (1862) that

even baptism will not redeem the German Jew from the nightmare of German Jew-hatred. The Germans hate less the religion of the Jews than their race, less their peculiar beliefs than their peculiar noses. . . . Jewish noses cannot be reformed, nor black, curly, Jewish hair be turned through baptism or combing into smooth hair. The Jewish race is a primal one, which had reproduced itself in its integrity despite climactic influences. . . . The Jewish type is indestructible.[60]

The theme of the Jew's immutability was directly tied to arguments about the permanence of the negative features of the Jewish race.

On one count, Hess seemed to be wrong—the external appearance of the Jew did seem to be shifting. His skin seemed to be getting whiter, at least in his own estimation, though it could never get white enough. Jews, at least in Western Europe, no longer suffered from the disgusting skin diseases of poverty that had once marked their skin. But on another account, Hess was right. The Jew's nose could not be "reformed." Interrelated with the meaning of skin was the meaning of the Jew's physiognomy, especially the

Jew's nose. And it was also associated with the Jew's nature. George Jabet, writing as Eden Warwick, in his *Notes on Noses* (1848) characterized the "Jewish, or Hawknose" as one that is "very convex, and preserves its convexity like a bow, throughout the whole length from the eyes to the tip. It is thin and sharp." Shape also carried here a specific meaning: "It indicates considerable Shrewdness in worldly matters; a deep insight into character, and facility of turning that insight to profitable account."[61] Physicians, drawing on such analogies, speculated that the difference of the Jew's language, the very mirror of his psyche, was the result of the form of his nose. Thus Bernhard Blechmann's rationale for the *Mauscheln* of the Jews, their inability to speak with other than a Jewish intonation, was that the "muscles, which are used for speaking and laughing are used inherently different from those of Christians and that this use can be traced . . . to the great difference in their nose and chin."[62] The nose became one of the central loci of difference in seeing the Jew.

It was the relationship between character and physiognomy that led Jewish social scientists, such as Joseph Jacobs, to confront the question of the "nostrility" of the Jews. He (and other Jewish scientists of the fin de siècle) saw that "the nose does contribute much toward producing the Jewish expression."[63] But how can one alter the "nostrility" of the Jewish nose, a sign that, unlike the skin color of the Jew, does not seem to vanish when the Jew is acculturated? Indeed, a detailed study of the anthropology of the "*Mischlinge* born to Jews and non-Jews" published in 1928 summarized the given view that there was a "Jew nose" and that this specific form of the nose was dominant in mixed marriages and was recognized to be a fixed, inherited sign of being Jewish.[64] In popular and medical imagery, the nose came to be the sign of the pathological Jewish character for Western Jews, replacing the pathognomonic sign of the skin, though closely linked to it. For the shape of the nose and the color of the skin, as we have seen, are related signs.

It seemed that one could "cure" the skin, could make it less "black," by eliminating the skin diseases that haunted the poverty of the ghetto, or one could simply see oneself as "white." With this, the "disease" of Jewishness could no longer be seen on the skin. But how could one eliminate the symptom of the "nostrility" of the Jew, that sign that everyone at the close of the nineteenth century associated with the Jew's visibility? An answer was supplied by Jacques Joseph, a highly acculturated young German-Jewish surgeon practicing in fin-de-siècle Berlin. Born Jakob Joseph, the physician had altered his Jewish name when he studied medicine in Berlin and Leipzig. Joseph was a typical acculturated Jew of the period. He had been a member of one of the conservative dueling fraternities and bore the scars of his sabre dueling with pride. Like many acculturated Jews, such as Theodor Herzl, Joseph "relished the test and adventure of the duel, the so-called *Mensur*, which was considered manly and edifying."[65] The scars (*Schmisse*) from the *Mensur* were intentionally created. Students challenged each other to duels as a matter of course, without any real need for insults to be exchanged. Being challenged was a process of social selection. "Without exclusivity—no corporation" was the code of the fraternities as late as 1912.[66]

The duelists had their eyes and throat protected, but their faces were purposefully exposed to the blade of the sabre. When a cut was made, there were guidelines as to how to repair it so as to maximize the resulting scar. The scar that Joseph bore his entire life marked him as someone who was *Satisfaktionsfähig* (worthy of satisfaction), someone who had been seen as an equal and had been challenged to a duel. Marked on the duelist's face was his integration into German culture. And the more marginal you were the more you wanted to be scarred. In 1874 William Osler, then a young Canadian medical student visiting Berlin, described "one hopeful young Spanish American of my acquaintance [who] has one half of his face—they are usually on the left half—laid out in the most irregular manner, the cicatrices running in all directions, enclosing areas of all shapes—the relics of fourteen duels!"[67] While such scarring was extreme among the medical students of the day, it was not unknown. The scar marked the individual, even within the medical faculty, who was seen as a hardy member of the body politic. Being a member of a Jewish fraternity (most of which did not duel) could reconstitute the sickly Jewish body into what Max Nordau called the "new muscle Jew." The Jewish fraternity organization stated in 1902 that "it desires the physical education of its members in order to collaborate in the physical regeneration of the Jewish people."[68]   A dueling scar marked the socially healthy individual.

The social status of the fraternity member, like that of the military officer, was contested for Jews at the close of the nineteenth century. In 1896 the following proposal had been accepted by the dueling fraternities:

> In full appreciation of the fact that there exists between Aryans
> and Jews such a deep moral and psychic difference, and that our
> qualities have suffered so much through Jewish mischief, in full
> consideration of the many proofs which the Jewish student has also
> given of his lack of honor and character and since he is completely
> void of honor according to our German concepts, today's conference
> . . . resolves: "No satisfaction is to be given to a Jew with any
> weapon, as he is unworthy of it."[69]

Jews are different. But with their facial scars, they look just like us.
The visibility of the scar is meant as an assurance of the purity of
the group. But Jews cannot be pure, so they must be excluded. For
a Jew to bear a facial scar is to hide his sickly essence from us. And
that is "mischief."

The scarred Jacques Joseph was a trained orthopedic surgeon
who had been the assistant of Julius Wolff, one of the leaders in that
field. Among Wolff's most important findings was the establishment
of the "law of the transformation of the skeleton," which argued that
every function of the skeleton could be described through the laws of
mechanics and that any change of the relationship between single
components of the skeleton would lead to a functional and physiological change of the external form of the entire skeleton.[70]   Wolff's
major contribution to the treatment of diseases of the leg was his
development of a therapeutic procedure by which a club foot could be
corrected through the use of a specialized dressing that altered the
very shape of the foot.[71]   Orthopedics, more than any other medical
specialty of the period, presented the challenge of altering the visible
errors of development so as to restore a "normal" function. Wolff's
approach also stressed the interrelationship among all aspects of the
body. Among his procedures were corrective surgery and the use of
appliances. Joseph's interests did not lie with the foot, another sign
of Jewish inferiority, but elsewhere in the anatomy. In 1896 Joseph
had undertaken a corrective procedure on a child with protruding
ears, which, while successful, caused him to be dismissed from
Wolff's clinic. This was cosmetic, not reconstructive, surgery.[72]
One simply did not undertake surgical procedures for vanity's sake,
he was told. This was not a case of a functional disability, such as
a club foot. The child was not suffering from any physical ailment
that could be cured through surgery. Here reconstructive surgery
became aesthetic surgery.

Joseph opened a private surgical practice in Berlin. In January 1898, a twenty-eight-year-old man came to him, having heard of the successful operation on the child's ears. He complained that "his nose was the source of considerable annoyance. Wherever he went, everybody stared at him; often, he was the target of remarks or ridiculing gestures. On account of this he became melancholic, withdrew almost completely from social life, and had the earnest desire to be relieved of this deformity."[73]   Joseph took the young man's case and proceeded to perform the first modern cosmetic rhinoplasty. On 11 May 1898 he reported on this operation before the Berlin Medical Society. In that report Joseph provided a "scientific" rationale for performing a medical procedure on what was an otherwise completely healthy individual: "The psychological effect of the operation is of utmost importance. The depressed attitude of the patient subsided completely. He is happy to move around unnoticed. His happiness in life has increased, his wife was glad to report; the patient who formerly avoided social contact now wishes to attend and give parties. In other words, he is happy over the results."[74]   The patient no longer felt himself marked by the form of his nose. He was cured of his "disease," which was his visibility. Joseph had undertaken a surgical procedure that had cured his patient's psychological disorder!

Here we can evoke Jean-Jacques Rousseau, who commented in his novel of education, *Emile* (1762), that "the way in which the Author of our being has shaped our heads does not suit us; we must have them modelled from without by midwives and from within by philosophers."[75]   For Joseph articulated the basic premise of modern aesthetic surgery, that the correction of perceived physical anomalies (not pathologies) was a means of repairing not the body but the psyche. And this at exactly the same moment in modern history when Sigmund Freud had begun to understand the basis for his own approach to curing the hysterical body, with all of its physical signs and symptoms, through the treatment of the psyche! Aesthetic surgery came to be understood as "organopsychic therapy" in which "it is exclusively the altered or defective form of the pathologically and anatomically normal organ that causes psychic conflicts."[76]   We see at the close of the nineteenth century a "modelling from within" by surgeons rather than philosophers, but surgeons whose role was to cure not the body but the psyche. But what if the source of the dis-ease with one's body came as much from an internalization of the society's image of oneself as from any private cause?   What if the anti-Semitic representation of the Jewish nose—so widely present in the literature of the fin de siècle—itself shaped the Jew's response to the Jew's own nose?   Thus, the French turn-of-the-century anti-Semitic pamphleteer "Dr. Celticus" presented an anatomy of the Jew in which the "hooked nose" represented the "true Jew."   "Nasality" here became the first visual representation of the "primitiveness of the Semitic race."[77]   It is in this context that the damaged psyche of the Jew was to be repaired.   But it was not unique within the annals of nineteenth-century medicine.

Joseph's procedure was not the first reduction rhinoplasty. Cosmetic nose surgery had been undertaken earlier in the century in Germany and France, before the introduction of modern surgical techniques of anesthesia and antisepsis, by such surgeons as Johann Friedrich Dieffenbach.   In the 1880s, John Orlando Roe in Rochester, New York, had performed an operation to "cure" the "pug nose."[78]   On the basis of the profile, Roe divided the image of the nose into five categories: Roman, Greek, Jewish, Snub or Pug, and Celestial.   Roe cited the "snub-nose" as "proof of a degeneracy of the human race."   It is, of course, the Irish profile that is characterized by the snub-nose in the caricatures of the period.[79]   Roe's procedure turned the Irish nose into "a thing of beauty."[80]   (In addition, work on reshaping the nose had been done by Robert Weir in New York, Vincenz von Czerny in Heidelberg, George Monks in Boston, and James Israel in Berlin.   All of these were primarily forms of reconstructive surgery with the emphasis on correcting underlying somatic rather than aesthetic problems.[81])   However, Joseph's was the first procedure of the type still carried out today.   The climate was ripe for the development of a quick and relatively simple procedure to alter the external form of the nose.   The earlier procedures were not only more complicated (as well as dangerous), but they also did not come at a time when the need to "cure" the disease of the visibility of the Other was so powerful.   Central to Joseph's process of nasal reduction was the fact that there was "no visible scar."[82]   Joseph's procedure began the craze for nose jobs in fin-de-siècle Germany and Austria.   In the history of medicine, Joseph was the "father of aesthetic rhinoplasty."   He came to be nicknamed "Nase-Josef=Nosef" in the German-Jewish community.[83]

It is unclear whether Joseph's first patient was Jewish, but the depiction of his psychological sense of social isolation due to the form of his nose certainly mirrors the meaning associated with anti-Semitic bias at the fin de siècle.   It is clear, however, that Joseph's initial clientele was heavily Jewish and that he regularly reduced "Jewish noses" to "gentile contours." Many of his patients underwent the operation "to conceal their origins."[84] In justifying the procedure, Joseph called upon the rationale of the psychological damage done by the nose's shape. He cured the sense of inferiority of his patients through changing the shape of their nose. His primary "cure" was to make them less visible in their world. This was one of the rationales cited by the other German-Jewish cosmetic surgeons of the period, such as the art historian–physician Eugen Holländer.[85] Joseph's orthopedic training served him well. He could holistically cure the ailments of the entire patient, including the patient's psyche, by operating on the patient's nose. Here was an extension of Wolff's law into the realm of the psychological. Joseph noted, at the conclusion of his first annual report (1917) as the director of the first department for "facial-plasty" at the *Charité*, the major teaching hospital in Berlin, that "the discharged patients have all been cured of their psychic depression which the consciousness of bodily deformity always involves."[86] These were for the most part patients horribly maimed in the war who were made whole, both physically and psychologically. How equally true of his private patients.

We have one very late case description of one of Joseph's rhinoplasties, dating from January 1933, soon after the Nazi seizure of power and after Jewish physicians were forbidden to operate on non-Jewish patients except with special permission. The sixteen-year-old Adolphine Schwarz followed the lead of her older brother and had "her nose bobbed." She commented that her brother had written to Joseph and informed him that he had very limited means. "Joseph was very charitable," she later said, "and when he felt that someone suffered from a 'Jewish nose,' he would operate for nothing."[87] The image of "suffering from a 'Jewish nose'" is a powerful one. Young men and women needed to become invisible, needed to alter their bodies, as their visibility became even more marked. For the virtual invisibility of the Jews in Germany vanished with the introduction of the yellow "Jewish star." "Nosef" died in February 1934 from a heart attack, before he was completely forbidden to practice medicine. His scarred face, at the last, did not make him invisible as a Jew, nor did his surgical interventions make those Jews whose noses he "bobbed" any less visible.

But Jacques Joseph was not the only Berlin physician who was operating on noses in the 1890s. Two Jewish scientists of fin-de-siècle Europe who were preoccupied with the nose argued that there is a direct relationship between the "nose" and the "genitalia." For Wilhelm Fliess and his Viennese collaborator, Sigmund Freud, the nose came to serve as a sign of universal development rather than as a specific sign of an "inferior" racial identity.[88] The nose was the developmental analogy to the genitalia. Evolving embryologically at the same stage, there was a shared relationship between the tissue of the nose and that of the genitalia. And, for Fliess and Freud, this was true of all human beings, not merely Jews. Thus one cure for sexual dysfunction, according to Fliess, was to operate on the nose, and that he regularly did. Fliess's views were shared by other physicians of the time, such as John Noland Mackensie at Johns Hopkins University.[89] But their interest was hypothetical; Fliess acted on his theories by operating upon the nose in order to cure perceived "nervous" illnesses. In reviewing the records, it is clear that Fliess's patients did not make up a cross-section of society. Of the 156 cases he recorded (some from the medical literature of the time), only a dozen were men.[90] All of the rest were women, who were operated upon for numerous complaints, primarily psychological ones. Fliess treated a wide range of mental illnesses, including hysteria, through the extensive use of cocaine, but he also applied acid to the internal structures of the nasal passages or surgically removed them. What Fliess managed to do in these years was to convert a quality of race into an attribute of gender. While his theoretical material covered both males and females, his clinical material (and one assumes this reflected his clinical practice) focused on the female's nasal cavities as the clinical substitute for the Jew's nose.

It was not merely that in turn-of-the-century Europe there was an association between the genitalia and the nose; there was, and had long been, a direct relationship drawn in popular and medical thought between the size of the nose and that of the penis. Ovid wrote, "Noscitur e naso quanta sit hast viro." The link between the Jew's sexuality and the Jew's nose was a similarly well-established one at century's end, but here the traditional pattern was reversed.[91] The specific shape of the Jew's nose indicated the damaged nature, the shortened form, of his penis. The traditional positive association between the size of the nose and that of the male genitalia was reversed and this reversal was made a pathological sign.[92] The association between the Jewish nose and the circumcised penis, as signs of Jewish difference, was made in the crudest and most revolting manner during the 1880s. In the streets of Berlin and Vienna, in penny-papers or on the newly installed "Litfassäulen," or advertising columns, caricatures of Jews could be seen.[93] An image of the essential Jew, little "Mr. Kohn," showed him drowned, only his nose and huge, over-sized feet showing above the waterline.[94] These extraordinary caricatures stressed one central aspect of the physiognomy of the Jewish male, his nose, which represented that hidden sign of his sexual difference, his circumcised penis. Jewish difference, as embodied in Jews' sexual selectivity, was an indicator of their identity. As Friedrich Nietzsche strikingly observed in *Beyond Good and Evil*, the focus of the Germans' fear of the superficiality of their recently created national identity was the Jewish difference.[95] This fear was represented in caricatures by the elongated nose. It also permeated the scientific discussions of the time. In the "anatomical-anthropological" study of the nose by Viennese anatomist Oskar Hovorka (1893), the form of the nose was seen as a sign of negative racial difference, as well as a sign of the "idiot and the insane."[96] Look at the nose of the Other and you will see the basic sign of the atavism. Thus, when Wilhelm Fliess attempted to alter the pathology of the genitalia by operating on the nose, at a point in time when national identity was extremely unsure of itself and scapegoats easy to find, he joined together the Enlightenment universalist theory to the German biology of race. Fliess's desire was to make this into a quality of all human beings, male and female, Jew and Aryan, not merely of Jewish males. He succeeded in generating an image of the woman as the sufferer from the pathologies of the nose that was equivalent to the general cultural view of the Jewish male.

Fliess's goal—as that of so many others of the time—was to alter the Jewish body so that the Jew could become invisible. Some Jews, such as the Berlin literary critic Ludwig Geiger, rebelled against this desire for a Jewish invisibility: "If one desires assimilation—and that can only mean becoming German in morals, language, actions, feelings—one needs neither mixed marriages nor baptism. No serious person would suggest an assimilation which demanded that all Jews had straight noses and blond hair."[97] But, of course, in arguing the point this way Geiger was reacting to precisely those pressures that caused Jews to dye their hair and "bob" their noses. Geiger implied that the changes were primarily made for cosmetic purposes, for vanity's sake. What he pointedly avoided discussing is the fact that they were actually meant to "cure" the disease of Jewishness, the anxiety of being seen as a Jew. Being seen as a Jew meant being persecuted, attacked, and harassed. The "cure" for this was the actual alteration of the body. The Jewish mind, which German culture saw as different from that of the Aryan, was afflicted by its sense of its own difference. In order to cure the Jew's mind, Joseph and Fliess had to operate on the Jew's nose.

One can cite another case of the severe psychological damage done by the internalization of this sense of the "Jewish nose," not from the surgical literature but from the psychoanalytic literature of the fin de siècle. It comes from the case file of Freud's first biographer and one of the first psychoanalysts, the Viennese-Jewish physician Fritz Wittels. At the meeting of the Viennese Psychoanalytic Society on 9 December 1908, Wittels recounted a case of a patient who had come to him specifically because of the publication of his polemical work on baptized Jews, on Jews who were trying to pass as Christians.[98] Wittels saw this as a form of insanity. His patient was a young man of about thirty who suffered from "anti-Semitic persecution, for which he holds his inconspicuously Semitic nose responsible. He therefore plans to have the shape of his nose changed by plastic surgery."[99] Wittels attempted to persuade him that his anxiety about his nose was merely a displacement for anxiety about his sexual identity. "This the patient declared to be a good joke." The evident analogy of Wittel's suggestions did not occur to him. If a patient came to him expressly because of his writing about the neurosis of conversion and wished to have his nose rebuilt to hide his Jewishness, then the question of his own "paranoid" relationship to his own circumcised penis, that invisible but omnipresent sign of the male's Jewishness was self-evident. Freud picked up on this directly and noted that "the man is evidently unhappy about being a Jew and wants to be baptized." "At this point Wittels remarks that the patient is an ardent Jew. Nevertheless, he does not undergo baptism. In this fact lies the conflict that has absorbed the meaning of other conflicts." To be a Jew and to be so intensely fixated on the public visibility of that identity was to be ill. Then Wittels revealed the name of the patient to the group and Freud recognized from the name that the patient's father was an engaged Zionist. He then read the desire to unmake himself as a Jew as a sign of the rejection of the father. Freud, however, did not comment on the link between a strong Jewish identity and the rejection of the visibility that that identity entailed. There was a real sense in Freud's comment that the Jewish body, represented by the skin or the nose, could never truly be changed. It was a permanent fixture, forever reflecting the Jew's racial identity. Altering the Jew's external form may have provided a wider margin in which the Jew could "pass," but the Jew could never be truly at peace with the sense of his or her invisibility.

But the Jew's internalization of society's image of the Jew's body leads to psychic damage, according to Joseph if not Freud. In post-Shoah Jewish tradition this connection is acknowledged in a straightforward manner. Traditional Judaism rejects surgical alteration of the body except for reconstructive surgery. (Circumcision is a religious and not a medical practice for traditional Jews.) Yet what is striking is that halakhic traditions would permit the alteration of the shape of the nose for men and for women, for such a procedure would fall within the interpretation that sees "a state of mind which prevents a person from mingling with people" as "pain." Joseph's rationale—that the reshaping of the nose cures the psyche —has become accepted among traditional Jews who in general would reject any merely cosmetic alteration of the body.[100] And this to what the Talmud sees as one of the central organs of the body. Abba Saul notes "that when an embryo is formed it is formed from the center, but with respect to existence all agree that its source is in the nose; for it is written, *All in whose nostrils was the breath of the spirit of life* [Gen. 7:22]."[101] The alteration of the nose is a serious procedure, but it is permitted if it eliminates "psychological anguish."

The image of a literally scarred Jacques Joseph operating on the literal image of the Jew is powerfully disturbing. Joseph reshaped the image of the Jew, but even that was not enough. The more the Jew desired to become invisible, the more the Jew's invisibility became a sign of difference. We can see this operation in effect once again in the writings of Walter Lippmann, one of the leading American-Jewish intellectuals of the first half of the twentieth century, who commented in the late 1920s that

> the rich and vulgar and pretentious Jews of our big American cities
> are perhaps the greatest misfortune that has ever befallen the
> Jewish people. They are the fountain of anti-Semitism. When they
> rush about in super automobiles, bejeweled and furred and painted
> and overbarbered, when they build themselves French chateaux
> and Italian palazzi, they stir up the latent hatred against crude

wealth in the hands of shallow people; and that hatred diffuses itself.[102]

The Jew remains a Jew even when disguised. It is in their "painted and overbarbered" essence. One cannot hide—nose job or no nose job—from the lessons of race. And the Jew is the most aware of this. Lippmann created in his mind's eye the image of his antithesis, the "bad" Jew to his "good" Jew. And this Jew was just as visible as he believed himself to be invisible. Lippmann, in his Wall Street suit and carefully controlled manners and appearance, looked just like everyone else—or so he hoped. But there is no hiding from the fact of a constructed difference. There is no mask, no operation, no refuge.

But the desire for invisibility, the desire to "look like everyone else," still shaped the Jew's desire to alter his/her body. The greatest growth in rhinoplasties in the United States occurred in the 1940s, at the point when the awareness of the dangers of being seen as a Jew was at its peak.[103] And, indeed, through the 1960s as many as more than half of the patients seeking rhinoplasty were first- or second-generation Americans.[104] In 1960 a Johns Hopkins survey of predominantly Jewish female adolescents saw their desire for rhinoplasty as rooted in their ethnic origin. Indeed, the assumption of this study was that these young women were articulating their negative identification with their parents, specifically their desire to alter the appearance of their noses, which they said seemed to resemble their fathers'. But it was the image of their fathers as Jews and the associations of this image that they were attempting to mask. But like Fritz Wittel's patient, these young women gave no sign of wishing to abandon their Jewish identity, only their Jewish visibility:

> We were interested to know whether the quest for rhinoplasty was perceived as a disavowal or disassociation from a Jewish identity. Whereas this would seem to be true at a superficial level, the patients came from practicing religious homes and there was no hint they wished to marry or have male friends outside of their religion or that they contemplated any deviation from the patterns of religious beliefs of the family. In the attitudes and response of parents also, there was no evidence of their being perceived as a desertion of religious or racial identifications.[105]

The internalization of the negative image of the Jew, the desire not to be seen as a Jew while retaining one's own identity as a Jew was one model of response to the sense of being seen as "too Jewish" or, indeed, being seen as Jewish at all.

The overt motivation for rhinoplasty still seemed to be "ethno-cultural considerations." "On a conscious level," wrote the best sociologist to deal with this question, Frances Cooke Macgregor, in 1989, "prejudice and discrimination—real or imagined—and the desire to 'look American,' played a substantial role in [the patient's] motivation for surgery."[106] And indeed almost 40 percent of Macgregor's 1989 sample were Jews. In another study Macgregor points out the radical impact of the image of the nose on patients whose own psychic makeup predisposed them to focus on their own inadequacies. Thus, in one case, an eighteen-year-old male student focused on his nose, a "typically Jewish nose," as the source of his social failings.[107] While this patient was advised not to have surgery, it was clear from the detailed case description that the social environment in which he had been raised marked his nose as the appropriate focus for his status anxieties. Such patients, who see their own sense of inadequacy mirrored in the society's image of the inadequacy of the Jew, as is shown in another of Macgregor's case studies, rarely see their surgery as successful. Yet for Jews in general the level of satisfaction with rhinoplasties is higher than the norm. John M. and Marcia Kraft Goin illustrate a significantly lower index of negative responses to rhinoplasty among Jews, with some 84 percent of their Jewish patients expressing a sense of the improvement of their appearance as opposed to approximately 50 percent of the other control groups.[108] Paul Schilder, one of Freud's original collaborators in Vienna, recounted in 1935 a case of a twenty-nine-year-old man whose "nose was particularly offensive to him since it was in his opinion too Jewish."[109] He associated this with "his father's family because of their very Semitic appearance and specific Jewish qualities." Appearance became associated for Schilder's patient with a specific negative disposition and this in turn with his own ugliness and his sexual rejection by a young woman. Jewishness sensed on the body became converted into the ugliness of the spirit. Schilder saw the patient only after his rhinoplasty. The patient "quoted others who said that before his operation his face was more characteristic [read: Jewish] than it was now, but seemed on the whole rather contented with the result." This patient eventually broke with his religious identity and converted to Catholicism, the ultimate form of invisibility in Catholic Vienna.

While in the course of the mid-twentieth century in the United States the "nose job" came to represent as much a gender distinction as a racial one, its roots remained within the internalization of the meaning of the Jew's body in Western culture. With the rise of a heightened feminist and Jewish consciousness during the late 1980s, this association became the focus of some concern. This is nowhere better illustrated than in the feminist "Wimmen's Comix" entitled "Little Girls" (1989), subtitled "Case Histories in Child Psychology." One of the most striking of these case histories is Aline Kominsky-Crumb's "Nose Job." Aline Kominsky-Crumb was one of the founders of the feminist comic book movement. In the late 1970s she created *Twisted Sisters* and is presently the editor of *Weirdo* magazine. "Nose Job" is a cautionary tale about a young woman "growing up with cosmetic surgery all around [her]" who avoids cosmetic surgery in her forties by recalling her earlier temptation as a teenager on Long Island in 1962. There "prominent noses, oily skin, and frizzy hair were the norm. . . . (No, we Jews are not a cute race!)" This self-conscious admission of the internalization of the norms of her society even in 1989 reveals the dangers lurking even for those who can articulate the meaning ascribed to the Jew's body. As all about her teenagers were having their noses restructured, she held out. She eventually fled to Greenwich Village, where she "felt hideously repulsive." Her "sensitive folks kicked this already beaten dog" by pushing their daughter to have a nose job. After she ran away, her parents agreed to postpone the procedure. And she "manages to make it through high school with [her] nose." The story, at least in the "comix," has a happy end: "6 months later styles had changed and she looks like the folk singers Joan Baez or Buffy St. Marie." In other words, one could look as "beat" as one wanted, as long as one did not look "Jewish." The "Jewish" nose came to signify the outsider, but that outsider was never identified as Jewish. The moral of Aline Kominsky-Crumb's tale is that fashions in appearance change and that women should not succumb to the pressures of fashion to homogenize their bodies. But the hidden meaning is that it is alright to look Jewish as long as you are visible as anything but a Jew. What is still left within the memory of Aline Kominsky-Crumb is the sense that looking Jewish is still looking different, looking marginal, not "looking cute." Even heightened feminist awareness does not overcome the power of the internalization of a culture's sense that one not only looks different, but also, as in Julian Barnes's portrait of the Jew, that one is associated with marginality, with being a beatnik folk singer who could in no way be understood as being "cute." This sense of the negative aspects of the body leads to the sense that some type of alteration of the body is a potential need, even if it is rejected.

Indeed, as the plastic surgeon Mark Gorney has recently noted,

> Patients seeking rhinoplasty . . . frequently show a guilt-tinged, second generation rejection of their ethnic background masked by excuses, such as not photographing well. Often it is not so much a desire to abandon the ethnic group as it is to be viewed as individuals and to rid themselves of specific physical attributes associated with their particular ethnic group.[110]

It is in being visible in "the body that betrays" that the Jew is most uncomfortable.[111]   This is still true even in the case of the new "ethnic-specific" aesthetic surgeries of the 1980s—for the fear there is not looking Jewish but looking "too Jewish."[112]   Ethnic identity—whether being Jewish-American or Asian-American or African-American—is validated as long as the general aesthetic norms of the society are not transgressed. For being too visible means being seen not as an individual but as an Other, one of the "ugly" race.

NOTES

1.   His comments are reported in Michael Specter, "The Oracle of Crown Heights," *New York Times Magazine*, 15 March 1992, 34–76, here 67 (my emphasis).
2.   Gilles Deleuze and Félix Guattari, *A Thousand Plateaus: Capitalism and Schizophrenia*, trans. Brian Massumi (Minneapolis: University of Minnesota Press, 1987), 291–92.
3.   *Washingtonian* 26, 4 (January 1991): 196.
4.   Mary Douglas, *Natural Symbols* (New York: Pantheon, 1970), 70.
5.   Theodosius Dobzhansky, "On Types, Genotypes, and the Genetic Diversity in Populations," in *Genetic Diversity and Human Behavior*, ed. J. N. Spuhler (Chicago: Aldine, 1967), 12.
6.   See, for example, Peter A. Bochnik, *Die mächtigen Diener: Die Medizin und die Entwicklung von Frauenfeindlichkeit und Antisemitismus in der europäischen Geschichte* (Reinbek bei Hamburg: Rowohlt, 1985).
7.   Robert Jay Lifton, *The Nazi Doctors: Medical Killing and the Psychology of Genocide* (New York: Basic, 1986).

8. See Oliver Ransford, *"Bid the Sickness Cease"*: *Disease in the History of Black Africa* (London: Murray, 1983).

9. François-Maximilien Mission, *A New Voyage to Italy* (London: Bonwicke, 1714), 2:139.

10. Johann Pezzl, *Skizze von Wien: Ein Kultur- und Sittenbild as der josephinischen Zeit*, ed. Gustav Gugitz and Anton Schlossar (Graz: Leykam-Verlag, 1923), 107–8.

11. On the meaning of this disease in the medical literature of the period, see the following dissertations on the topic: Michael Scheiba, *Dissertatio inauguralis medica, sistens quaedam plicae pathologica: Germ. Juden-Zopff, Polon. Koltun: quam . . . in Academia Albertina pro gradu doctoris . . . subjiciet defensurus Michael Scheiba . . .* (Regiomonti: Litteris Reusnerianis, 1739); and Hieronymus Ludolf, *Dissertatio inauguralis medica de plica, vom Juden-Zopff . . .* (Erfordiae: Typis Groschianis, 1724).

12. Harry Friedenwald, *The Jews and Medicine: Essays* (Baltimore: Johns Hopkins University Press, 1944), 2:531.

13. Joseph Rohrer, *Versuch über die jüdischen Bewohner der österreichischen Monarchie* (Vienna, 1804), 26. The debate about the special tendency of the Jews for skin disease, especially *plica polonica*, went on well into the twentieth century. See Richard Weinberg, "Zur Pathologie der Juden," *Zeitschrift für Demographie und Statistik der Juden* 1 (1905): 10–11.

14. Wolfgang Häusler, *Das galizische Judentum in der Habsburgermonarchie im Lichte der zeitgenössischen Publizistik und Reiseliteratur von 1772–1848* (Vienna: Verlag für Geschichte und Politik, 1979). On the status of the debates about the pathology of the Jews in the East after 1919, see *Voprosy biologii i patologii evreev* (Leningrad: State Publishing House, 1926).

15. Elcan Isaac Wolf, *Von den Krankheiten der Juden* (Mannheim: Schwan, 1777), 12.

16. James Cowles Pritchard, *Researches into the Physical History of Man* (Chicago: University of Chicago Press, 1973), 186.

17. Claudius Buchanan, *Christian Researches in Asia, with Notices of the Translation of the Scriptures into the Oriental Languages* (Boston: Armstrong, 1811), 169. On the background to these questions, see George W. Stocking, Jr., *Victorian Anthropology* (New York: Free Press, 1987).

18. Léon Poliakov, *The Aryan Myth: A History of Racist and Nationalist Ideas in Europe* (New York: Meridan, 1977), 155–82.

19. Sander L. Gilman, *On Blackness without Blacks: Essays on the Image of the Black in Germany*, Yale Afro-American Studies (Boston: Hall, 1982).

20. See Cheryl Herr, "The Erotics of Irishness," *Critical Inquiry* 17 (1990): 1–34.

21. Houston Stewart Chamberlain, *Foundations of the Nineteenth Century*, trans. John Lees (London: John Lane/The Bodley Head, 1913), 1:389.

22. Nathan Birnbaum, "Über Houston Stewart Chamberlain," in his *Ausgewählte Schriften zur jüdischen Frage* (Czernowitz: Verlag der Buchhandlung Dr. Birnbaum & Dr. Kohut, 1910), 2:201.

23. Peter Camper, *Der natürliche Unterschied der Gesichtszüge in Menschen verschiedener Gegenden und verschiedenen Alters*, trans. S. Th. Sömmering (Berlin: Voss, 1792), 62.

24. Ibid., 7.

25. Johann Caspar Lavater, *Physiognomische Fragment zur Beförderung des Menschenkenntnis und Menschenliebe* (Leipzig: Weidmann, 1775–78), 3:98 and 4:272–74. This reference is cited (and rebutted) in Paolo Mantegazza, *Physiognomy and Expression* (New York: Scott, 1904), 239.

26. Robert Knox, *The Races of Men: A Fragment* (Philadelphia: Lea & Blanchard, 1850), 134.

27. Ibid., 133.

28. A summary of this literature is offered in the chapter "Die negerische Rasse" in the standard racial anthropology of the Jew written during the first third of the twentieth century, Hans F. K. Günther, *Rassenkunde des jüdischen Volkes* (Munich: Lehmann, 1930), 143–49. These two quotes are taken from von Luschan and Judt.

29. Adam G. de Gurowski, *America and Europe* (New York: Appleton, 1857), 177.

30. Carl Huter, *Menschenkenntnis: Körperform- und Gesichts-Ausdruckskunde* (1904; Schwaig bei Nuremberg: Verlag für Carl Huters Werke, 1957). See the partisan discussion in Fritz Aerni, *Carl Huter (1861–1912): Leben und Werk* (Zurich: Kalos, 1986) and his *Huter und Lavater: Von der Gefühlsphysiognomik zur Psychologie und Psycho-Physiognomik* (Zurich: Kalos, 1984).

31. *Nasenform und Charakter* (1941; Zurich: Helioda, 1960).

32. On the question of the definition and meaning of the *Mischling,* see Paul Weindling, *Health, Race, and German Politics between National Unification and Nazism, 1870–1945* (Cambridge: Cambridge University Press, 1989), 531–32.

33. Chamberlain, *Foundations of the Nineteenth Century*, 1:332.

34. W. W. Kopp, "Beobachtung an Halbjuden in Berliner Schulen," *Volk und Rasse* 10 (1935): 392.

35. Joseph Jacobs, *Studies in Jewish Statistics, Social, Vital, and Anthropometric* (London: Nutt, 1891), xxiii.

36. Edgar Allan Poe, *Poetry and Tales* (New York: Library of America, 1984), 321 (my emphasis).

37. Jacob Wassermann, *My Life as German and Jew* (London: Allen & Unwin, 1933), 72.

38. All references are to Sigmund Freud, *Standard Edition of the Complete*

Psychological Works of Sigmund Freud, ed. and trans. J. Strachey, A. Freud, A. Strachey, and A. Tyson (London: Hogarth, 1955–74), 14:191.
39. Ibid., 11:199; 18:101; 21:114.
40. Ibid., 21:120.
41. Samuel Stanhope Smith, *An Essay on the Causes of the Variety of Complexion and Figure in the Human Species* (Cambridge: Belknap, 1965), 42.
42. William Lawrence, *Lectures on Physiology, Zoology, and the Natural History of Man* (London: Smith, 1823), 468.
43. Rudolf Virchow, "Gesamtbericht über die Farbe der Haut, der Haare und der Augen der Schulkinder in Deutschland," *Archiv für Anthropologie* 16 (1886): 275–475.
44. George L. Mosse, *Toward the Final Solution: A History of European Racism* (New York: Fertig, 1975), 90–91.
45. This report was submitted to Congress on 3 December 1910 and issued on 17 March 1911. A full text was published by Columbia University Press in 1912. Boas summarized his findings (and chronicles the objections to this report) in his *Race, Language, and Culture* (New York: Macmillan, 1940), 60–75.
46. Boas, *Race, Language, and Culture,* 83.
47. Cited from an interview by Neal Gabler, *An Empire of Their Own: How the Jews Invented Hollywood* (New York: Crown, 1988), 242.
48. "Types," *The Jewish Encyclopedia* (New York: Funk & Wagnalls, 1906), 12:295.
49. Heinrich Heine, *Werke,* ed. Klaus Briegleb (Berlin: Ullstein, 1981), 7:31.
50. Wassermann, *My Life,* 156.
51. Ibid.
52. David Berger, trans. and ed., *The Jewish-Christian Debate in the High Middles Ages* (Philadelphia: Jewish Publication Society of America, 1979), 224.
53. On the cultural background for this concept, see Jacob Katz, *Out of the Ghetto: The Social Background of Jewish Emancipation, 1770–1870* (Cambridge, Mass.: Harvard University Press, 1973); and Rainer Erb and Werner Bergmann, *Die Nachtseite der Judenemanzipation: Der Widerstand gegen die Integration der Juden in Deutschland, 1780–1860* (Berlin: Metropol, 1989).
54. Wilhelm Busch, *Gesamtausgabe,* ed. Friedrich Bohne (Wiesbaden: Vollmer, n.d.), 2:204; the English translation, which is very accurate to the tone, but not to the order of the parts of the Jew's body, is from Walter Arndt, comp. and trans., *The Genius of Wilhelm Busch* (Berkeley: University of California Press, 1982), 42.
55. Gordon Allport and Bernard M. Kramer, "Some Roots of Prejudice," *Journal of Psychology* 22 (1946): 9–39. See also Frederick H. Lund and Wilner C. Berg, "Identifiability of Nationality Characteristics," *Journal of Social Psychology* 24 (1946): 77–83; Launor F. Carter, "The Identifica-

tion of 'Racial' Membership," *Journal of Abnormal and Social Psychology* 43 (1948): 279–86; Gardner Lindzey and Saul Rogolsky, "Prejudice and Identification of Minority Group Membership," *Journal of Abnormal and Social Psychology* 45 (1950): 37–53; Donald N. Elliott and Bernard H. Wittenberg, "Accuracy of Identification of Jewish and Non-Jewish Photographs," *Journal of Abnormal and Social Psychology* 51 (1955): 339–41.

56. Leonard D. Savitz and Richard F. Tomasson, "The Identifiability of Jews," *American Journal of Sociology* 64 (1958): 468–75.

57. Alvin Scodel and Harvey Austrin, "The Perception of Jewish Photographs by Non-Jews and Jews," *Journal of Abnormal and Social Psychology* 54 (1957): 278–80.

58. Julian Barnes, *Metroland* (London: Cape, 1980), 32.

59. See the discussion in Hyman L. Muslin, "The Jew in Literature: The Hated Self," *Israel Journal of Psychiatry and Related Science* 27 (1990): 1–16.

60. Moses Hess, *Rom und Jerusalem*, 2d ed. (Leipzig: Kaufmann, 1899), brief 4. Cited in the translation from Paul Lawrence Rose, *Revolutionary Antisemitism in Germany from Kant to Wagner* (Princeton, N.J.: Princeton University Press, 1990), 323.

61. Eden Warwick, *Notes on Noses* (1848; London: Bentley, 1864), 11. On the general question of the representation of the physiognomy of the Jew in mid-nineteenth-century culture, see Mary Cowling, *The Artist as Anthropologist: The Representation of Type and Character in Victorian Art* (Cambridge: Cambridge University Press, 1989), 118–19, 332–33.

62. Bernhard Blechmann, *Ein Beitrag zur Anthropologie der Juden* (Dorpat: Just, 1882), 11.

63. Jacobs, *Studies in Jewish Statistics*, xxxii.

64. Hans Leicher, *Die Vererbung anatomischer Variationen der Nase, Ihrer Nebenhöhlen und des Gehörorgans* (Munich: Bergmann, 1928), 80–85.

65. Amos Elon, *Herzl* (New York: Holt, Rinehart & Winston, 1975), 63.

66. Quoted from Konrad H. Jarausch, *Students, Society, and Politics in Imperial Germany: The Rise of Academic Illiberalism* (Princeton, N.J.: Princeton University Press, 1982), 350. See also his *Deutsche Studenten, 1800–1970* (Frankfurt a. M.: Suhrkamp, 1984), 82–93; as well as Michael Kater, *Studentenschaft und Rechtsradikalismus in Deutschland, 1918–1933: Eine sozialgeschichtliche Studie zur Bildungskrise in der Weimarer Republik* (Hamburg: Hoffmann & Campe, 1975), 145–62.

67. W[illiam] O[sler], "Berlin Correspondence," *Canada Medical and Surgical Journal* 2 (1874): 308–15, here 310.

68. Jarausch, *Students*, 272.

69. Quoted by Peter Pulzer, *The Rise of Political Anti-Semitism in Germany and Austria* (London: Halband, 1988), 246.

70. Stephan Mencke, *Zur Geschichte der Orthopädie* (Munich: Beckstein, 1930), 68–69.

71. Bruno Valentin, *Geschichte der Orthopädie* (Stuttgart: Thieme, 1961), 101–2.

72. The traditional histories of reconstructive surgery still do not cover cosmetic surgery. See, for example, Joachim Gabka and Ekkehard Vaubel, *Plastic Surgery, Past and Present: Origin and History of Modern Lines of Incision* (Munich: Karger, 1983), which mentions Joseph in passing but does not even supply his biography in the biographical appendix. The only comprehensive history of cosmetic surgery discusses his role, without any social context: Mario González-Ulloa, ed., *The Creation of Aesthetic Plastic Surgery* (New York: Springer, 1985), 87–114.

73. "Über die operative Verkleinerung einer Nase (Rhinomiosis)," *Berliner klinische Wochenschrift* 40 (1898): 882–85. Translation from Jacques Joseph, "Operative Reduction of the Size of a Nose (Rhinomiosis)," trans. Gustave Aufricht, *Plastic and Reconstructive Surgery* 46 (1970): 178–81, here 178; reproduced in Frank McDowell, ed., *The Source Book of Plastic Surgery* (Baltimore: Williams & Wilkins, 1977), 164–67. See also Paul Natvig, *Jacques Joseph: Surgical Sculptor* (Philadelphia: Saunders, 1982), 23–24. On the general history of rhinoplasty, see Blair O. Rogers, "A Chronological History of Cosmetic Surgery," *Bulletin of the New York Academy of Medicine* 47 (1971): 265–302; Blair O. Rogers, "A Brief History of Cosmetic Surgery," *Surgical Clinics of North America* 51 (1971): 265–88; S. Milstein, "Jacques Joseph and the Upper Lateral Nasal Cartilages," *Plastic and Reconstructive Surgery* 78 (1986): 424; J. S. Carey, "Kant and the Cosmetic Surgeon," *Journal of the Florida Medical Association* 76 (1989): 637–43.

74. Joseph, "Operative Reduction," 180.

75. Jean-Jacques Rousseau, *Oeuvres completes*, ed. V. D. Musset-Pathay (Paris: Didot, 1823), 3:20.

76. Alfred Berndorfer, "Aesthetic Surgery as Organopyschic Therapy," *Aesthetic and Plastic Surgery* 3 (1979): 143–46, here 143. For a good critique of this problem, see David A. Hyman, "Aesthetics and Ethics: The Implications of Cosmetic Surgery," *Perspectives in Biology and Medicine* 33 (1990): 190–202.

77. Docteur Celticus, *Les 19 Tares corporelles visibles pour reconnaitre un juif* (Paris: Librairie Antisemite, 1903), chap. 1.

78. John O. Roe, "The Deformity Termed 'Pug Nose' and Its Correction, by a Simple Operation" (1887), reprinted in McDowell, *Source Book of Plastic Surgery*, 114–19, here 114.

79. Cowling, *Artist as Anthropologist*, 125–29. The image of the nose reproduced by Cowling from the physiognomic literature of the nineteenth century representing the Irish is identical with those in the "before" images reproduced by Roe.

80. Blair O. Rogers, "John Orlando Roe—Not Jacques Joseph—The Father of Aesthetic Rhinoplasty," *Aesthetic Plastic Surgery* 10 (1986): 63–88.

81. See the papers reproduced in McDowell, *Source Book of Plastic Surgery*, 136–64.

82. Jacques Joseph, "Nasenverkleinerungen," *Deutsche medizinische Wochenschrift* 30 (1904): 1095–98, here 1095; trans. Frank McDowell in McDowell, *Source Book of Plastic Surgery*, 174–76, here 184.

83. Natvig, *Jacques Joseph*, 94.

84. Ibid., 71.

85. See the comments by Eugen Holländer, "Die kosmetische Chirurgie," in *Handbuch der Kosmetik*, ed. Max Joseph (Leipzig: Veit, 1912), 669–712, here 673.

86. Natvig, *Jacques Joseph*, 179.

87. Ibid., 95.

88. See Sander L. Gilman, *Disease and Representation: Images of Illness from Madness to AIDS* (Ithaca, N.Y.: Cornell University Press, 1988), 182–201.

89. Frank J. Sulloway, *Freud, Biologist of the Mind: Beyond the Psychoanalytic Legend* (New York: Basic Books, 1979), 148–50.

90. Wilhelm Fliess, *Die Beziehungen zwischen Nase und weiblichen Geschlechtsorganen. In ihrer biologischen Bedeutung dargetellt* (Leipzig: Deuticke, 1897).

91. Hanns Bächtold-Stäubli, ed., *Handwörterbuch des deutschen Aberglaubens* (Berlin and Leipzig: Gruyter, 1934–35), 6:970–79; and Havelock Ellis, *Studies in the Psychology of Sex*. Vol. 4, *Sexual Selection in Man* (Philadelphia: Davis, 1905), 67–69.

92. On this principle of reversal and the meaning of the nose as a symbol of the castrated penis, see Otto Fenichel, "Die 'lange Nase,'" *Imago* 14 (1928): 502–4.

93. John Grand-Carteret, *L'affaire Dreyfus et l'image* (Paris: E. Flammarion, 1898); Eduard Fuchs, *Die Juden in der Karikatur* (Munich: Langen, 1921); and Judith Vogt, *Historien om et Image: Antisemitisme og Antizionisme i Karikaturer* (Copenhagen: Samieren, 1978).

94. See Dietz Bering, *Der Name als Stigma: Antisemitismus im deutschen Alltag, 1812–1933* (Stuttgart: Klett/Cotta, 1987), 211.

95. Friedrich Nietzsche, *Beyond Good and Evil*, trans. Marianne Cowan (Chicago: Regnery, 1955), 184–88.

96. Oskar Hovorka, *Die äussere Nase: Eine anatomisch-anthropologische Studie* (Vienna: Hölder, 1893), 130–40. On the pathological meaning of the nose in German science for the later period see Leicher, *Die Vererbung anatomischer Variationen der Nase*, 81.

97. Arthur Landsberger, ed., *Judentaufe* (Munich: Müller, 1912), 45.

98. See Sander L. Gilman, *Jewish Self-Hatred: Anti-Semitism and the Hidden Language of the Jews* (Baltimore, Md.: Johns Hopkins University Press, 1986), 193–94.

99. Herman Nunberg and Ernst Federn, ed., *Protokolle der Wiener Psychoanalytischen Vereinigung* (Frankfurt a. M.: Fischer, 1976–81), 1:66–67;

translation from *Minutes of the Vienna Psychoanalytic Society*, trans. M. Nunberg (New York: International Universities Press, 1962–75), 2:60–61.

100.   See J. David Bleich, *Judaism and Healing: Halakhic Perspectives* (New York: KTAV, 1981), 126–28.
101.   Sotah 45b.
102.   Ronald Steel, *Walter Lippmann and the American Century* (Boston: Little, Brown, 1980), 192.
103.   Frances Cooke Macgregor, "Social, Psychological and Cultural Dimensions of Cosmetic and Reconstructive Plastic Surgery," *Aesthetic Plastic Surgery* 13 (1989): 1–8, here 1.
104.   See the discussion in Joseph G. McCarthy, ed., *Plastic Surgery* (Philadelphia: Saunders, 1990), 1:122–24.
105.   Eugene Meyer, Wayne E. Jacobson, Milton T. Edgerton, and Arthur Canter, "Motivational Patterns in Patients Seeking Elective Plastic Surgery," *Psychosomatic Medicine* 22 (1960): 193–203, here 197.
106.   Macgregor, "Social, Psychological, and Cultural Dimensions," 2.
107.   Frances Cooke Macgregor and Bertram Schaffner, "Screening Patients for Nasal Plastic Operations," *Psychosomatic Medicine* 12 (1950): 277–91, here 283–84.
108.   John M. Goin and Macia Kraft Goin, *Changing the Body: Psychological Effects of Plastic Surgery* (Baltimore/London: Williams & Wilkins, 1981), 133.
109.   Paul Schilder, *The Image and Appearance of the Human Body: Studies in the Constructive Energies of the Psyche* (London: Paul, Trench, Trubner, 1935), 258.
110.   Mark Gorney, "Patient Selection and Medicolegal Responsibility for the Rhinoplasty Patient," in *Rhinoplasty: Problems and Controversies*, ed. Thomas D. Ress (St. Louis: Mosby, 1988), 2.
111.   Jean-Paul Sartre, *Anti-Semite and Jew*, trans. George J. Becker (New York: Schocken, 1965), 119.
112.   For example, see the discussion of "special considerations" in Eugene H. Courtiss, ed., *Male Aesthetic Surgery* (St. Louis: Mosby, 1991), 159–88, as well as "Ethnic Ideals: Rethinking Plastic Surgery," *New York Times*, 25 September 1991, C1.

Chapter 17

The Other in Levinas and Derrida: Society, Philosophy, Judaism

Jacob Meskin

In this essay I compare two very different views of the other, that of Emmanuel Levinas and that of Jacques Derrida.[1] Specifically, I want to argue that Levinas's view of the other offers us an important new way to understand concrete societal forms such as tradition, political institutions, and social institutions. My argument rests on two connected theses: (1) In Levinas's subtle and philosophically sophisticated approach, the other represents, above all, a profound, unqualified ethical urgency. (2) This conception of ethical immediacy generates a very different understanding of *mediation*: one in which the embodied, the institutional, the social, and the traditional are not opposed to the spiritual, or the "beyond."

To support these two theses, I shall focus on the issue of "asymmetry"—the Levinasian claim that the ethical relationship moves asymmetrically *from* the ego outward toward the other, and not vice versa, thus leaving the ego's obligations to the other unqualified by mutuality or reciprocal exchange. Critics have charged that this asymmetrical view is one-sided or excessive, and that it leads to negative consequences. I shall argue, however, that this notion of asymmetry actually generates (and secures) the powerful ethical orientation in Levinas's new understanding of social institutions, tradition, and politics.[2]

My theses concerning Levinas's work suggest an intricate interconnection between philosophy and Jewish tradition. In what follows I offer an initial reading of this intricate interconnection. Levinas's relation to the Jewish tradition raises a vast host of issues that fall outside the scope of this article. However, to ignore this interconnection is to lose the full complexity of Levinas's work and its vital resistance to easy categorization.

Introductory Digression: Derrida, Philosophy, and Culture

The work of Jacques Derrida proves to have excellent heuristic value in exploring the question of the uniqueness of Levinas's view of the other. In contrast with Levinas's conception of the other and the new, ethical understanding of the societal forms it engenders, Derrida's conception of the other demands of us, rather, unflagging critical vigilance concerning such notions as "tradition," "identity," and "religion." In keeping with the critical program generally associated with the Enlightenment, Derrida is concerned with freeing and distancing us from these "enthusiasms," thereby releasing us from determinate, committed forms of life, and the all-too-definite identities in which they may imprison us. One finds a very nuanced and complex form of just this refusal of enthusiasm in Derrida's prolific writing.[3]

As many recent readers of his work have argued, it is an error to view Derrida as the unconcerned, perpetually insouciant philosopher of play that some have taken him to be. Both Derrida's writings on political topics and his earlier deconstructive readings of the philosophical tradition evince a highly developed apprehension about the perils of immediate certainty, and the hazards of utopian moments of sheer, unqualified self-identity. The practice of deconstruction thus aims precisely to reveal the internal differentiations, or fissures, that complicate unity, homogeneity, and purity from within. This characteristic Derridean rejection of untroubled identity with oneself applies not only to the identity of the self or ego—but also and especially to the apparently unproblematic sort of identity that religious traditions, cultures, and ethnicities might seem to provide.[4]

Derrida's clear-eyed rejection of such nostalgic identity dreams similarly prevents deconstructive philosophy from becoming some sort of stable, priggish *apologia* for the Enlightenment's prejudice against the extrarational. On the contrary, Derrida seems intent to show philosophy's endless contamination by such extrarational factors as literature, and especially literary figures of speech. In so doing, as Norris has recently argued, Derrida neither abandons the genre of philosophy per se nor sacrifices the rigors of argumentation for the pleasures of inspired literary association. Rather, Derrida creates a rich, allusive, literary texture that also offers tight analysis and argumentation, thereby producing a provocative, multivalent grafting between the literary and the philosophical.[5]

We see here the classic sort of critical irresolution that marks many of Derrida's astute cultural interventions. Derrida's "oscillating nonposition" balances two important moments. In the first moment, Derrida argues for suspicion toward enthusiastic claims about unmediated identity (whether these refer to personal, ethnic, national, or religious identity). This moment reflects basic Enlightenment concerns and insists that any form of identity will be an internally multifarious and "impure" affair, with definite dependence on and connection to what is supposed to be "outside" of and other than this identity. In a second moment, however, Derrida's oscillating nonposition leads us to be suspicious precisely about the Enlightenment's own claim to have reached a fully mediated, discursive, rational point of view. Here Derrida reminds us that philosophical reflection itself is also an "impure" affair, necessarily contaminated by certain extrarational factors.

In exploring the notion of critically informed irresolution, our digression has helped to bring out one of the central differences between Derrida and Levinas. The Derridean attitude of critical detachment (which, to be sure, intends to remain distinct from any sort of quietism), and the emphasis on knowledge, especially knowledge of the tensions constituting any situation or reality, reveal a basic conception of philosophy as a kind of critical intervention. For Derrida, speaking most generally, philosophy interrupts the texts or events on which it comments, so as to rigorously question the apparent unity or identity of these texts or events. Without straightforwardly denying the identity in question, philosophy à la Derrida unearths additional and diverse moments *within* the identity in question, thus offering a complex and multifarious reading of what was taken to be simply and unitarily present.

As we will see in much more detail below, Levinas has a very different sense of what it is to do philosophy, one with its own set of implications for concrete cultural, social, and political realities. For Levinas, philosophy is an indispensable activity of commentary through which we reveal the "saying" that animates any said. Thus philosophy constantly "remembers" an immediate ethical moment that both echoes within and *helps to constitute* the decidedly mediated nature of our day-to-day life, with its institutions, laws, rules, procedures, and rituals. Indeed, in this way Levinas connects (not equates!) philosophy and prophecy, for philosophy helps us to "hear" an inherently ethical or relational moment *already* echoing in the ordinary world. By appealing to just this ethical moment, prophecy finds its own critical standard.

With this preliminary frame for understanding the differences between Levinas and Derrida, we can now explore the question of the uniqueness of Levinas's view of the other, an exploration in which the work of Derrida possesses great heuristic value. Accordingly, I shall now turn to their different views of otherness, the issue of asymmetry, and the question of tradition, society, and the everyday.

Levinas's View of the Other

One of Levinas's most important distinctions,[6] introduced in *Otherwise than Being*, is between the saying (*le dire*) and the said (*le dit*). On the simplest level, "saying" would be the commonplace *activity* through which we put linguistic meanings into circulation by speaking words, gesturing, making faces—or even by saying something to ourselves silently, as in thinking. By contrast, *the words or meanings themselves* that we actively contribute through our saying make up what Levinas calls "the said."

However, Levinas argues that the straightforward phenomenon of "saying" also possesses another dimension of significance. According to Levinas, when we bracket all the intentional qualities of the phenomenon of saying, whether they be active or passive, there nonetheless remains a feature of saying so primordial that, like Poe's famous purloined letter, we never notice it: the turning toward the other.

In the otherwise ordinary act of saying, Levinas points out, I *also* turn toward the other person, directing myself toward him or her in an orientation or focus that I certainly did not consciously choose or even think about. Indeed, Levinas argues that my conscious act of saying and its active and passive qualities presuppose this very basic directedness toward the other.

This unthought and unwilled level of saying reveals a deep fact about sociality: saying is the basic "frame" in which all interpersonal life takes place. Even when I intend to deceive another person, I still find myself to have moved somehow toward him, to have positioned myself in a way that manifests a primordial taking into account of the fact that he is there, nearby. Even the conscious intention to murder another rests upon the preintentional form of human sociality in which I turn toward the other—what one might call my "embodied registering" of the fact of his existence.[7]

To Levinas, precisely this basic "nonneutrality" toward the other is the hidden dimension of the phenomenon of saying. On its most primordial level, saying would reveal that I am somehow *affected by the other*, and not merely that I actively intend to affect him in some way. In this way, saying uncovers a certain vulnerability within me, since the other has *already* reached me on a different level than that of my conscious thinking, willing, and acting.

Levinas deepens this analysis by focusing on the fact that saying—as my unchosen and thus vulnerable orientation toward the other—involves my body, my very flesh. For over and above putting words and meanings into play, saying means that I find myself turned toward the other *in* and *with* my body. Thus, saying is not some sort of disembodied acknowledgment of the other, mediated by concepts, or strategies, or deliberations. Saying reveals, rather, that I am directly and immediately affected by the other, affected in the very body that I find myself to have turned toward him, in the very flesh with which I approach him.

In one of the most suggestive analyses in twentieth-century philosophy, Levinas argues that this prevolitional, extracognitive involvement with the other that we find in saying *takes place in, and as*, the human body. To explain this intriguing claim, Levinas attends to such corporeal phenomena as pain and aging. These phenomena help to show the way in which the body, precisely in its immediately lived (and living) aspect as *my* body, incarnates both a certain passivity and an uninitiated involvement with the other. Thus, in pain, for instance, my own ability to feel, my sensateness itself, betrays an unwilled, tactile receptivity, as I find myself unable to avoid undergoing my own sensations of pain. In aging, too, I discover myself passively vulnerable to an ongoing organic process that I not only must undergo but that I *am*.

Pain and aging reveal a sort of unwilled corporeal vulnerability that parallels that which we discovered in the primordial dimension of saying. But, even more importantly, pain and aging evoke the way in which I remain utterly and irremediably self-identical with myself *despite myself*. It is this aspect of corporeal identity, in particular, that helps to shed light on saying.

When I am in pain, I remain self-identical with myself during the spasmodic visitations of pain, *against my will*. Similarly, the contraction and relaxation of smooth muscle tissue, through which my body rhythmically registers the passage of its own unique time, has nothing to do with *my* conscious choice, or intention.

Thus pain and aging show me undergoing or suffering what we might call an extravolitional self-identity. Moreover, this extravolitional self-identity would seem to be demanded or called for by *an other than myself* who dwells within my very flesh. But I cannot recall or find this other within myself—I can only find the trace of such otherness in the "despite-myself" of pain and aging.

"Beneath" the powerful, active center of consciousness that I am, I am also a suffering, embodied response to an other who calls me from within my very flesh, an other whose call inevitably and irretrievably *precedes* my consciousness. Thus, my extravolitional, and often unwanted, ongoing identity with myself over time is a kind of response to a silent and never fully spoken summons. Prior to power, thought, and action, we might say that the self coagulates around the internal irritant of the other.[8] To be me is already to be *for* the other: I am for the other before I am for myself.

We can now see how the body realizes or incarnates the reality of saying. In saying, I find myself prevolitionally approaching the other. My unchosen openness and directedness toward the other in saying reflect the way in which my embodied being is, from the start, a response to an ancient call. Even in finding myself turned toward the other person in saying, I do not ever succeed in meeting the other to whom I ultimately aspire, the one for whom I seem bodily to exist, the other in my flesh. Human sociality and the interpersonal *repeat* a primordial and immemorial involvement, an involvement that we find in the human body and see most clearly in pain and aging.[9]

For these reasons, Levinas claims that saying represents a form of "folly," for how can I justify being ceaselessly occupied in turning toward an other whom I can never finally meet, an other with whom I can never be finished? Why should I endlessly lower my façade of impervious neutrality *to say* to the other? In saying, I senselessly risk revealing the fact that I have been involuntarily affected by the other. Displaying my vulnerability, I advertise that I can be wounded. Would it not be wiser to maintain a permanent self-enclosure?

For Levinas, saying, precisely in its apparent nonsensicality and lack of prudence, is "the grain of folly" that safeguards our humanity. "In my non-indifference to the neighbor," Levinas writes, "I am obedient as though to an order addressed to me. Such an order throws a 'seed of folly' into the universality of the ego."[10] The other within me *deranges* me, so to speak, forever transforming my natural concentric course into an eccentric solicitude for the other.[11]

In saying, then, we see the way in which Levinas *defines* the speaking subject as an unwilled being-concerned-with, an unchosen directedness toward the other. The other, we may say, is the one toward whom the speaking subject finds herself oriented in saying, even if the subject's face-to-face encounter with the other repeats a "preoriginal" encounter with an other with whom she can never be finished—an other who dwells in her flesh.

The Other and Writing in Derrida

Derrida, in his early books and articles, formulates a very different conception of otherness, and of our relation to the other.[12] Derrida's account of the other stems from an investigation of thought and language, rather than from an analysis of the pressing nature of the ethical relation. For Derrida both consciousness and language testify to what one might call an ongoing, self-promulgating differentiation. In Derrida's hands, reflection becomes the activity of uncovering this ongoing differentiation—or fissuring—within the apparent solidity and unity that it in fact makes possible.

Derrida's earliest work, the *Introduction to Husserl's Origin of Geometry*, focuses on the complex role that ideality, or the nature of ideas and concepts, plays in the constitution of unitary entities that retain their self-identity over time. Following suggestions in Husserl, Derrida argues that the ideas through which we grasp objectivity and spatio-temporal continuity depend on language. And it is particularly written language that preserves ideality, endowing it with an existence free from any contingent exchange of speech.[13]

In his subsequent text, *Speech and Phenomena*, Derrida builds on this conclusion. In this text Derrida argues that a differential system of written marks, which lacks the animating, immediate presence of consciousness we associate with speech, actually makes such presence possible in the first place. For a system of writing, as both the ongoing embodiment and the preservation of differentiation, plays an indispensable role in that internal, being-out-of-sync with itself through which consciousness of the present actually arises. This follows because our apparently immediately given consciousness of the present can be what it is only if it contains its own internal differentiation from memories of the past and anticipations of the future. Thus the conscious present must have, already constitutively inscribed within itself, its difference from past and future. And such constitutive inscription is writing in the deepest sense.

Finally, in both *Dissemination* and *Of Grammatology*, as well as in the article "Signature, Event, Context," Derrida posits that writing rests upon two conditions: (1) a meaningful mark differs from each and every other mark, and (2) a meaningful mark can be successfully removed from the presence of its referent or signifying intention. According to Derrida, both the white space between letters and the different spatial configuration of each letter allow a differential system of nonidentical symbols to come into being. In addition, the fact that the letters and words I write retain their various meanings in different contexts and retain their various meanings even after I am dead and gone, makes it possible for this differential system of signs to constitute a language.

Thus writing and the presence that it generates depend, paradoxically enough, upon absence. Absence is clearly manifest in the spacing, or gap, through which any mark is differentiated from another. Similarly, absence is manifest in the fact that the symbols I write can be ceaselessly transferred into contexts where I am no longer present. In both cases, something other than presence turns out to be a necessary condition for presence.

Derrida's early work offers us a tightly woven, Kantian argument that reveals the volatile, self-differentiating reality through which presence and substance come to be constituted. Starting with the nature of ideal objects and ideality generally, Derrida practically deduces, à la Kant, the pervasive otherness that is a prerequisite of the enduring sameness of identity.[14]

Among the most important consequences that follow from Derrida's position is a somewhat paradoxical view of identity: that in order for any thing to be what it is, it must be other than itself, and thus must also *not* be what it is! To be self-identical is to differ from oneself, without the possibility of any final, Hegelian homogenization.

The Issue of Asymmetry

From the deconstructive perspective, Levinas's emphatic insistence on the other, and on the self's asymmetrical solicitude for the other, appears to be a potentially dangerous and one-sided form of folly. Levinas, it would seem, refuses to balance the metaphysical foreignness of the other with descriptions that would also at the same time include the other within some embracing commonality with the self. The unqualified exteriority Levinas attributes to the other remains unmitigated by any overarching framework that would also establish similarity and community between self and other. This insistence on the other's exteriority and foreignness, without a second moment of inclusion and familiarity, seems to run the risk of mystifying the other, leading possibly to dangerously one-sided enthusiasms, and even violence.

As we have seen above, deconstructive writing intervenes precisely to supplement any *one-sided identity* by uncovering and adding the other, apparently absent side. In this way, deconstruction endeavors through reflection to restore the full and often difficult complexities inherent in any and all contexts. From the deconstructive point of view, Levinas seems to advocate just such a one-sided identity, since for Levinas the identity of the other—what it means to *be* the other—is to be a reality that can never be assimilated to any sort of common measure (whether conceptual or temporal) that might place self and other on the same plane. Thus we are left with an immediate, urgent, and utterly unreciprocal relation that moves from self toward other.

Indeed, as Derrida makes clear in "Violence and Metaphysics," the first of his two pieces on Levinas, the maintenance of such an absolute, asymmetrical difference between self and other would seem to deny that the other is also a thinking, feeling ego, *like* the self.[15] Nor does Levinas add on the supplementary affirmation that the other, while remaining other, is *also* a center of consciousness, an ego, like the self. Levinas excludes any kind of likeness or commonality from the self-other relation, thereby apparently *denying to the other the property of being an ego*. Thus when viewed from the deconstructive perspective, Levinas's philosophy would appear to border on a kind of violent usurpation of that very other that it set out to respect.

The complex relationship between Levinas's work and feminist thought also revolves, in large part, around the asymmetry issue. In

Totality and Infinity Levinas seemed to have produced a work that decisively inscribed the maleness of its author. As Derrida and others have pointed out, *Totality and Infinity* in this respect breaks new ground, since it refuses the seemingly ungendered language in which most if not all classic works of Western philosophy have been written. Yet this advance, which might be taken to denote a fundamental recognition of the reality of gender difference, thus acknowledging the independence and irreducibility of feminine alterity, has been criticized precisely because of its asymmetry. For once again, *absolute or total* alterity seems to deny any commonality between the masculine and the feminine, thereby opening up the way for mystification of the feminine other. This, in turn, seems to destroy the very respect for feminine alterity that was his apparent initial starting point.[16]

A. Asymmetry as the Source of Ethics

In order to effectively counter these criticisms, two aspects of Levinas's conception of asymmetry must be introduced at this point, one having to do with ethics and the other leading to a consideration of the social and institutional.

Throughout his long philosophical career, Levinas has constantly associated the other with "the orphan, the widow, and the poor." Through his frequent invocation of this biblical phrase, Levinas clearly means to suggest that insofar as I am I, I stand in a position of responsibility for the other, whose very otherness Levinas associates with the general context of disenfranchisement from society, influence, and power. In explaining this association of the other with disenfranchisement, I think we also uncover the basis for Levinas's insistence on maintaining the asymmetry between self and other.[17]

For Levinas, being in the subject position—being me—and facing another human being implies that I bear a unique and asymmetrical identity. Of course, in talking about my unique identity, Levinas certainly is aware that the ego's identity is shot through with difference, for Hegel haunts many pages of Levinas's work. Nevertheless, Levinas asserts that, in at least one peculiar sense, the ego's identity remains unitary and self-identical. In the face-to-face encounter with the other, I possess at least enough unity and identity to be a potential center of action. *My recurring to myself in a unity of sensation that I do not will* puts me in a position of relative integration, of sufficient coordination and connection with myself *to enable me to become* a center of willed action.

But we must be careful here, for Levinas clearly does not intend to advance a simple-minded view of the identity found in the subject position of potential agency. On the contrary, as we have seen, Levinas argues that my identity or selfhood is itself a being *deranged*, a being disrupted by an other who unsettlingly calls me from within. In other words, identity or selfhood (and the agency they make possible) remain permanently obsessed by the other who summons me. As we saw in Levinas's analysis of saying, my very possession of the integrated capacity to act is already being affected by the other; my ego itself is already in relation with the other, an eccentric gravitation toward him from within myself that maintains my identity despite myself.

Thus Levinas perpetrates the folly of an asymmetrical view of the other precisely so as to safeguard the other from being assimilated to any neutralizing, all-inclusive, common framework. If ab initio the other and I were to share in some reassuring network of mutual, symmetrical relations, then the unslakeable urgency and undeniable specificity of the ethical relationship disappears—for then calculation, prudence, and reason would constitute the *whole* of the interaction between self and other. Against this possibility, however, Levinas argues that the asymmetrical ethical relationship represents an immemorially ancient fountain of our humanity, and that the mediated commonality in which we always find ourselves cannot be fully severed from an ultimate wellspring of asymmetrical solicitude for the other.

Levinas thus concludes that the urgency of the ethical relation can neither be reduced to nor assimilated to the detached, universal neutrality of reflection. Far from threatening us with mystification or violence, Levinas's notion of the asymmetrical ethical relation in fact aims to displace and modify philosophical and ideological views of the self-other relation. Insofar as *my* untransferable obligation to the other keeps all subsequent interpretations of the other at one remove, *my* solicitude for the other both precedes and disrupts any theoretical understanding of the other.

Of course, remaining deaf to the other, I may refuse this irreplaceable ethical uniqueness and insist that he or she be subsumed within some reflective category, thereby relieving me of my direct and unqualifiable responsibility. But it is vital to understand that for Levinas such a move is not, *ultimately*, a philosophical or ideological failure. It is rather a negative way of relating to the other, a negative way of relating to the sometimes uncomfortable fact that to be human means to be turned toward the other. Theory and reflection may well help us understand the other, but we need the Levinasian folly of a pretheoretical, preideological, unchosen ethical directedness toward the other to be human. Cain's question remains unanswered on the level he asks it; on a level different from that of inquiry and theoretical activity, philosophy may help us to hear the answer to this question.

B. Asymmetry and the Understanding of Society, Institutions, and Tradition

Up to now, we have focused on that feature of asymmetry on which Levinas himself spends most of his time—the excessive ethical directedness toward the other that constitutes the "unabandonable post" of my identity. Yet asymmetry also has a vitally important "other side."

The ordinary world in which we live is a place of mediations, and comparisons, and equations, which portion out and distribute our relationships. Now this objectivity of the intersubjective world seems different from the asymmetrical intensity Levinas describes. For in our mundane sphere we make claims to general truths and organize beings into coherent, systematic arrangements, all of which seems to belie the incalculable and unsystematizably unique reality of the ethical relation.

However, for Levinas, the asymmetry of the ethical relation, even in the unslakeable urgency of my concern for the other, always includes what Levinas calls "the third party." The third party is neither myself nor the other; rather the third party is, as Levinas puts it, not the neighbor himself, but the neighbor of the neighbor. Thus something "larger" than the self-other relation is always already contained in—but *not* identical with—the asymmetry of the ethical relation.

This third party opens up the question of justice, the necessity to make decisions, formulate procedures, and build institutions in a world that exceeds the "intimate society" of two, of self concerned with other. The third party represents all those others who also come to obsess me as I stand face to face with the other. The third party, as a separable dimension of the face-to-face encounter with the other, demands system, calculation, and contemporaneity.[18] As

Levinas puts it, the "entry" of the third is the birth of consciousness, representation, and the said. Indeed, with the entry of the third, I too find myself always already to have entered an embracing order in which I stand as the object of another's concern—in which there is justice for me as well.[19]

Levinas's very subtle position has profound consequences. The third party reveals a new moment of asymmetry, one that complicates or enriches asymmetry, but by no means cancels or negates it. Levinas puts it this way: "The other is from the first the brother of all the other men. The neighbor that obsesses me is already a face, both comparable and incomparable, a unique face and in relationship with faces, which are visible in concern for justice."[20] To reiterate this significant idea, in light of the third, the face of the other is *both* comparable and incomparable, a unique face *and* one that is in relationship with other faces.

Here we see what the third reveals about asymmetry. The empirical face-to-face encounter takes place in the mundane world of comparison, objectification, and evaluation. In this ordinary encounter, the concrete, empirical, fleshly face that looks at me *also* evokes uniqueness, urgency, and immediacy in the very midst of mediation.

In other words, asymmetry is *not* something that needs to be balanced or corrected by the *dialectical addition* of an implied or needed "other side," but rather a basic, eccentric "goodness" (as Levinas calls it) that is implanted in reality from the start. Because asymmetry has always included the entry of the third party within itself, we do *not* "fall away" from the diachronic, primordial urgency of the immediate, ethical relation into the "sad necessity" of distributive justice and the "prudent pragmatism" of mediation. Rather, Levinas argues that mediation, comparison, synchronization, and distributive justice are the very forms that themselves resonate with the immediacy of unqualified, ethical solicitude. My irreplaceable closeness to the neighbor, my primordial or diachronic proximity to the other, remains distinct from, and yet is found only in, the flow of empirical time in our social world of laws, rules, and conventions.

Two singularly significant citations from *Otherwise than Being* illustrate the all-important claims being advanced here. In these two passages, Levinas speaks of proximity—what we have here been calling the immediate, ethical relation—and shows its connections with the world of mediation, i.e., our ordinary, day-to-day world.

The one for the other of proximity is not a deforming abstraction. In it justice is shown from the first. . . . This means concretely that justice is not a legality regulating human masses, from which a technique of social equilibrium is drawn, harmonizing antagonistic forces. That would be a justification of the State delivered over to its own necessities. *Justice is impossible without the one that renders it finding himself in proximity.* . . . Justice, society, the State and its institutions, exchanges and work are comprehensible out of proximity.[21]

Proximity, or the extreme, untransferable responsibility of the ethical relation, shows us "justice from the first." The mediated social forms and institutions within which human life takes place do *not* oppose nor contradict the ethical urgency of proximity. Indeed, these mediated forms, such as tradition, political procedures, and legal institutions, are a further development of the ethical relation.

In one of the most striking and suggestive passages in *Otherwise than Being*, Levinas describes this complex relation between asymmetry and the third party this way:

In no way is justice a degradation of obsession, a degeneration of the for-the-other, a diminution, a limitation of anarchic responsibility, a neutralization of the glory of the Infinite, a degeneration that would be produced to the extent that, for empirical reasons, the initial duo would become a trio. But the contemporaneity of the multiple is tied about the diachrony of the two: *justice remains justice only in a society where there is no distinction between those close by and those far off, but where there also remains the impossibility of passing by the closest. . . . The equality of all is borne by my inequality.*[22]

As noted above, far from being some sort of fall from grace, or some sort of wary compromise, justice and the mediation of human sociopolitical institutions actually incarnate the reality of the ethical relation without exhausting that reality. And now Levinas adds the intriguing claim that the mediated form of justice itself requires the immediacy of the ethical relation, the derangement of my identity by the other, in order that it be justice!

Without the ethical relation, and the prevolitional orientation toward the face of the other that it provides, justice would not remain justice, and other social arrangements, norms, and laws would similarly degenerate into something else. In order to make impartial decisions, and to distribute goods and services in an equal, impersonal, public manner, we need, paradoxically, the inequality of the ego that is uniquely responsible for the other. Otherwise, as Levinas says, we will "pass by the closest" (ignore or fail to notice those nearby us) as we go about applying rules and procedures, thereby enacting a coldness and detachment toward the flesh-and-blood people around us that ends up being the opposite of fairness and even-handedness. Levinas is not merely saying that we need ethics in order to make our institutions better (although of course this may be true). Rather, he is saying that even for our mediated forms of social organization and regulation to be what they are, and to accomplish their goals, the ethical relation is required.

Mediation itself contains—and is the form of—immediacy! This is the suggestive position to which Levinas's conception of asymmetry and the third lead us. The everyday world of institutions and legality, considered solely as organizational arrangements for accomplishing public life, already embody immediacy, urgency, and solicitude. Considered solely as mediated social or institutional forms per se, society's traditions and procedures do not stand in need of some external infusion of spiritual spontaneity.

Goodness is and always has been right here, Levinas would seem to be saying: mediated social forms of human organization do not stand in opposition to some beyond in which we could achieve immediate self-expression and realize our true identity. Rather this immediacy already echoes within and is reflected in the form of law, the general rule, the comprehensive institution, the tradition. Outside of these mediated forms there is no immediacy, despite our romantic delusions. Immediacy is to be found, rather, within them.

Indeed, to speculate, one might argue that it is precisely the romantic resort to something beyond the law, beyond the institution, that inevitability leads to injustice, violence, and the end of distributive justice. Levinas's position, because it finds goodness, immediacy, and the ethical *within* mediated social forms, might be able to avoid these sources of ontological violence. The entry of the third, and the mediated procedures that come with it, *emerge out of* the responsibility and solicitude of the ethical. This means that Levinas's prophetic, touchstone "principle"—despite its diachronic and philosophically anarchic character, in which we find ourselves called by an other we can never finally meet—is constantly circulating invisibly amidst our worldly doings.

Thus from Levinas's perspective, we need wreak no fundamental violence on the social, and we need no drastic escape from the human: societies may be evil and may need radical, even revolutionary changes, but there is no utopic, immediate, new society to create out of hitherto unimagined and unimaginably spontaneous social forms. Social forms per se (not necessarily any given set of concrete social forms) already realize the ethical. The question thus comes down to which of the existing social forms should be institutionalized, and how they should be modified. For Levinas, it cannot *ever* be a question of whether or not there ought to be social forms, for this otherworldly or romantic refusal of the mediated nature of human society and tradition represents exactly the sort of violence against which he is arguing.

Philosophy and the Jewish Commentarial Tradition

The preceding analysis suggests an extremely interesting parallel between philosophy and one aspect of the Jewish tradition, and I would like briefly to explore this here.[23] If the above account of Levinas's thought is correct, then it should be clear that Levinas sees reality as thoroughly mediated through institutions, traditions, and the like, in which the ethical relation reverberates and is concretized. Here we see a parallel to Levinas's initial distinction between the saying and the said: the said, in its organized, synchronized, or contemporaneous system, would nonetheless be "animated by" the diachronic, unruly, and never fully recapturable folly of saying.

However, human beings run the ongoing risk or temptation of trying to block out this echo of the saying that resounds in the said. Human freedom itself presupposes the possibility of reducing human interaction to mediated rules and procedures, whether in the form of the state or in the manipulations and stratagems through which I attempt to exploit the other. Indeed, Levinas, by refusing to make the ethical a visible, empirical part of our active world, allows for just this possibility. This leaves reality paradoxically "richer than it is" or, as Levinas puts it, *enigmatic*, since the transcendence of the ethical relation "appears" in its very invisibility and diachronic irrecuperability, in the form of institutions, laws, and traditions.[24]

In this situation philosophy itself, or even writing in general, takes on an extremely interesting significance for Levinas, one very different from that which we saw operating in Derrida's work. Where Derrida sees writing as the ceaseless restoration of the obscured "other side" of any one-sided identity or position, Levinas seems to appeal to a more specifically Jewish religious notion of writing. I say this because Levinas's philosophy endeavors, with great creativity and resourcefulness, to open our ears to a nonfoundational, eternally unsynchronizable, and anachronistic ethical resonance. For Levinas, philosophy, writing, and the book represent the vital reading and rereading of reality through which we can endlessly rediscover this ethical resonance—the saying—resounding in the said, the immediate invisibly animating the mediate.

In Levinas's hands, philosophy becomes the ceaseless task of reinterpreting the text of reality so as to bring out the ethical relation dissimulated within it. In writing we can momentarily induce the enigma with which reality confronts us to speak, thereby allowing us to hear, for a passing instant, the inaudible echo of responsibility resonating *in and as* the merely apparent neutrality and impersonality of society. This is why writing or philosophy or the book must be taken up again and again, for we can never be finished with the task of attempting to synchronize the urgent immediacy of ethics, however fleeting this momentary "re-presentation" of the ethical within reality may be.[25]

The mundane is the womb of the transcendent. Thus, the text of reality must be read and reread if we are not to lose whatever "contact" we can have with that primordial saying that *says* this text. In the face of changing historical conditions, and even the changing circumstances, moods, and habits of an individual person, we must repeatedly undertake interpretive forays in an effort to uncover the endlessly "new" lying within the accepted, ordinary text of reality.

Here we can see rather clearly the affinity between Levinas's understanding of philosophy and the Jewish hermeneutical tradition. Both conceptions presuppose the necessity of the text, for only through writing can we catch a glimpse, a face, a shadow of that never fully visible reality that lies in the text. In the Jewish tradition, commentary (*perush*) aims to uncover the *hiddush*, or new meaning forever glimmering in the familiar text. Levinas seems to be advancing a conception of philosophical writing in which much the same thing occurs.

For Levinas philosophy is a momentary attempt to evoke the saying within the said—an endeavor, of course, that may succeed only temporarily, for philosophical discourse itself is the said, even as it soars above the said. This too is similar to the search by the Jewish hermeneutical tradition for *hiddush*: each reader uncovers a new sense, only to have this new sense itself become incorporated within the very text that is to be interpreted.

In this sense, both Levinasian philosophy and *perush*, or Jewish commentary, embody the eternal and infinite work of renewal. They both strive to keep us aware of the ethical, the immediate, and the urgent amidst the ordinary regularities of life—regularities that are themselves a "blessing" and whose absence, in those areas torn by war, famine, poverty, or prejudice, must always evoke our most powerful, immediate ethical response.

NOTES

1. This essay represents an extensively revised version of a paper delivered at a conference, "The Other in Jewish Thought and History," held at the Berman Center for Jewish Studies at Lehigh University in May 1992. I would like to thank Elliot Wolfson, Daniel Boyarin, Jonathan Boyarin, Larry Silberstein, and Susan Shapiro for their helpful comments on the earlier version of this paper.

2. This discussion, focusing on certain concepts, cannot do full justice to the rich texts through which Derrida (in particular) and Levinas have engaged in intellectual conversation. A more complete account of the Levinas/Derrida relationship would demand both philosophical and literary analysis, especially of Derrida's most recent essay on Levinas, "At This Moment in This Work Here I Am" (which originally appeared in French as "En ce moment même dans cet ouvrage me voici," in *Textes pour Emmanuel Levinas*, ed. Francis Laruelle [Paris: Place, 1980], 21–60; and which has recently been translated into English by Ruben Berezdivin in *Re-reading Levinas*, ed. Robert Bernasconi and Simon Critchley [Bloomington: Indiana University Press, 1991], 11–48). I hope to address these texts in a future article.

3. Of course, Levinas also knows the dangers associated with enthusiasm, and it is not possible to read his fifty or so years of philosophical production as some sort of simplistic, or even subtle, paean to uncritical notions of "tradition," or "religion," or "identity." The differences between Levinas and Derrida do not lie in some sort of positive, versus some sort of negative, view of enthusiasm.

4. In one of Derrida's more recent works, translated into English under the title *The Other Heading: Reflections on Today's Europe (Autre cap)*, we read the following striking illustration of this important critical

distance through which Derrida views culture and identity: "What is proper to a culture is not to be identical to itself. Not to not have an identity, but not to be able to identify itself, to be able to say 'me' or 'we'; to be able to take the form of the subject only in the non-identity to itself or, if you prefer, only in difference with itself (*avec soi*). There is no cultural identity without this difference with itself" (trans. Pascale-Ann Brault and Michael B. Naas [Bloomington: Indiana University Press, 1992], 9). I would like to thank Rael Meyerowitz for this reference.

5. Christopher Norris, *What's Wrong with Postmodernism* (Baltimore, Md.: Johns Hopkins University Press, 1990), 49–76.

6. In presenting Levinas's view of the other here and, in particular, in discussing the role of corporeality in this view, I have made use of material taken from my essay "In the Flesh: Embodiment and Jewish Existence in the Thought of Emmanuel Levinas," *Soundings* 76, 1 (Spring 1993). The latter piece offers a far more detailed examination of Levinas's later philosophy, especially of his overall approach to questions of the body and the other. In the present context, I am more interested in sketching out Levinas's basic conception of the speaking subject as constitutively turned toward the other.

7. This helps to explain the complexity, for Levinas, of the relationship between human beings and animals. In the act of saying, I register the fact that another person is there, near me. It is not a matter of will—this directedness toward the other just seems to be the way we *are* whenever we are with other human beings. We certainly are *not* this way when we are with rocks, furniture, machines, and so on. But given Levinas's account of the primordiality of saying, animals remain a challenging intermediate case. On this topic see John Llewelyn's "Am I Obsessed by Bobby? (Humanism of the Other Animal)," in Bernasconi and Critchley, *Re-reading Levinas*, 234–45.

8. See Emmanuel Levinas, *Autrement qu'être ou au-delá de l'essence* (Dordrecht: Kluwer, 1988), 60 passim; idem, *Otherwise than Being or Beyond Essence*, trans. A. Lingis (The Hague: Nijhof, 1981), 50 passim.

9. As Levinas puts it, "A face . . . is a trace of itself . . . an anachronous immediacy" (*Autrement qu'être*, 115; *Otherwise than Being*, 91).

10. Ibid. Levinas employs the figure of "folly," and in particular that of "the all important grain of folly" in several crucial places in *Otherwise than Being*. Although I will have a few things to say about "folly" in this chapter, the detailed consideration of this metaphor or of the associated complex of similar metaphors in *Otherwise than Being* is beyond the scope of this essay and must await another opportunity.

11. So as to avoid any misunderstandings, it should be emphasized that when Levinas talks about saying, and about corporeality, he is not referring to intentional actions or active, physical undertakings by a volitional self. Rather, saying and corporeality would seem to resound

"below" (or diachronically with, or asynchronically with) the level on which actions are taken, intentions carried out. In *Otherwise than Being*, Levinas attempts to articulate this intriguing and involved relationship between the prevolitional openness of saying and the active, thinking, willing self. I will consider this question in the section on asymmetry below, in the context of Levinas's notion of "the third" (what one might call, loosely, the "continuous derivation" of intersubjectivity from the ethical relation).

12. It goes without saying, of course, that I am not attempting here to offer a comprehensive account of alterity in Derrida's work. Rather, what I present here is a brief sketch of some of Derrida's early, seminal texts, in the hope of indicating a few basic intellectual roots—whose fascinating efflorescence can be seen in Derrida's later work.

13. Jacques Derrida, *Edmund Husserl's Origin of Geometry: An Introduction*, trans. John P. Leavey (Stony Brook, N.Y.: Hays, 1978), 87.

14. This Kantian reading of Derrida can be found, inter alia, in Norris, *What's Wrong with Postmodernism*; and Irene Harvey, *Derrida and the Economy of Difference* (Bloomington: University of Indiana Press, 1986). It is also found, in a different sense, in Drucilla Cornell, *The Philosophy of the Limit* (New York: Routledge, 1992).

15. Jacques Derrida, "Violence and Metaphysics," in *Writing and Difference*, trans. Alan Bass (Chicago: University Chicago Press, 1978), esp. 118–33. Derrida's two essays on Levinas should not be read simply as a "critique" of Levinas. As Robert Bernasconi has pointed out, in several essays Derrida's work on Levinas follows the general deconstructive path of offering at least *two* readings—one a close, revealing commentary, and one that reads the very same material against the grain, showing how the piece in question depends upon those very things that it wants to subordinate, exclude, or minimize (digressions, figures of speech, metaphors, etc.) The latter reading generally uncovers the diremptive tensions that constitute certain arguments or rhetorical strategies. See, for instance, Bernasconi's "Deconstruction and the Possibility of Ethics," in *Deconstruction and Philosophy*, ed. John Sallis (Chicago: University of Chicago Press, 1987), 122–39; and his "The Trace of Levinas in Derrida," in *Derrida and Différance*, ed. David Wood and Robert Bernasconi (Evanston, Ill.: Northwestern University Press, 1988), 13–29.

It is clear from the tone of Derrida's essays on Levinas (and, for that matter, from the tone of Levinas's few writings about Derrida) that there is a strong element of *homage* in the relationship between these two thinkers. Derrida often credits Levinas with philosophical insights and advances of the first order of importance. Indeed, as indicated both by the early date of Derrida's "Violence and Metaphysics" essay (it was originally published in two parts in the *Revue de métaphysique et de morale* in 1964, and thus represents one of the earliest objects of

Derrida's intellectual attention) and Derrida's reference to Levinas as one the important forerunners of his own thought in the famous "Difference" essay, there is far more than "criticism" at play here.

16. The whole issue of Levinas's relation to feminist thought clearly deserves a separate, detailed study. The status of the metaphors of the feminine in *Totality and Infinity* remains controversial and unclear to say the least. In addition, Levinas makes a far more subtle use of the rhetoric of maternality, pregnancy, and fecundity (the ego bears the other within itself as in birth-travail) to express the nature of ethical solicitude in *Otherwise than Being*. The possibility of appropriating Levinas's work for constructive feminist thought per se also remains open. For recent divergent views on these topics, see the essays by Irigaray, Chalier, and Chanter in Bernasconi and Critchley, *Re-reading Levinas*. In addition, see Catherine Chalier's *Figures du féminin: Lecture d'Emmanuel Levinas* (Paris: La nuit surveillée, 1982); Drucilla Cornell's *The Philosophy of the Limit* (New York: Routledge, 1992); and the interesting analysis of Derrida's views on this issue in *Jacques Derrida*, ed. Geoffrey Bennington and Jacques Derrida (Paris: Seuil, 1991), 190–93, 198–212.

17. As we will see immediately below, to associate the other with the "poor, widow, and orphan" is not, despite appearances, to take up a condescending or patronizing stance toward the other. It is, rather, to give absolute "priority" to the ways in which I may be of help or service to the other. Certainly there are many other dimensions to the relationship between self and other. But if we do not grant a heterogeneous and independent priority to the subject's orientation of ethical solicitude toward the other, then indeed, we open the way to condescension, and imperialism. Here we see one of the most salient aspects of Levinasian asymmetry: it establishes an ethical sociality as the distinctive and ineliminable feature of being human, even if this ethical connection must be conceived of as an asynchronic echo—the ancient resonance of being human to which I may always stop my ears.

18. Of course, just as the ethical relation transpires on a level other than that of the empirical per se, this reference to the third person must not be taken to refer to an empirical individual suddenly materializing upon a stage.

19. Levinas originally worked out the concept of the third party as early as 1954 in an article entitled "Le moi et la totalité," *Revue de Métaphysique et de Morale* 59 (October/December 1954): 353–73. For the English translation, see Emmanuel Levinas, "The Ego and the Totality," in *Collected Philosophical Papers*, trans. A. Lingis (Dordrecht and Boston: Nijhoff, 1987), 25–47. See also Levinas, *Autrement qu'être*, 200–202; idem, *Otherwise than Being*, 158–59.

20. Levinas, *Autrement qu'être*, 201; idem, *Otherwise than Being*, 158.

21. Levinas, *Autrement qu'être*, 202–3; idem, *Otherwise than Being*, 159, emphasis added.

22. Levinas, *Autrement qu'être*, 203; idem, *Otherwise than Being*, 159, emphasis added. I have slightly altered the translation of this difficult passage, which reads in the original,

> En aucune façon la justice n'est une dégradation de l'obsession, une dégéné-rescence du *pour l'autre*, une diminution, une limitation de la responsabilité anarchique, une "neutralization" de la gloire de l'Infini, dégénérescence qui se produirant au fur et à mesure où, pour des raisons empiriques, le *duo* initial deviendrait *trio*. Mais la contemporanéité du multiple se noue autour de la dia-chronie de duex: la justice ne demeure que dans une société où il n'y a pas de distinction entre proches et lointains, mais où demeure aussi l'impossibilté de passer à côté du plus proche; oú l'égalité de tous est portée par mon inégalité.

23. I attempt an initial inquiry into this complex subject in "In the Flesh: The Body and Jewish Existence in the Thought of Emmanuel Levinas." Although this aspect of Levinas's work has not received that much attention, I believe it to be essential to a real understanding of Levinas's *oeuvre*. Some useful essays on this topic are Fabio Ciaramelli, "Le rôle du judaisme dans l'oeuvre de Levinas," *Revue Philosophique de Louvain* 81, 52 (1983): 580–99; Adriaan Peperzak, "Emmanuel Levinas: Jewish Experience and Philosophy," *Philosophy Today* 27 (1983): 297–306; David Banon, "Une herméneutique de la sollicitation: Levinas lecteur du Talmud," *Emmanuel Levinas: Les cahiers de la nuit surve-illée* (Lagrasse: Verdier, 1984), 99–115; Catherine Chalier, "Singularité juive et philosophie," *Emmanuel Levinas: Les cahiers de la nuit surveillée* (Lagrasse: Verdier, 1984), 78–98; Catherine Chalier, *Judaisme et alérité* (Lagrasse: Verdier, 1982); Catherine Chalier, "L'âme de la vie: Levinas, lectuer de R. Haim de Volozin," *Emmanuel Levinas* (Paris: Herne, 1991) 387–98; and Charles Mopsik, "La pensée d'Emmanuel Levinas et la Cabale," *Emmanuel Levinas* (Paris: Herne, 1991), 378–86.

24. See "Phenomenon and Enigma," *Collected Philosophical Papers of Emmanuel Levinas* (Dordrecht: Nijhoff, 1987), 61–74, originally published in French in *Revue de Métaphysique et de Morale* 62 (1957): 241–53. See also Levinas, *Autrement qu'être*, 194–207; idem, *Otherwise than Being*, 152–62.

25. Here, and in some degree in other parts of this paper, I have been influenced by Jean Greisch's "The Face and Reading: Immediacy and Mediation," in *Re-reading Levinas*, 67–81.

Chapter 18

The Other Within and the Other Without

Jonathan Boyarin

> I would like to ask whether [the idea] that it is necessary to
> conceive the Other as a radically separable and separate
> entity in order for it to command our respect . . . is a useful
> idea. Just how other, we need to force ourselves to specify,
> is the Other?
> —S. P. Mohanty, *Yale Journal of Criticism*

The quote from S. P. Mohanty that I have used as an epigraph for
this paper asks a wry question about the way non-Western identities
have recently been validated under the philosophical dictate of the
moral primacy of the Other. Mohanty questions, in effect, whether
it is desirable for the Other to be given attention under that rubric,
or whether the language of otherness might turn out to be another
ruse for excluding the vast majority of people from the dominant
notion of "the humanities." In the context of this volume, the focus
of the question must be shifted slightly: in what contexts do a
certain group of people become labeled as "the Other," and what are
the effects of that label in different situations?

While remembering Mohanty's warning that the label of otherness should not be embraced too hastily or uncritically, my project is
aimed at placing the question of Jewish identity (or what some

An earlier version of this chapter appeared in Jonathan Boyarin's *Storm
from Paradise: The Politics of Jewish Memory*. Copyright 1992 by the
Regents of the University of Minnesota.

critics might call "the Jewish subject position") into a critical dialogue with different explorations of the politics of identity, especially those grounded in the experience of colonialism and its aftermath. I will argue that the situation of Jews after World War II bears striking similarities to the postcolonial situation, but that these similarities have been occluded by an unthinking association of Jews with a monolithic "Europe" or a monolithic "West." The belated inclusion of Jews within a modern individualist and universalist culture of empathy is one of the main reasons for that occlusion, yet the record of modern Jews' agonistic encounter with and within Europe is not limited to assimilation and genocide. Therefore I will conclude by suggesting one literary model for a "Jewish ethnography" that displays a remarkable capacity for self-reflection without relying on the imperial pretensions of empathy.

Where did this monolithic "Europe" begin, then? In an essay on the Enlightenment search for Atlantis as one possible alternative to replace biblical Israel as the origin of European civilization, Pierre Vidal-Nacquet notes that "to be autochthonous means never having been instructed by an other; the theme is fundamental" (1982, 58, n. 80). Though the Enlightenment certainly predated what we usually think of as the period of "Romantic nationalism," Vidal-Nacquet shows that it nevertheless included several attempts to locate an "autochthonous" European civilization in such places as Sweden or Italy. Representing competing national visions, on a larger scale these Enlighteners collaborated in a larger project of "overcoming the Judeocentric vision of the history of the world" (14). After 1679, when Olof Rudbeck first published in Uppsala his *Atlantica*, attempting "to show that Sweden was the cradle of history, that it was Atlantis and its capital Uppsala . . . virtually no one who borrowed the myth failed to refer to the proud Swede" (19).

Most of us no longer believe in Atlantis. Most of us have overcome the passionate desire to claim pride of origin for a particular ethnic nation. Many of us, in fact, have come to question the very search for "the origins of civilization." After the horrors of colonialism committed in the name of civilization and the horrors of "autochthonous," blood-and-soil Aryanism, the Enlightenment twist on Christian supercessionism has been called into question. In some quarters, in some registers, moving beyond the question of origins, an explicitly Jewish voice has emerged in critical social thought, largely as a response to the apocalyptic eclipse of reason during World War II. This Jewish voice speaks of a knowledge that is always contingent and never ideal, always contaminated by its own interests, resources, and limitations, a knowledge that is always structured and restructured by the next contexts in which it is deployed, a knowledge that moves away from an emphasis on originality and progress toward critical commentary and dialogue. I am of course not speaking of a secular flowering of an esoteric or hermetic lore only available to those who call themselves Jews, but of a knowledge linked to precisely the vital sense that history and identity inextricably shape each other that also characterizes to a large degree the postmodern temper.

Yet for that voice to remain vital, to retain a connection to the memory of the cultural worlds it grows out of, it must be articulated with other emergent voices in the aftermath of colonialism and of triumphal modern progressivism. There are many such voices, offering an almost infinite number of points of initial contact. Here, I will take two strong voices in cultural critique as starting points for comparing Jewish and postcolonial difference, and for elucidating the ways that an ethnography has articulated or could otherwise articulate those differences. The first is several recent essays by Edward Said. In his article "Anthropology and Its Interlocutors" (1989a), Said responds to the various calls and proposed strategies for letting the voice of anthropology's object into the finished product of ethnography by insisting that the anthropological project still remains trapped in a situation of dominance over its object. The Other, in anthropological discourse, remains outside, as she must in a neocolonial situation where power/knowledge remains concentrated in the old imperial centers. Said believes that the imperial project, the control of the colonized world and the extraction of its labor power and material resources, was the most urgent task for white Christian ideology in Europe. The "interlocutors" of anthropology he is interested in are therefore the colonized and the formerly colonized. Nor will Said accept the simple equation of the colonized with other excluded groups, such as workers or women, whom he sees as equally implicated in enthusiasm for the imperialist project (1989b, 6).

However, although Said identifies the Eurocentric imperial vision as "the idea of white Christian Europe" (1989b), nowhere does he direct his attention to those inside Europe who were not Christian. Said is certainly right to suggest that hostility to Islam in the modern Christian West has historically gone hand in hand with, has stemmed from, the same source, has been nourished at the same stream as anti-Semitism, and that a critique of the orthodoxies, dogmas, and disciplinary procedures of Orientalism contribute to an enlargement of our understanding of the cultural mechanisms of anti-Semitism (1985, 99).

Though Said's critique of the discipline of Orientalism has been criticized in turn as monolithic (Clifford 1988, 255–76; Thom 1990), it nevertheless stands as a powerful model for a retrospective critique of the cultural and biological racism that has been employed in the service of nationalism at home and colonialism abroad. As Said has shown, the tendencies to essentialize self and Other, to buttress national collective identity with a fiction of majestic and pure origins, to create grand schemata of cultural history that cloak themselves in the rhetoric of scientific authority but appear in retrospect as ludicrously speculative—these were all practiced since the early modern period on various of Europe's Others, notably including Muslims and Jews (Olender 1989).

If the hangover of Orientalism—a rubric under which one can certainly include expertise on Jews—demands from us a dissolution of essences, a complication and contamination of origins, that demand challenges critical Jewish thought as well. Similarly, if Said insists that the object in contemporary ethnography remains trapped by the scientific ethos of controlling knowledge, Jews as object of ethnography should be trapped the same way. Or are they? I will return to this question toward the end of this essay.

A second voice with which a critical Jewish ethnography may be articulated is that of Gayatri Spivak. Her distinction between teaching as "information retrieval" and teaching as a politically enabling critical practice may help to inform the very idea of critical ethnography. According to Spivak, teaching Indian history outside India is information retrieval, but doing so inside India is truly active *teaching*. Conversely, for Spivak teaching critical theory in India is information retrieval; it is about "other people," whereas teaching theory in the United States "is a critique of imperialist cultural politics" (1990, 91).

Spivak's underlying assumption here is apparently that Indian students are not empowered to engage critical theory, either to change it or to apply it dynamically within their own situation; for them it can serve only as a means to acquiring legitimating academic authority. Spivak's dichotomy seems to preclude the possibility that scholars living and working in India might, through the common medium of the English language, have a critical effect on or through theory, or that pretentious theory developed within the former colonial metropole could "speak" powerfully to those in the postcolonial situation. Her dichotomy, like Said's critique, is based on a spatial distinction that mystifies as well as reveals.

But the force of Spivak's distinction here should not be lost, nor should we ignore the fact that some people are differently situated, and hence more empowered, to "take on" theory than others. Nor, as with Said, should the distinction Spivak makes between Others inside the metropole and the vast millions of the formerly colonized be minimized. Spivak is well aware that "the stories (or histories) of the postcolonial world" are not the same as "the way the metropolitan countries discriminate against disenfranchised groups in their midst" (1989, 274). Consequently, she acknowledges that postcolonial intellectuals can also be placed in positions of relative privilege vis-à-vis those "native" disenfranchised groups.

The lessons for a critical Jewish ethnography are twofold. First, it is important to distinguish between using theory to validate the study of Jews, to make their difference just as "sexy" as gender or colonialism (analogous to "information retrieval" type legitimation), and engaging theory in an effort to articulate a postfoundationalist Jewish identity (analogous to the engaged critical practice Spivak promotes). Second, Spivak's argument about the paradoxical position of the postcolonial intellectual in the metropole serves as a reminder that Jews, too, can serve as privileged Others in ways that mystify both anti-Semitism and the larger system of domination of which it is an integral part.

Nevertheless, there are a number of reasons why these analogies seem irrelevant or forced. The first is the conventional geographical specification of the Other as being outside Europe, or, since the nineteenth century, outside Europe and America (Baudet 1965; Fabian 1983; Barker, et al. 1985; Torgovnick 1990; Mason 1990; Cheyfitz 1990; Campbell 1988). The title of Spivak's earlier collection of essays, *In Other Worlds*, reinforces this spatial organization, emphasizing by a pun the way the English *word* is situated outside England. Even in the metaphoric sense of *"world"*—India and England as different cultural worlds—the two countries are located along a spatial axis; they are "distant" from each other. The spatial difference emphasized in Spivak's title is reinforced by the cover illustration, a reproduction from a seventeenth-century Indian illuminated manuscript.

Only inside the text do we read about Spivak's careful articulation of Marxist, deconstructivist, and feminist insights, and about her debt to Jacques Derrida for enabling her to live in other worlds (1987, author's note). Spivak, appropriately echoing Derrida's own discretion, says nothing about his Jewishness. She refers to herself by the official designation "nonresident Indian." Thus, she is defined and defines herself in relation to a territorial state from which she is absent, neatly signaling the problematic of spatial identity, nationalism, and postmodern diaspora.

This problematic is very much at the forefront of contemporary cultural studies, especially in literature and anthropology. However, the emphasis on the colonized non-European Other ironically complements ethnography's ingrained repression of the Other inside Europe. An instructive case in this regard is that of Richard Simon, a seventeenth-century priest, Christian Hebraist, and ethnographer of European Jewish communities. Simon was eventually excommunicated—not, apparently, for doing fieldwork, but for his argument, against Bossuet, that the Hebrew Bible as received had been falsified by the Jews after Jesus to remove the prophecies of his coming. At first Simon's accusation of Jewish textual distortion seems to contradict his sympathetic inquiries into contemporary Jewish community life.

Closer consideration suggests that, from the perspective of church doctrine, Simon's sin was consistent in both respects. By questioning the received text, he disrupted the efforts of centuries of Christian scholarship that had developed the doctrine of Christian supercession. At the same time, by arguing that "Jewish communities come to life, are transformed over time and according to the places where they settle" (Olender 1989, 111; see also van Gennep 1920 and Yardeni 1970), Simon challenged the notion that since Jesus' time, Jewish life and thought had been petrified. This conflicted with the church's effort to deal with the problem of its internal Jewish Other by distancing it in time, fixing it in the past. Simon threatened this temporal segregation that neutralized Jewish difference both by relegating it to the past and by removing the critical force of Judaism in the present.

The same mistake might well be made with regard to the impact of Judaism on the identities of thinkers in the present. We certainly do not want to make naive claims about the "Jewishness" of certain sets of ideas merely on the basis of the Jewish background of those who articulate them. On the other hand, neither should we assume that family and communal traditions have no bearing on high theory—or that a profound critical impulse cannot be fed by a legacy of events that happened half a century ago. Thus, we may hesitate to relegate the Jewishness of someone like Derrida to a mere "biography effect."[1]

Said's plausible insistence on imperialism as a *geographical* fact cancels out the significance of the temporal boundaries of domination, however: "Imperialism after all is an act of geographical violence through which virtually every space in the world is explored, charted, and finally brought under control" (1989b, 10). Said is correct, of course, but we are so accustomed to thinking of time and space as contrasting axes that this emphasis on spatiality tends to marginalize discourses of temporal othering.

Different places exist simultaneously, but different times do not exist in the same place—except in the minds and writings of extraordinary individuals such as Walter Benjamin. Thus, if the vast preponderance of Jews who resisted imperialism culturally or militarily and those who were victimized by imperialism are dead, rather than elsewhere, they seem irrelevant to the struggles of postcolonial people against (neo)imperialism. Thus the question arises whether those who are not in a position to be interlocutors (of anthropology, literary criticism, or any other form of contemporary critical thought) because they are dead could be a source of critical discursive power. Where Spivak asks, "Can the Subaltern Speak?" (1988), those who would revive a critical Jewish discourse might ask, "Can the dead speak?" Again, while our intuitive answer is no, an underground tradition says that our lives depend on our hearing them. At the same time, a new initiative in academic anthropology has begun to explore ways of relating to the Other through time (Ohnuki-Tierney 1990).

I consider Said and Spivak here because, largely thanks to their own efforts, they are now situated along relatively clearly established fault lines, or paradoxes, between excluded otherness (he as a Palestinian exile, she as a nonresident Indian) and authoritative scholarly privilege. I am trying to explore an analogous fault line between the marginalization and victimization of the Jew by European anti-Semitism and the prominent role of Jews at the heart of modern European culture. A better understanding of this complex of marginalization, victimization, and creative interaction, and its transformation in the aftermath of Nazi genocide, can lead to a better understanding of an analogous complex between colonial brutality and European humanism that claimed to unite the entire species under its benign purview. But this fault line between the Jew and the idea of Europe has been occluded in several ways. Because of this, the creative contribution of the Jewish Other to European critical thought has been hidden.

The first way is called "assimilation." This is a misnomer, since it assumes an unchanging nature on the part of the non-Jewish majority, which Jews can approach if they have the will and if they are given the chance. The assumption that Jews could or should assimilate was consistent with a liberal argument, enshrined in anthropological discourse, that differences between groups were "cultural" rather than "biological" inheritances (Kirshenblatt-Gimblett 1987; Gilman 1986, 219).

Moreover, the dissolution of distinctive Jewish communities presupposed similar processes of dissolution within the larger society, a society that was itself "dissolving," changing in unprecedented and unpredictable ways. Further, the anxiety over this dissolution fueled, in turn, the growth of both "cultural" and racialist anti-Semitism.[2] Still, even after the Nazi genocide, the myth of Enlightenment universalism remains whenever Jewish assimilation is tacitly assumed to be the modern norm, while Jewish separatism and exclusion are regarded as odd "holdovers" from tradition.

A second factor related to assimilation that contributes to the occlusion of Jewish otherness is the fact of annihilation. This obscures the Jewish difference in various ways. There are fewer poor Jews than there were in 1939, fewer Jewish radicals, fewer Jews who speak a nonstate Jewish language. Moreover, because many people in Europe and America were horrified by the genocide in their midst, anti-Semitism, at least until now, has been excluded from much polite company, and "Holocaust Memorials" have taken pride of place in a postmodern culture of imperial guilt. Likewise, "the Holocaust" itself sometimes comes to be seen as the one really dreadful thing that happened to Jews. This effectively precludes serious cultural criticism of the situation of Jews before or after World War II, as reflected in Renato Rosaldo's observation that "the humor in Marx's use of anti-Semitic stereotypes does not make one laugh out loud, particularly not after the Holocaust" (1989, 191). Thus, the shadow of the Holocaust makes it hard, even for those who acknowledge the power of the past, to see how seriously we must think about the pre-Holocaust temptation to laugh at anti-Semitic stereotypes (cf. Greenblatt 1990).

Much as "assimilation" assumes a fixed and approachable non-Jewish culture, fetishizing "the Holocaust" assumes an undifferentiated situation before and after—whether that situation is seen as endemic anti-Semitism, in the Zionist view, or as "normal" tolerance, in the assimilationist view. On the other hand, to see the Nazi genocide as dynamically connected to and part of the phenomena that both "precede" and "follow" it throws into question both the notion that it was an insane irruption of the irrational and the argument that it epitomized the abnormal and unhealthy situation of Jews in diaspora. Situating the genocide within a continuing history, but always in a contingent and provisional way, is a way to let the dead speak.

A third form of the occlusion of Jewish otherness is related to the formation of a Jewish state. Spivak may be a nonresident Indian, but I am not a nonresident Israeli—except in the Zionist dream. Nevertheless, radical critics continue to make the paradoxical claims that (1) Jews cannot be in a postcolonial situation because they are participants in a belated colonial venture, and (2) Jews are no longer a diaspora people because they now have a "homeland." Assumption (1) places Israel outside the pale of legitimate "new nations"; assumption (2) implies that the "Jewish question" has been solved by the creation of Israel. Thus we see confusion between the boundaries of inside and outside, between a positive emphasis on difference and a frequent presumption of unanimity among Jews.

The uncovering of all three of these forms of occlusion and the belief that they must be critically confronted if Jewish concerns are to be brought into dialogue with contemporary cultural studies form the double thematics of this essay. The first fault line I am exploring is that between the Other outside Europe and the Other inside Europe. My focus, of course, is on Jews, but the purview might well be extended in several directions. Peter Mason, for example, has considered the relation between the early colonialist representation of "Plinian" monstrous races in the New World and the construction of witches and the insane as explored by Foucault (Mason 1987). The problem, however, is that witches and the insane are understood in this paradigm as a reflexive effect of the self-constitution of civil society. Sartre notwithstanding, the scholarly consensus today holds that the continued existence of Jews cannot be reduced to an effect of anti-Semitism (Finkielkraut 1980; Friedlander 1990). Rather than pursuing this Foucauldian direction, it might be more helpful to consider under this rubric groups that have not yet been brought within the convocation of theory. One thinks immediately of the Romani, Others within Europe whose transnational (or at least nonnational) and stubbornly distinct minority identities make them at least to that extent analogous to Jews (Trumpener 1992).

There is also a second boundary between "within" and "without," between the collective with which one is conventionally identified and the presumably alien collective Other. The older catechism of American anthropological practice held that only the Other without was a fit subject for research, since "distance" encourages "objectivity." While the notion was self-evident a few years ago, it seems almost bizarre today.

At the same time, work was being carried out in many rural backyards and national archives in Europe on the Others within, often under the rubric of "folklore." Moreover, the boundaries separating ethnography of the Other without and folklore of the Other within were not necessarily rigid. Thus the manual produced by a member of S. Anski's ethnographic expedition studying the Jews of the Ukraine near the turn of the century was titled *Yidishe etnografye un folklor* (Rekhtman 1958). Long before Anski's expedition, however, the nineteenth-century German Jewish founders of *Wissenschaft des Judentums* (the historical study of Judaism), through objectivist research modeled on colonial ethnological science, maintained ties to their Jewish identity while distancing themselves from their "primitive" contemporaries and forebears. Wishing to purify Judaism of elements of folkloric "superstition," the proponents of *Wissenschaft* separated out those universal elements that could inform a modern Judaism compatible with ecumenical liberalism. Theirs was primarily a strategy of othering in time, allowing identity to draw on identification with a heritage that now can be dispensed with. Aiming to lay to rest "the savage in Judaism," *Wissenschaft des Judentums* thus complemented the efforts of contemporary Christian scholars of ancient Judaism, who aimed

> to radically differentiate Judaism and savage religion [as] part of an ongoing attempt to protect the privileged status of Judaism, and by extension, Christianity itself. This motivation informed the work of both Jewish and Christian interpreters from the Enlightenment until the present day. (Eilberg-Schwartz 1990, 4–5)

But under whose assumptions about the "savage" were Jewish interpreters working? The scholars of *Wissenschaft des Judentums* shared with many scholars in the late twentieth century the assumption that the duality of culture and nature was part of a shared Greek and "Judeo-Christian" mythology (Haraway 1989, 246). Pending more detailed archaeology, especially of the German tradition, it is safe to assert that *both* Christian and Jewish scholars, whether studying ancient Jews or colonized peoples, were motivated in complex and semiconscious ways by images of the colonized savage and the superseded Jew. Moreover, such scholarship could be a technique of self-defense as well as an aggression against the Other. Thus, cultural folkloristics arose in debate with, and partly as a defense against, the rise of physical/racialist anthropology (Belke 1971).

In a fundamental way, the projects of studying the Other within and of studying the Other without share a common goal: "Our ways of making the Other are ways of making ourselves" (Fabian 1990, 756).[3] But even this quotation reproduces a dichotomous logic—self and Other, Jew and Christian, ancient and modern, within and without. Thus, as argued by both structuralism and deconstruction, we tend, like our ancestors, to produce our world in binaries. François Hartog notes that this pattern, which at first appears as the "rule of the excluded middle," comes to seem

> not so much a rule obeyed by the narrator or procedures he deliberately adopts, as a rhythm, a beat which runs through the narrative. It appears that, in the end, in its efforts to translate the "other" the narrative proves unable to cope with more than two terms at a time. (1988, 258)

Or, as S. P. Mohanty puts it in the sentence I have used as an epigraph here, "Just how other . . . is the Other?"[4]

All of the foregoing suggests an archaeological project connecting questions about the formulation of modern cultural anthropology and the problematics of modern Jewish identity. Clearly there is something buried there that may be accessible at several points.[5]

My concern here, however, remains with the layers of topsoil overlaying that buried history. Why is it that the otherness of Jews has tended to be occluded in Europe and America since World War II? One reason, I suggest, is the obliteration of Otherness through the method of empathy. This occurs where humanism demands acknowledgment of the Other's suffering, but where conditions do not allow for what Eric Cheyfitz calls "the *difficult* poetics of translation"—that is, where the paradoxical linkage of shared humanity and cultural otherness cannot be expressed (1990). Thus, for example, in popular-culture representations of "the Holocaust," the particular horror of the Nazi genocide is emphasized by an image of Jews as normal Europeans, "just like us." In fact, we can only "empathize with," *feel ourselves into*, those we can imagine as ourselves. Thus, in the television docudrama "Holocaust," the Jewish protagonists are a middle-class, German-speaking nuclear family. Conceivably, such representations might make viewers marginally more alert to anti-Semitism in the present, but they do not really expand the space of the Other.[6]

If empathy turns out to be as problematic as a rhetoric for extending human concern and compassion, as I have just suggested, what implications does this have for the tradition of liberal cultural anthropology? This anthropology has postulated that by sharing for a time the lives of the Other, we can empathize with the Other and thus adequately represent the Other back to those who are like ourselves. However, if a strategy of empathy does not leave space for the Other, what alternative strategies would still allow for humane contact and not freeze the Other into that position of utter alienation that Mohanty warns against?

First it is necessary to historicize empathy. Is it Greek, Christian, imperial, generally universalist, or all of the above? In a painstaking though necessarily selective study of the sentence "I am you," Karl Morrison has begun to sketch out a history of the concept. Although Morrison's references go back to Vedic texts, he argues that

> within Western culture, the sentence and the patterns of thought that it epitomized originated in ancient Greece. Neither sentence nor patterns of thought owed essential meaning or content to the other two fonts of the Western intellectual tradition, Old Testament Judaism and Roman thought. .... True to that beginning, the sentence and its meaning retained their cogency among people who moved easily in the intellectual heritage of Greece, and who worked in inquiries of high abstraction, rather than the forensic and social inquiries in which both Old Testament Jews and Romans of the classical and postclassical periods most notably distinguished themselves. (1988, 27)

Morrison's scope is large, and he aims toward a redemptive critique that would demonstrate the intellectual and ethical vitality of "the hermeneutics of empathy." However, he remains virtually silent about the repressive effects of empathy on those who remain beyond the pale. Thus, he provocatively begins his preface with a discussion of the German philosopher Fichte's call for the removal of the Jews from Europe, since they are a stumbling block in the path of European brotherhood (xii–xiii), but does not criticize it except for the warning that "the example of Fichte . . . does not let us escape from the question of how doctrines of harmony justified conflict and even persecution" (137).

Besides Christ, the individual who appears most often and most consequentially in Morrison's account is Augustine. In an extended review of Augustine's interpretation of the Jacob and Esau story, Morrison reveals (though he fails to state) how Augustine appropriates the figure of Jacob for Christian theology while simultaneously distancing the Jews. For Augustine, Esau represents carnality, Jacob spirituality; Esau the Jews and Romans, Jacob the Christians; Esau the earthly Adam, Jacob the heavenly Christ; Esau the reprobate, Jacob the elect (82–83). In Jacob's struggle with the angel, by contrast, Jacob takes on a double moral persona: "In his withered member, Jacob personified . . . Jews and bad Christians, people of carnal vision, whereas in his blessedness, he personified true believers" (83).

We may well ask what has happened to empathy here; Augustine's treatment of the biblical narrative seems much more like an opportunistic appropriation of selected motifs to argue points determined in advance. Especially noteworthy here, as elsewhere in Augustine, is the contrast between Jewish carnality and Christian spirituality—one of the prime figures that will be carried forward into the thematics of colonialism, with the Christian remaining in place as the colonizer while the Jew is now replaced by "the savage." Traces of the Augustinian heritage may even be seen in the anti-Semitism of the idealist humanist Fichte: for spiritual empathy to take place, those who are trapped in base carnality must be removed.

However, Morrison does not explore any of these suggestions. In his effort to achieve such a broad reopening of a long-neglected theme, he exhibits selective blindness, along with strategic dichotomization. The latter is seen, for example, in the passage quoted above where he identifies empathy as "Greek," not "Jewish" or "Roman"—once again, as if these terms referred to three noncontingent cultural worlds.

For Morrison, the flaw in Western culture is the incomplete synthesis of the Greek theme "I am you" and the Jewish commandment "Love your neighbor as yourself." He attributes this failure to social structure—individuals' loyalties "to family, cult, class, party, nation, or state" (357). Curiously, whereas Morrison repeatedly emphasizes the aspect of domination inherent in metaphors of male empathetic acquisition and female reception, he has nothing to say about the role of power in the histories of the Greek theme and the Jewish commandment. He does not articulate what his account repeatedly suggests: that Greco-Christian empathy flowers within a situation of imperial triumphalism, while Jewish ethics works outward from particular identification with those who are closest to one.

We are left, then, with the impression that spiritual empathy is not a particularly Jewish theme, and that it tends to be deployed from a position of relative dominance. Because of the colonial context of classic ethnography, it would be important to explore in detail the role that an implicit hermeneutics of empathy plays in ethnographic fieldwork method, especially in the practice of "participant observation." The assumption—much diluted now, but still shaping our work—is that by doing what "they" do for long enough, the anthropologist can learn what it is like to be "one of them," thereby earning the right to articulate the experience of the inarticulate, to write the experience of the illiterate.[7]

This assumption not only informs the deployment of empathy in space; it also underlies empathetic historicism, the deployment of empathy in time. Historicism's goal is to sufficiently forget one's own context and sufficiently immerse oneself in a world "distant in time" so that one comes to share the experience of the dead. Given the link between empathy and empire, we can better understand Walter Benjamin's insistence that "the adherents of historicism actually empathize . . . with the victor" (1969, 256). Historicism implies control over the past, comprehension of all its aspects, confidence that it will not surprise us by coming to life in the present. In the triumphal view of universal history and unidirectional progress, the European can comprehend the spatially distant Other empathetically because the savage is contained in the history of civilization. In much the same way, the present-day historian can comprehend the past because he has developed out of it. Thus, the distinctions between the Other within and the Other without, the

Other in space and the Other in time, collapse at the pinnacle of *modern* European imperialism.

To return to the question posed earlier, what possible alternatives are there to the triumphalism of empathetic participant observation or empathetic historicism? First, it is not the case that because there are problems with empathy, other strategies will necessarily be benign. Rhetorics that are grounded in the assumption of "radical alterity" do not necessarily encourage a respect for the right to live differently. Instead, they often permit a more solipsistic, less self-reflexive deployment of tropes of otherness to suit selfish needs of the moment. We have seen something of this in Augustine's discussion of Jacob. François Hartog describes a similar case in Herodotus: when it is a question of the Greek identity, the Scythians appear as the opposite of the Greeks; when the Persians need to appear like Greeks, the Scythians are contrasted both to Greeks and to Persians (1988). They are available as an all-purpose topos; it little matters what they are "really" like.

Lack of "empathy," then—the lack of any demand for an attempt to comprehend the experience of the Other—may also feed into ethnocentrism. Ethnocentrism is consequential both within and without the boundaries of the ethnic group. Within, it is a powerful means of enforcing solidarity, often at the cost of repressing internal difference. Without, it legitimizes discrimination against those excluded from the group. I suspect, therefore, that we cannot blithely dispense with empathy, with some presumption that human experience is commonly approachable across the lines of difference (cf. Mohanty 1989). What we need to do instead, perhaps, is to reinscribe empathy more knowingly, with a critical awareness of the power relations and the tendencies to symbolic violence its usage implies.

Isn't a measure of empathetic identification inherent in the idea of postmodern criticism? As I understand it, "postmodernism" implies not a progressive supercession of the modern, but a critique from within that preserves the freedom of modernism while dismantling its progressivist pretensions to be the last and culminating word. Hence an eclectic diffusion of "participant observation," the sense that we are always susceptible to the cultural systems we analyze, characterizes the prominence of criticism in contemporary elite culture. Everything becomes fieldwork.

Yet as sympathetic as I am to the postmodern turn, it frequently betrays itself in a hubristic rhetoric of accomplishment: *finally* we have realized that we are what we write, *finally* we have realized that the observer cannot be separated from the observed, *finally* we know that the monstrous Other is the monster in our minds. Postmodernism, that is, denies Benjamin's claim that '"the state of emergency' in which we live is not the exception but the rule" (1969, 257).

If postmodernism is at least partly characterized by the anthropological stance of participant observation, then, it is vital that we explore the analogies within European cultural history to the insidious potentials of anthropology. This is one approach to finding the right questions about the relations among universalism, imperialism, and genocide.

One country where the continuing state of emergency has been particularly acute in the last couple of years is Germany—whose heritage contains, in the figure of Kant, the categorical imperative as the ultimate modern expression of the ethic of empathy, and in the living memory of Nazism, the greatest legacy of common humanity denied within Europe. Without raising the specter of a literal recurrence of Nazi rule and genocide, I find that German xenophobia toward foreign workers and refugees in the context of German reunification inescapably brings to mind past debates about integration and exclusivism in German cultural politics. Therefore, I want to focus briefly on the case of "Germany"—not so much the German state as a machine for wielding power as the project of creating a national German collective identity (see Renan, quoted in Olender 1989, 87).

Consideration of Germany helps to destabilize the rigid geographical distinction between the imperial world and the colonized world:[8] Germany is within Europe yet has an ambivalent relation to empire, coming late to colonization and eventually seeking empire within Europe. Doubtless the fact that the Nazi genocide against the Jews was committed by German speakers, rather than by the rulers of one of the great modern European empires, has helped to obscure the relationship between colonialism and genocide. But these are larger questions than I am equipped to pursue.

My particular interest in "Germany," following Sander Gilman's recent book, *Jewish Self-Hatred*, centers on the threat that Jewish linguistic difference within German-speaking lands posed to those advocating German national identity based on a common language. Gilman traces in painstaking detail the attitudes of non-Jewish scholars in German-speaking lands toward the Jews, their language, and their books, starting with the sixteenth-century Christian humanist Reuchlin, who held that the Jews were not worthy of their own books and did not know how to read them correctly (1986, 42–44). Do we not hear echoes of Richard Simon, who would claim a century later that the Jews had actually falsified the Bible? Much of what even Christian humanists knew about Jewish classical texts was learned, of course, from converts, and much that converts wrote took the form of virulent, scurrilous "exposés." Here is the dark side of the notion that the native is the one who truly knows; the convert's insider exposure of "the hidden language of the Jews" is the demonic reverse image of participant observation. Later, in the period when romantic and folkloristic nationalism flowered, the question of the holy texts ceded precedence to the search for a pure national vernacular. Yiddish came to be seen as a deliberate corruption and desecration of German, a secretive and lying code, and as a particular threat to the new pan-German political identity based on a standardized literary language (Gilman 1986, 71 ff.) Hence the manic anti-Semitic insistence on the "Jewishness" of the language of nineteenth-century journalists writing in German. And, as is well known, German Jews in their chimerical quest for assimilation distinguished themselves carefully from their Yiddish-speaking past and their Yiddish-speaking cousins to the east. One way to accomplish this was to collapse the two, to *localize* the past outside Germany. The Jewish convert Gottfried Selig did this in his Yiddish textbook of 1792 by claiming that Hebrew words are used in Yiddish in ways

> so deformed that they appear to be parts of the Hottentot language.
> . . . Thus, in the eyes of the formerly Yiddish-speaking convert,
> Yiddish moved from being a language of a "nation within nations"
> to a language of the "barbarian." But for the Jew, convert or not,
> these barbarians must be localized, like the Hottentot, in some
> remote geographic place to separate them from the image of the
> German Jew. Their locus is the East, specifically Poland, and the
> Yiddish-speaking Jew becomes identified with the Polish Jew.
> (Gilman 1986, 99)

It is worth bearing in mind that in the late seventeenth century, German speakers did not have a very direct ideological investment in "Hottentots"; the term was simply a metaphor for distance and incomprehensibility. When a converted Jew writing in German about Yiddish invoked it, it was indeed the Other within that he was trying to exorcise—the Jew inside himself and the Jew inside "Germany." Here again, we realize that there is no justification for a global insistence on either the priority of the colonized or the priority of marginal groups within Europe. Instead the interaction between the two in the dominant imagination should be made the priority.[9]

The need to set a boundary between "native" German Jewry and primitive Yiddish speakers became especially acute when East European Jews began migrating to Germany en masse, invading and unsettling the "metropole" much the way the Third World has come to work in Europe since World War II (see Wertheimer 1987; Kramer 1980). The German-speaking Jews' great investment in maintaining the distance between themselves and the immigrants doubtless helps to explain why many assumed that the Nazis would perceive the same distance, and thus spare them. This strenuous and sustained attempt by German Jews to become the same eventually encountered Nazism, an othering so violent that it resulted in annihilation.

This is a good point at which to turn the ethnographic gaze back on Europe—not to study "folk culture" or ethnicity inside Europe, but to employ a *Verfremdungseffect*, using the anthropologist's distant eye to see the most "rarified" ideas as culturally marked products. Perhaps the most general "idea"—indeed, so pervasive that it has only been articulated recently in the process of critique—is the notion that Europe is the point of reference, the topos of the same, an idea that is inseparable from the idea of progress. The linkage of the two produces the notion of a progressive world history culminating in post-Enlightenment Europe as the measure of all things, "universal history" à la Hegel. In some ways this picture of universal history, which was hegemonic until the middle of this century, already seems strange in light of the combined impact of decolonization outside Europe and genocide within. In other ways it persists, sustained by the reification of memory and history as fundamentally different modes of relating to the past, with the Jews serving as a favorite example of a "people of memory" as opposed to history (Yerushalmi 1982; Nora 1989; cf., however, Funkenstein 1989). The temptation to romanticize Jewish history in this fashion —ironically linked to a new validation of memory—reinforces the lingering assumption of a universal history that the Jews somehow fall outside of.

The greatest exponent in modern Europe of an all-encompassing, progressive, and universal history was Hegel. Although the mature Hegel supported the civil rights of Jews as part of his vision of civil society, as a young man he saw the biblical narrative as the origin of alienation. In his *Early Theological Writings,* figures such as Noah, Abraham, Joseph, and Moses are responsible for the eternal and unchanging nature of the Jews, removed from history and the human community. For the young Hegel, the Flood is the primordial event, destroying the organic unity of humankind with nature:

> It was in a thought-product that Noah built the distracted world together again; his thought-produced ideal he turned into a Being and then set everything else over against it, so that in this opposition realities were reduced to thoughts, i.e., to something mastered. (1977, 183)

This alienated relation to reality is further developed in Hegel's account of the history of Abraham. His leavetaking of Ur of the Chaldees, his wanderings, the act of circumcision, his insistence on paying for the field of Machpelah rather than accepting it as a gift—all are seen as evidences of Abraham's rejection of the general human community: "The whole world Abraham regarded as simply his opposite; if he did not take it to be a nullity, he looked on it as sustained by the God who was alien to it" (187). Abraham's Joseph, acquiring viceregal power in Egypt, introduces legislation whereby the subjects of the pharaoh are brought into the same relationship to him as Joseph stands to his Idea, that is, the relationship of slave to master. The diatribe continues, with Moses' role as liberator being ridiculed and his giving of the Law regarded as merely the laying on of another form of bondage.

In his summation, Hegel criticizes the Jews' dependence on an unseen God and their inability to worship Beauty:

> The subsequent circumstances of the Jewish people up to the mean, abject, wretched circumstances in which they still are today, have all of them been simply consequences and elaborations of their original fate. By this fate—an infinite power which they set over against themselves and could never conquer—they have been maltreated and will be continually maltreated until they appease it by the spirit of beauty and so annul it by reconciliation.[10] (200)

Hegel may have later dropped the overtly theological language, but contemporary Jews never fit into his scheme of providential world history. So I come to a zero point, where the Jews appear both superseded by a post-Christian account of providential history and obviated by a spatialist critique of imperialism that sees the population of Europe as an undifferentiated mass of colonizers.

At this point, it is time to bring in the literary model I promised at the beginning, an unprofessional, "unscientific" model for a Jewish ethnography that could restore Jews to their cultural specificity within Europe and reinforce the critical Jewish voice still contending against supersessionism and progress. It is time to bring in Kafka—a Jewish voice from the other side of the abyss. In Kafka, the relation to the Other within is quite different both from Hegel's myth of eternal Jewish servility and from the folklorism of the *Wissenschaft des Judentums*. Many of Kafka's texts challenge the genre-boundary claims of professional ethnography. They are produced on cultural borderlines, but not as "information retrieval." Kafka's ethnography of simultaneous Jewish loss and emancipation has much to teach us through its own active engagement.

Kafka's *Letter to His Father* is an obvious example. Several pages in the letter detail his childhood impressions of his father's Judaism, along with his retrospective analysis of those impressions. Kafka wants to understand how something that struck the child as utterly empty could have been significant to the father, and in the process he sketches the experience of countless Jewish parents and children in the modern period:

> You really had brought some traces of Judaism with you from the ghetto-like village community; it was not much and it dwindled a little more in the city and during your military service; but still, the impressions and memories of your youth did just about suffice for some sort of Jewish life. . . . Even in this there was Judaism enough, but it was too little to be handed on to the child; it all dribbled away while you were passing it on. . . . The whole thing is, of course, no isolated phenomenon. It was much the same with a large section of this transitional generation of Jews, which had migrated from the still comparatively devout countryside to the cities. (Kafka 1976, 79–83)

The content of Judaism in the "ghetto-like village community"—removed from Kafka's Prague childhood in both time and space—is not restored, but only hinted at through the marks of its absence.

Kafka neither exoticizes the traditional, rural Jewish Other nor attempts to obliterate the distance. The focus here is indeed on what Eric Cheyfitz calls "the difficult poetics of translation"—and in this case, the translation of Jewish intimacy from the village to the city has failed.

The impression is confirmed in a fragment called "The Animal in the Synagogue" (Kafka 1961, 49–59), where Kafka adopts the voice of a Jew in a small town, speaking perhaps to a visitor from the big city. The imaginary animal is described in some detail: "about the size of a marten," "pale blue-green in color," and so forth. It is located quite precisely within the architecture of the synagogue; like a child it prefers to stay near the women's section, but the beadle does not allow it to stay there. It is "more shy than a denizen of the forest, and seems to be attached only to the building." But the animal should know that soon it will be able to stay in the synagogue undisturbed:

> The congregation in this little town of ours in the mountains is becoming smaller every year and . . . it is already having trouble in raising the money for the upkeep of the synagogue. It is not impossible that before long the synagogue will have become a granary or something of the sort and the animal will then have the peace it now so sorely lacks. (51)

But meanwhile, curiously enough, the animal in the synagogue only appears when the Jews gather for services, although it probably would like best to remain in "some hole in the wall" where it lives when no one is there. When it does come out, it is drawn toward the Ark of the Covenant,

> but when it is there is always quiet, not even when it is right up close to the Ark can it be said to be causing a disturbance, it seems to be gazing at the congregation with its bright, unwinking, and perhaps lidless eyes, but it is certainly not looking at anybody, it is only facing the dangers by which it feels itself threatened. (55)

Why indeed would a shy animal, happiest when its dwelling is empty of people, only come out in terror when the synagogue is full? When we read this fragment in conjunction with the description of the Torah in *Letter to His Father*, the animal, as it faces the congregation, seems to be the Torah itself. In the *Letter*, the adult Kafka reminisces that at the moment when the Ark was opened, it "always reminded me of the shooting galleries where a cupboard door would open in the same way whenever one hit a bull's eye; except that there something interesting always came out and here it was always just the same old dolls without heads" (1976, 77).

The terror of the animal becomes quite understandable if we picture it exposed as a target at a shooting gallery; the image of the Torah scrolls as headless dolls is doubled by the image of the animal's unwinking eyes, unable to see anything but the dangers by which it feels itself threatened. The terrified animal could also be Kafka himself; he recalls being frightened "because of all the people one came into close contact with, but also because you once mentioned in passing that I too might be called to the Torah" (77). Is it mere coincidence that, in the collection of Kafka's *Parables and Paradoxes*, "The Animal in the Synagogue" is immediately followed by the famous fragment "Before the Law"? The child's terror at the prospect of being called upon to perform in public a ritual he utterly fails to understand need not be traced to any neurotic complex. The boredom Kafka remembers from the synagogue is familiar enough to me and to so many other Jewish children who were compelled to go by their parents' nostalgia for something that had once been alive—a furry, elusive animal perhaps. Kafka suggests, in sum, that his father's Judaism had come to be a frozen, defensive posture rather than an autonomous ground of selfhood that could serve as an opening toward the Other.

What Kafka could not quite anticipate was just how much cause there was for defensiveness. For the synagogues are granaries now, if they are still standing, not just in the little villages the Jews abandoned at the turn of the century but also in cities where there were thousands of Jews during Kafka's lifetime. It is not the awareness of a life that has slipped away, even before the great catastrophe, that distinguishes Kafka here; the theme of disappearing worlds has been prominent in Jewish writing since at least the nineteenth century (Kugelmass and Boyarin 1983). What makes the brief scene in the synagogue from *Letter to His Father* and the fragment on "The Animal in the Synagogue" so powerfully evocative is not that they *restore* a lost world to our vision, but precisely that they remind us that we are not the first generation to discover that loss is the heart of our connection.[11]

Dwelling in loss, rather than in a richly detailed space reconstituted through memory, is another term for what Deleuze and Guattari (1986) call "deterritorialization." This deterritorialization is not limited to the sociological fact of migration,[12] nor to the experience of being uprooted, but is an overcoming of the fixation on the metaphor of "roots."   The analysis of Deleuze and Guattari suggests that Kafka, having shed any expectations either of organically identifying as a Jew or of fitting with the non-Jewish German literary world, was freed to outline not just a "minor literature," as they call it, but more precisely a minor ethnography.   Kafka's ethnography writes a people's experience in history without presuming to circumscribe that experience, without turning persons into exemplars of a reified culture.   Refusing rigid identifications between tradition and place, treating space and time in the same phrase, he knows that a world can disappear in the village just when its echo is heard in Prague.

Kafka's writing of Jewishness contrasts most sharply with the rhetoric used by the convert Gottfried Selig, described above.   Selig writes a comprehensive and distancing grammar of Yiddish from the perspective of a former insider; Kafka, pretending to no expertise, senses that there once must have been something rich and living. Selig employs frozen racial stereotypes to brand Yiddish as a "Hottentot" tongue; Kafka turns animals into sacred texts and sacred texts into dolls, enhancing the otherness of the tradition without romantically exaggerating its place in his own history. Selig, likening the rejected Other within to the fantasized Other without, attempts to reterritorialize himself in a newly bounded time and space; Kafka chips away at the same boundaries without denying that they exist.

Kafka's minor ethnography moves us to look more closely at the silencing of Europe's Jewish Other within.   We may gain some desperately needed clues as to how that ominously "self-identical" continent managed for so long to contain the threat of the colonial Other without.   We may also come to see how the ultimate violent removal of the Jewish Other within is linked to Europe's loss of control over the colonial Other without.   The direction suggested by Kafka may enable us to further the projects of inserting a Jewish voice into cultural studies, while simultaneously invigorating Jewish studies with contemporary critical concerns.   In a world where the centrality of European power seems less and less a reality (although Eurocentric thought is remarkably durable), Kafka may even help us to understand how Jewish identity and Jewish difference are bound up with the unpredictable future of our planet.

NOTES

1. Relevant to this point, Avital Ronell insists that "Derrida had been listening for the murmurs of the Holocaust long before this became, for intellectuals, somewhat of a journalistic imperative" (1989, 63).

2. Howard Eilberg-Schwartz, in the introduction to a pioneering study of the historical suppression and analytic possibilities of comparative biblical anthropology, writes that "if nineteenth-century and early twentieth-century intellectuals discovered the savage in distant places, subsequent thinkers gradually learned that if savagery is to be found anywhere, it is at home among us" (1990, 23–24). If the savage was admitted to Europe in the twentieth century, what does this say about the expulsion of the Jew?

3. Whether or not the Other has an independent existence at all is a controversial issue. Fabian hopes for an independent "recognition of the Other that is not limited to representations of the Other" (1990, 771). Homi Bhabha, on the other hand, insists that "the 'other' is never outside or beyond us; it emerges forcefully, within cultural discourse, when we *think* we speak most intimately and indigenously 'between ourselves'" (1990, 4). Peter Mason, following Levinas, stresses the *radical* alterity of the Other and the problem of trying "to understand the other without using the violence of comprehension to do so" (1990, 2).

4. Anthony Appiah (1991) warns against the danger that those living in postcolonial nations may be once again frozen into the position of the West's "radically Other." The rhetoric of "radical alterity," therefore, is to be used with caution also by those who would "valorize the Other." For a dramatic example of the excesses binary rhetoric can lead to in feminism, see Martinez (1988).

5. Thus, Ivan Strenski has suggested to me that it would be worthwhile to consider material in the nineteenth-century *Revue des Etudes Juives* in the light of Said's *Orientalism* (1978). Such a project would help, for example, to explain the prominence of Jews in sociology and anthropology during the decades around the fin de siècle. Gyan Prakash has emphasized "the colonized's appeal to and affiliation with the subordinated selves of the colonizer" (Prakash 1990, 405); doubtless the appeal and affiliation have been made from the other direction as well, social scientists identifying with and seeking validation from the subalterns whom they write about. See also the historical essays in Barbara Kirshenblatt-Gimblett's forthcoming collection *Ashkenaz*.

6. See the articles on the reception of "Holocaust" in Germany in a special issue of *New German Critique* (Herf 1980; Markovits and Hayden 1980; Zielinski 1980).

7. As James Clifford observes, "This strategy has classically involved an

unquestioned claim to appear as the purveyor of truth in the text. A complex cultural experience is enunciated by an individual: *We the Tikopia* by Raymond Firth; *Nous avons mangè la forêt* by Georges Condominas; *Coming of Age in Samoa* by Margaret Mead; *The Nuer* by E. E. Evans-Pritchard" (1988, 25).

8.   Said, in response to critics who complained about his failure to discuss German Orientalism, retorts that "no one has given any reason for me to have *included* [it]" (1985, 90). If these were simply complaints that Said's groundbreaking study was not encyclopedic, he is justified in not taking them seriously. Nevertheless, given the quite different and in some ways "marginal" experience of German-speaking lands vis-à-vis the colonized world, a companion study of German Orientalism would be quite in order. Doubtless its elements are being produced right now.

9.   Most revealing, perhaps, is the coincidence of Columbus's departure on his voyage of discovery with the completion of the *Reconquista*: "The year 1492 already symbolizes, in the history of Spain, this double movement: in this same year the country repudiates its interior Other by triumphing over the Moors in the final battle of Granada and by forcing the Jews to leave its territory; and it discovers the exterior Other, that whole America which will become Latin. We know that Columbus himself constantly links the two events" (Todorov 1985, 50).

10.   Compare a comment by the mature Marx: "The chosen people bore in their features the sign that they were the property of Jehovah" (quoted in Gilman 1986, 205). By reference to a scurrilous description in a letter from Marx to Engels about the appearance of their Socialist rival, the Jew Ferdinand Lassalle, Gilman suggests that these are visible, external features, such as dark skin. I wonder whether Marx might not have been referring instead to circumcision.

11.   Significantly, the fragment about the animal breaks off precisely at the point where it is becoming a *story*:

> Many years ago, so it is recounted, attempts were really still made to drive the animal away. The beadle of the synagogue says he remembers how his grandfather, who was also beadle, liked to tell the story. As a small boy his grandfather had frequently heard talk about the impossibility of getting rid of the animal; and so, fired with ambition and being an excellent climber, one bright morning when the whole synagogue, with all its nooks and crannies, lay open in the sunlight, he had sneaked in, armed with a rope, a catapult, and a crook-handled stick. (Kafka 1961, 59)

It is unimportant whether Kafka originally intended to continue but found that the writing no longer interested him, or whether he intended precisely to suggest that positive storytelling was not the point here. What matters is that Kafka shows himself stopping just when narrative begins. Compare the ending of Sholem-Aleykhem's story "Stantsye

Baranovitsh," where a complicated tale of the narrator's grandfather is interrupted just as, according to the narrator, it is about to begin (see Boyarin 1986).
12. Although, as Pierre Vidal-Nacquet notes, *"l'exil rend lucide"* (1982, 21).

BIBLIOGRAPHY

Appiah, Kwame Anthony. 1991. "Is the Post- in Postmodernism the Post-in Postcolonial?" *Critical Inquiry* 17 (Winter): 336–57.

Barker, Francis, Peter Hulme, Margaret Iverson, and Diana Loxley, eds. 1985. *Europe and Its Others.* 2 vols. Colchester: University of Essex Press.

Baudet, Henri. 1965. *Paradise on Earth: Some Thoughts on European Images of Non-European Man.* New Haven and London: Yale University Press.

Belke, Ingrid, ed. 1971. *Moritz Lazarus und Heymann Steinthal: Die Begruender der Voelkerpsychologie in ihren Briefen. Mit einter Einleitung herausgegeben von Ingrid Belke.* Tuebingen: Mohr.

Benjamin, Walter. 1969. "Theses on the Philosophy of History." In *Illuminations.* New York: Schocken.

Bhabha, Homi. 1990. Introduction to *Nation and Narration,* ed. Homi Bhabha. New York: Routledge.

Boyarin, Jonathan. 1986. "Sholem-Aleykhem's Stantsye Baranovitsh." In *Identity and Ethos: A Festschrift for Sol Liptzin,* ed. Mark Gelber. New York: Lang.

Campbell, Mary B. 1988. *The Witness and the Other World: Exotic European Travel Writing, 400–1600.* Ithaca, N.Y.: Cornell University Press.

Cheyfitz, Eric. 1990. *The Poetics of Imperialism: Translation and Colonization from* The Tempest *to* Tarzan. New York: Oxford University Press.

Clifford, James. 1988. "On Orientalism." In *The Predicament of Culture: Twentieth-Century Ethnography, Literature, and Art.* Cambridge, Mass.: Harvard University Press.

Deleuze, Gilles, and Felix Guattari. 1986. *Kafka: Toward a Minor Literature.* Minneapolis: University of Minnesota Press.

Eilberg-Schwartz, Howard. 1990. *The Savage in Judaism: An Anthropology of Israelite Religion and Ancient Judaism.* Bloomington: Indiana University Press.

Fabian, Johannes. 1983. *Time and the Other: How Anthropology Makes Its Object.* New York: Columbia University Press.

————. 1990. "Presence and Representation: The Other and Anthropological Writing." *Critical Inquiry* 16:753–72.

Finkielkraut, Alain. 1980. *Le juif imaginaire*. Paris: Seuil.

Friedlander, Judith. 1990. *Vilna on the Seine*. New Haven, Conn.: Yale University Press.

Funkenstein, Amos. 1989. "Collective Memory and Historical Consciousness." *History and Memory* 1, 1:5–26.

Gilman, Sander. 1986. *Jewish Self-Hatred: Anti-Semitism and the Hidden Language of the Jews*. Baltimore, Md.: Johns Hopkins University Press.

Greenblatt, Stephen. 1990. "Marx, Marlowe, and Anti-Semitism." In *Learning to Curse: Essays in Early Modern Culture*. New York: Routledge.

Haraway, Donna. 1989. *Primate Visions*. New York: Routledge.

Hartog, Francois. 1988. *The Mirror of Herodotus: The Representation of the Other in the Writing of History*. Berkeley: University of California Press.

Hegel, G. W. F. 1977. *Early Theological Writings*. Philadelphia: University of Pennsylvania Press.

Herf, Jeffrey. 1980. "The 'Holocaust' Reception in West Germany: Right, Center, and Left." *New German Critique* 19:30–52.

Kafka, Franz. 1961. *Parables and Paradoxes*. New York: Schocken.

————. 1976 (1953). *Letter to His Father*. New York: Schocken. Books.

Kirshenblatt-Gimblett, Barbara. 1987. "Erasing the Subject: Franz Boas and the Anthropological Study of Jews in the United States." Paper presented at the annual meeting of the American Anthropological Association, Chicago.

————. Forthcoming. *Ashkenaz: Essays in Jewish Folkloristics*.

Kramer, Jane. 1980. *Unsettling Europe*. New York: Random House.

Kugelmass, Jack, and Jonathan Boyarin. 1983. *From a Ruined Garden: The Memorial Books of Polish Jewry*. New York: Schocken.

Markovitz, Andrei S., and Rebecca S. Hayden. 1980. "'Holocaust' before and after the Event: Reactions in West Germany and Austria." *New German Critique* 19:53–80.

Martinez, Z. Nelly. 1988. "From a Representational to a Holographic Paradigm: The Emergence of Female Power." *Atlantis* 14, 1:134–40.

Mason, Peter. 1987. "Seduction from Afar: Europe's Inner Indians." *Anthropos* 82:581–601.

————. 1990. *Deconstructing America*. New York: Routledge.

Mohanty, S. P. 1989. "Us and Them: On the Philosophical Bases of Political Criticism." *Yale Journal of Criticism* 2, 2:1–32.

Morrison, Karl F. 1988. *I Am You: The Hermeneutics of Empathy in Western Literature, Theology, and Art*. Princeton, N.J.: Princeton University Press.

Nora, Pierre. 1989. "Between Memory and History: Les Lieux de Memoire." *Representations* 26:7–25.

Ohnuki-Tierney, Emiko, ed. 1990. *Culture through Time: Anthropological Approaches*. Stanford, Calif.: Stanford University Press.

Olender, Maurice. 1989. *Les Langues du Paradis: Aryens et Semites: un couple providentiel*. Paris: Gallimard & Seuil.

Prakash, Gyan. 1990. "Writing Post-Orientalist Histories of the Third World: Perspective from Indian Historiography." *Comparative Studies in Society and History* 32:383–408.

Rekhtman, Avrom. 1958. *Yidishe etnografye un folklor: zikhroynes vegn der etnografisher ekspeditsye ongefirt fun Sh. Anski*. Buenos Aires: Yidisher Visnshaftlekher Institut.

Ronell, Avital. 1989. "The Differends of Man." *Diacritics* 19, 3–4: 25–37.

Rosaldo, Renato. 1989. *Culture and Truth*. Boston: Beacon.

Said, Edward. 1978. *Orientalism*. New York: Pantheon.

———. 1985. "Orientalism Reconsidered." *Cultural Critique* 1:89–107.

———. 1989a. "Anthropology and Its Interlocutors." *Critical Inquiry* 15:205–25.

———. 1989b. "Yeats and Decolonization." In *Remaking History*, ed. Barbara Kruger and Phil Mariani. Seattle: Bay,

Spivak, Gayatri. 1987. *In Other Worlds: Essays in Cultural Politics*. New York: Methuen.

———. 1988. "Can the Subaltern Speak?" In *Marxism and the Interpretation of Culture*, ed. Cary Nelson and Lawrence Grossberg. Urbana and Chicago: University of Illinois Press.

———. 1989. "Who Claims Alterity?" In *Remaking History*, ed. Barbara Kruger and Phil Mariani. Seattle: Bay.

———. 1990. *The Post-Colonial Critic*, ed. Sarah Harasym. New York: Routledge.

Thom, Martin. 1990. "Tribes within Nations: The Ancient Germans and the History of Modern France." In *Nation and Narration*, ed. Homi Bhabha. New York: Routledge.

Todorov, Tzvetan. 1985. *The Conquest of America: The Question of the Other*. New York: Harper & Row.

Torgovnick, Marianna. 1990. *Gone Primitive: Savage Intellects, Modern Lives*. Chicago: University of Chicago Press.

Trumpener, Katie. 1992. "The Time of the Gypsies: A People without History in the Narratives of the West." *Critical Inquiry* 18, 4:843–84.

van Gennep, A. 1920. "Nouvelles recherches sur l'histoire en France de la methode ethnographique: Claude Guichard, Richard Simon, Claude Fleury." *Revue de l'Histoire des Religions* 82–83:139–62.

Vidal-Naquet, Pierre. 1982. "Herodote et l'Atlantide: entre les Grecs et les Juifs. Reflexions sur l'historiographie du siecle des Lumieres." *Quaderni di storia* 16:5–74.

Wertheimer, Jack. 1987. *Unwelcome Strangers: East European Jews in Imperial Germany*. New York: Oxford University Press.

Yardeni, Myriam. 1970. "La Vision des Juifs et du judaisme dans l'oeuvre de Richard Simon." *Revue des etudes juives* 129:179– 203.

Yerushalmi, Yosef Haim. 1982. *Zakhor: Jewish History and Jewish Memory*. Seattle: University of Washington Press.

Zielinski, Siegfried. 1980. "History as Entertainment and Provocation: The TV Series 'Holocaust' in West Germany." *New German Critique* 19:81–96.

About the Editors

ROBERT L. COHN is Philip and Muriel Berman Professor of Jewish Studies in the Department of Religion at Lafayette College. Elected to Phi Beta Kappa in 1969, he earned his M.A. and Ph.D. at Stanford University. In 1982 he received the College of Arts and Sciences Award for Outstanding Teaching at Northwestern University and was designated Lafayette College's Thomas Roy and Lura Forrest Jones Faculty Lecturer for 1993–94. He is the coauthor of *Exploring the Hebrew Bible* and author of *The Shape of Sacred Space: Four Biblical Studies* and "1 Samuel" in *Harper's Bible Commentary*. His articles on biblical narrative have appeared in such journals as *Religion and Intellectual Life*, *Catholic Biblical Quarterly*, *Vetus Testamentum*, and *Journal of Biblical Literature*.

LAURENCE J. SILBERSTEIN is Philip and Muriel Berman Professor of Jewish Studies in the Department of Religion Studies, Lehigh University, and director of the Philip and Muriel Berman Center for Jewish Studies. He received his Ph.D. from Brandeis University and was the recipient of a fellowship for independent research from the National Endowment for the Humanities. He is author of *Martin Buber's Social and Religious Thought: Alienation and the Quest for Meaning* and editor of *New Perspectives on Israeli History: The Early Years of the State* and *Jewish Fundamentalism in Comparative Perspective: Religion, Ideology, and the Crisis of Modernity*. His articles on modern Jewish thought have appeared in *Soundings*, *The Encyclopedia of Religion*, *Journal of the American Academy of Religion*, *International Journal of Middle Eastern Studies*, and *Religious Studies Review*. His current research focuses on the emergence of post-Zionist discourse.

About the Contributors

JONATHAN BOYARIN is an independent scholar affiliated with the Center for Studies of Social Change, New School for Social Research, New York. Among his books are *Polish Jews in Paris: The Ethnography of Memory, Storm from Paradise: The Politics of Jewish Memory*, and a forthcoming volume on Palestine and Jewish history.

GERALD CROMER teaches in the Department of Criminology at Bar-Ilan University. He has published numerous articles on various aspects of political extremism in Israel and is currently engaged in research on religious zealotry among Israeli ultraorthodox Jews.

TRUDE DOTHAN is professor of archaeology and director of the Philip and Muriel Berman Center for Biblical Archaeology at the Hebrew University of Jerusalem. She is the author of numerous books and articles, including her seminal work *The Philistines and Their Material Culture* and *People of the Sea: The Search for the Philistines*, coauthored with Moshe Dothan.

ELIZABETH FIFER, professor of English at Lehigh University, teaches world literature, drama, and poetry. Her recent articles have appeared in such journals as *Signs, Contemporary Literature*, and *Texas Studies in Literature and Language*. In 1992 she published *Rescued Readings: A Reconstruction of Gertrude Stein's Difficult Texts*.

STEVEN D. FRAADE is Mark Taper Professor of the History of Judaism at Yale University. He was awarded the National Jewish Book Award for Scholarship in 1992. His books include *From Tradition to Commentary: Torah and Its Interpretation in the*

Midrash Sifre to Deuteronomy and *Targum and Torah: Early Rabbinic Views of Scriptural Translation in a Multilingual Society.*

SANDER L. GILMAN, author or editor of over thirty books, including *The Jew's Body* and *Jewish Self-Hatred*, is a cultural and literary historian. He is the Goldwin Smith Professor of Humane Studies at Cornell University and professor of the history of psychiatry at the Cornell Medical College.

HANNAN HEVER is senior lecturer in the Department of Poetics and Comparative Literature at Tel Aviv University. His publications include an academic edition of *The Collected Poems of Avraham Ben-Yitzhak, Studies in the Poetry of Avraham Ben-Yitzhak*, and *The Rise of the Political Hebrew Poem*, forthcoming.

ROSS S. KRAEMER is adjunct associate professor of religious studies and 1993–94 fellow at the Center for Judaic Studies at the University of Pennsylvania. Among her recent publications are *Her Share of the Blessings: Women's Religions among Pagans, Jews, and Christians in the Greco-Roman World* and *Maenads, Martyrs, Matrons, Monastics: A Sourcebook on Women's Religions in the Greco-Roman World.*

ORLY LUBIN teaches in the Department of Poetics and Comparative Literature and in the cinema studies program at Tel Aviv University. Her writings focus mainly on Israeli cinema and feminist theory and literature.

PETER MACHINIST, Hancock Professor of Hebrew and Other Oriental Languages in the Department of Near Eastern Languages and Civilizations at Harvard University, has written widely on the comparative history of the cultures of the ancient Near East, in particular Israel and Mesopotamia. His volume *Letters from Assyrian and Babylonian Priests to Kings Esarhaddon and Assurbanipal* is forthcoming in 1994, and he is currently completing a commentary on Nahum for the Anchor Bible Series.

JACOB MESKIN is an assistant professor of religion at Williams College. He is currently writing a monograph on the interrelationship between philosophy and Jewish religious texts in the work of Emmanual Levinas. His recent articles include "In the Flesh:

Embodiment and Jewish Existence in the Thought of Emmanual Levinas" and "From Phenomenology to Liberation: The Displacement of History and Theology in Levinas' *Totality and Infinity*."

ADI OPHIR, lecturer at the Cohn Institute for the History and Philosophy of Science and Ideas at Tel Aviv University, is author of *Plato's Invisible Cities: Discourse and Power in the Republic*, and editor of *Theoria ve-Bikoret*, an annual interdisciplinary journal for Israeli culture and society.

ILAN PELEG is Charles A. Dana Professor in Lafayette College's Department of Government and Law. He has written numerous articles on Israel and the Arab-Israeli conflict. His books include *Begin's Foreign Policy, 1977–1983*, *The Emergence of a Binational Israel* (coedited), and *Patterns of Censorship around the World*.

MIRIAM PESKOWITZ is assistant professor of religion at the University of Florida. In 1992–93 she was Samuel Kress Fellow at the W. F. Albright Institute and Graduate Research Fellow at the Annenberg Research Institute. She is currently engaged in the writing of a monograph, *Stories about Spinners and Weavers: Gendering the Everyday in Roman-period Judaism*.

NAOMI B. SOKOLOFF is associate professor of Hebrew in the Department of Near Eastern Languages and Civilization at the University of Washington. She is a coeditor of *Gender and Text in Modern Hebrew and Yiddish Literature* and *Imagining the Child in Modern Jewish Fiction*.

ELLIOT R. WOLFSON is associate professor of Hebrew and Judaic Studies at New York University and adjunct professor of Jewish History at Columbia University. His volumes *Through a Speculum That Shines: Vision and Imagination in Medieval Jewish Mysticism* and *Along the Path: Studies in Kabbalistic Hermeneutics, Myth, and Symbolism* will be available in 1995.

Index

Abraham, 78, 79, 81–82, 84–86; Hegel on, 442

Adam: androgyny of, 170–77, 197 n. 41

Against Judaizing Christians (Chrysostom), 127, 135–37, 138, 143 n. 57

Aggadah, 159 n. 4

Albright, William F., 35

Allport, Gordon, 379

Alt, Albrecht, 35

Alter, Robert, 342

America. *See* United States

American Citizen (Green), 309–10

Amihai, Yehuda, 326

Amir, Aharon, 240–41, 244

Amir, Yehuda, 269–70

Amorites, 50–51

Amos, 52–53, 59 n. 48

Ancestor *arche*: the Canaanite as Other in, 75, 77–85

Anderson, Benedict, 239

Androgyny: divine, 20, 168–71, 177–85, 197 n. 40, 199 n. 58, 199 n. 61, 199 n. 62, 202 n. 77, 203 n. 79; human, 170–77, 197 n. 37, 197 n. 41

"The Animal in the Synagogue" (Kafka), 26, 444, 445–46, 448 n. 11

Anski, S., 433

Apion of Alexandria, 124–25, 133

Appiah, Anthony, 447 n. 4

Arabs (Palestinians) and Arab political activity, 268–69; in the Canaanite Movement, 240–44, 246–50; in Israeli literature, 269; and Israeli right-wing political groups, 272–76, 278 n. 20; and Israeli youth, 267–68; and Jewish-Arab contact, 269–70; Kahane on, 283–87; compared to Nazis, 291, 304 n. 43; as Other, 14, 21–22, 209, 237–38, 260, 271–72; and Zionism, 21, 231 n. 14, 265–67, 268. *See also* Israeli-Arab conflict

Arche: ancestor, 75, 77–85; conquest, 75, 76–77

Ark of the Covenant, 64

Aseneth, 128–30

Ashkenazic Jews, 13, 14, 27 n. 2

Assimilation, 25, 28 n. 6, 431; and cosmetic surgery, 388–89, 391; and the Holocaust, 431–32, 435, 439, 441; and Jewish identity, 366; Kahane on, 284, 289–90, 292

Asymmetry, 402, 405, 410–11, 421 n. 11; and ethics, 411–13, 422 n. 17; and the third party, 413–17

Atlantis, 425

Augustine, 436

Avineri, Shlomo, 274

Babylonian Exile, 16, 51, 53–54, 60 n. 55

Bakhtin, M. M., 331–32, 334, 350 n. 5, 350 n. 7

Barbash, Uri, 309

Barnes, Julian, 379–80

Bartov, Hanoch, 327

Bat Adam, Michal, 305–8, 314–20

"Battle of Fort Williams" (Gafni), 244–46, 248, 253–57